Foundations of GTK+ Development

Andrew Krause

Foundations of GTK+ Development

Copyright © 2007 by Andrew Krause

ISBN-13 (pbk): 978-1-59059-793-4

ISBN-10 (pbk): 1-59059-793-1

ISBN-13 (electronic): 978-1-4302-0386-5

Printed and bound in the United States of America 9 8 7 6 5 4 3 2

Lead Editors: Jason Gilmore, Matt Wade
Technical Reviewers: Christiana Evelyn Johnson, Micah Carrick
Editorial Board: Steve Anglin, Ewan Buckingham, Gary Cornell, Jason Gilmore, Jonathan Gennick,
    Jonathan Hassell, James Huddleston, Chris Mills, Matthew Moodie, Jeff Pepper, Paul Sarknas,
    Dominic Shakeshaft, Jim Sumser, Matt Wade
Project Manager: Richard Dal Porto
Copy Edit Manager: Nicole Flores
Copy Editor: Heather Lang
Assistant Production Director: Kari Brooks-Copony
Production Editor: Katie Stence
Compositor: Pat Christenson
Proofreader: Elizabeth Berry
Indexer: Ann Rogers
Artist: April Milne
Cover Designer: Kurt Krames
Manufacturing Director: Tom Debolski

Distributed to the book trade worldwide by Springer-Verlag New York, Inc., 233 Spring Street, 6th Floor, New York, NY 10013. Phone 1-800-SPRINGER, fax 201-348-4505, e-mail orders-ny@springer-sbm.com, or visit http://www.springeronline.com.

For information on translations, please contact Apress directly at 2855 Telegraph Avenue, Suite 600, Berkeley, CA 94705. Phone 510-549-5930, fax 510-549-5939, e-mail info@apress.com, or visit http://www.apress.com.

The source code for this book is available to readers at http://www.apress.com in the Source Code/ Download section or at the official book site, http://www.gtkbook.com.

I dedicate this book to Mrs. Kaminsky, for never allowing me to settle for anything but my best. I hope you can look at this book and see everything that you have done for me, even though I have yet to broaden the scope of my writing beyond technology.

Contents at a Glance

Contents

About the Author

ANDREW KRAUSE is the creator of OpenLDev, an integrated development environment that focuses on C, C++, and GTK+ projects. He is currently attending Pennsylvania State University with a major in computer engineering. Since 1998, Andrew has been developing with many computer and web programming languages, including C, C++, Perl, and PHP, as well as the graphical design libraries GTK+, Gtkmm, and Qt. He also designed flight hardware for the Low Ionosphere Measurement Satellite project at Penn State. More information about Andrew can be found at www.andrewkrause.net.

Acknowledgments

I would like to express my gratitude to the many people who have made this book possible. Many thanks go to Josh Hoy and Aaron Sebold, whose assistance has certainly decreased the number of errors in the book. I would also like to thank Christiana Johnson and Micah Carrick for their fine technical reviewing skills. You were very tough on every paragraph I wrote and every example I coded, but this book is better today because of the hard work you put into the project.

In addition, I would like to thank the people at Apress who put so many hours of hard work into the book. I could not imagine writing for any other publisher. It is a great organization that makes the writing process enjoyable. I would especially like to thank Matt Wade, Jason Gilmore, Richard Dal Porto, Heather Lang, and Katie Stence, who put up with all of my questions and provided quick help whenever it was needed.

Finally, I need to acknowledge my family, who has supported me in every step of the process. Without all of you, I would not be who I am today and for that I am forever grateful.

Introduction

One of the most important aspects of an application is the interface that is provided to interact with the user. With the unprecedented popularity of computers in society today, people have come to expect those user interfaces to be graphical, and the question of which graphical toolkit to use quickly arises for any developer. For many, the cross-platform, feature-rich GTK+ library is the obvious choice.

Learning GTK+ can be a daunting task, because many features lack documentation, and even more are difficult to understand from only the API documentation. *Foundations of GTK+ Development* aims to decrease the learning curve and set you on your way to creating cross-platform graphical user interfaces for your applications.

Each chapter in this book contains multiple examples that will help you further your understanding. In addition to these examples, the final chapter of this book provides five complete applications that incorporate topics from the previous chapters. These applications will show you how to bring together what you have learned to accomplish various projects.

The beginning of each chapter provides an overview of what that chapter will cover, so that you are able to skip around if you want. Most chapters also contain exercises to test your understanding of the material. I recommend that you complete all of the exercises before continuing, because the best way to learn GTK+ is to use it.

At the end of this book, you will find multiple appendixes that can serve as references for various aspects of GTK+. These appendixes include tables listing signals, styles, and properties for every widget in GTK+ and a complete list of stock items and GError types. These appendixes will remain a useful reference even after you have finished reading the book and begin creating your own applications. In addition, Appendix F contains explanations of the solutions to all of the exercises throughout the book.

Who Should Read This Book

Because this book begins with the basics and works up to more difficult concepts, you do not need any previous knowledge of GTK+ development to use this book. This book *does* assume that you have a decent grasp of the C programming language. You should also be comfortable with running commands and terminating applications (Ctrl+C) in a Linux terminal.

In addition to a grasp of the C programming language, some parts of this book may be difficult to understand without some further knowledge about programming for Linux in general. You will get more out of this book if you already comprehend basic object-oriented concepts. It is also helpful to know how Linux handles processes.

You can still use this book if you do not already know how to implement object orientation or manage processes in Linux, but you may need to supplement this book with one or more online resources. A list of helpful links and tutorials can be found on the book's web site, which is located at www.gtkbook.com. You can also find more information about the book at www.apress.com.

How This Book Is Organized

Foundations of GTK+ Development is composed of 13 chapters. Each chapter will give you a broad understanding of its topic. For example, Chapter 3 covers container widgets and will introduce many of the most important widgets derived from the GtkContainer class.

Because of this structure, some chapters can be somewhat lengthy. Do not feel as though you have to complete a whole chapter in one sitting, because it can be difficult to remember all of the information presented. Also, because many examples span multiple pages, consider focusing on just a few examples at a time and really trying to understand their syntax and intent.

Each chapter provides important information and unique perspectives that will help you to become a proficient GTK+ developer. They are as follows:

Chapter 1 teaches you how to install the GTK+ libraries and their dependencies on your Linux system. It also gives an overview of each of the GTK+ libraries including GLib, GObject, GDK, GdkPixbuf, Pango, and ATK.

Chapter 2 steps through two "Hello World" applications. The first shows you the basic essentials that are required by every GTK+ application. The second expands on the first while also covering signals, callback functions, events, and child widgets. You will then learn about widget properties and the GtkButton widget.

Chapter 3 begins by introducing the GtkContainer structure. Next, it teaches you about horizontal and vertical boxes, tables, fixed containers, horizontal and vertical panes, notebooks, and event boxes.

Chapter 4 covers basic widgets that provide a way for you to interact with users. These include toggle buttons, specialized buttons, text entries, and spin buttons.

Chapter 5 introduces you to the vast array of built-in dialogs available to you. It also teaches you how to create your own custom dialogs.

Chapter 6 is a general overview of the most useful features in GLib. It covers many of the data types available to you. It also introduces idle functions, timeouts, spawning processes, loading dynamic modules, file utility functions, timers, and other general utility functions.

Chapter 7 introduces you to scrolled windows. It also gives in-depth instructions on using the text view widget. Other topics include the clipboard and the GtkSourceView library.

Chapter 8 covers two types of widgets that use the GtkTreeModel object. It gives an in-depth overview of the tree view widget and shows you how to use combo boxes with tree models or strings.

Chapter 9 provides two methods of menu creation: manual and dynamic. It covers menus, toolbars, pop-up menus, keyboard accelerators, and the status bar widget.

Chapter 10 is a short chapter about how to design user interfaces with the Glade User Interface Builder. It also shows you how to dynamically load your user interfaces using Libglade.

Chapter 11 teaches you how to create your own custom GTK+ widgets by deriving them from other widgets or creating them from scratch. It also introduces you to implementing and using interfaces.

Chapter 12 covers many of the remaining widgets that do not quite fit into other chapters. This includes several widgets that were introduced in GTK+ 2.10 including recent files and tray icon support.

Chapter 13 gives you a few longer, real-world examples. They take the concepts you have learned throughout the book and show you how they can be used together.

In addition to the chapters, six appendixes are provided as references to widget properties, signals, styles, stock items, GError types, and descriptions of exercise solutions.

Conventions

This book uses various typefaces to help you distinguish between GTK+ code and regular English phrases. Actual code is typeset in a monospace font. This can include whole lines of code or function names, signals, and properties in a paragraph.

There are other types of conventions used in this book, which follow.

Exercise 0-0. Sample Exercise

These boxes show exercises that test your understanding of the material in the section. They can include questions, code challenges, or various other types of material.

You should complete each of these exercises before proceeding, because they will help you practice the concepts you have learned throughout the current chapter and put them together with concepts from past chapters.

Note These boxes give important notes, tips, and cautions. It is essential that you pay attention to them, because they give you information that you will need when developing your own applications.

```
Textual output in the terminal is shown in a monospace font between these lines,
although most output will be in the form of an image, since GTK+ is graphical.
```

What You Need

Before proceeding, you will need a few things: a compiler, a text editor, a terminal emulator, the GTK+ libraries, the pkg-config application, and this book.

All compiler commands provided by this book are for the GCC compiler available at http://gcc.gnu.org or through your package manager. Most standard C or C++ compilers will work, but if you use a compiler other than GCC, you will have to use a different set of commands than those provided.

Any text editor will do, so you should choose the one that suits you best. Some popular text editors that you might consider include Vim, Emacs, Leafpad, and GEdit. Vim and Emacs are terminal-based editors, while Leafpad and GEdit are graphical text editors.

Instructions on installing the GTK+ libraries and the pkg-config application are provided in the last section of Chapter 1.

Official Web Site

You can find additional resources on the book's official web site, found at www.gtkbook.com. This web site includes up-to-date documentation, links to useful resources, and articles that will supplement what you learn in this book. You can also find at this site a link to the downloadable source code for every example in this book. The Apress web site, found at www.apress.com, is another great place to find more information about this book.

When you unzip the source code from the web site, you will find a folder that contains the examples in each chapter and an additional folder that holds exercise solutions. You can run make to build all of the files within the current folder. It is also possible to make a single file by using the compile command given in Chapter 2 or by running make sourcefile. For example, to build exercise2-1.c, you should type make exercise2-1.

CHAPTER 1

■■■

Getting Started

Welcome to *Foundations of GTK+ Development*! In this book, you will acquire a comprehensive understanding of GIMP Toolkit (GTK+) that can help you to become a proficient graphical programmer. Before continuing, you should be aware that this book is aimed at C programmers, so we will jump right into using GTK+. Time will not be spent covering information you already know.

To get the most out of this book, you should follow along with each of the examples and try the exercises found at the end of most chapters. Getting started with GTK+ on Linux is quite simple, because the majority of modern distributions are typically bundled with the necessary libraries and tools.

Nevertheless, you need to make sure that you already have a few tools installed including the GNU Compiler Collection (GCC), the GTK+ 2.0 libraries, and the associated development packages. Later in this chapter, you will learn how to install these applications. If you do not have a compiler, you can still use this book, but you will get more out of it if you do the exercises. The best way to learn GTK+ is to use it!

■Note The compiler of choice for this book is GCC, available for download at `http://gcc.gnu.org`. Any standard C or C++ compiler will work, but you will have to use a different set of commands than those provided. Alternative compiler commands will not be covered in this book.

At the end of most chapters, you will find one or two exercises that illustrate what you have learned up to that point. Make sure you complete each of the exercises before moving on to the next chapter, because they will help reaffirm your knowledge. Each chapter builds on concepts presented in previous chapters, so you will need a firm foundation in the basics to understand more complex examples.

In this chapter, you will learn the following:

- The history of GTK+ and the X Window System, which will provide you with some context regarding the tremendous impact these two technologies have had on developers

- What GTK+ and its supporting libraries provide to the graphical application developer

- What GTK+ language bindings are available and where to download them

- How to install GTK+ and its dependencies on your computer

A Brief History of GTK+

The GIMP Toolkit (GTK+) was originally designed for a raster graphics editor called the GNU Image Manipulation Program (GIMP). Three individuals, Peter Mattis, Spencer Kimball, and Josh MacDonald created GTK+ in 1997 while working in the eXperimental Computing Facility at the University of California, Berkeley.

Licensed under the Lesser General Public License (LGPL), GTK+ was adopted as the default graphical toolkit of GNOME and XFCE, two of the most popular Linux desktop environments. While it was originally used on the Linux operating system, GTK+ has since been expanded to support other UNIX-like operating systems: Microsoft Windows, BeOS, Solaris, Mac OS X, and others.

■**Note** The LGPL is one of the things that distinguish GTK+ from other open source graphical toolkits. The LGPL is easier to use alongside proprietary software, unlike many other popular open source licenses. This makes the GNOME desktop environment, which utilizes GTK+, a popular choice throughout commercial industry.

GTK+ is currently in its second stable release cycle, GTK+ 2. The original branch, GTK+ 1, needed to be changed dramatically to include new features and its developers saw fit to break API compatibility.

Since the two branches of GTK+ are not compatible, they can be installed in parallel. You will need to make the distinction to the compiler that you want to use the second branch instead of the first when building an application, which you will learn how to do with GCC in the next chapter.

GTK+ 2 introduced a lot of new features including a font-rendering engine called Pango and a newly enhanced theme engine. Furthermore, improved accessibility support was implemented through the Accessibility Toolkit (ATK).

This book uses version 2 of GTK+ for all code examples. While GTK+ 2.10 has already been released, most of the examples should work with any version in the second branch. GTK+ 2 maintains backward compatibility, which means that any application that works for an earlier release of GTK+ 2 will work on later releases of version 2.

The X Window System

In 1984, Jim Gettys and Bob Scheifler created the X Window System (X11) at Massachusetts Institute of Technology as a platform-independent display environment for debugging the Argus system. Currently developed by The X.Org Foundation, X11 is the standard display manager on Linux and other UNIX-like operating systems. In the most basic terms, X11 provides windowing functionality for bitmap displays.

While the X Window System is used on Linux, many other operating systems such as Microsoft Windows do not use it. Therefore, another advantage of GTK+ is that it masks the need to interact with the underlying rendering system, regardless of what it is. Your code will look the same whether you are writing it for Linux, Windows, or Mac OS X.

Returning to Linux, X11 manages windows in their most basic and abstract form. It draws windows on the screen and handles their movements. X11 also controls input devices, such as mice and keyboards, in graphical environments.

X11's basic programming interface, Xlib, provides the tools necessary to create graphical user interfaces. Although developing with Xlib is possible, most programmers prefer to use a graphical toolkit such as GTK+, since all of the low-level calls are hidden and managed by the library's methods.

One of the major features that makes X11 unique among display managers is that it assumes the client and server are treated independently of each other. This allows the client to exist at a remote location independent of the server.

___

■Note The definitions of client and server in the X Window System differ from their traditional ones. The client is the machine where the application is run. The server refers to the user's local display, rather than the remote machine.

___

Another advantage of the X Window System is that it does not strictly mandate user interfaces. This allows the graphical user interfaces (GUI) of window managers to be highly customizable. It is also why window managers can provide such differing interfaces and themes. This enables the freedom of choice Linux users enjoy today.

Ironically, this freedom is also one of the biggest criticisms of X11. Many people fear that it will encourage fragmentation within the community of Linux developers. But for now, we can continue to enjoy the ability to choose the window manager that best suits our own needs.

The GTK+ libraries were created so that you, as the programmer, do not need to interface with the X Window System directly. You can create windows and widgets, and you can handle interactions between those widgets and the user, but all direct rendering to the screen and Xlib function calls are handled automatically.

Therefore, this book will not cover the X Window System any further and will focus on the GTK+ libraries instead. You are welcome to find more information about X11 and the X.Org Foundation at www.x.org.

GTK+ and Supporting Libraries

GTK+ relies on multiple libraries, each providing the graphical application developer a specific class of functionality.

GTK+ is an object-oriented application programming interface (API) written in the C programming language. It is implemented with the concept of classes in mind to create an extensible system that builds upon itself. The object-oriented framework used was originally developed as a part of the GTK+ library itself, but has since been split from GTK+ and added to GLib as a separate supporting library called GObject. GObject enables full object-orientated development in C, including object inheritance, polymorphism, and, to the extent permissible in C, data hiding.

While making a great deal of functionality from the other libraries transparently available through its own API, the GTK+ library focuses only on providing the necessities of building graphical user interfaces. The elements implemented in GTK+ itself include widgets such as buttons, labels, text boxes, and windows. It also provides more abstract components used for application layout and extended event capturing functionality. For example, Figure 1-1 is a screenshot of the GIMP application, which uses GTK+.

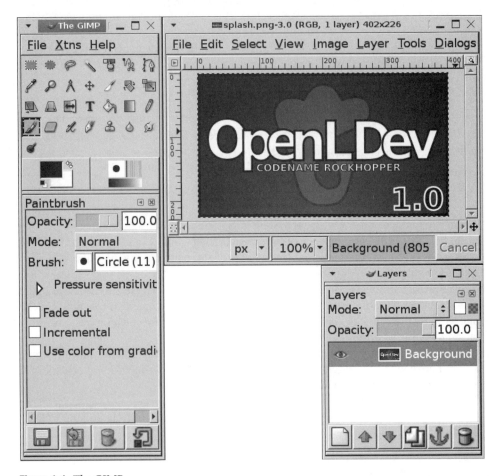

Figure 1-1. *The GIMP*

Other, less visible basics of GUI development, such as synchronous and asynchronous event processing, are supported mainly by other libraries. Yet, GTK+ does give access to many of them through its own API.

A 2-D vector graphics rendering library called Cairo has provided the rendering capabilities to GTK+ since the release of version 2.8. Cairo was created to render vector graphics consistently across all platforms and systems. It also allows the window manager to take advantage of hardware acceleration where available.

Cairo itself will not be covered in this book, with the exception of how it relates to GTK+'s printing API, since its calls lie underneath the layers of GTK+ that you will be interacting with. It is an important aspect you will want to explore if you later choose to hack the GTK+ source code. You can visit www.cairographics.org to find more information about Cairo.

GLib

GLib is a general-purpose utility library that is used to implement many useful nongraphical features. While it is required by GTK+, it can also be used independently. Because of this, some applications use GLib without the other GTK+ libraries for the many capabilities it provides.

One of the main benefits of using GLib is that it provides a cross-platform interface that allows your code to be run on any of its supported operating systems *with little to no rewriting of code!* Another advantageous aspect of GLib is the vast array of data types it provides to developers. A list of a few of the data types provided by GLib follows and will be covered in further detail in Chapter 6:

- GLib provides a number of data types to C programmers that are usually included by default in other languages, such as singly and doubly linked lists. Other basic data types include double-ended queues, self-balancing binary trees, and unbalanced n-ary trees.

- Hash tables allow you to create lists of pointers to data. They differ from linked lists, because, instead of accessing elements by an integer reference, you specify a second pointer as the key.

- Strings in GLib are similar to strings in C++, because they are text buffers that grow automatically as data is added. These are also easy to integrate with calls to the `printf()` function family.

- Memory slices are an efficient way to create chunks of memory that are all of the same size. They can be used to create arrays of evenly sized elements. This structure replaced memory chunks when it was introduced in the release of GLib 2.10.

- Caches allow you to share large, complex data structures in an easy API, which helps you to save space. These are used by GTK+ for styles and graphics contexts, since both of these objects consume a lot of resources.

GLib provides other data types, many of which will be introduced in Chapter 6. Furthermore, GLib implements other features besides data types. It also provides you with numerous types of utility functions. For instance, you'll find utility functions for file manipulation, internationalization support, strings, warnings, debugging flags, dynamic module loading, and automatic string completion, just to name a few.

In Chapter 6, you will also learn about idle functions, time-out functions, and timers—all of which open up a variety of interesting possibilities to developers. Idle functions allow you to call a function when the processor is not doing anything else for the application. Timeouts are used to call a function at a specified interval of time provided by you. A timer keeps track of how much time has passed since it was initiated. These could be used to check for updates when the application is idle, implement automatic save functionality, or track elapsed time, respectively.

Because of the cross-platform characteristics of GLib, it makes a convenient library to use for spawning processes, file manipulation, memory allocation, and threads. Any of these can be a nightmare when trying to develop for multiple platforms. GLib takes care of the hassles, so you do not have to worry about cross-platform compatibility issues.

GObject

The GLib Object System (GObject) was originally a part of the GTK+ 1 library in the form of the GtkObject class. With the release of GTK+ 2.0, it was moved into its own library, distributed along with GLib.

GObject is often criticized for its complexity, since its APIs can seem extremely drawn out. However, it was originally created to allow easy access to C objects from other programming languages. The ability to easily access C objects from other languages facilitates the large variety of bindings available for other programming languages, even though it is implemented in C.

This is so difficult because each programming language provides a different approach to data types, whether the differences appear on the surface or the internals of each language. For example, in C, you have data types including char, long, and integer. Other languages, such as Perl, do not have similar data types, since the type of each object is decided by how it is used. GObject gets around these limitations, the drawback being that deriving new objects is a convoluted process.

GObject also implements a fully featured object-oriented interface in C, which will be covered in detail throughout this section and the rest of this book. This system is the base for the GTK+ widget hierarchical structure as well as for many of the objects implemented in GTK+'s supporting libraries. GObject's object-oriented interface is implemented in part by a generic, dynamic type system called GType. GType allows programmers to implement many different dynamic data types through singly-inherited class structure. A singly-inherited class is an object hierarchy where each child class can only be derived directly from a single parent class. This will be discussed in more detail in Chapter 2, after you are introduced to GTK+ widgets.

Along with the ability to create extensible data types, GObject provides programmers with many nonclassed (or fundamental) data types. A nonclassed data type is a root class from which others are derived. It is important to note that the root class is not derived from any other classes itself.

Table 1-1 provides a list of the most important nonclassed data types. The GType macro, C variable descriptor, and a description is shown for each, along with its range if applicable.

Table 1-1. *Standard GObject Nonclassed Data Types*

GType	C Type	Description
G_TYPE_NONE		An empty type that is equivalent to void.
G_TYPE_CHAR	gchar	Equivalent to the standard C char type.
G_TYPE_INT	gint	Equivalent to the standard C int type. Values must be within the range of G_MININT to G_MAXINT.
G_TYPE_LONG	glong	Equivalent to the standard C long type. Values must be within the range of G_MINLONG to G_MAXLONG.
G_TYPE_BOOLEAN	gboolean	A standard Boolean type that holds either TRUE or FALSE.
G_TYPE_ENUM	GEnumClass	A standard enumeration equivalent to the C enum type.
G_TYPE_FLAGS	GFlagsClass	Bit fields holding Boolean flags.
G_TYPE_FLOAT	gfloat	Equivalent to the standard C float type. Values must be within the range of negative G_MAXFLOAT to G_MAXFLOAT.

GType	C Type	Description
G_TYPE_DOUBLE	gdouble	Equivalent to the standard C double type. Values must be within the range of negative G_MAXDOUBLE to G_MAXDOUBLE.
G_TYPE_STRING	gchar*	Equivalent to NULL-terminated C strings.
G_TYPE_POINTER	gpointer	An untyped pointer type similar to void*.

GObject provides GTK+ with two other vital data types: GValue and GObject. GValue is a generic container that can hold any structure of which the system is already aware. This allows functions to return a piece of data of an arbitrary type. Without GValue, the object-oriented nature of GTK+ would not be possible.

G_TYPE_GOBJECT, or GObject, is the fundamental type that the widget class inheritance structure of GTK+ is based on. It allows widgets to inherit the properties of their parents, including style properties and signals.

GObject is a singly-inherited system, where each child class can only have one parent class. The derived child inherits all characteristics of the parent, because in every way, the child *is* the parent. You will learn how to use this system to derive custom GTK+ widgets in Chapter 11.

GObject also provides widgets with a signal system, an object properties system, and memory management. We will explore all of these concepts in the next chapter.

GDK

The GIMP Drawing Kit (GDK) is a computer graphics library originally designed for the X Window System that wraps around low-level drawing and window functions. GDK acts as the intermediary between Xlib and GTK+.

It renders drawings, raster graphics, cursors, and fonts in all GTK+ applications. Also, since it is implemented in every GTK+ program, GDK provides drag-and-drop support and window events.

GDK provides GTK+ widgets the ability to be drawn to the screen. To do this, every widget has an associated GdkWindow object, except for a few widgets that will be discussed in a later chapter. A GdkWindow is essentially a rectangular area located on the screen in which the widget is drawn. GdkWindow objects also allow widgets to detect X Window System events, which will be covered in the next chapter.

GDK has been ported to Windows and Mac OS X. It has also included support for Cairo since the release of GTK+ 2.8.

GdkPixbuf

GdkPixbuf is a small library that provides client-side image manipulation functions. It was created as a replacement for the GNOME Imaging Model (Imlib). Images can be loaded from files or image data can be fed directly into the library functions. We will use this library when adding images to tree views and when creating new GtkImage widgets in later chapters.

One advantage of GdkPixbuf images is that images can be reference-counted. This means that a GdkPixbuf image can be displayed in multiple locations, while only being stored in memory once. It will only be destroyed when all reference counts are decremented.

The GdkPixbuf library takes advantage of Libart, a 2-D drawing library distributed with GNOME, to apply transformations to images. Because of this, you can shear, scale, and rotate images to your heart's delight. The images are then rendered using the GdkRGB library and drawable areas. By using such a wide variety of specialized tools, GdkPixbuf can provide image rendering of a very high class.

GdkPixbuf, while it is a small library, provides a wide variety of functions for manipulating and displaying images. The library will be put to only the most basic of uses throughout this book. For more information on advanced GdkPixbuf topics, you should reference its API documentation.

Pango

While GDK handles rendering images and windows, Pango controls text and font output in conjunction with Cairo or Xft, depending on your GTK+ version. It can also render directly to an in-memory buffer without the use of any secondary libraries.

■Note Pango originated from the Greek word pan, which means "all," and the Japanese word go, which means "language." It was chosen because one of the design goals of Pango is to support all languages by creating a fully internationalized font-rendering system.

On Linux, Pango uses the FreeType and fontconfig libraries for client-side fonts. The thing that makes Pango stand out from the crowd is that it supports a vast array of languages. Virtually all of the world's major scripts are supported, which makes rendering internationalized text a nonissue in your applications.

All text within Pango is represented internally with UTF-8 encoding. UTF-8 is used because it is compatible with 8-bit software, which is prevalent on UNIX platforms. Offsets in UTF-8 are calculated based on characters, not bits, because each character can take up more than one byte. This will be important in Chapter 7 when you learn how to use the `GtkTextView` widget, because you will have to step by character offset, which may not always be one byte.

Pango supports a wide variety of text attributes. These include but are not limited to language, font family, style, weight, stretch, size, foreground color, background color, underline, strikethrough, rise, shape, and scale. Many of these attributes support multiple options themselves.

For convenience, the Pango Text Markup Language provides a simple set of tags that represent the text attributes in a form similar to HTML. With this markup language, you can easily change the font styles for arbitrary parts of text in a widget. This is especially useful when creating user interfaces with Glade User Interface Builder, because you can type tags directly into a widget's textual content field.

We will utilize Pango for many examples in later chapters when we need to change the font of a widget to something other than the user's default. Using the `PangoFontDescription` object or the Pango Text Markup Language can do this.

ATK

When designing an application, it is important to take into consideration the disabilities that some of your users may have. Therefore, the Accessibility Toolkit (ATK) provides all GTK+ widgets with a built-in method of handling accessibility issues.

Some examples of things ATK adds support for are screen readers and high-contrast visual themes for people who are visually impaired and keyboard behavior modifiers, such as sticky keys, for those with diminished motor control.

Although this is an important part of designing an application for production use, this book will not cover ATK. You need to learn how to use GTK+ widgets and how to create your own custom widgets before you can use ATK. Therefore, I will focus on GTK+ and other essentials for the remainder of this book.

It is important that you keep accessibility in the back of your mind and revisit the library when you are ready to deal with ATK in your own applications.

Language Bindings

GTK+, in its original form, can be used with the C programming language, but bindings have been created for many others. The most popular language bindings are in the following list, although a full list is available at www.gtk.org/bindings.html:

- Gtkmm is the official set of C++ bindings. You can use GTK+ with C++ because of backward compatibility, but Gtkmm provides all of the GTK+ features in a series of classes, the style of which will be familiar to all C++ programmers. The sources for Gtkmm, GLibmm, Libglademm, and other dependencies are available at www.gtkmm.org.

- PyGTK, available at www.pygtk.org, provides Python bindings for the GTK+ libraries. The advantage of using PyGTK is that it takes care of memory management and type casting for you. This alleviates problems that can plague programmers using other language bindings.

- Gtk2-perl, available at http://gtk2-perl.sf.net, provides all of the GTK+ libraries in an object-oriented Perl toolkit. Each of the libraries is split into modules called Glib, Gtk2, and Gtk2::GladeXML. Like most GTK+ bindings for scripting languages, memory management is handled by the language's facilities.

- PHP-GTK allows for handling PHP language bindings for GTK+. The PHP bindings allow you to create client-side cross-platform GUI applications. PHP-GTK is available at http://gtk.php.net. This topic is also covered in the Apress book *Pro PHP-GTK*, authored by Scott Mattocks (Berkeley, 2006).

- Java-Gnome, much like Gtkmm, provides a true object-oriented platform for the GTK+ libraries. Available at http://java-gnome.sf.net, it provides all of the essential libraries for developing GTK+ applications in Java.

- Gtk# provides GTK+ bindings for C# applications on a wide variety of operating systems. It is provided by the Mono Project at www.mono-project.com.

Installing GTK+

Before you can begin programming, you must install GTK+ and its dependencies on your system. This section covers installing GTK+ on Linux and other UNIX-like operating systems.

It is important to note, if you are using a Linux distribution with a package manager including Ubuntu, Debian, Fedora Core, or one of many others, you should install the precompiled binaries provided. You will need the GTK+ 2 libraries, pkg-config, and their dependencies.

The development packages of GTK+ and each of its dependencies are also required. In Debian and Debian-based distributions, these packages will end in -dev. In Fedora Core and other distributions that use the RedHat Package Manager (RPM), they will end in -devel. If you install the development package of GTK+, most modern package managers will take care of all of the necessary dependencies automatically. You should reference your Linux distribution's documentation for more information on installing distributed packages.

If you are going to install GTK+ and its dependencies from the source archives, the rest of this section is for you. GTK+ uses the standard GNU tools for compiling: autoconf is used for configuration and dealing with portability issues, automake for building makefiles, libtool for building shared libraries, and make for compiling and installing binaries.

The most recent GTK+ sources can be found at `www.gtk.org/download`. You will need to download the latest versions of ATK, GLib, GTK+, and Pango. You will also need Cairo, JPEG, libpng, pkg-config, and tiff from the dependencies directory.

If you are using an older version of Linux, you will need to install libiconv. Most systems already have this package, so it is safe to continue without it and install the library in the future if you run into any problems. You may also need to install libintl, fontconfig, and FreeType, although these are packages provided as standard on most modern Linux distributions.

You should also note that these packages *must* be installed in a precise order for the following procedure to work. After installing all of the packages from the dependencies directory on the GTK+ FTP site, you will need to install GLib, Pango, ATK, and GTK+ in that specific order.

The following procedure should be used on each source package, one at a time. Each library must be successfully installed before continuing on to the next, or the procedure will not work.

You are now ready to install GTK+, so let's begin. Once you have downloaded a package from the GTK+ FTP site, you can use one of the following commands to extract the file, depending on the type of archive you downloaded.

```
tar -xvzf package-name.tar.gz
tar -xvjf package-name.tar.bz2
```

By moving into the directory of the extracted archive, you will see a shell script called `configure`. This script will recursively parse through each of the directories in the source distribution and create template makefiles that are customized for your operating system. Each template file will be named `Makefile.in`. The following is a sample configure command that you can use:

```
./configure --prefix=/usr
```

The configure script can be passed a number of options. By using --prefix=/usr, the preceding example tells make to install the package with /usr as the root directory. There are many other options that can be passed to the GTK+ configure script.

Table 1-2 shows a short list of parameters that can be passed specifically to the GTK+ configure. You can use ./configure --help to view a full list of parameters for any package.

Table 1-2. *GTK+ Configuration Options*

Option	Description
--enable-debug	If you set this to no, debugging and asserts are disabled. Setting it to yes enables runtime debugging. The default is minimum, which disables only cast checks.
--enable-shm	Turns on shared memory if available; disable it with --disable-shm.
--enable-xkb	Supports X Window System keyboard extension; disable it with --disable-xkb.
--disable-rebuilds	Disables all source autogeneration rules; enable it with --enable-rebuilds.
--enable-visibility	Uses ELF visibility attributes; disable it with --disable-visibility.
--with-xinput	Use yes to support XInput extension in your application or no to disable it.
--with-gdktarget=	Selects a non-default GDK target. Options for this parameter are x11, linux-fb, win32, quartz, and directfb.
--disable-shadowfb	Disable support for shadowfb in linux-fb or enable it with --enable-shadowfb.
--enable-fbmanager	Enable frame buffer manager support through GtkFB.
--disable-modules	This indicates that all image file format loaders for GdkPixbuf should be built statically into the GTK+ library. You can build them as shared libraries with --enable-modules.
--with-included-loaders	This allows you to specify which image loaders to include such as PNG and JPEG.

After configuring a package, you can build and install it using the following set of commands; it is important to note that make install and ldconfig need to be run as the root user:

```
make
make install
ldconfig
```

The ldconfig command is not necessary on all systems, but you should run it to be on the safe side. It will make sure your system recognizes the libraries you installed before compiling the next package.

Exercise 1-1. Verifying Your Install

If you install the GTK+ libraries from the source packages, you are provided with a simple way to verify a successful install. To do this, you have to run the gtk-demo application installed in /usr/bin. Run the following command from a terminal or by double-clicking the executable file:

```
/usr/bin/gtk-demo
```

If your install was successful, you will be presented with a window with the title "GTK+ Code Demos". In that window, you can view information and source code for each of the widgets listed. This also gives you a good opportunity to sample many of the widgets that you will be learning about.

If you run into any problems launching the application, pay close attention to the errors shown in your terminal. They will give you a good idea of which library is causing the problem.

Once you have all of the GTK+ libraries and their dependencies installed, you are ready to continue on to the next chapter, which begins with a simple example showing the most basic elements required by every GTK+ application.

Summary

In this chapter, you learned the history of the GTK+ libraries and the X Window System and for what each can be used.

You were then introduced to GTK+ as a graphical widget library as well as its supporting libraries. These libraries include the following:

- GLib is a general-purpose utility library that is used to implement many useful non-graphical features including data types, file management, pipes, threads, and more.

- The GLib Object System (GObject) implements the object-oriented GType system. It also provides signal and property systems.

- The GIMP Drawing Kit (GDK) is a computer graphics library originally designed for the X Window System that wraps around low-level drawing and window functions.

- GdkPixbuf is a small library that provides client-side image manipulation functions. It was created as a replacement for Imlib.

- Pango is used for font rendering. It uses UTF-8 encoding, so it is able to support all forms of internationalized text.

- The Accessibility Toolkit (ATK) provides all GTK+ widgets with a built-in method of handling accessibility.

The last two sections of the chapter showed you all of the available language bindings that implement GTK+ in other programming languages and how to install the GTK+ libraries. Language bindings are possible because of the way GObject was originally designed.

In Chapter 2, you will be introduced to the widget hierarchy system as well as window, label, and button widgets. You will learn how to use these widgets in basic GTK+ applications.

CHAPTER 2

■■■

Your First GTK+ Applications

In Chapter 1, you were given an overview of the things available to you in the GTK+ libraries as a graphical application developer. In this chapter, you'll learn how to write your own GTK+ applications.

While we will begin with simple examples, there are many important concepts presented in this chapter. We will cover the topics that every other GTK+ application you write will rely on. Therefore, as with any chapter, make sure you understand the concepts presented to you in the next few pages before continuing on.

In this chapter, you will learn the following:

- The basic function calls required by all GTK+ applications

- How to compile GTK+ code with GCC

- The object-oriented nature of the GTK+ widget system

- What role signals, callbacks, and events play in your applications

- How to alter textual styles with the Pango Text Markup Language

- Various other useful functions provided for the widgets presented in this chapter

- How to use the GtkButton widget to make a clickable GtkLabel

- How to get and set properties of objects using GObject methods

Hello World

Every programming book I have read in my lifetime has begun with a "Hello World" example application. I do not want to be the one to break with tradition.

Before we get to the example, you should know that all of the source code for every example is downloadable from this book's web site, found at www.gtkbook.com. You can compile each example with the method presented in a later section of this chapter or follow the instructions found in the base folder of the package.

Listing 2-1 is the first and most simple GTK+ application in this book. It initializes GTK+, creates a window, displays it to the user, and waits for the program to be terminated. It is very basic, but it shows the essential code that every GTK+ application you create must have!

■**Note** The application in Listing 2-1 does not provide a way for you to terminate it. If you click the X in the corner of the window, the window will close, but the application will remain running. Therefore, you will have to press Ctrl+C in your terminal window to force the application to exit!

Listing 2-1. *Greeting the World (helloworld.c)*

```
#include <gtk/gtk.h>

int main (int argc,
          char *argv[])
{
  GtkWidget *window;

  /* Initialize GTK+ and all of its supporting libraries. */
  gtk_init (&argc, &argv);

  /* Create a new window, give it a title and display it to the user. */
  window = gtk_window_new (GTK_WINDOW_TOPLEVEL);
  gtk_window_set_title (GTK_WINDOW (window), "Hello World");
  gtk_widget_show (window);

  /* Hand control over to the main loop. */
  gtk_main ();
  return 0;
}
```

The <gtk/gtk.h> file includes all of the widgets, variables, functions, and structures available in GTK+ as well as header files from other libraries that GTK+ depends on, such as <glib/glib.h> and <gdk/gdk.h>. In most of your applications, <gtk/gtk.h> will be the only GTK+ header file you will need to include for GTK+ development, although some more advanced applications may require further inclusions.

Listing 2-1 is one of the simplest applications that you can create with GTK+. It produces a top-level GtkWindow widget with a default width and height of 200 pixels. There is no way of exiting the application except to kill it in the terminal where it was launched. You will learn how to use signals to exit the application when necessary in the next example.

This example is rather simple, but it shows the bare essentials you will need for every GTK+ application you create. The first step in understanding the "Hello World" application is to look at the content of the main() function.

Initializing GTK+

Initializing the GTK+ libraries is extremely simple for most applications. By calling gtk_init(), all initialization work is automatically performed for you.

It begins by setting up the GTK+ environment, including obtaining the GDK display and preparing the GLib main event loop and basic signal handling. If gtk_init() does more than you need, you may create your own, small initialization function that calls fewer of the functions, such as gdk_init() and g_main_loop_new(), although this is not necessary for most applications.

One of the great benefits of using open source libraries is the ability to read the code yourself to see how things are done. You can easily view the GTK+ source code to figure out everything that is called by gtk_init() and choose what needs to be performed by your application. However, you should use gtk_init() for now until you learn more about how each of the libraries are used and how they interrelate.

You will also notice that we passed the standard main() argument parameters argc and argv to gtk_init(). The GTK+ initialization function parses through all of the arguments and strips out any it recognizes. Any parameters it uses will be removed from the list, so you should do any argument parsing of your own after calling gtk_init(). This means that a standard list of parameters can be passed and parsed by all GTK+ applications without any extra work performed by you, the developer.

It is important to call gtk_init() before any other function calls to the GTK+ libraries. Otherwise, your application will not function properly and will likely crash.

The gtk_init() function will terminate your application if it is unable to initialize the GUI or has any other significant problems that cannot be resolved. If you would like your application to fall back on a text interface when GUI initialization fails, you need to use gtk_init_check().

```
gboolean gtk_init_check (int *argc,
                         char ***argv);
```

If the initialization fails, FALSE is returned. Otherwise, gtk_init_check() will return TRUE. You should only use this function if you have a textual interface to fall back on!

Widget Hierarchy

I consider widget hierarchy one of the most important topics of discussion when learning GTK+. While it is not difficult to understand, without it, widgets would not be possible as they exist today.

To understand this topic, we will look at gtk_window_new(), the function used to create a new GtkWindow object. You will notice in the following line that, while we want to create a new GtkWindow, gtk_window_new() returns a pointer to a GtkWidget. This is because every widget in GTK+ is actually a GtkWidget itself.

```
GtkWidget* gtk_window_new (GtkWindowType type);
```

Widgets in GTK+ use the GObject hierarchy system, which allows you to derive new widgets from those that already exist. Child widgets inherit properties, functions, and signals from their parent, their grandparent, and so on, because they are actually implementations of their ancestors themselves.

Widget hierarchy in GTK+ is a singly inherited system, which means that each child can have only one direct parent. This creates a simple linear relationship that every widget implements. You will learn how to derive your own child widgets in Chapter 11. Until then, we will use widget hierarchy to take advantage of inherited methods and properties.

In Figure 2-2, a simple outline of the widget hierarchy of the GtkWindow class is illustrated.

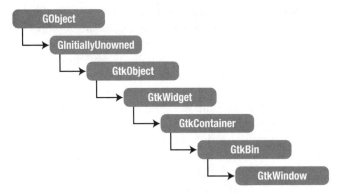

Figure 2-1. *The widget hierarchy of GtkWindow*

Figure 2-1 may look daunting at first, but let's look at each class type one at a time to make things easier to understand:

- GObject is the fundamental type providing common attributes for all libraries based on it including GTK+ and Pango. It allows objects derived from it to be constructed, destroyed, referenced, and unreferenced. It also provides the signal system and object property functions. You can cast an object as a GObject with G_OBJECT(). If you try to cast an object with G_OBJECT() that is not a GObject or derived from it, GLib will throw a critical error, and the cast will fail. This will occur with any other GTK+ casting function.

- GInitiallyUnowned should never be accessed by the programmer, since all of its members are private. It exists so that references can be floating. A floating reference is one that is not owned by anyone.

- GtkObject is the base class for all GTK+ objects. It was replaced as the absolute base class of all objects in GTK+ 2.0, but GtkObject was kept for backward compatibility of nonwidget classes like GtkAdjustment. You can cast an object as a GtkObject with GTK_OBJECT().

- GtkWidget is an abstract base class for all GTK+ widgets. It introduces style properties and standard functions that are needed by all widgets. The standard practice is to store all widgets as a GtkWidget, which can be seen in Listing 2-1. Therefore, you will rarely need to use GTK_WIDGET() to cast an object.

- GtkContainer is an abstract class that is used to contain one or more widgets. It is an extremely important structure, since you could not add any other widgets to a window without it. Therefore, the whole of Chapter 3 is dedicated to widgets derived from this class. You can cast an object as a GtkContainer with GTK_CONTAINER().

- GtkBin is another abstract class that allows a widget to contain only one child. It allows multiple widgets to have this functionality without the need for reproduction of code. You can cast an object as a GtkBin with GTK_BIN().

- GtkWindow is the standard window object you saw in Listing 2-1. You can use GTK_WINDOW() to cast an object.

Every widget in this book will use a similar widget hierarchy. It is useful to have the API documentation handy, so you can reference the hierarchy of the widgets you are using. The API documentation is available at www.gtk.org/api, if you did not install it along with the libraries.

For now, it is enough to know how to cast objects and what the basic abstract types are used for. In Chapter 11, you will learn how to create your own widgets. At that point, we will delve further into the workings of the GObject system.

GTK+ Windows

The code in Listing 2-1 creates a GtkWindow object that is set to the default width and height of 200 pixels. This default size was chosen because a window with a width and height of 0 pixels cannot be resized. You should note that the title bar and window border are included in the total size, so the working area of the window is smaller than 200 pixels by 200 pixels.

We passed GTK_WINDOW_TOPLEVEL to gtk_window_new(). This tells GTK+ to create a new top-level window. Top-level windows use window manager decorations, have a border frame, and allow themselves to be placed by the window manager. This means that you do *not* have absolute control over your window position and should not assume that you do.

```
GtkWidget *window = gtk_window_new (GTK_WINDOW_TOPLEVEL);
```

It is important to make the distinction between what GTK+ controls and what the window manager controls. You are able to make recommendations and requests for the size and placement of top-level widgets. However, the window manager has ultimate control of these features.

Conversely, you can use GTK_WINDOW_POPUP to create a pop-up window, although its name is somewhat misleading in GTK+. Pop-up windows are used for things that are not normally thought of as windows, such as tooltips and menus.

Pop-up windows are ignored by the window manager, and therefore, they have no decorations or border frame. There is no way to minimize or maximize a pop-up window, because the window manager does not know about them. Resize grips are not shown, and default key bindings will not work.

GTK_WINDOW_TOPLEVEL and GTK_WINDOW_POPUP are the only two elements available in the GtkWindowType enumeration. In most cases, you will want to use GTK_WINDOW_TOPLEVEL, unless there is a compelling reason not to.

■**Note** You should not use GTK_WINDOW_POPUP if you only want window manager decorations turned off for the window. Instead, use gtk_window_set_decorated (GtkWindow *window, gboolean show) to turn off window decorations.

The following function requests the title bar and taskbar to display "Hello World!" as the title of the window. Since gtk_window_set_title() requires a GtkWindow object as it's the first parameter, we must cast our window using the GTK_WINDOW() function.

```
void gtk_window_set_title (GtkWindow *window,
                           const gchar *title);
```

The second parameter of gtk_window_set_title() is the title that will be displayed by the window. It uses GLib's implementation of char, which is called gchar. When you see a parameter listed as gchar*, it will also accept const char*, because gchar* is defined as a typedef of the standard C string object.

The last function of interest in this section is gtk_widget_show(), which tells GTK+ to set the specified widget as visible. The widget may not be immediately shown when you call gtk_widget_show(), because GTK+ queues the widget until all preprocessing is complete before it is drawn onto the screen.

It is important to note that gtk_widget_show() will only show the widget it is called on. If the widget has children that are not already set as visible, they will not be drawn on the screen. Furthermore, if the widget's parent is not visible, it will not be drawn on the screen. Instead, it will be queued until its parent is set as visible as well.

In addition to showing a widget, it is also possible to use gtk_widget_hide() to hide a widget from the user's view.

```
void gtk_widget_hide (GtkWidget *widget);
```

This will hide all child widgets from view, but you should be careful. This function only sets the specified widget as hidden. If you show the widget at a later time, its children will be visible as well, since they were never marked as hidden. This will become an important distinction to make when you learn how to show and hide multiple widgets at once.

The Main Loop Function

After all initialization is complete and necessary signals are connected in a GTK+ application, there will come a time when you want to let the GTK+ main loop take control and start processing events. To do this, you will call gtk_main(), which will continue to run until you call gtk_main_quit() or the application terminates. This should be the last GTK+ function called in main().

After you call gtk_main(), it is not possible to regain control of the program until a callback function is initialized. In GTK+, signals and callback functions are triggered by user actions such as button clicks, asynchronous input-output events, programmable timeouts, and others. We will start exploring signals, events, and callback functions in the next example.

■**Note** It is also possible to create functions that are called at a specified interval of time; these are referred to as timeouts. Another type of callback function, referred to as an idle function, is called when the operating system is not busy processing other tasks. Both of these features are a part of GLib and will be explored in detail in Chapter 6.

Other than those few situations, control of the application is managed by signals, timeout functions, and various other callback functions once `gtk_main()` is called. Later in this chapter, you will see how to use signals and callbacks in your own applications.

Using GCC and pkg-config to Compile

Now that you understand how Listing 2-1 works, it is time to compile the code into an executable. To do this, you run the following command from a terminal:

```
gcc -Wall -g helloworld.c -o helloworld `pkg-config --cflags gtk+-2.0` \
     `pkg-config --libs gtk+-2.0`
```

This command can be used for all of the examples in this book except those in Chapter 10, which will require libglade as well. I decided to use the GCC compiler, because it is the standard C compiler on Linux, but most C and C++ compilers will work. To use another compiler, you will need to reference its documentation.

The previous compile command is parsed with multiple provided options. The -Wall option enables all types of compiler warnings. While this may not always be desirable, it can help you detect simple programming errors as you begin programming with GTK+. Debugging is enabled with -g, so that you will be able to use your compiled application with GDB or your debugger of choice.

The next set of commands, `helloworld.c -o helloworld`, compiles the specified file and outputs it to an executable file named `helloworld`. One or many source files may be specified for compilation by GCC.

■**Caution** The single, slanted quotation mark used in the compile command is a backquote, which is found on the key in the top-left corner of most keyboards. This tells your terminal that the command between the quotes should be run and replaced by the output before the rest of the line is executed.

In addition to the GCC compiler, you need to use the pkg-config application, which returns a list of specified libraries or paths.

The first instance, `pkg-config --cflags gtk+-2.0`, returns directory names to the compiler's include path. This will make sure that the GTK+ header files are available to the compiler. Try running `pkg-config --cflags gtk+-2.0` in your terminal to see an example of what is being output to the compiler.

The second call, `pkg-config --libs gtk+-2.0`, appends options to the command line used by the linker including library directory path extensions and a list of libraries needed for linking to the executable. The libraries that are returned in a standard Linux environment follow:

- GTK+ (`-lgtk`): Graphical widgets

- GDK (`-lgdk`): The standard graphics rendering library

- GdkPixbuf (`-lgdk_pixbuf`): Client-side image manipulation

- Pango (`-lpango`): Font rendering and output

- GObject (`-lgobject`): Object-oriented type system

- GModule (`-lgmodule`): Dynamically loading libraries

- GLib (`-lglib`): Data types and utility functions

- Xlib (`-lX11`): X Window System protocol library

- Xext (`-lXext`): X extensions library routines

- GNU math library (`-lm`): The GNU library from which GTK+ uses many routines

As you can see, pkg-config provides a convenient way for you to avoid hard-coding a long list of includes and libraries manually every time you compile a GTK+ application.

Listing 2-1 is one of the simplest applications that you can create with GTK+. It produces a top-level `GtkWindow` widget with a default width and height of 200 pixels, as displayed in Figure 2-2.

Figure 2-2. *The Hello World window at the default size*

Even though the window includes the standard X on the right side of the title bar, you'll notice that clicking that X will only cause the window to disappear. The application continues to wait for events, and control will not be returned to the launching terminal until you press Ctrl+C. You will learn how to implement a shutdown callback with signals in the next example.

Extending "Hello World"

Every GTK+ application you write requires the function calls shown in Listing 2-1, but the example on its own is clearly not exceptionally useful. Now that you understand how to get started, it is time for us to say "hello" to the world in a more useful manner.

Listing 2-2 expands upon our "Hello World" application in two ways. First, it connects callback functions to window signals, so the application can terminate itself. Secondly, this example introduces the GtkContainer structure, which allows a widget to contain one or more other widgets.

Listing 2-2. *Greeting the World Again (helloworld2.c)*

```
#include <gtk/gtk.h>

static void destroy (GtkWidget*, gpointer);
static gboolean delete_event (GtkWidget*, GdkEvent*, gpointer);

int main (int argc,
          char *argv[])
{
  GtkWidget *window, *label;

  gtk_init (&argc, &argv);

  window = gtk_window_new (GTK_WINDOW_TOPLEVEL);
  gtk_window_set_title (GTK_WINDOW (window), "Hello World!");
  gtk_container_set_border_width (GTK_CONTAINER (window), 10);
  gtk_widget_set_size_request (window, 200, 100);

  /* Connect the main window to the destroy and delete-event signals. */
  g_signal_connect (G_OBJECT (window), "destroy",
                    G_CALLBACK (destroy), NULL);
  g_signal_connect (G_OBJECT (window), "delete_event",
                    G_CALLBACK (delete_event), NULL);

  /* Create a new GtkLabel widget that is selectable. */
  label = gtk_label_new ("Hello World");
  gtk_label_set_selectable (GTK_LABEL (label), TRUE);

  /* Add the label as a child widget of the window. */
  gtk_container_add (GTK_CONTAINER (window), label);
  gtk_widget_show_all (window);

  gtk_main ();
  return 0;
}
```

```
/* Stop the GTK+ main loop function when the window is destroyed. */
static void
destroy (GtkWidget *window,
         gpointer data)
{
  gtk_main_quit ();
}

/* Return FALSE to destroy the widget. By returning TRUE, you can cancel
 * a delete-event. This can be used to confirm quitting the application. */
static gboolean
delete_event (GtkWidget *window,
              GdkEvent *event,
              gpointer data)
{
    return FALSE;
}
```

In Figure 2-3, you can see a screenshot of Listing 2-2 in action. It shows the GtkLabel contained by a GtkWindow. Let us now take a look at the new features presented by this example.

Figure 2-3. *The extended Hello World window*

The GtkLabel Widget

In Listing 2-2, a new type of widget called GtkLabel was created. As the name implies, GtkLabel widgets are normally used to label other widgets. However, they can also be used for such things as creating large blocks of noneditable, formatted, or wrapped text.

You can create a new label widget by calling gtk_label_new(). Passing NULL to gtk_label_new() is equivalent to passing an empty string. This will cause the label to be displayed without any text.

```
GtkWidget* gtk_label_new (const gchar *str);
```

It is not possible for users to edit a normal GtkLabel with the keyboard or mouse (without some extra work by the programmer, that is), but by using gtk_label_set_selectable(), the user will be able to select and copy the text. The widget will also be able to accept cursor focus, so you can use the Tab key to move between the label and other widgets.

```
void gtk_label_set_selectable (GtkLabel *label,
                               gboolean selectable);
```

The ability to select labels is turned off by default, because this feature should only be used when there is a need for the user to retain the information. For example, error messages should be set as selectable, so they can easily be copied into other applications such as a web browser.

The text in a GtkLabel does not have to remain in the same state as the text string you specified during creation. You can easily change it with gtk_label_set_text(). Any text currently contained by the label will be overwritten as well as any mnemonics.

```
void gtk_label_set_text (GtkLabel *label,
                         const gchar *str);
```

■**Note** A mnemonic is a combination of keys that, when pressed by the user, will perform some type of action. It is possible to add a mnemonic to a GtkLabel that will activate a designated widget when pressed.

The string currently being displayed by the label can be retrieved with gtk_label_get_text(). The returned string will not include any markup or mnemonic information. The label also uses it internally, so you should never modify the returned string!

The last GtkLabel method you should know about is gtk_label_set_markup(), which allows you to define custom styles for the displayed text. There are a number of tags provided by the Pango Text Markup Language, which can be found in Appendix C in the back of this book.

```
void gtk_label_set_markup (GtkLabel *label,
                           const gchar *str);
```

The Pango Text Markup Language provides two types of style methods. You can use the <span> tag with some attributes such as the font type, size, weight, foreground color, and others. It also provides various other tags such as <b>, <tt>, and <i>, which make the enclosed text bold, monospace, or italic.

Container Widgets and Layout

Recall from the first example in this chapter that the GtkWindow structure is derived indirectly from GtkContainer. This indicates that GtkWindow is a GtkContainer and inherits all of the GtkContainer functions, signals, and properties.

By using gtk_container_add(), you can add a widget as the child of the container. It follows that the container is now the widget's parent. The language popularly used to describe this container and contained relationship is "parent and child," where the parent is the containing widget, and the child is contained in the parent.

```
void gtk_container_add (GtkContainer *container,
                        GtkWidget *child);
```

This language unfortunately often causes confusion, because GTK+ is object oriented in every sense. Because of this, when using and talking about GTK+, one must be aware of the context in which "parent" and "child" is used. They are used to talk about both container widget relationships and about widget derivation relationships.

The purpose of the GtkContainer class is to allow a parent widget to contain one or more children. GtkWindow is derived from a type of container called GtkBin. GtkBin allows the parent to contain only one child. Windows, as containers, are therefore limited to directly containing a single child. Fortunately, that single child may be a more complex container widget itself, which, in turn, may contain more than one child widget.

It is important to notice that our window is no longer the default 200 by 200 pixels in size and that the square aspect ratio is not retained. This is because GTK+ uses, primarily, an automatic and dynamically sized layout system. This dynamic sizing is the reason behind the existence of container objects. The sizing system will be discussed in more detail in the next chapter, which covers container widgets.

Because our window is a GtkContainer, we can also use the function gtk_container_set_border_width() to place a 10-pixel border around the inside edge of the window. The border is set on all four sides of the child widget.

```
void gtk_container_set_border_width (GtkContainer *container,
                                     guint border_width);
```

Without adding the border, the layout manager would allow the window to shrink to the default size of the GtkLabel widget. In Listing 2-1, the window is set to a width of 200 pixels and a height of 100 pixels. With this size, there will be more than a 10-pixel border around the label on most systems. The border will prevent the user from resizing the window to a smaller size than allocated by the widget and the border.

We then call gtk_widget_show_all() on the window. This function recursively draws the window, its children, its children's children and so on. Without this function, you would have to call gtk_widget_show() on every single child widget. Instead, by using gtk_widget_show_all(), GTK+ does all of the work for you by showing each widget until they are all visible on the screen.

```
void gtk_widget_show_all (GtkWidget *widget);
```

Like the nonrecursive gtk_widget_show(), if you call this function on a widget whose parent is not set as visible, it will not be shown. The widget will be queued until its parent is set as visible.

GTK+ also provides gtk_widget_hide_all(), which will set the specified widget and all of its children as hidden. Because contained widgets are invisible when their container is hidden, it will appear that gtk_widget_hide(), when called on the containing object, does the same thing as gtk_widget_hide_all(), because both will hide the container and all of its children. However, there is an important difference. Calling gtk_widget_hide() sets the visible property to FALSE on only one widget, while gtk_widget_hide_all() changes that property on the passed widget and recursively on all contained widgets.

```
void gtk_widget_hide_all (GtkWidget *widget);
```

The gtk_widget_show() and gtk_widget_show_all() set of functions have the same relationship. So, if you use gtk_widget_hide_all() but call gtk_widget_show() on the same widget, all of its children will remain invisible.

Container widgets and managing the application layout will be covered in more detail in the next chapter. Since you have enough information to understand the GtkContainer in Listing 2-2, we will continue on to signals and callback functions.

Signals and Callbacks

GTK+ is a system that relies on signals and callback functions. A signal is a notification to your application that the user has performed some action. You can tell GTK+ to run a function when the signal is emitted. These are named callback functions.

■**Caution** GTK+ signals are not the same thing as POSIX signals! Signals in GTK+ are propagated by events from the X Window System. Each provides separate methods, and these two signal types should not be used interchangeably.

After you initialize your user interface, control is given to the gtk_main() function, which sleeps until a signal is emitted. At this point, control is passed to other functions called callback functions.

You, as the programmer, connect signals to their callback functions before calling gtk_main(). The callback function will be called when the action has occurred and the signal is emitted or when you have explicitly emitted the signal. You also have the capability of stopping signals from being emitted at all.

■**Note** It is possible to connect signals at any point within your applications. For example, new signals can be connected within callback functions. However, you should try to initialize mission-critical callbacks before calling gtk_main().

There are many types of signals, and just like functions, they are inherited from parent structures. Many signals are generic to all widgets such as hide and grab-focus or specific to the widget such as the GtkRadioButton signal group-changed. In either case, widgets derived from a class can use all of the signals available to all of its ancestors.

Connecting the Signal

The first instance of a signal you have encountered was in Listing 2-2. The GtkWindow was connected to the destroy() callback function. This function will be called when the destroy signal is emitted.

```
g_signal_connect (G_OBJECT (window), "destroy",
                  G_CALLBACK (destroy), NULL);
```

GTK+ emits the destroy signal when gtk_widget_destroy() is called on the widget or when FALSE is returned from a delete_event() callback function. If you reference the API documentation, you will see that the destroy signal belongs to the GtkObject class. This means that every class in GTK+ inherits the signal, and you can be notified of the destruction of any GTK+ structure.

There are four parameters to every g_signal_connect() call. The first is the widget that is to be monitored for the signal. Next, you specify the name of the signal you want to track. Each widget has many possible signals, all of which can be found in the API documentation. Remember that widgets are free to use the signals of their ancestors, since each widget is actually an implementation of each of its ancestors. You can use the "Object Hierarchy" section of the API to reference parent classes.

```
gulong g_signal_connect (gpointer object,
                         const gchar *signal_name,
                         GCallback handler,
                         gpointer data);
```

When typing the signal name, the underscore and dash characters are interchangeable. They will be parsed as the same character, so it does not make any difference which one you choose. I will use the underscore character for all of the examples in this book.

The third parameter in g_signal_connect() is the callback function that will be called when the signal is emitted, cast with G_CALLBACK(). The format of the callback function depends on the function prototype requirements of each specific signal. An example callback function is shown in the next section.

The last parameter in g_signal_connect() allows you to send a pointer to the callback function. In Listing 2-2, we passed NULL, so the pointer was void, but let us assume for a moment that we wanted to pass the GtkLabel to the callback function.

In this instance of g_signal_connect(), the GtkLabel was cast as a gpointer, which will be passed to the callback function. A gpointer is simply a type definition of a void pointer. You can recast this in the callback function, but g_signal_connect() requires a gpointer type.

```
g_signal_connect (G_OBJECT (window), "destroy",
                  G_CALLBACK (destroy),
                  (gpointer) label);
```

The return value for g_signal_connect() is the handler identifier of the signal. You can use this with g_signal_handler_block(), g_signal_hander_unblock(), and g_signal_handler_disconnect(). These functions will stop a callback function from being called, re-enable the callback function, and remove the signal handler from memory, respectively. More information can be found in the API documentation.

Callback Functions

Callback functions specified in g_signal_connect() will be called when the signal is emitted on the widget to which it was connected. For all signals, with the exception of events, which will be covered in the next section, callback functions are in the following form.

```
static void
callback_function (GtkWidget *widget,
                   ... /* Other Possible Arguments */ ...,
                   gpointer data);
```

You can find an example format of a callback function for each signal in the API documentation, but this is the generic format. The first parameter is the object from g_signal_connect(), except it must always be cast as the widget type for which the signal was created. If you need access to a widget type from which the widget was derived, you can use the built-in casting functions.

There are other possible arguments that may appear in the middle as well, although this is not always the case. For these parameters, you need to reference the documentation of the signal you are utilizing.

The last parameter of your callback function corresponds to the last parameter of g_signal_connect(). Since the data is passed as a void pointer, you can place the data type you want it cast to as the last parameter of the callback function. Let us assume that you passed a GtkLabel to the fourth parameter of g_signal_connect().

```
static void
destroy (GtkWidget *window,
         GtkLabel *label)
```

In this example, we were sure that the object was of the type GtkLabel, so we used GtkLabel as the last parameter of the callback function. This will avoid having to recast the object from a gpointer to the desired data type.

In Chapter 11, you will be covering how to create your own signals when you are taught how to create custom widgets.

Emitting and Stopping Signals

Before we move onto events, there are two interesting functions that you should know about that relate to signals. By using g_signal_emit_by_name(), you can emit a signal on an object by using its textual name. You can use the signal identifier to emit a signal as well, but it is much more likely that you will have access to the signal's name. If you have the signal identifier, you can emit the signal with g_signal_emit().

```
void g_signal_emit_by_name (gpointer instance,
                            const gchar *signal_name,
                            ...);
```

The last parameters of g_signal_emit_by_name() are a list of parameters that should be passed to the signal and the location to store the return value. The return value can safely be ignored if it is a void function.

You can also use g_signal_stop_emission_by_name() to stop the current emission of a signal. This allows you to temporarily disable a signal that will be emitting because of some action performed by your code.

```
void g_signal_stop_emission_by_name (gpointer instance,
                                     const gchar *signal_name);
```

Events

Events are special types of signals that are emitted by the X Window System. They are initially emitted by the X Window System and then sent from the window manager to your application to be interpreted by the signal system provided by GLib. For example, the destroy signal is emitted on the widget, but the delete-event event is first recognized by the underlying GdkWindow of the widget and then emitted as a signal of the widget.

The first instance of an event you encountered was delete-event in Listing 2-2. The delete-event signal is emitted when the user tries to close the window. The window can be exited by clicking the close button on the title bar, using the close pop-up menu item in the taskbar, or by any other means provided by the window manager.

Connecting events to a callback function is done in the same manner with g_signal_connect() as with other GTK+ signals. However, your callback function will be set up slightly differently.

```
static gboolean
callback_function (GtkWidget *widget,
                   GdkEvent *event,
                   gpointer data);
```

The first difference in the callback function is the gboolean return value. If TRUE is returned from an event callback, GTK+ assumes the event has already been handled and will not continue. By returning FALSE, you are telling GTK+ to continue handling the event. FALSE is the default return value for the function, so you do not need to use the delete-event signal in most cases. This is only useful if you want to override the default signal handler.

For example, in many applications, you may want to confirm the exit of the program. By using the following code, you can prevent the application from exiting if the user does not want to quit.

```
static gboolean
delete_event (GtkWidget *window,
              GdkEvent *event,
              gpointer data)
{
  gboolean answer = /* Ask the user if exiting is desired. */

  if (answer)
    return FALSE;
  else
    return TRUE;
}
```

By returning FALSE from the delete-event callback function, gtk_widget_destroy() is automatically called on the widget. As stated before, this signal will automatically continue with the action, so there is no need to connect to it unless you want to override the default.

In addition, the callback function includes the GdkEvent parameter. GdkEvent is a C union of the GdkEventType enumeration and all of the available event structures. Let's first look at the GdkEventType enumeration.

Event Types

The GdkEventType enumeration provides a list of available event types. These can be used to determine the type of event that has occurred, since you may not always know what has happened.

For example, if you connect the button-press-event signal to a widget, there are three differ-ent types of events that can cause the signal's callback function to be run: GDK_BUTTON_PRESS, GDK_2BUTTON_PRESS, and GDK_3BUTTON_PRESS. Double-clicks and triple-clicks emit the GDK_BUTTON_PRESS as a second event as well, so being able to distinguish between different types of events is necessary.

In Appendix B, you can see a complete list of the events available to you. It shows the signal name that is passed to g_signal_connect(), the GdkEventType enumeration value, and a description of the event.

Let's look at the delete-event callback function from Listing 2-2. We already know that delete-event is of the type GDK_DELETE, but let us assume for a moment that we did not know that. We can easily test this by using the following conditional statement:

```
static gboolean
delete_event (GtkWidget *window,
              GdkEvent *event,
              gpointer data)
{
  if (event->type == GDK_DELETE)
    return FALSE;

  return TRUE;
}
```

In this example, if the event type is GDK_DELETE, FALSE is returned, and gtk_widget_destroy() will be called on the widget. Otherwise, TRUE is returned, and no further action is taken.

Using Specific Event Structures

Sometimes, you may already know what type of event has been emitted. In the following exam-ple, we know that a key-press-event will always be emitted:

```
g_signal_connect (G_OBJECT (widget), "key-press-event"
                  G_CALLBACK (key_press), NULL);
```

In this case, it is safe to assume that the type of event will always be GDK_KEY_PRESS, and the callback function can be declared as such.

```
static gboolean
key_press (GtkWidget *widget,
           GdkEventKey *event,
           gpointer data)
```

Since we know that the type of event is a GDK_KEY_PRESS, we will not need access to all of the structures in GdkEvent. We will only have a use for GdkEventKey, which we can use instead of GdkEvent in the callback function. Since the event is already cast as GdkEventKey, we will have direct access to only the elements in that structure.

```
typedef struct
{
  GdkEventType type;            // GDK_KEY_PRESS or GDK_KEY_RELEASE
  GdkWindow *window;            // The window that received the event
  gint8 send_event;             // TRUE if the event used XSendEvent
  guint32 time;                 // The length of the event in milliseconds
  guint state;                  // The state of Control, Shift, and Alt
  guint keyval;                 // The key that was pressed <gdk/gdkkeysyms.h>
  gint length;                  // The length of string
  gchar *string;                // A string approximating the entered text
  guint16 hardware_keycode;     // Raw code of the key that was pressed or released
  guint8 group;                 // The keyboard group
  guint is_modifier : 1;        // Whether hardware_keycode was mapped (since 2.10)
} GdkEventKey;
```

There are many useful properties in the GdkEventKey structure that we will use throughout the book. At some point it would be useful for you to browse some of the GdkEvent structures in the API documentation. We will cover a few of the most important structures in this book, including GdkEventKey and GdkEventButton.

The only variable that is available in all of the event structures is the event type, which defines the type of event that has occurred. It is a good idea to always check the event type to avoid handling it in the wrong way.

Further GTK+ Functions

Before continuing on to further examples, I would like to draw your attention to a few functions that will come in handy in later chapters and when you create your own GTK+ applications.

GtkWidget Functions

The GtkWidget structure contains many useful functions that you can use with any widget. This section outlines a few that you will need in a lot of your applications.

It is possible to destroy a widget by explicitly calling gtk_widget_destroy() on the object. When invoked, gtk_widget_destroy() will drop the reference count on the widget and all of its children recursively. The widget, along with its children, will then be destroyed, and all memory freed.

```
void gtk_widget_destroy (GtkWidget *widget);
```

Generally, this is only called on top-level widgets. It is usually only used to destroy dialog windows and to implement menu items that quit the application. It will be used in the next example in this chapter to quit the application when a button is clicked

You can use gtk_widget_set_size_request() to set the minimum size of a widget. It will force the widget to be either smaller or larger than it would normally be. It will not, however, resize the widget so that it is too small to be functional or able to draw itself on the screen.

```
void gtk_widget_set_size_request (GtkWidget *widget,
                                  gint width,
                                  gint height);
```

By passing -1 to either parameter, you are telling GTK+ to use its natural size, or the size that the widget would normally be allocated to if you do not define a custom size. This can be used if you want to specify either only the height or only the width parameter. It will also allow you to reset the widget to its original size.

There is no way to set a widget with a width or height of less than 1 pixel, but by passing 0 to either parameter, GTK+ will make the widget as small as possible. Again, it will not be resized so small that it's nonfunctional or unable to draw itself.

Because of internationalization, there is a danger by setting the size of any widget. The text may look great on your computer, but on a computer using a German translation of your application, the widget may be too small or large for the text. Themes also present issues with widget sizing, because widgets are defaulted to different sizes depending on the theme. Therefore, it is best to allow GTK+ to choose the size of widgets and windows in most cases.

You can use gtk_widget_grab_focus() to force a widget to grab keyboard focus. This will only work on widgets that can handle keyboard interaction. One example of a use for gtk_widget_grab_focus() is sending the cursor to a text entry when the search toolbar is shown in Firefox. This could also be used to give focus to a GtkLabel that is selectable.

```
void gtk_widget_grab_focus (GtkWidget *widget);
```

Often, you will want to set a widget as inactive. By calling gtk_widget_set_sensitive(), the specified widget and all of its children are disabled or enabled. By setting a widget as inactive, the user will be prevented from interacting with the widget. Most widgets will also be grayed out when set as inactive.

```
void gtk_widget_set_sensitive (GtkWidget *widget,
                               gboolean sensitive);
```

If you want to re-enable a widget and its children, you need only to call this function on the same widget. Children are affected by the sensitivity of their parents, but they only reflect the parent's setting instead of changing their properties.

GtkWindow Functions

You have now seen two examples using the GtkWindow structure. You have learned how to add border padding between the inner edge of the window and its child. You have also learned how to set the title of a window and add a child widget. Now, let us explore a few more functions that will allow you to further customize windows.

All windows are set as resizable by default. This is desirable in most applications, because each user will have different size preferences. However, if there is a specific reason for doing so, you can use gtk_window_set_resizable() to prevent the user from resizing the window.

```
void gtk_window_set_resizable (GtkWindow *window,
                               gboolean resizable);
```

Caution You should note that the ability to resize is controlled by the window manager, so this setting may not be honored in all cases!

The note directly above brings up an important point. Much of what GTK+ does interacts with the functionality provided by the window manager. Because of this, not all of your window settings may be followed on all window managers. This is because your settings are merely hints given that are then either used or ignored. You should keep in mind that your requests may or may not be honored when designing applications with GTK+.

The default size of a GtkWindow can be set with gtk_window_set_default_size(), but there are a few things to watch out for when using this function. If the minimum size of the window is larger than the size you specify, this function will be ignored by GTK+. It will also be ignored if you have previously set a larger size request.

```
void gtk_window_set_default_size (GtkWindow *window,
                                  gint width,
                                  gint height);
```

Unlike gtk_widget_set_size_request(), gtk_window_set_default_size() only sets the initial size of the window—it does not prevent the user from resizing it to a larger or smaller size. If you set a height or width parameter to 0, the window's height or width will be set to the minimum possible size. If you pass -1 to either parameter, the window will be set to its natural size.

You can *request* that the window manager move the window to the specified location with gtk_window_move(). However, the window manager is free to ignore this request. This is true of all "request" functions that require action from the window manager.

```
void gtk_window_move (GtkWindow *window,
                      gint x,
                      gint y);
```

By default, the position of the window on the screen is calculated with respect to the top-left corner of the screen, but you can use gtk_window_set_gravity() to change this assumption.

```
void gtk_window_set_gravity (GtkWindow *window,
                             GdkGravity gravity);
```

This function defines the gravity of the widget, which is the point that layout calculations will consider (0, 0). Possible values for the GdkGravity enumeration include GDK_GRAVITY_NORTH_WEST, GDK_GRAVITY_NORTH, GDK_GRAVITY_NORTH_EAST, GDK_GRAVITY_WEST, GDK_GRAVITY_CENTER, GDK_GRAVITY_EAST, GDK_GRAVITY_SOUTH_WEST, GDK_GRAVITY_SOUTH, GDK_GRAVITY_SOUTH_EAST, and GDK_GRAVITY_STATIC.

North, south, east, and west refer to the top, bottom, right, and left edges of the screen. They are used to construct multiple gravity types. GDK_GRAVITY_STATIC refers to the top-left corner of the window itself, ignoring window decorations.

If your application has more than one window, you can set one as the parent with gtk_window_set_transient_for(). This allows the window manager to do things such as center the child above the parent or make sure one window is always on top of the other. We will explore the idea of multiple windows and transient relationships in Chapter 5 when discussing dialogs.

```
void gtk_window_set_transient_for (GtkWindow *window,
                                   GtkWindow *parent);
```

You can set the icon that will appear in the task bar and title bar of the window by calling gtk_window_set_icon_from_file(). The size of the icon does not matter, because it will be resized when the desired size is known. This allows for the best quality possible of the scaled icon.

```
gboolean gtk_window_set_icon_from_file (GtkWindow *window,
                                        const gchar *filename,
                                        GError **err); // NULL
```

TRUE is returned if the icon was successfully loaded and set. Therefore, unless you want in-depth information on why the icon loading failed, it is safe to pass NULL to the third parameter for now. We will discuss the GError structure in Chapter 4.

Process Pending Events

At times, you may want to process all pending events in an application. This is extremely useful when you are running a piece of code that will take a long time to process. This will cause your application to appear frozen, because widgets will not be redrawn if the CPU is taken up by another process. For example, in an integrated development environment that I have created called OpenLDev, I have to update the user interface while a build command is being processed. Otherwise, the window would lock up, and no build output would be shown until the build was complete.

The following loop is the solution for this problem. It is the answer to a great number of questions presented by new GTK+ programmers.

```
while (gtk_events_pending ())
  gtk_main_iteration ();
```

The loop calls gtk_main_iteration(), which will process the first pending event for your application. This is continued while gtk_events_pending() returns TRUE, which tells you whether there are events waiting to be processed.

Using this loop is an easy solution to the freezing problem, but a better solution would be to use coding strategies that avoid the problem altogether. For example, you can use idle functions, which will be covered in Chapter 6, to call a function only when there are no actions of greater importance to process.

Buttons

The GtkButton widget is a special type of container that turns its child into a clickable entity. It is only capable of holding one child. However, that child can be a container itself, so the button can theoretically be the ancestor of large amounts of children. This allows the button to hold, for example, a label and an image at the same time.

Because the purpose of a GtkButton widget is to make the child clickable, you will almost always need to use the clicked signal to get notification of when the button is activated. You will use this signal in the following example.

The GtkButton widget is usually initialized with gtk_button_new_with_label(), which creates a new button with a GtkLabel as its child. If you want to create an empty GtkButton and add your own child at a later time, you can use gtk_button_new(), although this is not what you will want to do in most cases.

Figure 2-4 shows a button with mnemonic capabilities. You can recognize a mnemonic label by the underlined character. In the case of the button below, when Alt+C is pressed, the button will be clicked.

Figure 2-4. *A GtkButton widget with a mnemonic label*

The function gtk_button_new_with_mnemonic() will initialize a new button with mnemonic label support. When the user presses the Alt key along with the specified accelerator key, the button will be activated. An accelerator is a key or set of keys that can be used to activate a predefined action.

■**Note** When the mnemonic option is available for a widget that provides some type of user interaction, it is recommended that you take advantage of that capability. Even if you do not use keyboard shortcuts, some users prefer to navigate user interfaces using a keyboard instead of a mouse.

Listing 2-3 is a simple demonstration of GtkButton capabilities using the clicked signal. When the button is pressed, the window will be destroyed, and the application will quit. The button in this example also takes advantage of the mnemonic and keyboard accelerator features. You saw a screenshot of this example in Figure 2-4.

Listing 2-3. *The GtkButton Widget (buttons.c)*

```
#include <gtk/gtk.h>

static void destroy (GtkWidget*, gpointer);

int main (int argc,
          char *argv[])
{
  GtkWidget *window, *button;

  gtk_init (&argc, &argv);

  window = gtk_window_new (GTK_WINDOW_TOPLEVEL);
  gtk_window_set_title (GTK_WINDOW (window), "Buttons");
  gtk_container_set_border_width (GTK_CONTAINER (window), 25);
  gtk_widget_set_size_request (window, 200, 100);

  g_signal_connect (G_OBJECT (window), "destroy",
                    G_CALLBACK (destroy), NULL);

  /* Create a new button that has a mnemonic key of Alt+C. */
  button = gtk_button_new_with_mnemonic ("_Close");
  gtk_button_set_relief (GTK_BUTTON (button), GTK_RELIEF_NONE);

  /* Connect the button to the clicked signal. The callback function receives the
   * window followed by the button because the arguments are swapped. */
  g_signal_connect_swapped (G_OBJECT (button), "clicked",
                            G_CALLBACK (gtk_widget_destroy),
                            (gpointer) window);

  gtk_container_add (GTK_CONTAINER (window), button);
  gtk_widget_show_all (window);

  gtk_main ();
  return 0;
}

/* Stop the GTK+ main loop function. */
static void
destroy (GtkWidget *window,
         gpointer data)
{
  gtk_main_quit ();
}
```

In Listing 2-3, gtk_widget_destroy() is called on the main window when the button is clicked. This is a very simple example, but it has a practical use in most applications.

The GNOME Human Interface Guidelines, which can be viewed or downloaded at `http://developer.gnome.org/projects/gup/hig`, state that preferences dialogs should apply settings immediately after a setting is changed.

Therefore, if you create a preferences dialog, there is a good chance that you will only need one button. The purpose of the button would be to destroy the window that contains the button and save the changes.

After creating the button, `gtk_button_set_relief()` can be used to add a certain magnitude of relief around the `GtkButton`. Relief is a type of 3-D border that distinguishes the button from surrounding widgets. Values of the `GtkReliefStyle` enumeration follow:

- `GTK_RELIEF_NORMAL`: Add relief around all edges of the button.

- `GTK_RELIEF_HALF`: Add relief around only half of the button.

- `GTK_RELIEF_NONE`: Add no relief around the button.

Listing 2-3 introduces `g_signal_connect_swapped()`, a new signal connection function. This function swaps the position of the object on which the signal is being emitted and the data parameter when running the callback function.

```
g_signal_connect_swapped (G_OBJECT (button), "clicked",
                          G_CALLBACK (gtk_widget_destroy),
                          (gpointer) window);
```

This allows you to use `gtk_widget_destroy()` on the callback function, which will call `gtk_widget_destroy (window)`. If the callback function only receives one parameter, the object will be ignored.

Widget Properties

GObject provides a property system, which allows you to customize how widgets interact with the user and how they are drawn on the screen. In this section, you will learn how to use styles, resource files and GObject's property system.

Every class derived from the `GObject` class can install any number of properties. In GTK+, these properties store information about how the widget will act. For example, `GtkButton` has a property called `relief` that defines the relief style used by the button.

In the following code, `g_object_get()` is used to retrieve the current value stored by the button's `relief` property. This function accepts a `NULL`-terminated list of properties and variables to store the returned value.

```
g_object_get (button, "relief", &value, NULL);
```

Each object can have many properties, so a full list will not be found in this book. For more information on properties available for a specific widget, you should reference the API documentation.

Setting Widget Properties

Setting a new value for a property is easily done with g_object_set(). In this example, the relief property of the button was set to GTK_RELIEF_NORMAL:

```
g_object_set (button, "relief", GTK_RELIEF_NORMAL, NULL);
```

Functions are provided to set and retrieve many of the properties of each widget. However, not every property has that option. These functions will become extremely important when you learn about the GtkTreeView widget in Chapter 8, because many objects used in that chapter do not provide get or set functions for any properties.

It is also possible to monitor a specific property with GObject's notify signal. You can monitor a property by connecting to the notify::property-name signal. The example in Listing 2-4 calls property_changed() when the relief property is changed.

Listing 2-4. *Using the Notify Property*

```
g_signal_connect (G_OBJECT (button), "notify::relief",
                  G_CALLBACK (property_changed), NULL);

...

static void
property_changed (GObject *button,
                  GParamSpec *property,
                  gpointer data)
{
  /* Handle the property change ... */
}
```

■**Caution** While it is acceptable to use either a dash or an underscore when typing signal names, you must always use dashes when using the notify signal. For example, if you need to monitor GtkWidget's can-focus property, notify::can_focus is not acceptable! Remember that notify is the signal name, and can-focus is the name of the widget property.

The callback function receives a new type of object called GParamSpec, which holds information about the property that was changed. For now, all you need to know is that you can retrieve the name of the property that was changed with property->name. You will learn more about the GParamSpec structure in Chapter 11 when you learn how to add properties to your own custom widgets.

In addition to the property system, every GObject has a table that associates a list of strings to a list of pointers. This allows you to add data to an object that can easily be accessed, which is useful when you need to pass additional data to a signal handler. To add a new data field to an object, all you have to do is call g_object_set_data(). This function accepts a unique string that will be used to point to data. If an association already exists with the same key name, the new data will replace the old.

```
void g_object_set_data (GObject *object,
                        const gchar *key,
                        gpointer data);
```

When you need to access the data, you can call g_object_get_data(), which returns the pointer associated with key. You should use this method of passing data instead of trying to pass arbitrary pieces of data with g_signal_connect().

Test Your Understanding

In Chapter 2, you have learned about the window and label widgets. It is time to put that knowledge into practice. In the following two exercises, you will employ your knowledge of the structure of GTK+ applications, signals, and the GObject property system.

Exercise 2-1. Using Events and Properties

This exercise will expand on the first two examples in this chapter by creating a GtkWindow that has the ability to destroy itself. You should set your first name as the title of the window. A selectable GtkLabel with your last name as its default text string should be added as the child of the window.

Other properties of this window are that it should not be resizable and the minimum size should be 300 pixels by 100 pixels. Functions to perform these tasks can be found in this chapter.

Next, by looking at the API documentation, connect the key-press-event signal to the window. In the key-press-event callback function, switch the window title and the label text. For example, the first time the callback function is called, the window title should be set to your last name and the label text to your first.

You may also find this function useful:

```
gint g_ascii_strcasecmp (const gchar *str1, const gchar *str2);
```

When the two strings in g_ascii_strcasesmp() are the same, 0 is returned. If str1 is less than str2, a negative number is returned. Otherwise, a positive number is returned.

Once you have completed Exercise 2-1, you can find a description of the solution in Appendix F, or the solution's complete source code is downloadable at www.gtkbook.com.

Exercise 2-2. GObject Property System

In this exercise, you will expand on Exercise 2-1, but the title, height, and width of the window should be set by using the functions provided by GObject. Also, within the callback function, all operations involving the window title and label text should be performed with the functions provided by GObject. Additionally, you should monitor the window's title with the notify signal. When the title is changed, you should notify the user in the terminal output.

Hint: You can use a function provided by GLib, `g_message()`, to output a message to the terminal. This function follows the same formatting supported by `printf()`.

Once you have completed both of these exercises, you are ready to move on to the next chapter, which covers container widgets. These widgets allow your main window to contain more than just a single widget, which was the case in all of the examples in this chapter.

However, before you continue, you should know about www.gtkbook.com, which can be used to supplement the content of *Foundations of GTK+ Development*. This web site is filled with downloads, links to further GTK+ information, C refresher tutorials, API documentation, and more. You can use it as you go through this book to aid in your quest to learn GTK+.

Summary

In this chapter, you learned about the most basic GTK+ widget and applications. The first application was a simple "Hello World" example that showed the fundamental calls required by all GTK+ applications. These include the following:

- Initialize GTK+ with `gtk_init()`.

- Create your top-level `GtkWindow`.

- Show the `GtkWindow`.

- Move into the main loop with `gtk_main()`.

In the second example, you learned the purpose of signals, events, and callback functions within GTK+ applications. The `GtkContainer` structure was introduced as it relates to `GtkWindow`. You also saw the purpose of the widget hierarchy system implemented by the GObject library.

You then saw useful functions that relate to `GtkWidget`, `GtkWindow`, and `GtkLabel`. Many of these will be used throughout the book. In fact, both of the exercises required that you put a few of them into practice.

The last example introduced you to the `GtkButton` widget. `GtkButton` is a type of container that makes its child widget a clickable button. It can be used to display labels, mnemonics, or arbitrary widgets. Buttons will be covered in further detail in Chapter 4.

In the next chapter, you will learn more about the `GtkContainer` structure and how it relates to the vast array of container widgets at your disposal.

CHAPTER 3

■■■

Container Widgets

Chapter 2 showed you the basic essentials you will need in every GTK+ application you create. It also introduced you to signals, events, callback functions, the GtkLabel widget, the GtkButton widget, and the GtkContainer class.

In this chapter, you will cover the two types of container widgets: decorators and layout containers. Then you will gain knowledge of many important container widgets including boxes, notebooks, handle boxes, and event boxes.

The last widget covered, GtkEventBox, allows all widgets that would otherwise be unable to do so to take advantage of GDK events.

In this chapter, you will learn the following:

- The purpose of the GtkContainer class and its descendents

- How to use layout containers including boxes, panes, and tables

- The pros and cons of using fixed containers

- How to create multipaged notebook containers

- How to provide events to all widgets using event boxes

GtkContainer

The GtkContainer class has briefly been covered in past sections, but more in-depth coverage of the class is required for you to become a competent GTK+ developer. Therefore, this section covers all of the important aspects of this abstract class.

The main purpose of a container class is to allow a parent widget to contain one or more children. There are two types of container widgets in GTK+, those used for laying out children and decorators and those that add some sort of functionality beyond positioning to a child.

Decorator Containers

In Chapter 2, you were introduced to GtkWindow, a widget derived from GtkBin. GtkBin is a type of container class that has the capability of holding only one child widget. Widgets derived from this class are called decorator containers, because they add some type of functionality to the child widget.

For example, a GtkWindow provides its child with the extra functionality of being placed in a top-level widget. Other examples of decorators include the GtkFrame widget, which draws a frame around its child, a GtkButton, which makes its child into a clickable button, and a GtkExpander, which can hide or show its child from the user. All of these widgets use gtk_container_add() for adding a child widget.

The GtkBin class only provides one function, gtk_bin_get_child(), which allows you to retrieve a pointer to the container's child widget. The actual purpose of the GtkBin class is to provide an instantiable widget from which all subclasses that only require one child widget can be derived. It is a central class used for a common base.

```
GtkWidget* gtk_bin_get_child (GtkBin *bin);
```

Widgets that derive from GtkBin include windows, alignments, frames, buttons, items, combo boxes, event boxes, expanders, handle boxes, scrolled windows, and tool items. Many of these containers will be covered in this chapter and later chapters.

Layout Containers

Another type of container widget provided by GTK+ is called a layout container. These are widgets that are used to arrange multiple widgets. Layout containers can be recognized by the fact that they are derived directly from GtkContainer.

As the name implies, the purpose of layout containers is to correctly arrange their children according to the user's preferences, your instructions, and built-in rules. User preferences include the use of themes and font preferences. These can be overridden, but in most cases, you should honor the user's preferences. There are also resizing rules that govern all container widgets, which will be covered in the next section.

Layout containers include boxes, fixed containers, paned widgets, icon views, layouts, menu shells, notebooks, sockets, tables, text views, toolbars, and tree views. We will be covering most of the layout widgets throughout this chapter and the rest of the book. More information on those we do not cover is available in the API documentation.

Resizing Children

In addition to arranging and decorating children, containers are tasked with resizing child widgets. Resizing is performed in two phases: size requisition and size allocation. In short, these two steps negotiate the size that is available to a widget. This is a recursive process of communication between the widget, its ancestors, and its children.

Size requisition refers to the desired size of the child. The process begins at the top-level widget, which asks its children for their preferred sizes. The children ask their children and so on, until the last child is reached.

At this point, the last child decides what size it wants to be based on the space it needs to be shown correctly on the screen and any size requests from the programmer. For example, a GtkLabel widget will ask for enough space to fully display its text on the screen or more space if you requested it to have a larger size.

The child then passes this size to its ancestors until the top-level widget receives the amount of space needed based on its children's requisitions.

```
typedef struct
{
  gint width;
  gint height;
} GtkRequisition;
```

Each widget stores its size preferences as width and height values in a GtkRequisition object. Keep in mind that a requisition is only a request; it does not have to be honored by the parent widget.

When the top-level widget has determined the amount of space it wants, size allocation begins. If you have set the top-level widget as nonresizable, the widget will never be resized; no further action will occur and requisitions will be ignored. Otherwise, the top-level widget will resize itself to the desired size. It will then pass the amount of available space to its child widget. This process is repeated until all widgets have resized themselves.

```
typedef struct
{
  gint x;
  gint y;
  gint width;
  gint height;
} GtkAllocation;
```

Size allocations for every widget are stored in one instance of the GtkAllocation structure for each child. This structure is passed to child widgets for resizing with gtk_widget_size_allocate(). This function can be called explicitly by the programmer as well, but doing so is not a good idea in the majority of cases.

In most situations, children will be given the space they request, but there are certain circumstances when this cannot happen. For example, a requisition will not be honored when the top-level widget cannot be resized.

Conversely, once a widget has been given a size allocation by its parent, the widget has no choice but to redraw itself with the new size. Therefore, you should be careful where you call gtk_widget_size_allocate(). In most cases, gtk_widget_set_size_request() is best to use for resizing widgets.

Container Signals

The GtkContainer class currently provides four signals. These are add, check_resize, remove, and set_focus_child:

- add: A child widget was added or packed into the container. This signal will be emitted even if you do not explicitly call gtk_container_add() but use the widget's built-in packing functions instead.

- check_resize: The container is checking whether it needs to resize for its children before taking further action.

- remove: A child has been removed from the container.

- set_focus_child: A child of the container has received focus from the window manager.

Now that you know the purpose of the GtkContainer class, we will progress onto other types of container widgets. You have already learned about windows, a type of GtkBin widget, so we will begin this chapter with a layout container called GtkBox.

Horizontal and Vertical Boxes

GtkBox is an abstract container widget that allows multiple children to be packed in a one-dimensional, rectangular area. There are two types of boxes: GtkVBox packs children into a single column, and GtkHBox packs them into a single row.

■**Note** For the rest of the book, code listings will only include portions of text significant to the section. Therefore, you will need to download the source code to view the full examples. For example, the destroy callback function will not be included in any further examples, because you should know how to use it by this point. It will, however, be included in the source code downloadable from www.gtkbook.com.

Listing 3-1. *Vertical Boxes with Default Packing (boxes.c)*

```
#include <gtk/gtk.h>

#define NUM_NAMES 4
const gchar* names[] = { "Andrew", "Joe", "Samantha", "Jonathan" };

int main (int argc,
          char *argv[])
{
  gint i;
  GtkWidget *window, *vbox;

  gtk_init (&argc, &argv);
```

```
window = gtk_window_new (GTK_WINDOW_TOPLEVEL);
gtk_window_set_title (GTK_WINDOW (window), "Boxes");
gtk_container_set_border_width (GTK_CONTAINER (window), 10);
gtk_widget_set_size_request (window, 200, -1);

vbox = gtk_vbox_new (TRUE, 5);

/* Add four buttons to the vertical box. */
for (i = 0; i < NUM_NAMES; i++)
{
  GtkWidget *button = gtk_button_new_with_label (names[i]);
  gtk_box_pack_start_defaults (GTK_BOX (vbox), button);

  g_signal_connect_swapped (G_OBJECT (button), "clicked",
                            G_CALLBACK (gtk_widget_destroy),
                            (gpointer) button);
}

gtk_container_add (GTK_CONTAINER (window), vbox);
gtk_widget_show_all (window);

gtk_main ();
return 0;
}
```

Listing 3-1 shows a simple illustration of a GtkVBox widget. The graphical output of the application is shown in Figure 3-1. Notice that the names are shown in the same order as they were added to the array, even though each was packed at the start position.

Figure 3-1. *A vertical box packed from the start position*

In analyzing Listing 3-1, you should note that the GtkVBox and GtkHBox widgets use the same set of functions, because they are both derived from the GtkBox class. The only difference is that vertical boxes are created with gtk_vbox_new() and horizontal boxes with gtk_hbox_new(), although the parameters of each function are the same.

As with every widget, you need to initialize GtkVBox before using the object. The first parameter in gtk_vbox_new() indicates whether all of the children in the box should be homogeneous. If it is set to TRUE, all of the children will be given the smallest amount of space that can fit every widget.

```
GtkWidget* gtk_vbox_new (gboolean homogeneous,
                         gint spacing);
```

The second parameter places a default number of pixels of spacing between each child and its neighbor. This value can be changed for individual cells as children are added, if the box is not set as equally spaced.

Since you do not need further access to the labels in Listing 3-1 after they are added to the GtkBox widget, the application does not store individual pointers to each object. They will all be cleaned up automatically when the parent is destroyed. Each button is then added to the box using a method called packing.

By adding widgets to the box with gtk_box_pack_start_defaults(), the child has three properties automatically set: Expanding is set to TRUE, which will automatically provide the cell with the extra space allocated to the box. This space is distributed evenly to all of the cells that request it. The fill property is also set to TRUE, which means the widget will expand into all of the extra space provided instead of filling it with padding. Lastly, the amount of padding placed between the cell and its neighbors is set to zero pixels.

```
void gtk_box_pack_start_defaults (GtkBox *box,
                                  GtkWidget *widget);
```

Packing boxes can be slightly unintuitive because of the naming of functions. The best way to think about it is in terms of where the packing begins. If you pack at the start position, children will be added with the first child appearing at the top or left. If you pack at the end position, the first child will appear at the bottom or right of the box.

In other words, the reference position for start moves as you add widgets. When adding widgets to the end position, the same process occurs. Therefore, you should use gtk_box_pack_end() or gtk_box_pack_end_defaults() to add elements in reverse order. An example of this can be seen in the code excerpt in Listing 3-2.

Listing 3-2. *Specifying Packing Parameters (boxes2.c)*

```
vbox = gtk_vbox_new (TRUE, 5);

/* Add four buttons to the vertical box, packing at the end. */
for (i = 0; i < NUM_NAMES; i++)
{
  GtkWidget *button = gtk_button_new_with_label (names[i]);
  gtk_box_pack_end (GTK_BOX (vbox), button, FALSE, FALSE, 5);

  g_signal_connect_swapped (G_OBJECT (button), "clicked",
                            G_CALLBACK (gtk_widget_destroy),
                            (gpointer) button);
}
```

Figure 3-2 shows the graphical output of Listing 3-2. Since we packed each of the widgets starting at the end, they are shown in reverse order. The packing began at the end of the box and packed each child before the previous one. You are free to intersperse calls to start and end packing functions. GTK+ keeps track of both reference positions.

Figure 3-2. *A vertical box packed from the end position*

If you do not want to use the default values for expanding, filling, and spacing, you can use gtk_box_pack_end() or gtk_box_pack_start() to specify different values for each packing property.

By setting the expand property to TRUE, the cell will expand so that it takes up additional space allocated to the box that is not needed by the widgets. By setting the fill property to TRUE, the widget itself will expand to fill extra space available to the cell. Table 3-1 offers a brief description of all possible combinations of the expand and fill properties.

Table 3-1. *expand and fill Properties*

expand	fill	Result
TRUE	TRUE	The cell will expand so that it takes up additional space allocated to the box, and the child widget will expand to fill that space.
TRUE	FALSE	The cell will expand so that it takes up additional space, but the widget will not expand. Instead, the extra space will be empty.
FALSE	TRUE	Neither the cell nor the widget will expand to fill extra space. This is the same thing as setting both properties to FALSE.
FALSE	FALSE	Neither the cell nor the widget will expand to fill extra space. If you resize the window, the cell will not resize itself.

In the previous gtk_box_pack_end() call, each cell is told to place five pixels of spacing between itself and any neighbor cells. Also, according to Table 3-1, neither the cell nor its child widget will expand to take up additional space provided to the box.

```
void gtk_box_pack_end (GtkBox *box,
                       GtkWidget *child,
                       gboolean expand,
                       gboolean fill,
                       guint padding);
```

■Note If you have experience programming with other graphical toolkits, the size negotiation system provided by GTK+ may seem odd. However, you will quickly learn its benefits. GTK+ automatically takes care of
resizing everything if you change a user interface, instead of requiring you to reposition everything programmatically. You will come to view this as a great benefit as you continue learning GTK+.

While you should try to finalize the order of elements in a GtkBox widget before displaying
it to the user, it is possible to reorder child widgets in a box with gtk_box_reorder_child().

```
void gtk_box_reorder_child (GtkBox *box,
                            GtkWidget *child,
                            gint position);
```

By using this function, you can move a child widget to a new position in the GtkBox. The
position of the first widget in a GtkBox container is indexed from zero. The widget will be placed
in the last position of the box if you specify a position value of -1 or a value greater than the
number of children.

Horizontal and Vertical Panes

GtkPaned is a special type of container widget that holds exactly two widgets. A resize bar is
placed between them, which allows the user to resize the two widgets by dragging the bar in
one direction or the other. When the bar is moved, either by user interaction or programmatic
calls, one of the two widgets will shrink while the other expands.

There are two types of paned widgets: GtkHPaned for horizontal resizing and GtkVPaned for
vertical resizing. As with boxes, the horizontal and vertical pane classes only provide functions
to create the widget. All other functionality is defined in the common parent class, GtkPaned.
Listing 3-3 shows a simple example where two GtkButton widgets are placed as the children of
a horizontal pane.

Listing 3-3. *Horizontal Pane (panes.c)*

```c
#include <gtk/gtk.h>

int main (int argc,
          char *argv[])
{
  GtkWidget *window, *hpaned, *button1, *button2;

  gtk_init (&argc, &argv);

  window = gtk_window_new (GTK_WINDOW_TOPLEVEL);
  gtk_window_set_title (GTK_WINDOW (window), "Panes");

  gtk_container_set_border_width (GTK_CONTAINER (window), 10);
  gtk_widget_set_size_request (window, 225, 150);

  hpaned = gtk_hpaned_new ();
  button1 = gtk_button_new_with_label ("Resize");
  button2 = gtk_button_new_with_label ("Me!");

  g_signal_connect_swapped (G_OBJECT (button1), "clicked",
                            G_CALLBACK (gtk_widget_destroy),
                            (gpointer) window);
  g_signal_connect_swapped (G_OBJECT (button2), "clicked",
                            G_CALLBACK (gtk_widget_destroy),
                            (gpointer) window);

  /* Pack both buttons as the two children of the GtkHPaned widget. */
  gtk_paned_add1 (GTK_PANED (hpaned), button1);
  gtk_paned_add2 (GTK_PANED (hpaned), button2);

  gtk_container_add (GTK_CONTAINER (window), hpaned);
  gtk_widget_show_all (window);

  gtk_main ();
  return 0;
}
```

As you can see in Figure 3-3, the GtkHPaned widget places a vertical bar between its two children. By dragging the bar, one widget will shrink while the other expands. In fact, it is possible to move the bar so that one child is completely hidden from the user's view. You will learn how to prevent this with gtk_paned_pack1() and gtk_paned_pack2().

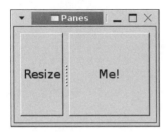

Figure 3-3. *The graphical output of Listing 3-3*

In Listing 3-3, we created a GtkHPaned object with gtk_hpaned_new(). If you want to use a vertical paned widget instead, you need only to call gtk_vpaned_new(). All of the GtkPaned functions will then work with either type of paned widget.

Since GtkPaned can only handle two children, GTK+ provides a function for packing each child. In the example below, gtk_paned_add1() and gtk_paned_add2() were used to add both children to hpaned. These functions use the default values for the resize and shrink properties of the GtkPaned widget.

```
gtk_paned_add1 (GTK_PANED (hpaned), button1);
gtk_paned_add2 (GTK_PANED (hpaned), button2);
```

The preceding gtk_paned_add1() and gtk_paned_add2() calls are from Listing 3-3 and are equivalent to the following:

```
gtk_paned_pack1 (GTK_PANED (hpaned), button1, FALSE, TRUE);
gtk_paned_pack2 (GTK_PANED (hpaned), button2, TRUE, TRUE);
```

The third parameter in gtk_paned_pack1() and gtk_paned_pack2() specifies whether the child widget should expand when the pane is resized. If you set this to FALSE, no matter how much larger you make the available area, the child widget will not be expanded.

The last parameter specifies whether the child can be made smaller than its size requisition. In most cases, you will want to set this to TRUE so that a widget can be completely hidden by the user by dragging the resize bar. If you want to prevent the user from doing this, set the fourth parameter to FALSE. Table 3-2 illustrates how the resize and shrink properties interrelate.

Table 3-2. *resize and shrink Properties*

resize	shrink	Result
TRUE	TRUE	The widget will take up all available space when the pane is resized, and the user will be able to make it smaller than its size requisition.
TRUE	FALSE	The widget will take up all available space when the pane is resized, but available space must be greater than or equal to the widget's size requisition.

resize	shrink	Result
FALSE	TRUE	The widget will not resize itself to take up additional space available in the pane, but the user will be able to make it smaller than its size requisition.
FALSE	FALSE	The widget will not resize itself to take up additional space available in the pane, and the available space must be greater than or equal to the widget's size requisition.

You can easily set the exact position of the resize bar with gtk_paned_set_position(). The position is calculated in pixels with respect to the top or left side of the container. If you set the position of the bar to zero, it will be moved all the way to the top or left if the widget allows shrinking.

```
void gtk_paned_set_position (GtkPaned *paned,
                             gint position);
```

Most applications will want to remember the position of the resize bar, so it can be restored to the same location when the user next loads the application. The current position of the resize bar can be retrieved with gtk_paned_get_position().

```
gint gtk_paned_get_position (GtkPaned *paned);
```

GtkPaned provides multiple signals, but one of the most useful is move-handle, which will tell you when the resizing bar has been moved. If you want to remember the position of the resize bar, this will tell you when you need to retrieve a new value. A full list of GtkPaned signals can be found in Appendix B.

Tables

So far, all of the layout container widgets I have covered only allow children to be packed in one dimension. The GtkTable widget, however, allows you to pack children in two-dimensional space.

One advantage of using the GtkTable widget over using multiple GtkHBox and GtkVBox widgets is that children in adjacent rows and columns are automatically aligned with each other, which is not the case with boxes within boxes. However, this is also a disadvantage, because you will not always want everything to be lined up in this way.

Figure 3-4 shows a simple table that contains three widgets. Notice that the single label spans two columns. This illustrates the fact that tables allow one widget to span multiple columns and/or rows as long as the region is rectangular.

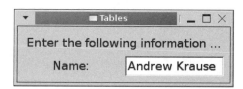

Figure 3-4. *A table containing a label widget that spans multiple columns*

Listing 3-4 creates the GtkTable widget shown in Figure 3-4, inserting two GtkLabel widgets and a GtkEntry widget into the two-by-two area (you will learn how to use the GtkEntry widget in Chapter 4, but this gives you a taste of what is to come).

Listing 3-4. *GtkTable Displaying Name (tables.c)*

```c
#include <gtk/gtk.h>

int main (int argc,
          char *argv[])
{
  GtkWidget *window, *table, *label, *label2, *name;

  gtk_init (&argc, &argv);

  window = gtk_window_new (GTK_WINDOW_TOPLEVEL);
  gtk_window_set_title (GTK_WINDOW (window), "Tables");
  gtk_container_set_border_width (GTK_CONTAINER (window), 10);
  gtk_widget_set_size_request (window, 150, 100);

  table = gtk_table_new (2, 2, TRUE);
  label = gtk_label_new ("Enter the following information ...");
  label2 = gtk_label_new ("Name: ");
  name = gtk_entry_new ();

  /* Attach the two labels and entry widget to their parent container. */
  gtk_table_attach (GTK_TABLE (table), label, 0, 2, 0, 1,
                    GTK_EXPAND, GTK_SHRINK, 0, 0);
  gtk_table_attach (GTK_TABLE (table), label2, 0, 1, 1, 2,
                    GTK_EXPAND, GTK_SHRINK, 0, 0);
  gtk_table_attach (GTK_TABLE (table), name, 1, 2, 1, 2,
                    GTK_EXPAND, GTK_SHRINK, 0, 0);

  /* Add five pixels of spacing between every row and every column. */
  gtk_table_set_row_spacings (GTK_TABLE (table), 5);
  gtk_table_set_col_spacings (GTK_TABLE (table), 5);

  gtk_container_add (GTK_CONTAINER (window), table);
  gtk_widget_show_all (window);

  gtk_main ();
  return 0;
}
```

Table Packing

When creating a table with gtk_table_new(), you must specify the number of columns, the number of rows, and whether table cells should be homogeneous.

```
GtkWidget* gtk_table_new (guint rows,
                          guint columns,
                          gboolean homogeneous);
```

The number of columns and rows can be changed after creating the table with gtk_table_resize(), but you should use the correct numbers initially, if possible, to avoid confusion on the part of the user. You do not want to get in the habit of liberally changing user interfaces when it is not completely necessary.

```
void gtk_table_resize (GtkTable *table,
                       guint rows,
                       guint columns);
```

The function gtk_table_set_homogeneous() can also be used to reset the homogeneous property after creation, but you should use the desired value initially here as well. The user should have control of resizing after the initial user interface is set.

```
void gtk_table_set_homogeneous (GtkTable *table,
                                gboolean homogeneous);
```

Packing a new widget is performed with gtk_table_attach(). The second parameter, child, refers to the child widget that you are adding to the table.

```
void gtk_table_attach (GtkTable *table,
                       GtkWidget *child,
                       guint left,
                       guint right,
                       guint top,
                       guint bottom,
                       GtkAttachOptions xoptions,
                       GtkAttachOptions yoptions,
                       guint xpadding,
                       guint ypadding);
```

The left, right, top, and bottom variables describe the location where the child widget should be placed within the table. For example, the first GtkLabel in Listing 3-4 was attached with the following command:

```
gtk_table_attach (GTK_TABLE (table), label, 0, 2, 0, 1,
                  GTK_EXPAND, GTK_SHRINK, 0, 0);
```

The GtkLabel widget is attached directly to the first column and row of the table, because x coordinates are added, followed by y coordinates. It is then attached to the second row on the bottom and the third column on the right. The packing from the example in Listing 3-4 is shown in Figure 3-5.

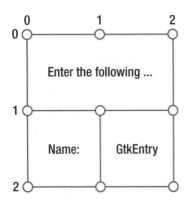

Figure 3-5. *Table packing*

If you choose to have two columns, there will be three zero-indexed column attach points labeled. The same logic applies to row attach points if there are two columns.

As previously stated, if a widget spans multiple cells, it must take up a rectangular area. A widget could span two rows and one column with (0,1,0,2) or the whole table with (0,2,0,2). The best way to remember the order in which the attach points are specified is that both x coordinates come first, followed by the y coordinates. After specifying attach points, you need to give attach options for the horizontal and vertical directions. In our example, children are set to expand in the x direction and shrink in the y direction. There are three values in the GtkAttachOptions enumeration:

- GTK_EXPAND: The widget should take up extra space allocated to it by the table. This space is allocated evenly between all children that specify this option.

- GTK_SHRINK: The widget should shrink so that it will only take up enough space to be rendered. This is often used so that extra space is taken up by other widgets.

- GTK_FILL: The widget should fill all allocated space instead of filling the extra space with padding.

It is possible to give multiple attach option parameters by using a bitwise or operator. For example, you can use GTK_EXPAND | GTK_FILL, so the child will take up extra space and fill it instead of adding padding.

The last two parameters of gtk_table_attach() specify pixels of horizontal and vertical padding that should be added between the child and its neighbor cells.

```
void gtk_table_attach_defaults (GtkTable *table,
                                GtkWidget *child,
                                guint left,
                                guint right,
                                guint top,
                                guint bottom);
```

As with boxes, you do not need to specify the full set of parameters when adding a child. You can use gtk_table_attach_defaults() to add a child without specifying attach and padding options. When using this function, GTK_EXPAND | GTK_FILL will be used for each attach option, and no padding will be added.

Table Spacing

You can specify the spacing between columns or rows with gtk_table_attach(), but GTK+ provides four methods for changing these after adding a child.

If you want to set the spacing for every column in a table, you can use gtk_table_set_col_spacings(). This function was used in Listing 3-4 to add five pixels of spacing. GTK+ also provides gtk_table_set_row_spacings() to add padding between rows. These functions will override any previous settings of the table.

```
void gtk_table_set_col_spacings (GtkTable *table,
                                 guint spacing);
```

You may also set the spacing of one specific column or row with gtk_table_set_col_spacing() or gtk_table_set_row_spacing(). These functions will add spacing between the child and its neighbors to the left and right of the widget or above and below it.

```
void gtk_table_set_col_spacing (GtkTable *table,
                                guint column,
                                guint spacing);
```

Fixed Containers

The GtkFixed widget is a type of layout container that allows you to place widgets by the pixel. There are many problems that can arise when using this widget, but before we explore the drawbacks, let us look at a simple example.

Listing 3-5 creates a GtkFixed widget that contains two buttons, one found at each of the locations (0,0) and (20,30), with respect to the top-left corner of the widget.

Listing 3-5. *Specifying Exact Locations (fixed.c)*

```
#include <gtk/gtk.h>

int main (int argc,
          char *argv[])
{
  GtkWidget *window, *fixed, *button1, *button2;

  gtk_init (&argc, &argv);

  window = gtk_window_new (GTK_WINDOW_TOPLEVEL);
  gtk_window_set_title (GTK_WINDOW (window), "Fixed");
  gtk_container_set_border_width (GTK_CONTAINER (window), 10);

  fixed = gtk_fixed_new ();
  button1 = gtk_button_new_with_label ("Pixel by pixel ...");
  button2 = gtk_button_new_with_label ("you choose my fate.");

  g_signal_connect_swapped (G_OBJECT (button1), "clicked",
                            G_CALLBACK (gtk_widget_destroy),
                            (gpointer) window);
  g_signal_connect_swapped (G_OBJECT (button2), "clicked",
                            G_CALLBACK (gtk_widget_destroy),
                            (gpointer) window);

  /* Place two buttons on the GtkFixed container. */
  gtk_fixed_put (GTK_FIXED (fixed), button1, 0, 0);
  gtk_fixed_put (GTK_FIXED (fixed), button2, 20, 30);

  gtk_container_add (GTK_CONTAINER (window), fixed);
  gtk_widget_show_all (window);

  gtk_main ();
  return 0;
}
```

The GtkFixed widget, initialized with gtk_fixed_new(), allows you to place widgets with a specific size in a specific location. Placing widgets is performed with gtk_fixed_put(), at specified horizontal and vertical positions.

```
void gtk_fixed_put (GtkFixed *fixed,
                    GtkWidget *child,
                    gint x,
                    gint y);
```

The top-left corner of the fixed container is referred to by location (0,0). You should only be able to specify *real* locations for widgets or locations in positive space. The fixed container will resize itself, so every widget is completely visible.

If you need to move a widget after it has been placed within a GtkFixed container, you can use gtk_fixed_move(). You need to be careful not to overlap a widget that has already been placed. The GtkFixed widget will not provide notification in the case of overlap. Instead, it will try to render the window with unpredictable results.

```
void gtk_fixed_move (GtkFixed *fixed,
                     GtkWidget *child,
                     gint x_position,
                     gint y_position);
```

This brings us to the inherent problems with using the GtkFixed widget. The first problem is that your users are free to use whatever theme they want. This means that the size of text on the user's machine may differ from the size of text on your machine unless you explicitly set the font. The sizes of widgets vary among different user themes as well. This can cause misalignment and overlap. This is illustrated in Figure 3-6, which shows two screenshots of Listing 3-5, one with a small font size and one with a larger font size.

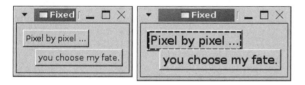

Figure 3-6. *Problems caused by different font sizes in a GtkFixed container*

You can explicitly set the size and font of text to avoid overlap, but this is not advised in most cases. Accessibility options are provided for users with low vision. If you change their fonts, some users may not be able to read the text on the screen.

Another problem with using GtkFixed arises when your application is translated into other languages. A user interface may look great in English, but the displayed strings in other languages may cause display problems, because the width will not be constant. Furthermore, languages that are read right to left, such as Hebrew and Arabic, cannot be properly mirrored with the GtkFixed widget. It is best to use a variable-sized container such as GtkBox or GtkTable in this case.

Finally, it can be quite a pain adding and removing widgets from your graphical interface when using a GtkFixed container. Changing the user interface will require you to reposition all of your widgets. If you have an application with a lot of widgets, this presents a long-term maintenance problem.

On the other hand, you have tables, boxes, and various other automatically formatting containers. If you need to add or remove a widget from the user interface, it is as easy as adding or removing a cell. This makes maintenance much more efficient, which is something you should consider in large applications.

Therefore, unless you know that none of the presented problems will plague your application, you should use variable-sized containers instead of GtkFixed. This container was presented only so you know it is available if a suitable situation arises. Even in suitable situations, flexible containers are almost always a better solution and are the proper way of doing things.

Expanders

The GtkExpander container can handle only one child. The child can be shown or hidden by clicking the triangle to the left of the expander's label. A before-and-after screenshot of this action can be viewed in Figure 3-7.

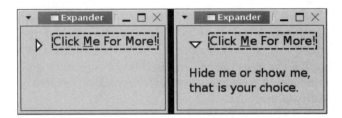

Figure 3-7. *A GtkExpander container*

Listing 3-6 was used to create Figure 3-7. The example introduces you to the most important GtkExpander methods.

Listing 3-6. *Showing and Hiding Widgets (expanders.c)*

```
#include <gtk/gtk.h>

int main (int argc,
          char *argv[])
{
  GtkWidget *window, *expander, *label;

  gtk_init (&argc, &argv);

  window = gtk_window_new (GTK_WINDOW_TOPLEVEL);
  gtk_window_set_title (GTK_WINDOW (window), "Expander");
  gtk_container_set_border_width (GTK_CONTAINER (window), 10);
  gtk_widget_set_size_request (window, 200, 100);

  expander = gtk_expander_new_with_mnemonic ("Click _Me For More!");
  label = gtk_label_new ("Hide me or show me,\nthat is your choice.");
```

```
gtk_container_add (GTK_CONTAINER (expander), label);
gtk_expander_set_expanded (GTK_EXPANDER (expander), TRUE);
gtk_container_add (GTK_CONTAINER (window), expander);

gtk_widget_show_all (window);

gtk_main ();
return 0;
}
```

Listing 3-6 uses gtk_expander_new_with_mnemonic() to initialize the GtkExpander. If you place an underscore in the initialization string of this function, a keyboard accelerator will be created. For example, whenever the user presses Alt+M on the keyboard in Listing 3-6, the widget will be activated. Activating a GtkExpander widget will cause it to be expanded or retracted depending on its current state.

▇Tip Mnemonics are available in almost every widget that displays a label. Where available, you should always use this feature, because some users prefer to navigate through applications with the keyboard.

If you wish to include an underscore character in the expander label, you should prefix it with a second underscore. If you do not want to take advantage of the mnemonic feature, you can use gtk_expander_new() to initialize the GtkExpander with a standard string as the label, but providing mnemonics as an option to the user is always a good idea. In normal expander labels, underscore characters will not be parsed but will be treated as just another character.

The GtkExpander widget itself is derived from GtkBin, which means that it can only contain one child. As with other containers that hold one child, you need to use gtk_container_add() to add the child widget.

In Listing 3-6, I wanted the child widget to be visible by default, so I set the GtkExpander widget to be expanded. The child widget of a GtkExpander container can be shown or hidden by calling gtk_expander_set_expanded().

```
void gtk_expander_set_expanded (GtkExpander *expander,
                                gboolean expanded);
```

By default, GTK+ does not add any spacing between the expander label and the child widget. To add pixels of spacing, you can use gtk_expander_set_spacing() to add padding.

```
void gtk_expander_set_spacing (GtkExpander *expander,
                               gint spacing);
```

Handle Boxes

The GtkHandleBox widget is another type of GtkBin container that allows its child to be removed from the parent window by dragging it with the mouse.

When removed, the child is placed in its own window that is without decorations. A ghost is placed where the widget was originally located. If there are other widgets in the window, they will be resized to fill the void of space if possible.

This widget is most commonly used to contain toolbars and other toolkit displays. An example of a GtkHandleBox widget is shown in Figure 3-8. It shows the handle box attached to the window and then removed. The handle box can be reattached by aligning it with the original location.

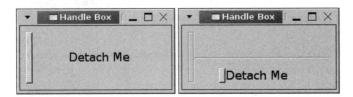

Figure 3-8. *A handle box attached and then detached*

In Listing 3-7, we create a GtkHandleBox widget that contains a GtkLabel child. The example shows all of the properties available to you through the GtkHandleBox class.

Listing 3-7. *Detachable Widgets (handleboxes.c)*

```
#include <gtk/gtk.h>

int main (int argc,
          char *argv[])
{
  GtkWidget *window, *handle, *label;

  gtk_init (&argc, &argv);

  window = gtk_window_new (GTK_WINDOW_TOPLEVEL);
  gtk_window_set_title (GTK_WINDOW (window), "Handle Box");
  gtk_container_set_border_width (GTK_CONTAINER (window), 10);
  gtk_widget_set_size_request (window, 200, 100);
```

```
  handle = gtk_handle_box_new ();
  label = gtk_label_new ("Detach Me");

  /* Add a shadow to the handle box, set the handle position on the left and
   * set the snap edge to the top of the widget. */
  gtk_handle_box_set_shadow_type (GTK_HANDLE_BOX (handle), GTK_SHADOW_IN);
  gtk_handle_box_set_handle_position (GTK_HANDLE_BOX (handle), GTK_POS_LEFT);
  gtk_handle_box_set_snap_edge (GTK_HANDLE_BOX (handle), GTK_POS_TOP);

  gtk_container_add (GTK_CONTAINER (handle), label);
  gtk_container_add (GTK_CONTAINER (window), handle);
  gtk_widget_show_all (window);

  gtk_main ();
  return 0;
}
```

When you create a GtkHandleBox widget, you need to decide where the handle and the snap edge will be placed. The handle is the area on the side of the child widget that you grab onto in order to detach the GtkHandleBox child from its parent. When the handle box is detached from the parent, a slim ghost is drawn in the original location.

The function gtk_handle_box_set_handle_position() is used to set the position of the handle. The GtkPositionType enumeration provides four options for the placement of the handle. By default, the handle position is set to GTK_POS_LEFT, but you can place it on any side with GTK_POS_RIGHT, GTK_POS_TOP, or GTK_POS_BOTTOM.

```
void gtk_handle_box_set_handle_position (GtkHandleBox *handle_box,
                                         GtkPositionType position);
```

Based on the handle position, GTK+ chooses the position for the snap edge, which is where the handle box must realign itself for it to be reattached to its parent. The snap edge is where the ghost will appear after detachment.

You can specify a new GtkPositionType value for the snap edge with gtk_handle_box_set_snap_edge(). It is important for you to pay attention to where you place the snap edge with respect to the handle to avoid confusing the user.

```
void gtk_handle_box_set_snap_edge (GtkHandleBox *handle_box,
                                   GtkPositionType position);
```

For example, if the handle box is at the top of a GtkVBox widget and the handle is on the left side, you should set the snap edge position as GTK_POS_TOP. This way, the ghost is in the same position as the snap edge without the need for resizing.

GtkHandleBox also provides gtk_handle_box_set_shadow_type(), which allows you to set the type of border to place around the child widget. Values for the GtkShadowType enumeration follow.

- GTK_SHADOW_NONE: No border will be placed around the child.

- GTK_SHADOW_IN: The border will be skewed inwards.

- GTK_SHADOW_OUT: The border will be skewed outwards, like a button.

- GTK_SHADOW_ETCHED_IN: The border will have a sunken 3-D appearance.

- GTK_SHADOW_ETCHED_OUT: The border will have a raised 3-D appearance.

Notebooks

The GtkNotebook widget organizes child widgets into a number of pages. The user can switch between these pages by clicking the tabs that appear along one edge of the widget.

You are able to specify the location of the tabs, although they appear along the top by default. You can also hide the tabs altogether. Figure 3-9 shows a GtkNotebook widget with two tabs that was created with the code in Listing 3-8.

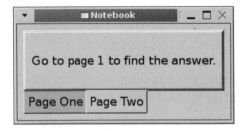

Figure 3-9. *A notebook container with two pages*

When creating a notebook container, you must specify a tab label widget and a child widget for each tab. Tabs can be added to the front or back, inserted, reordered, and removed.

Listing 3-8. *Container with Multiple Pages (notebooks.c)*

```
#include <gtk/gtk.h>

static void switch_page (GtkButton*, GtkNotebook*);

int main (int argc,
          char *argv[])
{
  GtkWidget *window, *notebook;
  GtkWidget *label1, *label2, *child1, *child2;
```

```
  gtk_init (&argc, &argv);

  window = gtk_window_new (GTK_WINDOW_TOPLEVEL);
  gtk_window_set_title (GTK_WINDOW (window), "Notebook");
  gtk_container_set_border_width (GTK_CONTAINER (window), 10);
  gtk_widget_set_size_request (window, 250, 100);

  notebook = gtk_notebook_new ();
  label1 = gtk_label_new ("Page One");
  label2 = gtk_label_new ("Page Two");
  child1 = gtk_label_new ("Go to page 2 to find the answer.");
  child2 = gtk_label_new ("Go to page 1 to find the answer.");

  /* Notice that two widgets were connected to the same callback function! */
  g_signal_connect (G_OBJECT (child1), "clicked",
                    G_CALLBACK (switch_page),
                    (gpointer) notebook);
  g_signal_connect (G_OBJECT (child2), "clicked",
                    G_CALLBACK (switch_page),
                    (gpointer) notebook);

  /* Append to pages to the notebook container. */
  gtk_notebook_append_page (GTK_NOTEBOOK (notebook), child1, label1);
  gtk_notebook_append_page (GTK_NOTEBOOK (notebook), child2, label2);

  gtk_notebook_set_tab_pos (GTK_NOTEBOOK (notebook), GTK_POS_BOTTOM);

  gtk_container_add (GTK_CONTAINER (window), notebook);
  gtk_widget_show_all (window);

  gtk_main ();
  return 0;
}

/* Switch to the next or previous GtkNotebook page. */
static void
switch_page (GtkButton *button,
             GtkNotebook *notebook)
{
  gint page = gtk_notebook_get_current_page (notebook);

  if (page == 0)
    gtk_notebook_set_current_page (notebook, 1);
  else
    gtk_notebook_set_current_page (notebook, 0);
}
```

After you create a GtkNotebook, it is not very useful until you add tabs to it. To add a tab to the end or beginning of the list of tabs, you can use gtk_notebook_append_page() or gtk_notebook_prepend_page(), respectively. Each of these functions accepts GtkNotebook, a child widget, and a widget to display in the tab as shown below.

```
gint gtk_notebook_append_page (GtkNotebook *notebook,
                               GtkWidget *child,
                               GtkWidget *tab_label);
```

■**Tip** The tab label does not have to be a GtkLabel widget. For example, you could use a GtkHBox widget that contains a label and a close button. This allows you to embed other useful widgets such as buttons and images into the tab label.

Each notebook page can only display one child widget. However, each of the children can be another container, so each page can display many widgets. In fact, it is possible to use GtkNotebook as the child widget of another GtkNotebook tab.

■**Caution** Placing notebooks within notebooks is possible but should be done with caution, because it can easily confuse the user. If you must do this, make sure that you place the child notebook's tabs on a different side of the notebook than its parent's tabs. By doing this, the user will be able to figure out what tabs belong to which notebook.

If you want to insert a tab in a specific location, you can use gtk_notebook_insert_page(). This function will allow you to specify the integer location of the tab. The index of all tabs located after the inserted tab will increase by one.

```
gint gtk_notebook_insert_page (GtkNotebook *notebook,
                               GtkWidget *child,
                               GtkWidget *tab_label,
                               gint position);
```

All three of the functions used to add tabs to a GtkNotebook will return the integer location of the tab you added or -1 if the action has failed.

GtkNotebook Properties

In Listing 3-8, the tab-position property was set for the GtkNotebook, which was done with the following call.

```
void gtk_notebook_set_tab_pos (GtkNotebook *notebook,
                               GtkPositionType position);
```

Tab position can be set in gtk_notebook_tab_pos() by using the GtkPositionType enumeration you used to set the handle and snap edge locations of a GtkHandleBox. These include GTK_POS_TOP, GTK_POS_BOTTOM, GTK_POS_LEFT, and GTK_POS_RIGHT.

Notebooks are useful if you want to give the user multiple options, but you want to show them in multiple stages. If you place a few in each tab and hide the tabs with gtk_notebook_set_show_tabs(), you can progress the user back and forth through the options. An example of this concept would be many of the wizards you see throughout your operating system, similar to the functionality provided by the GtkAssistant widget.

```
void gtk_notebook_set_show_tabs (GtkNotebook *notebook,
                                 gboolean show_tabs);
```

At some point, the GtkNotebook will run out of room to store tabs in the allocated space. In order to remedy this problem, you can set notebook tabs as scrollable with gtk_notebook_set_scrollable().

```
void gtk_notebook_set_scrollable (GtkNotebook *notebook,
                                  gboolean scrollable);
```

This property will force tabs to be hidden from the user. Arrows will be provided so that the user will be able to scroll through the list of tabs. This is necessary because tabs are only shown in one row or column.

If you resize the window so that all of the tabs cannot be shown, the tabs will be made scrollable. Scrolling will also occur if you make the font size large enough that the tabs cannot all be drawn. You should always set this property to TRUE if there is any chance that the tabs will take up more than the allotted space.

Tab Operations

GTK+ provides multiple functions that allow you to interact with tabs that already exist. Before learning about these methods, it is useful to know that most of these will cause the change-current-page signal to be emitted. This signal is emitted when the current tab that is in focus is changed.

If you can add tabs, there has to be a method to remove tabs as well. By using gtk_notebook_remove_page(), you can remove a tab based on its index reference. If you did not increase the reference count before adding the widget to the GtkNotebook, this function will release the last reference and destroy the child.

```
void gtk_notebook_remove_page (GtkNotebook *notebook,
                               gint page_number);
```

You can manually reorder the tabs by calling gtk_notebook_reorder_child(). You must specify the child widget of the page you want to move and the location to where it should be moved. If you specify a number that is greater than the number of tabs or a negative number, the tab will be moved to the end of the list.

```
void gtk_notebook_reorder_child (GtkNotebook *notebook,
                                 GtkWidget *child,
                                 gint position);
```

There are three methods provided for changing the current page. If you know the specific index of the page you want to view, you can use gtk_notebook_set_current_page() to move to that page.

```
void gtk_notebook_set_current_page (GtkNotebook *notebook,
                                    gint page_number);
```

At times, you may also want switch to the next or previous tab, which can be done with call gtk_notebook_next_page() or gtk_notebook_prev_page(). If a call to either of these functions would cause the current tab to drop below zero or go above the current number of tabs, nothing will occur; the call will be ignored.

When deciding what page to move to, it is often useful to know the current page and the total number of tabs. These values can be obtained with gtk_notebook_get_current_page() and gtk_notebook_get_n_pages() respectively.

Event Boxes

Various widgets including GtkLabel do not respond to GDK events, because they do not have an associated GDK window. To fix this, GTK+ provides a container widget called GtkEventBox. Event boxes catch events for the child widget by providing a GDK window for the object.

Listing 3-9 connects the button-press-event signal to a GtkLabel by using an event box. The text in the label is changed based on its current state when the label is double-clicked. Nothing visible happens when a single click occurs, although the signal is still emitted in that case.

Listing 3-9. *Adding Events to a GtkLabel (eventboxes.c)*

```
#include <gtk/gtk.h>

static gboolean button_pressed (GtkWidget*, GdkEventButton*, GtkLabel*);

int main (int argc,
          char *argv[])
{
  GtkWidget *window, *eventbox, *label;

  gtk_init (&argc, &argv);

  window = gtk_window_new (GTK_WINDOW_TOPLEVEL);
  gtk_window_set_title (GTK_WINDOW (window), "Event Box");
  gtk_container_set_border_width (GTK_CONTAINER (window), 10);
  gtk_widget_set_size_request (window, 200, 50);
```

```c
eventbox = gtk_event_box_new ();
label = gtk_label_new ("Double-Click Me!");

/* Set the order in which widgets will receive notification of events. */
gtk_event_box_set_above_child (GTK_EVENT_BOX (eventbox), FALSE);

g_signal_connect (G_OBJECT (eventbox), "button_press_event",
                  G_CALLBACK (button_pressed), (gpointer) label);

gtk_container_add (GTK_CONTAINER (eventbox), label);
gtk_container_add (GTK_CONTAINER (window), eventbox);

/* Allow the event box to catch button presses, realize the widget, and set the
 * cursor that will be displayed when the mouse is over the event box. */
gtk_widget_set_events (eventbox, GDK_BUTTON_PRESS_MASK);
gtk_widget_realize (eventbox);
gdk_window_set_cursor (eventbox->window, gdk_cursor_new (GDK_HAND1));
gtk_widget_show_all (window);

gtk_main ();
return 0;
}

/* This is called every time a button-press event occurs on the GtkEventBox. */
static gboolean
button_pressed (GtkWidget *eventbox,
                GdkEventButton *event,
                GtkLabel *label)
{
  if (event->type == GDK_2BUTTON_PRESS)
  {
    const gchar *text = gtk_label_get_text (label);

    if (text[0] == 'D')
      gtk_label_set_text (label, "I Was Double-Clicked!");
    else
      gtk_label_set_text (label, "Double-Click Me Again!");
  }

  return FALSE;
}
```

When using an event box, you need to decide whether the event box's GdkWindow should be positioned above the windows of its child or below them. If the event box window is above, all events inside the event box will go to the event box. If the window is below, events in windows of child widgets will first go to that widget and then to its parents.

Note If you set the window's position as below, events do go to child widgets first. However, this is only the case for widgets that have associated GDK windows. If the child is a GtkLabel widget, it does not have the ability to detect events on its own. Therefore, it does not matter whether you set the window's position as above or below in Listing 3-9.

The location of the event box window can be moved above or below its children with gtk_event_box_set_above_child(). By default, this property is set to FALSE for all event boxes. This means that all events will be handled by the widget for which the signal was first emitted. The event will then be passed to its parent after the widget is finished.

```
void gtk_event_box_set_above_child (GtkEventBox *event_box,
                                    gboolean above_child);
```

Next, you need to add an event mask to the event box so that it knows what type of events the widget will receive. Values for the GdkEventMask enumeration that specify event masks are shown in Table 3-3. A bitwise list of GdkEventMask values can be passed to gtk_widget_set_events() if you need to set more than one.

Table 3-3. *GdkEventMask Values*

Value	Description
GDK_EXPOSURE_MASK	Accept events when a widget is exposed.
GDK_POINTER_MOTION_MASK	Accept all pointer motion events.
GDK_POINTER_MOTION_HINT_MASK	Limit the number of GDK_MOTION_NOTIFY events, so they are not emitted every time the mouse moves.
GDK_BUTTON_MOTION_MASK	Accept pointer motion events while any button is pressed.
GDK_BUTTON1_MOTION_MASK	Accept pointer motion events while button 1 is pressed.
GDK_BUTTON2_MOTION_MASK	Accept pointer motion events while button 2 is pressed.
GDK_BUTTON3_MOTION_MASK	Accept pointer motion events while button 3 is pressed.
GDK_BUTTON_PRESS_MASK	Accept mouse button press events.
GDK_BUTTON_RELEASE_MASK	Accept mouse button release events.
GDK_KEY_PRESS_MASK	Accept key press events from a keyboard.
GDK_KEY_RELEASE_MASK	Accept key release events from a keyboard.

Value	Description
GDK_ENTER_NOTIFY_MASK	Accept events emitted when the proximity of the window is entered.
GDK_LEAVE_NOTIFY_MASK	Accept events emitted when the proximity of the window is left.
GDK_FOCUS_CHANGE_MASK	Accept change of focus events.
GDK_STRUCTURE_MASK	Accept events emitted when changes to window configurations occur.
GDK_PROPERTY_CHANGE_MASK	Accept changes to object properties.
GDK_VISIBILITY_NOTIFY_MASK	Accept change of visibility events.
GDK_PROXIMITY_IN_MASK	Accept events emitted when the mouse cursor enters the proximity of the widget.
GDK_PROXIMITY_OUT_MASK	Accept events emitted when the mouse cursor leaves the proximity of the widget.
GDK_SUBSTRUCTURE_MASK	Accept events that change the configuration of child windows.
GDK_SCROLL_MASK	Accept all scroll events.
GDK_ALL_EVENTS_MASK	Accept all types of events.

You *must* call gtk_widget_set_events() before you call gtk_widget_realize() on the widget. If a widget has already been realized by GTK+, you will have to instead use gtk_widget_add_events() to add event masks.

Before calling gtk_widget_realize(), your GtkEventBox does not yet have an associated GdkWindow or any other GDK widget resources. Normally, realization occurs when the parent is realized, but event boxes are an exception. When you call gtk_widget_show() on a widget, it is automatically realized by GTK+. Event boxes are not realized when you call gtk_widget_show_all(), because they are set as invisible. Calling gtk_widget_realize() on the event box is an easy way to work around this problem.

When you realize your event box, you need to make sure that it is already added as a child to a top-level widget, or it will not work. This is because, when you realize a widget, it will automatically realize its ancestors. If it has no ancestors, GTK+ will not be happy and realization will fail.

After the event box is realized, it will have an associated GdkWindow. GdkWindow is a class that refers to a rectangular region on the screen where a widget is drawn. It is not the same thing as a GtkWindow, which refers to a top-level window with a title bar and so on. A GtkWindow will contain many GdkWindow objects, one for each child widget. They are used for drawing widgets on the screen.

Since we are allowing the GtkLabel widget to be clicked, it makes sense to change the cursor to a hand when it is hovering over the label, which is done with gdk_window_set_cursor() and gdk_cursor_new(). There are many cursor types available in GDK. To see a full list of available cursors, view the GdkCursorType enumeration in the API documentation.

```
gdk_window_set_cursor (eventbox->window, gdk_cursor_new (GDK_HAND1));
```

■**Note** The GtkWidget structure includes multiple public members. One of them is window, which is the GdkWindow associated with the given widget. In the preceding code, the new cursor was associated with the event box's GdkWindow.

Test Your Understanding

This chapter has introduced you to a number of container widgets that are included in GTK+. The following two exercises will allow you to practice what you have learned about a few of these new widgets.

Exercise 3-1. Using Multiple Containers

One important characteristic of containers is that each container can hold other containers. To really drive this point home, in this example, you will use a large number of containers. The main window will show a GtkNotebook and two buttons along the bottom.

The notebook should have four pages. Each notebook page should hold a GtkButton that moves to the next page (The GtkButton on the last page should wrap around to the first page.)

Create two buttons along the bottom of the window. The first should move to the previous page in the GtkNotebook, wrapping to the last page if necessary. The second button should close the window and exit the application when clicked.

Exercise 3-1 is a simple application to implement, but it illustrates a few important points. First, it shows the usefulness of GtkVBox and GtkHBox, and how they can be used together to create complex user interfaces.

It is true that this same application could be implemented with a GtkTable as the direct child of the window, but it is significantly easier to align the buttons along the bottom with a horizontal box. You will notice that the buttons were packed at the end of the box, which aligns them to the right side of the box, and this is easier to implement with boxes.

Also, you saw that containers can, and should, be used to hold other containers. For example, in Exercise 3-1, a GtkWindow holds a GtkVBox, which holds a GtkHBox and a GtkNotebook. This structure can become even more complex as your application grows in size.

Once you have completed Exercise 3-1, move on to Exercise 3-2. In the next problem, you will use the paned container instead of a vertical box.

Exercise 3-2. Even More Containers

In this exercise, you will expand upon the code you wrote in Exercise 3-1. Instead of using a GtkVBox to hold the notebook and horizontal box of buttons, create a GtkVPaned widget.

In addition to this change, you should hide the GtkNotebook tabs, so the user is not able to switch between pages without pressing buttons. In this case, you will not be able to know when a page is being changed. Therefore, each button that is in a GtkNotebook page should be contained by its own expander. The expander labels will allow you to differentiate between notebook pages.

Once you have completed Exercise 3-2, you will have had practice with GtkBox, GtkPaned, GtkNotebook, and GtkExpander— four important containers that will be used throughout the rest of this book.

Before continuing on to the next chapter, you may want to test out a few of the containers covered in this chapter that you did not need for Exercises 3-1 and 3-2. This will give you practice using all of the containers, because later chapters will *not* review past information.

Summary

In this chapter, you learned about the two types of container widgets: decorators and layout containers. Types of decorators covered were expanders, handle boxes, and event boxes. Types of layout containers covered were boxes, panes, tables, fixed containers, and notebooks.

The event box container will be seen in later chapters, because there are other widgets besides GtkLabel that cannot handle GDK events. This will be specified when you learn about these widgets. You will see most of the containers covered in this chapter in later chapters as well.

While these containers are necessary for GTK+ application development, merely displaying GtkLabel and GtkButton widgets in containers is not very useful (or interesting) in most applications. This type of application does little to accommodate anything beyond basic user interaction.

Therefore, in the next chapter, you are going to learn about many widgets that allow you to interact with the user. These widgets include types of buttons, toggles, text entries, and spin buttons.

As mentioned before, make sure you understand container widgets before continuing on to Chapter 4. Later chapters will assume that you have a decent grasp of the most important container widgets and other concepts covered in this chapter.

■ ■ ■

Basic Widgets

So far, you have not learned about any widgets that are designed to facilitate user interaction except GtkButton. That changes in this chapter, as we will cover many types of widgets that allow the user to make choices, change settings, or input information.

These widgets include stock buttons, toggle buttons, check buttons, radio buttons, color selection buttons, file chooser buttons, font selection buttons, text entries, and number selection buttons.

The exercise at the end of the chapter will give you the opportunity to combine many of these widgets into larger applications.

In this chapter, you will learn the following:

- How to use clickable buttons with stock items

- How to use types of toggle buttons, including check buttons and radio buttons

- How to use the entry widget for one-line, free-form text input

- How to use the spin button widget for integer or floating-point number selection

- What sort of specialized buttons are available

Using Stock Items

When you create applications in GTK+, you will begin to notice that you are using the same buttons and menu items across many applications. Because of this, GTK+ includes stock items, which are pairs of images and strings that accommodate often-used menu items and buttons.

GTK+ provides gtk_button_new_from_stock(), which will create a new button using a predefined stock item. Each stock item contains an image and a mnemonic label that are applied to the button. A full list of stock items can be found in Appendix D. Each item is included in GTK+, because each is used by a wide number of applications.

While Appendix D includes all of the stock icons available in GTK+ 2.10, you may notice when running applications that the icons are not the same on your system. This is because, while you will always have these stock items available, the default image may be replaced by the user's theme of choice or by the developer.

■**Note** If the stock item provided to `gtk_button_new_from_stock()` or any other stock retrieval function in GTK+ is not found, it will be treated as a mnemonic label. This prevents buttons from being rendered in an unpredictable way.

It is possible for you to define your own stock icons, but this will not be covered until Chapter 9, which covers menus and toolbars. An example of a button using the `GTK_STOCK_CLOSE` stock item can be seen in Figure 4-1.

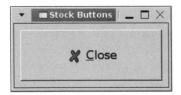

Figure 4-1. *A GTK_STOCK_CLOSE stock item*

Each stock item can be referred to by its string value or its macro definition. For example, the close stock item used in Listing 4-1 can be referred to as `gtk-close` or `GTK_STOCK_CLOSE`. However, the preprocessor directives are merely convenient aliases of the string values, so there is no reason to learn both identifiers.

■**Tip** You should always use the preprocessor directives, because unsupported items will be flagged when you compile the code. If you use the stock item's string, the compiler will not flag the error, and the invalid icon will be displayed.

Listing 4-1. *Stock Items (stockitems.c)*

```
button = gtk_button_new_from_stock (GTK_STOCK_CLOSE);

g_signal_connect_swapped (G_OBJECT (button), "clicked",
                          G_CALLBACK (gtk_widget_destroy),
                          (gpointer) window);
```

There are 98 stock items provided by GTK+ as of the release of 2.10. A list of these items can be viewed in Appendix D. We will use stock items again when covering menus and toolbars in Chapter 9.

It is important to note that some stock items have been added since the release of GTK+ 2.0, so a few items may not be available to you if you are not running the most current version of GTK+. This is essential to keep in mind when creating new applications. Your users may not have the most current version of GTK+!

Toggle Buttons

The GtkToggleButton widget is a type of GtkButton that holds its active or inactive state after it is clicked. It is shown as pressed down when active. Clicking an active toggle button will cause it to return to its normal state. There are two widgets derived from GtkToggleButton: GtkCheckButton and GtkRadioButton.

You can create a new GtkToggleButton with one of three functions. To create an empty toggle button, use gtk_toggle_button_new(). If you want the toggle button to include a label by default, use gtk_toggle_button_new_with_label(). Lastly, GtkToggleButton also supports mnemonic labels with gtk_toggle_button_new_with_mnemonic().

Figure 4-2 shows two GtkToggleButton widgets that were created with two mnemonic labels by calling the gtk_toggle_button_new_with_mnemonic() initializer. The widgets in the screenshot were created with the code in Listing 4-2.

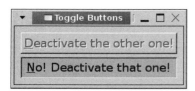

Figure 4-2. *Two GtkToggleButton widgets*

In the example in Listing 4-2, when one toggle button is activated, the other is disabled. The only way to make it sensitive is to deactivate the original toggle button.

Listing 4-2. *Using Toggle Buttons (togglebuttons.c)*

```
#include <gtk/gtk.h>

static void button_toggled (GtkToggleButton*, GtkWidget*);

int main (int argc,
          char *argv[])
{
  GtkWidget *window, *vbox, *toggle1, *toggle2;

  gtk_init (&argc, &argv);

  window = gtk_window_new (GTK_WINDOW_TOPLEVEL);
  gtk_window_set_title (GTK_WINDOW (window), "Toggle Buttons");
  gtk_container_set_border_width (GTK_CONTAINER (window), 10);

  vbox = gtk_vbox_new (TRUE, 5);
  toggle1  = gtk_toggle_button_new_with_mnemonic ("_Deactivate the other one!");
  toggle2 = gtk_toggle_button_new_with_mnemonic ("_No! Deactivate that one!");
```

```
  g_signal_connect (G_OBJECT (toggle1), "toggled",
                    G_CALLBACK (button_toggled),
                    (gpointer) toggle2);
  g_signal_connect (G_OBJECT (toggle2), "toggled",
                    G_CALLBACK (button_toggled),
                    (gpointer) toggle1);

  gtk_box_pack_start_defaults (GTK_BOX (vbox), toggle1);
  gtk_box_pack_start_defaults (GTK_BOX (vbox), toggle2);

  gtk_container_add (GTK_CONTAINER (window), vbox);
  gtk_widget_show_all (window);

  gtk_main ();
  return 0;
}

/* If the toggle button was activated, set the other as disabled. Otherwise,
 * enable the other toggle button. */
static void
button_toggled (GtkToggleButton *toggle,
                GtkWidget *other_toggle)
{
  if (gtk_toggle_button_get_active (toggle))
    gtk_widget_set_sensitive (other_toggle, FALSE);
  else
    gtk_widget_set_sensitive (other_toggle, TRUE);
}
```

The only signal added by the GtkToggleButton class is toggled, which is emitted when the user activates or deactivates the button. This signal was triggered in Listing 4-2 by one toggle button in order to disable the other.

In Listing 4-2, another important piece of information was shown: multiple widgets can use the same callback function. We did not need to create a separate callback function for each toggle button, since each required the same functionality. It is also possible to connect one signal to multiple callback functions, although this is not recommended. Instead, you should just implement the whole functionality in a single callback function.

Managing Widget Flags

One important property of a widget is its ability to become disabled or inactive. This is managed by the sensitive property, which will disable the widget when set to FALSE with gtk_widget_set_sensitive().

```
gtk_widget_set_sensitive (other_toggle, FALSE);
```

Sensitivity is actually only one of many widget flags provided by the GtkWidgetFlags enumeration. Widget flags, which are in the following list, can be set with GTK_WIDGET_SET_FLAGS() or disabled with GTK_WIDGET_UNSET_FLAGS(). You can also get a list of the flags that are set for a widget with GTK_WIDGET_FLAGS().

- GTK_TOPLEVEL: The widget does not have a parent widget. This is usually set for widgets such as windows and menus. This flag should always be set throughout a top-level widget's lifetime.

- GTK_NO_WINDOW: The widget does not have its own GdkWindow, so drawing is done with the GdkWindow of the parent. You can use this flag to test whether a widget needs a GtkEventBox to catch GDK events.

- GTK_REALIZED: The widget was realized with gtk_widget_realize(). This flag will be automatically unset when you unrealize the widget.

- GTK_MAPPED: The widget was mapped with gtk_widget_map(). This basically means that the widget was shown to the user if its parent is visible.

- GTK_VISIBLE: This flag does not mean that the user is able to see the widget, but that the widget will only be visible if its parent is also visible to the user.

- GTK_SENSITIVE: The widget is able to interact with the user and receive certain events such as button and key-press events.

- GTK_PARENT_SENSITIVE: A widget's parent must be sensitive for the widget itself to be set as sensitive. Therefore, GTK_SENSITIVE is dependent on this property.

- GTK_CAN_FOCUS: The widget is able to grab focus if requested.

- GTK_HAS_FOCUS: The widget has focus, which can be set with gtk_widget_grab_focus(). This property depends on GTK_CAN_FOCUS.

- GTK_CAN_DEFAULT: The widget is able to become the default widget of the window.

- GTK_HAS_DEFAULT: The widget is the default widget of the window. You can set the default widget with gtk_widget_grab_default().

- GTK_HAS_GRAB: The widget is in the stack of grab widgets, which shows preference for receiving events.

- GTK_RC_STYLE: GTK+ searched for a style for the widget in a resource (RC) definition. This can be set even if no style was found for the widget.

- GTK_COMPOSITE_CHILD: The widget exists to give details about the implementation of its parent widget and should not be shown to the user.

- GTK_APP_PAINTABLE: If set, the application should be able to draw on the widget. This prevents GTK+ from overwriting the current content.

- GTK_RECEIVES_DEFAULT: If set, the widget will automatically receive the default action even if it is not the default widget of the window.

- GTK_DOUBLE_BUFFERED: When the widget is exposed to the user, it should be double-buffered. This helps the window to be updated for the user in one step, which is smoother to the eye.

- GTK_NO_SHOW_ALL: If you set this flag, calls to gtk_widget_show_all() will not affect the widget. You will need to manually show the widget yourself. This allows you to prevent a widget from being shown with the rest of the application.

When the toggled signal is emitted, you will most often want to check whether a toggle button is active, because it is emitted both when the widget is activated and deactivated. This can be performed with gtk_toggle_button_get_active(). TRUE is returned if the button is active or FALSE if it is inactive. The current state of a toggle button can also be set with gtk_toggle_button_set_active().

```
void gtk_toggle_button_set_active (GtkToggleButton *toggle,
                                   gboolean active);
```

Check Buttons

In most cases, you will not want to use the GtkToggleButton widget, because it looks exactly like a normal GtkButton. Instead, GTK+ provides the GtkCheckButton widget, which places a discrete toggle next to the display text. GtkCheckButton is derived from the GtkToggleButton class. Two instances of this widget can be viewed in Figure 4-3.

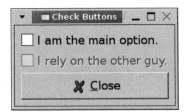

Figure 4-3. *Check buttons*

As with toggle buttons, three functions are provided for GtkCheckButton initialization. These include gtk_check_button_new(), gtk_check_button_new_with_label(), and gtk_check_button_new_with_mnemonic(). GtkCheckButton also inherits the important toggled signal, which is used in Listing 4-3.

Listing 4-3. *Check Button Interaction (checkbuttons.c)*

```
#include <gtk/gtk.h>

static void check_toggled (GtkToggleButton*, GtkWidget*);

int main (int argc,
          char *argv[])
```

```
{
  GtkWidget *window, *vbox, *check1, *check2, *close;

  gtk_init (&argc, &argv);

  window = gtk_window_new (GTK_WINDOW_TOPLEVEL);
  gtk_window_set_title (GTK_WINDOW (window), "Check Buttons");
  gtk_container_set_border_width (GTK_CONTAINER (window), 10);

  check1 = gtk_check_button_new_with_label ("I am the main option.");
  check2 = gtk_check_button_new_with_label ("I rely on the other guy.");

  /* Only enable the second check button when the first is enabled. */
  gtk_widget_set_sensitive (check2, FALSE);
  g_signal_connect (G_OBJECT (check1), "toggled",
                    G_CALLBACK (check_toggled),
                    (gpointer) check2);

  close = gtk_button_new_from_stock (GTK_STOCK_CLOSE);
  g_signal_connect_swapped (G_OBJECT (close), "clicked",
                            G_CALLBACK (gtk_widget_destroy),
                            (gpointer) window);

  vbox = gtk_vbox_new (FALSE, 5);
  gtk_box_pack_start (GTK_BOX (vbox), check1, FALSE, TRUE, 0);
  gtk_box_pack_start (GTK_BOX (vbox), check2, FALSE, TRUE, 0);
  gtk_box_pack_start (GTK_BOX (vbox), close, FALSE, TRUE, 0);

  gtk_container_add (GTK_CONTAINER (window), table);
  gtk_widget_show_all (window);

  gtk_main ();
  return 0;
}

/* If the main check button is active, enable the other. Otherwise, disable
 * the supplementary check button. */
static void
check_toggled (GtkToggleButton *check1,
               GtkWidget *check2)
{
  if (gtk_toggle_button_get_active (check1))
    gtk_widget_set_sensitive (check2, TRUE);
  else
    gtk_widget_set_sensitive (check2, FALSE);
}
```

Excluding the initialization methods, all functionality for check boxes is implemented in the GtkToggleButton class and its ancestors. GtkCheckButton is merely a convenience widget, which provides the graphical differences from standard GtkButton widgets.

Radio Buttons

The second type of widget derived from GtkToggleButton is the radio button widget. In fact, GtkRadioButton is actually derived from GtkCheckButton. Radio buttons are toggles that are generally grouped together.

In a group, when one radio button is selected, all others will be deselected. The group forbids selecting multiple radio buttons at once. This allows you to provide multiple options to the user where only one should be selected.

■**Note** There is no way provided by GTK+ to deselect a radio button, so a group of one radio button is not desirable. The user will not be able to deselect the option! In the case that you only need one button, you should use a GtkCheckButton or GtkToggleButton widget.

Radio buttons are drawn as a discrete circular toggle to the side of the label widget, so they can be differentiated from other types of toggle buttons. It is possible to draw radio buttons with the same toggle as GtkCheckButton, but this should not be done, because it can confuse and frustrate the user. A group of four radio buttons in a vertical box is shown in Figure 4-4.

Figure 4-4. *Radio buttons*

For radio buttons to work correctly, they must all be referenced to another radio button in the group. Otherwise, all of the buttons would act as independent toggle buttons. An example of how to use multiple radio buttons is shown in Listing 4-4.

Listing 4-4. *Selfish Toggle Buttons (radiobuttons.c)*

```
#include <gtk/gtk.h>

int main (int argc,
          char *argv[])
{
  GtkWidget *window, *vbox, *radio1, *radio2, *radio3;

  gtk_init (&argc, &argv);

  window = gtk_window_new (GTK_WINDOW_TOPLEVEL);
  gtk_window_set_title (GTK_WINDOW (window), "Radio Buttons");
  gtk_container_set_border_width (GTK_CONTAINER (window), 10);

  /* Create three radio buttons where the second two join radio1's group. */
  radio1 = gtk_radio_button_new_with_label (NULL, "I want to be clicked!");
  radio2 = gtk_radio_button_new_with_label_from_widget (GTK_RADIO_BUTTON (radio1),
                                                        "Click me instead!");
  radio3 = gtk_radio_button_new_with_label_from_widget (GTK_RADIO_BUTTON (radio1),
                                                        "No! Click me!");

  /* Note: The radio button you create the new widget from does not matter as
   *       long as it is already a member of the group! */
  radio4 = gtk_radio_button_new_with_label_from_widget (GTK_RADIO_BUTTON (radio3),
                                                        "No! Click me instead!");

  vbox = gtk_vbox_new (FALSE, 5);
  gtk_box_pack_start_defaults (GTK_BOX (vbox), radio1);
  gtk_box_pack_start_defaults (GTK_BOX (vbox), radio2);
  gtk_box_pack_start_defaults (GTK_BOX (vbox), radio3);
  gtk_box_pack_start_defaults (GTK_BOX (vbox), radio4);

  gtk_container_add (GTK_CONTAINER (window), vbox);
  gtk_widget_show_all (window);

  gtk_main ();
  return 0;
}
```

The first radio button in a group can be created with any of the following three functions. However, if you want to use a GtkLabel widget as the child, it is also possible to use a mnemonic widget, so the toggle can be activated from the keyboard.

```
GtkWidget* gtk_radio_button_new              (GSList *group);
GtkWidget* gtk_radio_button_new_with_label   (GSList *group,
                                               const gchar *label);
GtkWidget* gtk_radio_button_new_with_mnemonic (GSList *group,
                                               const gchar *label);
```

You will notice that NULL is specified for the radio group in each call. This is because the simplest way to create a group of radio buttons is to associate them to another widget in the group. By using this method, you avoid having to use the GLib with singly linked lists, since the list will be created and managed for you automatically. (GSList data structures will be covered later in Chapters 5 and 6.)

You can create any type of toggle button, including radio buttons, without a label, in which case you would add your own child widget with gtk_container_add(). You can also create radio buttons with a programmatically defined label or a mnemonic label.

The easiest way to create the rest of the radio buttons is with one of the following three _from_widget() functions. Similar to creating the first radio button, these can be created with a label, a mnemonic label, or without an initial child widget.

```
GtkWidget* gtk_radio_button_new_from_widget              (GtkRadioButton *group);
GtkWidget* gtk_radio_button_new_with_label_from_widget   (GtkRadioButton *group,
                                                           const gchar *label);
GtkWidget* gtk_radio_button_new_with_mnemonic_from_widget (GtkRadioButton *group,
                                                           const gchar *label);
```

Referring the initialization function to a radio button that already exists creates each of these. GTK+ will add the new radio button to the group from the specified widget. Because of this, you need only refer to any widget that already exists within the desired radio group.

Lastly, every radio button in the group must be connected to the toggled signal. When a radio button is selected, only two radio buttons will emit the toggled signal, because one will be selected, and another will be deselected. You will not be able to catch all radio button signals if you do not connect every radio button to toggled.

Text Entries

The GtkEntry widget is a single line, free-form text entry widget. It is implemented in a general manner, so that it can be molded to fit many types of solutions. It can be used for text entry, password entry, and even number selections.

GtkEntry also implements the GtkEditable interface, which provides a large number of functions that are created to handle selections of text. An example GtkEntry widget is shown in Figure 4-5. This text entry is used for password entry.

Figure 4-5. *A password text entry*

■**Note** GtkEditable is a special type of object called an interface. An interface is a set of APIs that are implemented by multiple widgets and used for consistency. You will learn how to implement and utilize interfaces in your own widgets in Chapter 11.

The GtkEntry widget considers all text to be standard strings. The only way it differentiates between normal text and passwords is that a special character called an invisibility character is shown instead of password content. Listing 4-5 shows you how to use a GtkEntry widget for password entry. If you want to use a GtkEntry widget for normal text entry, you need only to turn visibility on.

Listing 4-5. *Retrieving User Information (entries.c)*

```
#include <gtk/gtk.h>

int main (int argc,
          char *argv[])
{
  GtkWidget *window, *vbox, *hbox, *question, *label, *pass;
  gchar* str;

  gtk_init (&argc, &argv);

  window = gtk_window_new (GTK_WINDOW_TOPLEVEL);
  gtk_window_set_title (GTK_WINDOW (window), "Password?");
  gtk_container_set_border_width (GTK_CONTAINER (window), 10);

  str = g_strconcat ("What is the password for ", g_get_user_name(), "?", NULL);
  question = gtk_label_new (str);
  label = gtk_label_new ("Password:");

  /* Create a new GtkEntry widget and hide its content from view. */
  pass = gtk_entry_new ();
  gtk_entry_set_visibility (GTK_ENTRY (pass), FALSE);
  gtk_entry_set_invisible_char (GTK_ENTRY (pass), '*');
```

```
    hbox = gtk_hbox_new (FALSE, 5);
    gtk_box_pack_start_defaults (GTK_BOX (hbox), label);
    gtk_box_pack_start_defaults (GTK_BOX (hbox), pass);

    vbox = gtk_vbox_new (FALSE, 5);
    gtk_box_pack_start_defaults (GTK_BOX (vbox), question);
    gtk_box_pack_start_defaults (GTK_BOX (vbox), hbox);

    gtk_container_add (GTK_CONTAINER (window), vbox);
    gtk_widget_show_all (window);

    gtk_main ();
    return 0;
}
```

Entry Properties

The GtkEntry widget is a highly flexible widget, because it was designed to be employed in the maximum number of instances. This can be seen from the wide array of properties provided by the class. A sampling of the most important of those is included in this section. For a full list of properties, you should reference Appendix A.

Text does not always have to be editable in a GtkEntry widget. If you set the entry as non-editable with gtk_editable_set_editable(), the user will not be able to edit the text. However, the user *will* still be able to use the selection and copy functionality of the GtkEntry widget, because this property is not the same thing as setting the widget as insensitive.

```
void gtk_editable_set_editable (GtkEditable *editable,
                                gboolean is_editable);
```

Oftentimes, you will want to restrict the length of the free-form text entered into an entry widget because of string limitations of the value. In the following function prototype, gtk_entry_set_max_length() limits the text of the entry to max_length characters. This can be useful when you want to limit the length of user names, passwords, or other length-sensitive information.

```
void gtk_entry_set_max_length (GtkEntry *entry,
                               gint max_length);
```

Invisibility characters facilitate password entries in GTK+. The invisibility character is the character that will replace the actual password content in the entry, which can be set with gtk_entry_set_invisible_char(). The default character for the entry is an asterisk.

```
void gtk_entry_set_invisible_char (GtkEntry *entry,
                                   gunichar inv_char);
void gtk_entry_set_visibility     (GtkEntry *entry,
                                   gboolean visible);
```

After specifying the invisibility character, you can hide all entered text by setting visibility to FALSE with gtk_entry_set_visiblity(). You will still be able to retrieve the actual content of the entry programmatically even though it is hidden from view.

Inserting Text into a GtkEntry Widget

There are multiple ways to insert text to a GtkEntry widget. The simplest way is to use gtk_entry_set_text(), which will overwrite the whole content of the text entry with the given string. However, this is only useful if you no longer care about the current text displayed by the widget.

```
void gtk_entry_set_text (GtkEntry *entry,
                         const gchar *text);
```

The current text displayed by GtkEntry can be retrieved with gtk_entry_get_text(). This string is used internally by the widget and must *never* be freed or modified in any way.

It is also possible to use gtk_editable_insert_text() to insert text into a GtkEntry widget. This function accepts the text to insert, the length of the text in bytes, and the position where the text should be inserted.

```
void gtk_editable_insert_text (GtkEditable *editable,
                               const gchar *text,
                               gint length_of_text,
                               gint *position);
```

There are also functions provided for prepending and appending text, but these are not needed, since you can perform these functions by providing positions of 0 and -1, respectively, to gtk_editable_insert_text().

Manipulating GtkEntry Text

Deleting specific content from a text entry is easy with gtk_editable_delete_text(). It will remove all of the text between the two positions specified but not the character at the end position.

```
void gtk_editable_delete_text (GtkEditable *editable,
                               gint start_pos,
                               gint end_pos);
```

When using gtk_editable_delete_text(), the order of the positions that you specify does not matter. Also, if you specify -1 as the end position, the characters from the start position to the end of the text will be deleted.

If you need a specific region of text to be selected automatically, this can be done with gtk_editable_select_region(). As with deleting text, an end position of -1 will select all of the text from the start position to the end of the content. Manual and automatic selections are what facilitate the following few functions.

```
void gtk_editable_select_region (GtkEditable *editable,
                                 gint start_pos,
                                 gint end_pos);
```

Once you are able to select text, it would be useful to be able to delete the selection. This is very easy to do with gtk_editable_delete_selection(). This function will delete all of the selected text, leaving any nonselected text.

```
void gtk_editable_delete_selection (GtkEditable *editable);
```

In addition to retrieving the whole textual content of the widget, it is possible to retrieve only a section of the text with gtk_editable_get_chars(). This will return a copy of the specified string, which must be freed with g_free() when you are finished with it.

```
gchar* gtk_editable_get_chars (GtkEditable *editable,
                               gint start_pos,
                               gint end_pos);
```

The following three functions perform various clipboard functions. There are keyboard accelerators for cutting (Ctrl+X), copying (Ctrl+C), and pasting (Ctrl+V) built into entries by default. Therefore, you will not usually need to implement clipboard functionality when using a GtkEntry widget.

```
void gtk_editable_cut_clipboard   (GtkEditable *editable);
void gtk_editable_copy_clipboard  (GtkEditable *editable);
void gtk_editable_paste_clipboard (GtkEditable *editable);
```

Spin Buttons

The GtkSpinButton widget is a number selection widget that is capable of handling integers and floating-point numbers. It is derived from GtkEntry, so GtkSpinButton inherits all of its functions and signals.

Adjustments

Before covering the GtkSpinButton widget, you must understand the GtkAdjustment class. GtkAdjustment is one of the few classes in GTK+ that is not considered a widget, because it is derived directly from GtkObject. It is used for several widgets including spin buttons, view ports, and the multiple widgets derived from GtkRange.

New adjustments are created with gtk_adjustment_new(), although they are usually cast with GTK_ADJUSTMENT() upon initialization, because storage as a GtkObject is not practical. Once added to a widget, memory management of the adjustment is handled by the widget, so you do not have to worry about this aspect of the object.

```
GtkObject* gtk_adjustment_new (gdouble initial_value,
                               gdouble lower_range,
                               gdouble upper_range,
                               gdouble step_increment,
                               gdouble page_increment,
                               gdouble page_size);
```

New adjustments are initialized with six parameters. A list of these parameters follows.

- initial_value: The value stored by the adjustment when it is initialized. This corresponds to the value property of the GtkAdjustment class.

- lower_range: The minimum value the adjustment will be allowed to hold. This corresponds to the lower property of the GtkAdjustment class.

- upper_range: The maximum value the adjustment will be allowed to hold. This corresponds to the upper property of the GtkAdjustment class.

- step_increment: The increment to make the smallest change possible. If you want to count all integers between 1 and 10, the increment would be set to 1.

- page_increment: The increment to make when Page Up or Page Down is pressed. This is almost always larger than the step_increment.

- page_size: The size of a page. This value does not have much use in a GtkSpinButton, so it should be set to the same value as page_increment or to 0.

There are two useful signals provided by the GtkAdjustment class: changed and value-changed. The changed signal is emitted when one or more properties of the adjustment have been altered, excluding the value property. The value-changed signal is emitted when the current value of the adjustment has been altered.

A Spin Button Example

The spin button widget allows the user to select an integer or floating-point number by incrementing or decrementing with the up or down arrows. The user can still type in a value with the keyboard, and it will be displayed as the nearest acceptable value if it is out of range. Figure 4-6 shows two spin buttons in action that display an integer and a floating-point number.

Figure 4-6. *Spin buttons*

As previously stated, spin buttons can be used to show integer or floating-point numbers. In actuality, numbers are stored as gdouble values. The spin button handles rounding the number to the correct number of decimal places. Listing 4-6 is a simple example that creates both integer and floating-point number spin buttons.

Listing 4-6. *Integer and Floating-point Number Selection (spinbuttons.c)*

```
#include <gtk/gtk.h>

int main (int argc,
          char *argv[])
{
  GtkWidget *window, *spin_int, *spin_float, *vbox;
  GtkAdjustment *integer, *float_pt;

  gtk_init (&argc, &argv);

  window = gtk_window_new (GTK_WINDOW_TOPLEVEL);
  gtk_window_set_title (GTK_WINDOW (window), "Spin Buttons");
  gtk_container_set_border_width (GTK_CONTAINER (window), 10);
  gtk_widget_set_size_request (window, 150, 100);

  /* Create two new adjustments. The first spans between 0 and 10, starting at 5 and
   * moves in increments of 1. The second spans between 0 and 1, starting at 0.5 and
   * moves in increments of 0.1. */
  integer = GTK_ADJUSTMENT (gtk_adjustment_new (5.0, 0.0, 10.0, 1.0, 2.0, 2.0));
  float_pt = GTK_ADJUSTMENT (gtk_adjustment_new (0.5, 0.0, 1.0, 0.1, 0.5, 0.5));

  /* Create two new spin buttons. The first will display no decimal places and the
   * second will display one decimal place. */
  spin_int = gtk_spin_button_new (integer, 1.0, 0);
  spin_float = gtk_spin_button_new (float_pt, 0.1, 1);

  vbox = gtk_vbox_new (FALSE, 5);
  gtk_box_pack_start_defaults (GTK_BOX (vbox), spin_int);
  gtk_box_pack_start_defaults (GTK_BOX (vbox), spin_float);

  gtk_container_add (GTK_CONTAINER (window), vbox);
  gtk_widget_show_all (window);

  gtk_main ();
  return 0;
}
```

Before creating the spin buttons, you should create the adjustments. You can also initialize the spin button with a NULL adjustment, but it will be set as insensitive.

After your adjustments are initialized, you can create new spin buttons with gtk_spin_button_new(). The other two parameters in the initialization function specify the climb rate of the spin button and the number of decimal places to display. The climb rate is how much the value should be incremented or decremented when an arrow button is pressed.

```
GtkWidget *gtk_spin_button_new (GtkAdjustment *adjustment,
                                gdouble climb_rate,
                                guint digits);
```

Alternatively, you can create a new spin button with gtk_spin_button_new_with_range(), which will automatically create a new adjustment based on the minimum, maximum, and step values you specify. The initial value is set to the minimum value plus a page increment of ten times the step_increment by default. The precision of the widget is automatically set to the value of step_increment.

```
GtkWidget* gtk_spin_button_new_with_range (gdouble minimum_value,
                                           gdouble maximum_value,
                                           gdouble step_increment);
```

You can call gtk_spin_button_set_digits() to set a new precision of the spin button and gtk_spin_button_set_value() to set a new value. The value will automatically be altered if it is out of bounds of the spin button.

```
void gtk_spin_button_set_value (GtkSpinButton *spin_button,
                                gdouble value);
```

Horizontal and Vertical Scales

Another type of widget called a scale allows you to provide a horizontal or vertical slider that can choose an integer or a floating-point number. GtkHScale is a horizontal scale widget, and GtkVScale is a vertical scale widget. Both of these classes are derived from GtkScale, which provides properties, signals, and functions.

The functionality of the GtkScale widget is not much different from GtkSpinButton. It is often used when you want to restrict the user from entering values, since the value is chosen by moving the slider. Figure 4-7 shows a screenshot of two horizontal scale widgets.

Figure 4-7. *Horizontal scale widgets*

Scales provide essentially the same functionality as spin buttons, except using a slider chooses the number. To show the similarities between the widgets, Listing 4-7 implements the same functionality as Listing 4-6: two sliders allow the user to select an integer and a floating-point number.

Listing 4-7. *Integer and Floating-point Number Selection with Scales (scales.c)*

```c
#include <gtk/gtk.h>

int main (int argc,
          char *argv[])
{
  GtkWidget *window, *scale_int, *scale_float, *vbox;

  gtk_init (&argc, &argv);

  window = gtk_window_new (GTK_WINDOW_TOPLEVEL);
  gtk_window_set_title (GTK_WINDOW (window), "Scales");
  gtk_container_set_border_width (GTK_CONTAINER (window), 10);
  gtk_widget_set_size_request (window, 250, -1);

  /* Create a scale that scrolls integers and one that scrolls floating point. */
  scale_int = gtk_hscale_new_with_range (0.0, 10.0, 1.0);
  scale_float = gtk_hscale_new_with_range (0.0, 1.0, 0.1);

  /* Set the number of decimal places to display for each widget. */
  gtk_scale_set_digits (GTK_SCALE (scale_int), 0);
  gtk_scale_set_digits (GTK_SCALE (scale_float), 1);

  /* Set the position of the value with respect to the widget. */
  gtk_scale_set_value_pos (GTK_SCALE (scale_int), GTK_POS_RIGHT);
  gtk_scale_set_value_pos (GTK_SCALE (scale_float), GTK_POS_LEFT);

  vbox = gtk_vbox_new (FALSE, 5);
  gtk_box_pack_start_defaults (GTK_BOX (vbox), scale_int);
  gtk_box_pack_start_defaults (GTK_BOX (vbox), scale_float);

  gtk_container_add (GTK_CONTAINER (window), vbox);
  gtk_widget_show_all (window);

  gtk_main ();
  return 0;
}
```

There are two ways to create new scale widgets. The first is with gtk_hscale_new() or gtk_vscale_new(), which accepts a GtkAdjustment that defines how the scale will work.

```c
GtkWidget *gtk_hscale_new (GtkAdjustment *adjustment);
```

Alternatively, you can create scales with gtk_hscale_new_with_range() or gtk_vscale_new_with_range(). This function accepts the minimum value, the maximum value, and the step increment of the scale.

```
GtkWidget *gtk_hscale_new_with_range (gdouble minimum,
                                      gdouble maximum,
                                      gdouble step);
```

Since the value of the scale is always stored as a gdouble, you will need to define the number of decimal places to show with gtk_scale_set_digits() if the default value is not what you want. The default number of decimal places is calculated based on the number of decimal places provided for the step increment. For example, if you provide a step increment of 0.01, two decimal places will be displayed by default.

```
void gtk_scale_set_digits (GtkScale *scale,
                           gint digits);
```

Depending on what type of scale widget you are using, you may want to change where the value is displayed with gtk_scale_set_value_pos(). Positions are defined by the GtkPositionType enumeration, and they are GTK_POS_LEFT, GTK_POS_RIGHT, GTK_POS_TOP, and GTK_POS_BOTTOM. You can also use gtk_scale_set_draw_value() to hide the value from the user's view altogether.

```
void gtk_scale_set_value_pos (GtkScale *scale,
                              GtkPositionType pos);
```

GtkScale is derived from a widget called GtkRange. This widget is an abstract type that provides the ability to handle an adjustment. Because of this, you should use gtk_range_get_value() to retrieve the current value of the scale. GtkRange also provides the value-changed signal, which is emitted when the user changes the position of the scale.

Widget Styles

In the next few sections, you will be editing widget style properties, so it is time to learn about the GtkStyle structure and resource files. Resource files are external collections of style settings that can be loaded and applied to your application during runtime to allow for further customization.

The GtkStyle Structure

Every GtkWidget has five public members, which are shown in the following code snippet. These are style information, size requisition, size allocation, a GdkWindow that is used to draw the widget on the screen, and a pointer to the parent widget.

```
typedef struct
{
  GtkStyle *style;
  GtkRequisition requisition;
  GtkAllocation allocation;
  GdkWindow *window;
  GtkWidget *parent;
} GtkWidget;
```

The GtkStyle structure stores drawing information about the widget. The content of the structure follows:

```
typedef struct
{
  GdkColor fg[5]            /* The foreground color for most widgets. */
  GdkColor bg[5]            /* The background color for most widgets. */
  GdkColor light[5]         /* Lighter colors used for creating widget shadows. */
  GdkColor dark[5]          /* Darker colors used for creating widget shadows. */
  GdkColor mid[5]           /* The color midway between light and dark. */
  GdkColor text[5]          /* The text color for most text widgets. */
  GdkColor base[5]          /* The background color used for text-editing widgets. */
  GdkColor text_aa[5];      /* Used for anti-aliased text colors. */
  GdkColor black, white;    /* Colors that represent "Black" and "White". */

  PangoFontDescription *font_desc;  /* The default text font. */
  gint xthickness, ythickness;      /* Thickness of lines. */
  GdkPixmap *bg_pixmap[5];          /* Background image to use for a widget. */

  /* Graphics contexts that hold drawing properties for each color and state. */
  GdkGC *fg_gc [5], *bg_gc [5], *light_gc[5], *dark_gc[5], *mid_gc[5], *text_gc[5],
       *base_gc[5], *text_aa_gc[5];
  GdkGC *black_gc, *white_gc;
} GtkStyle;
```

There are many objects in the GtkStyle structure. Each of these will have a default value set by the user's style, so overriding them may not always be a good idea. However, if it is necessary, editing a widget's GtkStyle is a simple way to change how it is displayed.

You will notice that many of the style properties are arrays of file elements. This is because each of these elements can have different values for one of the following five possible widget states:

- GTK_STATE_NORMAL: The widget during normal operation.

- GTK_STATE_ACTIVE: An active widget, such as when a toggle is depressed.

- GTK_STATE_PRELIGHT: A widget when the mouse pointer is over the widget; it will respond to button clicks.

- GTK_STATE_SELECTED: A widget when the widget or its text has been selected.

- GTK_STATE_INSENSITIVE: A widget is deactivated and will not respond to the user.

Resource Files

GTK+ provides a way for applications to use user-defined styles called resource files (RC files). RC files allow the user to define styles for widget types or individual widgets, which can be changed to fit the user's preferences. These are usually stored in the user's home directory along with other application data, so that the user has permissions to alter the settings.

To load a resource file, you should call gtk_rc_parse() when loading your application. This will automatically apply the styles on all appropriate widgets.

```
void gtk_rc_parse (const gchar *filename);
```

Also, if you want to directly reference a widget from an RC file, you need to use gtk_widget_set_name() to set a unique name for the widget. This name will be used in the RC file to set the widget's style and/or the styles of its children.

In Listing 4-8, a simple example RC file is shown. In this example, multiple widget styles are created, each style containing a number of properties.

Listing 4-8. *Defining Widget Styles (.gtkrc)*

```
style "widgets"
{
  xthickness = 2
  ythickness = 2

  fg[ACTIVE] = "#FFFFFF"
  fg[SELECTED] = "#003366"
  fg[NORMAL] = "#CCCCCC"
  fg[PRELIGHT] = "#FFFFFF"
  fg[INSENSITIVE] = "#999999"

  bg[ACTIVE] = "#003366"
  bg[SELECTED] = "#FFFFFF"
  bg[NORMAL] = "#666666"
  bg[PRELIGHT] = "#003366"
  bg[INSENSITIVE] = "#666666"
}

style "labels" = "widgets" {
  font_name = "Sans Bold 14"
}

style "buttons" = "widgets" {
  GtkButton::inner-border = { 10, 10, 10, 10 }
}

style "checks" = "buttons" {
  GtkCheckButton::indicator-size = 25
}

class "GtkWindow" style "widgets"
class "GtkLabel" style "labels"
class "GtkCheckButton" style "checks"
class "Gtk*Button" style "buttons"
```

Figure 4-8 shows an application that is taking advantage of the RC file shown in Listing 4-8. The colors and font are different from the examples found in the past few chapters.

Figure 4-8. *An example application using .gtkrc*

If you would like to explore the standard styles available to all widgets in RC files, you should read Appendix C. This section will teach you how to apply those styles in your own applications.

Styles can be applied by the widget type with the class directive as shown in the preceding example. In this example, the buttons style is applied to all Gtk*Button* widgets, where the asterisk is used as a wildcard. This is applied to every widget in the application that has a matching class name.

```
class "Gtk*Button" style "buttons"
```

The second method for applying a widget style is based on a hierarchy pattern with the widget directive. This example applies the stylename style to all direct and indirect children of widgetname that are of the type GtkButton.

```
widget "widgetname.*.GtkButton" style "stylename"
```

In addition to the asterisk wildcard that matches zero or more of any character, you can use a question mark wildcard to match one or more of any character. Also, widget hierarchy is shown by using a period, where the widget to the right of the period is the child of the widget to the left.

The problem with the widget directive is that if a name is specified for the widget, it must be used instead of the class name. If you only want to use widget classes, you can use the widget_class directive. This allows you to ignore all widget names and apply a style to all widgets that follow the specified pattern.

```
widget_class "GtkWindow.*.GtkLabel" style "stylename"
```

In addition to basic style directives, the following list shows other top-level directives supported in RC files:

- `include`: Include another resource file. You can specify either an absolute or relative filename.

- `module_path`: A list of paths separated by colons that will be searched for theme engines referenced by the RC file.

- `*pixmap_path`: A list of paths separated by colons that will be searched for theme engines referenced by the RC file.

If you are planning on using RC files in an application, you should make sure to provide an example file to the user. You can use the pound (#) symbol to add comments to an RC file to give the user help in editing the content.

This section only gave you a very basic introduction to RC files. For more information, you should reference Appendix C. There are also a lot of resources for learning about RC files and themes with GTK+ found at `http://art.gnome.org`.

Additional Buttons

While the `GtkButton` widget allows you to create your own custom buttons, GTK+ provides three additional button widgets that are at your disposal: the color selection button, file chooser button, and font selection button.

Each of the sections covering these three widgets will also cover other important concepts such as the `GdkColor` structure, file filters, and Pango fonts. These concepts will be used in later chapters, so it is a good idea to get a grasp of them now.

Color Buttons

The `GtkColorButton` widget provides a simple way for you to allow your users to select a specific color. These colors can be specified as six-digit hexadecimal values or the RGB value. The color button itself displays the selected color in a rectangular block set as the child widget of the button. An example of this can be viewed in Figure 4-9.

Figure 4-9. *A color selection dialog*

A GtkColorButton Example

When clicked, the color button opens a dialog that allows the user to enter in the color value or browse for a choice on the color wheel. The color wheel is provided so the user is not required to know the numeric values of the colors. Listing 4-9 shows how to use the GtkColorButton widget in an application.

Listing 4-9. *Color Buttons and GdkColors (colorbuttons.c)*

```
#include <gtk/gtk.h>

static void color_changed (GtkColorButton*, GtkWidget*);

int main (int argc,
          char *argv[])
{
  GtkWidget *window, *button, *label, *hbox;
  GdkColor color;

  gtk_init (&argc, &argv);
```

```
  window = gtk_window_new (GTK_WINDOW_TOPLEVEL);
  gtk_window_set_title (GTK_WINDOW (window), "Color Button");
  gtk_container_set_border_width (GTK_CONTAINER (window), 10);

  /* Set the initial color as #003366 and set the dialog title. */
  gdk_color_parse ("#003366", &color);
  button = gtk_color_button_new_with_color (&color);
  gtk_color_button_set_title (GTK_COLOR_BUTTON (button), "Select a Color");

  label = gtk_label_new ("Look at my color!");
  gtk_widget_modify_fg (label, GTK_STATE_NORMAL, &color);

  g_signal_connect (G_OBJECT (button), "color_set",
                    G_CALLBACK (color_changed),
                    (gpointer) label);

  hbox = gtk_hbox_new (FALSE, 5);
  gtk_box_pack_start_defaults (GTK_BOX (hbox), button);
  gtk_box_pack_start_defaults (GTK_BOX (hbox), label);

  gtk_container_add (GTK_CONTAINER (window), hbox);
  gtk_widget_show_all (window);

  gtk_main ();
  return 0;
}

/* Retrieve the selected color and set it as the GtkLabel's foreground color. */
static void
color_changed (GtkColorButton *button,
               GtkWidget *label)
{
  GdkColor color;
  gtk_color_button_get_color (button, &color);
  gtk_widget_modify_fg (label, GTK_STATE_NORMAL, &color);
}
```

In most cases, you will want to create a GtkColorButton with an initial color value, which is done by specifying a GdkColor object to gtk_color_button_new_with_color(). The default color, if none is provided, is opaque black with the alpha option disabled.

Storing Colors in GdkColor

GdkColor is a structure that stores red, green, and blue values for a color as shown in the following code snippet. The pixel object automatically stores the index of the color when it is allocated in a color map, so there is usually no need for you to alter this value.

```
struct GdkColor
{
  guint32 pixel;
  guint16 red;
  guint16 green;
  guint16 blue;
};
```

After creating a new GdkColor object, if you already know the red, green, and blue values of the color, you can specify them in the following manner. Red, green, and blue values are stored as unsigned integer values ranging from 0 to 65,535, where 65,535 indicates full color intensity. For example, the following color refers to white:

```
color.red = 65535;
color.green = 65535;
color.blue = 65535;
```

In most cases, you will be more familiar with the six-digit hexadecimal value for the color, such as #FFFFFF that refers to the color white. Therefore, GDK provides gdk_color_parse(), which parses the hexadecimal color into the correct RGB values. This function was used in Listing 4-9.

```
gboolean gdk_color_parse (const gchar *color_string,
                          GdkColor *color);
```

Using the Color Button

After setting your initial color, you can choose the title that will be given to the color selection dialog with gtk_color_button_set_title(). By default, the title is "Pick a Color", so it is not necessary to set this value if you are content with this title.

```
void gtk_color_button_set_title (GtkColorButton *button,
                                 const gchar *title);
```

The color selection dialog, covered in the next chapter in more detail, is shown when the user clicks the button. It allows the user to change the selected color. You can view the color selection dialog in Figure 4-9.

When the color value is changed, the color-set signal is emitted for the widget. In Listing 4-5, the signal is caught and the foreground color of a GtkLabel changed with gtk_widget_modify_fg() as follows:

```
gtk_color_button_get_color (button, &color);
gtk_widget_modify_fg (label, GTK_STATE_NORMAL, &color);
```

In Listing 4-9, the foreground color was set in the normal widget state, which is what state all labels will be in, by and large, unless they are selectable. There are five options for the GtkStateType enumeration that can be used in gtk_widget_modify_fg(), which were presented in the "Widget Styles" section. You can reset the widget's foreground color to the default value by passing a NULL color.

File Chooser Buttons

The GtkFileChooserButton widget provides an easy method for you to ask users to choose a file or a folder. It implements the functionality of the GtkFileChooser interface, the file selection framework provided by GTK+. Figure 4-10 shows a file chooser button set to select a folder and a button set to select a file.

Figure 4-10. *File chooser buttons*

When the user clicks a GtkFileChooserButton, an instance of GtkFileChooserDialog is opened that allows the user to browse and select one file or one folder, depending on the type of button you created.

■**Note** You will not learn how to use the GtkFileChooserDialog widget until Chapter 5, but you do not need to directly interface with it at this point, because GtkFileChooserButton will handle all interactions with the dialog.

A GtkFileChooserButton Example

You are able to change basic settings such as the currently selected file, the current folder, and the title of the file selection window. Listing 4-10 shows you how to use both types of file chooser buttons.

Listing 4-10. *Using the File Chooser Button (filechooserbuttons.c)*

```
#include <gtk/gtk.h>

static void folder_changed (GtkFileChooser*, GtkFileChooser*);
static void file_changed (GtkFileChooser*, GtkLabel*);

int main (int argc,
          char *argv[])
{
  GtkWidget *window, *chooser1, *chooser2, label, *vbox;
  GtkFileFilter *filter1, *filter2;

  gtk_init (&argc, &argv);

  window = gtk_window_new (GTK_WINDOW_TOPLEVEL);
  gtk_window_set_title (GTK_WINDOW (window), "File Chooser Button");
  gtk_container_set_border_width (GTK_CONTAINER (window), 10);

  label = gtk_label_new ("");

  /* Create two buttons, one to select a folder and one to select a file. */
  chooser1 = gtk_file_chooser_button_new ("Choose a Folder",
                                    GTK_FILE_CHOOSER_ACTION_SELECT_FOLDER);
  chooser2 = gtk_file_chooser_button_new ("Choose a Folder",
                                    GTK_FILE_CHOOSER_ACTION_OPEN);

  /* Monitor when the selected folder or file are changed. */
  g_signal_connect (G_OBJECT (chooser1), "selection_changed",
                    G_CALLBACK (folder_changed),
                    (gpointer) chooser2);
  g_signal_connect (G_OBJECT (chooser2), "selection_changed",
                    G_CALLBACK (file_changed),
                    (gpointer) label);

  /* Set both file chooser buttons to the location of the user's home directory. */
  gtk_file_chooser_set_current_folder (GTK_FILE_CHOOSER (chooser1),
                                       g_get_home_dir());
  gtk_file_chooser_set_current_folder (GTK_FILE_CHOOSER (chooser2),
                                       g_get_home_dir());
```

```
    /* Provide a filter to show all files and one to show only 3 types of images. */
    filter1 = gtk_file_filter_new ();
    filter2 = gtk_file_filter_new ();
    gtk_file_filter_set_name (filter1, "Image Files");
    gtk_file_filter_set_name (filter2, "All Files");
    gtk_file_filter_add_pattern (filter1, "*.png");
    gtk_file_filter_add_pattern (filter1, "*.jpg");
    gtk_file_filter_add_pattern (filter1, "*.gif");
    gtk_file_filter_add_pattern (filter2, "*");

    /* Add both the filters to the file chooser button that selects files. */
    gtk_file_chooser_add_filter (GTK_FILE_CHOOSER (chooser2), filter1);
    gtk_file_chooser_add_filter (GTK_FILE_CHOOSER (chooser2), filter2);

    vbox = gtk_vbox_new (FALSE, 5);
    gtk_box_pack_start_defaults (GTK_BOX (vbox), chooser1);
    gtk_box_pack_start_defaults (GTK_BOX (vbox), chooser2);
    gtk_box_pack_start_defaults (GTK_BOX (vbox), label);

    gtk_container_add (GTK_CONTAINER (window), vbox);
    gtk_widget_show_all (window);

    gtk_main ();
    return 0;
}

/* When a folder is selected, use that as the new location of the other chooser. */
static void
folder_changed (GtkFileChooser *chooser1,
                GtkFileChooser *chooser2)
{
  gchar *folder = gtk_file_chooser_get_filename (GTK_FILE_CHOOSER (chooser1));
  gtk_file_chooser_set_current_folder (GTK_FILE_CHOOSER (chooser2), folder);
}

/* When a file is selected, display the full path in the GtkLabel widget. */
static void
file_changed (GtkFileChooser *chooser2,
              GtkLabel *label)
{
  gchar *file = gtk_file_chooser_get_filename (GTK_FILE_CHOOSER (chooser2));
  gtk_label_set_text (label, file);
}
```

File chooser button widgets are created with `gtk_file_chooser_button_new()`. This widget is able to serve two purposes: selecting a single file or a single folder. There are four types of file choosers that can be created (the remaining two are covered in Chapter 5), but file chooser buttons support only `GTK_FILE_CHOOSER_ACTION_OPEN` and `GTK_FILE_CHOOSER_ACTION_SELECT_FOLDER`.

- `GTK_FILE_CHOOSER_ACTION_OPEN`: The user will be able to select a single file that already exists on the system. You are able to provide filters to this type of action so that only specific file patterns are shown to the user.

- `GTK_FILE_CHOOSER_ACTION_SELECT_FOLDER`: The user will be able to select a single folder that already exists on the system.

The other parameter in `gtk_file_chooser_button_new()` allows you to set the title of the file chooser dialog that is shown when the user clicks the button. By default, the title is "Select A File," so you will want to make sure to reset the title if you use `GTK_FILE_CHOOSER_ACTION_SELECT_FOLDER`.

GtkFileChooser

The `GtkFileChooserButton` widget is an implementation of the functionality provided by the `GtkFileChooser` interface. This means that, while the button is not derived from `GtkFileChooser`, it can be treated as a file chooser if you cast it with `GTK_FILE_CHOOSER()`. You will notice that quite a few of the functions in Listing 4-10 utilize functions provided by `GtkFileChooser`.

In Listing 4-10, `gtk_file_chooser_set_current_folder()` was used to set the current folder of each file chooser button to the user's home directory. The contents of this folder will be shown when the user initially clicks a file chooser button unless it is changed through some other means. This function will return `TRUE` if the folder was successfully changed.

```
gboolean gtk_file_chooser_set_current_folder (GtkFileChooser *chooser,
                                              const gchar *filename);
```

The `g_get_home_dir()` function is a utility function provided by GLib that returns the current user's home directory. As with most features in GLib, this function is cross platform.

This brings up a useful characteristic of the file chooser interface; it can be used to browse many types of file structures, whether it is on a UNIX or Windows machine. This is especially useful if you want your application to be compiled for multiple operating systems.

Since the file chooser button only allows one file to be selected at a time, you can use `gtk_file_chooser_get_filename()` to retrieve the currently selected file or folder, depending on the type of file chooser button. If no file is selected, this function will return `NULL`. The returned string should be freed with `g_free()` when you are finished with it.

```
gchar* gtk_file_chooser_get_filename (GtkFileChooser *chooser);
```

At this point, you have enough information about the `GtkFileChooser` interface to implement file chooser buttons. `GtkFileChooser` will be covered in more depth in the next chapter when you learn about the `GtkFileChooserDialog` widget.

File Filters

GtkFileFilter objects allow you to restrict the files shown in the file chooser. For example, in Listing 4-10, only PNG, JPG, and GIF files could be viewed and chosen by the user when the Image Files filter was selected.

File filters are created with gtk_file_filter_new(). Therefore, you need to use gtk_file_filter_set_name() to set a displayed name for the filter type. If you provide more than one filter, this name will allow the user to switch between them.

```
GtkFileFilter* gtk_file_filter_new ();
void gtk_file_filter_set_name (GtkFileFilter *filter,
                               const gchar *name);
```

Lastly, for a filter to be complete you need to add types of files to show. The standard way of doing this is with gtk_file_filter_add_pattern() as shown in the following code snippet. This function allows you to specify a format for the filenames that are to be shown. Usually identifying file extensions that should be shown does this. You can use the asterisk character as a wildcard for any type of filtering function.

```
void gtk_file_filter_add_pattern (GtkFileFilter *filter,
                                  const gchar *pattern);
```

■**Tip** As in Listing 4-10, you may want to provide an All Files filter that shows every file in the directory. To do this, you should create a filter with only one pattern set to the wildcard character. If you do not provide this filter, the user will never be able to view any files that do not match a pattern provided by another filter.

You can also specify filter patterns with gtk_file_filter_add_mime_type() by specifying the Multipurpose Internet Mail Extensions (MIME) type. For example, image/* will show all files that are an image MIME type. The problem with this function is that you need to be familiar with MIME types. However, the advantage of using MIME types is that you do not need to specify every file extension for a filter. It allows you to generalize to all files in a specific MIME category.

```
void gtk_file_filter_add_mime_type (GtkFileFilter *filter,
                                    const char *mime_type);
```

After you create the filter, it needs to be added to the file chooser, which can be done with gtk_file_chooser_add_filter(). Once you supply the filters, the first specified filters will be used by default in the file chooser. The user will be able to switch between types if you have specified multiple filters.

```
void gtk_file_chooser_add_filter (GtkFileChooser *chooser,
                                  GtkFileFilter *filter);
```

Font Buttons

GtkFontButton is another type of specialized button that allows the user to select font parameters that correspond to fonts currently residing on the user's system. Font options are chosen in a font selection dialog that is displayed when the user clicks the button. These options include the font name, style options, and font size. An example GtkFontButton widget is displayed in Figure 4-11.

Figure 4-11. *Font selection buttons*

Font button widgets are initialized with gtk_font_button_new_with_font(), which allows you to specify the initial font. The font is provided as a string in the following format: Family Style Size. Each of the parameters is optional; the default font for GtkFontButton is Sans 12, which provides no style parameters.

"Family" refers to the formal font name such as "Sans", "Serif" or "Arial". Style options can vary between fonts, but they normally include "Italic", "Bold" and "Bold Italic". If you choose a font style of Regular, no font style will be specified. The size is point size of the text to be shown, such as "12" or "12.5".

A GtkFontButton Example

Listing 4-11 creates a GtkFontButton widget that is initialized with a font of "Sans Bold 12". When the chosen font in the button is changed, the new font is applied to a GtkLabel widget packed below the font button.

Listing 4-11. *Using the Font Selection Button (fontbuttons.c)*

```
#include <gtk/gtk.h>

static void font_changed (GtkFontButton*, GtkWidget*);

int main (int argc,
          char *argv[])
{
  GtkWidget *window, *vbox, *button, *label;
  PangoFontDescription *initial_font;

  gtk_init (&argc, &argv);
```

```
  window = gtk_window_new (GTK_WINDOW_TOPLEVEL);
  gtk_window_set_title (GTK_WINDOW (window), "Font Button");
  gtk_container_set_border_width (GTK_CONTAINER (window), 10);

  label = gtk_label_new ("Look at the font!");
  initial_font = pango_font_description_from_string ("Sans Bold 12");
  gtk_widget_modify_font (label, initial_font);

  /* Create a new font selection button with the given default font. */
  button = gtk_font_button_new_with_font ("Sans Bold 12");
  gtk_font_button_set_title (GTK_FONT_BUTTON (button), "Choose a Font");

  /* Monitor for changes to the font chosen in the font button. */
  g_signal_connect (G_OBJECT (button), "font_set",
                    G_CALLBACK (font_changed),
                    (gpointer) label);

  vbox= gtk_vbox_new (FALSE, 5);
  gtk_box_pack_start_defaults (GTK_BOX (vbox), button);
  gtk_box_pack_start_defaults (GTK_BOX (vbox), label);

  gtk_container_add (GTK_CONTAINER (window), vbox);
  gtk_widget_show_all (window);

  gtk_main ();
  return 0;
}


/* When the font is changed, display the font both as the text of a label and as
 * the label's physical font. */
static void
font_changed (GtkFontButton *button,
              GtkWidget *label)
{
  const gchar *font, buffer[512];
  PangoFontDescription *desc;

  font = gtk_font_button_get_font_name (button);
  desc = pango_font_description_from_string (font);

  g_snprintf (buffer, sizeof (buffer), "Font: %s", font);
  gtk_label_set_text (GTK_LABEL (label), buffer);
  gtk_widget_modify_font (label, desc);
}
```

Using Font Selection Buttons

The code in Listing 4-11 gives the first sampling of the PangoFontDescription type that you have run across. The PangoFontDescription structure is used to parse font style strings. You can create a new font description from a font string such as "Sans Bold 12" by calling pango_font_description_from_string() as follows:

```
initial_font = pango_font_description_from_string ("Sans Bold 12");
gtk_widget_modify_font (label, initial_font);
```

After creating a font description, gtk_widget_modify_font() can be called to set the font of the widget's text. This function will edit the font description object stored by the widget's GtkStyle property.

In Listing 4-11, the label's text was set to the font stored by the GtkFontButton when the font-set signal was emitted. You can retrieve the whole font description string stored by the font button with gtk_font_button_get_font_name(), which was used to retrieve the font string displayed by the label. The returned string should never be modified or freed.

```
const gchar* gtk_font_button_get_font_name (GtkFontButton *button);
```

In Listing 4-11, the new font style was applied to the GtkLabel. However, if you set gtk_font_button_set_use_font() and gtk_font_button_set_use_size() to TRUE, the font button will use the font family and size when rendering its text. This allows the user to preview the text in the font button. This is turned off for font buttons by default.

```
void gtk_font_button_set_use_font (GtkFontButton *button,
                                   gboolean use_font);
void gtk_font_button_set_use_size (GtkFontButton *button,
                                   gboolean use_size);
```

Test Your Understanding

In this chapter, you learned about a number of basic widgets such as GtkEntry, GtkSpinButton, and various types of toggles and buttons. In the following two exercises, you will be creating two applications to practice using these widgets.

Exercise 4-1. Renaming Files

In this exercise, use a GtkFileChooserButton widget to allow the user to choose a file on the system. Next, use a GtkEntry widget that allows the user to specify a new name for the file. (Note that you can find functions for the file utilities required by this exercise in the GLib API documentation.)

If the file was successfully renamed, you should disable the GtkEntry widget and button until the user chooses a new file. If the user does not have permission to rename the file that is selected, then the GtkEntry widget and button should be set as insensitive as well. When you complete this exercise, you can find the solution in Appendix F.

This exercise makes use of two widgets covered in this chapter: GtkEntry and GtkFileChooserButton. It also requires you to use multiple utility functions provided by GLib, including functions to rename a file and retrieve information about the permissions of an existing file.

While you will not be learning about GLib until Chapter 6, you may also want to experiment with some other file-related utility functions such as the ability to create directories, change file permissions, and move throughout a directory structure. GLib provides a lot of functionality, and it is worth your while to explore the API documentation in your free time.

Exercise 4-2. Spin Buttons and Scales

In this exercise, create three widgets: a spin button, a horizontal scale, and a check button. The spin button and horizontal scale should be set with the same initial value and bounds. If the check button is selected, the two adjustment widgets should be synchronized to the same value. This means that when the user changes the value of one widget, the other will be changed to the same value.

Since both widgets support integers and floating-point numbers, you should implement this exercise with various numbers of decimal places. You should also practice creating spin buttons and scales both with adjustments and by using the convenience initializers.

Since there were a large number of widgets introduced in this chapter, the exercises do not require you to use every one. However, after you have completed both exercises, you should make sure that you understand each of the widgets covered thus far.

I encourage you to continue to experiment with these basic widgets, since you will use many of them throughout the rest of this book and in your future applications. You should also visit the API documentation to learn about features provided by these widgets that were not covered in this chapter.

Summary

In this chapter, you have learned about the following nine new widgets that provide you with a meaningful way to interact with your users:

- GtkToggleButton: A type of GtkButton widget that holds its active or inactive state after it is clicked. It is shown as pressed down when it is active.

- GtkCheckButton: Derived from GtkToggleButton, this widget is drawn as a discrete toggle next to the displayed text. This allows it to be differentiated from a GtkButton.

- GtkRadioButton: You can group multiple radio button widgets together so that only one toggle can be activated at once.

- GtkEntry: This widget allows the user to enter free-form text on a single line. It also facilitates password entry.

- GtkSpinButton: Derived from GtkEntry, spin buttons allow the user to select or enter an integer or floating-point number within a predefined range.

- GtkScale: Similar to the spin button, this widget allows the user to select an integer or floating-point number by moving a vertical or horizontal slider.

- GtkColorButton: This special type of button allows the user to select a specific color along with an optional alpha value.

- GtkFileChooserButton: This special type of button allows the user to select a single file or folder that already exists on the system.

- GtkFontButton: This special type of button allows the user to select a font family, style, and size.

In the next chapter, you will learn how to create your own custom dialogs using the GtkDialog class and about a number of dialogs that are built into GTK+. By the end of Chapter 5, you will have a decent grasp of the most important simple widgets available to you in GTK+. From there, we will continue on to more complex topics.

CHAPTER 5

■■■

Dialogs

This chapter introduces you to a special type of window called a dialog. Dialogs are windows that supplement the top-level window. The dialog is provided by GtkDialog, a child class of GtkWindow, extended with additional functionality. This means it is possible to implement your entire interface in one or more dialogs, while leaving the main window hidden.

You can do anything with a dialog, such as display a message or prompt the user to select an option. Their purpose is to enhance user experience by providing some type of transient functionality.

In the first part of the chapter, you will learn how to use GtkDialog to create your own custom dialogs. The next section will introduce you to the large number of built-in dialogs provided by GTK+. Lastly, you will learn about a widget called GtkAssistant that allows you to create dialogs with multiple pages; assistants are meant to help the user through a multistage process.

In this chapter, you will learn the following:

- How to create your own custom dialogs using the GtkDialog widget

- How to give general information, error messages, and warnings to the user with the GtkMessageDialog widget

- How to provide information about your application with GtkAboutDialog

- What types of file chooser dialogs are available

- The ways to collect information with font and color selection dialogs

- How to create dialogs with multiple pages using the GtkAssistant widget

Creating Your Own Dialogs

A dialog is a special type of GtkWindow that is used to supplement the top-level window. It can be used to give the user a message, retrieve information from the user, or provide some other transient type of action.

Dialog widgets are split in half by a horizontal separator. The top part is where you place the main part of the dialog's user interface. The bottom half is called the action area, and it holds a collection of buttons. When clicked, each button will emit a unique response identifier that tells the programmer which button was clicked.

In most ways, the dialog widget can be treated as a window, because it is derived from the GtkWindow class. However, when you have multiple windows, a parent-child relationship should be established between the dialog and the top-level window when the dialog is meant to supplement the top-level window.

```
typedef struct
{
  GtkWidget *vbox;
  GtkWidget *action_area;
} GtkDialog;
```

GtkDialog provides two public members that include a horizontal button box called the action area and a vertical box. The action area holds all of the buttons along the bottom of the dialog. You can manually add buttons to this with GtkHButtonBox, but you should usually use the functions provided by GtkDialog for adding action area widgets.

■**Note** It is possible to manually implement the functionality of GtkDialog by creating a GtkWindow with all of the same widgets and establishing window relationships with gtk_window_set_transient_for() in addition to other functions provided by GtkWindow. GtkDialog is simply a convenience widget that provides standard methods.

Both the action area and a separator are packed at the end of the dialog's vertical box. The GtkVBox (vbox) is used to hold all of the dialog content. Because the action area is packed at the end, you should use gtk_box_pack_start() or gtk_box_pack_start_defaults() to add widgets to a GtkDialog as follows:

```
gtk_box_pack_start_defaults (GTK_BOX (dialog->vbox), child);
```

By packing widgets at the start of the box, the action area and the separator will always remain at the bottom of the dialog.

Creating a Message Dialog

One advantage of GtkDialog is that, no matter how complex the content of your dialog is, the same basic concepts can be applied to every dialog. To illustrate this, we will begin by creating a very simple dialog that gives the user a message. Figure 5-1 is a screenshot of this dialog.

Figure 5-1. *A message dialog created programmatically*

Listing 5-1 creates a simple dialog that notifies the user when the clicked signal is emitted by the button. This functionality is provided by the GtkMessageDialog widget, which will be covered in a later section of this chapter.

Listing 5-1. *Your First Custom Dialog (dialogs.c)*

```c
#include <gtk/gtk.h>

static void button_clicked (GtkButton*, GtkWindow*);

int main (int argc,
          char *argv[])
{
  GtkWidget *window, *button;

  gtk_init (&argc, &argv);

  window = gtk_window_new (GTK_WINDOW_TOPLEVEL);
  gtk_window_set_title (GTK_WINDOW (window), "Dialogs");
  gtk_container_set_border_width (GTK_CONTAINER (window), 10);

  button = gtk_button_new_with_mnemonic ("_Click Me");

  g_signal_connect (G_OBJECT (button), "clicked",
                    G_CALLBACK (button_clicked),
                    (gpointer) window);

  gtk_container_add (GTK_CONTAINER (window), button);
  gtk_widget_show_all (window);

  gtk_main ();
  return 0;
}

/* Create a new GtkDialog that will tell the user that the button was clicked. */
static void
button_clicked (GtkButton *button,
                GtkWindow *parent)
{
  GtkWidget *dialog, *label, *image, *hbox;

  /* Create a new dialog with one OK button. */
  dialog = gtk_dialog_new_with_buttons ("Information", parent,
                                        GTK_DIALOG_MODAL,
                                        GTK_STOCK_OK, GTK_RESPONSE_OK,
                                        NULL);
```

```
gtk_dialog_set_has_separator (GTK_DIALOG (dialog), FALSE);

label = gtk_label_new ("The button was clicked!");
image = gtk_image_new_from_stock (GTK_STOCK_DIALOG_INFO,
                                  GTK_ICON_SIZE_DIALOG);

hbox = gtk_hbox_new (FALSE, 5);
gtk_container_set_border_width (GTK_CONTAINER (hbox), 10);
gtk_box_pack_start_defaults (GTK_BOX (hbox), image);
gtk_box_pack_start_defaults (GTK_BOX (hbox), label);

/* Pack the dialog content into the dialog's GtkVBox. */
gtk_box_pack_start_defaults (GTK_BOX (GTK_DIALOG (dialog)->vbox), hbox);
gtk_widget_show_all (dialog);

/* Create the dialog as modal and destroy it when a button is clicked. */
gtk_dialog_run (GTK_DIALOG (dialog));
gtk_widget_destroy (dialog);
}
```

Creating the Dialog

The first thing you need to do when the button in the main window is clicked is create the GtkDialog widget with gtk_dialog_new_with_buttons(). The first two parameters of this function specify the title of the dialog and a pointer to the parent window.

```
GtkWidget* gtk_dialog_new_with_buttons (const gchar *title,
                                        GtkWindow *parent,
                                        GtkDialogFlags flags,
                                        const gchar *first_button_text,
                                        ...);
```

The dialog will be set as the transient window of the parent window, which allows the window manager to center the dialog over the main window and keep it on top if necessary. This can be achieved for arbitrary windows by calling gtk_window_set_transient_for(). You can also provide NULL if you do not want the dialog to have or recognize a parent window.

Next, you can specify one or more dialog flags. Options for this parameter are given by the GtkDialogFlags enumeration. There are three available values, which are shown in the following list:

- GTK_DIALOG_MODAL: Force the dialog to remain in focus on top of the parent window until closed. The user will be prevented from interacting with the parent.

- GTK_DIALOG_DESTROY_WITH_PARENT: Destroy the dialog when the parent is destroyed, but do not force the dialog to be in focus. This will create a nonmodal dialog unless you call gtk_dialog_run().

- GTK_DIALOG_NO_SEPARATOR: If set, a separator will not be placed between the action area and the dialog content.

In Listing 5-1, specifying GTK_DIALOG_MODAL created a modal dialog. It is not necessary to specify a title or parent window; the values can be set to NULL. However, you should always set the title, so it can be drawn in the window manager. Otherwise, the user will have difficulties choosing the desired window.

Lastly, a NULL-terminated list of action area buttons and their response identifiers should be specified. In Listing 5-1, an OK button with a response of GTK_RESPONSE_OK was added to the dialog.

Alternatively, you can create an empty dialog with gtk_dialog_new(), but in that case, you will need to manually add buttons with gtk_dialog_add_button() or gtk_dialog_add_buttons(). In most cases, it is easier to create dialogs in the same manner as shown in Listing 5-1.

By default, all dialogs place a horizontal separator between the main content and the action area of the dialog. However, in some cases, as shown in this example, it is desirable to hide the separator. This can be done with gtk_dialog_set_has_separator().

```
void gtk_dialog_set_has_separator (GtkDialog *dialog,
                                   gboolean has_separator);
```

After the child widgets are created, they need to be added to the dialog. As I previously stated, child widgets are added to the dialog by calling gtk_box_pack_start_defaults() or gtk_box_pack_start(). The dialog has a public member called vbox into which child widgets are packed as follows:

```
gtk_box_pack_start_defaults (GTK_BOX (GTK_DIALOG (dialog)->vbox), hbox);
gtk_widget_show_all (dialog);
```

At this point, you need to show the dialog and its child widgets, because gtk_dialog_run() will only call gtk_widget_show() on the dialog itself. To do this, call gtk_widget_show_all() on the dialog or its GtkVBox. If you do not show the widgets, only the separator and action area will be visible when gtk_dialog_run() is called.

Response Identifiers

When a dialog is fully constructed, one method of showing the dialog is by calling gtk_dialog_run(). This function will return an integer called a response identifier when complete. It will also prevent the user from interacting with anything outside of the dialog until it is destroyed or an action area button is clicked.

```
gint gtk_dialog_run (GtkDialog *dialog);
```

Internally, gtk_dialog_run() creates a new main loop for the dialog, which prevents you from interacting with its parent window until a response identifier is emitted or the user closes the dialog. Regardless of what dialog flags you set, the dialog will always be modal when you call this function, because it calls gtk_window_set_modal().

If the dialog is manually destroyed by using a method provided by the window manager, GTK_RESPONSE_NONE is returned. Otherwise, gtk_dialog_run() returns the response identifier referring to the button that was clicked. A full list of available response identifiers from the GtkResponseType enumeration is shown in Table 5-1. You should always use the identifier's preprocessor directive instead of random integer values, since they could change in future versions of GTK+.

Table 5-1. *GtkResponseType Enumeration Values*

Identifier	Value	Description
GTK_RESPONSE_NONE	-1	The dialog was destroyed by the window manager or programmatically destroyed with gtk_widget_destroy(). This is also returned if a response widget does not have a response identifier set.
GTK_RESPONSE_REJECT	-2	This identifier is not associated with buttons in built-in dialogs, but you are free to use it yourself.
GTK_RESPONSE_ACCEPT	-3	This identifier is not associated with buttons in built-in dialogs, but you are free to use it yourself.
GTK_RESPONSE_DELETE_EVENT	-4	Each dialog is automatically connected to the delete-event signal. While gtk_dialog_run() is running, this identifier will be returned, and delete-event will be stopped from destroying the window as usual.
GTK_RESPONSE_OK	-5	A GTK_STOCK_OK button was clicked in a built-in dialog. You are free to use this button or any of the following in your own dialogs.
GTK_RESPONSE_CANCEL	-6	A GTK_STOCK_CANCEL button was clicked in a built-in dialog.
GTK_RESPONSE_CLOSE	-7	A GTK_STOCK_CLOSE button was clicked in a built-in dialog.
GTK_RESPONSE_YES	-8	A GTK_STOCK_YES button was clicked in a built-in dialog.
GTK_RESPONSE_NO	-9	A GTK_STOCK_NO button was clicked in a built-in dialog.
GTK_RESPONSE_APPLY	-10	A GTK_STOCK_APPLY button was clicked in a built-in dialog.
GTK_RESPONSE_HELP	-11	A GTK_STOCK_HELP button was clicked in a built-in dialog.

Of course, when you create your own dialogs and when using many of the built-in dialogs that will be covered in the next few pages, you are free to choose which response identifier to use. However, you should try to resist the urge to apply a GTK_RESPONSE_CANCEL identifier to an OK button, or some other type of absurdity along those lines.

Note You are free to create your own response identifiers, but you should use positive numbers, since all of the built-in identifiers are negative. This will allow you to avoid conflicts when more identifiers are added in future versions of GTK+.

After the dialog returns a response identifier, you need to make sure to call gtk_widget_destroy(), or it will cause a memory leak. GTK+ will make sure all of the dialog's children are destroyed, but you need to remember to initiate the process.

By calling gtk_widget_destroy(), all of the parent's children will be destroyed and its reference count will drop. When an object's reference count reaches zero, the object is finalized, and its memory freed.

The GtkImage Widget

Listing 5-1 introduces another new widget called GtkImage. Images can be loaded in a wide variety of ways, but one advantage of GtkImage is that it will display the GTK_STOCK_MISSING_IMAGE icon if the loading has failed. It is also derived from GtkWidget, so it can be added as a child of a container unlike other image objects, such as GdkPixbuf.

In our example, gtk_image_new_from_stock() created the GtkImage widget from a stock item.

```
GtkWidget* gtk_image_new_from_stock (const gchar *stock_id,
                                     GtkIconSize size);
```

When loading an image, you also need to specify a size for the image. GTK+ will automatically look for a stock icon for the given size and resize the image to that size if none is found. Available size parameters are specified by the GtkIconSize enumeration and can be viewed in the following list:

- GTK_ICON_SIZE_INVALID: Unspecified size

- GTK_ICON_SIZE_MENU: 16 ×16 pixels

- GTK_ICON_SIZE_SMALL_TOOLBAR: 18 ×18 pixels

- GTK_ICON_SIZE_LARGE_TOOLBAR: 24 × 24 pixels

- GTK_ICON_SIZE_BUTTON: 24 × 24 pixels

- GTK_ICON_SIZE_DND: 32 × 32 pixels

- GTK_ICON_SIZE_DIALOG: 48 × 48 pixels

As you can see, stock GtkImage objects are usually used for smaller images, such as those that appear in buttons, menus, and dialogs, since stock images are provided in a discrete number of standard sizes. In Listing 5-1, the image was set to GTK_ICON_SIZE_DIALOG or 48 × 48 pixels.

Multiple initialization functions for GtkImage are provided, which can be viewed in the API documentation, but gtk_image_new_from_file() and gtk_image_new_from_pixbuf() are especially important to future examples in this book.

```
GtkWidget *gtk_image_new_from_file (const gchar *filename);
```

GtkImage will automatically detect the image type of the file specified to gtk_image_new_from_file(). If the image cannot be loaded, it will display a broken-image icon. Therefore, this function will never return a NULL object. GtkImage also supports animations that occur within the image file.

Calling gtk_image_new_from_pixbuf() creates a new GtkImage widget out of a previously initialized GdkPixbuf. Unlike gtk_image_new_from_file(), you can use this function to easily figure out whether the image is successfully loaded since you first have to create a GdkPixbuf.

```
GtkWidget *gtk_image_new_from_pixbuf (GdkPixbuf *pixbuf);
```

You need to note that the GtkImage will create its own references to the GdkPixbuf, so you will need to release your reference to the object if it should be destroyed with the GtkImage.

Nonmodal Message Dialog

By calling gtk_dialog_run(), your dialog will always be set as modal, which is not always desirable. In order to create a nonmodal dialog, you need to connect to GtkDialog's response signal.

In Listing 5-2, the message dialog from Figure 5-1 is reimplemented as a nonmodal dialog. You should try clicking the button in the main window multiple times in a row. This will show how you can not only create multiple instances of the same dialog but also access the main window from a nonmodal dialog.

Listing 5-2. *A Nonmodal Message Dialog (dialogs2.c)*

```
static void
button_clicked (GtkButton *button,
                GtkWindow *parent)
{
  GtkWidget *dialog, *label, *image, *hbox;

  /* Create a nonmodal dialog with one OK button. */
  dialog = gtk_dialog_new_with_buttons ("Information", parent,
                                        GTK_DIALOG_DESTROY_WITH_PARENT,
                                        GTK_STOCK_OK, GTK_RESPONSE_OK,
                                        NULL);

  gtk_dialog_set_has_separator (GTK_DIALOG (dialog), FALSE);

  label = gtk_label_new ("The button was clicked!");
  image = gtk_image_new_from_stock (GTK_STOCK_DIALOG_INFO,
                                    GTK_ICON_SIZE_DIALOG);

  hbox = gtk_hbox_new (FALSE, 5);
  gtk_container_set_border_width (GTK_CONTAINER (hbox), 10);
  gtk_box_pack_start_defaults (GTK_BOX (hbox), image);
  gtk_box_pack_start_defaults (GTK_BOX (hbox), label);

  gtk_box_pack_start_defaults (GTK_BOX (GTK_DIALOG (dialog)->vbox), hbox);
  gtk_widget_show_all (dialog);

  /* Call gtk_widget_destroy() when the dialog emits the response signal. */
  g_signal_connect (G_OBJECT (dialog), "response",
                    G_CALLBACK (gtk_widget_destroy), NULL);
}
```

Creating a nonmodal dialog is very similar to the previous example, except you do not want to call gtk_dialog_run(). By calling this function, a modal dialog is created by blocking the parent window's main loop regardless of the dialog flags.

■**Tip** You can still create a modal dialog without using `gtk_dialog_run()` by setting the `GTK_DIALOG_MODAL` flag. You can then connect to the `response` signal. This function simply provides a convenient way to create modal dialogs and handle response identifiers within one function.

By connecting to GtkDialog's `response` signal, you can wait for a response identifier to be emitted. By using this method, the dialog will not automatically be unreferenced when a response identifier is emitted. The `response` callback function receives the dialog, the response identifier that was emitted, and the optional data parameter.

One of the most important decisions you have to make when designing a dialog is whether it will be modal or nonmodal. As a rule of thumb, if the action needs to be completed before the user can continue working with the application, the dialog should be modal. Examples of this would be message dialogs, dialogs that ask the user a question, and dialogs to open a file.

If there is no reason why the user cannot continue working while the dialog is open, you should use a nonmodal dialog. You also need to remember that multiple instances of non-modal dialogs can be created unless you prevent this programmatically, so dialogs that must have only one instance should be created as modal.

Another Dialog Example

Now that you have created a simple message dialog from scratch, it is time to produce a more complex dialog. In Listing 5-3, a few pieces of basic information about the user are propagated using GLib's utility functions. A dialog, which is shown in Figure 5-2, allows you to edit each piece of information.

Figure 5-2. *A simple GtkDialog widget*

This information is, of course, not actually changed within the user's system; the new text is simply output to the screen. This example illustrates the fact that, regardless of the complexity of the dialog, the basic principles of how to handle response identifiers are still the only ones that are necessary.

You could easily implement this as a nonmodal dialog as well, although this would not be of much use since the dialog itself is the application's top-level window.

Listing 5-3. *Editing Information in a Dialog (dialogs3.c)*

```c
#include <gtk/gtk.h>

int main (int argc,
          char *argv[])
{
  GtkWidget *dialog, *table, *user, *real, *home, *host;
  GtkWidget *lbl1, *lbl2, *lbl3, *lbl4;
  gint result;

  gtk_init (&argc, &argv);

  dialog = gtk_dialog_new_with_buttons ("Edit User Information", NULL
                                        GTK_DIALOG_MODAL,
                                        GTK_STOCK_OK, GTK_RESPONSE_OK,
                                        GTK_STOCK_CANCEL, GTK_RESPONSE_CANCEL,
                                        NULL);

  gtk_dialog_set_default_response (GTK_DIALOG (dialog), GTK_RESPONSE_OK);

  /* Create four entries that will tell the user what data to enter. */
  lbl1 = gtk_label_new ("User Name:");
  lbl2 = gtk_label_new ("Real Name:");
  lbl3 = gtk_label_new ("Home Dir:");
  lbl4 = gtk_label_new ("Host Name:");

  user = gtk_entry_new ();
  real = gtk_entry_new ();
  home = gtk_entry_new ();
  host = gtk_entry_new ();

  /* Retrieve the user's information for the default values. */
  gtk_entry_set_text (GTK_ENTRY (user), g_get_user_name());
  gtk_entry_set_text (GTK_ENTRY (real), g_get_real_name());
  gtk_entry_set_text (GTK_ENTRY (home), g_get_home_dir());
  gtk_entry_set_text (GTK_ENTRY (host), g_get_host_name());

  table = gtk_table_new (4, 2, FALSE);
  gtk_table_attach_defaults (GTK_TABLE (table), lbl1, 0, 1, 0, 1);
  gtk_table_attach_defaults (GTK_TABLE (table), lbl2, 0, 1, 1, 2);
  gtk_table_attach_defaults (GTK_TABLE (table), lbl3, 0, 1, 2, 3);
  gtk_table_attach_defaults (GTK_TABLE (table), lbl4, 0, 1, 3, 4);
```

```
gtk_table_attach_defaults (GTK_TABLE (table), user, 1, 2, 0, 1);
gtk_table_attach_defaults (GTK_TABLE (table), real, 1, 2, 1, 2);
gtk_table_attach_defaults (GTK_TABLE (table), home, 1, 2, 2, 3);
gtk_table_attach_defaults (GTK_TABLE (table), host, 1, 2, 3, 4);

gtk_table_set_row_spacings (GTK_TABLE (table), 5);
gtk_table_set_col_spacings (GTK_TABLE (table), 5);
gtk_container_set_border_width (GTK_CONTAINER (table), 5);

gtk_box_pack_start_defaults (GTK_BOX (GTK_DIALOG (dialog)->vbox), table);
gtk_widget_show_all (dialog);

/* Run the dialog and output the data if the user clicks the OK button. */
result = gtk_dialog_run (GTK_DIALOG (dialog));
if (result == GTK_RESPONSE_OK)
{
  g_print ("User Name: %s\n", gtk_entry_get_text (GTK_ENTRY (user)));
  g_print ("Real Name: %s\n", gtk_entry_get_text (GTK_ENTRY (real)));
  g_print ("Home Folder: %s\n", gtk_entry_get_text (GTK_ENTRY (home)));
  g_print ("Host Name: %s\n", gtk_entry_get_text (GTK_ENTRY (host)));
}

gtk_widget_destroy (dialog);
return 0;
}
```

The proper way to handle any modal dialog is to use the response identifiers, deriving the correct response based on the clicked button. Since there was only one response that needed to be deliberately detected, a conditional if statement was used in Listing 5-3.

However, let us assume that you need to handle multiple response identifiers. In this case, a switch() statement would be a better solution, since it was created to compare a single variable to multiple selections, as shown in the following code snippet.

```
result = gtk_dialog_run (GTK_DIALOG (dialog));
switch (result)
{
  case (GTK_RESPONSE_OK):
    /* ... Handle the response ... */
    break;
  case (GTK_RESPONSE_APPLY):
    /* ... Handle the response ... */
    break;
  default:
    break;
}

gtk_widget_destroy (dialog);
```

Since the dialog will need to be destroyed in each case, you can break from the `switch()` statement. If you only needed to check one case with a `switch()` statement, you could fall through to the default case, which would be set to destroy the dialog no matter what response identifier is emitted.

Built-in Dialogs

There are many types of dialogs already built into GTK+. Although not all of the available dialogs will be covered in this chapter, you will be given a strong understanding of the concepts needed to use any built-in dialog. This section will cover `GtkMessageDialog`, `GtkAboutDialog`, `GtkFileChooserDialog`, `GtkFontSelectionDialog`, and `GtkColorSelectionDialog`.

Message Dialogs

Message dialogs are used to give one of four types of informational messages: general information, error messages, warnings, and questions. The type of dialog is used to decide the icon to display, the title of the dialog, and the buttons to add.

There is also a general type provided that makes no assumption as to the content of the message. In most cases, you will not want to use this, since the four provided types will fill most of your needs.

It is very simple to re-create the `GtkMessageDialog` widget. The first two examples implemented a simple message dialog, but `GtkMessageDialog` already provides this functionality, so you should not need to re-create the widget. Using `GtkMessageDialog` saves on typing and avoids the need to recreate this widget many times, since most applications make heavy use of `GtkMessageDialog`. It also provides a uniform look for message dialogs across all GTK+ applications.

Figure 5-3 shows an example of a `GtkMessageDialog` (compare this to Figure 5-1) that is being used to give the user visual notification of a button's `clicked` signal.

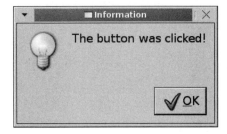

Figure 5-3. *A GtkMessageDialog widget*

Since the content of the message is not critical, its type is set to a general message. This message dialog can be produced using the code shown in Listing 5-4.

Listing 5-4. *Using a GtkMessageDialog (messagedialogs.c)*

```
#include <gtk/gtk.h>

static void button_clicked (GtkButton*, GtkWindow*);

int main (int argc,
          char *argv[])
{
  GtkWidget *window, *button;

  gtk_init (&argc, &argv);

  window = gtk_window_new (GTK_WINDOW_TOPLEVEL);
  gtk_window_set_title (GTK_WINDOW (window), "Message Dialogs");
  gtk_container_set_border_width (GTK_CONTAINER (window), 10);

  button = gtk_button_new_with_mnemonic ("_Click Me");

  g_signal_connect (G_OBJECT (button), "clicked",
                    G_CALLBACK (button_clicked),
                    (gpointer) window);

  gtk_container_add (GTK_CONTAINER (window), button);
  gtk_widget_show_all (window);

  gtk_main ();
  return 0;
}

/* Create a new message dialog that tells the user that the button was clicked. */
static void
button_clicked (GtkButton *button,
                GtkWindow *parent)
{
  GtkWidget *dialog;

  dialog = gtk_message_dialog_new (parent, GTK_DIALOG_MODAL,
                                   GTK_MESSAGE_INFO, GTK_BUTTONS_OK,
                                   "The button was clicked!");
  gtk_window_set_title (GTK_WINDOW (dialog), "Information");

  gtk_dialog_run (GTK_DIALOG (dialog));
  gtk_widget_destroy (dialog);
}
```

After the button in the main window is clicked, this example creates a new GtkMessageDialog with gtk_message_dialog_new(). The first parameter in this function is the dialog's parent GtkWindow.

The parent window can be set to NULL if necessary, but in most cases, a parent-child relationship should be established. If you do not set a parent widget, the message dialog will not be centered above the parent window.

Message dialogs are meant to be addressed by the user immediately, because they present some type of important message or critical question that needs the user's attention. By not setting a parent window, the message dialog can be easily ignored, which is not the desired action in most cases.

```
GtkWidget* gtk_message_dialog_new (GtkWindow *parent,
                                   GtkDialogFlags flags,
                                   GtkMessageType type,
                                   GtkButtonsType buttons,
                                   const gchar *message_format,
                                   ...);
```

Next, you can specify one or more dialog flags. Options for this parameter are given by the GtkDialogFlags enumeration that was used when creating custom dialogs in the previous three examples.

The third parameter of gtk_message_dialog_new() is used to specify what type of message dialog you want to create. The title and image shown in the dialog are set based on the type you choose. For instance, in Listing 5-4 a GTK_MESSAGE_INFO dialog was created. Therefore, a light-bulb image (GTK_STOCK_DIALOG_INFO) is placed in the dialog and the title is set to "Information". The five available types of messages from the GtkMessageType enumeration follow:

- GTK_MESSAGE_INFO: General message that provides information to the user.

- GTK_MESSAGE_WARNING: A warning that a nonfatal error has happened.

- GTK_MESSAGE_QUESTION: Asks the user a question that requires a choice. You need to provide multiple buttons for this type of message.

- GTK_MESSAGE_ERROR: A warning that a fatal error has happened.

- GTK_MESSAGE_OTHER: Generic type of message that makes no assumptions as to the content of the message.

The next decision you need to make is what type of button or buttons will appear in the dialog. This decision is based on the type of message dialog you have created. For example, if you choose GTK_MESSAGE_QUESTION as the type, it is logical to choose either GTK_BUTTONS_YES_NO or GTK_BUTTONS_OK_CANCEL so that the user will be able to provide a response for the question. A list of the six available GtkButtonsType values follows:

- GTK_BUTTONS_NONE: No buttons will be added.

- GTK_BUTTONS_OK: Add the button GTK_STOCK_OK.

- GTK_BUTTONS_CLOSE: Add the button GTK_STOCK_CLOSE.

- GTK_BUTTONS_CANCEL: Add the button GTK_STOCK_CANCEL.

- GTK_BUTTONS_YES_NO: Add the buttons GTK_STOCK_YES and GTK_STOCK_NO.

- GTK_BUTTONS_OK_CANCEL: Add the buttons GTK_STOCK_OK and GTK_STOCK_CANCEL.

■**Note** While dialog flags can be a bitwise list, in addition to many enumeration parameters in GTK+, it is not possible to do the same with the buttons you choose for a GTK_MESSAGE_DIALOG. If you are not happy with the available button selection, you can remove the buttons from the dialog's GtkHButtonBox container and add your own with the functions provided by GtkDialog.

The last parameter (or parameters depending on your needs) of gtk_message_dialog_new() is the message that will be displayed by the dialog. The string should be formatted similarly to those supported by printf(). For more information on the available printf() options, you should reference your preferred C language manual or book.

You have no control over the visual formatting of the message provided to gtk_message_dialog_new(). If you would like to use the Pango Text Markup Language to format the message dialog's text, you can use gtk_message_dialog_new_with_markup() to create the dialog. This is the same as creating the dialog with gtk_message_dialog_new() and setting its text with gtk_message_dialog_set_markup().

```
void gtk_message_dialog_set_format_secondary_text (GtkMessageDialog *dialog,
                                                   const gchar *message_format,
                                                   ...);
```

It is possible to add a secondary text to the message dialog, which will cause the first message to be set as bold with `gtk_message_dialog_set_format_secondary_text()`. The text string provided to this function should be similar to the format supported by `printf()`.

This feature is very useful, because it allows you to give a quick summary in the primary text and go into detail with the secondary text. You can also set the markup of the secondary text with `gtk_message_dialog_set_format_secondary_markup()`.

The About Dialog

The `GtkAboutDialog` widget provides you with a simple way to provide the user with information about an application. This dialog is usually displayed when the `GTK_STOCK_ABOUT` item in the Help menu is chosen. However, since menus will not be covered until Chapter 9, our example dialog will be used as the top-level window.

There are many types of information that can be shown with the `GtkAboutDialog`. These include the name of the application, copyright, current version, license content, authors, documenters, artists, and translators. Because every application will not have all of these, every property is optional. The main window displays only the basic information, which can be viewed along with the author credits in Figure 5-4.

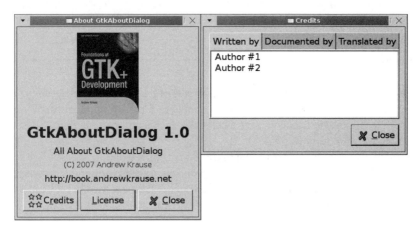

Figure 5-4. *An About dialog and author credits*

By clicking the Credits button, the user will be presented with any authors, documenters, translators, and artists that are provided. Each category of contributors is shown in a separate tab.

The License button will pop up a new dialog that shows the given license content. Listing 5-5 is a simple example that shows you how to use every available property of the `GtkAboutDialog` widget.

Listing 5-5. *Using a GtkAboutDialog (aboutdialogs.c)*

```c
#include <gtk/gtk.h>

int main (int argc,
          char *argv[])
{
  GtkWidget *dialog;
  GdkPixbuf *logo;
  GError *error = NULL;

  gtk_init (&argc, &argv);

  const gchar *authors[] = {
    "Author #1",
    "Author #2",
    NULL
  };

  const gchar *documenters[] = {
    "Documenter #1",
    "Documenter #2",
    NULL
  };

  dialog = gtk_about_dialog_new ();

  /* You should edit '/path/to/logo.png' to point to the location of logo.png
   * from the chapter_5 source directory on your system. */
  logo = gdk_pixbuf_new_from_file ("/path/to/logo.png", &error);

  /* Set the application logo or handle the error. */
  if (error == NULL)
    gtk_about_dialog_set_logo (GTK_ABOUT_DIALOG (dialog), logo);
  else
  {
    if (error->domain == GDK_PIXBUF_ERROR)
      g_print ("GdkPixbufError: %s\n", error->message);
    else if (error->domain == G_FILE_ERROR)
      g_print ("GFileError: %s\n", error->message);
    else
      g_print ("An error in the domain: %d has occurred!\n", error->domain);

    g_error_free (error);
  }
```

```
/* Set application data that will be displayed in the main dialog. */
gtk_about_dialog_set_name (GTK_ABOUT_DIALOG (dialog), "GtkAboutDialog");
gtk_about_dialog_set_version (GTK_ABOUT_DIALOG (dialog), "1.0");
gtk_about_dialog_set_copyright (GTK_ABOUT_DIALOG (dialog),
                                "(C) 2007 Andrew Krause");
gtk_about_dialog_set_comments (GTK_ABOUT_DIALOG (dialog),
                               "All About GtkAboutDialog");

/* Set the license text, which is usually loaded from a file. Also, set the
 * web site address and label. */
gtk_about_dialog_set_license (GTK_ABOUT_DIALOG (dialog), "Free to all!");
gtk_about_dialog_set_website (GTK_ABOUT_DIALOG (dialog),
                              "http://book.andrewkrause.net");
gtk_about_dialog_set_website_label (GTK_ABOUT_DIALOG (dialog),
                                    "book.andrewkrause.net");

/* Set the application authors, documenters and translators. */
gtk_about_dialog_set_authors (GTK_ABOUT_DIALOG (dialog), authors);
gtk_about_dialog_set_documenters (GTK_ABOUT_DIALOG (dialog), documenters);
gtk_about_dialog_set_translator_credits (GTK_ABOUT_DIALOG (dialog),
                                         "Translator #1\nTranslator #2");

gtk_dialog_run (GTK_DIALOG (dialog));
gtk_widget_destroy (dialog);
return 0;
}
```

Many properties are available for you to set when creating your own GtkAboutDialog instance. Table 5-2 summarizes those options that were used in Listing 5-5. If the license is not specified, the License button will not be visible. The Credits button will not be visible if there are no credits.

Table 5-2. *GtkAboutDialog Options*

Option	Description
Name	The application's name.
Version	The current version of the application the user is running.
Copyright	A short copyright string that should not span more than one or two lines.
Comments	A short description of the application that should not span more than one or two lines.

Option	Description
License	License information that is displayed in a secondary dialog. Setting this to NULL hides the License button.
Web Site	The homepage URL of the application.
Web Site Label	A label that is displayed instead of the URL.
Authors	A NULL-terminated array of authors who have contributed code to the project.
Artists	A NULL-terminated array of artists who have created graphics for the project.
Documenters	A NULL-terminated array of documenters who have written documentation.
Translator Credits	A string that specifies the translator(s) of the current language.
Logo	Usually loaded from a file, this GdkPixbuf object is the application's logo.

Unlike author, artist, and documenter credits, the translator credits are only a single string. The reason for this is because the translator string should be set to the person that translated the language currently in use. Internationalization and gettext are not topics for this book. For more information, you should visit www.gnu.org/software/gettext.

GdkPixbuf

GdkPixbuf is a class that contains information about an image stored in memory. It allows you to build images manually by placing shapes or pixels or to load a prebuilt image from a file. The latter is preferred in most cases, so that is what will be covered in this book.

Since GdkPixbuf is derived from GObject, it supports referencing. This means that the same image can be used in multiple locations in a program by increasing the reference count with g_object_ref(). Dereferencing GdkPixbuf objects (pixbufs) is performed automatically in almost all cases.

To load a pixbuf from a file, you can use gdk_pixbuf_new_from_file(), which was used in Listing 5-5. This function will load the image with an initial size set to the actual size of the image.

```
GdkPixbuf* gdk_pixbuf_new_from_file (const char *filename,
                                     GError **error);
```

After you load the image, you can resize it with gdk_pixbuf_scale_simple(). This function accepts the new size parameters of the GdkPixbuf and the interpolation mode to use for the scaling.

```
GdkPixbuf* gdk_pixbuf_scale_simple (const GdkPixbuf *src,
                                    int destination_width,
                                    int destination_height,
                                    GdkInterpType interpolation);
```

The four GdkInterpType modes follow:

- GDK_INTERP_NEAREST: Sampling is performed on the nearest neighboring pixel. This mode is very fast, but it produces the lowest quality of scaling. It should never be used for scaling an image to a smaller size!

- GDK_INTERP_TILES: This mode renders every pixel as a shape of color and uses anti-aliasing for the edges. This is similar to using GDK_INTERP_NEAREST for making an image larger or GDK_INTERP_BILINEAR for reducing its size.

- GDK_INTERP_BILINEAR: This mode is the best mode for resizing images in both directions, because it has a balance between its speed and the quality of the image.

- GDK_INTERP_HYPER: While it is very high quality, this method is also very slow. It should only be used when speed is not a concern. Therefore, it should never be used for any application that the user would expect a fast display time. For your convenience, gtk_pixbuf_new_from_file_at_size() can be used to resize the image to the new size immediately after it is loaded from the file in one function call.

Many other features are provided in the GdkPixbuf library, but only a few of these will be covered, as needed. For further information on GdkPixbuf, you should reference the API documentation.

GError

Runtime errors are something that every programmer has to contend with. To make your life easier, GLib provides a standard method for error propagation called the GError structure, which follows:

```
struct GError
{
  GQuark domain;
  gchar *message;
  gint code;
};
```

The GError structure contains three values. The domain is a group that encompasses similar types of errors. In Listing 5-5, we check for errors in the GDK_PIXBUF_ERROR and G_FILE_ERROR domains.

■**Caution** You may be tempted to check the domain of an error in a switch() statement. However, you should not do so, because it will not work. The error domains are resolved at runtime, so this will not compile, because case statements must already be determined at this time.

The message is a human-readable string that describes the specific error that has occurred. If the error requires you to give visual feedback to the user, this message should be used. This string is freed when you call g_error_free().

The last element, code, is an error code that falls under the specified domain. For example, Table 5-3 shows the six types of errors that can occur under the GDK_PIXBUF_ERROR domain. This is a full list of possible errors, but not all of the errors can occur in every GdkPixbuf function.

Table 5-3. *GdkPixbufError Enumeration Values*

Error Value	Description
GDK_PIXBUF_ERROR_CORRUPT_IMAGE	The image file is broken in some way.
GDK_PIXBUF_ERROR_INSUFFICIENT_MEMORY	Not enough memory is available to store the image.
GDK_PIXBUF_ERROR_BAD_OPTION	A bad option was passed. This error can occur while saving an image.
GDK_PIXBUF_ERROR_UNKNOWN_TYPE	GdkPixbuf was unable to detect the image type.
GDK_PIXBUF_ERROR_UNSUPPORTED_OPERATION	GdkPixbuf does not know how to perform the operation on the specified image.
GDK_PIXBUF_ERROR_FAILED	A generic failure code for all other errors.

GLib uses a standard type of naming for error elements. The error domain is always formatted <NAMESPACE>_<MODULE>_ERROR, where the namespace is the library containing the function and the module is the widget or object type.

Appending the error type to the end of the domain's name creates the error code. Every error code enumeration also includes <NAMESPACE>_<MODULE>_ERROR_FAILED, a generic fail code called. This will be returned if a specific error is not available.

If you are checking error codes, you should pick and choose the most likely to occur, because checking every error type is neither efficient nor sensible. You should only check the types of errors that you can recover from. In all other cases, the human-readable message is provided for more precise user feedback.

There is one pitfall with the GError structure called piling up. If you use the same GError structure in two consecutive functions, the second error will replace the first. The original error will be forever lost.

To prevent this problem, you should handle errors immediately after the first function call. Then use g_clear_error() to reset the GError structure values to their initial states. At that point, you can reuse the GError structure for the next function.

```
if (error && * error)
{
  g_error_free (*error);
  *error = NULL;
}
```

You should note that g_clear_error() is simply a convenience function, which performs the functionality shown in the preceding code snippet. If the error is set, call g_error_free(), which frees first the message string and then the slice allocated by the GError object. It then points the error to NULL.

A complete list of error domains in GTK+ and its supporting libraries, along with the corresponding error types, can be found in Appendix E.

File Chooser Dialogs

In the last chapter, you learned about GtkFileChooser and the GtkFileChooserButton widget. Recall that GtkFileChooser is not a widget, but an interface. Interfaces differ from classes, because you cannot derive from them, and they do not implement the functionality they declare.

GTK+ provides the following three widgets that implement the GtkFileChooser interface:

- GtkFileChooserButton: The file chooser button was covered in the previous chapter. It allows the user to choose one file or folder by displaying a GtkFileChooser dialog when clicked.

- GtkFileChooserDialog: This widget is simply a dialog that uses a GtkFileChooserWidget as its child. Since it implements the GtkFileChooser interface, you do not ever have to directly access its child widget.

- GtkFileChooserWidget: This is the actual widget that allows the user to choose a file or folder. It can also facilitate the creation of a folder or saving of a file. When you use a GtkFileChooserDialog, you are actually using a file chooser widget packed into a GtkDialog.

You have already learned about GtkFileChooserButton and have used a file chooser to open one file and to select a directory. There are three other abilities provided by the file chooser widget. In the next three examples, you will learn how to use a file chooser dialog to save a file, create a directory, and choose multiple files.

Saving Files

Figure 5-5 shows a GtkFileChooserDialog widget that is being used to save a file. You will notice that it is similar to the next two figures as well, because all types of file chooser dialogs have a consistent look so that it is minimally confusing to new users and maximally efficient to all. The widget also uses the same code to implement each dialog type to minimize the amount of necessary code.

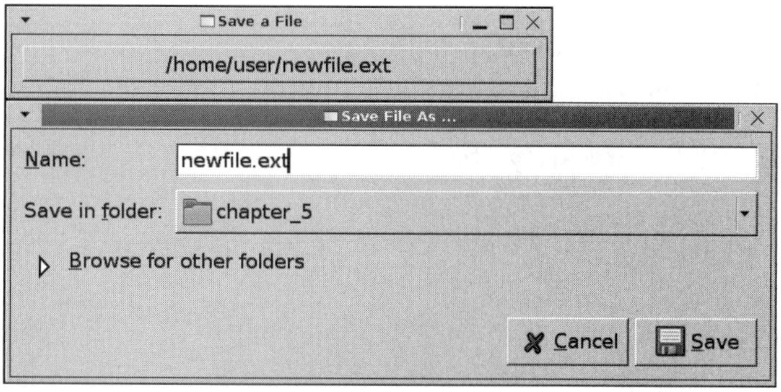

Figure 5-5. *A file chooser dialog for saving*

File chooser dialogs are used in the same way as the previous two dialogs covered in this chapter, except you need to handle the response code returned by gtk_dialog_new(). Listing 5-6 allows the user to choose a file name and sets the button's text to that file name if the correct response identifier is returned.

Listing 5-6. *Using a GtkFileChooserDialog to Save a File (savefile.c)*

```
#include <gtk/gtk.h>

static void button_clicked (GtkButton*, GtkWindow*);

int main (int argc,
          char *argv[])
{
  GtkWidget *window, *button;

  gtk_init (&argc, &argv);

  window = gtk_window_new (GTK_WINDOW_TOPLEVEL);
  gtk_window_set_title (GTK_WINDOW (window), "Save a File");
  gtk_container_set_border_width (GTK_CONTAINER (window), 10);

  gtk_widget_set_size_request (window, 200, 100);

  button = gtk_button_new_with_label ("Save As ...");
```

```
    g_signal_connect (G_OBJECT (button), "clicked",
                        G_CALLBACK (button_clicked),
                        (gpointer) window);

    gtk_container_add (GTK_CONTAINER (window), button);
    gtk_widget_show_all (window);

    gtk_main ();
    return 0;
}

/* Allow the user to enter a new file name and location for the file and
 * set the button to the text of the location. */
static void
button_clicked (GtkButton *button,
                GtkWindow *window)
{
  GtkWidget *dialog;
  gchar *filename;


  dialog = gtk_file_chooser_dialog_new ("Save File As ...", window,
                                GTK_FILE_CHOOSER_ACTION_SAVE,
                                GTK_STOCK_CANCEL, GTK_RESPONSE_CANCEL,
                                GTK_STOCK_SAVE, GTK_RESPONSE_ACCEPT,
                                NULL);

  gint result = gtk_dialog_run (GTK_DIALOG (dialog));
  if (result == GTK_RESPONSE_ACCEPT)
  {
    filename = gtk_file_chooser_get_filename (GTK_FILE_CHOOSER (dialog));
    gtk_button_set_label (button, filename);
  }

  gtk_widget_destroy (dialog);
}
```

All file chooser dialogs are created with the gtk_file_chooser_dialog_new() regardless of what options you choose. As with other dialogs, you begin by setting the title of the dialog and the parent window. The parent window should always be set, because file chooser dialogs should be modal.

```
GtkWidget* gtk_file_chooser_dialog_new (const gchar *title,
                                        GtkWindow *parent,
                                        GtkFileChooserAction action,
                                        const gchar *first_button_text,
                                        ...);
```

Next, as with file chooser buttons, you have to choose the action of file chooser that will be created. All four action types provided by the GtkFileChooser interface are available to GtkFileChooserDialog. These can be viewed in the following list:

- GTK_FILE_CHOOSER_ACTION_SAVE: The user is prompted to enter a file name and browse throughout the file system for a location. The returned file will be the chosen path with the new file name appended to the end. GtkFileChooser provides methods that allow you to ask for confirmation if the user enters a file name that already exists.

- GTK_FILE_CHOOSER_ACTION_OPEN: The file chooser will only allow the user to select one or more files that already exist on the user's system. The user will be able to browse throughout the file system or choose a bookmarked location.

- GTK_FILE_CHOOSER_ACTION_SELECT_FOLDER: The file chooser will only allow the user to select a folder that already exists. Since the user can only select a folder, other files on the file system will not be displayed.

- GTK_FILE_CHOOSER_ACTION_CREATE_FOLDER: This is very similar to the save action, because it allows the user to choose a location and specify a new folder name. The user can enter a new folder name that will be created when the file chooser returns or click the Create Folder button, shown in Figure 5-6, which will create a new folder in the current directory.

Lastly, you have to provide a NULL-terminated list of buttons along with their response identifiers that will be added to the action area. In Listing 5-6, when the Cancel button is clicked, GTK_RESPONSE_CANCEL is emitted, and when the Save button is clicked, GTK_RESPONSE_ACCEPT is emitted.

Creating a Folder

GTK+ allows you not only to select a folder but also to create a folder. A GtkFileChooserDialog widget using this type can be seen in Figure 5-6, which is a screenshot of Listing 5-7.

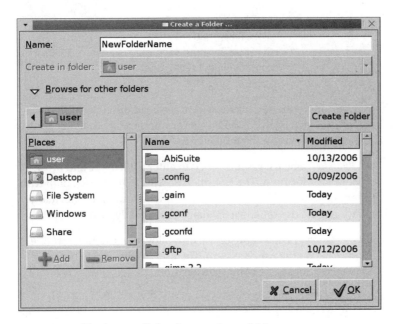

Figure 5-6. *A file chooser dialog for creating a folder*

The dialog in Listing 5-7 will handle creating the new folder when accepted by the user, so you do not need to take any further action beyond destroying the dialog.

Listing 5-7. *Using a GtkFileChooserDialog to Create a Folder (createfolder.c)*

```c
#include <gtk/gtk.h>

int main (int argc,
          char *argv[])
{
  GtkWidget *dialog;
  gchar *filename;
  gint result;

  gtk_init (&argc, &argv);
```

```
/* Create a new GtkFileChooserDialog that will be used to create a new folder. */
dialog = gtk_file_chooser_dialog_new ("Create a Folder ...", NULL,
                                       GTK_FILE_CHOOSER_ACTION_CREATE_FOLDER,
                                       GTK_STOCK_CANCEL, GTK_RESPONSE_CANCEL,
                                       GTK_STOCK_OK, GTK_RESPONSE_OK,
                                       NULL);

result = gtk_dialog_run (GTK_DIALOG (dialog));
if (result == GTK_RESPONSE_OK)
{
  filename = gtk_file_chooser_get_filename (GTK_FILE_CHOOSER (dialog));
  g_print ("Creating directory: %s\n", filename);
}

gtk_widget_destroy (dialog);
return 0;
}
```

The full folder name of the dialog can be retrieved by using the same function that retrieved the file name in the previous example, gtk_file_chooser_get_filename(). The standard GLib function g_mkdir() will create a folder in the specified location on all supported operating systems.

Selecting Multiple Files

Figure 5-7 shows a standard file chooser dialog that will allow the user to choose a file. The difference between GtkFileChooserDialog and GtkFileChooserButton using the GTK_FILE_CHOOSER_ACTION_OPEN type is that dialogs are capable of selecting multiple files while buttons are restricted to one file.

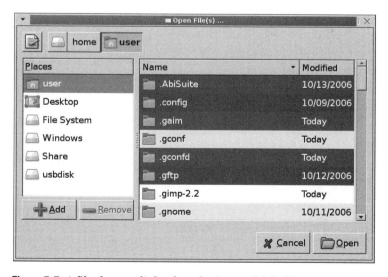

Figure 5-7. *A file chooser dialog for selecting multiple files*

Listing 5-8 shows you how to handle multiple file selections. It is very similar to single file selections except for the fact that selections are returned in a singly linked list.

Listing 5-8. *Using a GtkFileChooserDialog to Select Multiple Files (multiplefiles.c)*

```
static void
button_clicked (GtkButton *button,
                GtkWindow *window)
{
  GtkWidget *dialog;
  GSList *filenames;

  dialog = gtk_file_chooser_dialog_new ("Open File(s) ...", window,
                                 GTK_FILE_CHOOSER_ACTION_OPEN,
                                 GTK_STOCK_CANCEL, GTK_RESPONSE_CANCEL,
                                 GTK_STOCK_OPEN, GTK_RESPONSE_ACCEPT,
                                 NULL);

  /* Allow the user to choose more than one file at a time. */
  gtk_file_chooser_set_select_multiple (GTK_FILE_CHOOSER (dialog), TRUE);

  gint result = gtk_dialog_run (GTK_DIALOG (dialog));

  if (result == GTK_RESPONSE_ACCEPT)
  {
    filenames = gtk_file_chooser_get_filenames (GTK_FILE_CHOOSER (dialog));

    while (filenames != NULL)
    {
      gchar *file = (gchar*) filenames->data;
      g_print ("%s was selected.\n", file);
      filenames = filenames->next;
    }
  }

  gtk_widget_destroy (dialog);
}
```

The gtk_file_chooser_get_filenames() function returns a new GLib data type called GSList, a singly linked list. These are linked lists that can only iterate in one direction. Each element in the list contains a piece of data and a link to the next element.

```
gchar *file = (gchar*) filenames->data;
```

Linked lists in GLib store data as gpointers, so that all types of data can be stored. Because of this, data returned from g_slist_nth_data() has to be cast as its original data type. The first element in the list is indexed as zero.

The GSList structure also provides functions for retrieving the length, appending, prepending, inserting, and removing elements. More information on singly and doubly linked lists can be found in the next chapter.

Color Selection Dialogs

In the previous chapter, you learned about the GtkColorButton widget, which allowed the user to select a color. After clicking that button, the user was presented with a dialog. Although not specified at the time, that dialog was a GtkColorSelectionDialog widget.

Similar to GtkFileChooserDialog, the color selection dialog is actually a GtkDialog container with a GtkColorSelection widget packed as its child widget. GtkColorSelection can easily be used on its own. However, since a dialog is a natural way of presenting the widget, GTK+ provides GtkColorSelectionDialog. A color selection dialog is shown in Figure 5-8.

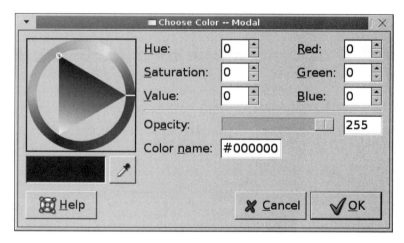

Figure 5-8. *A color selection dialog*

Listing 5-9 contains a top-level window that has two buttons. When the first button is clicked, a modal GtkColorSelectionDialog is created. The other button will create a nonmodal GtkColorSelectionDialog. Each is used to choose global color and opacity values.

This example also loops through program arguments, setting the initial color value if provided. This allows you to pass an initial color when launching the application.

Listing 5-9. *Using a GtkColorSelectionDialog (colorselection.c)*

```c
#include <gtk/gtk.h>

static void run_color_selection_dialog (GtkButton*, GtkWindow*, gboolean);
static void modal_clicked (GtkButton*, GtkWindow*);
static void nonmodal_clicked (GtkButton*, GtkWindow*);
static void dialog_response (GtkDialog*, gint, gpointer);

static GdkColor global_color;
static guint global_alpha = 65535;

int main (int argc,
          char *argv[])
{
  GtkWidget *window, *hbox, *modal, *nonmodal;
  gint i;

  gtk_init (&argc, &argv);

  /* Loop through the parameters.  The first color name that is specified and
   * successfully parsed, it will be used as the initial color of the selection. */
  for (i=1; i < argc; i++)
    if (gdk_color_parse (argv[i], &global_color))
      break;

  window = gtk_window_new (GTK_WINDOW_TOPLEVEL);
  gtk_window_set_title (GTK_WINDOW (window), "Color Selection Dialogs");
  gtk_container_set_border_width (GTK_CONTAINER (window), 10);
  gtk_widget_set_size_request (window, 200, 75);

  modal = gtk_button_new_with_label ("Modal");
  nonmodal = gtk_button_new_with_label ("Non-Modal");

  g_signal_connect (G_OBJECT (modal), "clicked",
                    G_CALLBACK (modal_clicked),
                    (gpointer) window);
  g_signal_connect (G_OBJECT (nonmodal), "clicked",
                    G_CALLBACK (nonmodal_clicked),
                    (gpointer) window);

  hbox = gtk_hbox_new (TRUE, 10);
  gtk_box_pack_start_defaults (GTK_BOX (hbox), modal);
  gtk_box_pack_start_defaults (GTK_BOX (hbox), nonmodal);
```

```
gtk_container_add (GTK_CONTAINER (window), hbox);
gtk_widget_show_all (window);

gtk_main ();
return 0;
}

/* Create a new color selection dialog that is modal. */
static void
modal_clicked (GtkButton *button,
               GtkWindow *window)
{
  run_color_selection_dialog (button, window, TRUE);
}

/* Create a new color selection dialog that is nonmodal. */
static void
nonmodal_clicked (GtkButton *button,
                  GtkWindow *window)
{
  run_color_selection_dialog (button, window, FALSE);
}

/* Create a new color selection dialog and allow the user to choose a color
 * and an opacity value. */
static void
run_color_selection_dialog (GtkButton *button,
                            GtkWindow *window,
                            gboolean domodal)
{
  GtkWidget *dialog, *colorsel;
  gchar *title;

  if (domodal)
    title = "Choose Color -- Modal";
  else
    title = "Choose Color -- Non-Modal";

  dialog = gtk_color_selection_dialog_new (title);
  gtk_window_set_modal (GTK_WINDOW (dialog), domodal);

  colorsel = GTK_COLOR_SELECTION_DIALOG (dialog)->colorsel;
  gtk_color_selection_set_has_opacity_control (GTK_COLOR_SELECTION (colorsel),
                                               TRUE);
```

```c
  gtk_color_selection_set_current_color (GTK_COLOR_SELECTION (colorsel),
                                         &global_color);
  gtk_color_selection_set_current_alpha (GTK_COLOR_SELECTION (colorsel),
                                         global_alpha);

  g_signal_connect (G_OBJECT (dialog), "response",
                    G_CALLBACK (dialog_response), NULL);
  gtk_widget_show_all (dialog);
}

/* Handle the response identifier from the assistant. Either tell the user to
 * read the manual, retrieve the new color value or destroy the dialog. */
static void
dialog_response (GtkDialog *dialog,
                 gint result,
                 gpointer data)
{
  GtkWidget *colorsel;
  GdkColor color = { 0, };
  guint16 alpha = 0;

  switch (result)
  {
  case GTK_RESPONSE_HELP:
    g_print("Read the GTK+ API documentation.\n");
    break;

  case GTK_RESPONSE_OK:
    colorsel = GTK_COLOR_SELECTION_DIALOG (dialog)->colorsel;
    alpha = gtk_color_selection_get_current_alpha (GTK_COLOR_SELECTION (colorsel));
    gtk_color_selection_get_current_color (GTK_COLOR_SELECTION (colorsel), &color);

    g_print ("#%04X%04X%04X%04X\n", color.red, color.green, color.blue, alpha);

    global_color = color;
    global_alpha = alpha;

  default:
    gtk_widget_destroy (GTK_WIDGET(dialog));
  }
}
```

The only function provided by the GtkColorSelectionDialog class is gtk_color_ selection_dialog_new(), which will return a new color selection dialog with the specified title.

```
struct GtkColorSelectionDialog
{
  GtkWidget *colorsel;
  GtkWidget *ok_button;
  GtkWidget *cancel_button;
  GtkWidget *help_button;
};
```

GtkColorSelectionDialog provides direct access to its four available child widgets. The first, colorsel is the GtkColorSelection widget that facilitates color selection. The other three are GTK_STOCK_OK, GTK_STOCK_CANCEL, and GTK_STOCK_HELP buttons. By default, the Help button is hidden. You can use gtk_widget_show() to set it as visible.

As with Listing 5-2, this example connects to the response signal, which is used to receive all of the response identifiers regardless of whether the dialog is modal or nonmodal. The dialog is set as modal or nonmodal with gtk_window_set_modal().

Listing 5-9 shows a fourth color property apart from its RGB values, its opacity (alpha value). Ranging between 0 and 65,535, this value regulates how transparent the color will be drawn, where 0 is fully transparent and 65,535 is opaque. By default, the opacity control is turned off within color selection widgets. You can call the function gtk_color_selection_set_has_opacity_control() to enable the feature.

```
void gtk_color_selection_set_has_opacity_control (GtkColorSelection *colorsel,
                                                  gboolean has_opacity);
```

When opacity is turned on, the hexadecimal color value is sixteen digits long, four digits for each of the values: red, green, blue, and alpha. The opacity is not stored in the GdkColor structure, so you must use gtk_color_selection_get_current_alpha() to retrieve its value from the color selection widget.

```
g_print ("#%04X%04X%04X%04X\n", color.red, color.green, color.blue, alpha);
```

Font Selection Dialogs

The font selection dialog is a dialog that allows the user to select a font and is the dialog shown when a GtkFontButton button is clicked. As with GtkColorSelectionDialog, direct access to the action area buttons is provided through the GtkFontSelectionDialog structure. An example font selection dialog can be viewed in Figure 5-9, which should look similar to the one you saw in the last chapter.

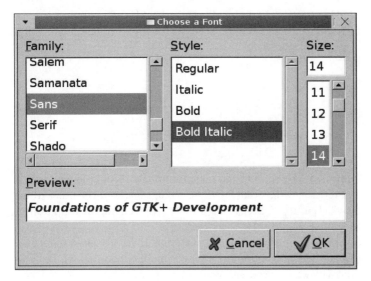

Figure 5-9. *A font selection dialog*

Listing 5-10 uses GtkFontSelectionDialog as the top-level widget. You should note that this dialog is used as a top-level window in this example, which is possible for any dialog. However, you should not get in the habit of doing this, because while it is possible, it is poor programming practice.

Listing 5-10. *Using GtkFontSelectionDialog (fontselection.c)*

```c
#include <gtk/gtk.h>

static void ok_clicked (GtkButton*, GtkWidget*);
static void font_dialog_response (GtkFontSelectionDialog*, gint, gpointer);

int main (int argc,
          char *argv[])
{
  GtkWidget *dialog;

  gtk_init (&argc, &argv);

  /* Use the font selection dialog as the top-level widget. */
  dialog = gtk_font_selection_dialog_new ("Choose a Font");
  gtk_font_selection_dialog_set_font_name (GTK_FONT_SELECTION_DIALOG (dialog),
                                           "Sans Bold Italic 12");
```

```
  gtk_font_selection_dialog_set_preview_text (GTK_FONT_SELECTION_DIALOG (dialog),
                                      "Foundations of GTK+ Development");

  g_signal_connect (G_OBJECT (dialog), "response",
                    G_CALLBACK (font_dialog_response), NULL);

  gtk_widget_show_all (dialog);

  gtk_main ();
  return 0;
}

/* If the user clicks "Apply", display the font, but do not destroy the dialog. If
 * "OK" is pressed, display the font and destroy the dialog. Otherwise, just destroy
 * the dialog. */
static void
font_dialog_response (GtkFontSelectionDialog *dialog,
                      gint response,
                      gpointer data)
{
  gchar *font;
  GtkWidget *message;

  switch (response)
  {
  case (GTK_RESPONSE_APPLY):
  case (GTK_RESPONSE_OK):
    font = gtk_font_selection_dialog_get_font_name (dialog);
    message = gtk_message_dialog_new (NULL, GTK_DIALOG_MODAL,
                                      GTK_MESSAGE_INFO, GTK_BUTTONS_OK, font);
    gtk_window_set_title (GTK_WINDOW (message), "Selected Font");

    gtk_dialog_run (GTK_DIALOG (message));
    gtk_widget_destroy (message);
    g_free (font);
    break;
  default:
    gtk_widget_destroy (GTK_WIDGET (dialog));
  }

  if (response == GTK_RESPONSE_OK)
    gtk_widget_destroy (GTK_WIDGET (dialog));
}
```

The font selection dialog initialization function, gtk_font_selection_dialog_new(), returns a new GtkFontSelectionDialog widget with the specified title.

```
struct GtkFontSelectionDialog
{
  GtkWidget *ok_button;
  GtkWidget *apply_button;
  GtkWidget *cancel_button;
};
```

The dialog itself contains three buttons: GTK_STOCK_OK, GTK_STOCK_APPLY, and GTK_STOCK_CANCEL.

There is no need to create a modal dialog, because the font selection dialog is already the top-level widget. Therefore, the dialog is connected to the response signal.

If the user clicks the OK button, the user is presented with the selected font, and the dialog is destroyed. By clicking Apply, the selected font will be presented to the user, but the dialog is not destroyed. This will allow you to apply the new font so the user can view the changes without closing the dialog.

The font selection widget contains a GtkEntry widget that allows the user to preview the font. By default, the preview text is set to "abcdefghijk ABCDEFGHIJK". This is somewhat boring, so I decided to reset it to "Foundations of GTK+ Development," the title of this book.

The last functions provided by GtkFontSelectionDialog allow you to set and retrieve the current font string. The font string used by gtk_font_selection_dialog_set_font_name() and gtk_font_selection_dialog_get_font_name() is in the same format that we parsed with PangoFontDescription in the previous chapter.

Dialogs with Multiple Pages

With the release of GTK+ 2.10, a widget called GtkAssistant was introduced, which makes it easier to create dialogs with multiple stages, because you do not have to programmatically create the whole dialog. This allows you to split otherwise complex dialogs, into steps that guide the user. This functionality is implemented in what are often referred to as wizards throughout various applications.

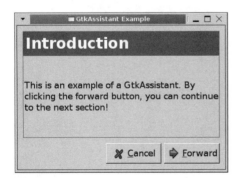

Figure 5-10. *The first page of a GtkAssistant widget*

Figure 5-10 shows the first page of a simple GtkAssistant widget, which was created using the code in Listing 5-11. This example begins by giving the user general information. The next page will not allow the user to proceed until text is entered in a GtkEntry widget. The third page will not allow the user to proceed until a GtkCheckButton button is activated. The fourth page will not let you do anything until the progress bar is filled, and the last page gives a summary of what has happened. This is the general flow that every GtkAssistant widget should follow.

Listing 5-11. *The GtkAssistant Widget (assistant.c)*

```c
#include <gtk/gtk.h>
#include <string.h>

static void entry_changed (GtkEditable*, GtkAssistant*);
static void button_toggled (GtkCheckButton*, GtkAssistant*);
static void button_clicked (GtkButton*, GtkAssistant*);
static void assistant_cancel (GtkAssistant*, gpointer);
static void assistant_close (GtkAssistant*, gpointer);

typedef struct {
    GtkWidget *widget;
    gint index;
    const gchar *title;
    GtkAssistantPageType type;
    gboolean complete;
} PageInfo;

int main (int argc,
          char *argv[])
{
  GtkWidget *assistant, *entry, *label, *button, *progress, *hbox;
  guint i;
  PageInfo page[5] = {
      { NULL, -1, "Introduction",          GTK_ASSISTANT_PAGE_INTRO,   TRUE},
      { NULL, -1, NULL,                     GTK_ASSISTANT_PAGE_CONTENT, FALSE},
      { NULL, -1, "Click the Check Button", GTK_ASSISTANT_PAGE_CONTENT, FALSE},
      { NULL, -1, "Click the Button",       GTK_ASSISTANT_PAGE_PROGRESS, FALSE},
      { NULL, -1, "Confirmation",           GTK_ASSISTANT_PAGE_CONFIRM, TRUE},
  };

  gtk_init (&argc, &argv);
```

```
/* Create a new assistant widget with no pages. */
assistant = gtk_assistant_new ();
gtk_widget_set_size_request (assistant, 450, 300);
gtk_window_set_title (GTK_WINDOW (assistant), "GtkAssistant Example");

g_signal_connect (G_OBJECT (assistant), "destroy",
                  G_CALLBACK (gtk_main_quit), NULL);

page[0].widget = gtk_label_new ("This is an example of a GtkAssistant. By\n"\
                                "clicking the forward button, you can continue\n"\
                                "to the next section!");
page[1].widget = gtk_hbox_new (FALSE, 5);
page[2].widget = gtk_check_button_new_with_label ("Click Me To Continue!");
page[3].widget = gtk_alignment_new (0.5, 0.5, 0.0, 0.0);
page[4].widget = gtk_label_new ("Text has been entered in the label and the\n"\
                                "combo box is clicked. If you are done, then\n"\
                                "it is time to leave!");

/* Create the necessary widgets for the second page. */
label = gtk_label_new ("Your Name: ");
entry = gtk_entry_new ();
gtk_box_pack_start (GTK_BOX (page[1].widget), label, FALSE, FALSE, 5);
gtk_box_pack_start (GTK_BOX (page[1].widget), entry, FALSE, FALSE, 5);

/* Create the necessary widgets for the fourth page. Then, attach the progress bar
 * to the GtkAlignment widget for later access.*/
button = gtk_button_new_with_label ("Click me!");
progress = gtk_progress_bar_new ();
hbox = gtk_hbox_new (FALSE, 5);
gtk_box_pack_start (GTK_BOX (hbox), progress, TRUE, FALSE, 5);
gtk_box_pack_start (GTK_BOX (hbox), button, FALSE, FALSE, 5);
gtk_container_add (GTK_CONTAINER (page[3].widget), hbox);
g_object_set_data (G_OBJECT (page[3].widget), "pbar", (gpointer) progress);

/* Add five pages to the GtkAssistant dialog. */
for (i = 0; i < 5; i++)
{
  page[i].index = gtk_assistant_append_page (GTK_ASSISTANT (assistant),
                                             page[i].widget);
  gtk_assistant_set_page_title (GTK_ASSISTANT (assistant),
                                page[i].widget, page[i].title);
  gtk_assistant_set_page_type  (GTK_ASSISTANT (assistant),
                                page[i].widget, page[i].type);
```

```
      /* Set the introduction and conclusion pages as complete so they can be
       * incremented or closed. */
      gtk_assistant_set_page_complete (GTK_ASSISTANT (assistant),
                                       page[i].widget, page[i].complete);
  }

  /* Update whether pages 2 through 4 are complete based upon whether there is
   * text in the GtkEntry, the check button is active, or the progress bar
   * is completely filled. */
  g_signal_connect (G_OBJECT (entry), "changed",
                    G_CALLBACK (entry_changed), (gpointer) assistant);
  g_signal_connect (G_OBJECT (page[2].widget), "toggled",
                    G_CALLBACK (button_toggled),  (gpointer) assistant);
  g_signal_connect (G_OBJECT (button), "clicked",
                    G_CALLBACK (button_clicked), (gpointer) assistant);

  g_signal_connect (G_OBJECT (assistant), "cancel",
                    G_CALLBACK (assistant_cancel), NULL);
  g_signal_connect (G_OBJECT (assistant), "close",
                    G_CALLBACK (assistant_close), NULL);

  gtk_widget_show_all (assistant);

  gtk_main ();
  return 0;
}

/* If there is text in the GtkEntry, set the page as complete. Otherwise,
 * stop the user from progressing to the next page. */
static void
entry_changed (GtkEditable *entry,
               GtkAssistant *assistant)
{
  const gchar *text = gtk_entry_get_text (GTK_ENTRY (entry));
  gint num = gtk_assistant_get_current_page (assistant);
  GtkWidget *page = gtk_assistant_get_nth_page (assistant, num);

  gtk_assistant_set_page_complete (assistant, page, (strlen (text) > 0));
}

/* If the check button is toggled, set the page as complete. Otherwise,
 * stop the user from progressing the next page. */
static void
button_toggled (GtkCheckButton *toggle,
                GtkAssistant *assistant)
```

```
{
  gboolean active = gtk_toggle_button_get_active (GTK_TOGGLE_BUTTON (toggle));
  gtk_assistant_set_page_complete (assistant, GTK_WIDGET (toggle), active);
}

/* Fill up the progress bar, 10% every second when the button is clicked. Then,
 * set the page as complete when the progress bar is filled. */
static void
button_clicked (GtkButton *button,
                GtkAssistant *assistant)
{
  GtkProgressBar *progress;
  GtkWidget *page;
  gdouble percent = 0.0;

  gtk_widget_set_sensitive (GTK_WIDGET (button), FALSE);
  page = gtk_assistant_get_nth_page (assistant, 3);
  progress = GTK_PROGRESS_BAR (g_object_get_data (G_OBJECT (page), "pbar"));

  while (percent <= 100.0)
  {
    gchar *message = g_strdup_printf ("%.0f%% Complete", percent);
    gtk_progress_bar_set_fraction (progress, percent / 100.0);
    gtk_progress_bar_set_text (progress, message);

    while (gtk_events_pending ())
      gtk_main_iteration ();

    g_usleep (500000);
    percent += 5.0;
  }

  gtk_assistant_set_page_complete (assistant, page, TRUE);
}

/* If the dialog is cancelled, delete it from memory and then clean up after
 * the Assistant structure. */
static void
assistant_cancel (GtkAssistant *assistant,
                  gpointer data)
```

```
{
  gtk_widget_destroy (GTK_WIDGET (assistant));
}

/* This function is where you would apply the changes and destroy the assistant. */
static void
assistant_close (GtkAssistant *assistant,
                 gpointer data)
{
  g_print ("You would apply your changes now!\n");
  gtk_widget_destroy (GTK_WIDGET (assistant));
}
```

Creating GtkAssistant Pages

A GtkAssistant widget is a dialog with multiple pages, although it is actually not derived from GtkDialog. By calling gtk_assistant_new(), you create a new GtkAssistant widget with no initial pages.

```
index = gtk_assistant_append_page (GTK_ASSISTANT (assistant), widget);
```

There is no actual page widget for assistants, because each page is actually a child widget that is added with gtk_assistant_prepend_page(), gtk_assistant_append_page(), or gtk_assistant_insert_page(). Each of these functions accepts the child widget that is added as the content of the page and returns the new page's index. Each page has a number of properties that can be set, each of which is optional. A list of these options follows:

- Page title: Every page should have a title, so the user knows what it is for. Your first page should be an introductory page that tells the user information about the assistant. The last page must be a summary or confirmation page that makes sure the user is ready to apply the previous changes.

- Header image: In the top panel, you can display an optional image to the left of the title. This is often the application's logo or an image that complements the assistant's purpose.

- Side image: This optional image is placed along the left side of the assistant beside the main page content. It is meant to be used for aesthetic appeal.

- Page type: The page type must always be set, or it will default to GTK_ASSISTANT_ PAGE_CONTENT. The last page must always be a confirmation or summary page. You should also make the first page an introductory page that gives the user information about what task the assistant performs.

After you have set the page's properties, you must choose what type of page it is. There are five types of pages. The first page should always be GTK_ASSISTANT_PAGE_INTRO. The last page should always be GTK_ASSISTANT_PAGE_CONFIRM or GTK_ASSISTANT_PAGE_SUMMARY—if your assistant does not end with one of those two types of pages, it will not work correctly. All of the available page types can be viewed in the following list:

- GTK_ASSISTANT_PAGE_CONTENT: This type of page has general content, which means it will be used for almost every page in the assistant. It should never be used for the last page in an assistant.

- GTK_ASSISTANT_PAGE_INTRO: This type of page has introductory information for the user. This should only be set for the first page in the assistant. While not required, introductory pages give the user direction and should be used in most assistants.

- GTK_ASSISTANT_PAGE_CONFIRM: The page allows the user to confirm or deny a set of changes. This is usually used for changes that cannot be undone or may cause something to break if not set correctly. This should only be set for the last page of the assistant.

- GTK_ASSISTANT_PAGE_SUMMARY: The page gives a summary of the changes that have occurred. This should only be set for the last page of the assistant.

- GTK_ASSISTANT_PAGE_PROGRESS: When a task takes a long time to complete, this will block the assistant until the page is marked as complete. The difference between this page and a normal content page is that all of the buttons are disabled and the user is prevented from closing the assistant.

■**Caution** If you do not set the last page type as GTK_ASSISTANT_PAGE_CONFIRM or GTK_ASSISTANT_PAGE_SUMMARY, your application will abort with a GTK+ error when computing the last button state.

Since GtkAssistant is not derived from GtkDialog, you cannot use gtk_dialog_run() (or any other GtkDialog function) on this widget. Instead, the following four signals are provided for you to handle button clicked signals:

- apply: This signal is emitted when the Apply button or Forward button is clicked on any assistant page.

- cancel: This signal is emitted when the Cancel button is clicked on any assistant page.

- close: This signal is emitted when the Close button or Apply button on the last page in the assistant is clicked.

- prepare: Before making a new page visible, this signal is emitted so that you can do any preparation work before it is visible to the user.

You can connect to all GtkAssistant signals with g_signal_connect() or any other signal connection function provided by GLib. Excluding prepare, the callback functions for GtkAssistant signals receive the assistant and the user data parameter. The callback function for the prepare signal also accepts the child widget of the current page.

By default, every page is set as incomplete. You have to manually set each page as complete when the time is right with gtk_assistant_set_page_complete() or the GtkAssistant will not be able to progress to the next page.

```
void gtk_assistant_set_page_complete (GtkAssistant *assistant,
                                      GtkWidget *page,
                                      gboolean complete);
```

On every page, a Cancel button is displayed in addition to a few others. On pages other than the first one, a Back button is displayed that is always sensitive. This allows you to visit the previously displayed page and make changes.

Note The page that is visited when the user clicks the Back button is not always the previous page according to the page index. It is the previously displayed page, which may be different based on how you defined the page flow of your assistant.

On every page except the last page, a Forward button is placed, which allows the user to move to the next page. On the last page an Apply button is displayed that allows the user to apply the changes. However, until the page is set as complete, the assistant will set the Forward or Apply button as insensitive. This allows you to prevent the user from proceeding until some action is taken.

In Listing 5-11, the first and last pages of the assistant were set as complete, because they were merely informative pages. This is the case in most assistants since they should begin with an introduction page and end with a confirmation or summary page.

The other two pages are where it becomes interesting. On the second page, we want to make sure that the user cannot proceed until text is entered in the GtkEntry widget. It would seem that that we should just check when text has been inserted and be done with it.

However, what happens if the user deletes all of the text? In this case, the forward button should be disabled yet again. To handle both of these actions, you can use GtkEditable's changed signal. This will allow you to check the current state of the text in the entry upon every change, as in Listing 5-11.

On the third page, we want to enable the forward button only when the check button is active. To do this, we used the toggled signal of GtkToggleButton to check the current state of the check button. Based on this state, the forward button's sensitivity was set.

The fourth page has a type of GTK_ASSISTANT_PAGE_PROGRESS, which disables all actions until the page is set as complete. The user is instructed to click a button, which begins the process of filling a GtkProgressBar widget 10 percent every second. When the progress bar is filled, the page is set as complete.

GtkProgressBar

The GtkAssistant example introduced another new widget called GtkProgressBar. Progress bars are a simple way to show how much of a process has been completed and is useful for processes that take a long time to handle. Progress bars give the user a visual cue that progress is being made, so they do not think the program has frozen.

New progress bars are created with gtk_progress_bar_new(). The implementation of GtkProgressBar was made a lot simpler with the release of GTK+ 2.0, so be careful when using the API documentation, because a number of the displayed functions and properties are depreciated. The two examples following show you how to correctly use the GtkProgressBar widget.

There are two ways to use the GtkProgressBar widget. If you are sure of how much progress a process has made, you should use gtk_progress_bar_set_fraction() to set a discrete value. This function accepts values between 0.0 and 1.0, where 1.0 sets the progress bar as 100 percent complete.

```
while (percent <= 100.0)
{
  gchar *message = g_strdup_printf ("%.0f%% Complete", percent);
  gtk_progress_bar_set_fraction (progress, percent / 100.0);
  gtk_progress_bar_set_text (progress, message);

  while (gtk_events_pending ())
    gtk_main_iteration ();

  g_usleep (500000);
  percent += 5.0;
}
```

You may also want to display text that can be used to complement the progress bar. In the preceding example, gtk_progress_bar_set_text() was used to display the percent complete statistic, which is superimposed on the progress bar widget.

If you are not able to detect the progress of the process, you can use pulses. In the preceding example, gtk_progress_bar_pulse() was used to move the progress bar one step for every pending event that was processed. You can set the pulse step with gtk_progress_bar_set_pulse_step().

```
gtk_progress_bar_set_pulse_step (GTK_PROGRESS_BAR (bar), 0.1);
while (gtk_events_pending ())
{
  gtk_main_iteration ();
  gtk_progress_bar_pulse ();
}
```

By setting the pulse step to 0.1, the progress bar will fill itself up in the first ten steps and clear itself out in the next ten. This process will continue for as long as you continue pulsing the progress bar.

Page Forward Functions

There are times that you may want to skip to specific assistant pages if conditions are correct. For example, let us assume your application is creating a new project. Depending on the chosen language, you want to jump to either the third or fourth page. In this case, you will want to define your own GtkAssistantPageFunc function for forward motion.

You can use gtk_assistant_set_forward_page_func() to define a new page forward function for the assistant. By default, GTK+ will increment directly through the pages in order, one page at a time. By defining a new forward function, you can define the flow.

```
void gtk_assistant_set_forward_page_func (GtkAssistant *assistant,
                                          GtkAssistantPageFunc page_func,
                                          gpointer data,
                                          GDestroyNotify destroy_func);
```

For example, assistant_forward() is a simple GtkAssistantPageFunc implementation that moves from page two to either three or four depending on the condition returned by decide_next_page().

```
static gint
assistant_forward (gint current_page,
                   gpointer data)
{
  gint next_page = 0;

  switch (current_page)
  {
    case 0:
      next_page = 1;
      break;
    case 1:
      next_page = (decide_next_page() ? 2 : 3);
      break;
    case 2:
    case 3:
      next_page = 4;
      break;
    default:
      next_page = -1;
  }

  return next_page;
}
```

■**Note** By returning -1 from a page forward function, the user will be presented with a critical error and the assistant will not move to another page. The critical error message will tell the user that the page flow is broken.

In the assistant_forward() function, flow is changed based on the Boolean value returned by the fictional function decide_next_page(). In either case, the last page will be page 4. If the current page is not within bounds, -1 is returned, so an exception is thrown by GTK+.

While this GtkAssistant example is very simple, implementations of this widget can become very complex as they expand in number of pages. This widget could be re-created with a dialog, a GtkNotebook with hidden tabs, and a few buttons (I have had to do that very thing multiple times!), but it makes the process a lot easier.

Test Your Understanding

In the exercise for this chapter, you will be creating custom dialogs of your own. Each of the dialogs will be implementations of different types of file chooser dialogs. However, you will be embedding a GtkFileChooserWidget into a GtkDialog to recreate the functionality of the built-in dialogs.

Exercise 5-1. Implementing File Chooser Dialogs

In this exercise, create a window with four buttons. Each button will open a different dialog when clicked that implements one of the four GtkFileChooser actions. You should use GtkFileChooserWidget added to a GtkDialog instead of the prebuilt GtkFileChooserDialog.

1. Your dialog will implement a GTK_FILE_CHOOSER_ACTION_SAVE file chooser dialog. The chosen file name should be printed to the screen.

2. Your dialog will implement a GTK_FILE_CHOOSER_ACTION_CREATE_FOLDER file chooser dialog. The new folder name should be printed to the screen. You will have to manually create the new folder with g_mkdir().

3. Your dialog will implement a GTK_FILE_CHOOSER_ACTION_OPEN file chooser dialog. The chosen file names should be printed to the screen.

4. Your dialog will implement a GTK_FILE_CHOOSER_ACTION_SELECT_FOLDER file chooser dialog. The chosen folder path should be printed to the screen.

For each of the dialogs, you need to make sure to set it to a decent size so that the whole content can be visible to the user. If you get stuck on this exercise, you can find one possible solution in Appendix F.

Summary

In this chapter, you learned how to create your own custom dialogs. To do this, you need to first initialize the dialog. Then, action area buttons need to be added as well as the main content to the dialog's GtkVBox.

Dialogs can be created as modal or nonmodal. A modal dialog created with gtk_dialog_run() blocks the user from interacting with the parent window until it is destroyed by creating a main loop for the dialog. It also centers the dialog above its parent window. Nonmodal dialogs allow the user to interact with any other window in the application and will not force focus on the dialog.

After learning about the built-in dialogs, you learned about multiple types of built-in dialogs provided by GTK+:

- Message dialog (GtkMessageDialog): Provide a general message, error message, warning, or simple yes-no question to the user.

- About dialog (GtkAboutDialog): Show information about the application including version, copyright, license, authors, and others.

- File chooser dialog (GtkFileChooserDialog): Allow the user to choose a file, choose multiple files, save a file, choose a directory, or create a directory.

- Color selection dialog (GtkColorSelectionDialog): Allow the user to choose a color along with an optional opacity value.

- Font selection dialog (GtkFontSelectionDialog): Allow the user to choose a font and its size and style properties.

The last section of this chapter showed you a widget called GtkAssistant, which was introduced in GTK+ 2.10. It allows you to create dialogs with multiple stages. It is important to note that assistants are not actually a type of GtkDialog widget but are directly derived from the GtkWindow class. This means that you have to handle these by connecting signals in the main loop instead of calling gtk_dialog_run().

You now have a firm understanding of many important aspects of GTK+. Before we continue on to more advanced widgets, the next chapter will give you a thorough understanding of GLib. Chapter 6 will cover many GLib data types, idle functions, timeouts, process spawning, threads, dynamic modules, file utilities, and timers, as well as other important topics.

CHAPTER 6

■ ■ ■

Using GLib

Now that you have a reasonable grasp of GTK+ and a number of simple widgets, it is time to move to another library. GTK+ depends on GLib, a general-purpose library that provides many kinds of utility functions, data types, and wrapper functions. In fact, you have already used some aspects of GLib in previous chapters.

GLib can be run independently of any other library, which means that some of the examples in this chapter do not require the GTK+, GDK, and Pango libraries. However, GTK+ does depend on GLib.

Not all of the topics throughout this chapter will be used in later chapters, but all are useful in many GTK+ applications in the real world. Many of the topics are used for very specific tasks. For example, GModule can be used to create a plug-in system for your application or open a binary's symbol table.

The goal of Chapter 6 is not to be a comprehensive guide to everything in GLib. When using a feature shown in this chapter, you should reference the GLib API documentation for more information. However, this chapter *will* introduce you to a wide array of important features so that you have a general understanding of what GLib provides.

In this chapter, you will learn the following:

- The basic data types, macros, and utility functions provided by GLib

- How to give textual feedback to the user about errors and warnings that occur within your application

- Memory management schemes provided by GLib such as memory slices, g_malloc(), and friends

- Various utility functions provided by GLib for timing, file manipulation, reading directory contents, and working with the file system

- How the main loop is implemented in GLib and how it implements timeout and idle functions

- Data structures provided by GLib including strings, linked lists, binary trees, arrays, hash tables, quarks, keyed data lists, and n-ary trees

- How to us GIOChannel to manipulate files and create pipes as well as how to spawn asynchronous and synchronous processes

- How to dynamically load shared libraries with GModule

GLib Basics

GLib is a general-purpose utility library that is used to implement many useful nongraphical features. While it is required by GTK+, it can also be used independently. Because of this, some applications use GLib without GTK+ and other supporting libraries for the many capabilities it provides.

One of the main benefits of using GLib is that it provides a cross-platform interface that allows your code to be run on any of its supported operating systems *with little to no rewriting of code.* You will see this illustrated in the examples throughout the rest of this chapter.

Basic Data Types

You have been using many data types in previous chapters that originate in GLib. These data types provide a set of common data types that are portable to not only other platforms, but also other programming languages wrapping GTK+.

Table 6-1 is a list of the basic data types provided by GLib. You can find all of the type definitions in the gtypes.h header file. More advanced data structures will be covered later, in the "Data Types" section.

Table 6-1. *GLib Data Types*

Type	Description
gboolean	Since C does not provide a Boolean data type, GLib provides gboolean, which is set to either TRUE or FALSE.
gchar (guchar)	Signed and unsigned data types corresponding to the standard C character type.
gconstpointer	A pointer to constant data that is untyped. The data that this type points to should not be changed. Therefore, it is typically used in function prototypes to indicate that the function will not alter the data to which it points.
gdouble	A data type corresponding to the standard C double type. Possible values are within the range from -G_MAXDOUBLE to G_MAXDOUBLE. G_MINDOUBLE refers to the minimum positive value that gdouble can hold.
gfloat	A data type corresponding to the standard C float type. Possible values are within the range from -G_MAXFLOAT to G_MAXFLOAT. G_MINFLOAT refers to the minimum positive value that gfloat can hold.
gint (guint)	Signed and unsigned data types corresponding to the standard C int type. Signed gint values must be within the range from G_MININT to G_MAXINT. The maximum guint value is given by G_MAXUINT.
gint8 (guint8)	Signed and unsigned integers that are designed to be 8 bits on all platforms. Signed values are within the range from -128 to 127 (G_MININT8 to G_MAXINT8) and unsigned values from 0 to 255 (G_MAXUINT8).
gint16 (guint16)	Signed and unsigned integers that are designed to be 16 bits on all platforms. Signed values are within the range from -32,768 to 32,767 (G_MININT16 to G_MAXINT16) and unsigned values from 0 to 65,535 (G_MAXUINT16).

Type	Description
gint32 (guint32)	Signed and unsigned integers that are designed to be 32 bits on all platforms. Signed values are within the range from -2,147,483,648 to 2,147,483,647 (G_MININT32 to G_MAXINT32) and unsigned values from 0 to 4,294,967,295 (G_MAXUINT32).
gint64 (guint64)	Signed and unsigned integers that are designed to be 64 bits on all platforms. Signed values are within the range from -2^{63} to 2^{63}-1 (G_MININT64 to G_MAXINT64) and unsigned values from 0 to 2^{64}-1 (G_MAXUINT64).
glong (gulong)	Signed and unsigned data types corresponding to the standard C long type. Signed glong values must be within the range from G_MINLONG to G_MAXLONG. The maximum gulong value is given by G_MAXULONG.
gpointer	A generic, untyped pointer that is defined as void*. It is simply meant to look more appealing than the standard void* type.
gshort (gushort)	Signed and unsigned data types corresponding to the standard C short type. Signed gshort values must be within the range from G_MINSHORT to G_MAXSHORT. The maximum gushort value is given by G_MAXUSHORT.
gsize (gssize)	Unsigned and signed 32-bit integers that are used by many data structures to represent sizes. The gsize data type is defined as unsigned int and gssize as signed int.

You used to be able to check whether gint64 and guint64 were supported on the platform by using the G_HAVE_GINT64 macro. However, since the release of GLib 2.0, 64-bit integers have been required, so this macro is always defined, as well as both data types. These two types have the following definitions:

```
G_GNUC_EXTENSION typedef signed long long gint64;
G_GNUC_EXTENSION typedef unsigned long long guint64;
```

■**Note** Some options such as -pedantic cause warnings for extensions in GNU C. Typing __extension__ before the expression can prevent this. G_GNUC_EXTENSION is equivalent to __extension__.

GLib also provides G_GINT64_CONSTANT() and G_GUINT64_CONSTANT(), which can be used to insert 64-bit literals into the source code. For example, G_MAXINT64 is defined as G_GINT64_CONSTANT(0x7fffffffffffffff).

Standard Macros

In addition to the basic data types, GLib provides a number of predefined values and standard macros that you can use throughout your applications. While most applications will not make wide use of every macro, they are here to make your life easier. For instance, there are macros for checking the GLib version and various type conversions.

At times, you may want to check the user's version of GLib to decide whether or not to compile a certain feature. GLib provides version information for use during compile time and runtime, shown in Table 6-2.

Table 6-2. *GLib Version Information*

Value	Description
GLIB_MAJOR_VERSION	The major version of the GLib headers that is included. To get the major version of the library that you linked against, you can use glib_major_version. In GLib 2.12.1, "2" indicates the major version.
GLIB_MINOR_VERSION	The minor version of the GLib headers that is included. To get the minor version of the library that you linked against, you can use glib_minor_version. In GLib 2.12.1, "12" indicates the minor version.
GLIB_MICRO_VERSION	The micro version of the GLib headers that is included. To get the micro version of the library that you linked against, you can use glib_micro_version. In GLib 2.12.1, "1" indicates the micro version.
GLIB_CHECK_VERSION (major, minor, micro)	Returns TRUE if the version of the GLib header files that you are using is the same or a newer version than specified. You can use this to make sure that the user has a compatible version of GLib when compiling a specific feature.

In addition to the version information presented in Table 6-2, you can also use glib_check_version() to check the version of GLib currently in use at runtime. This function returns NULL, if the library is compatible, or a string that gives more information about the incompatibility. This function makes sure that the runtime version is the same or a more recent release.

```
const gchar* glib_check_version (guint major,
                                 guint minor,
                                 guint micro);
```

GLib also provides a number of additional macros that do everything from numerical operations, type conversions, and memory referencing to simply defining Boolean values for TRUE and FALSE. A list of some of the most useful macros can be found in Table 6-3.

Table 6-3. *Standard GLib Macros*

Macro	Description
ABS (a)	Return the absolute value of argument a. This function simply returns any negative number without the negative sign and does nothing to positive numbers.
CLAMP (a, low, high)	Make sure that a is between low and high. If a is not between low and high, the returned value will be the closest of the two. Otherwise, the returned value will be left unchanged.
G_DIR_SEPARATOR G_DIR_SEPARATOR_S	On UNIX machines, directories are separated by a slash (/), and on Windows machines, they are separated by a backslash (\). G_DIR_SEPARATOR will return the appropriate separator as a character, and G_DIR_SEPARATOR_S will return the separator as a string.

Macro	Description
GINT_TO_POINTER (i) GPOINTER_TO_INT (p)	Convert an integer to a gpointer or a gpointer to an integer. Only 32 bits of the integer will be stored, so you should avoid using integers that will take up more than that amount of space when using these macros. Remember that you cannot store pointers in integers. This only allows you to store an integer as a pointer.
GSIZE_TO_POINTER (s) GPOINTER_TO_SIZE (p)	Convert a gsize value to a gpointer or a gpointer to gsize value. The gsize data type must have been stored as a pointer with GSIZE_TO_POINTER() to convert it back. See GINT_TO_POINTER() for more information.
GUINT_TO_POINTER (u) GPOINTER_TO_UINT (p)	Convert an unsigned integer to a gpointer or a gpointer to an unsigned integer. The integer must have been stored as a pointer with GUINT_TO_POINTER() to convert it back. See GINT_TO_POINTER() for more information.
G_OS_WIN32 G_OS_BEOS G_OS_UNIX	These three macros allow you to define code that will only be run on a specific platform. Only the macro corresponding to the user's system will be defined, so you can bracket code specific to the user's operating system with #ifdef G_OS_*.
G_STRUCT_MEMBER (type, struct_p, offset)	Returns the member of the structure located at the specified offset. This offset must be within struct_p. type defines the data type of the field you are retrieving.
G_STRUCT_MEMBER_P (struct_p, offset)	Returns an untyped pointer to the member of the structure located at the specified offset. The offset must be within struct_p.
G_STRUCT_OFFSET (type, member)	Returns the byte offset of a member within a structure. The structure type is defined by type.
MIN (a, b) MAX (a, b)	Calculates the minimum or maximum value of the two arguments a and b respectively.
TRUE and FALSE	FALSE is defined as zero, and TRUE is set to the logical not of FALSE. These values are used for the gboolean type.

GLib also provides a number of macros for standard mathematical units, with precision up to 50 decimal places in some cases. Those included in GLib 2.12 follow:

- G_E: The base of the natural logarithm with a precision of 49 decimal places

- G_LN2: The natural logarithm of 2 with a precision of 50 decimal places

- G_LN10: The natural logarithm of 10 with a precision of 49 decimal places

- G_PI: The value of pi with a precision of 49 decimal places

- G_PI_2: The value of pi divided by 2 with a precision of 49 decimal places

- G_PI_4: The value of pi divided by 4 with a precision of 50 decimal places

- G_SQRT2: The square root of 2 with a precision of 49 decimal places

- G_LOG_2_BASE_10: The logarithm of 2 with base 10 with a precision of 20 decimal places

Message Logging

Throughout this chapter and later chapters, you will need a way to report textual errors, information, and warnings to the user. It is possible to use g_print() for all of these messages, but GLib provides a logging system with some useful features.

Any type of textual message can be conveyed using g_log(). The first parameter of this function allows you to define a custom log domain. The log domain is a string that is passed to GLogFunc that is used to help the user to differentiate messages that were output by your application from those outputted by other libraries.

```
void g_log (const gchar *log_domain,
            GLogLevelFlags log_level,
            const gchar *message,
            ...);
```

Unless you are creating a library, you should use G_LOG_DOMAIN as the domain. Any text specified to the log domain parameter will be prepended to the beginning of messages before they are output. If you do not specify a log domain, G_LOG_DOMAIN will be used. For example, the GTK+ library specifies "Gtk" as the domain so the user will know from where the messages have been emitted.

The second parameter of g_log() allows you to specify what type of message is being reported. For example, if you are reporting an error message that should cause the application to be terminated, you should use G_LOG_LEVEL_ERROR. A list of GLogLevelFlags follows:

- G_LOG_FLAG_RECURSION: A flag used for recursive messages.

- G_LOG_FLAG_FATAL: Log levels that are set with this flag will cause the application to quit and the core to be dumped when called.

- G_LOG_LEVEL_ERROR: A type of error that is always fatal.

- G_LOG_LEVEL_CRITICAL: A nonfatal error that is more important than a warning but does not need the application to quit.

- G_LOG_LEVEL_WARNING: A warning of something that will not cause the application to be unable to continue.

- G_LOG_LEVEL_MESSAGE: Used to log normal messages that are not critical.

- G_LOG_LEVEL_INFO: Any other type of message not covered by the other levels, such as general information.

- G_LOG_LEVEL_DEBUG: A general message used for debugging purposes.

- G_LOG_LEVEL_MASK: Equal to (G_LOG_FLAG_RECURSION | G_LOG_FLAG_FATAL).

Note As an example, g_malloc() terminates the application when memory allocation fails, because G_LOG_LEVEL_ERROR is used. On the other hand, g_try_malloc() will not output any message when allocation fails. Instead, it returns a NULL pointer.

The actual error message reported to g_log() should be in the same format reported to g_print().

For the sake of convenience, GLib also provides five functions that allow you to bypass the domain and flag parameters of g_log(). The message reported by these functions should also be formatted in the same manner as g_print().

These functions correspond directly to the specified log flags and will be emitted under the G_LOG_DOMAIN domain. The functions, along with their associated log flags, follow:

```
void g_message (...);    /* G_LOG_LEVEL_MESSAGE */
void g_warning (...);    /* G_LOG_LEVEL_WARNING */
void g_critical (...);   /* G_LOG_LEVEL_CRITICAL */
void g_error (...);      /* G_LOG_LEVEL_ERROR */
void g_debug (...);      /* G_LOG_LEVEL_DEBUG */
```

Lastly, depending on how your application handles messages, you may want to make other types of messages fatal. By default, only the G_LOG_LEVEL_ERROR flag will cause the application to be terminated. No matter what, this level is always fatal.

To make another type of message fatal, you can call g_log_set_always_fatal(). This will associate the G_LOG_FLAG_FATAL flag with the specified level.

```
g_log_set_always_fatal (G_LOG_LEVEL_DEBUG | G_LOG_LEVEL_WARNING);
```

For example, the preceding example command will force the application to terminate when you report debugging and warning messages to the user. This feature should be used sparingly, because not all errors or warnings should cause the application to terminate!

Memory Management

Memory management is an extremely important aspect of any application and becomes increasingly significant as your application grows in size and complexity. While there are a large number of functions provided for memory management in GLib, this section will cover only those that are used most often.

Memory Slices

Prior to GLib 2.10 memory allocators and memory chunks were used for the allocation of pieces of memory. However, a much more efficient method has been introduced in the current release in the form of memory slices. Therefore, memory slices are the only type of allocator that will be covered in this section. If you are using an older version of GLib for any reason, you should check out GMemChunk in the API documentation.

The advantage of using memory slices is that they avoid excessive memory waste and fix scalability and performance problems that plagued memory chunks. This is achieved by using slab allocation.

Memory slices very efficiently allocate memory as equally sized chunks. This means that they can be used to allocate individual objects as small as two pointers or many objects of the same size.

SLAB ALLOCATION OF MEMORY

The slab allocator was originally designed by Jeff Bonwick of Sun Microsystems. It is a memory management scheme that helps reduce the problem of fragmentation of internal memory, which is caused by the system allocating a larger block of memory than was originally requested.

To understand slab allocation, you need to know the meaning of slab and cache in context. A slab is one contiguous chunk of memory that represents one memory allocation. A cache is a very efficient chunk of memory that is used to hold only one type of data. Each cache is made out of one or more slabs.

Each object is initially marked as free, which means that the slab is empty. When a process requests a new object from the kernel, the system will attempt to find a location on a partially filled slab, which will be used to place the object. If a partial slab is not found that will fit the object, a new slab is allocated from contiguous physical memory and that slab is added to the cache. When a slab becomes full, it is then marked as used.

Slab allocation has many benefits, but one major benefit is that the requested memory allocation size is the same as the actual allocation. This avoids fragmentation of memory and makes allocation very efficient. For more information, you should read Jeff Bonwick's paper on the slab allocator, which is available online.

When you need to allocate large blocks of memory, the system's implementation of malloc() will automatically be used. Although we will briefly discuss using g_malloc() and its related functions in the next section, you should use memory slices for memory allocation in new code as long as you do not plan on resizing objects after allocation. One constraint of memory slices is that the size of the object must be the same size when it was allocated and when it is freed.

There are two ways to use slice allocators: to allocate a single object of any size greater than two pointers or to allocate multiple objects of the same size. The code in Listing 6-1 shows you how to allocate multiple objects; it allocates an array of one hundred objects with the slice allocator and then frees them.

Listing 6-1. *Allocating Multiple Objects*

```
#define SLICE_SIZE 10

gchar *strings[100];
gint i;

for (i = 0; i < 100; i++)
  strings[i] = g_slice_alloc (SLICE_SIZE);

/* ... Use the strings in some way ... */

/* Free all of the memory after you are done using it. */
for (i = 0; i < 100; i++)
  g_slice_free1 (SLICE_SIZE, strings[i]);
```

In Listing 6-1, g_slice_alloc() was used to allocate 100 strings of length SLICE_SIZE. Slice allocation is very simple—all you need to do is supply the size of memory that the slice should be. Similar to malloc(), this function returns a gpointer to the memory instead of an object that is cast.

Internally, GLib decides whether to use slab allocation or delegate the memory allocation to g_malloc(). Memory allocation is performed by g_malloc() when the desired memory slice is very large. GLib also provides g_slice_alloc0(), which will initialize the returned memory chunk to 0.

■**Note** Memory slices will choose the most efficient method of memory allocation for the current case during runtime, whether that is slab allocation, g_malloc(), or some other method. However, you can force it to always use g_malloc() by setting the G_SLICE environment variable to always-malloc.

When you are finished using the memory, you should free it with g_slice_free1() so that it can be used by another part of your application. This function frees a memory block of size SLICE_SIZE, located at strings[i].

```
g_slice_free1 (SLICE_SIZE, strings[i]);
```

Internally, memory will be freed using the same method as it was allocated. Therefore, to use this function, you must have allocated the memory with g_slice_alloc() or g_slice_alloc0().

When you need to allocate only a single instance of an object, g_slice_new() is available. An example of using this function to allocate one object is shown in Listing 6-2.

Listing 6-2. *Allocating a Single Object*

```
typedef struct
{
  GtkWidget *window;
  GtkWidget *label;
} Widgets;

Widgets *w = g_slice_new (Widgets);

/* Use the structure just as you would any other structure. */
w->window = gtk_window_new (GTK_WINDOW_TOPLEVEL);
w->label = gtk_label_new ("I belong to widgets!");

/* Free the block of memory of size "Widgets" so it can be reused. */
g_slice_free (Widgets, w);
```

If you need to allocate a single block of memory with a slice allocation, instead of using the method presented in Listing 6-1, you can call g_slice_new(). This function is defined as follows; it casts the value returned by g_slice_alloc() as the desired type.

```
#define g_slice_new(type)  ((type*) g_slice_alloc (sizeof (type))
```

In addition to g_slice_new(), GLib provides g_slice_new0(), which uses g_slice_alloc0() to initialize the returned slice to 0.

After you are finished with the memory, you need to free it. Since we only allocated one piece of memory in Listing 6-2, we can use g_slice_free(), which freed one piece of memory of the size Widgets and at the location w.

Memory Allocation

GLib provides a number of functions that wrap functionality provided by the standard C library. A description of a few of these functions is presented in this section.

■**Note** It is important to note that you do not need to verify that any of the following calls were successful. If any call to allocate memory fails, the application will automatically be terminated by Glib, and a message will be printed to standard error, displaying the error that has occurred.

To allocate one or more new structures, you should use g_new(). This function receives the type of data and the number of structures to allocate. It then returns a pointer to the new memory.

```
struct_type* g_new (struct_type, number_of_structs);
```

The returned data is already cast to the correct type, so there is no need to recast the object. If you want all of the structures to be initialized to 0 by default, you should use g_new0() instead.

A method most C programmers are familiar with is malloc(). GLib provides a portable wrapped version of this function called g_malloc(). This function receives the number of bytes to allocate and returns a pointer to the allocated memory.

```
gpointer g_malloc (gulong number_of_bytes);
```

The easiest way to calculate the number of bytes of memory to allocate is to use the sizeof() function on the data type. The returned object is not automatically cast, so you will want to immediately take care of casting in most cases. The g_malloc0() function is also provided if you want the newly allocated memory to be initialized with a value of 0.

When memory allocation with g_malloc() fails, the application will abort. Alternatively, you can use g_try_malloc(), which will return NULL instead of aborting when memory allocation fails. This should only be used when your application can recover from an unsuccessful memory allocation. When using g_try_malloc(), it is important to handle the NULL case.

```
gpointer g_try_malloc (gulong number_of_bytes);
```

After you are finished with a piece of memory, you should always free it so it can be used again. If not, it will cause a memory leak in your application, which is never a good thing. To free a piece of memory, you can call g_free(). This is needed to free strings returned from many functions available in the GTK+ API.

```
void g_free (gpointer memory);
```

This function should be used on objects that you explicitly allocated memory for or objects that do not provide their own destroy or free function calls. For example, you should never use g_free() on a chunk of memory that was allocated with memory slices. If the piece of data provides its own free function, you should *always* use that function. If NULL memory is sent to g_free(), it will be ignored, and the function will return.

One more important memory function is g_memmove(), which is used to move pieces of memory. For example, the following call to g_memmove() can be used to remove a section of a string beginning at pos and continuing on len characters.

```
g_memmove (str + pos, str + pos + len, strlen(str) - (pos + len));
str[strlen(str) - len] = 0;
```

With the exception of g_memmove(), I would like to reiterate one last time that you should always use memory slices when allocating one object or multiple objects of the same size instead of g_malloc() and friends.

Memory Profiling

GLib provides a simple way to output a summary of memory usage within your application. This can be done by calling g_mem_profile() at any point within your application.

Before using memory profiling, you must always set the GMemVTable. Listing 6-3 shows you how to set up the default GMemVTable and output memory profiling information on application termination.

■**Note** By using the default GMemVTable, only calls to g_malloc(), g_free(), and friends will be counted. Calls to malloc() and free() will not be counted. Also, to profile memory slices, you need to set the G_SLICE environment variable to always-malloc to force it to always use g_malloc(). GLib's memory profiler will not count allocations with the slab allocator. To monitor all memory, you should use an external tool such as Valgrind.

Listing 6-3. *Memory Profiling (memprofile.c)*

```
#include <glib.h>

int main (int argc,
          char *argv[])
{
  GSList *list = NULL;

  /* Set the GMemVTable to the default table. This needs to be called before
   * any other call to a GLib function. */
  g_mem_set_vtable (glib_mem_profiler_table);

  /* Call g_mem_profile() when the application exits. */
  g_atexit (g_mem_profile);

  list = (GSList*) g_malloc (sizeof (GSList));
  list->next = (GSList*) g_malloc (sizeof (GSList));

  /* Only free one of the GSList objects to see the memory profiler output. */
  g_free (list->next);

  return 0;
}
```

Before you can output a memory usage summary, you have to set the GMemVTable with g_mem_set_vtable(). The GMemVTable defines new versions of memory allocation functions with profiling enabled, so they can be tracked by GLib. These include malloc(), realloc(), free(), calloc(), try_malloc(), and try_realloc().

Although it is possible to create your own GMemVTable, GLib provides a prebuilt version named glib_mem_profiler_table. In almost every case, the default memory table should be used.

After defining the GMemVTable, Listing 6-3 uses g_atexit() so g_mem_profile() will be called when the application is exiting. Functions specified to g_atexit() must accept no parameters and return no value.

The output of the application in Listing 6-3 follows. This output will vary depending on your GLib version, your system type, and various other factors.

```
GLib Memory statistics (successful operations):
 blocks of | allocated  | freed       | allocated  | freed       | n_bytes
  n_bytes  | n_times by | n_times by  | n_times by | n_times by  | remaining
           | malloc()   | free()      | realloc()  | realloc()   |
===========|============|=============|============|=============|===========
         8 |          2 |           1 |          0 |           0 |        +8
GLib Memory statistics (failing operations):
 --- none ---
Total bytes: allocated=16, zero-initialized=0 (0.00%), freed=8 (50.00%), remaining=8
```

The preceding table shows the size of memory that is allocated, followed by how many times malloc() was called on it. It shows that two blocks of 8 bytes that represent the two GSList objects were allocated. It then shows how many blocks of memory were freed with free(), allocated with realloc(), and freed with realloc(). The last column shows the number of bytes of memory that are not freed. Since only one GSList object was freed, it shows that 8 bytes were leaked.

The table illustrates only successful operations, because nothing failed within the application. If some type of failure in memory allocation or deallocation had occurred, there would be a second table to show those operations.

A summary is given at the end of the output that shows totals of all of the information shown in the tables.

Utility Functions

As you may have already noticed, GLib provides you with a very wide array of functionality. This section should further show you that it is an indispensable library when developing GTK+ applications.

In this section, you will learn about many types of functionality provided by GLib including access to environment variables, timers, directory functions, and file manipulation.

Environment Variables

If you create an application that is going to be run on multiple platforms, it can be quite a chore to deal with environment-dependent values such as the user's home directory or the host name. Table 6-4 offers a short list of functions that return important environment variables.

Table 6-4. *Environment Utility Functions*

Function	Description
g_get_current_dir()	Get the current working directory. The returned string should be freed when it is no longer needed.
g_get_home_dir()	Get the home directory of the current user. On Windows, the HOME or USERPROFILE environment variable is used, or the root Windows directory is used if neither is set. On UNIX-like systems, the user's entry in passwd will be used.
g_get_host_name()	Get the host name of the system. If the name of the system cannot be determined, localhost is returned. You should not rely on this variable being consistent across systems, because administrators have the option of setting this to whatever they want in some systems.
g_get_real_name()	Get the real name of the user. On UNIX-like machines, this usually comes from the user's information in the passwd file. The string "Unknown" is returned if the real name cannot be determined.
g_get_tmp_dir()	Get the directory used to store temporary files. The environment variables TMPDIR, TMP, and TEMP will be checked. If none of those are defined, "/tmp" will be returned on UNIX and "c:\" on Windows.
g_get_user_name()	Get the user name of the current user. On Windows, the returned string will always be UTF-8. On UNIX-like systems, it depends on the preferred encoding for file names and will differ depending on the system.

In addition to the functions in Table 6-4, it is possible to retrieve the value of any environment variable with g_getenv(). If the environment variable is not found, NULL is returned. You should note that the returned string may be overwritten by calling g_getenv() again, so you should store a new copy of the string if it needs to stay around.

```
gboolean g_setenv (const gchar *variable,
                   const gchar *value,
                   gboolean overwrite);
```

It is also possible to give a new value to an environment variable with g_setenv(). You should provide TRUE to the function if you want the value to be overwritten if it already exists. FALSE will be returned by g_setenv() if the environment variable could not be set. You can also unset an environment variable with g_unsetenv(), which accepts the name of the variable.

Timers

In many applications, you will want to keep track of elapsed time. An example of this would be applications that download files from the Internet or process a complex task. For this, GLib provides the GTimer structure.

GTimer objects keep track of elapsed time in microseconds and fractions of seconds. To retrieve the number of seconds, you can use the returned gdouble value. This value can then be used to calculate the elapsed minutes. Higher precision is also available since time is counted in microseconds.

Listing 6-4 offers a simple timer example that counts the elapsed time between two button clicks. Since the timer is always counting, it works by storing the starting and ending times when the button is clicked.

Listing 6-4. *Elapsed Time Between Toggling (timers.c)*

```
#include <gtk/gtk.h>

static void button_clicked (GtkButton*, GTimer*);

int main (int argc,
          char *argv[])
{
  GtkWidget *window, *button;
  GTimer *timer;

  gtk_init (&argc, &argv);

  window = gtk_window_new (GTK_WINDOW_TOPLEVEL);
  gtk_window_set_title (GTK_WINDOW (window), "Timers");
  gtk_container_set_border_width (GTK_CONTAINER (window), 10);
  gtk_widget_set_size_request (window, 150, 75);

  /* Initialize the timer. */
  timer = g_timer_new ();
  button = gtk_button_new_with_label ("Start Timer");

  g_signal_connect (G_OBJECT (button), "clicked",
                    G_CALLBACK (button_clicked),
                    (gpointer) timer);

  gtk_container_add (GTK_CONTAINER (window), button);
  gtk_widget_show_all (window);

  gtk_main ();
  return 0;
}

/* Count the amount of elapsed time between two button clicks. */
static void
button_clicked (GtkButton *button,
                GTimer *timer)
{
  static gdouble start_time = 0.0;
  static gdouble end_time = 0.0;
  static gboolean running = FALSE;
```

```
  if (!running)
  {
    start_time = g_timer_elapsed (timer, NULL);
    gtk_button_set_label (button, "Stop Timer");
  }
  else
  {
    end_time = g_timer_elapsed (timer, NULL);
    gtk_button_set_label (button, "Start Timer");
    g_print ("Elapsed Time: %.2f\n", end_time - start_time);
  }

  running = !running;
}
```

Timers are a relatively easy topic to digest. They are handled differently on different platforms, but GLib provides a portable interface for dealing with them. New timers are created with g_timer_new(). When you create a new timer, it will automatically start by calling g_timer_start() for you.

You can stop or continue a stopped timer with g_timer_stop() or g_timer_continue() respectively. At any point in your application, you can use g_timer_elapsed() to retrieve the elapsed time.

```
gdouble g_timer_elapsed (GTimer *timer,
                         gulong *microseconds);
```

If the timer has been started but not stopped, then the time elapsed will be calculated based on the start time. However, if g_timer_continue() was used to restart the timer, the two times will be added together to calculate the total time elapsed.

The return value of g_timer_elapsed() is the number of seconds that have elapsed along with any fractional time. There is also a microseconds parameter that returns the number of elapsed microseconds, which is essentially useless since you can already retrieve the number of seconds as a floating-point value.

You can use g_timer_reset() to set the timer back to 0 seconds. You can also reset the timer with g_timer_start(), but the timer will continue to count automatically.

If you are finished using a timer object before you exit your application, you can call g_timer_destroy()to destroy the timer and deallocate any associated resources.

File Manipulation

Reading and writing from files are very important aspects of almost every application. There are two ways in GTK+ to work with files: with IO channels and with file utility functions.

Listing 6-5 illustrates how to use file utility functions to read and write data to a file. You should note that the functions presented read the whole contents of a file and overwrite the whole contents of a file. Therefore, this method is not the solution for all applications. This example also introduces a way to perform file tests.

Listing 6-5. *Write and Read a File (files.c)*

```c
#include <glib.h>

static void handle_error (GError*);

int main (int argc,
          char *argv[])
{
  gchar *filename, *content;
  gsize bytes;
  GError *error = NULL;

  /* Build a filename in the user's home directory. */
  filename = g_build_filename (g_get_home_dir(), "temp", NULL);

  /* Set the contents of the given file and report any errors. */
  g_file_set_contents (filename, "Hello World!", -1, &error);
  handle_error (error);

  if (!g_file_test (filename, G_FILE_TEST_EXISTS))
    g_error ("Error: File does not exist!");

  /* Get the contents of the given file and report any errors. */
  g_file_get_contents (filename, &content, &bytes, &error);
  handle_error (error);
  g_print ("%s\n", content);

  g_free (content);
  g_free (filename);

  return 0;
}

static void
handle_error (GError *error)
{
  if (error != NULL)
  {
    g_printf (error->message);
    g_clear_error (&error);
  }
}
```

Before using any of the file utility functions, g_build_filename() was used to build the path to the desired file. This function uses a NULL-terminated list of strings to build a path to a file name. No effort is made by the function to force the path to be absolute, so relative paths can be built as well. It will also use the correct type of slashes for the user's platform.

In Listing 6-5, g_file_set_contents() was called to write the string "Hello World!" to a file. The whole contents of a file, if it already exists, will be overwritten. The function requires you to specify the length of the text string unless it is NULL-terminated. In that case, you can use -1 as the length of the string.

```
gboolean g_file_set_contents (const gchar *filename,
                              const gchar *contents,
                              gssize length,
                              GError **error);
```

Two methods of error checking are provided by g_file_set_contents(). TRUE is returned if the action was successful and FALSE if it failed. Also, errors under the G_FILE_ERROR domain will be returned through the GError parameter. A full list of possible errors under this error domain can be found in Appendix E.

Reading the contents of a file is performed, in a similar manner as writing, by calling the g_file_get_contents() function. This function returns TRUE if the action was successful and FALSE if it failed. The length of the text string read from the file is also set by the function. Errors under the G_FILE_ERROR domain will be reported.

```
gboolean g_file_get_contents (const gchar *filename,
                              gchar **contents,
                              gsize *length,
                              GError **error);
```

Before reading a file, it is a good idea to do some sort of testing to make sure that it already exists. For this, GLib provides file testing with g_file_test(). This function receives a file or directory name as well as the type of test to perform. It returns TRUE if the test was successful and FALSE if it was not. Test parameters are provided by the following GFileTest enumeration:

- G_FILE_TEST_IS_REGULAR: The file is not a symbolic link or a directory, which means that it is a regular file.

- G_FILE_TEST_IS_SYMLINK: The file you specified is actually a symbolic link.

- G_FILE_TEST_IS_DIR: The path points to the location of a directory.

- G_FILE_TEST_IS_EXECUTABLE: The specified file is executable.

- G_FILE_TEST_EXISTS: Some type of object exists at the specified location. However, this test does not determine whether it is a symbolic link, a directory, or a regular file.

It is possible to perform multiple tests at the same time by using a bitwise operation. For example, (G_FILE_TEST_IS_DIR | G_FILE_TEST_IS_REGULAR) will return TRUE if the path points to a directory or a regular file.

There are a few cases with symbolic links in which you need to take caution. First, all tests will follow through symbolic links. So, G_FILE_TEST_IS_REGULAR will return TRUE if a symbolic link points to a regular file.

You should be careful when using g_file_test() to test whether it is safe to perform some type of action on a file or directory. The state of the file may change before you perform the action, so you can never be sure whether the action was acceptable until after it has been performed. This is why it is a good idea to check G_FILE_ERROR_EXIST in the returned GError.

Directories

In some applications, you may need to retrieve the contents of a directory. There are functions provided by C that can do this, but a much easier method is to use GLib's GDir structure. Listing 6-6 shows you how to read the full contents of the user's home directory and print them to the screen.

Listing 6-6. *Get the Contents of a Directory (directories.c)*

```
#include <glib.h>

int main (int argc,
          char *argv[])
{
  /* Open the user's home directory for reading. */
  GDir *dir = g_dir_open (g_get_home_dir (), 0, NULL);
  const gchar *file;

  if (!g_file_test (g_get_home_dir (), G_FILE_TEST_IS_DIR))
    g_error ("Error: You do not have a home directory!");

  while ((file = g_dir_read_name (dir)))
    g_print ("%s\n", file);

  g_dir_close (dir);

  return 0;
}
```

Directories are opened with g_dir_open(). The first parameter of the function specifies the directory to open. The second parameter of g_dir_open() is reserved for future use and should be set to 0 at this time. The last parameter returns a GError, although you will know if the function fails, because NULL is returned if the directory was not successfully loaded.

```
while ((file = g_dir_read_name (dir)))
  g_print ("%s\n", file);
```

A simple while loop can be used to retrieve all of the files and folders in the directory. This list is returned one element at a time with g_dir_read_name() in the order the elements appear on the disk. NULL is returned when no more entries exist. You must not free the returned string, because it is owned by GLib.

Note When using g_dir_read_name(), the "." and ".." file entries will not be returned, since they are assumed to exist if the directory exists.

If you need to return to the first entry in the list in order to loop through the entries again, g_dir_rewind() should be called on the GDir object. This will reset the structure so that it again points to the first file or folder.

When you are finished with the GDir object, you should always call g_dir_close() to deallocate the GDir and free all of its related resources.

File System

GLib provides a few other utility functions that wrap the functionality of UNIX operating systems. You need to include <glib/gstdio.h> for any of these functions to work. Many of the most important functions are shown in this section. For a full list, you should reference the "File Utilities" section of the GLib API documentation.

For all of the functions in this section, 0 is returned if the action was successful or -1 if it was unsuccessful.

Note All of the functions covered in this section were introduced in GLib 2.6, so if you are using an older version of GLib, this section is irrelevant.

Use g_rename() to move a file or a folder to a new location. If the old and new filenames are both the same string, 0 will be returned with no further action. If a file already exists in the location of the new filename, the file will be replaced on UNIX machines. Filenames for directories and files cannot be mixed.

```
int g_rename (const gchar *old_filename,
              const gchar *new_filename);
```

There are a few permissions issues surrounding g_rename() as well. The user owns the file and the directory containing the file. The user must also be able to write to the file.

Removing a file or directory is as easy as calling g_remove() or g_rmdir(). It is actually possible to remove a directory with g_remove(), because it will make a call to the directory removal function. However, for the sake or portability to other operating systems, you should always use g_rmdir() to remove directories. Both of these functions will fail if the directory is not empty.

```
int g_remove (const gchar *filename);
int g_rmdir  (const gchar *filename);
```

You can use g_mkdir() to create a new directory. You should specify permissions in a four-digit integer. For example, acceptable permissions would be 0755, 0700, and so on.

```
int g_mkdir (const gchar *filename,
             int permissions);
```

When using many of these file utility functions, you can use relative paths as well as absolute paths. However, to use relative paths, you will need to ensure that you are in the correct directory. You can use g_chdir() to move throughout the directory structure of your hard drive. This function will accept relative and absolute paths as well.

```
int g_chdir (const gchar *path);
```

You may need to change the permissions of a file or a folder from within your application. This can be done with g_chmod(). Permissions integers should be specified with four digits, as they were to g_mkdir().

```
int g_chmod (const gchar *filename,
             int permissions);
```

The Main Loop

In past chapters, we have used GTK+'s main loop without any thought of the fact that GLib has its own main loop. It could be ignored in all other examples, because gtk_init() will automatically create a GLib main loop for you.

In fact, most of the main loop functionality is actually implemented in GLib; GTK+ simply provides widget signals to the system. The GTK+ main loop also connects GDK's X server events to the GLib system.

The purpose of the main loop is to sleep until some event has occurred. At that point, a callback function will be invoked, if available. GLib's main loop is implemented in Linux using the poll() system call. Events and signals are associated with file descriptors, which are watched using poll().

The advantage of using poll() is that GLib does not need to continuously check for new events. Rather, it can sleep until some signal or event is emitted. By doing this, your application will take up almost no processor time until it is needed.

The GTK+ main loop is invoked with gtk_main(). This function can actually be called multiple times; the call on the top of the stack is removed when you call gtk_main_quit(). You can retrieve the current main loop stack level with gtk_main_level().

Contexts and Sources

The GLib main loop is implemented as a number of structures, which allow multiple instances to be run concurrently. GMainContext is used to represent a number of event sources. Each thread has its own context, which can be retrieved with g_main_context_get(). You can also retrieve the default context with g_main_context_get_default().

Each event source in the context is given a priority, defaulting to G_PRIORITY_DEFAULT or zero. Sources with a higher priority will be given precedence over those with a negative priority. Examples of event sources are timeouts and idle functions.

GLib also provides GMainLoop, which represents one instance of the main loop. A new main loop can be created with g_main_loop_new(), where a NULL context will use the default. Setting is_running to TRUE states that the main loop is running, although this will automatically be set when you call g_main_loop_run().

```
GMainLoop* g_main_loop_new (GMainContext *context,
                            gboolean is_running);
```

■**Tip** The gtk_dialog_run() function blocks the main loop from continuing by creating its own GLib main loop with g_main_loop_new(). It will continue to run until g_main_loop_quit() is called on the loop.

The GTK+ main loop implements the GLib main loop by creating a GMainLoop with the default context in gtk_main(). In short, the main loop functionality provided by functions in GTK+ is implemented in GLib.

GLib supports the ability to create new event sources. Deriving from GSource creates new sources. GLib provides the ability to create new timeout and idle function sources with g_timeout_source_new() and g_idle_source_new(). These can be associated with your contexts.

It is also possible to create a custom source with g_source_new(). This function accepts a table of functions and the structure size of the new source. These functions are used to define the behavior of the new source type.

```
GSource* g_source_new (GSourceFuncs *source_funcs,
                       guint struct_size);
```

You should then associate the source with a GMainContext by calling g_source_attach(). This will return a unique integer identifier of the source within the context.

For the scope of this book, you have learned enough about the main loop to understand the examples in the rest of this section. There is much more to the complexities of the main loop that will not be covered in this book. Therefore, if you have a need to create your own sources and contexts, you should reference the GLib API documentation.

Timeouts

Timeout functions are methods that are called at a certain interval of time until FALSE is returned. They are added to the main loop with g_timeout_add_full() or g_timeout_add().

Listing 6-7 is a simple example that pulses a progress bar every tenth of a second. Since the progress bar is set to have a pulse step of 0.1, it will take approximately one second for the progress indicator to travel from one end of the progress bar to the other. The timeout is removed after 25 calls.

Listing 6-7. *Adding a Timeout (timeouts.c)*

```c
#include <gtk/gtk.h>

static gboolean pulse_progress (GtkProgressBar*);

int main (int argc,
          char *argv[])
{
  GtkWidget *window, *progress;

  gtk_init (&argc, &argv);

  window = gtk_window_new (GTK_WINDOW_TOPLEVEL);
  gtk_window_set_title (GTK_WINDOW (window), "Timeouts");
  gtk_container_set_border_width (GTK_CONTAINER (window), 10);
  gtk_widget_set_size_request (window, 200, -1);

  progress = gtk_progress_bar_new ();
  gtk_progress_bar_set_pulse_step (GTK_PROGRESS_BAR (progress), 0.1);

  g_timeout_add (100, (GSourceFunc) pulse_progress, (gpointer) progress);

  gtk_container_add (GTK_CONTAINER (window), progress);
  gtk_widget_show_all (window);

  gtk_main ();
  return 0;
}

/* Pulse the progress bar and return TRUE so the timeout is called again. */
static gboolean
pulse_progress (GtkProgressBar *progress)
{
  static gint count = 0;

  gtk_progress_bar_pulse (progress);
  i++;

  return (i < 25);
}
```

Timeout functions are added with g_timeout_add() or g_timeout_add_full(). The only difference between these two functions is that the latter allows you to specify a GDestroyNotify function, which will be called when you return FALSE to remove the timeout function.

```
guint g_timeout_add_full (gint priority,
                          guint interval_in_milliseconds,
                          GSourceFunc timeout_function,
                          gpointer data,
                          GDestroyNotify destroy_function);
```

The first parameter of g_timeout_add_full() allows you to define the priority of the timeout. In most cases, you will want to use G_PRIORITY_DEFAULT as the timeout function's priority. A list of the available priorities follows:

- G_PRIORITY_HIGH: This priority is not used anywhere within GLib or GTK+, so this type of function will take precedence over all others. Therefore, it should *not* be used in most cases, because CPU-intensive computations could cause the user interface to be temporarily unresponsive.

- G_PRIORITY_DEFAULT: This priority is used for most timeouts and X events in GDK. It should not be used with idle functions, because they could disrupt more important function calls needed by the application.

- G_PRIORITY_HIGH_IDLE: High priority idle functions use this. Redrawing widgets has a slightly higher priority, so this will not interfere with or slow most GTK+ actions.

- G_PRIORITY_DEFAULT_IDLE: You should use this priority for most idle functions.

- G_PRIORITY_LOW: This is not used anywhere within GLib or GTK+, so everything will take precedence over these actions.

The second parameter of g_timeout_add_full() defines the interval of time in milliseconds between every call to the function. In Listing 6-7, the timeout was called every tenth of a second, or 100 milliseconds.

There is no reason to worry about the overlapping of timeout function calls, because the next interval is calculated based on when the previous call returns. Therefore, if the timeout function takes 3 seconds to return, that time will be added to the interval.

■**Caution** Timeout functions can be delayed by function calls with a higher priority and how long it takes to run the callback function. Therefore, it cannot be relied on as a source of precise timing. If a timeout gets behind in time, the next call will recalculate the interval. The function will not try to make up lost time from delays.

The third parameter in g_timeout_add_full() is the actual timeout function. Timeout functions receive a gpointer and return a gboolean value. By returning FALSE from the timeout function, it will be removed. The gpointer parameter is defined by the fourth parameter of g_timeout_add_full().

The last parameter defines a destroy function that should be called when the idle function is removed, which occurs when FALSE is returned from the idle function. It is safe to set this parameter as NULL.

Destroy functions defined in g_timeout_add_full() should not return any value, but do receive a gpointer as their parameter. This gpointer is the same value originally received by the timeout function, which gives you an opportunity to free it from memory if necessary.

Idle Functions

As mentioned in Chapter 1, GLib provides a special type of function called an idle function that will be called when there are no events pending with a higher priority. They run over and over when there is nothing else to do in the main loop.

Idle functions are added with g_idle_add() or g_idle_add_full(). The only difference between these two functions is that the latter allows you to specify a destroy function and a priority instead of using the default of G_PRIORITY_DEFAULT_IDLE.

The first parameter of this function is the priority of the idle function. The idle function is only called when there are no events pending with a higher priority. Therefore, the higher the priority, the more often the function will be called. In almost all cases, idle functions should have a priority of G_PRIORITY_HIGH_IDLE or G_PRIORITY_DEFAULT_IDLE.

```
guint g_idle_add_full (gint priority,
                       GSourceFunc idle_function,
                       gpointer data,
                       GDestroyNotify destroy_function);
```

The second parameter in g_idle_add_full() is the actual idle function. Similar to timeouts, idle functions receive a gpointer and return a gboolean value. By returning FALSE from the idle function, it will be removed. The gpointer parameter is defined by the third parameter of g_idle_add_full().

The last parameter defines a destroy function that will be called when the idle function is removed, which occurs when FALSE is returned from the idle function. It is safe to set this parameter as NULL.

Destroy functions defined in g_idle_add_full() should not return any value, but do receive a gpointer as their parameter. This gpointer is the same value originally received by the idle function, which gives you an opportunity to free it from memory.

While you can remove an idle function be returning FALSE from the callback, you can also remove it from any place in your application with g_idle_remove_data(). This function accepts the data that was used for the idle function's callback and will return TRUE if it was successfully removed.

```
gboolean g_idle_remove_by_data (gpointer data);
```

■**Caution** You should never call g_idle_remove_by_data() on an idle function within its callback. This can cause corruption in the idle function list. Instead, return FALSE to remove the idle function within the callback.

Data Types

One of the most useful features provided by GLib is the vast collection of data types. This chapter will introduce you to the most important data types, many of which are used in concurrence with GTK+ widgets. You should pay special attention to singly and doubly linked lists, since these are widely used throughout GTK+.

You will notice as you go through the rest of this section that each of the data types presented is used in a similar way. This uniform API reduces the number of design patterns you need to learn. In doing this, many of the types were endowed with similar functions. However, each of these types has specific advantages and disadvantages that you should pay close attention to when deciding what type to use.

Strings

Strings are nothing new to most programmers, but the GString structure can be very useful to the C programmer. It provides an easy way to create strings that automatically grow in size when text is added. This helps you avoid problems such as buffer overflows and other runtime errors that plague standard C strings.

GLib strings also provide some memory management, easy access to the current state of the C string, and useful functions for manipulating the string. This makes dealing with C strings a lot easier for the programmer than doing so without GString.

The GString structure consists of three members: the C string that holds the current state of the string, the length of str excluding the terminating byte, and the amount of memory currently allocated for the string. If the string needs to grow beyond this allocated length, GString will automatically allocate more memory.

```
typedef struct
{
  gchar *str;
  gsize  len;
  gsize  allocated_len;
} GString;
```

■**Caution** You should not make a permanent reference to the str member of a GString. It may be moved to a different location as text is added or inserted or removed from the string because of a change in the allocated length of the string!

There are three ways to create a new GString object. Calling g_string_new(), you can create a new GString out of an initial string. GString will copy the content of initial_str, so you can free the string afterwards if it is no longer needed. If you specify NULL as the initial string, g_string_new() will automatically create an empty GString.

```
GString* g_string_new       (const gchar *initial_str);
GString* g_string_new_len   (const gchar *initial_str,
                              gssize length);
GString* g_string_sized_new (gsize default_size);
```

Another way to create a new GString is with g_string_new_len(), which will initialize the GString with length characters of initial_str or the whole string if length is -1. Another advantage of using GString is that it can handle embedded null bytes.

The last GString initialization function is g_string_sized_new(), which will create a new string with a length of default_size. You can use this function to allocate a large string so that it will not have to be reallocated very often.

One very useful function is g_string_printf(), which allows you to use a sprintf()-style format to construct the content of a GString. The only difference is that the GString will automatically expand if necessary. Any previous contents contained by the GString buffer are destroyed.

```
void g_string_printf (GString *string,
                      const gchar *format,
                      ...);
```

You can also use g_string_append_printf(), which will append the formatted string to the end of the GString, leaving its current contents unchanged. There are a large number of functions for appending text to a GString, shown in the following example. These functions allow you to append the whole content of val, the first len characters of val, a single character, or a single UCS-4 character respectively.

```
GString* g_string_append         (GString *string,
                                   const gchar *val);
GString* g_string_append_len     (GString *string,
                                   const gchar *str,
                                   gssize len);
GString* g_string_append_c       (GString *string,
                                   gchar c);
GString* g_string_append_unichar (GString *string,
                                   gunichar wc);
```

In addition to these four functions, there are versions of these functions for prepending and inserting into a GString. For example, g_string_prepend_c() will add a character to the beginning of a GString, and g_string_insert() will insert a string into a specified position in the GString. For more information on these functions, you should visit the "Strings" section of the GLib API documentation.

It is useful to be able to insert text into a GString, but it is just as important to be able to remove text. You can remove a number of characters from a GString, starting at a given position by calling g_string_erase(). This function will shift the end of the string to fill the void, place a terminating character at the new end position, and update the length of the string.

```
GString* g_string_erase (GString *string,
                         gssize pos,
                         gssize len);
```

When you are finished with the GString, you should free the memory with g_string_free(). If you set free_segment to TRUE, it will also free the C string and return NULL. Otherwise, it will return the C string, which you must later free yourself.

```
gchar* g_string_free (GString *string,
                      gboolean free_segment);
```

You should note that, while GString does provide a number of useful functions, you would still have to use the standard string functions provided by GLib to search through a string. GString implements functions that are not already available on your system to avoid reinventing the wheel. Therefore, you will still need to be comfortable with interacting with C strings directly.

Linked Lists

You have already seen instances of GLib linked lists in examples from past chapters. There are two types of linked lists provided by GLib: singly linked and doubly linked lists. GLib provides functions for these two data types with the prefixes of g_slist_foo() and g_list_foo() respectively.

Singly linked lists (GSList) are the simplest kind of linked list, where each node has a piece of data and a pointer to the next node. A pointer to NULL designates the last node. The GSList structure, which follows, represents one node within the list.

```
typedef struct
{
  gpointer data;
  GSList *next;
} GSList;
```

Doubly linked lists (GList) provide the same functionality as singly linked lists except a pointer is provided that points to the previous element in the list. This allows them to be traversed in either direction. A previous pointer to NULL designates the first element in the list.

```
typedef struct
{
  gpointer data;
  GList *next;
  GList *prev;
} GList;
```

Except for the ability to traverse a doubly linked list in reverse, both types of lists provide the same functionality. Therefore, while the rest of the information in this section will be given about doubly linked lists, it applies to singly linked lists as long as you first change the function prefix.

In addition, most of the functions in this section return a new GList pointer. This value should be stored, because the location of the beginning of the list may have changed because of some action performed by the function.

To add a new element to the beginning of the list, you can use g_list_prepend(). It is also possible to append an element with g_list_append(), but this function should not be used, because it has to traverse the list to find where to insert the element. Instead, you should prepend all of the elements and then call g_list_reverse() to reverse the order of the list.

```
GList* g_list_prepend (GList *list,
                       gointer data);
```

In addition to appending and prepending new nodes, you can insert a node at an arbitrary position of the list with g_list_insert(). If the position is negative or it is larger than the number of nodes in the list, it will act as g_list_append(). You can also insert a new node immediately before another with g_list_insert_before(). You can get the length of the list with g_list_length(), which returns an unsigned integer.

```
GList* g_list_insert (GList *list,
                      gpointer data,
                      gint position);
```

It is possible to remove an element from the list with g_list_remove(). The first node encountered that contains the same data will be removed, unless a matching node is not found.

```
GList* g_list_remove (GList *list,
                      gconstgpointer data);
```

If you would like to remove a node without freeing its data, you should call g_list_remove_link(), which accepts a pointer to the element you want to remove. The previous and next pointers are set to NULL, so the node becomes a list of one element.

While g_list_remove() will only remove the first occurrence of a node with matching data, g_list_remove_all() can be used to remove every node that has a matching data member. If no matching node is found, nothing will be done to the list.

When you are finished with a linked lists, you should free it with g_list_free(). You should note that only the linked list is freed. Therefore, you will need to make sure to free any dynamically allocated data before you call this function, or it will cause a memory leak.

```
void g_list_free (GList *list);
```

Sorting a linked list is very easy because of g_list_sort(). You need only to specify a GCompareFunc. Comparison functions receive two constant pointers (gconstpointer), which refer to the two nodes currently being compared. You need to compare the two, returning a negative number if the first should be sorted before the second, a positive number to sort the second before the first, and zero if they are equal.

```
GList* g_list_sort (GList *list,
                    GCompareFunc compare_func);
```

There are two functions provided for searching through a linked list. The default function is g_list_find(), which will find the first element in the list with the given data. If a matching node was not found, then this function returns NULL.

```
GList* g_list_find (GList *list,
                    gconstpointer data);
```

It is also possible to specify your own find function through g_list_find_custom() if each item contains a complex data type. This method uses the same format of comparison function as g_list_sort() and will return the corresponding GList node when you return 0 from the GCompareFunc. This function will also return NULL if no match is found.

One big problem with linked lists has already been alluded to—many actions are very inefficient when dealing with large lists, including sorting. The problem is that many functions require a traversal of the linked list, which can take a long time when there are many nodes in the list. Therefore, they should only be used when you know there will not be a lot of nodes necessary, which is why they are used for radio groups.

However, it is possible to use linked lists efficiently if you know how to avoid traversing the list as much as possible. One possible solution is to save your last list position, or those that are going to be commonly used. This can reduce the amount of time it takes to find certain elements.

It is impossible to completely avoid traversing a linked list. If you need to perform an operation on every element in the list, you should use g_list_foreach(), which will call your instance of GFunc for every node in the list.

```
void g_list_foreach (GList *list,
                     GFunc func,
                     gpointer data);
```

The GFunc prototype accepts the data member of the node and the data parameter in g_list_foreach(). By avoiding traversing linked lists many times, they can be effectively utilized for many different applications.

Balanced Binary Trees

A balanced binary tree is a tree that tries to automatically keep its height as low as possible. By doing this, the distance between any two elements is minimized. This keeps average times for lookup, traversal, insertion, and removal at a minimum.

Unlike linked lists and strings, the GTree structure does not have any public members. Instead, you should use the provided functions for performing operations on the tree. The functions will automatically handle balancing the binary tree if you perform an operation that alters the tree.

Each node in a binary tree consists of a key and a value. The key is used to calculate the position of the node within the tree and the value to hold the associated data. Each node can also have a maximum of two children. If a node does not have any children, it is called a leaf.

There are three functions provided for creating a new GTree. The simplest function is g_tree_new(), which will create a new empty tree with the specified comparison function. This function will be used to compare keys when inserting an element into the tree or reordering nodes. This function returns a negative integer if the first element is less than the second, a positive integer if the second element is less than the first, and zero if they are the same.

```
GTree* g_tree_new (GCompareFunc key_compare_func);
```

If you need to send data to the comparison function, you can create the binary tree with g_tree_new_with_data(). The key_compare_data pointer will be sent as a third parameter to the comparison function, defined by GCompareDataFunc.

```
GTree* g_tree_new_with_data (GCompareDataFunc key_compare_func,
                             gpointer key_compare_data);
```

Furthermore, you can create a new tree with g_tree_new_full(), which accepts two additional parameters. Each is a GDestroyNotify function that will be called to destroy a key or value when necessary. You should specify these functions if you are using dynamically allocated keys and/or values. Otherwise, the memory will be lost when the tree is destroyed.

```
GTree* g_tree_new_full (GCompareDataFunc key_compare_func,
                        gpointer key_compare_data,
                        GDestroyNotify key_destroy_func,
                        GDestroyNotify value_destroy_func);
```

Since GTree automatically calculates the position of new key-value pairs, GLib only provides two functions for adding new nodes into a tree including g_tree_insert(). If the key already exists within the tree, the old data will be freed with the destroy function if provided and replaced with the new value. The tree is then automatically balanced after the new node is inserted.

```
void g_tree_insert (GTree *tree,
                    gpointer key,
                    gpointer value);
```

You can also use g_tree_replace() to add a node to a binary tree. The only difference between this function and g_tree_insert() is that if the key already exists within the tree, the key itself will also be replaced. If the key does not already exist, it will be inserted into a new position in the tree, and the tree will automatically be balanced.

At times, you may need to know basic information about the structure of the tree. For example, you can get the number of nodes with g_tree_nnodes() and the current height of the tree with g_tree_height(). With these two pieces of information, you should be able to figure out the general structure of the tree.

To retrieve the value associated with a key in a binary tree, you need to call g_tree_lookup(). If the key is found, the associated value will be returned. Otherwise, this function will return NULL.

```
gpointer g_tree_lookup (GTree *tree,
                        gconstpointer key);
```

Alternatively, you can use g_tree_lookup_extended(), which will also return pointers to the original key and its associated value by reference. This function will return TRUE if the key was found.

This brings us to one big advantage of binary trees. Since the tree is automatically balanced, finding a key is very fast, even if there are a large number of elements in the list. In the worst case, it will take the number of comparisons equal to the height of the tree to find the node.

If you need to perform some operation on every node in a binary tree, you need to specify a traversal function to g_tree_foreach(). The GTraverseFunc prototype accepts three gpointer parameters corresponding to a key, its associated value, and the user data from g_tree_foreach(). In order to stop the traversal, you should return TRUE from the function. The nodes of the tree are traversed in sorted order.

```
void g_tree_foreach (GTree *tree,
                     GTraverseFunc func,
                     gpointer data);
```

As with linked lists, it is possible to search through a binary tree with g_tree_search(). However, there is a major advantage of using the binary tree over the linked list when you need to search.

```
gpointer g_tree_search (GTree *tree,
                        GCompareFunc search_func,
                        gconstpointer value);
```

When you search for an element in a linked list, every element will be visited until the match is found. If the match is the last node in the list, the value will be compared with every element in the list.

Since balanced binary trees in GList are automatically sorted, the maximum number of comparisons will be equal to the height of the tree if the match is a leaf that is as far from the root node as possible. Even if your tree has over 32,000 nodes, there will only be a maximum of 16 comparisons! This is why balanced binary trees should be used if you need to be able to quickly search through the data structure for a match.

The disadvantage of using binary trees is that you must know the key value of a node in order to directly reference an element. If you need to get instant access to a specific node, you should use a data structure that uses index referencing.

If you need to remove an item from the list, you should call g_tree_remove(). This function will return TRUE if the key was found in the list. The tree will be rebalanced if a node was removed.

```
gboolean g_tree_remove (GTree *tree,
                        gconstpointer key);
```

After you are finished with the tree, you should call g_tree_destroy(). This function will destroy the tree along with all of its elements. There is no need to free any of the keys or values after this is called.

N-ary Trees

The other type of tree data type provided by GLib is the n-ary tree, which allows a node to have any number of children. This data type is not balanced automatically; you perform management of its structure.

N-ary trees are actually a collection of GNode structures. Each structure contains five objects. The first, data, is a pointer to the actual piece data stored by the node. As with most of the data types provided by GLib, you can store any type of pointer data type.

```
typedef struct
{
  gpointer data;
  GNode *next;
  GNode *prev;
  GNode *parent;
  GNode *children;
} GNode;
```

The other members point to other nodes within the tree. These include the next node on the same level, the previous node on the same level, the parent node, and the first child. To help you understand this relationship, Figure 6-1 shows a simple association.

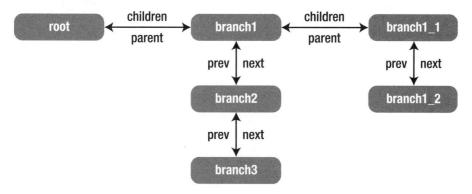

Figure 6-1. *GNode relationships*

There is one root element in the figure, which has three children. The first child also has two children of its own. The root node points only to the first child. To access its other children, each child points to the next and previous child. Each child will also point to its parent node.

You should notice that there is no pointer between the root child and its second and third children, because the parent node only points to its first child. You will need to use the next and prev pointer to access the rest of the children of a node.

A new n-ary tree is created with g_node_new(), which creates a tree with a single root node. Initially, all of the GNode pointers will be set to NULL for the new tree. You will need to use the function to create every node for the tree.

```
GNode* g_node_new (gpointer data);
```

After you create the nodes, you can use the functions shown in Table 6-5 to construct the tree with the desired structure.

Table 6-5. *N-ary Tree Construction Functions*

Function	Description
g_node_append()	Insert a node as the last child of the parent node. This is the same thing as calling g_node_insert_before() with a sibling node of NULL.
g_node_append_data()	This is the same thing as calling g_node_append(), except a new node is created with the specified data.
g_node_insert()	Insert a node as the child of the parent node at the specified position. If the position is -1, the node will be appended as the last child.
g_node_insert_after()	Insert a node as the child of the parent node immediately after a sibling. If the sibling is set to NULL, the node will be prepended as the first child of the parent.
g_node_insert_before()	Insert a node as the child of the parent node immediately before a sibling. If the sibling is set to NULL, the node will be appended as the last child of the parent.
g_node_insert_data()	This is the same thing as calling g_node_insert(), except a new node is created with the specified data.
g_node_insert_data_before()	This is the same thing as calling g_node_insert_before(), except a new node is created with the specified data.
g_node_prepend()	Insert a node as the first child of the parent node.
g_node_prepend_data()	This is the same thing as calling g_node_prepend(), except a new node is created with the specified data.

The structure of an n-ary tree can become quite complex. Therefore, GLib provides g_node_traverse(), which allows you to visit the nodes of a tree and call a function for each node.

```
void g_node_traverse (GNode *root,
                      GTraverseType order,
                      GTraverseFlags flags,
                      gint max_depth,
                      GNodeTraverseFunc func,
                      gpointer data);
```

When you call g_node_traverse(), you first need to specify the root node to begin search-ing from. This node does not necessarily have to be the root node of the tree. You next need to specify what type of traversal will occur, defined by the GTraverseType enumeration shown in the following list:

- G_IN_ORDER: Visit the leftmost child of the node first, moving from left to right. This is the order that nodes should be visited if you want to traverse the tree in sorted order after using a comparison function.

- G_PRE_ORDER: Visit the root node before visiting the left and right subtrees. The subtrees are then visited from left to right in that order.

- G_POST_ORDER: Visit the children of a node followed by the root node itself. This will visit all of the nodes, ending at the root node.

- G_LEVEL_ORDER: Visit a node and then all of its children, followed by its grandchildren, and so on. This traversal type is much more inefficient than the others, since it will not follow a natural recursive approach to traversal.

The next parameter in g_node_traverse() specifies what types of child nodes will be vis-ited, as defined by the following GTraverseFlags enumeration:

- G_TRAVERSE_LEAVES: Visit all of the leaves, which are the nodes with no children. This is identical to the G_TRAVERSE_LEAFS flag.

- G_TRAVERSE_NON_LEAVES: Visit all of the nodes that have children. This is identical to the G_TRAVERSE_NON_LEAFS flag.

- G_TRAVERSE_ALL: Traverse all of the nodes. This is identical to the bitwise mask of (G_TRAVERSE_LEAVES | G_TRAVERSE_NON_LEAVES).

- G_TRAVERSE_MASK: Include all of the traversal flags.

The fourth parameter of g_node_traverse() gives the maximum depth of children from the root node that will be visited. For example, a depth of three would only visit the root node, its children, and its grandchildren. You can set the maximum depth to -1 to visit all children.

You then need to specify a GNodeTraverseFunc callback that will be run for every traversed node. This function accepts a GNode corresponding to the current node and the pointer data parameter from g_node_traverse(). By returning TRUE from the traversal function, the traversal will stop. If you return FALSE, the traversal will continue if a node has not yet been visited.

As with binary trees, after you are finished with the n-ary tree, you should call g_node_destroy() on the root node. This will recursively destroy all of the elements in the tree, including every child of a child and so on.

```
g_node_destroy (node_root);
```

GLib provides a number of other functions for interacting with trees of GNode objects. If you have a need for this object, you should reference the API documentation on the GNode data type.

Arrays

There are three types of array data types provided by GLib, which are used to store pointers, bytes, or arbitrary types of data. There are multiple advantages of using arrays in GLib. First, they provide very fast memory access, because direct indexing is supported. This is because of the fact that the GArray structure holds data in an internal array.

Another advantage of GLib array types is that they will automatically expand in size if a new element will not fit. However, you do need to keep in mind that every time you change the number of elements in the array, it can call g_memmove() and memcpy(), which can be expensive if you do this too often. Therefore, GLib arrays are not optimal for applications that will need to constantly add and remove elements.

GArray

Each of the three types of arrays provided by GLib has similar APIs. Therefore, only GArray will be covered in detail. For more information on GPtrArray and GByteArray, you should supplement the instructions given in this section with the API documentation of each data type.

The GArray structure contains two public members: a pointer to the element data stored by the array and the current length of the array in elements. You should note that, as you change the number of elements stored by the array, data might not stay in a constant position. Therefore, you should not make a permanent reference to this pointer. Also, every element in the array must always be the same length.

```
typedef struct
{
  gchar *data;
  guint len;
} GArray;
```

GLib provides two functions for creating a new GArray. g_array_sized_new() allows you to create an array with an initial number of elements (reserved_size) already allocated. This allows you to avoid reallocating the array too many times.

```
GArray* g_array_sized_new (gboolean zero_terminated,
                           gboolean set_to_zero,
                           guint element_size
                           guint reserved_size);
```

If you set zero_terminated to TRUE, one extra element will be added to the array where every bit is set to zero. Setting set_to_zero to TRUE will clear all bits in the array to zero when allocated. You also need to specify the size that every element will be allocated. Every element must always have a size that is less than or equal to element_size.

Alternatively, you can create a new GArray with g_array_new(), which simply calls g_array_sized_new() with an initial allocated size of zero elements. You should only use this initialization function if the array will not be adding too many elements to the array, because adding a large number of elements will cause it to be reallocated many times.

```
GArray* g_array_new (gboolean zero_terminated,
                     gboolean set_to_zero,
                     guint element_size);
```

In order to append multiple new elements to a GArray, you should call g_array_append_vals(). This function will add len number of elements out of data to the end of the array. If you need to append one element to the array, you can use g_array_append_val(). It is defined by the following macro, so there is no difference between calling this function and g_array_append_vals() with a length of 1.

```
GArray* g_array_append_vals (GArray *array,
                             gconstpointer data,
                             guint len);
```

■**Caution** You cannot add literal values such as 13 to a GArray with g_array_append_val(), because it references the value parameter. You must always use variables when adding elements to an array!

In addition to appending values, GLib provides function for prepending and inserting a single value or multiple values in the same way as g_array_append_val() and g_array_append_vals().

```
#define g_array_append_val(a,v)  g_array_append_vals (a, &(v), 1)
```

You can remove an element with the given index with g_array_remove_index(). This function will then shift all of the elements that are located after the removed element one place forward. You should then store the new location of the GArray object.

```
GArray* g_array_remove_index (GArray *array,
                              guint index);
```

You can also use g_array_remove_index_fast(), which will shift the last element into the position of the removed element. This is considerably faster than g_array_remove_index(), but it will not preserve the order of the array. Therefore, it may not always be the optimal solution.

If you need to remove a block of elements in one call, you should use g_array_remove_range(). This function will remove length elements beginning at index and shift the following elements into the empty spaces. You should use this function when removing elements if possible, because it will require far fewer memory shifts than g_array_remove_index().

```
GArray* g_array_remove_range (GArray *array,
                              guint index);
                              guint length);
```

When using GArray, you will most likely need to access elements by their index. One advantage of this data structure is that indexing is performed very quickly, since elements are evenly sized. You can index an element with g_array_index(), which accepts the GArray object, the data type that will be used to cast the return value, and the element index. The returned value will automatically be cast to the data type you provided to the second parameter.

As with other data types in GLib, you are able to sort a GArray with g_array_sort(). This function accepts a standard GCompareFunc callback that is used to compare two elements. In addition, you can use g_array_sort_data(), which allows you to send an additional pointer data parameter to the comparison function.

```
void g_array_sort (GArray *array,
                   GCompareFunc compare_func);
```

When you are finished with the GArray object, you should free it with g_array_free(). As with other data structures, if the array contains dynamically allocated memory, you should free it before calling this function.

```
gchar* g_array_free (GArray *array,
                     gboolean free_segment);
```

If you set free_segment to true, the element memory will also be freed and the function will return NULL. Otherwise, the function will return the internal element array. This allows you to continue to use the array elsewhere, even after the GArray object is freed.

Pointer Arrays

GPtrArray is very similar to GArray in the API except the structure stores an array of pointers. This means that it does not matter what type of data is held by each element in the array; they do not have to be evenly sized. The GPtrArray structure holds an internal array of pointers and the current length of the array.

```
typedef struct
{
  gpointer *pdata;
  guint len;
} GPtrArray;
```

Only one function is provided for inserting an element into a GPtrArray, g_ptr_array_add(). This function appends the array element to the end of the list.

Removing elements is also very similar except two additional functions are provided: g_ptr_array_remove() and g_ptr_array_remove_fast(). Instead of removing an element by its index, each of these functions removes an element that matches the given data. TRUE is returned if an element was successfully found and removed.

```
gboolean g_ptr_array_remove (GPtrArray *array,
                             gpointer data);
```

GPtrArray provides an additional function, g_ptr_array_foreach(), which will call foreach_func() for every element within the array. This function accepts the pointer associated with the current element and the g_ptr_array_foreach() user data parameter.

```
void g_ptr_array_foreach (GPtrArray *array,
                          GFunc foreach_func,
                          gpointer data);
```

When you are finished with a pointer array, you should free it with g_ptr_array_free(). This function also gives you the option of whether to free the internal element array or to return it.

Byte Arrays

Byte arrays are simply a type of GArray that stores a guint8. Functions are provided for appending and prepending a single element. While, unlike GArray, GByteArray does not provide a function for inserting an element, it does allow you to append and prepend new elements.

```
typedef struct
{
  guint8 *data;
  guint len;
} GByteArray;
```

With the exception of the absence of insert functions and those that allow you to prepend or append multiple elements, GByteArray is exactly the same as GArray. In fact, GByteArray uses the GArray functions internally for its implementation.

When you are finished using a byte array, you should free it with g_byte_array_free(). You have the option of whether to free the internal byte array or for it to be returned by the function. If you specify for it to be freed, g_byte_array_free() will return NULL.

Hash Tables

A hash table is a data type that is optimized so that its elements can be found very quickly. Data is stored as a number of key-value pairs. Neither the key nor the value is actually stored by GHashTable in GLib, so the pair must exist for the lifetime of the hash table itself.

That means you should not use temporary strings such as those returned from GTK+ widgets. If you need to use a temporary string, you should call g_strdup() to make a permanent copy of the string.

Hash tables are useful when you are storing a large number of elements, because they provide constant lookup time on average. This average is independent of the number of elements. The lookup time can be longer in some cases, but that is rare.

New hash tables are created in GLib with g_hash_table_new(), which accepts two functions. The hash function is used to create a new hash value out of a key, which can be NULL. The second function is used to check whether two keys are equal to each other.

```
GHashTable* g_hash_table_new (GHashFunc hash_func,
                              GEqualFunc key_equal_func);
```

Hash functions are defined by the function prototype for GHashFunc, shown previously. It accepts the key value and returns the corresponding hash value. You are free to write your own hash functions, but GLib already provides three for commonly used values. These are g_direct_hash(), g_int_hash(), and g_str_hash(), which can be used when the key is a gpointer, gint, and a string respectively.

```
guint (*GHashFunc) (gconstpointer key);
```

The key comparison function is defined by the following GEqualFunc prototype. These functions should return TRUE if a and b are equal and FALSE if they are not. GLib already provides three functions: g_direct_equal(), g_int_equal(), and g_str_equal(), which act as comparison functions for gpointer, gint, and string type keys.

```
gboolean (*GEqualFunc) (gconstpointer a,
                        gconstpointer b);
```

In addition to g_hash_table_new(), GLib provides g_hash_table_new_full(), which allows you to supply destroy callback functions for keys and values when they are removed from the hash table.

There are two ways to insert a new key-value pair into a hash table. The first is by calling g_hash_table_insert(). If the key already exists within the table, value will replace its current value. You can also call g_hash_table_replace(), which provides the same functionality. However, if the key already exists within the table, both the key and value objects will be replaced.

```
void g_hash_table_insert (GHashTable *hash_table,
                          gpointer key,
                          gpointer value);
```

Removing a key-value pair from a hash table is done with g_hash_table_remove(). If you supplied destroy functions for the key and value, they will be called at this time. Otherwise, you will have to make sure to destroy any dynamically allocated data yourself. This function will return TRUE if the key was successfully removed. You can also remove every key-value pair from a hash table with g_hash_table_remove_all().

```
gboolean g_hash_table_remove (GHashTable *hash_table,
                              gconstpointer key);
```

As previously stated, one advantage of hash tables is that looking up a value occurs in constant time, regardless of the number of elements in the hash table. You can search for a value corresponding to the key given to g_hash_table_lookup(). The associated value will be returned, or NULL will be returned if the key could not be found.

```
gpointer g_hash_table_lookup (GHashTable *hash_table,
                              gconstpointer key);
```

Additionally, you can call g_hash_table_lookup_extended(). This function returns TRUE if the key was found within the GHashTable. It will then set the original key and the value, which are two additional parameters sent to the function.

When you are finished with the hash table, it should be freed with g_hash_table_destroy(). If you supplied destroy functions for the keys and values, they will be called on every object at this time.

```
void g_hash_table_destroy (GHashTable *hash_table);
```

One thing that makes this function unique is that, in addition to destroying all keys and values, it decrements its reference count by one. It is possible to increase and decrease the reference count of a hash table with g_hash_table_ref() and g_hash_table_unref() respectively. So, the hash table may still exist as an object if the reference count did not reach zero.

Quarks

A quark is a two-way association between a 32-bit integer and a string. This means that you can access the string by using the integer and vice versa. Quarks are calculated at runtime and are available globally throughout the application. You can set a new quark at any point in your program, and it will be available in any other aspect of the application.

Internally, quarks are implemented as a hash table and an array of strings. The quark itself is a 32-bit integer that is used as the index of the array, which is used to look up the associated string. The string is used to find the quark in the hash table. This means that all strings and integers must be unique.

```
typedef guint32 GQuark;
```

To get the GQuark of the given string, use g_quark_from_string(). If the string is not already associated with a GQuark, using a copy of the string will create one. If you are sure that the string will always exist, you can use g_quark_from_string_static(), which will use the string itself instead of a copy.

```
GQuark g_quark_from_string (const gchar *string);
```

To test whether a string already has an associated quark, you can use g_quark_try_string(). This function accepts a string and returns the associated GQuark. If the string has not been added, it will return 0.

If a string already exists within the global table, you can retrieve it from the quark with g_quark_to_string(). If the quark does not already exist, then this function will return NULL.

```
const gchar* g_quark_to_string (GQuark quark);
```

Keyed Data Lists

A keyed data list is a special type of linked list that uses quarks for indexing. GData does not have any public members. Its private members include a quark, a data pointer, an optional destroy function to call when the node is removed, and a pointer to the next node.

Data lists use the quark relationship to store another arbitrary data type, which can be retrieved by specifying either the string or the quark. Keyed data lists are initialized as an empty list with g_datalist_init(). This function will fail if the GData object is not NULL.

```
void g_datalist_init (GData **datalist);
```

GLib provides a large number of functions for adding and removing elements from a data list, but most of them are simply defined as calls to g_datalist_id_set_data_full(). If the key_id already exists within the data list, then the previous data will be removed and replaced by the new pointer.

```
void g_datalist_id_set_data_full (GData **datalist,
                                  GQuark key_id,
                                  gpointer data,
                                  GDestroyNotify destroy_func);
```

This function also allows you to specify a GDestroyNotify callback function that will be called when the node is removed. GDestroyNotify callback functions accept a pointer to the data member of the node.

You can also use g_datalist_id_set_data_full() to remove an element from the data list by specifying NULL to the data parameter. A number of other functions are provided that wrap the functionality provided by g_datalist_id_set_data_full() with multiple different prototypes.

When you remove an item with g_datalist_id_set_data_full(), the destroy-notify callback will be run if it was set. However, if you would like to prevent this, you can remove a node with g_datalist_id_remove_no_notify(). This function will the node and return the data stored that was specified at that location.

```
gpointer g_datalist_id_remove_no_notify (GData **datalist,
                                         GQuark key_id);
```

If you need to traverse through all of the nodes in a data list, you should use g_datalist_foreach(). The GDataForeachFunc prototype accepts the quark and element data of one node along with the data pointer specified in g_datalist_foreach().

```
void g_datalist_foreach (GData **datalist,
                         GDataForeachFunc func,
                         gpointer user_data);
```

After you are finished with the keyed data list, you need to clear all of its elements with g_datalist_clear(). This will make the list ready for the next use. There is no need to call a destroy function on the data list itself, since it will now take up no memory.

```
void g_datalist_clear (GData **datalist);
```

When the elements are being removed, a destroy function will be called on the data parameter if it was specified.

Input-Output Channels

The GIOChannel structure allows you to handle files, pipes, and sockets. The following sections will cover how to use the structure with files and pipes. You should only use the method covered in the pipes section when working on a UNIX-like operating system, because file descriptor and socket domains overlap in Windows.

You will be given an alternative for spawning processes in the "Spawning Processes" part of this section, which will cover both synchronous and asynchronous processes.

GIOChannels and Files

One way to create a new input-output (IO) channel is to use g_io_channel_new_file(). This method removes the need for UNIX file descriptors, so it can be safely used on non-UNIX operating systems.

This function opens a new file or pipe as a GIOChannel. Listing 6-8 uses g_io_channel_new_file() function twice. First, a file is created with some initial text. A second channel then opens the file, reads its contents, and prints the text to standard output. Contrast this with Listing 6-5, which implements the same functionality with file utility functions.

Listing 6-8. *Using IO Channels for Files (files2.c)*

```c
#include <glib.h>

static void handle_error (GError*);

int main (int argc,
          char *argv[])
{
  gchar *filename, *content;
  GIOChannel *write, *read;
  GError *error = NULL;
  gsize bytes;

  /* Build a filename in the user's home directory. */
  filename = g_build_filename (g_get_home_dir(), "temp", NULL);

  /* Set the contents of the given file and report any errors. */
  write = g_io_channel_new_file (filename, "w", &error);
  handle_error (error);
  g_io_channel_write_chars (write, "Hello World!", -1, &bytes, NULL);
  g_io_channel_close (write);
```

```
  if (!g_file_test (filename, G_FILE_TEST_EXISTS))
    g_error ("Error: File does not exist!\n");

  /* Get the contents of the given file and report any errors. */
  read = g_io_channel_new_file (filename, "r", &error);
  handle_error (error);
  g_io_channel_read_to_end (read, &content, &bytes, NULL);
  g_print ("%s\n", content);

  g_io_channel_close (read);
  g_free (content);
  g_free (filename);

  return 0;
}

static void
handle_error (GError *error)
{
  if (error != NULL)
  {
    g_print (error->message);
    g_clear_error (&error);
  }
}
```

The second parameter of g_io_channel_new_file() specifies the mode. This mode is a string in the same format as specified to fopen(). Table 6-6 shows the possible modes that g_io_channel_new_file() accepts. Files opened with g_io_channel_new_file() can have an error under the domain G_FILE_ERROR.

Table 6-6. *GIOChannel File Modes*

Mode	Description
r	Open the file for reading only and place the pointer at the beginning of the file.
w	Open the file for writing only and place the pointer at the beginning of the file. The file is also erased, so its length is zero characters, or created if it does not exist.
a	Open the file for writing only and place the pointer at the end of the file so that new text is appended. If the file does not exist, attempt to create it.
r+	Open the file for reading and writing and place the pointer at the beginning of the file.
w+	Open the file for reading and writing and place the pointer at the beginning of the file. The file is also erased, so its length is zero characters, or created if it does not exist.
a+	Open the file for reading and writing and place the pointer at the end of the file so that new text is appended. If the file does not exist, attempt to create it.

If you specified w, a, r+, w+, or a+ as the mode, you can use g_io_channel_write_chars() to write text to the file.

```
GIOStatus g_io_channel_write_chars (GIOChannel *channel,
                                    const gchar *text,
                                    gssize size_of_buffer,
                                    gsize *bytes_written,
                                    GError **error);
```

This function takes five parameters: the opened IO channel, text to write or append to the file, the size of the text, an integer to store the number of bytes written, and a GError structure. The size of the buffer can be set to -1 if the text string is NULL-terminated. The number of bytes written to the file is set by the function itself.

After you are finished with an IO channel, it needs to be closed with g_io_channel_shutdown(). By setting the second parameter to TRUE, any pending data will be flushed. Otherwise, GLib will continue the current action and close when it is completed. The third parameter will catch any errors of type GIOChannelError that occur.

```
GIOStatus g_io_channel_shutdown (GIOChannel *channel,
                                 gboolean flush,
                                 GError **error);
```

GIOChannel provides functions for reading a single character, a whole line, or a whole file. When dealing with files, g_io_channel_read_to_end() can be used to read the entire contents of the file. This function also sets the length of the text that is returned. Errors can be of type GIOChannelError or GConvertError.

```
GIOStatus g_io_channel_read_to_end (GIOChannel *channel,
                                    gchar **text,
                                    gsize *length,
                                    GError **error);
```

GIOChannels and Pipes

Since most objects on UNIX systems are treated as files, it is possible to use the same method covered in the previous section to open pipes. Pipes allow communication between applications. The only difference is that you would need to add watches so that you will know when data is ready to be read from or written to the pipe.

■**Note** While this book does provide an introduction to UNIX pipes, this is by no means an in-depth tutorial. After reading this section, you are encouraged to learn more about pipes from the C programming language tutorial of your choice.

INTERPROCESS COMMUNICATION USING PIPES

A process in UNIX is, fundamentally, a single, running application that has its own stack, memory pages, and file descriptors table. When the process is run, it is given a unique identifier called a process ID (pid). New processes can be created with a wide array of functions, but they all make calls to the fork() command.

A process is not a program, because multiple processes can be run as an instance of the same application at the same time. For example, you can open up multiple instances of your web browser at the same time.

Forking turns a single process into two identical processes: the parent and the child. Various UNIX commands can then be used to run another application from the forked process, although in our example, we want the same application to be created twice.

```
switch (fork())
{
  case -1:
    g_error ("Error: The fork() failed!");
    exit (1);
  case 0:
    g_message ("We are currently running the child process!");
    exit (0);
  default:
    gint status_of_child;
    wait (&status_of_child);
}
```

After a process has been forked, it returns a process identifier. If this identifier is -1, it means that the function has failed. An identifier of 0 lets you know that you are currently in the child process. You can perform the desired functionality for the child. The default case catches the main application, which waits for the child to exit.

Usually when you fork your application, you want a way to communicate with the child process, which is provided by pipes. Pipes are set up by calling the pipe() command. pipe() accepts an array of two integers and returns 0 on success or –1 on failure. After it's initialized, the first integer in the array refers to the read pipe and the second to the write pipe.

If you need to communicate in both directions between the child and the parent, you will need to set up two sets of pipes. You are able to write data to one pipe, which be read by the other instance of the application and vice versa. Our example will use the UNIX method for forking processes and creating pipes, but will use GLib's functions for interacting with the pipes.

Listing 6-9 uses UNIX's method of pipe creation in conjunction with the functions provided by the GIOChannel structure. To do this, watches are created.

A watch is like a signal, because it waits for an event to occur by integrating itself into GLib's main loop. It then invokes a callback function. Types of watch events include when the pipe has data that is ready to read and when it can accept data to be written.

Listing 6-9 creates a parent and child process, both with a GtkEntry widget. When you type into either entry widget, the new content is written to the pipe. The other entry is then set to have the same content as the first.

> **Note** You will notice that the pipes were set up and the application forked in a UNIX-specific way. The
> next section will show you a way to set up pipes and fork your application that is supported across platforms.

Listing 6-9. *Using IO Channels for Pipes (iochannels.c)*

```c
#include <gtk/gtk.h>
#include <stdlib.h>
#include <stdio.h>
#include <errno.h>
#include <unistd.h>
#include <string.h>

static void entry_changed (GtkEditable*, GIOChannel*);
static void setup_app (gint input[], gint output[], gint pid);
static gboolean iochannel_read (GIOChannel*, GIOCondition, GtkEntry*);

gulong signal_id = 0;

int main (int argc,
          char* argv[])
{
  gint child_to_parent[2], parent_to_child[2], pid, ret_value;

  /* Set up read and write pipes for the child and parent processes. */
  ret_value = pipe (parent_to_child);
  if (ret_value == -1)
  {
    g_error ("Error: %s\n", g_strerror (errno));
   exit (1);
  }

  ret_value = pipe (child_to_parent);
  if (ret_value == -1)
  {
    g_error ("Error: %s\n", g_strerror (errno));
    exit (1);
  }

  /* Fork the application, setting up both instances accordingly. */
  pid = fork ();
  switch (pid)
  {
    case -1:
      g_error ("Error: %s\n", g_strerror (errno));
      exit (1);
```

```
    case 0:
      gtk_init (&argc, &argv);
      setup_app (parent_to_child, child_to_parent, pid);
      break;
    default:
      gtk_init (&argc, &argv);
      setup_app (child_to_parent, parent_to_child, pid);
  }

  gtk_main ();
  return 0;
}

/* Set up the GUI aspects of each window and setup IO channel watches. */
static void
setup_app (gint input[],
           gint output[],
           gint pid)
{
  GtkWidget *window, *entry;
  GIOChannel *channel_read, *channel_write;

  window = gtk_window_new (GTK_WINDOW_TOPLEVEL);
  entry = gtk_entry_new ();

  gtk_container_add (GTK_CONTAINER (window), entry);
  gtk_container_set_border_width (GTK_CONTAINER (window), 10);
  gtk_widget_set_size_request (window, 200, -1);
  gtk_widget_show_all (window);

  /* Close the unnecessary pipes for the given process. */
  close (input[1]);
  close (output[0]);

  /* Create read and write channels out of the remaining pipes. */
  channel_read = g_io_channel_unix_new (input[0]);
  channel_write = g_io_channel_unix_new (output[1]);

  if (channel_read == NULL || channel_write == NULL)
    g_error ("Error: The GIOChannels could not be created!\n");

  /* Watch the read channel for changes. This will send the appropriate data. */
  if (!g_io_add_watch (channel_read, G_IO_IN | G_IO_HUP,
      iochannel_read, (gpointer) entry))
    g_error ("Error: Read watch could not be added to the GIOChannel!\n");
```

```
  signal_id = g_signal_connect (G_OBJECT (entry), "changed",
                                G_CALLBACK (entry_changed),
                                (gpointer) channel_write);

  /* Set the window title depending on the process identifier. */
  if (pid == 0)
    gtk_window_set_title (GTK_WINDOW (window), "Child Process");
  else
    gtk_window_set_title (GTK_WINDOW (window), "Parent Process");
}

/* Read the message from the pipe and set the text to the GtkEntry. */
static gboolean
iochannel_read (GIOChannel *channel,
                GIOCondition condition,
                GtkEntry *entry)
{
  GIOStatus ret_value;
  gchar *message;
  gsize length;

  /* The pipe has died unexpectedly, so exit the application. */
  if (condition & G_IO_HUP)
    g_error ("Error: The pipe has died!\n");

  /* Read the data that has been sent through the pipe. */
  ret_value = g_io_channel_read_line (channel, &message, &length, NULL, NULL);
  if (ret_value == G_IO_STATUS_ERROR)
    g_error ("Error: The line could not be read!\n");

  /* Synchronize the GtkEntry text, blocking the changed signal. Otherwise, an
   * infinite loop of communication would ensue. */
  g_signal_handler_block ((gpointer) entry, signal_id);
  message[length-1] = 0;
  gtk_entry_set_text (entry, message);
  g_signal_handler_unblock ((gpointer) entry, signal_id);

  return TRUE;
}

/* Write the new contents of the GtkEntry to the write IO channel. */
static void
entry_changed (GtkEditable *entry,
               GIOChannel *channel)
```

```
{
  gchar *text;
  gsize length;
  GIOStatus ret_value;

  text = g_strconcat (gtk_entry_get_text (GTK_ENTRY (entry)), "\n", NULL);

  /* Write the text to the channel so that the other process will get it. */
  ret_value = g_io_channel_write_chars (channel, text, -1, &length, NULL);
  if (ret_value = G_IO_STATUS_ERROR)
    g_error ("Error: The changes could not be written to the pipe!\n");
  else
    g_io_channel_flush (channel, NULL);
}
```

Setting Up IO Channels

If you are working on a UNIX-like machine, you can use the pipe() function to create new file descriptors. In Listing 6-9, two pairs of pipes are set up: one for sending messages from the parent to the child and one for sending messages in the other direction. Two GIOChannels can then be created from these file descriptors by calling the following function on each.

After the pipes are created, the application is forked with fork(). If the fork is successful, the application is set up for both the child and the parent process.

Within setup_app(), we begin by closing the pipes that are not needed by the child or parent applications with close(). Each process will only need one read and one write pipe in order to send and receive messages.

Next, we use the two remaining pipes in each application and set up a GIOChannel for each. We will use channel_read to receive data from the other process and channel_write to send the new content of the GtkEntry.

```
channel_read  = g_io_channel_unix_new (input[0]);
channel_write = g_io_channel_unix_new (output[1]);
```

After initializing your IO channels, you need to set up a watch on channel_read. The watch will monitor the channel for the specified events, which is setup with g_io_add_watch().

```
guint g_io_add_watch (GIOChannel *channel,
                      GIOCondition condition,
                      GIOFunc func,
                      gpointer data);
```

The second parameter of g_io_add_watch() adds one or more events that should be watched. You need to make sure to set up the correct conditions with each channel. You will never get a G_IO_IN event from a channel used for writing data, so monitoring for that event is useless. Possible values for the GIOCondition enumeration follow; these can be piped to the condition parameter of g_io_add_watch():

- G_IO_IN: Read data is pending.

- G_IO_OUT: Data can be written without the worry of blocking.

- G_IO_PRI: Read data is pending and urgent.

- G_IO_ERR: An error has occurred.

- G_IO_HUP: The connection has been hung up or broken.

- G_IO_NVAL: An invalid request has occurred because the file descriptor is not open.

When one of the specified conditions occurs, the GIOFunc callback function is called. The last parameter gives data that will be passed to the callback function. IO channel callback functions receive three parameters: the GIOChannel, the condition that occurred, and the data passed from g_io_add_watch(). TRUE should always be returned from the callback function unless you want it to be removed. The function prototype follows:

```
gboolean (*GIOFunc) (GIOChannel *source, GIOCondition condition, gpointer data);
```

Reading from and writing to a GIOChannel is done in the same manner regardless of whether it is a file or a pipe. Therefore, the g_io_channel_read_(*) and g_io_channel_write_*() functions covered in the previous section can still be used.

Many of the GIOChannel functions provide two ways to check for errors. The first is the GError structure that we have used in past chapters. Secondly, many functions return a GIOStatus value, which will report one of the following four values:

- G_IO_STATUS_ERROR: Some type of error has occurred. You should still track errors even if you are checking for this value.

- G_IO_STATUS_NORMAL: The action was successfully completed.

- G_IO_STATUS_EOF: The end of the file has been reached.

- G_IO_STATUS_AGAIN: Resources are temporarily unavailable. You should try again later.

Depending on the GIOStatus value, you should either continue or give an error message. The only exception is G_IO_STATUS_AGAIN, in which case you should return to poll() in the main loop and wait for the file descriptor to become ready.

To send the data to the read buffer, you need to flush the write buffer of the GIOChannel with g_io_channel_flush(). This function, along with all of the functions in this section, can cause an error of the type GIOChannelError.

```
GIOStatus g_io_channel_flush (GIOChannel *channel,
                              GError **error);
```

Spawning Processes

The GIOChannel example in the previous section used pipe() and fork() to set up the communication between the applications. However, this example is not cross-platform, because some commands will not be supported on Microsoft Windows.

To spawn processes in a way supported by multiple platforms, GLib provides three functions. Since all three work in a similar way, we will only talk about the following function, g_spawn_async_with_pipes():

```
gboolean g_spawn_async_with_pipes (const gchar *working_directory,
                                   gchar **argv,
                                   gchar **envp,
                                   GSpawnFlags flags,
                                   GSpawnChildSetupFunc child_setup,
                                   gpointer data,
                                   GPid *child_pid,
                                   gint *standard_input,
                                   gint *standard_output,
                                   gint *standard_error,
                                   GError **error);
```

This function asynchronously runs a child program, which means that the program will continue to run even if the child has not exited. The first parameter specifies the working directory for the child process or NULL to set it as the parent's working directory.

The argv list is a NULL-terminated array of strings. The first string in this list is the name of the application, followed by any additional parameters. This application must be a full path unless you use the G_SPAWN_SEARCH_PATH flag, which will be shown later. Another NULL-terminated array of strings is envp, each in the form KEY=VALUE. These will be set as the child's environment variables.

You can then specify one or more of the following GSpawnFlags:

- G_SPAWN_LEAVE_DESCRIPTORS_OPEN: The child will inherit the open file descriptors of the parent. If this flag is not set, all file descriptors except the standard input, output, and error will be closed.

- G_SPAWN_DO_NOT_REAP_CHILD: Stop the child from automatically becoming reaped. If you do not call waitpid() or handle SIGCHLD, it will become a zombie.

- G_SPAWN_SEARCH_PATH: If this flag is set, argv[0] will be searched for in the user's path if it is not an absolute location.

- G_SPAWN_STDOUT_TO_DEV_NULL: Discard the standard output from the child. If this flag is not set, it will go to the same location as the parent's standard output.

- G_SPAWN_STDERR_TO_DEV_NULL: Discard the standard error from the child.

- G_SPAWN_CHILD_INHERITS_STDIN: If this flag is not set, the standard input for the child is attached to /dev/null. You can use this flag so the child will inherit the standard input of the parent.

- G_SPAWN_FILE_AND_ARGV_ZERO: Use the first argument as the executable and only pass the remaining strings as the actual arguments. If this flag is not set, argv[0] will also be passed to the executable.

The next parameter of g_spawn_async_with_pipes() is the GSpawnChildSetupFunc callback function that will be run after GLib sets up pipes but before calling exec(). This function accepts the data parameter from g_spawn_async_with_pipes().

The next four parameters allow you to retrieve information about the new child process. These are the child's process identifier, standard input, standard output, and standard error. Any of these four parameters can be set to NULL if you want to ignore it.

If the application was successfully launched, g_spawn_async_with_pipes() will return TRUE. Otherwise, the error will be set under the GSpawnError domain, and it will return FALSE.

When you are finished with a GPid, you should use g_spawn_close_pid() to close it. This is especially important when spawning processes on Microsoft Windows.

```
void g_spawn_close_pid (GPid pid);
```

Dynamic Modules

One extremely useful feature provided by GLib is the ability to dynamically load libraries and explicitly call functions from those libraries using the GModule structure. This functionality is not performed in the same way across platforms, so a cross-platform solution for dynamic libraries makes things much easier. This functionality facilitates, for one, the creation of a plug-in system. In Listing 6-10, a simple theoretical plug-in system will be created.

The example is split into two separate files: one for the plug-in and one for the main application. To run this application, you first need to compile and link modules-plugin.c as a library. You can use the following two commands to create the library and install it into the standard location.

```
gcc –shared modules-plugin.c –o plugin.so `pkg-config --libs glib-2.0` \
    `pkg-config --cflags glib-2.0`
sudo mv plugin.so /usr/lib
```

Library creation is generally performed by the GNU linker (ld), but by using the -shared flag, GCC can create shared libraries. Also, on some systems it is necessary to run ldconfig after you move the plug-in library so it will be registered. You will need to do this if you want to use the library for purposes other than loading with GModule.

Listing 6-10. *The Plug-in (modules-plugin.c)*

```
#include <glib.h>
#include <gmodule.h>

G_MODULE_EXPORT gboolean
print_the_message (gpointer data)
{
  g_printf ("%s\n", (gchar*) data);
  return TRUE;
}

G_MODULE_EXPORT gboolean
print_another_one (gpointer data)
{
  g_printf ("%s\n", (gchar*) data);
  return TRUE;
}
```

The plug-in source only contains one or more functions that will be loaded by the main application. Therefore, there is no need to include a main() function within the plug-in's source file.

The only important aspect of the plug-in file is that you should include G_MODULE_EXPORT before any function you want to export. If you do not use this macro, GModule will be unable to load the function from the library.

Functions dynamically loaded from a library are called symbols. A symbol is merely a pointer to a function in the library. You call symbol functions in the same way you would call any other function. The only difference is that, when called, GLib searches out the actual function in the library and executes it from there.

The advantage of this method is that multiple applications can load a library at the same time. A library that allows itself to be loaded by multiple applications is called a shared library. Most libraries compiled on Linux are shared libraries.

When compiling the main file of Listing 6-11, you will need to use an altered compile line as well, because you need to link against the GModule library.

```
gcc modules.c -o modules `pkg-config --cflags --libs glib-2.0` \
    `pkg-config --cflags --libs gmodule-2.0`
```

GModule can easily be included by adding `pkg-config --cflags --libs gmodule-2.0` to the compile command. The following example illustrates how to load the library that we have just created and installed. Listing 6-11 is an application that takes advantage of the dynamic module from Listing 6-10.

Listing 6-11. *Loading the Plug-in (modules.c)*

```
#include <gmodule.h>
#include <glib.h>

typedef gboolean (* PrintMessageFunc) (gpointer data);
typedef gboolean (* PrintAnotherFunc) (gpointer data);

int main (int argc,
          char *argv[])
{
  GModule *module;
  PrintMessageFunc print_the_message;
  PrintAnotherFunc print_another_one;
  gchar *text = "This is some text";

  /* Make sure module loading is supported on the user's machine. */
  g_assert (g_module_supported ());

  /* Open the library and resolve symbols only when necessary. Libraries on
   * Windows will have a .dll appendix. */
  module = g_module_open ("/usr/lib/plugin.so", G_MODULE_BIND_LAZY);

  if (!module)
  {
    g_error ("Error: %s\n", (gchar*) g_module_error ());
    return -1;
  }
```

```
/* Load the print_the_message() function. */
if (!g_module_symbol (module, "print_the_message",
                      (gpointer*) &print_the_message))
{
  g_error ("Error: %s\n", (gchar*) g_module_error ());
  return -1;
}

/* Load the destroy_the_evidence() function. */
if (!g_module_symbol (module, "print_another_one",
                      (gpointer*) &print_another_one))
{
  g_error ("Error: %s\n", (gchar*) g_module_error ());
  return -1;
}

/* Run both loaded functions since there were no errors reported loading
 * neither the module nor the symbols. */
print_the_message ((gpointer) text);
print_another_one ("Another Message!");

/* Close the module and free allocated resources. */
if (!g_module_close (module))
  g_error ("Error: %s\n", (gchar*) g_module_error ());

return 0;
}
```

Not all platforms support the GModule structure. Therefore, if you are creating an application that will be compiled for multiple platforms, it is a good idea to make sure support is available.

Support for GModule can be checked with g_module_supported(), which will return TRUE if the feature is available. By using g_assert(), you can ensure that the application will terminate if GModule is not supported.

Once you are sure GModule is supported on the user's system, you can open a library with g_module_open(). If opening a module fails, NULL is returned by the function. However, before failing, the function will attempt multiple formats of the given library name to find a library that will load. This includes appending G_MODULE_SUFFIX, the system's default library suffix, to the specified path.

```
GModule* g_module_open (const gchar *library,
                        GModuleFlags flags);
```

The second parameter in g_module_open() specified one or more module flags, which instruct GModule how to deal with symbols. There are currently three available GModuleFlags enumeration values:

- G_MODULE_BIND_LAZY: Symbols should all be bound when the module is loaded by default. However, this tells GLib to only resolve symbols when needed.

- G_MODULE_BIND_LOCAL: Do not place symbols on the global namespace, which is the default on most systems.

- G_MODULE_BIND_MASK: Mask for all GModule flags.

At any point within your application, you can call g_module_error(), which will return a human-readable string describing the last error that has occurred. If any function returns an unexpected value, it is a good idea to output this message to the screen.

If the module was successfully loaded, g_module_symbol() can then be used to load any functions in the library that were made available with G_MODULE_EXPORT. If the symbol is successfully loaded, the function will return TRUE.

```
gboolean g_module_symbol (GModule *module,
                          const gchar *symbol_name,
                          gpointer *symbol);
```

The second parameter of g_module_symbol() should be the full name of the function you want to load from the library. The last parameter is a pointer that will store where to find the function in memory. It is essential that you specify the same parameter and return values for both the loaded function and the pointer, or problems will arise.

After you are finished with the GModule object, which is usually when the application is closing or the plug-in is being unloaded, g_module_close() should be called. TRUE is returned upon a successful destruction of the object.

If you are sure that the module should never be unloaded, you can ignore all calls to g_module_close() by calling g_module_make_resident(). Be careful with this function, because it will be impossible to unload the module after this is called!

Test Your Understanding

Since this chapter covers such a wide array of topics, it would be too time consuming to provide exercises for each thing you have learned. Therefore, in addition to doing the following two exercises, you should create your own applications using various other topics you learned in this chapter to practice.

Making your own examples, in addition to the following two exercises, should give you enough experience to easily be able to use what you have learned in future chapters. The following two exercises will allow you to practice file management, error handling, message reporting, and timeout functions.

Exercise 6-1. Working With Files

For this exercise, create a window that contains a GtkEntry widget. The entry can contain any text that the user wants. The window will also contain a GtkFileChooserButton that will allow the user to choose a folder.

A third widget, a button, should be placed within the window. Upon clicking that button, the text from the GtkEntry should be written to an arbitrary file in the folder chosen by the GtkFileChooserButton. You should handle all errors that can occur in this exercise.

Exercise 6-1 is straightforward. You need to create a normal GTK+ application as always. In the main window, the entry, file chooser button, and Save button should be added and packed by a GtkVBox. The exercise solution can be found in Appendix F.

When the button is pressed, you need to save the text in the entry to a file. That file should be created in the specified location under whatever name you choose. Then, you need to use the GError structure to make sure the file was successfully created.

Exercise 6-2. Timeout Functions

For this exercise, create a window that contains a GtkLabel and a button. The label should initially display the number "0". The timeout function should be called every second, incrementing the label up one digit. When the button is pressed, the counter should be reset and begin counting again.

As stated before, you should never use timeouts to count time if you need accuracy. Therefore, you should reimplement this example using timers. Consider placing two labels in the window, one using a timeout function for counting and one using a timer. What can you conclude from this example?

Exercise 6-2 is a little more difficult than the previous one, because you need to figure out how to get both the GtkLabel and the current count to the timeout function. Of course, you could use a global variable, but this is not the preferred method in most cases.

In the solution in Appendix F, both elements were stored in a structure that could easily be passed to the timeout function. This is the method that you should use in most of your applications, because it will make them easier to manage when they grow in size.

The purpose of the application was to count the number of seconds that have gone by using a timeout function. Whenever the Clear button is clicked, the count should be reset to 0 seconds for each button.

Both of these exercises are meant to stimulate your imagination. You have learned a great deal in this chapter as well as previous chapters. You should experiment with integrating your previous knowledge of GTK+ with the topics in this chapter.

Summary

Congratulations! You have made it through the longest chapter in the book. This chapter has given you a thorough understanding of many of the most important features provided by GLib.

Of course, there were topics that were not covered, and those that provide options not shown in this chapter's examples. Therefore, when you need one of these features in an application, you should reference the API documentation for further information.

The beginning of this chapter gave a quick overview of GLib basics including data types, macros, message logging, environment variables, timers, file manipulation, directory management, and file system work. You then learned about memory management in GLib. In addition to wrapping `malloc()` and friends, you can also use the slab allocator provided by `GSlice`. GLib provides a method for profiling memory usage within an application as well.

Another important topic in this chapter was the main loop. You learned that the main loop is actually implemented in GLib by `GMainLoop`, `GMainContext`, and `GSource`. Two types of sources already built-in are timeouts and idle functions. Timeout functions are called at a predefined interval of time and idle functions are called when there are no more actions with a higher priority to perform.

GLib provides a wide array of data types. You learned about ten different data types, including the following:

- Strings provide character arrays that automatically grow as text is added. These are similar to the string class provided by C++'s Standard Template Library.

- Linked lists allow you to traverse, search, and sort a large list of data of an arbitrary type. Both doubly and singly linked variations are provided by GLib.

- Balanced binary trees are tree structures that are optimized for traversing and searching. N-ary trees allow each node to have as many branches as you want. They can very quickly become complex.

- Arrays, byte arrays, and pointer arrays provide lists of elements that automatically grow when items are added.

- Quarks provide an integer pointer to an associated string. Keyed data lists use them as a reference to stored data of an arbitrary type.

- Hash tables are similar to linked lists, except items are accessed through a pointer of an arbitrary type. They are optimized so data can be found very quickly.

GLib provides many file and directory utility functions. These can read or write files, read the contents of a directory, or wrap UNIX file system functionality. The `GIOChannel` structure is used to deal with files or pipes, which provide interprocess communication.

An easy way to create a plug-in system is to use GLib's `GModule` structure. This structure allows you to dynamically load libraries and retrieve symbols from the files. This can also be used to make an application more modular.

At this point, you should have a decent grasp of many important GTK+ widgets and GLib features. Many of these features are going to be used in the next few chapters, which will cover more advanced widgets.

Chapter 7 will explain the multiline text entry widget called `GtkTextView`. Other topics include the clipboard and the GtkSourceView library.

CHAPTER 7

■■■

The Text View Widget

In Chapter 6, you learned about a large number of utilities, data structures, and other types of functionality provided by GLib, so there are very few further things about GLib that you will learn throughout the book. Instead, you will apply the knowledge that you have gained in Chapter 6 to future examples and exercises.

Chapter 7 will teach you how to use the GtkTextView widget. The text view widget is similar to a GtkEntry widget, except it is capable of holding text that spans multiple lines. Scrolled windows will be used to allow the document to exist beyond the bounds of the screen.

Before you learn about GtkTextView, Chapter 7 begins by introducing a few new widgets. The first two widgets are scrolled windows and viewports. Scrolled windows are composed of two scrollbars that are used to scroll the child widget. A few widgets support scrolling already, including GtkLayout, GtkTreeView, and GtkTextView. For all other widgets that you want to scroll, you will need to add them first to a GtkViewport widget, which gives its child widget scrolling abilities.

In this chapter, you will learn the following:

- How to use scrolled windows and viewports

- How to use the GtkTextView widget and apply text buffers

- What function text iterators and text marks perform when dealing with buffers

- Methods for applying styles to the whole or part of a document

- How to cut, copy, and paste to and from the clipboard

- How to insert images and child widgets into a text view

Scrolled Windows

Before you can learn about the GtkTextView widget, you need to learn about two container widgets called GtkScrolledWindow and GtkViewport. Scrolled windows use two scrollbars to allow a widget to take up more space than is visible on the screen. This widget will allow the GtkTextView widget to contain documents that expand beyond the bounds of the window.

Both scrollbars in the scrolled window have associated GtkAdjustment objects. These adjustments are used to track the current position and range of a scrollbar. However, you will not need to directly access the adjustments in most cases.

```
typedef struct
{
  gdouble value;
  gdouble upper;
  gdouble lower;
  gdouble step_increment;
  gdouble page_increment;
  gdouble page_size;
} GtkAdjustment;
```

A scrollbar's GtkAdjustment holds information about scroll bounds, steps, and its current position. The value variable is the current position of the scrollbar between the bounds. This variable must always be between the lower and upper values, which are the bounds of the adjustment. The page_size is the area that can be visible on the screen at one time, depending on the size of the widget. The step_increment and page_increment variables are used for stepping when an arrow is pressed or when the Page Down key is pressed.

Figure 7-1 is a screenshot of the window created with the code in Listing 7-1. Both scrollbars are enabled, because the table containing the buttons is larger than the visible area.

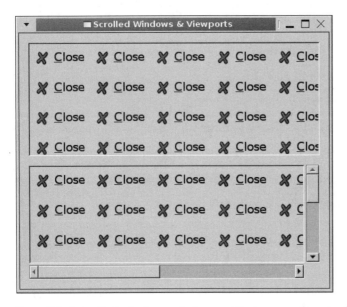

Figure 7-1. *A scrolled window and viewport that are synchronized*

Listing 7-1 shows how to use scrolled windows and viewports. As a scrollbar is moved, the viewport will scroll as well, because the adjustments are synchronized. Try to resize the window to see how the scrollbars react to becoming larger and smaller than the child widget.

Listing 7-1. *Using Scrolled Windows (scrolledwindows.c)*

```c
#include <gtk/gtk.h>

int main (int argc,
          char *argv[])
{
  GtkWidget *window, *swin, *viewport, *table1, *table2, *vbox;
  GtkAdjustment *horizontal, *vertical;
  GtkWidget *buttons1[10][10], *buttons2[10][10];
  unsigned int i, j;

  gtk_init (&argc, &argv);

  window = gtk_window_new (GTK_WINDOW_TOPLEVEL);
  gtk_window_set_title (GTK_WINDOW (window), "Scrolled Windows & Viewports");
  gtk_container_set_border_width (GTK_CONTAINER (window), 10);
  gtk_widget_set_size_request (window, 500, 400);

  g_signal_connect (G_OBJECT (window), "destroy",
                    G_CALLBACK (gtk_main_quit), NULL);

  table1 = gtk_table_new (10, 10, TRUE);
  table2 = gtk_table_new (10, 10, TRUE);
  gtk_table_set_row_spacings (GTK_TABLE (table1), 5);
  gtk_table_set_row_spacings (GTK_TABLE (table2), 5);
  gtk_table_set_col_spacings (GTK_TABLE (table1), 5);
  gtk_table_set_col_spacings (GTK_TABLE (table2), 5);

  /* Pack each table with 100 buttons. */
  for (i = 0; i < 10; i++)
  {
    for (j = 0; j < 10; j++)
    {
      buttons1[i][j] = gtk_button_new_from_stock (GTK_STOCK_CLOSE);
      buttons2[i][j] = gtk_button_new_from_stock (GTK_STOCK_CLOSE);
      gtk_button_set_relief (GTK_BUTTON (buttons1[i][j]), GTK_RELIEF_NONE);
      gtk_button_set_relief (GTK_BUTTON (buttons2[i][j]), GTK_RELIEF_NONE);

      gtk_table_attach_defaults (GTK_TABLE (table1), buttons1[i][j],
                                 i, i + 1, j, j + 1);
      gtk_table_attach_defaults (GTK_TABLE (table2), buttons2[i][j],
                                 i, i + 1, j, j + 1);
    }
  }
```

```
/* Create a scrolled window and a viewport, each with one table. Use the
 * adjustments in the scrolled window to synchronize both containers. */
swin = gtk_scrolled_window_new (NULL, NULL);
horizontal = gtk_scrolled_window_get_hadjustment (GTK_SCROLLED_WINDOW (swin));
vertical = gtk_scrolled_window_get_vadjustment (GTK_SCROLLED_WINDOW (swin));
viewport = gtk_viewport_new (horizontal, vertical);

gtk_container_set_border_width (GTK_CONTAINER (swin), 5);
gtk_container_set_border_width (GTK_CONTAINER (viewport), 5);

gtk_scrolled_window_set_policy (GTK_SCROLLED_WINDOW (swin),
                                GTK_POLICY_AUTOMATIC, GTK_POLICY_AUTOMATIC);
gtk_scrolled_window_add_with_viewport (GTK_SCROLLED_WINDOW (swin), table1);
gtk_container_add (GTK_CONTAINER (viewport), table2);

/* Pack the widgets into a GtkVBox and then into the window. */
vbox = gtk_vbox_new (TRUE, 5);
gtk_box_pack_start_defaults (GTK_BOX (vbox), viewport);
gtk_box_pack_start_defaults (GTK_BOX (vbox), swin);

gtk_container_add (GTK_CONTAINER (window), vbox);
gtk_widget_show_all (window);

gtk_main ();
return 0;
}
```

New scrolled windows are created with gtk_scrolled_window_new(). In Listing 7-1, each parameter is set to NULL, which will cause the scrolled window to create two default adjustments for you. In most cases, you will want to use the default adjustments, but it is also possible to specify your own horizontal and vertical adjustments for the scroll bars.

The adjustments are used in this example when the new viewport is created with gtk_viewport_new(). The viewport adjustments are initialized with those from the scrolled window, which makes sure that both containers will be scrolled at the same time.

The first decision you need to make when setting up a scrolled window is when the scrollbars will be visible. In this example, GTK_POLICY_AUTOMATIC was used for both scrollbars so that each will only be shown when needed. GTK_POLICY_ALWAYS is the default policy for both scrollbars. The three enumeration values provided by GtkPolicyType follow:

- GTK_POLICY_ALWAYS: The scrollbar will always be visible. It will be displayed as disabled or grayed out if scrolling is not possible.

- GTK_POLICY_AUTOMATIC: The scrollbar will only be visible if scrolling is possible. If it is not needed, the scrollbar will temporarily disappear.

- GTK_POLICY_NEVER: The scrollbar will never be shown.

Another property, although not used by very many applications, is the placement of the scrollbars. In most applications, you will want the scrollbars to appear along the bottom and the right side of the widget, which is the default functionality.

However, if you want to change this, you can call `gtk_scrolled_window_set_placement()`. This function receives a `GtkCornerType` value, which defines where the content is placed with respect to the scrollbars. For example, the default value is `GTK_CORNER_TOP_LEFT`, because the content normally appears above and to the left of the scrollbars.

```
void gtk_scrolled_window_set_placement (GtkScrolledWindow *swin
                                        GtkCornerType window_placement);
```

Available `GtkCornerType` values include `GTK_CORNER_TOP_LEFT`, `GTK_CORNER_BOTTOM_LEFT`, `GTK_CORNER_TOP_RIGHT`, and `GTK_CORNER_BOTTOM_RIGHT`, which define where the content is placed with respect to the scrollbars.

■**Caution** It is a very rare occasion when `gtk_scrolled_window_set_placement()` should be used! In almost every possible case, you should not use this function, because it can confuse the user. Unless you have a good reason for changing the placement, use the default value.

It is possible to set the shadow type of the widget with respect to the child widget by calling `gtk_scrolled_window_set_shadow_type()`.

```
void gtk_scrolled_window_set_shadow_type (GtkScrolledWindow *swin,
                                          GtkShadowType type);
```

In Chapter 3, you learned how to use the `GtkShadowType` enumeration along with handle boxes to set the type of border to place around the child widget. The same values as before are used to set the shadow type of a scrolled window.

After you have set up a scrolled window, you should add a child widget for it to be of any use. There are two possible ways to do this, and the method is chosen based on the type of child widget. If you are using a `GtkTextView`, `GtkTreeView`, `GtkIconView`, `GtkViewport`, or `GtkLayout` widget, you should use the default `gtk_container_add()` function, since all five of these widgets include native scrolling support.

All other GTK+ widgets do not have native scrolling support. For those widgets, `gtk_scrolled_window_add_with_viewport()` should be used. This function will give the child scrolling support by first packing it into a container widget called a `GtkViewport`. This widget implements scrolling ability for the child widget that lacks its own support. The viewport is then automatically added to the scrolled window.

■**Caution** You should never pack `GtkTextView`, `GtkTreeView`, `GtkIconView`, `GtkViewport`, or `GtkLayout` widgets into a scrolled window with `gtk_scrolled_window_add_with_viewport()`, because scrolling may not be performed correctly on the widget!

It is possible to manually add a widget to a new GtkViewport and then add that viewport to a scrolled window with gtk_container_add(), but the convenience function allows you to ignore the viewport completely.

The scrolled window is simply a container with scrollbars. Neither the container nor the scrollbars perform any action by themselves. Scrolling is handled by the child widget, which is why the child must already have native scrolling support to work correctly with the GtkScrolledWindow widget.

When you add a child widget that has scrolling support, a function is called to add adjustments for each axis. Nothing will be done unless the child widget has scrolling support, which is why a viewport is required by most widgets. When the scrollbar is clicked and dragged by the user, the value in the adjustment changes, which causes the value-changed signal to be emitted. This action will also cause the child widget to render itself accordingly.

Because the GtkViewport widget did not have any scrollbars of its own, it relied completely on the adjustments to define its current position on the screen. The scrollbars are used in the GtkScrolledWindow widget as an easy mechanism for adjusting the current value of the adjustment.

Text Views

The GtkTextView widget is used to display multiple lines of text of a document. It provides many ways to customize the whole of a document or individual portions of it. It is even possible to insert GdkPixbuf objects and child widgets into a document. GtkTextView is the first reasonably involved widget you have encountered up to this point, so the rest of this chapter is dedicated to many aspects of the widget. It is a very versatile widget that you will need to use in many GTK+ applications.

The first few examples of this chapter may lead you to believe that GtkTextView can only be used to display simple documents, but that is not the case. It can also be used to display many types of rich text, word-processing, and interactive documents that are used by a wide variety of applications. You will learn how to do this in the sections that follow.

Figure 7-2 shows a simple GtkTextView widget contained by a GtkScrolledWindow widget.

Figure 7-2. *A GtkTextView widget*

Text views are used in every type of text and document editing application that uses GTK+. If you have ever used AbiWord, Gedit, or most other text editors created for GNOME, you have used the GtkTextView widget. It is also used in the Gaim application in instant message windows. (In fact, all of the examples in this book were created in the OpenLDev application, which uses GtkTextView for source code editing!)

Text Buffers

Each text view is used to display the contents of a class called `GtkTextBuffer`. Text buffers are used to store the current state of the content within a text view. They hold text, images, child widgets, text tags, and all other information necessary for rendering the document.

A single text buffer is capable of being displayed by multiple text views, but each text view has only one associated buffer. Most programmers do not take advantage of this feature, but it will become important when you learn how to embed child widgets into a text buffer in a later section.

As with all text widgets in GTK+, text is stored as UTF-8 strings. UTF-8 is a type of character encoding that uses from 1 byte to 4 bytes for every character. In order to differentiate how many bytes a character will take up, "0" always precedes a character that is 1 byte, "110" precedes 2-byte characters, "1110" comes before 3-byte sequences, and so on. UTF-8 characters that span multiple bytes have "10" in the two most significant bits of the rest of the bytes.

By doing this, the basic 128 ASCII characters are still supported, because an additional 7 bits are available in a single-byte character after the initial "0". UTF-8 also provides support for characters in many other languages. This method also avoids small byte sequences occurring within larger byte sequences.

When handling text buffers, you need to know two terms: offset and index. The word "offset" refers to one character. UTF-8 characters may span one or more bytes within the buffer, so a character offset in a `GtkTextBuffer` may not be a single byte long.

Caution The word "index" refers to an individual byte. You need to be careful when stepping through a text buffer in later examples, because you cannot refer to an index that is between two character offsets.

Listing 7-2 illustrates one of the simplest text view examples you could create. A new `GtkTextView` widget is created. Its buffer is retrieved, and text is inserted into the buffer. A scrolled window is then used to contain the text view.

Listing 7-2. *A Simple GtkTextView Example (textview.c)*

```
#include <gtk/gtk.h>

int main (int argc,
          char *argv[])
{
  GtkWidget *window, *scrolled_win, *textview;
  GtkTextBuffer *buffer;

  gtk_init (&argc, &argv);

  window = gtk_window_new (GTK_WINDOW_TOPLEVEL);
  gtk_window_set_title (GTK_WINDOW (window), "Text Views");
  gtk_container_set_border_width (GTK_CONTAINER (window), 10);
  gtk_widget_set_size_request (window, 250, 150);
```

```
textview = gtk_text_view_new ();
buffer = gtk_text_view_get_buffer (GTK_TEXT_VIEW (textview));
gtk_text_buffer_set_text (buffer, "Your 1st GtkTextView widget!", -1);

scrolled_win = gtk_scrolled_window_new (NULL, NULL);
gtk_container_add (GTK_CONTAINER (scrolled_win), textview);
gtk_container_add (GTK_CONTAINER (window), scrolled_win);
gtk_widget_show_all (window);

gtk_main();
return 0;
}
```

Most new GtkTextView widgets are created with gtk_text_view_new(). By using this function, an empty buffer will be created for you. This default buffer can be replaced at a later time with gtk_text_view_set_buffer() or retrieved with gtk_text_view_get_buffer().

If you want to set the initial buffer to one that you have already created, you can create the text view with gtk_text_view_new_with_buffer(). In most cases, it will be easier to simply use the default text buffer.

Once you have access to a GtkTextBuffer object, there are many ways to add content, but the easiest method is to call gtk_text_buffer_set_text(). This function receives a text buffer, a UTF-8 text string to set as the buffer's new text, and the length of the text.

```
void gtk_text_buffer_set_text (GtkTextBuffer *buffer,
                               const gchar *text,
                               gint length);
```

If the text string is NULL-terminated, you can use -1 as the length of the string. This function will silently fail if a null character is found before the specified length of text.

The current contents of the buffer will be completely replaced by the new text string. In the "Text Iterators and Marks" section, you will be introduced to functions that allow you to insert text into a buffer without overwriting the current content that are more suitable for inserting large amounts of text.

Recall from the previous section that there are five widgets that have native scrolling abilities, including the GtkTextView widget. Because text views already have the facilities to manage adjustments, gtk_container_add() should always be used to add them to scrolled windows.

Text View Properties

GtkTextView was created to be a very versatile widget. Because of this, many properties are provided for the widget. In this section, you will learn about a number of these widget properties.

One feature that makes the text view widget extremely useful is that you are able to apply changes to the whole or only an individual part of the widget. Text tags are used to change the properties of a segment of text. Customizing only a part of the document will be covered in a later section of this chapter.

Listing 7-3 shows many of the properties that can be used to customize the whole content of a GtkTextBuffer. You should note that many of these properties could be overridden in individual sections of a document with text tags.

Listing 7-3. *Using GtkTextView Properties (textview2.c)*

```
#include <gtk/gtk.h>

int main (int argc,
          char *argv[])
{
  GtkWidget *window, *scrolled_win, *textview;
  GtkTextBuffer *buffer;
  PangoFontDescription *font;

  gtk_init (&argc, &argv);

  window = gtk_window_new (GTK_WINDOW_TOPLEVEL);
  gtk_window_set_title (GTK_WINDOW (window), "Text Views Properties");
  gtk_container_set_border_width (GTK_CONTAINER (window), 10);
  gtk_widget_set_size_request (window, 250, 150);

  font = pango_font_description_from_string ("Monospace Bold 10");
  textview = gtk_text_view_new ();
  gtk_widget_modify_font (textview, font);

  gtk_text_view_set_wrap_mode (GTK_TEXT_VIEW (textview), GTK_WRAP_WORD);
  gtk_text_view_set_justification (GTK_TEXT_VIEW (textview), GTK_JUSTIFY_RIGHT);

  gtk_text_view_set_editable (GTK_TEXT_VIEW (textview), TRUE);
  gtk_text_view_set_cursor_visible (GTK_TEXT_VIEW (textview), TRUE);

  gtk_text_view_set_pixels_above_lines (GTK_TEXT_VIEW (textview), 5);
  gtk_text_view_set_pixels_below_lines (GTK_TEXT_VIEW (textview), 5);
  gtk_text_view_set_pixels_inside_wrap (GTK_TEXT_VIEW (textview), 5);

  gtk_text_view_set_left_margin (GTK_TEXT_VIEW (textview), 10);
  gtk_text_view_set_right_margin (GTK_TEXT_VIEW (textview), 10);

  buffer = gtk_text_view_get_buffer (GTK_TEXT_VIEW (textview));
  gtk_text_buffer_set_text (buffer, "This is some text!\nChange me!\nPlease!", -1);

  scrolled_win = gtk_scrolled_window_new (NULL, NULL);
  gtk_scrolled_window_set_policy (GTK_SCROLLED_WINDOW (scrolled_win),
                                  GTK_POLICY_AUTOMATIC, GTK_POLICY_ALWAYS);
```

```
gtk_container_add (GTK_CONTAINER (scrolled_win), textview);
gtk_container_add (GTK_CONTAINER (window), scrolled_win);
gtk_widget_show_all (window);

gtk_main();
return 0;
}
```

The best way to explain what each of GtkTextView's properties does is to show you a screenshot of the result, which can be viewed in Figure 7-3. You should compile the application on your own machine and try changing the values used in Listing 7-3 to get a feel for what they do as well.

Figure 7-3. *GtkTextView with nondefault properties*

It is possible to change the font and colors of individual parts of the text view content, but as shown in Listing 7-3, it is still possible to use the functions from past chapters to change the content of the whole widget. This is useful when editing documents that have a consistent style, such as text files.

When dealing with a widget that displays text on multiple lines, you need to decide if and how text will be wrapped. In Listing 7-3, the wrap mode was set to GTK_WRAP_WORD with gtk_text_view_set_wrap_mode(). This setting wraps the text but does not split a word over two lines. There are four types of wrap modes available in the GtkWrapMode enumeration:

- GTK_WRAP_NONE: No wrapping will occur. If a scrolled window contains the view, the scrollbar will expand. Otherwise, the text view will expand on the screen. If a scrolled window does not contain the GtkTextView widget, it will expand the widget horizontally.

- GTK_WRAP_CHAR: Wrap to the character, even if the wrap point occurs in the middle of a word. This is usually not a good choice for a text editor, since it will split words over two lines.

- GTK_WRAP_WORD: Fill up the line with the largest number of words possible but do not break a word to wrap. Instead, bring the whole word onto the next line.

- GTK_WRAP_WORD_CHAR: Wrap in the same way as GTK_WRAP_WORD, but if a whole word takes up more than one visible width of the text view, wrap it by the character.

At times, you may want to prevent the user from editing the document. The `editable` property can be changed for the whole text view with `gtk_text_view_set_editable()`. It is worth noting that with text tags, you can override this for certain sections of the document, so this is not always an end-all solution.

Contrast this with `gtk_widget_set_sensitive()`, which is used to prevent the user from interacting with the widget at all. If a text view is set as not editable, the user will still be able to perform operations on the text that do not require the text buffer to be edited, such as selecting text. Setting a text view as insensitive will prevent the user from performing any of these actions.

When you disable editing within a document, it is also useful to stop the cursor from being visible with `gtk_text_view_set_cursor_visible()`. By default, both of these properties are set to `TRUE`, so both will need to be changed to keep them in sync.

By default, there is no extra spacing placed between lines, but Listing 7-3 shows you how to add spacing above a line, below a line, and between wrapped lines. These functions add *extra* space between lines, so you can assume that there will already be enough spacing between lines. In most cases, you should not use this feature, because spacing may not look correct to the user.

Justification is another important property of text views, especially when dealing with rich text documents. There are four default justification values: `GTK_JUSTIFY_LEFT`, `GTK_JUSTIFY_RIGHT`, `GTK_JUSTIFY_CENTER`, and `GTK_JUSTIFY_FILL`.

Justification can be set for the whole text view with `gtk_text_view_set_justification()`, but it can be overridden for specific sections of text with text tags. In most cases, you will want to use the default `GTK_JUSTIFY_LEFT` justification unless the user wants it to be changed. Text is aligned to the left of the view by default.

```
void gtk_text_view_set_justification (GtkTextView *textview,
                                      GtkJustification justification);
```

The last properties set by Listing 7-3 were the left and right margins. By default, there is no extra margin space added to either the left or right side, but you can add a certain number of pixels to the left with `gtk_text_view_set_left_margin()` or to the right with `gtk_text_view_set_right_margin()`.

Pango Tab Arrays

Tabs added to a text view are set to a default width, but there are times when you will want to change that. For example, in a source code editor, one user may want to indent two spaces while another may want to indent five spaces. GTK+ provides the `PangoTabArray` object, which defines a new tab size.

When changing the default tab size, you first calculate the number of horizontal pixels the tab will take up based on the current font. The following `make_tab_array()` function can be used to calculate a new tab size. The function begins by creating a string out of the desired number of spaces. That string is then translated into a `PangoLayout` object, which is used to retrieve the pixel width of the displayed string. Lastly, the `PangoLayout` is translated into a `PangoTabArray`, which can be applied to a text view.

```
static void
make_tab_array (PangoFontDescription *fd,
                gsize tab_size,
                GtkWidget *textview)
{
  PangoTabArray *tab_array;
  PangoLayout *layout;
  gchar *tab_string;
  gint width, height;

  g_return_if_fail (tab_size < 100);

  tab_string = g_strnfill (tab_size, ' ');
  layout = gtk_widget_create_pango_layout (textview, tab_string);
  pango_layout_set_font_description (layout, fd);
  pango_layout_get_pixel_size (layout, &width, &height);

  tab_array = pango_tab_array_new (1, TRUE);
  pango_tab_array_set_tab (tab_array, 0, PANGO_TAB_LEFT, width);
  gtk_text_view_set_tabs (GTK_TEXT_VIEW (textview), tab_array);

  g_free (tab_string);
}
```

The PangoLayout object is used to represent a whole paragraph of text. Normally, Pango uses it internally for laying out text within a widget. However, it can be employed by this example to calculate the width of the tab string.

We begin by creating a new PangoLayout object from the GtkTextView and creating the tab string with gtk_widget_create_pango_layout(). This uses the default font description of the text view. This is fine if the whole document will have the same font applied to it. PangoLayout is used to describe how to render a paragraph of text.

```
PangoLayout* gtk_widget_create_pango_layout (GtkWidget *textview,
                                             const gchar *text);
```

If the font varies within the document or is not already applied to the text view, you will want to specify the font to use for the calculations. You can set the font of a Pango layout with pango_layout_set_font_description(). This uses a PangoFontDescription object to describe the layout's font.

```
void pango_layout_set_font_description (PangoLayout *layout,
                                        const PangoFontDescription *fd);
```

Once you have correctly configured your PangoLayout, the width of the string can be retrieved with pango_layout_get_pixel_size(). This is the calculated space that the string will take up within the buffer, which should be added when the user presses the Tab key within the widget.

```
void pango_layout_get_pixel_size (PangoLayout *layout,
                                  int *width,
                                  int *height);
```

Now that you have retrieved the width of the tab, you need to create a new PangoTabArray with pango_tab_array_new(). This function receives the number of elements that should be added to the array and notification of whether the size of each element is going to be specified in pixels.

```
void pango_tab_array_new (gint initial_size,
                          gboolean positions_in_pixels);
```

You should always create the tab array with only one element, because there is only one tab type supported at this time. If TRUE is not specified for the second parameter, tabs will be stored as Pango units; 1 pixel is equal to 1,024 Pango units.

Before applying the tab array, you need to add the width. This is done with pango_tab_array_set_tab(). The integer "0" refers to the first element in the PangoTabArray, the only one that should ever exist. PANGO_TAB_LEFT must always be specified for the third parameter, because it is currently the only supported value. The last parameter is the width of the tab in pixels.

```
void pango_tab_array_set_tab (PangoTabArray *tabarray,
                              gint tab_index,
                              PangoTabAlign alignment,
                              gint location);
```

When you receive the tab array back from the function, you need to apply it to the whole of the text view with gtk_text_view_set_tabs(). This will make sure that all tabs within the text view are set to the same width. However, as with all other text view properties, this value can be overridden for individual paragraphs or sections of text.

```
void gtk_text_view_set_tabs (GtkTextView *textview,
                             PangoTabArray *tabs);
```

When you are finished with the tab array, it can be freed with pango_tab_array_free() if it is no longer needed.

Text Iterators and Marks

When manipulating text within a GtkTextBuffer, there are two objects that can be used to keep track of a position within the buffer: GtkTextIter and GtkTextMark. Functions are provided by GTK+ to translate between these two types of objects.

Text iterators are used to represent a position between two characters in a buffer. They are utilized when manipulating text within a buffer. The problem presented by text iterators is that they automatically become invalidated when a text buffer is edited. Even if the same text is inserted and then removed from the buffer, the text iterator will still become invalidated, because iterators are meant to be allocated on the stack and used immediately.

For keeping track of a position throughout changes within a text buffer, the GtkTextMark object is provided. Text marks remain intact while buffers are manipulated and will move position based on how the buffer is manipulated. You can retrieve an iterator pointing to a text mark with gtk_text_buffer_get_iter_at_mark(), which makes marks ideal for tracking a position in the document.

```
void gtk_text_buffer_get_iter_at_mark (GtkTextBuffer *buffer,
                                       GtkTextIter *iter,
                                       GtkTextMark *mark);
```

Text marks act as though they are invisible cursors within the text, changing position depending on how the text is edited. If text is added before the mark, it will move to the right so that it will remain in the same textual position.

By default, text marks have a gravity set to the right. This means that it moves to the right as text is added. Let us assume that the text surrounding a mark is deleted. The mark will move to the position between the two pieces of text on either side of the deleted text. Then, if text is inserted at the text mark, because of its right gravity setting, it will remain on the right side of the inserted text. This is similar to the cursor, because as text is inserted, the cursor remains to the right of the inserted text.

■**Tip** By default, text marks are invisible within the text. However, you can set a text mark as visible by calling gtk_text_mark_set_visible(), which will place a vertical bar to indicate where it is located.

Text marks can be accessed in two ways. You can retrieve a text mark at a specific GtkTextIter location. It is also possible to set up a text mark with a string as its name, which makes marks easy to keep track of.

Two default text marks are always provided by GTK+ for every GtkTextBuffer: insert and selection_bound. The insert text mark refers to the current cursor position within the buffer. The selection_bound text mark refers to the boundary of selected text if there is any selected text. If no text is selected, these two marks will point to the same position.

The insert and selection_bound text marks are extremely useful when manipulating buffers. They can be manipulated to automatically select or deselect text within a buffer and help you figure out where text should logically be inserted within a buffer.

Editing the Text Buffer

GTK+ provides a wide array of functions for retrieving text iterators as well as manipulating text buffers. In this section, you will see a few of the most important of these methods in use in Listing 7-4 and then be introduced to many more. Figure 7-4 displays an application that will insert and retrieve the text with a GtkTextBuffer.

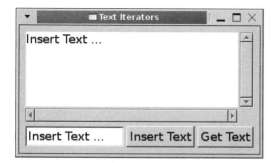

Figure 7-4. *Screenshot of an application using a GtkTextView widget*

Listing 7-4 is a simple example that performs two functions. When the Insert Text button shown in Figure 7-4 is clicked, the string shown in the GtkEntry widget is inserted at the current cursor position. When the Get Text button is clicked, any selected text is output with g_print().

Listing 7-4. *Using Text Iterators (iterators.c)*

```
#include <gtk/gtk.h>

typedef struct
{
  GtkWidget *entry, *textview;
} Widgets;

static void insert_text (GtkButton*, Widgets*);
static void retrieve_text (GtkButton*, Widgets*);

int main (int argc,
          char *argv[])
{
  GtkWidget *window, *scrolled_win, *hbox, *vbox, *insert, *retrieve;
  Widgets *w = g_slice_new (Widgets);

  gtk_init (&argc, &argv);

  window = gtk_window_new (GTK_WINDOW_TOPLEVEL);
  gtk_window_set_title (GTK_WINDOW (window), "Text Iterators");
  gtk_container_set_border_width (GTK_CONTAINER (window), 10);
  gtk_widget_set_size_request (window, -1, 200);

  w->textview = gtk_text_view_new ();
  w->entry = gtk_entry_new ();
  insert = gtk_button_new_with_label ("Insert Text");
  retrieve = gtk_button_new_with_label ("Get Text");
```

```
  g_signal_connect (G_OBJECT (insert), "clicked",
                     G_CALLBACK (insert_text),
                     (gpointer) w);
  g_signal_connect (G_OBJECT (retrieve), "clicked",
                     G_CALLBACK (retrieve_text),
                     (gpointer) w);

  scrolled_win = gtk_scrolled_window_new (NULL, NULL);
  gtk_container_add (GTK_CONTAINER (scrolled_win), w->textview);

  hbox = gtk_hbox_new (FALSE, 5);
  gtk_box_pack_start_defaults (GTK_BOX (hbox), w->entry);
  gtk_box_pack_start_defaults (GTK_BOX (hbox), insert);
  gtk_box_pack_start_defaults (GTK_BOX (hbox), retrieve);

  vbox = gtk_vbox_new (FALSE, 5);
  gtk_box_pack_start (GTK_BOX (vbox), scrolled_win, TRUE, TRUE, 0);
  gtk_box_pack_start (GTK_BOX (vbox), hbox, FALSE, TRUE, 0);

  gtk_container_add (GTK_CONTAINER (window), vbox);
  gtk_widget_show_all (window);

  gtk_main();
  return 0;
}

/* Insert the text from the GtkEntry into the GtkTextView. */
static void
insert_text (GtkButton *button,
             Widgets *w)
{
  GtkTextBuffer *buffer;
  GtkTextMark *mark;
  GtkTextIter iter;
  const gchar *text;

  buffer = gtk_text_view_get_buffer (GTK_TEXT_VIEW (w->textview));
  text = gtk_entry_get_text (GTK_ENTRY (w->entry));

  mark = gtk_text_buffer_get_insert (buffer);
  gtk_text_buffer_get_iter_at_mark (buffer, &iter, mark);
  gtk_text_buffer_insert (buffer, &iter, text, -1);
}
```

```
/* Retrieve the selected text from the GtkTextView and display it
 * to the user. */
static void
retrieve_text (GtkButton *button,
               Widgets *w)
{
  GtkTextBuffer *buffer;
  GtkTextIter start, end;
  gchar *text;

  buffer = gtk_text_view_get_buffer (GTK_TEXT_VIEW (w->textview));
  gtk_text_buffer_get_selection_bounds (buffer, &start, &end);
  text = gtk_text_buffer_get_text (buffer, &start, &end, FALSE);

  g_print ("%s\n", text);
}
```

You should notice from Listing 7-4 that, unlike most objects in GTK+, text iterators are stored as nonpointer objects. This means that they are allocated directly on the stack. Pointers to the iterators are then passed to functions using the address operator.

Another important property of iterators is that the same iterator can be used over and over, because iterators become invalidated every time you edit a text buffer. In this way, you can continue to reuse the same GtkTextIter object instead of creating a huge number of variables.

Retrieving Text Iterators and Marks

As stated before, there are quite a number of functions available for retrieving text iterators and text marks, many of which will be used throughout this chapter.

Listing 7-4 begins by retrieving the insert mark with gtk_text_buffer_get_insert(). It is also possible to use gtk_text_buffer_get_selection_bound() to retrieve the selection_bound text mark.

```
mark = gtk_text_buffer_get_insert (buffer);
gtk_text_buffer_get_iter_at_mark (buffer, &iter, mark);
```

Once you have retrieved a mark, you can translate it into a text iterator with gtk_text_buffer_get_iter_at_mark(), so that it can be used to manipulate the buffer.

The other function presented by Listing 7-4 for retrieving text iterators is gtk_text_buffer_get_selection_bounds(), which returns the iterators located at the insert and selection_bound marks. You can set one or both of the text iterator parameters to NULL, which will prevent the value from returning, although it would make more sense to use the functions for the specific mark if you only need one or the other.

When retrieving the contents of a buffer, you will need to specify a start and end iterator for the slice of text. If you want to get the whole contents of the document, you will need iterators pointing to the beginning and end of the document, which can be retrieved with gtk_text_buffer_get_bounds().

```
void gtk_text_buffer_get_bounds (GtkTextBuffer *buffer,
                                 GtkTextIter *start,
                                 GtkTextIter *end);
```

It is also possible to retrieve only the beginning or end iterator for the text buffer independently of the other with gtk_text_buffer_get_start_iter() or gtk_text_buffer_get_end_iter().

Text within a buffer can be retrieved with gtk_text_buffer_get_text(). It returns all of the text between the start and end iterators. If the last parameter is set to TRUE, then invisible text will also be returned.

```
gchar* gtk_text_buffer_get_text (GtkTextBuffer *buffer,
                                 const GtkTextIter *start,
                                 const GtkTextIter *end,
                                 gboolean include_hidden_chars);
```

■**Caution** You should only use gtk_text_buffer_get_text() for retrieving the whole contents of a buffer. It ignores any image or widget objects embedded in the text buffer, so character indexes may not correspond to the correct location. For retrieving individual parts of a text buffer, use gtk_text_buffer_get_slice() instead.

Recall that the offset refers to the number of individual characters within the buffer. These characters can be one or more bytes long. The gtk_text_buffer_get_iter_at_offset() function allows you to retrieve the iterator at the location of a specific offset from the beginning of the buffer.

```
void gtk_text_buffer_get_iter_at_offset (GtkTextBuffer *buffer,
                                         GtkTextIter *iter,
                                         gint character_offset);
```

GTK+ also provides gtk_text_buffer_get_iter_at_line_index(), which will choose a position of an individual byte on the specified line. You should be extremely careful when using this function, because the index must always point to the beginning of a UTF-8 character. Remember that characters in UTF-8 may not be only a single byte!

Rather than choosing a character offset, you can retrieve the first iterator on a specified line with gtk_text_buffer_get_iter_at_line().

```
void gtk_text_buffer_get_iter_at_line (GtkTextBuffer *buffer,
                                       GtkTextIter *iter,
                                       gint character_offset);
```

If you want to retrieve the iterator at an offset from the first character of a specific line, gtk_text_buffer_get_iter_at_line_offset() will do the trick.

Changing Text Buffer Contents

You have already learned how to reset the contents of a whole text buffer, but it is also useful to edit only a portion of a document. There are a number of functions provided for this purpose. Listing 7-4 shows you how to insert text into a buffer.

If you need to insert text in an arbitrary position of the buffer, you should use gtk_text_buffer_insert(). To do this, you will need a GtkTextIter pointing to the insertion point, the text string to insert into the buffer that must be UTF-8, and the length of the text. If the text string is NULL-terminated, you can specify -1 as its length.

```
GtkTextMark* gtk_text_buffer_get_insert (GtkTextBuffer *buffer);
```

When this function is called, the text buffer will emit the insert-text signal, and the text iterator will be invalidated. However, the text iterator will then be reinitialized to the end of the inserted text.

A convenience function named gtk_text_buffer_insert_at_cursor() can be used to call gtk_text_buffer_insert() at the cursor's current position. This can easily be implemented by using the insert text mark, but it helps you avoid repetitive calls.

```
void gtk_text_buffer_insert_at_cursor (GtkTextBuffer *buffer,
                                       const gchar *text,
                                       gint length);
```

You can delete the text between two text iterators with gtk_text_buffer_delete(). The order in which you specify the iterators is irrelevant, because the function will automatically place them in the correct order.

```
void gtk_text_buffer_delete (GtkTextBuffer *buffer,
                             GtkTextIter *start,
                             GtkTextIter *end);
```

This function will emit the delete-range signal, and both iterators will be invalidated. However, the start and end iterators will both be reinitialized to the start location of the deleted text.

Cutting, Copying, and Pasting Text

When you right-click a GtkTextView widget, you are presented with a pop-up menu containing multiple options. An example of this menu is shown in Figure 7-5, although the content may vary depending on your system.

Figure 7-5. *A GtkTextView menu displayed on a right-click*

Three of these options are cut, copy, and paste, which are standard to almost all text editors. They are built into every GtkTextView widget. However, there are times that you will want to implement your own versions of these functions to include in an application menu or toolbar.

Listing 7-5 gives an example of each of these methods. When one of the three GtkButton widgets is clicked, some action is initialized. Try using the buttons and the right-click menu to show that both use the same GtkClipboard object. These functions can also be called by using the built-in keyboard accelerators, which are Ctrl+C, Ctrl+X, and Ctrl+V.

Listing 7-5. *Using the Cut, Copy, and Paste Operations (cutcopypaste.c)*

```
#include <gtk/gtk.h>

static void cut_clicked (GtkButton*, GtkTextView*);
static void copy_clicked (GtkButton*, GtkTextView*);
static void paste_clicked (GtkButton*, GtkTextView*);

int main (int argc,
          char *argv[])
```

```c
{
  GtkWidget *window, *scrolled_win, *textview, *cut, *copy, *paste, *hbox, *vbox;

  gtk_init (&argc, &argv);

  window = gtk_window_new (GTK_WINDOW_TOPLEVEL);
  gtk_window_set_title (GTK_WINDOW (window), "Cut, Copy & Paste");
  gtk_container_set_border_width (GTK_CONTAINER (window), 10);

  textview = gtk_text_view_new ();

  cut = gtk_button_new_from_stock (GTK_STOCK_CUT);
  copy = gtk_button_new_from_stock (GTK_STOCK_COPY);
  paste = gtk_button_new_from_stock (GTK_STOCK_PASTE);

  g_signal_connect (G_OBJECT (cut), "clicked",
                    G_CALLBACK (cut_clicked),
                    (gpointer) textview);
  g_signal_connect (G_OBJECT (copy), "clicked",
                    G_CALLBACK (copy_clicked),
                    (gpointer) textview);
  g_signal_connect (G_OBJECT (paste), "clicked",
                    G_CALLBACK (paste_clicked),
                    (gpointer) textview);

  scrolled_win = gtk_scrolled_window_new (NULL, NULL);
  gtk_widget_set_size_request (scrolled_win, 300, 200);
  gtk_container_add (GTK_CONTAINER (scrolled_win), textview);

  hbox = gtk_hbox_new (TRUE, 5);
  gtk_box_pack_start (GTK_BOX (hbox), cut, TRUE, TRUE, 0);
  gtk_box_pack_start (GTK_BOX (hbox), copy, TRUE, TRUE, 0);
  gtk_box_pack_start (GTK_BOX (hbox), paste, TRUE, TRUE, 0);

  vbox = gtk_vbox_new (FALSE, 5);
  gtk_box_pack_start (GTK_BOX (vbox), scrolled_win, TRUE, TRUE, 0);
  gtk_box_pack_start (GTK_BOX (vbox), hbox, FALSE, TRUE, 0);

  gtk_container_add (GTK_CONTAINER (window), vbox);
  gtk_widget_show_all (window);

  gtk_main();
  return 0;
}
```

```
/* Copy the selected text to the clipboard and remove it from the buffer. */
static void
cut_clicked (GtkButton *cut,
             GtkTextView *textview)
{
  GtkClipboard *clipboard = gtk_clipboard_get (GDK_SELECTION_CLIPBOARD);
  GtkTextBuffer *buffer = gtk_text_view_get_buffer (textview);

  gtk_text_buffer_cut_clipboard (buffer, clipboard, TRUE);
}

/* Copy the selected text to the clipboard. */
static void
copy_clicked (GtkButton *copy,
              GtkTextView *textview)
{
  GtkClipboard *clipboard = gtk_clipboard_get (GDK_SELECTION_CLIPBOARD);
  GtkTextBuffer *buffer = gtk_text_view_get_buffer (textview);

  gtk_text_buffer_copy_clipboard (buffer, clipboard);
}

/* Insert the text from the clipboard into the text buffer. */
static void
paste_clicked (GtkButton *paste,
               GtkTextView *textview)
{
  GtkClipboard *clipboard = gtk_clipboard_get (GDK_SELECTION_CLIPBOARD);
  GtkTextBuffer *buffer = gtk_text_view_get_buffer (textview);

  gtk_text_buffer_paste_clipboard (buffer, clipboard, NULL, TRUE);
}
```

GtkClipboard is a central class where data can be transferred easily between applications. To retrieve a clipboard that has already been created, you should use gtk_clipboard_get(). Since a default clipboard is provided, this book will not teach you how to create your own clipboard object.

■Note While it is possible to create your own GtkClipboard objects, when performing basic tasks, you should use the default clipboard. You can retrieve it by passing GDK_SELECTION_CLIPBOARD to gtk_clipboard_get().

It is feasible to directly interact with the GtkClipboard object that you have created, adding and removing data from it. However, when performing simple tasks including copying and retrieving text strings for a GtkTextView widget, it makes more sense to use GtkTextBuffer's built-in functions.

The simplest of GtkTextBuffer's three clipboard actions is copying text, which can be done with the following:

```
void gtk_text_buffer_copy_clipboard (GtkTextBuffer *buffer,
                                     GtkClipboard *clipboard);
```

The second clipboard function, gtk_text_buffer_cut_clipboard() copies the selection to the clipboard as well as removing it from the buffer. If any of the selected text does not have the editable flag set, it will be set to the third parameter of this function. This function will copy not only text but also embedded objects such as images and text tags.

```
void gtk_text_buffer_cut_clipboard (GtkTextBuffer *buffer,
                                    GtkClipboard *clipboard,
                                    gboolean default_editable);
```

The last clipboard function, gtk_text_buffer_paste_clipboard() first retrieves the content of the clipboard. Next, the function will do one of two things. If the third parameter, which accepts a GtkTextIter, has been specified, the content will be inserted at the point of that iterator. If you specify NULL for the third parameter, the content will be inserted at the cursor.

```
void gtk_text_buffer_paste_clipboard (GtkTextBuffer *buffer,
                                      GtkClipboard *clipboard,
                                      GtkTextIter *override_location,
                                      gboolean default_editable);
```

If any of the content that is going to be pasted does not have the editable flag set, then it will be set automatically to default_editable. In most cases, you will want to set this parameter to TRUE, because it will allow the pasted content to be edited. You should also note that the paste operation is asynchronous.

Searching the Text Buffer

In most applications that use the GtkTextView widget, you will need to search through a text buffer in one or more instances. GTK+ provides two functions for finding text in a buffer: gtk_text_iter_forward_search() and gtk_text_iter_backward_search().

The following example shows you how to use the first of these functions to search for a text string in a GtkTextBuffer; a screenshot of the example is shown in Figure 7-6. The example begins when the user clicks the GTK_STOCK_FIND button.

Figure 7-6. *Screenshot of an application that searches a text buffer*

The application in Listing 7-6 searches for all instances of the specified string within the text buffer. A dialog is presented to the user, displaying how many times the string was found in the document.

Listing 7-6. *Using the GtkTextIter Find Function (find.c)*

```
#include <gtk/gtk.h>

typedef struct
{
  GtkWidget *entry, *textview;
} Widgets;

static void search (GtkButton*, Widgets*);

int main (int argc,
          char *argv[])
{
  GtkWidget *window, *scrolled_win, *vbox, *hbox, *find;
  Widgets *w = g_slice_new (Widgets);

  gtk_init (&argc, &argv);
```

```
    window = gtk_window_new (GTK_WINDOW_TOPLEVEL);
    gtk_window_set_title (GTK_WINDOW (window), "Searching Buffers");
    gtk_container_set_border_width (GTK_CONTAINER (window), 10);

    w->textview = gtk_text_view_new ();
    w->entry = gtk_entry_new ();
    gtk_entry_set_text (GTK_ENTRY (w->entry), "Search for ...");
    find = gtk_button_new_from_stock (GTK_STOCK_FIND);

    g_signal_connect (G_OBJECT (find), "clicked",
                      G_CALLBACK (search),
                      (gpointer) w);

    scrolled_win = gtk_scrolled_window_new (NULL, NULL);
    gtk_widget_set_size_request (scrolled_win, 250, 200);
    gtk_container_add (GTK_CONTAINER (scrolled_win), w->textview);

    hbox = gtk_hbox_new (FALSE, 5);
    gtk_box_pack_start (GTK_BOX (hbox), w->entry, TRUE, TRUE, 0);
    gtk_box_pack_start (GTK_BOX (hbox), find, FALSE, TRUE, 0);

    vbox = gtk_vbox_new (FALSE, 5);
    gtk_box_pack_start (GTK_BOX (vbox), scrolled_win, TRUE, TRUE, 0);
    gtk_box_pack_start (GTK_BOX (vbox), hbox, FALSE, TRUE, 0);

    gtk_container_add (GTK_CONTAINER (window), vbox);
    gtk_widget_show_all (window);

    gtk_main();
    return 0;
}


/* Search for the entered string within the GtkTextView. Then tell the user
 * how many times it was found. */
static void
search (GtkButton *button,
        Widgets *w)
{
    const gchar *find;
    gchar *output;
    GtkWidget *dialog;
    GtkTextBuffer *buffer;
    GtkTextIter start, begin, end;
    gboolean success;
    gint i = 0;
```

```
  find = gtk_entry_get_text (GTK_ENTRY (w->entry));
  buffer = gtk_text_view_get_buffer (GTK_TEXT_VIEW (w->textview));

  gtk_text_buffer_get_start_iter (buffer, &start);
  success = gtk_text_iter_forward_search (&start, (gchar*) find, 0,
                                          &begin, &end, NULL);

  while (success)
  {
    gtk_text_iter_forward_char (&start);
    success = gtk_text_iter_forward_search (&start, (gchar*) find, 0,
                                            &begin, &end, NULL);
    start = begin;
    i++;
  }

  output = g_strdup_printf ("The string '%s' was found %i times!", find, i);
  dialog = gtk_message_dialog_new (NULL, GTK_DIALOG_MODAL, GTK_MESSAGE_INFO,
                                   GTK_BUTTONS_OK, output, NULL);

  gtk_dialog_run (GTK_DIALOG (dialog));
  gtk_widget_destroy (dialog);
  g_free (output);
}
```

The first thing the search function needs to do is retrieve the lower search bound of the document with gtk_text_buffer_get_start_iter(). We do not need the bounding position of the buffer, because by leaving the search unbounded, it will automatically set the end of the document as the limit of the search.

Forward searching through a buffer is performed with gtk_text_iter_forward_search(), where TRUE is returned if the text is found. Otherwise, FALSE is returned by the function.

```
success = gtk_text_iter_forward_search (&start, find, 0, &begin, &end, NULL);
```

You must begin by specifying the start position iterator. Only text after that position will be searched. Next, you specify the text that is being searched for. The third parameter allows you to specify a GtkTextSearchFlags enumeration value if you want; the enumeration value is comprised of the following:

- GTK_TEXT_SEARCH_VISIBLE_ONLY: Do not search hidden elements within the buffer.

- GTK_TEXT_SEARCH_TEXT_ONLY: Ignore images, child widgets, or any other type of nontextual objects when searching.

If you do not specify the GTK_TEXT_SEARCH_TEXT_ONLY flag, you will need to use the special 0xFFFC character to represent child widgets and embedded pixbufs. Matches must be exact, so ignoring nontextual elements with a flag is usually a good idea. By default, all searching is case sensitive, although a flag may be introduced in the future that supports case-insensitive searches.

The next two iterators specify the start and end positions of the first match, if one is found. If you do not want to track the position of the match, you have the option to specify NULL for both iterators.

The last parameter allows you to specify a bounding iterator for the search. The function will only search up to the limit for matches. If your program must deal with large buffers, limiting searches is a good idea. Otherwise, you could risk locking up the screen until the search is complete. If you want to search until the end of the buffer, use NULL for the bounding iterator.

Searching with gtk_text_iter_backward_search() will work in the same way as gtk_text_iter_forward_search(), except limit must occur before start_pos. If you do not set a limiting iterator, the function will assume it is the start of the buffer. You should be careful when doing this, because searching the whole buffer repeatedly, or searching a large buffer, can take some time.

```
gboolean gtk_text_iter_backward_search (const GtkTextIter *start_pos,
                                        const gchar *text_string,
                                        GtkTextSearchFlags flags,
                                        GtkTextIter *match_start,
                                        GtkTextIter *match_end,
                                        const GtkTextIter *limit);
```

When searching in most applications, you will want to mark a match by selecting it. You can do this with gtk_text_buffer_select_range(). This function moves the insert and selection_bound marks at the same time to the locations of the two iterators.

```
void gtk_text_buffer_select_range (GtkTextBuffer *buffer,
                                   const GtkTextIter *ins,
                                   const GtkTextIter *sel_bound);
```

If you manually move the marks in two steps, you will cause commotion on the screen as the selected text is changed multiple times. This function avoids the confusion by forcing the selection to be recalculated only once.

Scrolling Text Buffers

GTK+ will not automatically scroll to search matches that you select. To do this, you need to first call gtk_text_buffer_create_mark() to create a temporary GtkTextMark at the location of the found text.

```
GtkTextMark* gtk_text_buffer_create_mark (GtkTextBuffer *buffer,
                                          const gchar *name,
                                          const GtkTextIter *location,
                                          gboolean left_gravity);
```

The second parameter of gtk_text_buffer_create_mark() allows you to specify a text string as a name for the mark. This name can be used to reference the mark at a later time without the actual mark object. The mark is created at the location of the specified text iterator. The last parameter will create a mark with left gravity if set to TRUE.

Then, use `gtk_text_view_scroll_mark_onscreen()` to scroll the buffer, so the mark is on the screen. After you are finished with the mark, you can remove it from the buffer with `gtk_text_buffer_delete_mark()`.

```
void gtk_text_view_scroll_mark_onscreen (GtkTextView *textview,
                                         GtkTextMark *mark);
```

The problem with `gtk_text_view_scroll_mark_onscreen()` is that it will only scroll the minimum distance to show the mark on the screen. For example, you may want the mark to be centered within the buffer. To specify alignment parameters for where the mark appears within the visible buffer, call `gtk_text_view_scroll_to_mark()`.

```
void gtk_text_view_scroll_to_mark (GtkTextView *textview,
                                   GtkTextMark *mark,
                                   gdouble margin,
                                   gboolean use_align,
                                   gdouble xalign,
                                   gdouble yalign);
```

You begin by placing a margin, which will reduce the scrollable area. The margin must be specified as a floating-point number, which will reduce the area by that factor. In most cases, you will want to use 0.0 as the margin so the area is not reduced at all.

If you specify `FALSE` for the `use_align` parameter, the function will scroll the minimal distance to get the mark onscreen. Otherwise, the function will use the two alignment parameters as guides, which allows you to specify horizontal and vertical alignment of the mark within the visible area.

An alignment of 0.0 refers to the left or top of the visible area, 1.0 refers to the right or bottom and 0.5 refers to the center. The function will scroll as far as possible, but it may not be able to scroll the mark to the specified position. For example, it is impossible to scroll the last line in a buffer to the top if the buffer is larger than one character tall.

There is another function, `gtk_text_view_scroll_to_iter()`, which behaves in the same manner as `gtk_text_view_scroll_to_mark()`. The only difference is that it receives a `GtkTextIter` instead of a `GtkTextMark` for the location, although in most cases, you should use text marks.

Text Tags

There are many functions provided for changing properties of all of the text within a `GtkTextBuffer`, which have been covered in previous sections. But, as previously mentioned, it is also possible to change the display properties of only an individual section of text with the `GtkTextTag` object.

Text tags allow you to create documents where the text style varies among different parts of the text, which is commonly called rich text editing. A screenshot of a `GtkTextView` that uses multiple text styles is shown in Figure 7-7.

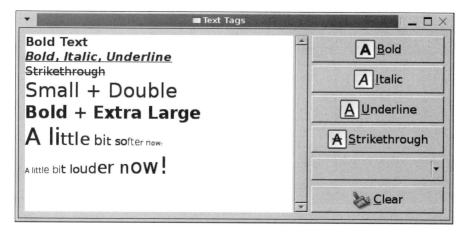

Figure 7-7. *Formatted text within a text buffer*

Text tags are actually a very simple concept to apply. In Listing 7-7, an application is created that allows the user to apply multiple styles or remove all of the tags from the selection. After reading the rest of this section, you might want to try out other text properties by altering Listing 7-7 to include different style options.

Listing 7-7. *Using Text Tags (texttags.c)*

```c
#include <gtk/gtk.h>

typedef struct
{
  gchar *str;
  double scale;
} text_to_double;

const text_to_double text_scales[] =
{
  { "Quarter Sized", (double) 0.25 },
  { "Double Extra Small", PANGO_SCALE_XX_SMALL},
  { "Extra Small", PANGO_SCALE_X_SMALL},
  { "Small", PANGO_SCALE_SMALL },
  { "Medium", PANGO_SCALE_MEDIUM },
  { "Large", PANGO_SCALE_LARGE},
  { "Extra Large", PANGO_SCALE_X_LARGE},
  { "Double Extra Large", PANGO_SCALE_XX_LARGE},
  { "Double Sized", (double) 2.0 },
  { NULL, 0 }
};
```

```
static void format (GtkWidget*, GtkTextView*);
static void scale_changed (GtkComboBox*, GtkTextView*);
static void clear_clicked (GtkButton*, GtkTextView*);

int main (int argc,
          char *argv[])
{
  GtkWidget *window, *scrolled_win, *textview, *hbox, *vbox;
  GtkWidget *bold, *italic, *underline, *strike, *scale, *clear;
  GtkTextBuffer *buffer;
  gint i = 0;

  gtk_init (&argc, &argv);

  window = gtk_window_new (GTK_WINDOW_TOPLEVEL);
  gtk_window_set_title (GTK_WINDOW (window), "Text Tags");
  gtk_container_set_border_width (GTK_CONTAINER (window), 10);
  gtk_widget_set_size_request (window, 500, -1);

  textview = gtk_text_view_new ();
  buffer = gtk_text_view_get_buffer (GTK_TEXT_VIEW (textview));

  gtk_text_buffer_create_tag (buffer, "bold", "weight", PANGO_WEIGHT_BOLD, NULL);
  gtk_text_buffer_create_tag (buffer, "italic", "style", PANGO_STYLE_ITALIC, NULL);
  gtk_text_buffer_create_tag (buffer, "strike", "strikethrough", TRUE, NULL);
  gtk_text_buffer_create_tag (buffer, "underline", "underline",
                              PANGO_UNDERLINE_SINGLE, NULL);

  bold = gtk_button_new_from_stock (GTK_STOCK_BOLD);
  italic = gtk_button_new_from_stock (GTK_STOCK_ITALIC);
  underline = gtk_button_new_from_stock (GTK_STOCK_UNDERLINE);
  strike = gtk_button_new_from_stock (GTK_STOCK_STRIKETHROUGH);
  clear = gtk_button_new_from_stock (GTK_STOCK_CLEAR);
  scale = gtk_combo_box_new_text();

  /* Add choices to the GtkComboBox widget. */
  for (i = 0; text_scales[i].str != NULL; i++)
  {
    gtk_combo_box_append_text (GTK_COMBO_BOX (scale), text_scales[i].str);
    gtk_text_buffer_create_tag (buffer, text_scales[i].str, "scale",
                                text_scales[i].scale, NULL );
  }
```

```
/* Add the name of the text tag as a data parameter of the object. */
g_object_set_data (G_OBJECT (bold), "tag", "bold");
g_object_set_data (G_OBJECT (italic), "tag", "italic");
g_object_set_data (G_OBJECT (underline), "tag", "underline");
g_object_set_data (G_OBJECT (strike), "tag", "strike");

/* Connect each of the buttons and the combo box to the necessary signals. */
g_signal_connect (G_OBJECT (bold), "clicked",
                  G_CALLBACK (format), (gpointer) textview);
g_signal_connect (G_OBJECT (italic), "clicked",
                  G_CALLBACK (format), (gpointer) textview);
g_signal_connect (G_OBJECT (underline), "clicked",
                  G_CALLBACK (format), (gpointer) textview);
g_signal_connect (G_OBJECT (strike), "clicked",
                  G_CALLBACK (format), (gpointer) textview);
g_signal_connect (G_OBJECT (scale), "changed",
                  G_CALLBACK (scale_changed),
                  (gpointer) textview);
g_signal_connect (G_OBJECT (clear), "clicked",
                  G_CALLBACK (clear_clicked),
                  (gpointer) textview);

/* Pack the widgets into a GtkVBox, GtkHBox, and then into the window. */
vbox = gtk_vbox_new (TRUE, 5);
gtk_box_pack_start (GTK_BOX (vbox), bold, FALSE, FALSE, 0);
gtk_box_pack_start (GTK_BOX (vbox), italic, FALSE, FALSE, 0);
gtk_box_pack_start (GTK_BOX (vbox), underline, FALSE, FALSE, 0);
gtk_box_pack_start (GTK_BOX (vbox), strike, FALSE, FALSE, 0);
gtk_box_pack_start (GTK_BOX (vbox), scale, FALSE, FALSE, 0);
gtk_box_pack_start (GTK_BOX (vbox), clear, FALSE, FALSE, 0);

scrolled_win = gtk_scrolled_window_new (NULL, NULL);
gtk_container_add (GTK_CONTAINER (scrolled_win), textview);
gtk_scrolled_window_set_policy (GTK_SCROLLED_WINDOW (scrolled_win),
                                GTK_POLICY_AUTOMATIC, GTK_POLICY_ALWAYS);

hbox = gtk_hbox_new (FALSE, 5);
gtk_box_pack_start (GTK_BOX (hbox), scrolled_win, TRUE, TRUE, 0);
gtk_box_pack_start (GTK_BOX (hbox), vbox, FALSE, TRUE, 0);

gtk_container_add (GTK_CONTAINER (window), hbox);
gtk_widget_show_all (window);
```

```
  gtk_main ();
  return 0;
}

/* Retrieve the tag from the "tag" object data and apply it to the selection. */
static void
format (GtkWidget *widget,
        GtkTextView *textview)
{
  GtkTextIter start, end;
  GtkTextBuffer *buffer;
  gchar *tagname;

  tagname = (gchar*) g_object_get_data (G_OBJECT (widget), "tag");
  buffer = gtk_text_view_get_buffer (textview);
  gtk_text_buffer_get_selection_bounds (buffer, &start, &end);
  gtk_text_buffer_apply_tag_by_name (buffer, tagname, &start, &end);
}

/* Apply the selected text size property as the tag. */
static void
scale_changed (GtkComboBox *combo,
               GtkTextView *textview)
{
  const gchar *text;

  if (gtk_combo_box_get_active (combo) == -1)
    return;

  text = gtk_combo_box_get_active_text (combo);
  g_object_set_data (G_OBJECT (combo), "tag", (gpointer) text);
  format (GTK_WIDGET (combo), textview);
  gtk_combo_box_set_active (combo, -1);
}

/* Remove all of the tags from the selected text. */
static void
clear_clicked (GtkButton *button,
               GtkTextView *textview)
{
  GtkTextIter start, end;
  GtkTextBuffer *buffer;
```

```
  buffer = gtk_text_view_get_buffer (textview);
  gtk_text_buffer_get_selection_bounds (buffer, &start, &end);
  gtk_text_buffer_remove_all_tags (buffer, &start, &end);
}
```

When you create a text tag, you normally have to add it to a GtkTextBuffer's tag table, an object that holds all of the tags available to a text buffer. You can create a new GtkTextTag object with gtk_text_tag_new() and then add it to the tag table. However, you can do this all in one step with gtk_text_buffer_create_tag().

```
GtkTextTag* gtk_text_buffer_create_tag (GtkTextBuffer *buffer,
                                        const gchar *tag_name,
                                        const gchar *first_property_name,
                                        ...);
```

The first two parameters of the function allow you to specify the text buffer to whose tag table the GtkTextTag will be added and a name to give the text tag. This name can be used to reference a tag for which you do not have the GtkTextTag object anymore. The next set of parameters is a NULL-terminated list of GtkTextTag style properties and their values.

For example, if you wanted to create a text tag that sets the background and foreground colors as black and white respectively, you could use the following function. This function returns the text tag that was created, although it will have already been added to the text buffer's tag table.

```
tag = gtk_text_buffer_create_tag (buffer, "colors", "background", "#000000",
                                  "foreground", "#FFFFFF", NULL);
```

There are a large number of style properties available in GTK+. A full list of GtkTextTag styles is shown in Appendix C. The table shows the name of each property, a short description of its use, and what type of value it accepts.

Once you have created a text tag and added it to a GtkTextBuffer's tag table, you can apply it to ranges of text. In Listing 7-7, the tag is applied to selected text when a button is clicked. If there is no selected text, the cursor position will be set to the style. All text typed at that position would have the tag applied as well.

Tags are generally applied to text with gtk_text_buffer_apply_tag_by_name(). The tag is applied to the text between the start and end iterators. If you still have access to the GtkTextTag object, you can also apply a tag with gtk_text_buffer_apply_tag().

```
void gtk_text_buffer_apply_tag_by_name (GtkTextBuffer *buffer,
                                        const gchar *tag_name,
                                        const GtkTextIter *start,
                                        const GtkTextIter *end);
```

Although not used in Listing 7-7, it is possible to remove a tag from an area of text with gtk_text_buffer_remove_tag_by_name(). This function will remove all instances of the tag between the two iterators if they exist.

```
void gtk_text_buffer_remove_tag_by_name (GtkTextBuffer *buffer,
                                         const gchar *name,
                                         const GtkTextIter *start,
                                         const GtkTextIter *end);
```

■**Note** These functions only remove tags from a certain range of text. If the tag was added to a larger range of text than the range specified, the tag will be removed for the smaller range, and new bounds will be created on either side of the selection. You can test this with the application in Listing 7-7.

If you have access to the GtkTextTag object, you can remove the tag with gtk_text_buffer_remove_tag(). It is also possible to remove every tag within a range with gtk_text_buffer_remove_all_tags().

Inserting Images

In some applications, you may want to insert images into a text buffer. This can easily be done with GdkPixbuf objects. In Figure 7-8, two images were inserted into a text buffer as GdkPixbuf objects.

Figure 7-8. *GdkPixbuf objects in a text buffer*

Adding a pixbuf to a GtkTextBuffer is performed in three steps. First, you must create the pixbuf object and retrieve the GtkTextIter where it will be inserted. Then, you can use gtk_text_buffer_insert_pixbuf() to add it to the buffer. Listing 7-8 shows the process of creating a GdkPixbuf object from a file and adding it to a text buffer.

Listing 7-8. *Inserting Images into Text Buffers (images.c)*

```c
#include <gtk/gtk.h>

#define IMAGE_UNDO "/path/to/undo.png"
#define IMAGE_REDO "/path/to/redo.png"

int main (int argc,
          char *argv[])
{
  GtkWidget *window, *scrolled_win, *textview;
  GdkPixbuf *undo, *redo;
  GtkTextIter line;
  GtkTextBuffer *buffer;

  gtk_init (&argc, &argv);

  window = gtk_window_new (GTK_WINDOW_TOPLEVEL);
  gtk_window_set_title (GTK_WINDOW (window), "Pixbufs");
  gtk_container_set_border_width (GTK_CONTAINER (window), 10);
  gtk_widget_set_size_request (window, 200, 150);

  textview = gtk_text_view_new ();
  buffer = gtk_text_view_get_buffer (GTK_TEXT_VIEW (textview));
  gtk_text_buffer_set_text (buffer, " Undo\n Redo", -1);

  /* Create two images and insert them into the text buffer. */
  undo = gdk_pixbuf_new_from_file (IMAGE_UNDO, NULL);
  gtk_text_buffer_get_iter_at_line (buffer, &line, 0);
  gtk_text_buffer_insert_pixbuf (buffer, &line, undo);

  redo = gdk_pixbuf_new_from_file (IMAGE_REDO, NULL);
  gtk_text_buffer_get_iter_at_line (buffer, &line, 1);
  gtk_text_buffer_insert_pixbuf (buffer, &line, redo);

  scrolled_win = gtk_scrolled_window_new (NULL, NULL);
  gtk_container_add (GTK_CONTAINER (scrolled_win), textview);
  gtk_container_add (GTK_CONTAINER (window), scrolled_win);
  gtk_widget_show_all (window);

  gtk_main();
  return 0;
}
```

Inserting a GdkPixbuf object into a text buffer is done with gtk_text_buffer_insert_pixbuf(). The GdkPixbuf object is inserted at the specified location, which can be any valid text iterator in the buffer.

```
void gtk_text_buffer_insert_pixbuf (GtkTextBuffer *buffer,
                                    GtkTextIter *iter,
                                    GdkPixbuf *pixbuf);
```

Pixbufs are handled differently by various functions. For example, gtk_text_buffer_get_slice() will place the 0xFFFC character where a pixbuf is located. However, the 0xFFFC character can occur as an actual character in the buffer, so that is not a reliable indicator of the location of a pixbuf.

Another example is gtk_text_buffer_get_text(), which will completely ignore nontextual elements, so there is no way to check for pixbufs within the text using this function.

Therefore, if you are using pixbufs in a GtkTextBuffer, it is best to retrieve text from the buffer with gtk_text_buffer_get_slice(). You can then use gtk_text_iter_get_pixbuf() to check whether the 0xFFFC character represents a GdkPixbuf object; it will return NULL if a pixbuf is not found at that location.

```
GdkPixbuf* gtk_text_iter_get_pixbuf (const GtktTextIter *iter);
```

Inserting Child Widgets

Inserting widgets into a text buffer is a little more complicated than pixbufs, because you must notify both the text buffer and the text view to embed the widget. You begin by creating a GtkTextChildAnchor object, which will be used to mark the placement of the widget within the GtkTextBuffer. Then, you add the widget to the GtkTextView widget.

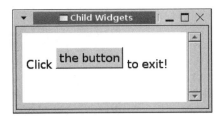

Figure 7-9. *A child widget inserted into a text buffer*

Figure 7-9 shows a GtkTextView widget that contains a child GtkButton widget. Listing 7-9 can be used to create this window. When the button is pressed, gtk_main_quit() is called, which terminates the application.

Listing 7-9. *Inserting Child Widgets into a Text Buffer (childwidgets.c)*

```
#include <gtk/gtk.h>

int main (int argc,
          char *argv[])
{
  GtkWidget *window, *scrolled_win, *textview, *button;
  GtkTextChildAnchor *anchor;
  GtkTextIter iter;
  GtkTextBuffer *buffer;

  gtk_init (&argc, &argv);

  window = gtk_window_new (GTK_WINDOW_TOPLEVEL);
  gtk_window_set_title (GTK_WINDOW (window), "Child Widgets");
  gtk_container_set_border_width (GTK_CONTAINER (window), 10);
  gtk_widget_set_size_request (window, 250, 100);

  textview = gtk_text_view_new ();
  buffer = gtk_text_view_get_buffer (GTK_TEXT_VIEW (textview));
  gtk_text_buffer_set_text (buffer, "\n Click  to exit!", -1);

  /* Create a new child widget anchor at the specified iterator. */
  gtk_text_buffer_get_iter_at_offset (buffer, &iter, 8);
  anchor = gtk_text_buffer_create_child_anchor (buffer, &iter);

  /* Insert a GtkButton widget at the child anchor. */
  button = gtk_button_new_with_label ("the button");
  gtk_text_view_add_child_at_anchor (GTK_TEXT_VIEW (textview), button, anchor);

  g_signal_connect_swapped (G_OBJECT (button), "clicked",
                            G_CALLBACK (gtk_widget_destroy),
                            (gpointer) window);

  scrolled_win = gtk_scrolled_window_new (NULL, NULL);
  gtk_container_add (GTK_CONTAINER (scrolled_win), textview);
  gtk_scrolled_window_set_policy (GTK_SCROLLED_WINDOW (scrolled_win),
                                  GTK_POLICY_AUTOMATIC, GTK_POLICY_ALWAYS);

  gtk_container_add (GTK_CONTAINER (window), scrolled_win);
  gtk_widget_show_all (window);

  gtk_main();
  return 0;
}
```

When creating a GtkTextChildAnchor, you need to initialize it and insert it into a GtkTextBuffer. You can do this by calling gtk_text_buffer_create_child_anchor().

```
GtkTextChildAnchor* gtk_text_buffer_create_child_anchor (GtkTextBuffer *buffer,
                                                         GtkTextIter *iter);
```

A child anchor is created at the location of the specified text iterator. This child anchor is simply a mark that tells GTK+ that a child widget can be added to that point within the text buffer.

Next, you need to use gtk_text_view_add_child_at_anchor() to add a child widget to the anchor point. As with GdkPixbuf objects, child widgets appear as the 0xFFFC character. This means that, if you see that character, you need to check whether it is a child widget or a pixbuf, because they will be indistinguishable otherwise.

```
void gtk_text_view_add_child_at_anchor (GtkTextView *textview,
                                        GtkWidget *child,
                                        GtkTextChildAnchor *anchor);
```

To check whether a child widget is at the location of an 0xFFFC character, you should call gtk_text_iter_get_child_anchor(), which will return NULL if a child anchor is not located at that position.

```
GtkTextChildAnchor* gtk_text_iter_get_child_anchor (const GtkTextIter *iter);
```

You can then retrieve a list of the widgets added at the anchor point with gtk_text_child_anchor_get_widgets(). You need to note that only one child widget can be added at a single anchor, so the returned list will usually contain only one element.

```
GList* gtk_text_child_anchor_get_widgets (GtkTextChildAnchor *anchor);
```

The exception is when you are using the same buffer for multiple text views. In this case, multiple widgets can be added to the same anchor in the text views, as long as no text view contains more than one widget. This is because of the fact that the child widget is attached to an anchor handled by the text view instead of the text buffer. When you are finished with the list of widgets, you need to free it with g_list_free().

GtkSourceView

GtkSourceView is a widget that is not actually a part of the GTK+ libraries. It is an external library used to extend the GtkTextView widget. If you have ever used GEdit, you will have experienced the GtkSourceView widget.

There is a large list of features that the GtkSourceView widget adds to text views. A few of the most notable ones follow:

- Line numbering

- Syntax highlighting for many programming and scripting languages

- Printing support for documents containing syntax highlighting

- Automatic indentation

- Bracket matching

- Undo/Redo support

- Source markers for denoting locations in source code

- Highlighting the current line

Figure 7-10 shows a screenshot of GEdit using the GtkSourceView widget. It has line numbering, syntax highlighting, bracket matching, and line highlighting turned on.

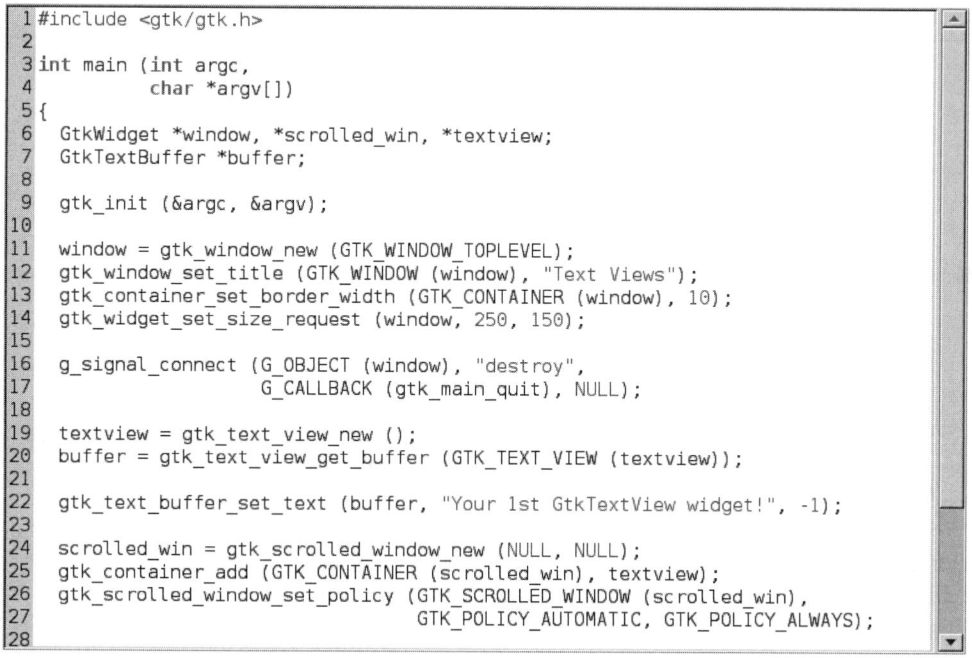

```
1 #include <gtk/gtk.h>
2
3 int main (int argc,
4          char *argv[])
5 {
6   GtkWidget *window, *scrolled_win, *textview;
7   GtkTextBuffer *buffer;
8
9   gtk_init (&argc, &argv);
10
11   window = gtk_window_new (GTK_WINDOW_TOPLEVEL);
12   gtk_window_set_title (GTK_WINDOW (window), "Text Views");
13   gtk_container_set_border_width (GTK_CONTAINER (window), 10);
14   gtk_widget_set_size_request (window, 250, 150);
15
16   g_signal_connect (G_OBJECT (window), "destroy",
17                     G_CALLBACK (gtk_main_quit), NULL);
18
19   textview = gtk_text_view_new ();
20   buffer = gtk_text_view_get_buffer (GTK_TEXT_VIEW (textview));
21
22   gtk_text_buffer_set_text (buffer, "Your 1st GtkTextView widget!", -1);
23
24   scrolled_win = gtk_scrolled_window_new (NULL, NULL);
25   gtk_container_add (GTK_CONTAINER (scrolled_win), textview);
26   gtk_scrolled_window_set_policy (GTK_SCROLLED_WINDOW (scrolled_win),
27                     GTK_POLICY_AUTOMATIC, GTK_POLICY_ALWAYS);
28
```

Figure 7-10. *Screenshot of a GtkSourceView widget*

The GtkSourceView library has a whole separate API documentation, which can be viewed at http://gtksourceview.sourceforge.net. If you need to compile an application that uses this library, you need to add `pkg-config --cflags --libs gtksourceview-1.0` to the compile command.

If you need syntax highlighting in a GTK+ application, the GtkSourceView library is one viable option, rather than creating your own widget from scratch.

Test Your Understanding

The following exercise instructs you to create a text editing application with basic functionality. It will give you practice on interacting with a GtkTextView widget.

Exercise 7-1. Text Editor

Use the GtkTextView widget to create a simple text editor. You should provide the ability to perform multiple text editing functions, including creating a new document, opening a file, saving a file, searching the document, cutting text, copying text, and pasting text.

When creating a new document, you should make sure the user actually wants to continue, because all changes will be lost. When the Save button is pressed, it should always ask where to save the file. Once you have finished this exercise, one possible solution is shown in Appendix F.

Hint: This is a much larger GTK+ application than any that has previously been created in this book, so you may want to take a few minutes to plan out your solution on paper before diving right into the code. Then, implement one function at a time, making sure it works before continuing on to the next feature. We will expand on this exercise in later chapters as well, so keep your solution handy!

This is the first instance of the Text Editor application that you will be creating throughout this book. In the last few chapters of this book, you will learn new elements that will help you create a fully featured text editor.

The application will first be expanded in Chapter 9; you will add a menu and toolbar. In Chapter 12, you will add printing support and the ability to remember past open files and searches.

You can view one possible solution to Exercise 7-1 in Appendix F. Much of the functionality of the text editor solution has been implemented by other examples in this chapter. Therefore, most of the solution should look familiar to you. The solution is also a bare minimum solution, and I encourage you to expand on the basic requirements of the exercise for more practice.

Summary

In this chapter, you learned all about the GtkTextView widget, which allows you to display multiple lines of text. Text views are usually contained by a special type of GtkBin container called GtkScrolledWindow that gives scrollbars to the child widget to implement scrolling abilities.

A GtkTextBuffer handles text within a view. Text buffers allow you to change many different properties of the whole or portions of the text using text tags. They also provide cut, copy, and paste functions.

You can move throughout a text buffer by using GtkTextIter objects, but text iterators become invalid once the text buffer is changed. Text iterators can be used to search forward or backward throughout a document. To keep a location over changes of a buffer, you need to use text marks. Text views are capable of displaying not only text but also images and child widgets. Child widgets are added at anchor points throughout a text buffer.

The last section of the chapter briefly introduced the GtkSourceView widget, which extends the functionality of the GtkTextView widget. It can be used when you need features such as syntax highlighting and line numbering.

In Chapter 8, you will be introduced to two new widgets: combo boxes and tree views. Combo boxes allow you to select one option from a drop-down list. Tree views allow you to select one or more options from a list usually contained by a scrolled window. GtkTreeView is the most difficult widget that will be covered in this book, so take your time with the next chapter.

CHAPTER 8

■■■

The Tree View Widget

This chapter will show you how to use the GtkScrolledWindow widget in combination with another powerful widget known as GtkTreeView. The tree view widget can be used to display data in lists or trees that span one or many columns. For example, a GtkTreeView can be used to implement a file browser or display the build the output of an integrated development environment.

GtkTreeView is an involved widget, because it provides a wide variety of features, so be sure to carefully read through each section of this chapter. However, once you learn this powerful widget, you will be able to apply it in many applications.

This chapter will introduce you to a large number of features provided by GtkTreeView. The information presented in this chapter will enable you to mold the tree view widget to meet your needs. Specifically, in this chapter, you will learn the following:

- What objects are used to create a GtkTreeView and how its model-view-controller design makes it unique

- How to create lists and tree structures with the GtkTreeView widget

- When to use GtkTreePath, GtkTreeIter, or GtkTreeRowReference to reference rows within a GtkTreeView

- How to handle double-clicks, single row selections, and multiple row selections

- How to create editable tree view cells or customize individual cells with cell renderer functions

- The widgets you can embed within a cell, including toggle buttons, pixbufs, spin buttons, combo boxes, progress bars, and keyboard accelerator strings

Parts of a Tree View

The GtkTreeView widget is used to display data organized as a list or a tree. The data displayed in the view is organized into columns and rows. The user is able to select one or multiple rows within the tree view using the mouse or keyboard. A screenshot of the Nautilus application using GtkTreeView can be viewed in Figure 8-1.

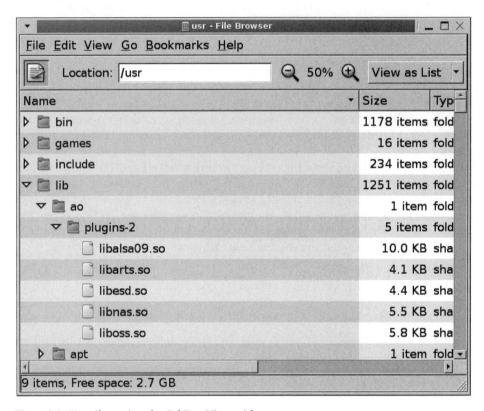

Figure 8-1. *Nautilus using the GtkTreeView widget*

GtkTreeView is a difficult widget to use and an even more difficult widget to understand, so this whole chapter is dedicated to using it. However, once you understand how the widget works, you will be able to apply it to a wide variety of applications, because it is possible to customize almost every aspect of the way the widget is displayed to the user.

What makes GtkTreeView unique is that it follows a design concept that is commonly referred to as model-view-controller (MVC) design. MVC is a design method where the information and the way it is rendered are completely independent of each other, similar to the relationship between GtkTextView and GtkTextBuffer.

GtkTreeModel

Data itself is stored within classes that implement the GtkTreeModel interface. GTK+ provides four types of built-in tree model classes, but only GtkListStore and GtkTreeStore will be covered in this chapter.

The GtkTreeModel interface provides a standard set of methods for retrieving general information about the data that is stored. For example, it allows you to get the number of rows in the tree and the number of children of a certain row. GtkTreeModel also gives you a way to retrieve the data that is stored in a specific row of the store.

■**Note** Models, renderers, and columns are referred to as objects instead of widgets, even though they are a part of the GTK+ library. This is an important distinction—since they are not derived from GtkWidget, they do not have the same set of functions, properties, and signals that are available to GTK+ widgets.

GtkListStore allows you to create a list of elements with multiple columns. Each row is a child of the root node, so only one level of rows is displayed. Basically, GtkListStore is a tree structure that has no hierarchy. It is only provided because faster algorithms exist for interacting with models that do not have any child items.

GtkTreeStore provides the same functionality as GtkListStore, except the data can be organized into a multilayered tree. GTK+ provides a method for creating your own custom model types as well, but the two available types should be suitable in most cases.

While GtkListStore and GtkTreeStore should fit most applications, a time may come when you need to implement your own store object. For example, if it needs to hold a huge number of rows, you should create a new model that will be more efficient. In Chapter 11, you will learn how to create new classes derived from GObject, which can be used as a guide to get you started deriving a new class that implements the GtkTreeModel interface.

After you have created the tree model, the view is used to display the data. By separating the tree view and its model, you are able to display the same set of data in multiple views. These views can be exact copies of each other, or the data can be displayed in varying ways. All of the views will be updated simultaneously as you make alterations to a model.

■**Tip** While it may not immediately seem beneficial to display the same set of data in multiple tree views, consider the case of a file browser. If you need to display the same set of files in multiple file browsers, using the same model for each view would save memory as well as make your program run considerably faster. This is also useful when you want to provide multiple display options for the file browser. When switching between display modes, you will not need to alter the data itself.

Models are composed of columns that contain the same data type and rows that hold each set of data. Each model column can hold a single type of data. A tree model column should not be confused with a tree view column, which is composed of a single header but may be rendered with data from multiple model columns. For example, a tree column may display a text string that has a foreground color defined by a model column that is not visible to the user. Figure 8-2 illustrates the difference between model columns and tree columns.

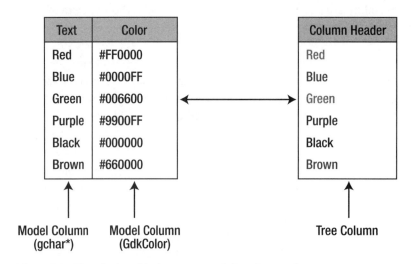

Figure 8-2. *The relationship between model and tree columns*

Each row within a model contains one piece of data corresponding to each model column. In Figure 8-2, each row contains a text string and a GdkColor value. These two values are used to display the text with the corresponding color in the tree column. You will learn how to implement this in code later in this chapter. For now, you should simply understand the differences between the two types of columns and how they relate.

New list and tree stores are created with a number of columns, each defined by an existing GType. Usually, you will need to use only those already implemented in GLib. For example, if you want to display text you can use G_TYPE_STRING, G_TYPE_BOOLEAN, and a few of the number types like G_TYPE_INT.

■**Tip** Since it is possible to store an arbitrary data type with G_TYPE_POINTER, one or more tree model columns can be used to simply store information about every row. You just need to be careful when there are a large number of rows, because memory usage will quickly escalate. You will also have to take care of freeing the pointers yourself.

GtkTreeViewColumn and GtkCellRenderer

As previously mentioned, a tree view displays one or more GtkTreeViewColumn objects. Tree columns are composed of a header and cells of data that are organized into one column. Each tree view column also contains one or more visible columns of data. For example, in a file browser, a tree view column may contain one column of images and one column of file names.

The header of the GtkTreeViewColumn widget contains a title that describes what data is held in the cells below. If you make the column sortable, the rows will be sorted when one of the column headers is clicked.

Tree view columns do not actually render anything to the screen. This is done with an object derived from GtkCellRenderer. Cell renderers are packed into tree view columns similar to how you add widgets into a horizontal box. Each tree view column can contain one or more cell renderers, which are used to render the data. For example, in a file browser, the image column would be rendered with GtkCellRendererPixbuf and the file name with GtkCellRendererText. An example of this was shown in Figure 8-1.

Each cell renderer is responsible for rendering a column of cells, one for every row in the tree view. It begins with the first row, rendering its cell and then proceeding to the next row down until the whole column, or part of the column, is rendered.

Cell renderers are composed of properties that define how each cell of data is rendered to the screen. There are a number of ways to set cell renderer properties. The easiest is to use g_object_set(), which will apply the setting to every cell in the column that the cell renderer is acting on. This is very fast, but often you will need to set attributes for specific cells.

Another way is to add attributes to the renderer. Column attributes correspond to tree model columns and are associated with cell renderer properties, as shown in Figure 8-3. These properties are applied to each cell as it is rendered.

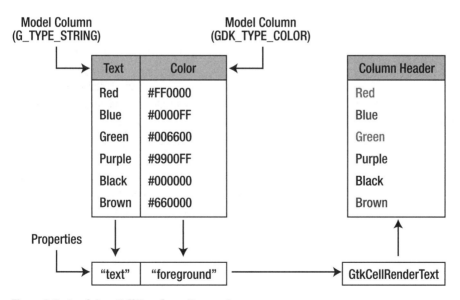

Figure 8-3. *Applying Cell Renderer Properties*

In Figure 8-3, there are two tree model columns with the types G_TYPE_STRING and GDK_TYPE_COLOR. These are applied to GtkCellRendererText's text and foreground properties and used to render the tree view column accordingly.

An additional way to change cell renderer properties is by defining a cell data function. This function will be called for every row in the tree view before it is rendered. This allows you to customize how every cell is rendered without the need for the data to be stored in a tree model. For example, a cell data function can be used to define how many decimal places of a floating point number to display. Cell data functions will be covered in detail in the "Cell Data Functions" section of this chapter.

Later on, this chapter also covers cell renderers that are used to display text (strings, numbers, and Boolean values), toggle buttons, spin buttons, progress bars, pixbufs, combo boxes, and keyboard accelerators. In addition, you can create custom cell renderer types, but this is usually not needed, since GTK+ now provides such a wide variety of types.

This section has taught you what objects are needed to use the GtkTreeView widget, what they do, and how they interrelate. Now that you have a basic understanding of the GtkTreeView widget, the next section will give a simple example using the GtkListStore tree model.

Using GtkListStore

Recall from the previous section that GtkTreeModel is simply an interface implemented by data stores such as GtkListStore. GtkListStore is used to create lists of data that have no hierarchical relationship among rows.

In this section, a simple Grocery List application will be implemented that contains three columns, all of which use GtkCellRendererText. A screenshot of this application can be viewed in Figure 8-4. The first column is a gboolean value displaying TRUE or FALSE that defines whether or not the product should be purchased.

■**Tip** You usually do not want to display Boolean values as text, because if you have many Boolean columns, it will become unmanageable for the user. Instead, you will want to use toggle buttons. You will learn how to do this with GtkCellRendererToggle in a later section. Boolean values are often also used as column attributes in order to define cell renderer properties.

The second column displays the quantity of the product to buy as an integer and the third a text string describing the product. All of the columns use GtkCellRendererText for rendering; GtkCellRendererText is a cell renderer capable of displaying Boolean values and various number formats (int, double, and float) as text strings.

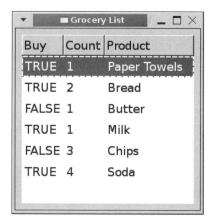

Figure 8-4. *A tree view widget using a GtkListStore tree model*

Listing 8-1 creates a GtkListStore object, which displays a list of groceries. In addition to displaying the products, the list store also displays whether to buy the product and how many of them to buy.

This Grocery List application will be used for many examples throughout the rest of the chapter. Therefore, the content of some functions may be excluded later on if it is presented in previous examples. Also, to keep things organized, in every example setup_tree_view() will be used to set up columns and renderers. Full code listings for every example can be downloaded at www.gtkbook.com.

Listing 8-1. *Creating a GtkTreeView (liststore.c)*

```
#include <gtk/gtk.h>

enum
{
  BUY_IT = 0,
  QUANTITY,
  PRODUCT,
  COLUMNS
};

typedef struct
{
  gboolean buy;
  gint quantity;
  gchar *product;
} GroceryItem;
```

```c
const GroceryItem list[] =
{
  { TRUE, 1, "Paper Towels" },
  { TRUE, 2, "Bread" },
  { FALSE, 1, "Butter" },
  { TRUE, 1, "Milk" },
  { FALSE, 3, "Chips" },
  { TRUE, 4, "Soda" },
  { FALSE, 0, NULL }
};

static void setup_tree_view (GtkWidget*);

int main (int argc,
          char *argv[])
{
  GtkWidget *window, *treeview, *scrolled_win;
  GtkListStore *store;
  GtkTreeIter iter;
  guint i = 0;

  gtk_init (&argc, &argv);

  window = gtk_window_new (GTK_WINDOW_TOPLEVEL);
  gtk_window_set_title (GTK_WINDOW (window), "Grocery List");
  gtk_container_set_border_width (GTK_CONTAINER (window), 10);
  gtk_widget_set_size_request (window, 250, 175);

  treeview = gtk_tree_view_new ();
  setup_tree_view (treeview);

  /* Create a new tree model with three columns, as string, gint and guint. */
  store = gtk_list_store_new (COLUMNS, G_TYPE_BOOLEAN, G_TYPE_INT, G_TYPE_STRING);

  /* Add all of the products to the GtkListStore. */
  while (list[i].product != NULL)
  {
    gtk_list_store_append (store, &iter);
    gtk_list_store_set (store, &iter, BUY_IT, list[i].buy,
                        QUANTITY, list[i].quantity, PRODUCT, list[i].product, -1);
    i++;
  }
```

```c
  /* Add the tree model to the tree view and unreference it so that the model will
   * be destroyed along with the tree view. */
  gtk_tree_view_set_model (GTK_TREE_VIEW (treeview), GTK_TREE_MODEL (store));
  g_object_unref (store);

  scrolled_win = gtk_scrolled_window_new (NULL, NULL);
  gtk_scrolled_window_set_policy (GTK_SCROLLED_WINDOW (scrolled_win),
                                  GTK_POLICY_AUTOMATIC, GTK_POLICY_AUTOMATIC);

  gtk_container_add (GTK_CONTAINER (scrolled_win), treeview);
  gtk_container_add (GTK_CONTAINER (window), scrolled_win);
  gtk_widget_show_all (window);

  gtk_main ();
  return 0;
}


/* Add three columns to the GtkTreeView. All three of the columns will be
 * displayed as text, although one is a gboolean value and another is
 * an integer. */
static void
setup_tree_view (GtkWidget *treeview)
{
  GtkCellRenderer *renderer;
  GtkTreeViewColumn *column;

  /* Create a new GtkCellRendererText, add it to the tree view column and
   * append the column to the tree view. */
  renderer = gtk_cell_renderer_text_new ();
  column = gtk_tree_view_column_new_with_attributes
                        ("Buy", renderer, "text", BUY_IT, NULL);
  gtk_tree_view_append_column (GTK_TREE_VIEW (treeview), column);

  renderer = gtk_cell_renderer_text_new ();
  column = gtk_tree_view_column_new_with_attributes
                        ("Count", renderer, "text", QUANTITY, NULL);
  gtk_tree_view_append_column (GTK_TREE_VIEW (treeview), column);

  renderer = gtk_cell_renderer_text_new ();
  column = gtk_tree_view_column_new_with_attributes
                        ("Product", renderer, "text", PRODUCT, NULL);
  gtk_tree_view_append_column (GTK_TREE_VIEW (treeview), column);
}
```

Creating the Tree View

Creating the GtkTreeView widget is the easiest part of the process. You need only to call
gtk_tree_view_new(). If you want to add the default tree model on initialization, you can
use gtk_tree_view_new_with_model(), but a tree model can easily be applied to a GtkTreeView
after initialization with gtk_tree_view_set_model(). The gtk_tree_view_new_with_model()
function is simply a convenience function.

There are many functions that allow you to customize a GtkTreeView to fit your needs. For
example, above each GtkTreeViewColumn, a header label is rendered that tells the user more
about the column contents. You can set gtk_tree_view_set_headers_visible() to FALSE in
order to hide them.

```
void gtk_tree_view_set_headers_visible (GtkTreeView *treeview,
                                        gboolean visible);
```

■**Note** You should be careful when hiding tree view headers, because they help the user know the contents
of each column. They should only be hidden if there is no more than one column or the contents of each column are clearly explained in some other manner.

GtkTreeViewColumn headers provide more functionality beyond column titles for some tree
views. In sortable tree models, clicking the column header can initiate sorting of all of the rows
according to the data held in the corresponding column. It also gives a visual indication of the
sort order of the column if applicable. You should not hide the headers if the user will need
them to sort the tree view rows.

Another GtkTreeView function, gtk_tree_view_set_rules_hint() requests a GTK+ theme
to differentiate between alternating rows. This is often done by changing the background color
of adjacent rows. However, as the function name suggests, this property is only a hint for the
theme engine and may not be honored. Also, some theme engines alternate background colors
automatically regardless of this setting.

```
void gtk_tree_view_set_rules_hint (GtkTreeView *treeview,
                                   gboolean alternate_colors);
```

This property should only be used if it is a necessity. For example, if your tree view contains many rows, it could help the user navigate throughout its contents. In contrast, it should
not be used for aesthetic purposes, because those settings should always be dictated by the
user's theme.

As a GTK+ developer, you should be very careful about changing visual properties. Users
have the ability to choose themes that fit their needs, and you can make your application unusable by changing how widgets are displayed.

Renderers and Columns

After creating the GtkTreeView, you need to add one or more columns to the view for it to be of any use. Each GtkTreeViewColumn is composed of a header, which displays a short description of its content, and at least one cell renderer. Tree view columns do not actually render any content. Tree view columns hold one or more cell renderers that are used to draw the data on the screen.

All cell renderers are derived from the GtkCellRenderer class and are referred to as objects in this chapter, because GtkCellRenderer is derived directly from GtkObject, not from GtkWidget. Each cell renderer contains a number of properties that determine how the data will be drawn within a cell.

The GtkCellRenderer class provides common properties to all derivative renderers including background color, size parameters, alignments, visibility, sensitivity, and padding. A full list of GtkCellRenderer properties can be found in Appendix A. It also provides the editing-canceled and editing-started signals, which allow you to implement editing in custom cell renderers.

In Listing 8-1, you were introduced to GtkCellRendererText, which is capable of rendering strings, numbers, and gboolean values as text. Textual cell renderers are initialized with gtk_cell_renderer_text_new().

GtkCellRendererText provides a number of additional properties that dictate how each cell will be rendered. You should always set the text property, which is the string that will be displayed in the cell. The rest of the properties are similar to those used with text tags.

GtkCellRendererText contains a large number of properties that dictate how every row will be rendered. g_object_set() was used in the following example to set the foreground color of every piece of text in the renderer to orange. Some properties have a corresponding set property as well, which must be set to TRUE if you want the value to be used. For example, you should set foreground-set to TRUE for the changes will take effect.

```
g_object_set (G_OBJECT (renderer), "foreground", "Orange",
              "foreground-set", TRUE, NULL);
```

After you create a cell renderer, it needs to be added to a GtkTreeViewColumn. Tree view columns can be created with gtk_tree_view_column_new_with_attributes() if you only want the column to display one cell renderer. In the following code, a tree view column is created with the title "Buy" and a renderer with one attribute. This attribute will be referred to as BUY_IT when the GtkListStore is populated.

```
column = gtk_tree_view_column_new_with_attributes ("Buy", renderer,
                                    "text", BUY_IT, NULL);
```

The preceding function accepts a string to display in the column header, a cell renderer, and a NULL-terminated list of attributes. Each attribute contains a string that refers to the renderer property and the tree view column number. The important thing to realize is that the column number provided to gtk_tree_view_column_new_with_attributes() refers to the tree model column, which may not be the same as the number of tree model columns or cell renderers used by the tree view.

The following four lines of code implement the same functionality that is provided by gtk_tree_view_column_new_with_attributes(). An empty column is created with gtk_tree_view_column_new(), and the column title is set to "Buy".

```
column = gtk_tree_view_column_new ();
gtk_tree_view_column_set_title (column, "Buy");
gtk_tree_view_column_pack_start (column, renderer, FALSE);
gtk_tree_view_column_set_attributes (column, renderer, "text", BUY_IT, NULL);
```

Next, a cell renderer is added to the column. gtk_tree_view_column_pack_start() accepts a third Boolean parameter, which instructs the column to expand horizontally to fill extra space if set to TRUE. The last function, gtk_tree_view_column_set_attributes() adds the NULL-terminated list of attributes that will be customized for every row you add to the tree view. These attributes are applied to the specified renderer.

Calling gtk_tree_view_column_pack_start() will remove all attributes previously associated with the specified cell renderer. To circumvent this, you can use gtk_tree_view_column_add_attribute() to add attributes to a column for a specific cell renderer one at a time. Both of these functions are useful when a GtkTreeViewColumn will contain more than one cell renderer.

```
void gtk_tree_view_column_add_attribute (GtkTreeViewColumn *column,
                                         GtkCellRenderer *renderer,
                                         const gchar *attribute,
                                         gint column);
```

If you want to add multiple renderers to the tree view column, you will need to pack each renderer and set its attributes separately. For example, in a file manager, you might want to include a text and an image renderer in the same column. However, if every column only needs one cell renderer, it is easiest to use gtk_tree_view_column_new_with_attributes().

■**Note** If you want a property, such as the foreground color, set to the same value for every row in the column, you should apply that property directly to the cell renderer with g_object_set(). However, if the property will vary depending on the row, you should add it as an attribute of the column for the given renderer.

After you have finished setting up a tree view column, it needs to be added to the tree view with gtk_tree_view_append_column(). Columns may also be added into an arbitrary position of the tree view with gtk_tree_view_insert_column() or removed from the view with gtk_tree_view_remove_column().

Creating the GtkListStore

The tree view columns are now set up with the desired cell renderers, so it is time to create the tree model that will interface between the renderers and the tree view. For the example found in Listing 8-1, we used GtkListStore so that the items would be shown as a list of elements.

New list stores are created with gtk_list_store_new(). This function accepts the number of columns and the type of the data each column will hold. In Listing 8-1, the list store has three columns that store gboolean, integer, and string data types.

```
GtkListStore* gtk_list_store_new (gint n_columns,
                                  /* List of column types */);
```

After creating the list store, you need to add rows with gtk_list_store_append() for it to be of any use. This function will append a new row to the list store, and the iterator will be set to point to the new row. You will learn more about tree iterators in a later section of this chapter. For now, it is adequate for you to know that it points to the new tree view row.

```
void gtk_list_store_append (GtkListStore *store,
                            GtkTreeIter *iter);
```

There are multiple other functions for adding rows to a list store including gtk_list_store_prepend() and gtk_list_store_insert(). A full list of available functions can be found in the GtkListStore API documentation.

In addition to adding rows, you can also remove them with gtk_list_store_remove(). This function will remove the row that GtkTreeIter refers to. After the row is removed, the iterator will point to the next row in the list store, and the function will return TRUE. If the last row was just removed, the iterator will become invalid, and the function will return FALSE.

```
gboolean gtk_list_store_remove (GtkListStore *store,
                                GtkTreeIter *iter);
```

In addition, gtk_list_store_clear() is provided, which can be used to remove all rows from a list store. You will be left with a GtkListStore that contains no data. If the object will not be used beyond this point, it should then be unreferenced.

Now that you have a row, you need to add data to it with gtk_list_store_set(). The gtk_list_store_set() function receives a list of pairs of column numbers and value parameters. For example, the first column in the following function call, referenced with BUY_IT, accepts a Boolean value that defines whether the product should be purchased. These values correspond to those set by gtk_list_store_new().

```
gtk_list_store_set (store, &iter, BUY_IT, list[i].buy,
                    QUANTITY, list[i].quantity, PRODUCT, list[i].product, -1);
```

The last element of gtk_list_store_set() must be set to -1 so that GTK+ knows that there are no more parameters. Otherwise, your users will be presented with an endless list of warnings and errors in the terminal output.

■**Note** GtkCellRendererText automatically converts Boolean values and numbers into text strings that can be rendered on the screen. Therefore, the type of data applied to a text attribute column does not have to be text itself, but just has to be consistent with the list store column type that was defined during initialization of the GtkListStore.

After the list store is created, you need to call gtk_tree_view_set_model() to add it to the tree view. By calling this function, the reference count of the tree model will be incremented by one. Therefore, if you want the tree model to be destroyed when the tree view is destroyed, you will need to call g_object_unref() on the list store.

Using GtkTreeStore

There is one other type of built-in tree model called GtkTreeStore, which organizes rows into a multilevel tree structure. It is possible to implement a list with a GtkTreeStore tree model as well, but this is not recommended because some overhead is added when the object assumes that the row may have one or more children.

Figure 8-5 shows an example tree store, which contains two root elements, each with children of its own. By clicking the expander to the left of a row with children, you can show or hide its children. This is similar to the functionality provided by the GtkExpander widget.

Figure 8-5. *A tree view widget using a GtkTreeStore tree model*

The only difference between a GtkTreeView implemented with a GtkTreeStore instead of a GtkListStore is in the creation of the store. Adding columns and renderers is performed in the same manner with both models, because columns are a part of the view not the model, so Listing 8-2 excludes the implementation of setup_tree_view().

Listing 8-2 revises the original Grocery List application, splitting the products into categories. This list includes two categories: Cleaning Supplies and Food, which both have children of their own. The quantity of each category is set initially to zero, because this is calculated during runtime.

Listing 8-2. *Creating a GtkTreeStore (treestore.c)*

```c
#include <gtk/gtk.h>

enum
{
  BUY_IT = 0,
  QUANTITY,
  PRODUCT,
  COLUMNS
};

enum
{
  PRODUCT_CATEGORY,
  PRODUCT_CHILD
};

typedef struct
{
  gint product_type;
  gboolean buy;
  gint quantity;
  gchar *product;
} GroceryItem;

GroceryItem list[] =
{
  { PRODUCT_CATEGORY, TRUE, 0, "Cleaning Supplies" },
  { PRODUCT_CHILD, TRUE, 1, "Paper Towels" },
  { PRODUCT_CHILD, TRUE, 3, "Toilet Paper" },
  { PRODUCT_CATEGORY, TRUE, 0, "Food" },
  { PRODUCT_CHILD, TRUE, 2, "Bread" },
  { PRODUCT_CHILD, FALSE, 1, "Butter" },
  { PRODUCT_CHILD, TRUE, 1, "Milk" },
  { PRODUCT_CHILD, FALSE, 3, "Chips" },
  { PRODUCT_CHILD, TRUE, 4, "Soda" },
  { PRODUCT_CATEGORY, FALSE, 0, NULL }
};

/* The implementation of this function is the same as in Listing 8-1. */
static void setup_tree_view (GtkWidget*);
```

```
int main (int argc,
          char *argv[])
{
  GtkWidget *window, *treeview, *scrolled_win;
  GtkTreeStore *store;
  GtkTreeIter iter, child;
  guint i = 0, j;

  gtk_init (&argc, &argv);

  window = gtk_window_new (GTK_WINDOW_TOPLEVEL);
  gtk_window_set_title (GTK_WINDOW (window), "Grocery List");
  gtk_container_set_border_width (GTK_CONTAINER (window), 10);
  gtk_widget_set_size_request (window, 275, 300);

  treeview = gtk_tree_view_new ();
  setup_tree_view (treeview);

  store = gtk_tree_store_new (COLUMNS, G_TYPE_BOOLEAN, G_TYPE_INT, G_TYPE_STRING);

  while (list[i].product != NULL)
  {
    /* If the product type is a category, count the quantity of all of the products
     * in the category that are going to be bought. */
    if (list[i].product_type == PRODUCT_CATEGORY)
    {
      j = i + 1;

      /* Calculate how many products will be bought in the category. */
      while (list[j].product != NULL && list[j].product_type != PRODUCT_CATEGORY)
      {
        if (list[j].buy)
          list[i].quantity += list[j].quantity;
        j++;
      }

      /* Add the category as a new root element. */
      gtk_tree_store_append (store, &iter, NULL);
      gtk_tree_store_set (store, &iter, BUY_IT, list[i].buy,
                          QUANTITY, list[i].quantity, PRODUCT, list[i].product, -1);
    }
```

```
    /* Otherwise, add the product as a child of the category. */
    else
    {
      gtk_tree_store_append (store, &child, &iter);
      gtk_tree_store_set (store, &child, BUY_IT, list[i].buy,
                          QUANTITY, list[i].quantity, PRODUCT, list[i].product, -1);
    }

    i++;
  }

  gtk_tree_view_set_model (GTK_TREE_VIEW (treeview), GTK_TREE_MODEL (store));
  gtk_tree_view_expand_all (GTK_TREE_VIEW (treeview));
  g_object_unref (store);

  scrolled_win = gtk_scrolled_window_new (NULL, NULL);
  gtk_scrolled_window_set_policy (GTK_SCROLLED_WINDOW (scrolled_win),
                                  GTK_POLICY_AUTOMATIC, GTK_POLICY_AUTOMATIC);

  gtk_container_add (GTK_CONTAINER (scrolled_win), treeview);
  gtk_container_add (GTK_CONTAINER (window), scrolled_win);
  gtk_widget_show_all (window);

  gtk_main ();
  return 0;
}
```

Tree stores are initialized with gtk_tree_store_new(), which accepts the same parameters as gtk_list_store_new(). These include the number of columns of data followed by a list of the data types corresponding to each tree model column.

Adding rows to a tree store is a little different than adding rows to a list store. You add rows to a tree store with gtk_tree_store_append(), which accepts two iterators instead of one. The first iterator will point to the inserted row when the function returns, and the second iterator should point to the parent row of the new row.

```
gtk_tree_store_append (store, &iter, NULL);
```

In the preceding call to gtk_tree_store_append(), a root element was appended to the list by passing NULL as the parent iterator. The iter tree iterator was set to the location of the new row. The first iterator does not need to already be initialized, because its current contents will be overwritten when the function returns.

In the second call to gtk_tree_store_append(), which follows, the row will be added as a child of iter. Next, the child tree iterator will be set to the current location of the new row within the tree store when the function returns.

```
gtk_tree_store_append (store, &child, &iter);
```

As with list stores, there are many functions available for adding rows to a tree store. These include gtk_tree_store_insert(), gtk_tree_store_prepend(), and gtk_tree_store_insert_before() to name a few. For a full list of functions, you should reference the GtkTreeStore API documentation.

After you add a row to the tree store, it is simply an empty row with no data. To add data to the row, call gtk_tree_store_set(). This function works in the same way as gtk_list_store_set(). It accepts the tree store, a tree iterator pointing to the location of the row, and a list of column-data pairs terminated by -1. These column numbers correspond to those you used when setting up the cell renderer attributes.

```
gtk_tree_store_set (store, &child, BUY_IT, list[i].buy, QUANTITY, list[i].quantity,
                    PRODUCT, list[i].product, -1);
```

In addition to adding rows to a tree store, you can also remove them with gtk_tree_store_remove(). This function will remove the row that is referred to by GtkTreeIter. After the row is removed, iter will point to the next row in the tree store, and the function will return TRUE. If the row that you removed was the last in the tree store, the iterator will become invalid, and the function will return FALSE.

```
gboolean gtk_tree_store_remove (GtkTreeStore *store,
                                GtkTreeIter *iter);
```

In addition, gtk_tree_store_clear() is provided, which can be used to remove all rows from a tree store. You will be left with a GtkTreeStore that contains no data. If the object will not be used beyond this point, it should then be unreferenced.

Before gtk_main() is called in Listing 8-2, gtk_tree_view_expand_all() is called to expand all of the rows. This is a recursive function that will expand every possible row, although it will only affect tree models that have child-parent row relationships. In addition, you can collapse all of the rows with gtk_tree_view_collapse_all(). By default, all rows will be collapsed.

Referencing Rows

Three objects are available for referring to a specific row within a tree model; each has its own unique advantages. They are GtkTreePath, GtkTreeIter, and GtkTreeRowReference. In the following sections, you will learn how each object works and how to use them within your own programs.

Tree Paths

GtkTreePath is a very convenient object for referring to rows within a tree model, because it can be easily represented as a human-readable string. It can also be represented as an array of unsigned integers.

For example, if you are presented with the string 3:7:5, you would start at the fourth root element (recall that indexing begins at zero, so element three is actually the fourth element in the level). You would next proceed to the eighth child of that root element. The row in question is that child's sixth child.

To illustrate this graphically, Figure 8-6 shows the tree view created in Listing 8-2 with the tree paths labeled. Each root element is referred to as only one element, 0 and 1. The first root element has two children, referred to as 0:0 and 0:1.

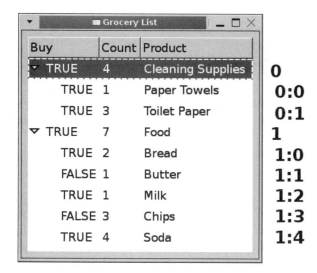

Figure 8-6. *Tree paths for a tree view using GtkTreeStore*

Two functions are provided that allow you to convert back and forth between a path and its equivalent string: gtk_tree_path_to_string() and gtk_tree_path_new_from_string(). You usually will not have to deal with the string path directly unless you are trying to save the state of a tree view, but using it helps in understanding the way tree paths work.

Listing 8-3 gives a short example of using tree paths. It begins by creating a new path that points to the Bread product row. Next, gtk_tree_path_up() moves up one level in the path. When you convert the path back into a string, you will see that the resulting output is 1, pointing to the Food row.

Listing 8-3. *Converting Between Paths and Strings*

```
GtkTreePath *path;
gchar *str;

path = gtk_tree_path_new_from_string ("1:0"); /* Point to bread */
gtk_tree_path_up (path);
str = gtk_tree_path_to_string (path);
g_print (str);
g_free (str);
```

■**Tip** If you need to get a tree iterator and only have the path string available, you can convert the string into a GtkTreePath and then to a GtkTreeIter. However, a better solution would be to skip the intermediate step with gtk_tree_model_get_iter_from_string(), which converts a tree path string directly into a tree iterator.

In addition to gtk_tree_path_up(), there are other functions that allow you to navigate throughout a tree model. You can use gtk_tree_path_down() to move to the child row and gtk_tree_path_next() or gtk_tree_path_prev() to move to the next or previous row in the same level. When you move to the previous row or parent row, FALSE will be returned if it was not successful.

At times, you may need to have a tree path as a list of integers instead of a string. The gtk_tree_path_get_indices() function will return the integers that compose the path string.

```
gint* gtk_tree_path_get_indices (GtkTreePath *path);
```

Problems can arise with tree paths when a row is added or removed from the tree model. The path could end up pointing to a different row within the tree or, worse, a row that does not exist anymore! For example, if a tree path points to the last element of a tree and you remove that row, it will now point beyond the limits of the tree. To get around this problem, you can convert the tree path into a tree row reference.

Tree Row References

GtkTreeRowReference objects are used to watch a tree model for changes. Internally, they connect to the row-inserted, row-deleted, and rows-reordered signals, updating the stored path based on the changes.

New tree row references are created with gtk_tree_row_reference_new() from an existing GtkTreeModel and GtkTreePath. The tree path copied into the row reference will be updated as changes occur within the model.

```
GtkTreeRowReference* gtk_tree_row_reference_new (GtkTreeModel *model,
                                                 GtkTreePath *path);
```

When you need to retrieve the path, you can use gtk_tree_row_reference_get_path(), which will return NULL if the row no longer exists within the model. Tree row references are able to update the tree path based on changes within the tree model, but if you remove all elements from the same level as the tree path's row, it will no longer have a row to point to.

The returned tree path should be freed with gtk_tree_path_free() when you are finished with it. The tree row reference can be freed with gtk_tree_row_reference_free().

You should be aware that tree row references do add a small bit of overhead processing when adding, removing, or sorting rows within a tree model, since the references will have to handle all of the signals emitted by these actions. This overhead does not matter for most applications, because there will not be enough rows for the user to notice. However, if your application contains a large number of rows, you should use tree row references wisely.

Tree Iterators

GTK+ provides the GtkTreeIter object, which can be used to reference a specific row within a GtkTreeModel. These iterators are used internally by models, which means that you should *never* directly alter the content of a tree iterator.

You have already seen multiple instances of GtkTreeIter, from which you can discern that tree iterators are used in a similar way to GtkTextIter. Tree iterators are used for manipulation of tree models. Tree paths, however, are used to point to rows within a tree model in a way that provides a human-readable interface. Tree row references can be used to make sure that tree paths adjust where they point throughout changes of a tree model.

GTK+ provides a number of built-in functions to perform operations on the tree iterators. Typically, iterators are used to add rows to a model, set the content of a row, and retrieve the content of a model. In Listings 8-1 and 8-2, tree iterators were used to add rows to GtkListStore and GtkTreeStore models and then set the initial content of each row.

GtkTreeModel provides a number of gtk_tree_model_iter_*() functions, which can be used to move iterators and retrieve information about them. For example, to move to the next iterator position, you could use gtk_tree_model_iter_next(), which returns TRUE if the action was successful. A full list of available functions can be found in the GtkTreeModel API documentation.

It is easy to convert between tree iterators and tree paths with the use of gtk_tree_model_get_path() and gtk_tree_model_get_iter(). The tree path or iterator must be valid for either of these functions to work correctly. Listing 8-4 gives a short example of how to convert between GtkTreeIter and GtkTreePath.

Listing 8-4. *Converting Between Paths and Iterators*

```
path = gtk_tree_model_get_path (model, &iter);
gtk_tree_model_get_iter (model, &iter, path);
gtk_tree_path_free (path);
```

The first function in Listing 8-4, gtk_tree_model_get_path() converts a valid tree iterator into a tree path. That path is then sent to gtk_tree_model_get_iter(), which converts it back into an iterator. Notice that the second function accepts three parameters, because the tree iterator must be treated as a pointer.

One problem presented by GtkTreeIter is that the iterator is not guaranteed to exist after a model is edited. This is not true in all cases, and you can use gtk_tree_model_get_flags() to check the GTK_TREE_MODEL_ITERS_PERSIST flag, which is turned on by default for GtkListStore and GtkTreeStore. If this flag is set, the tree iterator will always be valid as long as the row exists.

```
GtkTreeModelFlags gtk_tree_model_get_flags (GtkTreeModel *model);
```

Even if the iterator is set to persist, it is not a good idea to store tree iterator objects, since they are used internally by tree models. Instead, you should use tree row references to keep track of rows over time, since references will not become invalidated when the tree model changes.

Adding Rows and Handling Selections

Both of the examples that you have been given up to this point define the tree model during startup. The content does not change after it is initially set. In this section, the Grocery List application will be expanded to allow the user to add and remove products. Before the example is introduced, you will learn how to handle single and multiple selections.

Single Selections

Selection information is held for each tree view by a GtkTreeSelection object. You can retrieve this object with gtk_tree_view_get_selection(). A GtkTreeSelection object will automatically be created for you for every GtkTreeView, so there is never a need to create your own tree selection.

■**Caution** GtkTreeSelection provides one signal, changed, which is emitted when the selection has changed. You should be careful when using this signal, because it is not always reliable. It can be emitted when no changes occur by the user selecting a row that is already selected. Therefore, it is best to use the signals provided by GtkTreeView for selection handling, which can be found in Appendix B.

Tree views support multiple types of selections. You can change the selection type with gtk_tree_selection_set_mode(). Selection types are defined by the GtkSelectionMode enumeration, which includes the following values:

- GTK_SELECTION_NONE: The user will be prohibited from selecting any rows.

- GTK_SELECTION_SINGLE: The user may select up to one row, though it is possible that no row will be selected. By default, tree selections are initialized with GTK_SELECTION_SINGLE.

- GTK_SELECTION_BROWSE: The user will be able to select exactly one row. In some rare cases, there may be not be a selected row. This option actually prohibits the user from deselecting a row except when the selection is moved to another row.

- GTK_SELECTION_MULTIPLE: The user may select any number of rows. The user will be able to use the Ctrl and Shift keys to select additional elements or ranges of elements.

If you have defined the selection type as GTK_SELECTION_SINGLE or GTK_SELECTION_BROWSE, you can be sure that only one row will be selected. For tree views with one selection, you can use gtk_tree_selection_get_selected() to retrieve the selected row.

```
gboolean gtk_tree_selection_get_selected (GtkTreeSelection *selection,
                                          GtkTreeModel **model,
                                          GtkTreeIter *iter);
```

The gtk_tree_selection_get_selected() function can be used to retrieve the tree model associated with the GtkTreeSelection object and a tree iterator pointing to the selected row. TRUE is returned if the model and iterator were successfully set. This function will *not* work with a selection mode of GTK_SELECTION_MULTIPLE!

If no row has been selected, the tree iterator will be set to NULL, and FALSE will be returned from the function. Therefore, gtk_tree_selection_get_selected() can also be used as a test to check whether or not there is a selected row.

Multiple Selections

If your tree selection allows multiple rows to be selected (GTK_SELECTION_MULTIPLE), you have two options for handling selections, calling a function for every row or retrieving all of the selected rows as a GList. Your first option is to call a function for every selected row with gtk_tree_selection_selected_foreach().

```
gtk_tree_selection_selected_foreach (selection, foreach_func, NULL);
```

This function allows you to call foreach_func() for every selected row, passing an optional gpointer data parameter. In the preceding example, NULL was passed to the function. The function must be of the type GtkTreeSelectionForeachFunc, an example of which can be viewed in Listing 8-5. The following GtkTreeSelectionForeachFunc retrieves the product string and prints it to the screen.

Listing 8-5. *Selected For-Each Function*

```
static gboolean
foreach_func (GtkTreeModel *model,
              GtkTreePath *path,
              GtkTreeIter *iter,
              gpointer data)
{
  gchar *text;

  gtk_tree_model_get (model, iter, PRODUCT, &text, -1);
  g_print ("Selected Product: %s\n", text);
  g_free (text);
}
```

■**Note** You should not modify the tree model or selection from within a GtkTreeSelectionForeachFunc implementation! GTK+ will give critical errors to the user if you do so, because invalid tree paths and iterators may result.

One problem with using tree selection foreach functions is that you are not able to manipulate the selection from within the function. To remedy this problem, a better solution would be to use gtk_tree_selection_get_selected_rows(), which returns a GList of GtkTreePath objects, each pointing to a selected row.

```
GList* gtk_tree_selection_get_selected_rows (GtkTreeSelection *selection,
                                             GtkTreeModel **model);
```

You can then perform some operation on each row within the list. However, you need to be careful. If you need to edit the tree model within the GList foreach function, you will want to first convert all of the tree paths to tree row references, so they will continue to be valid throughout the duration of your actions.

If you want to loop through all of the rows manually, you are also able to use gtk_tree_selection_count_selected_rows(), which will return the number of rows that are currently selected. After you are finished with the list, you need to make sure to iterate through it and free all of the tree paths before freeing the list itself.

Adding New Rows

Now that you have been introduced to selections, it is time to add the ability to add new products to the list. Much of the application has been excluded from the following three listings, because it is the same as Listing 8-2.

The only difference in the main() function in this example in comparison to the previous Grocery List application is visible in Figure 8-7, which shows that GTK_STOCK_ADD and GTK_STOCK_REMOVE buttons were added along the bottom of the tree view. Also, the selection mode was changed to allow the user to select multiple rows at a time.

Figure 8-7. *Editing an item in the grocery list*

Listing 8-6 is the implementation of the callback function that will be run when the user clicks on the Add button. It presents the user with a GtkDialog that asks the user to choose a category, enter a product name and quantity of products to buy, and select whether or not to purchase the product.

If all of the fields are valid, the row is added under the chosen category. Also, if the user specified that the product should be purchased, the quantity is added to the total quantity of the category.

Listing 8-6. *Adding a New Product (selections.c)*

```
static void
add_product (GtkButton *add,
             GtkTreeView *treeview)
{
  GtkWidget *dialog, *table, *combobox, *entry, *spin, *check;
  GtkTreeIter iter, child;
  GtkTreePath *path;
  GtkTreeModel *model;
  const gchar *product;
  gchar *category, *name;
  gint quantity, i = 0;
  gboolean buy;

  /* Create a dialog that will be used to create a new product. */
  dialog = gtk_dialog_new_with_buttons ("Add a Product", NULL,
                                         GTK_DIALOG_MODAL,
                                         GTK_STOCK_ADD, GTK_RESPONSE_OK,
                                         GTK_STOCK_CANCEL, GTK_RESPONSE_CANCEL,
                                         NULL);

  /* Create widgets that will be packed into the dialog. */
  combobox = gtk_combo_box_new_text ();
  entry = gtk_entry_new ();
  spin = gtk_spin_button_new_with_range (0, 100, 1);
  check = gtk_check_button_new_with_mnemonic ("_Buy the Product");
  gtk_spin_button_set_digits (GTK_SPIN_BUTTON (spin), 0);

  /* Add all of the categories to the combo box. */
  while (list[i].product != NULL)
  {
    if (list[i].product_type == PRODUCT_CATEGORY)
      gtk_combo_box_append_text (GTK_COMBO_BOX (combobox), list[i].product);
    i++;
  }
}
```

```
table = gtk_table_new (4, 2, FALSE);
gtk_table_set_row_spacings (GTK_TABLE (table), 5);
gtk_table_set_col_spacings (GTK_TABLE (table), 5);
gtk_container_set_border_width (GTK_CONTAINER (table), 5);

/* Pack the table that will hold the dialog widgets. */
gtk_table_attach (GTK_TABLE (table), gtk_label_new ("Category:"), 0, 1, 0, 1,
                  GTK_SHRINK | GTK_FILL, GTK_SHRINK | GTK_FILL, 0, 0);
gtk_table_attach (GTK_TABLE (table), combobox, 1, 2, 0, 1, GTK_EXPAND | GTK_FILL,
                  GTK_SHRINK | GTK_FILL, 0, 0);
gtk_table_attach (GTK_TABLE (table), gtk_label_new ("Product:"), 0, 1, 1, 2,
                  GTK_SHRINK | GTK_FILL, GTK_SHRINK | GTK_FILL, 0, 0);
gtk_table_attach (GTK_TABLE (table), entry, 1, 2, 1, 2, GTK_EXPAND | GTK_FILL,
                  GTK_SHRINK | GTK_FILL, 0, 0);
gtk_table_attach (GTK_TABLE (table), gtk_label_new ("Quantity:"), 0, 1, 2, 3,
                  GTK_SHRINK | GTK_FILL, GTK_SHRINK | GTK_FILL, 0, 0);
gtk_table_attach (GTK_TABLE (table), spin, 1, 2, 2, 3, GTK_EXPAND | GTK_FILL,
                  GTK_SHRINK | GTK_FILL, 0, 0);
gtk_table_attach (GTK_TABLE (table), check, 1, 2, 3, 4, GTK_EXPAND | GTK_FILL,
                  GTK_SHRINK | GTK_FILL, 0, 0);

gtk_box_pack_start_defaults (GTK_BOX (GTK_DIALOG (dialog)->vbox), table);
gtk_widget_show_all (dialog);

/* If the user presses OK, verify the entries and add the product. */
if (gtk_dialog_run (GTK_DIALOG (dialog)) == GTK_RESPONSE_OK)
{
  quantity = (gint) gtk_spin_button_get_value (GTK_SPIN_BUTTON (spin));
  product = gtk_entry_get_text (GTK_ENTRY (entry));
  category = gtk_combo_box_get_active_text (GTK_COMBO_BOX (combobox));
  buy = gtk_toggle_button_get_active (GTK_TOGGLE_BUTTON (check));

  if (g_ascii_strcasecmp (product, "") || category == NULL)
  {
    g_warning ("All of the fields were not correctly filled out!");
    gtk_widget_destroy (dialog);

    if (category != NULL)
      g_free (category)
    return;
  }
```

```
model = gtk_tree_view_get_model (treeview);
gtk_tree_model_get_iter_from_string (model, &iter, "0");

/* Retrieve an iterator pointing to the selected category. */
do
{
  gtk_tree_model_get (model, &iter, PRODUCT, &name, -1);

  if (g_ascii_strcasecmp (name, category) == 0)
  {
    g_free (name);
    break;
  }

  g_free (name);
} while (gtk_tree_model_iter_next (model, &iter));

/* Convert the category iterator to a path so that it will not become invalid
 * and add the new product as a child of the category. */
path = gtk_tree_model_get_path (model, &iter);
gtk_tree_store_append (GTK_TREE_STORE (model), &child, &iter);
gtk_tree_store_set (GTK_TREE_STORE (model), &child, BUY_IT, buy,
                    QUANTITY, quantity, PRODUCT, product, -1);

/* Add the quantity to the running total if it is to be purchased. */
if (buy)
{
  gtk_tree_model_get_iter (model, &iter, path);
  gtk_tree_model_get (model, &iter, QUANTITY, &i, -1);
  i += quantity;
  gtk_tree_store_set (GTK_TREE_STORE (model), &iter, QUANTITY, i, -1);
}

gtk_tree_path_free (path);
g_free (category);
}

gtk_widget_destroy (dialog);
}
```

Retrieving Row Data

Retrieving the values stored in a tree model row is very similar to adding a row. In Listing 8-6, gtk_tree_model_get_iter_from_string() is first used to retrieve a tree iterator that points to the first row in the tree view. This corresponds to the first category.

Next, gtk_tree_model_iter_next() is used to loop through all of the root-level rows. For each root-level row, the following code is run. First, the product name is retrieved with gtk_tree_model_get(). This function works like gtk_tree_store_set(), which accepts a GtkTreeModel, an iterator pointing to a row, and a list of pairs of column numbers and variables to store the data. This list should be terminated with -1 and the returned value freed by the programmer.

```
gtk_tree_model_get (model, &iter, PRODUCT, &name, -1);
if (g_ascii_strcasecmp (name, category) == 0)
  break;
```

Then g_ascii_strcasecmp() is used to compare the current product to the chosen category name. If the two strings match, the loop is exited, because the correct category was found. The iter variable now points to the selected category.

Adding a New Row

Adding new rows to the tree model is done in the same way as they were originally added during startup. In the following code, the GtkTreeIter that points to the chosen category is first converted into a tree path, since it will become invalidated when the tree store is changed. Note that it does not have to be converted to a tree row reference, because its location will not possibly change.

```
path = gtk_tree_model_get_path (model, &iter);
gtk_tree_store_append (GTK_TREE_STORE (model), &child, &iter);
gtk_tree_store_set (GTK_TREE_STORE (model), &child, BUY_IT, buy,
                    QUANTITY, quantity, PRODUCT, product, -1);
```

Next, a new row is appended with gtk_tree_store_append(), where iter is the parent row. That row is populated with gtk_tree_store_set(), using the data entered by the user in the dialog.

Combo Boxes

Listing 8-6 introduces a new widget called GtkComboBox. GtkComboBox is a widget that allows the user to choose from a number of options in a drop-down list. The combo box displays the selected choice in its normal state.

Combo boxes can be used in two different ways, depending on what function you use to instantiate the widget, either with a custom GtkTreeModel or with a default model with only a single column of strings.

In Listing 8-6, a new GtkComboBox was created with gtk_combo_box_new_text(), which creates a specialized combo box that contains only one column of strings. This is simply a convenience function, because the drop-down list of a combo box is internally handled with a GtkTreeModel. Combo boxes created with gtk_combo_box_new_text() have a GtkTreeModel automatically created that can accepts only strings. This allows you to easily append and prepend options and insert new options with the following functions:

```
void gtk_combo_box_append_text  (GtkComboBox *combobox,
                                 const gchar *text);
void gtk_combo_box_prepend_text (GtkComboBox *combobox,
                                 const gchar *text);
void gtk_combo_box_insert_text  (GtkComboBox *combobox,
                                 gint position,
                                 const gchar *text);
```

In addition, you can remove choices with gtk_combo_box_remove_text() and retrieve a copy of the currently selected string with gtk_combo_box_get_active_text(). However, these functions can *only* be used when you initialize the GtkComboBox with gtk_combo_box_new_text().

Most combo boxes are created with gtk_combo_box_new(), which requires you to create a tree model to hold the selections and add it with gtk_combo_box_set_model(). This does not assume anything about the content of the tree model or the types of each column. Also, tree models with multiple columns are supported.

With combo boxes created with gtk_combo_box_new(), there is no need to provide functions for adding or removing choices because that is handled completely by the tree model. However, there are two functions for retrieving the current selection.

```
gint     gtk_combo_box_get_active      (GtkComboBox *combobox);
gooblean gtk_combo_box_get_active_iter (GtkComboBox *combobox,
                                        GtkTreeIter *iter);
```

The first function gtk_combo_box_get_active() returns an integer that refers to the index of the current row or -1 if there is no selection. This can be converted into a string and then into a GtkTreePath. Also, gtk_combo_box_get_active_iter() will retrieve an iterator pointing to the selected row, returning TRUE if the iterator was set.

Removing Multiple Rows

The next step is to add the ability to remove products from the list. Since we have added the ability for multiple rows to be selected, the code must also be able to remove more than one row.

Listing 8-7 implements two functions. The first function, remove_row(), is called for every selected row, removing the row if it is not a category. If the removed row was to be purchased, its quantity is removed from the category's running total. The second function, remove_products(), is the callback function that is run when the GTK_STOCK_REMOVE button is clicked.

Listing 8-7. *Removing One or More Products (selections.c)*

```
static void
remove_row (GtkTreeRowReference *ref,
            GtkTreeModel *model)
{
  GtkTreeIter parent, iter;
  GtkTreePath *path;
  gboolean buy;
  gint quantity, pnum;

  /* Convert the tree row reference to a path and retrieve the iterator. */
  path = gtk_tree_row_reference_get_path (ref);
  gtk_tree_model_get_iter (model, &iter, path);

  /* Only remove the row if it is not a root row. */
  if (gtk_tree_model_iter_parent (model, &parent, &iter))
  {
    gtk_tree_model_get (model, &iter, BUY_IT, &buy, QUANTITY, &quantity, -1);
    gtk_tree_model_get (model, &parent, QUANTITY, &pnum, -1);

    if (buy)
    {
      pnum -= quantity;
      gtk_tree_store_set (GTK_TREE_STORE (model), &parent, QUANTITY, pnum, -1);
    }

    gtk_tree_model_get_iter (model, &iter, path);
    gtk_tree_store_remove (GTK_TREE_STORE (model), &iter);
  }
}

static void
remove_products (GtkButton *remove,
                 GtkTreeView *treeview)
{
  GtkTreeSelection *selection;
  GtkTreeRowReference *ref;
  GtkTreeModel *model;
  GList *rows, *ptr, *references = NULL;

  selection = gtk_tree_view_get_selection (treeview);
  model = gtk_tree_view_get_model (treeview);
  rows = gtk_tree_selection_get_selected_rows (selection, &model);
```

```
/* Create tree row references to all of the selected rows. */
ptr = rows;
while (ptr != NULL)
{
  ref = gtk_tree_row_reference_new (model, (GtkTreePath*) ptr->data);
  references = g_list_prepend (references, gtk_tree_row_reference_copy (ref));
  gtk_tree_row_reference_free (ref);
  ptr = ptr->next;
}

/* Remove each of the selected rows pointed to by the row reference. */
g_list_foreach (references, (GFunc) remove_row, model);

/* Free the tree paths, tree row references and lists. */
g_list_foreach (references, (GFunc) gtk_tree_row_reference_free, NULL);
g_list_foreach (rows, (GFunc) gtk_tree_path_free, NULL);
g_list_free (references);
g_list_free (rows);
}
```

When the GTK_STOCK_REMOVE button is pressed, remove_products() will be called. This function begins by calling gtk_tree_selection_get_selected_rows() in order to retrieve a doubly linked list of tree paths that point to the selected rows. Since the application will be altering the rows, the list of paths is converted into a list of row references. This will make sure that all of the tree paths will remain valid.

■Note Remember that gtk_tree_selection_selected_foreach() cannot be used for this application, because it should not be used when rows will be altered! This is very important to remember, because it can cause many headaches if iterators are unexpectedly invalid because a tree model was changed.

After the paths are converted to tree row references, g_list_foreach() is used to call remove_row() for every item. Within remove_row(), a new function is used to check whether the row is a category.

If the selected row is a category, we know that it will be a root element and will have no parents. Therefore, the following gtk_tree_model_iter_parent() call performs two tasks. First, if the parent iterator is not set, this function will return FALSE, and the category row will not be removed. If the row has a parent, which means that it is a product, the parent iterator will be set and used later in the function.

```
if (gtk_tree_model_iter_parent (model, &parent, &iter))
```

Second, the function retrieves information about the selected product and its parent category. If the product was set to be purchased, its quantity is subtracted from the total product count displayed by the category. Since changing this data will invalidate the iterator, the path is converted into an iterator, and the row is removed from the tree model.

Handling Double-clicks

Double-clicks are handled with the row-activated signal of the GtkTreeView. The signal is emitted when the user double-clicks a row, when the user presses the spacebar, Shift+spacebar, Return, or Enter on a noneditable row, or when you call gtk_tree_view_row_activated().

Listing 8-8. *Editing a Clicked Row*

```
static void
row_activated (GtkTreeView *treeview,
               GtkTreePath *path,
               GtkTreeViewColumn *column,
               gpointer data)
{
  GtkTreeModel *model;
  GtkTreeIter iter;

  model = gtk_tree_view_get_model (treeview);
  if (gtk_tree_model_get_iter (model, &iter, path))
  {
    /* Handle the selection ... */
  }
}
```

In Listing 8-8, the callback function row_activated() is called when the user activates a row within the tree view. The activated row is retrieved from the tree path object with gtk_tree_model_get_iter(). From there, you are free to use whatever functions you have learned thus far to retrieve or alter the content of the row.

Editable Text Renderers

It would be very useful to allow the user to edit the contents of a tree view. This could be accomplished by presenting a dialog that contains a GtkEntry in which the user would be able to edit the content of a cell. However, GTK+ provides a much simpler way to edit textual components that is integrated into the tree cell by using GtkCellRendererText's edited signal.

When a user clicks on a cell in the selected row that is marked as editable, a GtkEntry will be placed in the cell that contains the current contents of the cell. An example of a cell being edited can be viewed in Figure 8-8.

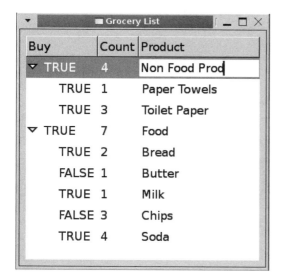

Figure 8-8. *An editable cell*

After the user presses the Enter key or removes focus from the text entry, the edited widget
will be emitted. You need to connect to this signal and apply the changes once it is emitted.
Listing 8-9 shows you how to create the GtkListStore Grocery List application where the product column is editable.

Listing 8-9. *Editing a Cell's Text (editable.c)*

```
static void
setup_tree_view (GtkWidget *treeview)
{
  GtkCellRenderer *renderer;
  GtkTreeViewColumn *column;

  renderer = gtk_cell_renderer_text_new ();
  column = gtk_tree_view_column_new_with_attributes
                        ("Buy", renderer, "text", BUY_IT, NULL);
  gtk_tree_view_append_column (GTK_TREE_VIEW (treeview), column);

  renderer = gtk_cell_renderer_text_new ();
  column = gtk_tree_view_column_new_with_attributes
                        ("Count", renderer, "text", QUANTITY, NULL);
  gtk_tree_view_append_column (GTK_TREE_VIEW (treeview), column);
```

```
  /* Set up the third column in the tree view to be editable. */
  renderer = gtk_cell_renderer_text_new ();
  g_object_set (renderer, "editable", TRUE, "editable-set", TRUE, NULL);

  g_signal_connect (G_OBJECT (renderer), "edited",
                    G_CALLBACK (cell_edited),
                    (gpointer) treeview);

  column = gtk_tree_view_column_new_with_attributes
                        ("Product", renderer, "text", PRODUCT, NULL);
  gtk_tree_view_append_column (GTK_TREE_VIEW (treeview), column);
}

/* Apply the changed text to the cell if it is not an empty string. */
static void
cell_edited (GtkCellRendererText *renderer,
             gchar *path,
             gchar *new_text,
             GtkTreeView *treeview)
{
  GtkTreeIter iter;
  GtkTreeModel *model;

  if (g_ascii_strcasecmp (new_text, "") != 0)
  {
    model = gtk_tree_view_get_model (treeview);
    if (gtk_tree_model_get_iter_from_string (model, &iter, path))
      gtk_list_store_set (GTK_LIST_STORE (model), &iter, PRODUCT, new_text, -1);
  }
}
```

Creating editable GtkCellRendererText cells is a very simple process. The first thing you need to do is set the editable and editable-set properties of the text renderer to TRUE.

```
g_object_set (renderer, "editable", TRUE, "editable-set", TRUE, NULL);
```

Remember that setting the editable property with g_object_set() will apply it to the whole column of data that is drawn by the renderer. If you want to specify row by row whether the cell should be editable, you should add it as an attribute of the column.

The next thing you need to do is connect the cell renderer to the edited signal provided by GtkCellRendererText. The callback function for this signal receives the cell renderer, a GtkTreePath string pointing to the edited row, and the new text that was entered by the user. This signal is emitted when the user presses the Enter key or moves focus from the cell's GtkEntry while the cell is being edited.

The edited signal is necessary, because changes are not automatically applied to the cell. This allows you to filter out invalid entries. For example, in Listing 8-9, the new text is not applied when the new string is empty.

```
if (gtk_tree_model_get_iter_from_string (model, &iter, path))
  gtk_list_store_set (GTK_LIST_STORE (model), &iter, PRODUCT, new_text, -1);
```

Once you are ready to apply the text, you can convert the GtkTreePath string directly into a GtkTreeIter with gtk_tree_model_get_iter_from_string(). This function returns TRUE if the iterator was successfully set, which means that the path string points to a valid row.

■**Caution** You will always want to check that the path is valid, even though it is supplied by GTK+, because there is a chance that the row has been removed or moved since the callback function was initialized.

After you retrieve the GtkTreeIter, you can use gtk_list_store_set() to apply the new text string to the column. In Listing 8-9, new_text was applied to the PRODUCT column of the GtkListStore.

Cell Data Functions

If you need to further customize every cell before it is rendered to the screen, you can use cell data functions. They allow you to tinker with every property of each individual cell. For example, you can set the foreground color based on the content of the cell or restrict the number of decimal places a floating point number that are shown. It can also be used to set properties that are calculated during runtime.

Figure 8-9 shows an application that uses cell data functions to set the background color of each cell based on the text property of the GtkCellRendererText.

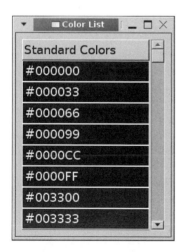

Figure 8-9. *Screenshot of Listing 8-10, which creates a color list*

■**Caution** Make sure not to use cell data functions if you have a large number of rows in your tree model. Cell data functions process every cell in the column before it is rendered, so they can significantly slow down tree models with many rows.

In Listing 8-10, a cell data function is used to set the background color to the value of the color string stored by the cell. The foreground color is also set to white for every cell, although this could also be applied to the whole renderer with g_object_set(). This application shows a list of the 256 web-safe colors.

Listing 8-10. *Using Cell Data Functions (celldatafunctions.c)*

```
#include <gtk/gtk.h>

enum
{
  COLOR = 0,
  COLUMNS
};

const gchar *clr[6] = { "00", "33", "66", "99", "CC", "FF" };

static void setup_tree_view (GtkWidget*);
static void cell_data_func (GtkTreeViewColumn*, GtkCellRenderer*,
                            GtkTreeModel*, GtkTreeIter*, gpointer);

int main (int argc,
          char *argv[])
{
  GtkWidget *window, *treeview, *scrolled_win;
  GtkListStore *store;
  GtkTreeIter iter;
  guint i, j, k;

  gtk_init (&argc, &argv);

  window = gtk_window_new (GTK_WINDOW_TOPLEVEL);
  gtk_window_set_title (GTK_WINDOW (window), "Color List");
  gtk_container_set_border_width (GTK_CONTAINER (window), 10);
  gtk_widget_set_size_request (window, 250, 175);

  treeview = gtk_tree_view_new ();
  setup_tree_view (treeview);
  store = gtk_list_store_new (COLUMNS, G_TYPE_STRING);
```

```
  /* Add all of the products to the GtkListStore. */
  for (i = 0; i < 6; i++)
    for (j = 0; j < 6; j++)
      for (k = 0; k < 6; k++)
      {
        gchar *color = g_strconcat ("#", clr[i], clr[j], clr[k], NULL);
        gtk_list_store_append (store, &iter);
        gtk_list_store_set (store, &iter, COLOR, color, -1);
        g_free (color);
      }

  gtk_tree_view_set_model (GTK_TREE_VIEW (treeview), GTK_TREE_MODEL (store));
  g_object_unref (store);

  scrolled_win = gtk_scrolled_window_new (NULL, NULL);
  gtk_scrolled_window_set_policy (GTK_SCROLLED_WINDOW (scrolled_win),
                                  GTK_POLICY_AUTOMATIC, GTK_POLICY_AUTOMATIC);

  gtk_container_add (GTK_CONTAINER (scrolled_win), treeview);
  gtk_container_add (GTK_CONTAINER (window), scrolled_win);
  gtk_widget_show_all (window);

  gtk_main ();
  return 0;
}


/* Add three columns to the GtkTreeView. All three of the columns will be
 * displayed as text, although one is a gboolean value and another is
 * an integer. */
static void
setup_tree_view (GtkWidget *treeview)
{
  GtkCellRenderer *renderer;
  GtkTreeViewColumn *column;

  renderer = gtk_cell_renderer_text_new ();
  column = gtk_tree_view_column_new_with_attributes
                      ("Standard Colors", renderer, "text", COLOR, NULL);
  gtk_tree_view_append_column (GTK_TREE_VIEW (treeview), column);

  gtk_tree_view_column_set_cell_data_func (column, renderer,
                                           cell_data_func, NULL, NULL);

}
```

```
static void
cell_data_func (GtkTreeViewColumn *column,
                GtkCellRenderer *renderer,
                GtkTreeModel *model,
                GtkTreeIter *iter,
                gpointer data)
{
  gchar *text;

  /* Get the color string stored by the column and make it the foreground color. */
  gtk_tree_model_get (model, iter, COLOR, &text, -1);
  g_object_set (renderer, "foreground", "#FFFFFF", "foreground-set", TRUE,
                "background", text, "background-set", TRUE, "text", text, NULL);
  g_free (text);
}
```

Another example of a useful cell data function is when you are using floating point numbers, and you need to control the number of decimal places that are displayed. In fact, that example will be used when you learn about spin button cell renderers in the "Spin Button Cell Renderer" section of this chapter.

Once you have set up your cell data function, you need to connect it to a specific column by calling gtk_tree_view_column_set_cell_data_func(). The last two parameters of this function allow you to supply data that will be passed to the cell data function and an additional function that will be called to destroy the data. You can set both of these parameters to NULL if they are not necessary.

```
void gtk_tree_view_column_set_cell_data_func (GtkTreeViewColumn *column,
                                              GtkCellRenderer *renderer,
                                              GtkTreeCellDataFunc cell_data_func,
                                              gpointer data,
                                              GtkDestroyNotify destroy_data);
```

If you have added a cell data function to a column that you now want to remove, you should call gtk_tree_view_column_set_cell_data_func() with the cell_data_func parameter set to NULL.

As previously stated, cell data functions should only be used when you have a definite need for fine-tuning the rendering of the data. In most cases, you will want to use additional column attributes or g_object_set() to change properties, depending on the scope of the settings. As a rule of thumb, cell data functions should only be used to apply settings that cannot be handled with column attributes or may not be set for every cell.

Cell Renderers

Up to this point, you have only learned about one type of cell renderer, GtkCellRendererText. This renderer allows you to display strings, numbers, and Boolean values as text. You are able to customize how the text is displayed with cell renderer attributes and cell data functions and allow it to be edited by the user.

GTK+ provides a large number of cell renderers that can display other types of widgets besides text. These are toggle buttons, images, spin buttons, combo boxes, progress bars, and accelerators, which will all be covered in this section.

Toggle Button Renderers

Displaying Boolean values as "TRUE" or "FALSE" with GtkCellRendererText is a bit tacky, and it takes up a large amount of valuable space in each row, especially when there are a lot of visible Boolean columns. You might be thinking that it would be nice if you could display a check button for Boolean values instead of text strings. It turns out that you can—with the help of a type of cell renderer named GtkCellRendererToggle.

By default, toggle button cell renderers are drawn as a check button, as shown in Figure 8-10. You can also set up toggle button renderers to be drawn as radio buttons, but you will need to manage the radio button functionality yourself.

Figure 8-10. *Toggle button renderers*

As with editable text renderers, you have to manually apply the changes performed by the user. Otherwise, the button will not toggle visually on the screen. Because of this, GtkCellRendererToggle provides the toggled signal, which is emitted when the user presses the check button. Listing 8-11 presents a toggled callback function for the Grocery List application. In this version of the application, the BUY_IT column is rendered with GtkCellRendererToggle.

Listing 8-11. *GtkCellRendererToggle Toggled Callback Function*

```
static void
buy_it_toggled (GtkCellRendererToggle *renderer,
                gchar *path,
                GtkTreeView *treeview)
{
  GtkTreeModel *model;
  GtkTreeIter iter;
  gboolean value;

  /* Toggle the cell renderer's current state to the logical not. */
  model = gtk_tree_view_get_model (treeview);
  if (gtk_tree_model_get_iter_from_string (model, &iter, path))
  {
    gtk_tree_model_get (model, &iter, BUY_IT, &value, -1);
    gtk_list_store_set (GTK_LIST_STORE (model), &iter, BUY_IT, !value, -1);
  }
}
```

Toggle cell renderers are created with gtk_cell_renderer_toggle_new(). After creating a toggle cell renderer, you will want to set its activatable property to TRUE so that it is able to be toggled. Otherwise, the user will not be able to toggle the button (which can be useful if you only want to display a setting but not allow it to be edited). g_object_set() can be used to apply this setting to every cell.

Next, the active property should be added as a column attribute instead of text, which was used by GtkCellRendererText. This property is set to TRUE or FALSE, depending on the desired state of the toggle button.

Then, you should connect the GtkCellRendererToggle cell renderer to a callback function for the toggled signal. Listing 8-11 gives an example callback function for the toggled signal. This callback function receives the cell renderer and a GtkTreePath string pointing to the row that contains the toggle button.

Within the callback function, you will need to manually toggle the current value displayed by the toggle button as shown in the following two lines of code. The emission of a toggled signal only tells you that the user *wants* the button to be toggled; it does not perform the action for you.

```
gtk_tree_model_get (model, &iter, BUY_IT, &value, -1);
gtk_list_store_set (GTK_LIST_STORE (model), &iter, BUY_IT, !value, -1);
```

To toggle the value, you can use gtk_tree_model_get() to retrieve the current value stored by the cell. Since the cell will be storing a Boolean value, you can set the new value to the opposite of the current in gtk_list_store_set().

As previously mentioned, GtkCellRendererToggle also allows you to render the toggle as a radio button. This can be initially set to the renderer by changing the radio property with gtk_cell_renderer_toggle_set_radio().

```
void gtk_cell_renderer_toggle_set_radio (GtkCellRendererToggle *toggle,
                                         gboolean radio);
```

You need to realize that the only thing that is changed by setting radio to TRUE is the rendering of the toggle button! You will have to manually implement the functionality of a radio button through your toggled callback function. This includes activating the new toggle button and deactivating the previously selected toggle button.

Pixbuf Renderers

Adding images in the form of GdkPixbuf objects as a column in a GtkTreeView is a very useful feature provided by GtkCellRendererPixbuf. An example of a pixbuf renderer can be viewed in Figure 8-11, which shows a small icon to the left of each item.

Figure 8-11. *Pixbuf renderers*

You have already learned almost everything necessary to add GdkPixbuf images to a tree view in previous sections, but Listing 8-12 presents a simple example to guide you. There is no need to create a separate column header for pixbufs in most cases, so Listing 8-12 shows you how to include multiple renderers in one column. Pixbuf cell renderers are extremely useful in types of tree view implementations such as file system browsers.

Listing 8-12. *GdkPixbuf Cell Renderers*

```
static void
setup_tree_view (GtkWidget *treeview)
{
  GtkCellRenderer *renderer;
  GtkTreeViewColumn *column;

  /* Create a tree view column with two renderers, one a pixbuf and one text. */
  column = gtk_tree_view_column_new ();
  gtk_tree_view_column_set_title (column, "Products");

  renderer = gtk_cell_renderer_pixbuf_new ();
  gtk_tree_view_column_pack_start (column, renderer, FALSE);
  gtk_tree_view_column_set_attributes (column, renderer, "pixbuf", ICON, NULL);

  renderer = gtk_cell_renderer_text_new ();
  gtk_tree_view_column_pack_start (column, renderer, TRUE);
  gtk_tree_view_column_set_attributes (column, renderer, "text", PRODUCT, NULL);

  gtk_tree_view_append_column (GTK_TREE_VIEW (treeview), column);
}
```

New GtkCellRendererPixbuf objects are created with gtk_cell_renderer_pixbuf_new(). You will then want to add the renderer to the column. Since there will be multiple renderers in our column, you can use gtk_tree_view_column_pack_start() to add the renderer to the column.

Next, you need to add attributes to the column for the GtkCellRendererPixbuf object. In Listing 8-12, the pixbuf property was used so that we could load a custom icon from a file. However, pixbufs are not the only type of image supported by GtkCellRendererPixbuf. You can also use the stock-id property, which will allow you to provide a stock icon identifier. This will display the stock icon instead of a custom GdkPixbuf image. A full list of stock icons available as of GTK+ 2.10 is shown in Appendix D.

If you are using a GtkTreeStore, it is useful to display a different pixbuf when the row is expanded and when it is retracted. To do this, you can specify two GdkPixbuf objects to pixbuf-expander-open and pixbuf-expander-closed. For example, you may want to do this to display an open folder when the row is expanded and a closed folder when the row is retracted.

When you create the tree model, you will need to use a new type called GDK_TYPE_PIXBUF, which will store GdkPixbuf objects in each model column. Every time you add a GdkPixbuf to a tree model column, its reference count is incremented by one. You should call g_object_unref() on the GdkPixbuf object after you are finished with it, so it will be destroyed at the same time as the tree view.

Spin Button Renderers

In Chapter 4, you learned how to use the GtkSpinButton widget. While GtkCellRendererText can display numbers, a better option is to use GtkCellRendererSpin. Instead of displaying a

GtkEntry when the content is to be edited, a GtkSpinButton is used. An example of a cell rendered with GtkCellRendererSpin that is being edited is shown in Figure 8-12.

Figure 8-12. *Spin Button renderers*

You will notice that the floating point numbers in the first column in Figure 8-12 show multiple decimal places. You can set the number of decimal places shown in the spin button but not the displayed text. To decrease or eliminate the number of decimal places, you should use a cell data function. An example of a cell data function that hides decimal places is shown in Listing 8-13.

Listing 8-13. *Cell Data Function for Floating Point Numbers*

```
static void
cell_data_func (GtkTreeViewColumn *column,
                GtkCellRenderer *renderer,
                GtkTreeModel *model,
                GtkTreeIter *iter,
                gpointer data)
{
  gfloat value;
  gchar *text;

  /* Retrieve the current value and render it with no decimal places. */
  gtk_tree_model_get (model, iter, QUANTITY, &value, -1);
  text = g_strdup_printf ("%.0f", value);
  g_object_set (renderer, "text", text, NULL);
  g_free (text);
}
```

Recall that if you want to dictate the number of decimal places shown by a floating point number in a column using GtkCellRendererText or another derived renderer, you need to use a cell data function. In Listing 8-13, a sample cell data function was shown that reads in the current floating point number and forces the renderer to display no decimal places. This is necessary because GtkCellRendererSpin stores numbers as floating point numbers.

GtkCellRendererSpin is compatible with both integers and floating point numbers, because its parameters are stored in a GtkAdjustment. Listing 8-14 is an implementation of the Grocery List application in which the Quantity column is rendered with GtkCellRendererSpin.

Listing 8-14. *Spin Button Cell Renderers*

```
static void
setup_tree_view (GtkWidget *treeview)
{
  GtkCellRenderer *renderer;
  GtkTreeViewColumn *column;
  GtkAdjustment *adj;

  adj = GTK_ADJUSTMENT (gtk_adjustment_new (0.0, 0.0, 100.0, 1.0, 2.0, 2.0));

  renderer = gtk_cell_renderer_spin_new ();
  g_object_set (renderer, "editable", TRUE, "adjustment", adj, "digits", 0, NULL);

  g_signal_connect (G_OBJECT (renderer), "edited",
                    G_CALLBACK (cell_edited),
                    (gpointer) treeview);

  column = gtk_tree_view_column_new_with_attributes
                        ("Count", renderer, "text", QUANTITY, NULL);
  gtk_tree_view_append_column (GTK_TREE_VIEW (treeview), column);

  /* ... Add a cell renderer for the PRODUCT column ... */
}

/* Apply the changed text to the cell. */
static void
cell_edited (GtkCellRendererText *renderer,
             gchar *path,
             gchar *new_text,
             GtkTreeView *treeview)
{
  GtkTreeIter iter;
  GtkTreeModel *model;
  GtkAdjustment *adjustment;
  gdouble value;

  /* Retrieve the current value stored by the spin button renderer's adjustment. */
  g_object_get (renderer, "adjustment", &adjustment, NULL);
  value = gtk_adjustmnet_get_value (adjustment);
```

```
    model = gtk_tree_view_get_model (treeview);
    if (gtk_tree_model_get_iter_from_string (model, &iter, path))
        gtk_list_store_set (GTK_LIST_STORE (model), &iter, QUANTITY, value, -1);
}
```

New GtkCellRendererSpin objects are created with gtk_cell_renderer_spin(). After you create the renderer, you should set the editable, adjustment, and digits properties of the object with g_object_set().

```
g_object_set (renderer, "editable", TRUE, "adjustment", adj, "digits", 0, NULL);
```

GtkCellRendererSpin provides three properties: adjustment, climb-rate, and digits. These are stored in a GtkAdjustment defining the spin button's properties, the acceleration rate when an arrow button is held down, and the number of decimal places to display in the spin button respectively. The climb rate and number of decimals to display are both set to zero by default.

GtkCellRendererSpin is derived from GtkCellRendererText, so you also have all of GtkCellRendererText's properties available, including editable, which must be set to TRUE to allow the content of the cell to be edited.

After setting up the cell renderer, you should then connect to the edited signal to the cell renderer, which will be used to apply the new value chosen by the user to the cell. There is usually no need to filter this value, because the adjustment will already limit the values allowed by the cell. The callback function will be run after the user presses the Enter key or moves focus from the spin button of a cell that is being edited.

Within the cell_edited() callback function in Listing 8-14, you need to first retrieve the adjustment of the spin button renderer, because it will store the new value that is to be displayed. This new value can then be applied to the given cell.

■ Note Although the edited signal of a GtkCellRendererText still receives the new_text parameter, this should not be used. The parameter will not store a textual version of the spin button's value. Furthermore, the value used in gtk_list_store_set() that will replace the current value must be supplied as a floating point number, so a string will not be acceptable regardless of its contents.

You can retrieve the adjustment's value with gtk_adjustment_get_value(), applying it to the appropriate column. Since the QUANTITY column is used to display a floating point number (G_TYPE_FLOAT), you can use the returned type in its current state.

When creating the tree model, the column must be of the type G_TYPE_FLOAT, even if you want to store an integer. You should use cell data functions to limit the number of decimal places displayed by each cell.

Combo Box Renderers

GtkCellRendererCombo provides a cell renderer for a widget that you have just learned about, GtkComboBox. Combo box cell renderers are useful, because they allow you to present multiple predefined options to the user. GtkCellRendererCombo renders text in a similar way to

GtkCellRendererText, but instead of showing a GtkEntry widget when editing, a GtkComboBox widget is presented to the user. An example of a GtkCellRendererCombo cell being edited can be viewed in Figure 8-13.

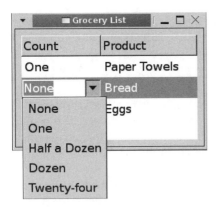

Figure 8-13. *A combo box cell renderer*

To use GtkCellRendererCombo, you need to create a GtkTreeModel for every cell in the column. In Listing 8-15, the QUANTITY column of the Grocery List application from Listing 8-1 is rendered with GtkCellRendererCombo.

Listing 8-15. *Combo Box Cell Renderers*

```
static void
setup_tree_view (GtkWidget *treeview)
{
  GtkCellRenderer *renderer;
  GtkTreeViewColumn *column;
  GtkListStore *model;
  GtkTreeIter iter;

  /* Create a GtkListStore that will be used for the combo box renderer. */
  model = gtk_list_store_new (1, G_TYPE_STRING);

  gtk_list_store_append (model, &iter);
  gtk_list_store_set (model, &iter, 0, "None", -1);
  gtk_list_store_append (model, &iter);
  gtk_list_store_set (model, &iter, 0, "One", -1);
  gtk_list_store_append (model, &iter);
  gtk_list_store_set (model, &iter, 0, "Half a Dozen", -1);
  gtk_list_store_append (model, &iter);
  gtk_list_store_set (model, &iter, 0, "Dozen", -1);
  gtk_list_store_append (model, &iter);
  gtk_list_store_set (model, &iter, 0, "Two Dozen", -1);
```

```
  /* Create the GtkCellRendererCombo and add the tree model. Then, add the
   * renderer to a new column and add the column to the GtkTreeView. */
  renderer = gtk_cell_renderer_combo_new ();
  g_object_set (renderer, "text-column", 0, "editable", TRUE,
                "has-entry", TRUE, "model", model, NULL);
  column = gtk_tree_view_column_new_with_attributes
                        ("Count", renderer, "text", QUANTITY, NULL);
  gtk_tree_view_append_column (GTK_TREE_VIEW (treeview), column);

  g_signal_connect (G_OBJECT (renderer), "edited",
                    G_CALLBACK (cell_edited),
                    (gpointer) treeview);

  renderer = gtk_cell_renderer_text_new ();
  column = gtk_tree_view_column_new_with_attributes
                        ("Product", renderer, "text", PRODUCT, NULL);
  gtk_tree_view_append_column (GTK_TREE_VIEW (treeview), column);
}

/* Apply the changed text to the cell. */
static void
cell_edited (GtkCellRendererText *renderer,
             gchar *path,
             gchar *new_text,
             GtkTreeView *treeview)
{
  GtkTreeIter iter;
  GtkTreeModel *model;

  /* Make sure the text is not empty. If not, apply it to the tree view cell. */
  if (g_ascii_strcasecmp (new_text, "") != 0)
  {
    model = gtk_tree_view_get_model (treeview);
    if (gtk_tree_model_get_iter_from_string (model, &iter, path))
      gtk_list_store_set (GTK_LIST_STORE (model), &iter, QUANTITY, new_text, -1);
  }
}
```

New combo box cell renderers are created with gtk_cell_renderer_combo_new(). GtkCellRendererCombo has three properties in addition to those inherited from GtkCellRendererText: has-entry, model, and text-column.

```
g_object_set (renderer, "text-column", 0, "editable", TRUE,
              "has-entry", TRUE, "model", model, NULL);
```

The first property you need to set is text-column, which refers to the column in the combo box's tree model that will be displayed in the cell renderer. This must be a type supported by GtkCellRendererText, such as G_TYPE_STRING, G_TYPE_INT, or G_TYPE_BOOLEAN. The model property is a GtkTreeModel that will be used as the content of the combo box. You must also set the editable property to TRUE, so the cell content may be edited.

Lastly, there is a widget called GtkComboBoxEntry that gives the user choices like a normal combo box, but it also uses a GtkEntry widget to allow the user to enter a custom string instead of choosing an existing option. To allow this functionality with a combo box cell renderer, you must set the has-entry property to TRUE. This is turned on by default, which means that you must turn it off to restrict the choices to those that appear in GtkCellRendererCombo's tree model.

As with other cell renderers derived from GtkCellRendererText, you will want to use the text field as the column attribute and set its initial text when creating the tree view's model. You can then use the edited signal to apply the text to the tree model. In Listing 8-15, the changes are only applied when the new_text string is not empty, since the user is free to enter free-form text as well.

Progress Bar Renderers

Another type of cell renderer is GtkCellRendererProgress, which implements the GtkProgressBar widget. While progress bars support pulsing, GtkCellRendererProgress only allows you to set the current value of the progress bar. Figure 8-14 shows a GtkTreeView widget that has a progress bar cell renderer in the second column, which displays textual feedback.

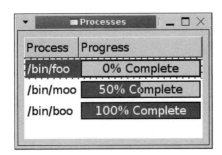

Figure 8-14. *Progress bar cell renderers*

Progress bar cell renderers are another easy feature to implement in a program. You can use gtk_cell_renderer_progress_new() to create new GtkCellRendererProgress objects. GtkCellRendererProgress provides two properties: text and value.

The progress bar state is defined by the value property, which is an integer with a value between 0 and 100. A value of 0 refers to an empty progress bar, and 100 refers to a full progress bar. Since it is stored as an integer, the tree model column corresponding to the value of the progress bar should have the type G_TYPE_INT.

The second property provided by GtkCellRendererProgress is text. This property is a string that will be drawn over the top of the progress bar. This property can be ignored in some cases, but it is usually a good idea to give the user more information about the progress of a process. Examples of possible progress bar strings are "67% Complete", "3 of 80 Files Processed", "Installing foo . . .", and so on.

GtkCellRendererProgress is a useful cell renderer in some cases, but you should be careful when you deploy it. You should avoid using multiple progress bars in one row, because doing so could confuse the user and will take up a lot of horizontal space. Also, tree views with many rows will appear messy. In many cases, it would be better for the user to use a textual cell renderer instead of a progress bar cell renderer.

However, there are some cases where GtkCellRendererProgress is a good choice. For example, if your application has to manage multiple downloads at the same time, progress bar cell renderers are an easy way to give coherent feedback about progress for each download.

Keyboard Accelerator Renderers

GTK+ 2.10 introduced a new type of cell renderer called GtkCellRendererAccel, which displays a textual representation of a keyboard accelerator. An example of an accelerator cell renderer can be viewed in Figure 8-15.

Figure 8-15. *Accelerator cell renderers*

Listing 8-16 creates a list of actions along with their keyboard accelerators. This type of tree view could be used to allow the user to edit the accelerators for an application. The accelerator is displayed as text, since the renderer is derived from GtkCellRendererText.

To edit the accelerator, the user needs to click the cell once. The cell will then show a string asking for a key. The new key code will be added, along with any mask keys such as Ctrl and Shift into the cell. Basically, the first keyboard shortcut pressed will be displayed by the cell.

Listing 8-16. *Keyboard Accelerator Cell Renderers (accelerators.c)*

```c
#include <gtk/gtk.h>
#include <gdk/gdkkeysyms.h>

enum
{
  ACTION = 0,
  MASK,
  VALUE,
  COLUMNS
};

typedef struct
{
  gchar *action;
  GdkModifierType mask;
  guint value;
} Accelerator;

const Accelerator list[] =
{
  { "Cut", GDK_CONTROL_MASK, GDK_X },
  { "Copy", GDK_CONTROL_MASK, GDK_C },
  { "Paste", GDK_CONTROL_MASK, GDK_V },
  { "New", GDK_CONTROL_MASK, GDK_N },
  { "Open", GDK_CONTROL_MASK, GDK_O },
  { "Print", GDK_CONTROL_MASK, GDK_P },
  { NULL, NULL, NULL }
};

static void setup_tree_view (GtkWidget*);
static void accel_edited (GtkCellRendererAccel*, gchar*, guint,
                          GdkModifierType, guint, GtkTreeView*);

int main (int argc,
          char *argv[])
{
  GtkWidget *window, *treeview, *scrolled_win;
  GtkListStore *store;
  GtkTreeIter iter;
  guint i = 0;

  gtk_init (&argc, &argv);
```

```
  window = gtk_window_new (GTK_WINDOW_TOPLEVEL);
  gtk_window_set_title (GTK_WINDOW (window), "Accelerator Keys");
  gtk_container_set_border_width (GTK_CONTAINER (window), 10);
  gtk_widget_set_size_request (window, 250, 250);

  treeview = gtk_tree_view_new ();
  setup_tree_view (treeview);

  store = gtk_list_store_new (COLUMNS, G_TYPE_STRING, G_TYPE_INT, G_TYPE_UINT);

  /* Add all of the keyboard accelerators to the GtkListStore. */
  while (list[i].action != NULL)
  {
    gtk_list_store_append (store, &iter);
    gtk_list_store_set (store, &iter, ACTION, list[i].action,
                        MASK, (gint) list[i].mask, VALUE, list[i].value, -1);
    i++;
  }

  gtk_tree_view_set_model (GTK_TREE_VIEW (treeview), GTK_TREE_MODEL (store));
  g_object_unref (store);

  scrolled_win = gtk_scrolled_window_new (NULL, NULL);
  gtk_scrolled_window_set_policy (GTK_SCROLLED_WINDOW (scrolled_win),
                                  GTK_POLICY_AUTOMATIC, GTK_POLICY_AUTOMATIC);

  gtk_container_add (GTK_CONTAINER (scrolled_win), treeview);
  gtk_container_add (GTK_CONTAINER (window), scrolled_win);
  gtk_widget_show_all (window);

  gtk_main ();
  return 0;
}

/* Create a tree view with two columns. The first is an action and the
 * second is a keyboard accelerator. */
static void
setup_tree_view (GtkWidget *treeview)
{
  GtkCellRenderer *renderer;
  GtkTreeViewColumn *column;

  renderer = gtk_cell_renderer_text_new ();
  column = gtk_tree_view_column_new_with_attributes
                        ("Buy", renderer, "text", ACTION, NULL);
  gtk_tree_view_append_column (GTK_TREE_VIEW (treeview), column);
```

```
    renderer = gtk_cell_renderer_accel_new ();
    g_object_set (renderer, "accel-mode", GTK_CELL_RENDERER_ACCEL_MODE_GTK,
                  "editable", TRUE, NULL);

    column = gtk_tree_view_column_new_with_attributes ("Buy", renderer,
                            "accel-mods", MASK, "accel-key", VALUE, NULL);
    gtk_tree_view_append_column (GTK_TREE_VIEW (treeview), column);

    g_signal_connect (G_OBJECT (renderer), "accel_edited",
                      G_CALLBACK (accel_edited),
                      (gpointer) treeview);
}

/* Apply the new keyboard accelerator key and mask to the cell. */
static void
accel_edited (GtkCellRendererAccel *renderer,
              gchar *path,
              guint accel_key,
              GdkModifierType mask,
              guint hardware_keycode,
              GtkTreeView *treeview)
{
  GtkTreeModel *model;
  GtkTreeIter iter;

  model = gtk_tree_view_get_model (treeview);
  if (gtk_tree_model_get_iter_from_string (model, &iter, path))
    gtk_list_store_set (GTK_LIST_STORE (model), &iter,
                        MASK, (gint) mask, VALUE, accel_key, -1);
}
```

You can use gtk_cell_renderer_accel_new() to create new GtkCellRendererAccel objects. GtkCellRendererAccel provides the following four properties that can be accessed with g_object_get():

- accel-key: The key value that corresponds to the accelerator. A full list of key values can be found in <gdk/gdkkeysyms.h>.

- accel-mode: A GtkCellRendererAccelMode value—GTK_CELL_RENDERER_ACCEL_MODE_GTK or GTK_CELL_RENDERER_ACCEL_MODE_OTHER. This defines how the accelerators are rendered within the cell. You should usually use GTK+'s version of rendering.

- accel-mods: An accelerator modifier of the type GdkModifierType. This allows you to detect Shift, Ctrl, Alt, and other masking keys.

- keycode: The hardware keycode of the accelerator, which is not usually used. This is only necessary if you do not define a key value.

The `accel-mods` value allows you to detect keys that usually do not cause any immediate action from an application by themselves. These values are defined by the `GdkModifierType` enumeration, although not all values can occur when dealing with keyboard accelerators. A list of important values follows:

- `GDK_SHIFT_MASK`: The Shift key.

- `GDK_CONTROL_MASK`: The Ctrl key.

- `GDK_MOD_MASK`, `GDK_MOD2_MASK`, `GDK_MOD3_MASK`, `GDK_MOD4_MASK`, `GDK_MOD5_MASK`: The first modifier usually represents the Alt key, but these are interpreted based on your X server mapping of the keys. They can also correspond to the Meta, Super, or Hyper key.

- `GDK_SUPER_MASK`: Introduced in 2.10, this allows you to explicitly state the Super modifier. This modifier may not be available on all systems!

- `GDK_HYPER_MASK`: Introduced in 2.10, this allows you to explicitly state the Hyper modifier. This modifier may not be available on all systems!

- `GDK_META_MODIFIER`: Introduced in 2.10, this allows you to explicitly state the Meta modifier. This modifier may not be available on all systems!

In most cases, you will want to set the modifier mask (`acel-mods`) and the accelerator key value (`accel-key`) as two attributes of the tree view column using `GtkCellRendererAccel`. In this case, the modifier mask will be of they type `G_TYPE_INT`, and the accelerator key value `G_TYPE_UINT`. Because of this, you will want to make sure to case the `GdkModifierType` value to a `gint` when setting the content of the modifier mask column.

```
store = gtk_list_store_new (COLUMNS, G_TYPE_STRING, G_TYPE_INT, G_TYPE_UINT);
```

`GtkCellRendererAccel` provides two signals. The first, `accel-cleared`, allows you to reset the accelerator when the user removes the current value. In most cases, you will not need to do this unless you have a default value that you want the accelerator to revert to.

Of greater importance, `accel-edited` allows you to apply changes that the user makes to the keyboard accelerator, as long as you set the `editable` property to `TRUE`. The callback function receives a path string to the row in question along with the accelerator key code, mask and hardware key code. In the callback function, you can apply the changes with `gtk_list_store_set()`, as you would with any other editable type of cell.

Test Your Understanding

In Exercise 8-1, you will have the opportunity to practice using the `GtkTreeView` widget, along with multiple types of cell renderers. This is an extremely important exercise for you to try, because you will need to use the `GtkTreeView` widget in many applications. As always, when you are finished, you can find one possible solution in Appendix F.

Exercise 8-1. File Browser

By now, you have probably had enough of Grocery List applications, so let us try something different. In this exercise, create a file browser using the GtkTreeView widget. You should use GtkListStore for the file browser and allow the user to browse throughout the file system.

The file browser should show images to differentiate among directories and files. Images can be found in the downloadable source code at www.gtkbook.com. You can also use the GLib directory utility functions to retrieve directory content. Double-clicking a directory should move to that location.

Summary

In this chapter, you learned how to use the GtkTreeView widget. This widget allows you to display lists and tree structures of data with GtkListStore and GtkTreeStore respectively. You also learned the relationship among the tree view, tree model, columns, and cell renderers and how to use each of the objects.

Next, you learned about the types of objects that can be used to refer to a row within the tree view. These include tree iterators, paths, and row references. Each of these objects has its own advantages and disadvantages. Tree iterators can be used directly with models, but they become invalid when the tree model changes. Tree paths are easily understandable, because they have associated human-readable strings, but may not point to the same row if the tree model is changed. Lastly, tree row references are useful, because they remain valid for as long as the row exists, even when the model is changed.

You next learned how to handle selections of one row or multiple rows. With multiple row selections, you can use a for-each function, or you can get a GList list of the selected rows. A useful signal when dealing with selections is GtkTreeView's row-activated signal, which allows you to handle double-clicks.

After that, you learned how to create editable cells with GtkCellRendererText's edited signal, which displays a GtkEntry to allow the user to edit the content in the cell. Cell data functions can also be connected to columns. These cell data functions allow you to customize each cell before it is rendered to the screen.

Lastly, you learned about a number of cell renderers that allow you to display toggle buttons, pixbufs, spin buttons, combo boxes, progress bars, and keyboard accelerator strings. You were also introduced to the GtkComboBox widget.

Congratulations! You are now familiar with one of the hardest and most versatile widgets provided by GTK+. In the next chapter, you will learn how to create menus, toolbars, and pop-up menus. You will also learn how to automate menu creation with user interface (UI) files.

CHAPTER 9

■ ■ ■

Menus and Toolbars

This chapter will teach you how to create pop-up menus, menu bars, and toolbars. You will begin by creating each manually, so you learn how the widgets are constructed. This will give you a firm understanding of all of the concepts on which menus and toolbars rely.

After you understand each widget, you will be introduced to GtkUIManager, which allows you to dynamically create menus and toolbars through custom XML files. Each user interface file is loaded, and each element applied to a corresponding action object, which tells the item how it will be displayed and how it will act.

In this chapter, you will learn the following:

- How to create pop-up menus, menu bars, and toolbars

- How to apply keyboard accelerators to menu items

- What the GtkStatusBar widget is and how you can use it to provide more information to the user about a menu item

- What types of menu and toolbar items are provided by GTK+

- How to dynamically create menus and toolbars with UI files

- How to create custom stock items with GtkIconFactory

Pop-up Menus

You will begin this chapter by learning how to create a pop-up menu. A pop-up menu is a GtkMenu widget that is displayed to the user when the right mouse button is clicked while hovering above certain widgets. Some widgets, such as GtkEntry and GtkTextView, already have pop-up menus built into the widget by default.

If you want to change the pop-up menu of a widget that offers one by default, you should edit the supplied GtkMenu widget in the pop-up callback function. For example, both GtkEntry and GtkTextView have a populate-popup signal, which receives the GtkMenu that is going to be displayed. You can edit this menu in any way you see fit before displaying it to the user.

Creating a Pop-up Menu

For most widgets, you will need to create your own pop-up menu. In this section, you are going to learn how to supply a pop-up menu to a GtkProgressBar widget. The pop-up menu we are going to implement is presented in Figure 9-1.

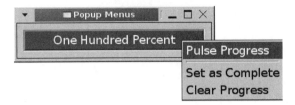

Figure 9-1. *A simple pop-up menu with three menu items*

The three pop-up menu items are used to pulse the progress bar, set it as 100 percent complete, and clear it. You will notice that, in Listing 9-1, an event box contains the progress bar. Because GtkProgressBar, like GtkLabel, is not able to detect GDK events by itself, we need to catch button-press-event signals using an event box.

Listing 9-1. *Simple Pop-up Menu (popupmenus.c)*

```
#include <gtk/gtk.h>

static void create_popup_menu (GtkWidget*, GtkWidget*);
static void pulse_activated (GtkMenuItem*, GtkProgressBar*);
static void clear_activated (GtkMenuItem*, GtkProgressBar*);
static void fill_activated (GtkMenuItem*, GtkProgressBar*);
static gboolean button_press_event (GtkWidget*, GdkEventButton*, GtkWidget*);

int main (int argc,
          char *argv[])
{
  GtkWidget *window, *progress, *eventbox, *menu;

  gtk_init (&argc, &argv);

  window = gtk_window_new (GTK_WINDOW_TOPLEVEL);
  gtk_window_set_title (GTK_WINDOW (window), "Pop-up Menus");
  gtk_container_set_border_width (GTK_CONTAINER (window), 10);
  gtk_widget_set_size_request (window, 250, -1);
```

```c
/* Create all of the necessary widgets and initialize the pop-up menu. */
menu = gtk_menu_new ();
eventbox = gtk_event_box_new ();
progress = gtk_progress_bar_new ();
gtk_progress_bar_set_text (GTK_PROGRESS_BAR (progress), "Nothing Yet Happened");
create_popup_menu (menu, progress);

gtk_progress_bar_set_pulse_step (GTK_PROGRESS_BAR (progress), 0.05);
gtk_event_box_set_above_child (GTK_EVENT_BOX (eventbox), FALSE);

g_signal_connect (G_OBJECT (eventbox), "button_press_event",
                  G_CALLBACK (button_press_event), menu);

gtk_container_add (GTK_CONTAINER (eventbox), progress);
gtk_container_add (GTK_CONTAINER (window), eventbox);

gtk_widget_set_events (eventbox, GDK_BUTTON_PRESS_MASK);
gtk_widget_realize (eventbox);

gtk_widget_show_all (window);
gtk_main ();
return 0;
}

/* Create the pop-up menu and attach it to the progress bar. This will make sure
 * that the accelerators will work from application load. */
static void
create_popup_menu (GtkWidget *menu,
                   GtkWidget *progress)
{
  GtkWidget *pulse, *fill, *clear, *separator;

  pulse = gtk_menu_item_new_with_label ("Pulse Progress");
  fill = gtk_menu_item_new_with_label ("Set as Complete");
  clear = gtk_menu_item_new_with_label ("Clear Progress");
  separator = gtk_separator_menu_item_new ();

  g_signal_connect (G_OBJECT (pulse), "activate",
                    G_CALLBACK (pulse_activated), progress);
  g_signal_connect (G_OBJECT (fill), "activate",
                    G_CALLBACK (fill_activated), progress);
  g_signal_connect (G_OBJECT (clear), "activate",
                    G_CALLBACK (clear_activated), progress);
```

```
    gtk_menu_shell_append (GTK_MENU_SHELL (menu), pulse);
    gtk_menu_shell_append (GTK_MENU_SHELL (menu), separator);
    gtk_menu_shell_append (GTK_MENU_SHELL (menu), fill);
    gtk_menu_shell_append (GTK_MENU_SHELL (menu), clear);

    gtk_menu_attach_to_widget (GTK_MENU (menu), progress, NULL);
    gtk_widget_show_all (menu);
}
```

In most cases, you will want to use button-press-event to detect when the user wants the pop-up menu to be shown. This allows you to check whether the right mouse button was clicked. If the right mouse button was clicked, GdkEventButton's button member will be equal to 3.

However, GtkWidget also provides the popup-menu signal, which is activated when the user presses built-in key accelerators to activate the pop-up menu. Most users will use the mouse to activate pop-up menus, so this is not usually a factor in GTK+ applications. Nevertheless, if you would like to handle this signal as well, you should create a third function that displays the pop-up menu that is called by both callback functions.

New menus are created with gtk_menu_new(). The menu is initialized with no initial content, so the next step is to create menu items.

In this section, we will cover two types of menu items. The first is the base class for all other types of menu items, GtkMenuItem. There are three initialization functions provided for GtkMenuItem: gtk_menu_item_new(), gtk_menu_item_new_with_label(), and gtk_menu_item_new_with_mnemonic().

```
GtkWidget* gtk_menu_item_new_with_label (const gchar *label);
```

In most cases, you will not need to use the gtk_menu_item_new(), because a menu item with no content is not of much use. If you use that function to initialize the menu item, you will have to construct each aspect of the menu in code instead of allowing GTK+ to handle the specifics.

■**Note** Menu item mnemonics are not the same thing as keyboard accelerators. A mnemonic will activate the menu item when the user presses Alt and the appropriate alphanumeric key while the menu has focus. A keyboard accelerator is a custom key combination that will cause a callback function to be run when the combination is pressed. You will learn about keyboard accelerators for menus in the next section.

The other type of basic menu item is GtkSeparatorMenuItem, which places a generic separator at its location. You can use gtk_separator_menu_item_new() to create a new separator menu item.

Separators are extremely important when designing a menu structure, because they organize menu items into groups so that the user can easily find the appropriate item. For example, in the File menu, menu items are often organized into groups that open files, save files, print files, and close the application. Rarely should you have many menu items listed without a separator in between them (e.g., a list of recent files might appear without a separator). In most cases, you should group similar menu items together and place a separator between adjacent groups.

After the menu items are created, you need to connect each menu item to the `activate` signal, which is emitted when the user selects the item. Alternatively, you can use the `activate-item` signal, which will additionally be emitted when a submenu of the given menu item is displayed. There will be no discernable difference between the two unless the menu item expands into a submenu.

Each `activate` and `activate-item` callback function receives the `GtkMenuItem` widget that initiated the action and any data you need to pass to the function. In Listing 9-2, three menu item callback functions are provided. They are used to pulse the progress bar, fill it to 100 percent complete, and clear all progress.

Now that you have created all of the menu items, you need to add them to the menu. `GtkMenu` is derived from `GtkMenuShell`, which is an abstract base class that contains and displays submenus and menu items. Menu items can be added to a menu shell with `gtk_menu_shell_append()`. This function appends each item to the end of the menu shell.

```
void gtk_menu_shell_append (GtkMenuShell *menu_shell,
                            GtkWidget *child);
```

Additionally, you can use `gtk_menu_shell_prepend()` or `gtk_menu_shell_insert()` to add a menu item to the beginning of the menu or insert it into an arbitrary position respectively. Positions accepted by `gtk_menu_shell_insert()` begin with an index of zero.

After setting all of the `GtkMenu`'s children as visible, you should call `gtk_menu_attach_to_widget()` so that the pop-up menu is associated to a specific widget. This function accepts the pop-up menu and the widget it will be attached to.

```
void gtk_menu_attach_to_widget (GtkMenu *menu,
                                GtkWidget *attach_widget,
                                GtkMenuDetachFunc detacher);
```

The last parameter of `gtk_menu_attach_widget()` accepts a `GtkMenuDetachFunc`, which can be used to call a specific function when the menu is detached from the widget.

Pop-up Menu Callback Functions

After creating the necessary widgets, you need to handle the `button-press-event` signal, which is shown in Listing 9-2. In this example, the pop-up menu is displayed every time the right mouse button is clicked on the progress bar.

Listing 9-2. *Callback Functions for the Simple Pop-up Menu (popupmenus.c)*

```
static gboolean
button_press_event (GtkWidget *eventbox,
                    GdkEventButton *event,
                    GtkWidget *menu)
{
  if ((event->button == 3) && (event->type == GDK_BUTTON_PRESS))
  {
    gtk_menu_popup (GTK_MENU (menu), NULL, NULL, NULL, NULL,
                    event->button, event->time);
    return TRUE;
  }

  return FALSE;
}

static void
pulse_activated (GtkMenuItem *item,
                 GtkProgressBar *progress)
{
  gtk_progress_bar_pulse (progress);
  gtk_progress_bar_set_text (progress, "Pulse!");
}

static void
fill_activated (GtkMenuItem *item,
                GtkProgressBar *progress)
{
  gtk_progress_bar_set_fraction (progress, 1.0);
  gtk_progress_bar_set_text (progress, "One Hundred Percent");
}

static void
clear_activated (GtkMenuItem *item,
                 GtkProgressBar *progress)
{
  gtk_progress_bar_set_fraction (progress, 0.0);
  gtk_progress_bar_set_text (progress, "Reset to Zero");
}
```

In the `button-press-event` callback function in Listing 9-2, you can use `gtk_menu_popup()` to display the menu on the screen.

```
void gtk_menu_popup (GtkMenu *menu,
                     GtkWidget *parent_menu_shell,
                     GtkWidget *parent_menu_item,
                     GtkMenuPositionFunc func,
                     gpointer func_data,
                     guint button,
                     guint32 event_time);
```

In Listing 9-2, all parameters were set to `NULL` except for the mouse button that was clicked to cause the event (`event->button`) and the time when the event occurred (`event->time`). If the pop-up menu was activated by something other than a button, you should supply 0 to the button parameter.

■Note If the action was invoked by a `popup-menu` signal, the event time will not be available. In that case, you can use `gtk_get_current_event_time()`. This function returns the timestamp of the current event or `GDK_CURRENT_TIME` if there are no recent events.

Usually, `parent_menu_shell`, `parent_menu_item`, `func`, and `func_data` are set to `NULL`, because they are used when the menu is a part of a menu bar structure. The `parent_menu_shell` widget is the menu shell that contains the item that caused the pop-up initialization. Alternatively, you can supply `parent_menu_item`, which is the menu item that caused the pop-up initialization.

`GtkMenuPositionFunc` is a function that decides at what position on the screen the menu should be drawn. It accepts `func_data` as an optional last parameter. As previously stated, these parameters are not frequently used in applications, so they can safely be set to `NULL`. In our example, the pop-up menu was already associated with the progress bar, so it will be drawn in the correct location.

Keyboard Accelerators

When creating a menu, one of the most important things to do is to set up keyboard accelerators. A keyboard accelerator is a key combination created from one accelerator key and one or more modifiers such as Ctrl or Shift. When the user presses the key combination, the appropriate signal is emitted.

Listing 9-3 is an extension of the progress bar pop-up menu application that adds keyboard accelerators to the menu items. The progress bar is pulsed when the user presses Ctrl+P, filled with Ctrl+F, and cleared with Ctrl+C.

Listing 9-3. *Adding Accelerators to Menu Items (accelerators.c)*

```
static void
create_popup_menu (GtkWidget *menu,
                   GtkWidget *window,
                   GtkWidget *progress)
{
  GtkWidget *pulse, *fill, *clear, *separator;
  GtkAccelGroup *group;

  /* Create a keyboard accelerator group for the application. */
  group = gtk_accel_group_new ();
  gtk_window_add_accel_group (GTK_WINDOW (window), group);
  gtk_menu_set_accel_group (GTK_MENU (menu), group);

  pulse = gtk_menu_item_new_with_label ("Pulse Progress");
  fill = gtk_menu_item_new_with_label ("Set as Complete");
  clear = gtk_menu_item_new_with_label ("Clear Progress");
  separator = gtk_separator_menu_item_new ();

  /* Add the necessary keyboard accelerators. */
  gtk_widget_add_accelerator (pulse, "activate", group, GDK_P,
                              GDK_CONTROL_MASK, GTK_ACCEL_VISIBLE);
  gtk_widget_add_accelerator (fill, "activate", group, GDK_F,
                              GDK_CONTROL_MASK, GTK_ACCEL_VISIBLE);
  gtk_widget_add_accelerator (clear, "activate", group, GDK_C,
                              GDK_CONTROL_MASK, GTK_ACCEL_VISIBLE);

  g_signal_connect (G_OBJECT (pulse), "activate",
                    G_CALLBACK (pulse_activated), progress);
  g_signal_connect (G_OBJECT (fill), "activate",
                    G_CALLBACK (fill_activated), progress);
  g_signal_connect (G_OBJECT (clear), "activate",
                    G_CALLBACK (clear_activated), progress);

  gtk_menu_shell_append (GTK_MENU_SHELL (menu), pulse);
  gtk_menu_shell_append (GTK_MENU_SHELL (menu), separator);
  gtk_menu_shell_append (GTK_MENU_SHELL (menu), fill);
  gtk_menu_shell_append (GTK_MENU_SHELL (menu), clear);

  gtk_menu_attach_to_widget (GTK_MENU (menu), progress, NULL);
  gtk_widget_show_all (menu);
}
```

Keyboard accelerators are stored as an instance of GtkAccelGroup. In order to implement accelerators in your application, you need to create a new accelerator group with gtk_accel_group_new(). This accelerator group must be added to the GtkWindow where the menu will appear for it to take effect. It must also be associated with any menus that take advantage of its accelerators. In Listing 9-3, this is performed immediately after creating the GtkAccelGroup with gtk_window_add_accel_group() and gtk_menu_set_accel_group().

It is possible to manually create keyboard accelerators with GtkAccelMap, but in most cases, gtk_widget_add_accelerator() will provide all of the necessary functionality. The only problem that this method presents is that the user cannot change keyboard accelerators created with this function during runtime.

```
void gtk_widget_add_accelerator (GtkWidget *widget,
                                 const gchar *signal_name,
                                 GtkAccelGroup *group,
                                 guint accel_key,
                                 GdkModifierType mods,
                                 GtkAccelFlags flags);
```

To add an accelerator to a widget, you can use gtk_widget_add_accelerator(), which will emit the signal specified by signal_name on the widget when the user presses the key combination. You need to specify your accelerator group to the function, which must be associated with the window and the menu as previously stated.

An accelerator key and one or more modifier keys form the complete key combination. A list of available accelerator keys is available in <gdk/gdkkeysyms.h>. This header file is not included in <gtk/gtk.h>, so it must explicitly be included. Modifiers are specified by the GdkModifierType enumeration. The most often used modifiers are GDK_SHIFT_LOCK, GDK_CONTROL_MASK, and GDK_MOD1_MASK, which correspond to the Shift, Ctrl, and Alt keys respectively.

■**Tip** When dealing with key codes, you need to be careful because you many need to supply multiple keys for the same action in some cases. For example, if you want to catch the number 1 key, you will need to watch for GDK_1 and GDK_KP_1—they correspond to the 1 key at the top of the keyboard and the 1 key on the numeric keypad.

The last parameter of gtk_widget_add_accelerator() is an accelerator flag. There are three flags defined by the GtkAccelFlags enumeration. The accelerator will be visible in a label if GTK_ACCEL_VISIBLE is set. GTK_ACCEL_LOCKED will prevent the user from modifying the accelerator. GTK_ACCEL_MASK will set both flags for the widget accelerator.

Status Bar Hints

Usually placed along the bottom of the main window, the GtkStatusbar widget can be used to give the user further information about what is going on in the application. A status bar can also be very useful with menus, because you can provide more information to the user about the functionality of the menu item that the mouse cursor is hovering over. A screenshot of a status bar can be viewed in Figure 9-2.

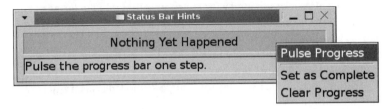

Figure 9-2. *A pop-up menu with status bar hints*

The Status Bar Widget

While the status bar can only display one message at a time, the widget actually stores a stack of messages. The currently displayed message is on the top of the stack. When you pop a message from the stack, the previous message is displayed. If there are no more strings left on the stack after you pop a message from the top, no message is displayed on the status bar.

New status bar widgets are created with gtk_statusbar_new(). This will create a new GtkStatusbar widget with an empty message stack. Before you are able to add or remove a message from the new status bar's stack, you must retrieve a context identifier with gtk_status_bar_get_context_id():

```
guint gtk_statusbar_get_context_id (GtkStatusBar *statusbar,
                                    const gchar *description);
```

The context identifier is a unique unsigned integer that is associated with a context description string. This identifier will be used for all messages of a specific type, which allows you to categorize messages on the stack.

For example, if your status bar will hold hyperlinks and IP addresses, you could create two context identifiers from the strings "URL" and "IP". When you push or pop messages to and from the stack, you have to specify a context identifier. This allows separate parts of your application to push and pop messages to and from the status bar message stack without affecting each other.

■**Tip** It is important to use different context identifiers for different categories of messages. If one part of your application is trying to give a message to the user while the other is trying to remove its own message, you do not want the wrong message to be popped from the stack!

After you generate a context identifier, you can add a message to the top of the status bar's stack with gtk_statusbar_push(). This function returns a unique message identifier for the string that was just added. This identifier can be used later to remove the message from the stack, regardless of its location.

```
guint gtk_statusbar_push (GtkStatusBar *statusbar,
                          guint context_id,
                          const gchar *message);
```

There are two ways to remove a message from the stack. If you want to remove a message from the top of the stack for a specific context ID, you can use gtk_statusbar_pop(). This function will remove the message that is highest on the status bar's stack with a context identifier of context_id.

```
void gtk_statusbar_pop (GtkStatusBar *statusbar,
                        guint context_id);
```

It is also possible to remove a specific message from the status bar's message stack with gtk_statusbar_remove(). To do this, you must provide the context identifier of the message and the message identifier of the message you want to remove, which was returned by gtk_statusbar_push() when it was added.

```
void gtk_statusbar_remove (GtkStatusBar *statusbar,
                           guint context_id,
                           guint message_id);
```

GtkStatusbar has one property, has-resize-grip, which will place a graphic in the corner of the status bar for resizing the window. The user will be able to grab the resize grip and drag it to resize its parent window. You can also use the built-in function gtk_statusbar_set_has_resize_grip() to set this property.

Menu Item Information

One useful role of the status bar is to give the user more information about the menu item the mouse cursor is currently hovering over. An example of this was shown in the previous section in Figure 9-2, which is a screenshot of the progress bar pop-up menu application in Listing 9-4.

To implement status bar hints, you should connect each of your menu items to GtkWidget's enter-notify-event and leave-notify-event signals. Listing 9-4 shows the progress bar pop-up menu application you have already learned about, except status bar hints are provided when the mouse cursor moves over a menu item.

Listing 9-4. *Displaying More Information About a Menu Item (statusbarhints.c)*

```
static void
create_popup_menu (GtkWidget *menu,
                   GtkWidget *progress,
                   GtkWidget *statusbar)
{
  GtkWidget *pulse, *fill, *clear, *separator;

  pulse = gtk_menu_item_new_with_label ("Pulse Progress");
  fill = gtk_menu_item_new_with_label ("Set as Complete");
  clear = gtk_menu_item_new_with_label ("Clear Progress");
  separator = gtk_separator_menu_item_new ();

  g_signal_connect (G_OBJECT (pulse), "activate",
                    G_CALLBACK (pulse_activated), progress);
  g_signal_connect (G_OBJECT (fill), "activate",
                    G_CALLBACK (fill_activated), progress);
  g_signal_connect (G_OBJECT (clear), "activate",
                    G_CALLBACK (clear_activated), progress);

  /* Connect signals to each menu item for status bar messages. */
  g_signal_connect (G_OBJECT (pulse), "enter-notify-event",
                    G_CALLBACK (statusbar_hint), statusbar);
  g_signal_connect (G_OBJECT (pulse), "leave-notify-event",
                    G_CALLBACK (statusbar_hint), statusbar);
  g_signal_connect (G_OBJECT (fill), "enter-notify-event",
                    G_CALLBACK (statusbar_hint), statusbar);
  g_signal_connect (G_OBJECT (fill), "leave-notify-event",
                    G_CALLBACK (statusbar_hint), statusbar);
  g_signal_connect (G_OBJECT (clear), "enter-notify-event",
                    G_CALLBACK (statusbar_hint), statusbar);
  g_signal_connect (G_OBJECT (clear), "leave-notify-event",
                    G_CALLBACK (statusbar_hint), statusbar);

  g_object_set_data (G_OBJECT (pulse), "menuhint",
                     (gpointer) "Pulse the progress bar one step.");
  g_object_set_data (G_OBJECT (fill), "menuhint",
                     (gpointer) "Set the progress bar to 100%.");
  g_object_set_data (G_OBJECT (clear), "menuhint",
                     (gpointer) "Clear the progress bar to 0%.");

  gtk_menu_shell_append (GTK_MENU_SHELL (menu), pulse);
  gtk_menu_shell_append (GTK_MENU_SHELL (menu), separator);
  gtk_menu_shell_append (GTK_MENU_SHELL (menu), fill);
  gtk_menu_shell_append (GTK_MENU_SHELL (menu), clear);
```

```
  gtk_menu_attach_to_widget (GTK_MENU (menu), progress, NULL);
  gtk_widget_show_all (menu);
}


/* Add or remove a status bar menu hint, depending on whether this function
 * is initialized by a proximity-in-event or proximity-out-event. */
static gboolean
statusbar_hint (GtkMenuItem *menuitem,
                GdkEventProximity *event,
                GtkStatusbar *statusbar)
{
  gchar *hint;
  guint id = gtk_statusbar_get_context_id (statusbar, "MenuItemHints");

  if (event->type == GDK_ENTER_NOTIFY)
  {
    hint = (gchar*) g_object_get_data (G_OBJECT (menuitem), "menuhint");
    gtk_statusbar_push (statusbar, id, hint);
  }
  else if (event->type == GDK_LEAVE_NOTIFY)
    gtk_statusbar_pop (statusbar, id);

  return FALSE;
}
```

When implementing status bar hints, you first need to figure out what signals are necessary. We want to be able to add a message to the status bar when the mouse cursor moves over the menu item and remove it when the mouse cursor leaves. From this description, using enter-notify-event and leave-notify-event is a good solution.

One advantage of using these two signals is that we only need one callback function, because the prototype for each receives a GdkEventProximity object. From this object, we can discern between GDK_ENTER_NOTIFY and GDK_LEAVE_NOTIFY events. You will want to return FALSE from the callback function, because you do not want to prevent GTK+ from handling the event; you only want to enhance what is performed when it is emitted.

Within the statusbar_hint() callback function, you should first retrieve a context identifier for the menu item messages. You can use whatever string you want, as long as your application remembers what was used. In Listing 9-4, "MenuItemHints" was used to describe all of the menu item messages added to the status bar. If other parts of the application used the status bar, using a different context identifier would leave the menu item hints untouched.

```
guint id = gtk_statusbar_get_context_id (statusbar, "MenuItemHints");
```

If the event type is GDK_ENTER_NOTIFY, you need to show the message to the user. In the create_popup_menu() function, a data parameter was added to each menu item called "menuhint". This is a more in-depth description of what the menu item does, which will be displayed to the user.

```
hint = (gchar*) g_object_get_data (G_OBJFCT (menuitem), "menuhint");
gtk_statusbar_push (statusbar, id, hint);
```

Then, with gtk_statusbar_push(), the message can be added to the status bar under the "MenuItemHints" context identifier. This message will be placed on the top of the stack and displayed to the user. You may want to consider processing all GTK+ events after calling this function, since the user interface should reflect the changes immediately.

However, if the event type is GDK_LEAVE_NOTIFY, you need to remove the last menu item message that was added with the same context identifier. The most recent message can be removed from the stack with gtk_statusbar_pop().

Menu Items

Thus far, you have learned about flat menus that display label and separator menu items. It is also possible to add a submenu to an existing menu item. GTK+ also provides a number of other GtkMenuItem objects. Figure 9-3 shows a pop-up menu that contains a submenu along with image, check, and radio menu items.

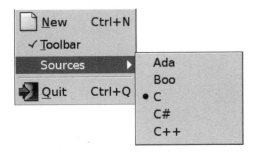

Figure 9-3. *Image, check, and radio menu items*

Submenus

Submenus in GTK+ are not created by a separate type of menu item widget but by calling gtk_menu_item_set_submenu(). This function calls gtk_menu_attach_to_widget() to attach the submenu to the menu item and places an arrow beside the menu item to show that it now has a submenu. If the menu item already has a submenu, it will be replaced with the given GtkMenu widget.

```
void gtk_menu_item_set_submenu (GtkMenuItem *menuitem,
                                GtkWidget *submenu);
```

Submenus are very useful if you have a list of very specific options that would clutter an otherwise organized menu structure. When using a submenu, you can use the activate-item signal provided by the GtkMenuItem widget, which will be emitted when the menu item displays its submenu.

In addition to GtkMenuItem and menu item separators, there are three other types of menu item objects: image, check, and radio menu items; these are covered in the remainder of this section.

Image Menu Items

GtkImageMenuItem is very similar to its parent class GtkMenuItem except it shows a small image to the left of the menu item label. There are four functions provided for creating a new image menu item.

The first function, gtk_image_menu_item_new() creates a new GtkImageMenuItem object with an empty label and no associated image. You can use image menu item's image property to set the image displayed by the menu item.

```
GtkWidget* gtk_image_menu_item_new ();
```

Additionally, you can create a new image menu item from a stock identifier with gtk_image_menu_item_new_from_stock(). This function creates the GtkImageMenuItem with the label and image associated with stock_id. This function accepts stock identifier strings that are listed in Appendix D.

```
GtkWidget* gtk_image_menu_item_new_from_stock (const gchar *stock_id,
                                               GtkAccelGroup *accel_group);
```

The second parameter of this function accepts an accelerator group, which will be set to the default accelerator of the stock item. If you want to manually set the keyboard accelerator for the menu item as we did in Listing 9-3, you can specify NULL for this parameter.

Also, you can use gtk_image_menu_item_new_with_label() to create a new GtkImageMenuItem initially with only a label. Later, you can use the image property to add an image widget. GTK+ also provided the function gtk_image_menu_item_set_image(), which allows you to edit the image property of the widget.

```
GtkWidget* gtk_image_menu_item_new_with_label (const gchar *label);
```

Also, GTK+ provides gtk_image_menu_item_new_with_mnemonic(), which will create an image menu item with a mnemonic label. As with the previous function, you will have to set the image property after the menu item is created.

Check Menu Items

GtkCheckMenuItem allows you to create a menu item that will display a check symbol beside the label, depending on whether its Boolean active property is TRUE or FALSE. This would allow the user to view whether an option is activated or deactivated.

As with GtkMenuItem, three initialization functions are provided: gtk_check_menu_item_new(), gtk_check_item_new_with_label(), and gtk_check_menu_item_new_with_mnemonic(). These functions create a GtkCheckMenuItem with no label, with an initial label, or with a mnemonic label, respectively.

```
GtkWidget* gtk_check_menu_item_new ();
GtkWidget* gtk_check_menu_item_new_with_label    (const gchar *label);
GtkWidget* gtk_check_menu_item_new_with_mnemonic (const gchar *label);
```

As previously stated, the current state of the check menu item is held by the active property of the widget. GTK+ provides two functions, gtk_check_menu_item_set_active() and gtk_check_menu_item_get_active() to set and retrieve the active value.

As with all check button widgets, you are able to use the `toggled` signal, which is emitted when the user toggles the state of the menu item. GTK+ takes care of updating the state of the check button, so this signal is simply to allow you to update your application to reflect the changed value.

`GtkCheckMenuItem` also provides `gtk_check_menu_item_set_inconsistent()`, which is used to alter the `inconsistent` property of the menu item. When set to `TRUE`, the check menu item will display a third, "in between" state that is neither active nor inactive. This can be used to show the user that a choice must be made that has yet to be set or that the property is both set and unset for different parts of a selection.

Radio Menu Items

`GtkRadioMenuItem` is a widget derived from `GtkCheckMenuItem`. It is rendered as a radio button instead of a check button by setting check menu item's `draw-as-radio` property to `TRUE`. Radio menu items work the same way as normal radio buttons.

The first radio button should be created with one of the following functions. You can set the radio button group to `NULL`, because it is not necessary since requisite elements will be added to the group by referencing the first element. These functions create an empty menu item, a menu item with a label, and a menu item with a mnemonic, respectively.

```
GtkWidget* gtk_radio_menu_item_new             (GSList *group);
GtkWidget* gtk_radio_menu_item_new_with_label  (GSList *group,
                                                const gchar *text);
GtkWidget* gtk_radio_menu_item_new_with_mnemonic (GSList *group,
                                                const gchar *text);
```

All other radio menu items should be created with one of the following three functions, which will add it to the radio button group associated with group. These functions create an empty menu item, a menu item with a label, and a menu item with a mnemonic, respectively.

```
GtkWidget* gtk_radio_menu_item_new_from_widget            (GtkRadioMenuItem *group);
GtkWidget* gtk_radio_menu_item_new_with_label_from_widget (GtkRadioMenuItem *group,
                                                           const gchar *text);
GtkWidget* gtk_radio_menu_item_new_with_mnemonic_from_widget
                                                          (GtkRadioMenuItem *group,
                                                           const gchar *text);
```

Menu Bars

`GtkMenuBar` is a widget that organizes multiple pop-up menus into a horizontal or vertical row. Each root element is a `GtkMenuItem` that pops down into a submenu. An instance of `GtkMenuBar` is usually displayed along the top of the main application window to provide access to functionality provided by the application. An example menu bar is shown in Figure 9-4.

Figure 9-4. *A menu bar with three menus*

In Listing 9-5, a GtkMenuBar widget is created with three menus: File, Edit, and Help. Each of the menus is actually a GtkMenuItem with a submenu. A number of menu items are then added to each submenu.

Listing 9-5. *Creating Groups of Menus (menubars.c)*

```
#include <gtk/gtk.h>

int main (int argc,
          char *argv[])
{
  GtkWidget *window, *menubar, *file, *edit, *help, *filemenu, *editmenu, *helpmenu;
  GtkWidget *new, *open, *cut, *copy, *paste, *contents, *about;
  GtkAccelGroup *group;

  gtk_init (&argc, &argv);

  window = gtk_window_new (GTK_WINDOW_TOPLEVEL);
  gtk_window_set_title (GTK_WINDOW (window), "Menu Bars");
  gtk_widget_set_size_request (window, 250, -1);

  group = gtk_accel_group_new ();
  menubar = gtk_menu_bar_new ();
  file = gtk_menu_item_new_with_label ("File");
  edit = gtk_menu_item_new_with_label ("Edit");
  help = gtk_menu_item_new_with_label ("Help");
  filemenu = gtk_menu_new ();
  editmenu = gtk_menu_new ();
  helpmenu = gtk_menu_new ();

  gtk_menu_item_set_submenu (GTK_MENU_ITEM (file), filemenu);
  gtk_menu_item_set_submenu (GTK_MENU_ITEM (edit), editmenu);
  gtk_menu_item_set_submenu (GTK_MENU_ITEM (help), helpmenu);
```

```
gtk_menu_shell_append (GTK_MENU_SHELL (menubar), file);
gtk_menu_shell_append (GTK_MENU_SHELL (menubar), edit);
gtk_menu_shell_append (GTK_MENU_SHELL (menubar), help);

/* Create the File menu content. */
new = gtk_image_menu_item_new_from_stock (GTK_STOCK_NEW, group);
open = gtk_image_menu_item_new_from_stock (GTK_STOCK_OPEN, group);
gtk_menu_shell_append (GTK_MENU_SHELL (filemenu), new);
gtk_menu_shell_append (GTK_MENU_SHELL (filemenu), open);

/* Create the Edit menu content. */
cut = gtk_image_menu_item_new_from_stock (GTK_STOCK_CUT, group);
copy = gtk_image_menu_item_new_from_stock (GTK_STOCK_COPY, group);
paste = gtk_image_menu_item_new_from_stock (GTK_STOCK_PASTE, group);
gtk_menu_shell_append (GTK_MENU_SHELL (editmenu), cut);
gtk_menu_shell_append (GTK_MENU_SHELL (editmenu), copy);
gtk_menu_shell_append (GTK_MENU_SHELL (editmenu), paste);

/* Create the Help menu content. */
contents = gtk_image_menu_item_new_from_stock (GTK_STOCK_HELP, group);
about = gtk_image_menu_item_new_from_stock (GTK_STOCK_ABOUT, group);
gtk_menu_shell_append (GTK_MENU_SHELL (helpmenu), contents);
gtk_menu_shell_append (GTK_MENU_SHELL (helpmenu), about);

gtk_container_add (GTK_CONTAINER (window), menubar);
gtk_window_add_accel_group (GTK_WINDOW (window), group);

gtk_widget_show_all (window);
gtk_main ();
return 0;
}
```

New GtkMenuBar widgets are created with gtk_menu_bar_new(). This will create an empty menu shell into which you can add content.

After you create the menu bar, you can define the pack direction of the menu bar items with gtk_menu_bar_set_pack_direction(). Values for the pack-direction property are defined by the GtkPackDirection enumeration and include GTK_PACK_DIRECTION_LTR, GTK_PACK_DIRECTION_RTL, GTK_PACK_DIRECTION_TTB, or GTK_PACK_DIRECTION_BTT. These will pack the menu items from left to right, right to left, top to bottom, or bottom to top, respectively. By default, child widgets are packed from left to right.

GtkMenuBar also provides another property called child-pack-direction, which sets what direction the menu items of the menu bar's children are packed. In other words, it controls how submenu items are packed. Values for this property are also defined by the GtkPackDirection enumeration.

Each child item in the menu bar is actually a GtkMenuItem widget. Since GtkMenuBar is derived from GtkMenuShell, you can use gtk_menu_shell_append() to add an item to the bar as shown in the following line.

```
gtk_menu_shell_append (GTK_MENU_SHELL (menubar), file);
```

You can also use gtk_menu_shell_prepend() or gtk_menu_shell_insert() to add an item to the beginning or in an arbitrary position of the menu bar.

You next need to call gtk_menu_item_set_submenu() to add a submenu to each of the root menu items. Each of the submenus is a GtkMenu widget created in the same way as pop-up menus. GTK+ will then take care of showing submenus to the user when necessary.

```
gtk_menu_item_set_submenu (GTK_MENU_ITEM (file), filemenu);
```

Toolbars

A GtkToolbar is a type of container that holds a number of widgets in a horizontal or vertical row. It is meant to allow easy customization of a large number of widgets with very little trouble. Typically, toolbars hold tool buttons that can display an image along with a text string. However, toolbars are actually able to hold any type of widget. A toolbar holding four tool buttons and a separator is shown in Figure 9-5.

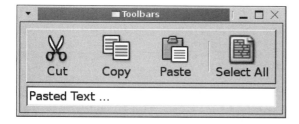

Figure 9-5. *A toolbar showing both images and text*

In Listing 9-6, a simple toolbar is created that shows five tool items in a horizontal row. Each toolbar item displays an icon and a label that describes the purpose of the item. The toolbar is also set to display an arrow that will provide access to toolbar items that do not fit in the menu.

In this example, a toolbar is used to provide cut, copy, paste, and select-all functionality to a GtkEntry widget. The main() function creates the toolbar, packing it above the GtkEntry. It then calls create_toolbar(), which populates the toolbar with tool items and connects the necessary signals.

Listing 9-6. *Creating a GtkToolbar Widget (toolbars.c)*

```
static void select_all (GtkEditable*);

/* Create a toolbar with Cut, Copy, Paste and Select All toolbar items. */
static void
create_toolbar (GtkWidget *toolbar,
                GtkWidget *entry)
{
  GtkToolItem *cut, *copy, *paste, *selectall, *separator;

  cut = gtk_tool_button_new_from_stock (GTK_STOCK_CUT);
  copy = gtk_tool_button_new_from_stock (GTK_STOCK_COPY);
  paste = gtk_tool_button_new_from_stock (GTK_STOCK_PASTE);
  selectall = gtk_tool_button_new_from_stock (GTK_STOCK_SELECT_ALL);
  separator = gtk_separator_tool_item_new ();

  gtk_toolbar_set_show_arrow (GTK_TOOLBAR (toolbar), TRUE);
  gtk_toolbar_set_style (GTK_TOOLBAR (toolbar), GTK_TOOLBAR_BOTH);

  gtk_toolbar_insert (GTK_TOOLBAR (toolbar), cut, 0);
  gtk_toolbar_insert (GTK_TOOLBAR (toolbar), copy, 1);
  gtk_toolbar_insert (GTK_TOOLBAR (toolbar), paste, 2);
  gtk_toolbar_insert (GTK_TOOLBAR (toolbar), separator, 3);
  gtk_toolbar_insert (GTK_TOOLBAR (toolbar), selectall, 4);

  g_signal_connect_swapped (G_OBJECT (cut), "clicked",
                            G_CALLBACK (gtk_editable_cut_clipboard), entry);
  g_signal_connect_swapped (G_OBJECT (copy), "clicked",
                            G_CALLBACK (gtk_editable_copy_clipboard), entry);
  g_signal_connect_swapped (G_OBJECT (paste), "clicked",
                            G_CALLBACK (gtk_editable_paste_clipboard), entry);
  g_signal_connect_swapped (G_OBJECT (selectall), "clicked",
                            G_CALLBACK (select_all), entry);
}

/* Select all of the text in the GtkEditable. */
static void
select_all (GtkEditable *entry)
{
  gtk_editable_select_region (entry, 0, -1);
}
```

New toolbars are created with `gtk_toolbar_new()`, which was called before the `create_toolbar()` function shown in Listing 9-6. This creates an empty `GtkToolbar` widget in which you can add tool buttons.

`GtkToolbar` provides a number of properties for customizing how it appears and interacts with the user including the orientation, button style, and the ability to give access to items that do not fit in the toolbar.

If all of the toolbar items cannot be displayed on the toolbar because there is not enough room, then an overflow menu will appear if you set `gtk_toolbar_set_show_arrow()` to `TRUE`. If all of the items can be displayed on the toolbar, the arrow will be hidden from view.

```
void gtk_toolbar_set_show_arrow (GtkToolbar *toolbar,
                                 gboolean show_arrow);
```

Another `GtkToolbar` property is the style by which all of the menu items will be displayed, which is set with `gtk_toolbar_set_style()`. You should note that this property can be overridden by the theme, so you should provide the option of using the default style by calling `gtk_toolbar_unset_style()`. There are four toolbar styles, which are defined by the `GtkToolbarStyle` enumeration:

- `GTK_TOOLBAR_ICONS`: Show only icons for each tool button in the toolbar.

- `GTK_TOOLBAR_TEXT`: Show only labels for each tool button in the toolbar.

- `GTK_TOOLBAR_BOTH`: Show both icons and labels for each tool button, where the icon is located above its label.

- `GTK_TOOLBAR_BOTH_HORIZ`: Show both icons and labels for each tool button, where the icon is to the left of the label. The label text of a tool item will only be shown if the `is-important` property for the item is set to `TRUE`.

Another important property of the toolbar is the orientation that can be set with `gtk_toolbar_set_orientation()`. There are two possible values defined by the `GtkOrientation` enumeration, `GTK_ORIENTATION_HORIZONTAL` and `GTK_ORIENTATION_VERTICAL`, which can be used to make the toolbar horizontal (default) or vertical.

Toolbar Items

Listing 9-6 introduces three important tool item types: `GtkToolItem`, `GtkToolButton`, and `GtkSeparatorToolItem`. All tool buttons are derived from the `GtkToolItem` class, which holds basic properties that are used by all tool items.

If you are using the `GTK_TOOLBAR_BOTH_HORIZ` style, then an essential property installed in `GtkToolItem` is the `is-important` setting. The label text of the toolbar item will only be shown for this style if this property is set to `TRUE`.

As with menus, separator tool items are provided by `GtkSeparatorToolItem` and are created with `gtk_separator_tool_item_new()`. Separator tool items have a `draw` property, which will draw a separator when set to `TRUE`. If you set `draw` to `FALSE`, it will place padding at its location without any visual separator.

Tip If you set the expand property of a GtkSeparatorToolItem to TRUE and its draw property to FALSE, you will force all tool items after the separator to the end of the toolbar.

Most toolbar items are of the type GtkToolButton. GtkToolButton provides a number of initialization functions including gtk_tool_button_new_from_stock(). This function accepts a stock identifier; a list of stock items available in GTK+ 2.10 can be found in Appendix D. Unlike most initialization functions, this method returns a GtkToolItem object instead of a GtkWidget.

Alternatively, you can use gtk_tool_button_new() to create a GtkToolButton with a custom icon and label. Each of these properties can be set to NULL.

```
GtkToolItem* gtk_tool_button_new (GtkWidget *icon,
                                  const gchar* label);
```

It is possible to manually set the label, stock identifier, and icon after initialization with gtk_tool_button_set_label(), gtk_tool_button_set_stock_id(), and gtk_tool_button_set_icon_widget(). These functions provide access to tool button's label, stock-id, and icon-widget properties.

Additionally, you can define your own widget to use instead of the default GtkLabel widget of the tool button with gtk_tool_button_set_label_widget(). This will allow you to embed an arbitrary widget, such as an entry or combo box, into the tool button. If this property is set to NULL, the default label will be used.

```
void gtk_tool_button_set_label_widget (GtkToolButton *button,
                                       GtkWidget *label_widget);
```

After you create the toolbar items, you can insert each GtkToolItem into the toolbar with gtk_toolbar_insert(). You do not have to cast the GtkToolItem, since the initialization functions do not return a GtkWidget.

```
void gtk_toolbar_insert (GtkToolbar *toolbar,
                         GtkToolItem *item,
                         gint pos);
```

The third parameter of gtk_toolbar_insert() accepts the position to insert the item into the toolbar. Tool button positions are indexed from zero. A negative position will append the item to the end of the toolbar.

Toggle Tool Buttons

GtkToggleToolButton is derived from GtkToolButton and, therefore, only implements initialization and toggle abilities itself. Toggle tool buttons provide the functionality of a GtkToggleButton widget in the form of a toolbar item. It allows the user to view whether the option is set or unset.

Toggle tool buttons are tool buttons that remain depressed when the active property is set to TRUE. You can use the toggled signal to receive notification when the state of the toggle button has been changed.

There are two ways to create a new GtkToggleToolButton. The first is with gtk_toggle_tool_button_new(), which will create an empty tool button. You can then use the functions provided by GtkToolButton to add a label and image.

```
GtkToolItem* gtk_toggle_tool_button_new ();
GtkToolItem* gtk_toggle_tool_button_new_from_stock (const gchar *stock_id);
```

Alternatively, you can use gtk_toggle_tool_button_new_from_stock(), which will create a tool button with the label and image associated with the stock identifier. If the stock identifier is not found, the image and label will be set to the error stock item.

Radio Tool Buttons

GtkRadioToolButton is derived from GtkToggleToolButton, so it inherits the active property and toggled signal. Therefore, the widget only needs to give a way for you to create new radio tool buttons and add them to a radio group.

The first radio tool button should be created with gtk_radio_tool_button_new() or gtk_radio_tool_button_new_from_stock(), where the radio group is set to NULL. This will create a default initial radio group for the radio tool button.

```
GtkToolItem* gtk_radio_tool_button_new              (GSList *group);
GtkToolItem* gtk_radio_tool_button_new_from_stock (GSList *group,
                                                    const gchar *stock_id);
```

GtkRadioToolButton inherits functions from GtkToolButton, which provides functions and properties that can then be used to set the label of the radio tool button if necessary.

All requisite elements should be created with gtk_radio_tool_button_from_widget() or gtk_radio_tool_button_new_with_stock_from_widget(). Setting group as the first radio tool button will add all requisite items added to the same group.

```
GtkToolItem* gtk_radio_tool_button_new_from_widget (GtkRadioToolButton *group);
GtkToolItem* gtk_radio_tool_button_new_with_stock_from_widget
                                                    (GtkRadioToolButton *group,
                                                     const gchar *stock_id);
```

GtkRadioToolButton provides one property, group, which is another radio tool button that belongs to the radio group. This allows you to link all of the radio buttons together so that only one will be selected at a time.

Menu Tool Buttons

GtkMenuToolButton, derived from GtkToolButton, allows you to attach a menu to a tool button. The widget places an arrow beside the image and label that provides access to the associated menu. For example, you could use GtkMenuToolButton to add a list of recently opened files to a GTK_STOCK_OPEN toolbar button. Figure 9-6 is a screenshot of a menu tool button that is used for this purpose.

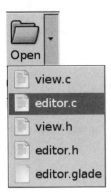

Figure 9-6. *A menu tool button showing recently opened files*

Listing 9-7 shows you how to implement a menu tool button. The actual tool button is created in a similar way as any other GtkToolButton except there is an extra step of attaching a menu to the GtkMenuToolButton widget.

Listing 9-7. *Using GtkMenuToolButton*

```
GtkToolItem *open;
GtkWidget *recent;

recent = gtk_menu_new ();
/* Add a number of menu items where each corresponds to one recent file. */

open = gtk_menu_tool_button_new_from_stock (GTK_STOCK_OPEN);
gtk_menu_tool_button_set_menu (GTK_MENU_TOOL_BUTTON (open), GTK_MENU (recent));
```

In Listing 9-7, the menu tool button was created with a default stock icon and label with gtk_menu_tool_button_new_from_stock(). This function accepts a stock identifier and will apply the appropriate label and icon.

Alternatively, you can create a menu tool button with gtk_menu_tool_button_new(), which accepts an icon widget and the label text. You can set either of these parameters to NULL if you want to set them at a later time using GtkToolButton properties.

```
GtkToolItem* gtk_menu_tool_button_new (GtkWidget *icon,
                                       const gchar *label);
```

What makes GtkMenuToolButton unique is that an arrow to the right of the tool button provides the user with access to a menu. The tool button's menu is set with gtk_menu_tool_button_set_menu() or by setting the menu property to a GtkMenu widget. This menu is displayed to the user when the arrow is clicked.

Dynamic Menu Creation

While it is possible to manually create every menu and toolbar item, doing so can take up a large amount of space and cause you to have to code monotonously for longer than necessary. In order to automate menu and toolbar creation, GTK+ allows you to dynamically create menus from XML files.

Creating UI Files

User interface files are constructed in XML format. All of the content has to be contained between <ui> and </ui> tags. One type of dynamic UI that you can create is a GtkMenuBar with the <menubar> tag shown in Listing 9-8.

Listing 9-8. *Menu UI File (menu.ui)*

```
<ui>
  <menubar name="MenuBar">
    <menu name="FileMenu" action="File">
      <menuitem name="FileOpen" action="Open"/>
      <menuitem name="FileSave" action="Save"/>
      <separator/>
      <menuitem name="FileQuit" action="Quit"/>
    </menu>
    <menu name="EditMenu" action="Edit">
      <menuitem name="EditCut" action="Cut"/>
      <menuitem name="EditCopy" action="Copy"/>
      <menuitem name="EditPaste" action="Paste"/>
      <separator/>
      <menuitem name="EditSelectAll" action="SelectAll"/>
      <menuitem name="EditDeselect" action="Deselect"/>
    </menu>
    <menu name="HelpMenu" action="Help">
      <menuitem name="HelpContents" action="Contents"/>
      <menuitem name="HelpAbout" action="About"/>
    </menu>
  </menubar>
</ui>
```

While not necessary, you should add the name attribute to every menubar, menu, and menuitem. The name attribute can be used to access the actual widget. If name is not specified, using the "action" field can access the widget.

Each `<menubar>` can have any number of `<menu>` children. Both of these tags must be closed according to normal XML rules. If a tag does not have a closing tag (e.g., `<menuitem/>`), you must place a forward slash character (/) at the end of the tag so the parser knows the tag has ended.

The `action` attribute is applied to all elements except top-level widgets and separators. When loading the UI file to associate a `GtkAction` object to each element, `GtkUIManager` uses the `action` attributes. `GtkAction` holds information about how the item is drawn and what callback function should be called, if any, when the item is activated.

Separators can be placed in a menu with the `<separator/>` tag. You do not need to provide name or action information for separators, because a generic `GtkSeparatorMenuItem` will be added.

In addition to menu bars, you can create toolbars in a UI file with the `<toolbar>` tag, as shown in Listing 9-9.

Listing 9-9. *Toolbar UI File (toolbar.ui)*

```
<ui>
  <toolbar name="Toolbar">
    <toolitem name="FileOpen" action="Open"/>
    <toolitem name="FileSave" action="Save"/>
    <separator/>
    <toolitem name="EditCut" action="Cut"/>
    <toolitem name="EditCopy" action="Copy"/>
    <toolitem name="EditPaste" action="Paste"/>
    <separator/>
    <toolitem name="EditSelectAll" action="SelectAll"/>
    <toolitem name="EditDeselect" action="Deselect"/>
    <separator/>
    <toolitem name="HelpContents" action="Contents"/>
    <toolitem name="HelpAbout" action="About"/>
  </toolbar>
</ui>
```

Each toolbar can contain any number of `<toolitem>` elements. Tool items are specified in the same manner as menu items, with an `"action"` and an optional `"name"`. You can use the same `"name` for elements in separate UI files, but you should not use the same names if, for example, the toolbar and menu bar are located in the same file.

However, you *can* and should use the same `"action"` for multiple elements. This will cause each element to be drawn in the same way and to be connected to the same callback function. The advantage of this is that you need to define only one `GtkAction` for each item type. For example, the same `"action"` will be used for the Cut element in the UI files in Listings 9-8 through 9-10.

■Tip While the toolbar, menu bar, and pop-up menu were split into separate UI files, you can include as many of these widgets as you want in one file. The only requirement is that the whole file content is contained between the `<ui>` and `</ui>` tags.

In addition to toolbars and menu bars, it is possible to define pop-up menus in a UI file, as illustrated in Listing 9-10. Notice that there are repeated actions in Listings 9-8, 9-9, and 9-10. Repeating actions allows you to define only a single `GtkAction` object instead of separate objects for each instance of an `"action"`.

Listing 9-10. *Pop-up UI File (popup.ui)*

```
<ui>
  <popup name="EntryPopup">
    <menuitem name="EditCut" action="Cut"/>
    <menuitem name="EditCopy" action="Copy"/>
    <menuitem name="EditPaste" action="Paste"/>
    <separator/>
    <menuitem name="EditSelectAll" action="SelectAll"/>
    <menuitem name="EditDeselect" action="Deselect"/>
  </popup>
</ui>
```

The last type of top-level widget supported by UI files is the pop-up menu, denoted by the `<popup>` tag. Since a pop-up menu is the same thing as a normal menu, you can still use `<menuitem>` elements as children.

Loading UI Files

After you create your UI files, you need to load them into your application and retrieve the necessary widgets. To do this, you need to utilize the functionality provided by `GtkActionGroup` and `GtkUIManager`.

`GtkActionGroup` is a set of items with name, stock identifier, label, keyboard accelerator, tooltip, and callback functions. The name of the each action can be set to an `action` parameter from a UI file to associate it with a UI element.

`GtkUIManager` is an object that allows you to dynamically load one or more user interface definitions. It will automatically create an accelerator group based on associated action groups and allow you to reference widgets based on the `name` parameter from the UI file.

In Listing 9-11 `GtkUIManager` is used to load the menu bar and toolbar from the UI files in Listings 9-8 and 9-9. The resulting application is shown in Figure 9-7.

Figure 9-7. *A menu bar and a toolbar that are dynamically loaded*

Each of the menu and tool items in the application are connected to empty callback functions, because this example is only meant to show you how to dynamically load menus and toolbars from UI definitions. You will implement callback functions with actual content in the two exercises found at the end of this chapter.

Listing 9-11. *Loading a Menu with GtkUIManager (uimanager.c)*

```c
#include <gtk/gtk.h>

/* All of the menu item callback functions have a GtkMenuItem parameter, and
 * receive the same gpointer value. There is only one callback function shown
 * since all of the rest will be formatted in the same manner. */
static void open (GtkMenuItem *menuitem, gpointer data);

#define NUM_ENTRIES 13
static GtkActionEntry entries[] =
{
  { "File", NULL, "_File", NULL, NULL, NULL },
  { "Open", GTK_STOCK_OPEN, NULL, NULL,
     "Open an existing file", G_CALLBACK (open) },
  { "Save", GTK_STOCK_SAVE, NULL, NULL,
     "Save the document to a file", G_CALLBACK (save) },
  { "Quit", GTK_STOCK_QUIT, NULL, NULL,
     "Quit the application", G_CALLBACK (quit) },
  { "Edit", NULL, "_Edit", NULL, NULL, NULL },
  { "Cut", GTK_STOCK_CUT, NULL, NULL,
     "Cut the selection to the clipboard", G_CALLBACK (cut) },
  { "Copy", GTK_STOCK_COPY, NULL, NULL,
     "Copy the selection to the clipboard", G_CALLBACK (copy) },
  { "Paste", GTK_STOCK_PASTE, NULL, NULL,
     "Paste text from the clipboard", G_CALLBACK (paste) },
  { "SelectAll", GTK_STOCK_SELECT_ALL, NULL, NULL,
     "Select all of the text", G_CALLBACK (selectall) },
  { "Deselect", NULL, "_Deselect", "<control>d",
     "Deselect all of the text", G_CALLBACK (deselect) },
  { "Help", NULL, "_Help", NULL, NULL, NULL },
  { "Contents", GTK_STOCK_HELP, NULL, NULL,
     "Get help on using the application", G_CALLBACK (help) },
```

```
  { "About", GTK_STOCK_ABOUT, NULL, NULL,
      "More information about the application", G_CALLBACK (about) }
};

int main (int argc,
          char *argv[])
{
  GtkWidget *window, *menubar, *toolbar, *vbox;
  GtkActionGroup *group;
  GtkUIManager *uimanager;

  gtk_init (&argc, &argv);

  window = gtk_window_new (GTK_WINDOW_TOPLEVEL);
  gtk_window_set_title (GTK_WINDOW (window), "UI Manager");
  gtk_widget_set_size_request (window, 250, -1);

  /* Create a new action group and add all of the actions to it. */
  group = gtk_action_group_new ("MainActionGroup");
  gtk_action_group_add_actions (group, entries, NUM_ENTRIES, NULL);

  /* Create a new UI manager and build the menu bar and toolbar. */
  uimanager = gtk_ui_manager_new ();
  gtk_ui_manager_insert_action_group (uimanager, group, 0);
  gtk_ui_manager_add_ui_from_file (uimanager, "menu.ui", NULL);
  gtk_ui_manager_add_ui_from_file (uimanager, "toolbar.ui", NULL);

  /* Retrieve the necessary widgets and associate accelerators. */
  menubar = gtk_ui_manager_get_widget (uimanager, "/MenuBar");
  toolbar = gtk_ui_manager_get_widget (uimanager, "/Toolbar");
  gtk_toolbar_set_style (GTK_TOOLBAR (toolbar), GTK_TOOLBAR_ICONS);
  gtk_window_add_accel_group (GTK_WINDOW (window),
                              gtk_ui_manager_get_accel_group (uimanager));

  vbox = gtk_vbox_new (FALSE, 0);
  gtk_box_pack_start_defaults (GTK_BOX (vbox), menubar);
  gtk_box_pack_start_defaults (GTK_BOX (vbox), toolbar);

  gtk_container_add (GTK_CONTAINER (window), vbox);
  gtk_widget_show_all (window);

  gtk_main ();
  return 0;
}
```

The first thing you need to do when using GtkUIManager to dynamically load menus and toolbars is to create an array of actions. It is possible to manually create every GtkAction, GtkToggleAction, or GtkRadioAction object, but there is a much easier way.

GtkActionEntry is a structure that holds an action name, stock identifier, label, accelerator, tooltip, and callback function. The content of the GtkActionEntry structure can be viewed in the following code snippet.

```
typedef struct
{
  const gchar *name;
  const gchar *stock_id;
  const gchar *label;
  const gchar *accelerator;
  const gchar *tooltip;
  GCallback    callback;
} GtkActionEntry;
```

The action name string must be the same as the action attribute of a menu or tool item in a UI definition for it to be used. Any of the attributes except for the action name can safely be set to NULL if they are not needed. If you specify a stock identifier, you do not need to specify a label or an accelerator unless you want to override their default values.

The keyboard accelerator is specified as a string that spells out its value. Acceptable keyboard accelerators include "<Control>a", "<Shift><Control>x", "F3", and so on. Some of the modifiers can also be abbreviated. For example, the Control key can be referenced with "<Ctrl>" or "<Ctl>". In short, the accelerator must be of the form that it can be parsed by gtk_accelerator_parse().

After you create lists of actions, you need to create a new GtkActionGroup that will hold all of the actions with gtk_action_group_new(). The name specified to this function will be used when associating key bindings with the actions.

An array of GtkActionEntry objects can be added to a GtkActionGroup by calling gtk_action_group_add_actions(). This function accepts the array of entries, the number of entries, and an optional data parameter that will be passed to each callback function.

```
void gtk_action_group_add_actions (GtkActionGroup *group,
                                   const GtkActionEntry *entries,
                                   guint n_entries,
                                   gpointer data);
```

If you need to pass different data parameters to different callback functions, you will have to manually create each GtkAction and add it to the group with gtk_action_group_add_action() or gtk_action_group_add_action_with_accel().

The next step is to create the GtkUIManager with gtk_ui_manager_new(). This object will be used to load the UI definitions and connect each item to its corresponding GtkAction. You then need to use gtk_ui_manager_insert_action_group() to add all of your action groups to the GtkUIManager. This function will add all of the actions from the group to the UI manager. Then, it will be able to match actions to elements in UI definitions to create appropriate widgets.

```
void gtk_ui_manager_insert_action_group (GtkUIManager *uimanager,
                                         GtkActionGroup *group,
                                         gint pos);
```

The third parameter of this function is an integer that states the position of the action group within the UI manager. Actions with the same name in groups with a lower position will take preference over those with higher positions.

Next, you will want to use gtk_ui_manager_add_ui_from_file() to load any number of UI files. In Listing 9-11, the menu.ui and toolbar.ui files were loaded with respect to the executable. The third parameter of this function is an optional GError object.

```
guint gtk_ui_manager_add_ui_from_file (GtkUIManager *uimanager,
                                       const gchar *filename,
                                       GError **error);
```

This function will load the content of each file. Each element is then matched up with objects added from an action group. The UI manager will then create all of the appropriate widgets according to the UI definition. An error will be output to the terminal if an action does not exist.

After the UI manager creates the widgets, you can load them based on name paths or the action if the name parameter does not exist, as shown in the following code. The two top-level widgets were the menu bar and toolbar found at "/MenuBar" and "/Toolbar". They are loaded with gtk_ui_manager_get_widget().

```
GtkWidget* gtk_ui_manager_get_widget (GtkUIManager *self,
                                      const gchar *path);
```

You have to give the absolute path to any widget when a path is required. In the absolute path, the <ui> element is omitted. The path is then built with the name attribute of each item. For example, if you wanted to access the GTK_STOCK_OPEN element in the menu bar, you call gtk_ui_manager_get_widget(), which would return the "/MenuBar/FileMenu/FileOpen" menu item.

Additional Action Types

Menu and toolbar items with stock images and keyboard accelerators are great, but what about using toggle buttons and radio buttons with GtkUIManager? For this, GTK+ provides GtkToggleActionEntry and GtkRadioActionEntry. The content of GtkToggleActionEntry follows:

```
typedef struct
{
  const gchar *name;
  const gchar *stock_id;
  const gchar *label;
  const gchar *accelerator;
  const gchar *tooltip;
  GCallback callback;
  gboolean is_active;
} GtkToggleActionEntry;
```

■**Note** One advantage of using UI definitions is that the actual definition does not know anything about how the action is going to be implemented in your application. Because of this, the user can redesign a menu structure without needing to know how each action will be implemented.

In addition to GtkActionEntry, GTK+ provides GtkToggleActionEntry, which will create a toggle menu or tool item. This structure includes an additional member—is_active, which defines whether the button is initially set as active.

Adding an array of GtkToggleActionEntry objects is similar to adding normal actions except you have to use gtk_action_group_add_toggle_actions(). This function accepts an array of GtkToggleActionEntry objects, the number of actions in the array, and a pointer that will be passed to every callback function.

```
void gtk_action_group_add_toggle_actions (GtkActionGroup *group,
                                           const GtkToggleActionEntry *entries,
                                           guint num_entries,
                                           gpointer data);
```

Additionally, GtkRadioActionEntry allows you to create a group of radio actions. The value member is a unique integer that can be used to activate a specific radio menu item or radio tool button.

```
typedef struct
{
  const gchar *name;
  const gchar *stock_id;
  const gchar *label;
  const gchar *accelerator;
  const gchar *tooltip;
  gint value;
} GtkRadioActionEntry;
```

The radio actions are added to the action group with gtk_action_group_add_radio_actions(), which will group all of the radio buttons together. This function works the same as gtk_action_group_add_toggle_actions() except you need to specify two additional parameters.

```
void gtk_action_group_add_radio_actions (GtkActionGroup *group,
                                          const GtkRadioActionEntry *entries,
                                          guint num_entries,
                                          gint value,
                                          GCallback on_change,
                                          gpointer data);
```

The value parameter is the identifier assigned to the action that should be initially activated or set to -1 to deactivate all by default. The callback function on_change() is called when the changed signal is emitted on a radio button.

Placeholders

When creating UI files, you may want to mark a location in a menu where other menu items can be added at a later time. For example, if you want to add a list of recent files to the File menu, you may not know how many files will be available for the list.

For this situation, GTK+ provides the `<placeholder>` tag. In the following line of code, a `<placeholder>` tag is defined that can be used to mark the location in the File menu that recent file menu items can be added.

```
<placeholder name="FileRecentFiles"/>
```

Within your application, you can use `gtk_ui_manager_add_ui()` to add new user interface information at the location of the placeholder. This function first accepts a unique unsigned integer that was returned by a call to `gtk_ui_manager_new_merge_id()`. You have to retrieve a new merge identifier every time you add a widget to the user interface.

```
void gtk_ui_manager_add_ui (GtkUIManager *uimanager,
                            guint merge_id,
                            const gchar *path,
                            const gchar *name,
                            const gchar *action,
                            GtkUIManagerItemType type,
                            gboolean top);
```

The next parameter of `gtk_ui_manager_add_ui()` is a path to the point where the new item should be added; this would be `"/MenuBar/File/FileRecentFiles"`, which is the path to the placeholder. Then, you should specify a name and action for the new widget followed by the type of UI item that is being added. UI item types are defined by the following `GtkUIManagerItemType` enumeration options:

- `GTK_UI_MANAGER_AUTO`: GTK+ will determine what type of widget is to be added.

- `GTK_UI_MANAGER_MENUBAR`: Add a `GtkMenuBar` widget. The location of the placeholder should be a direct child of a `<ui>` tag.

- `GTK_UI_MANAGER_MENU`: Add a `GtkMenu` as a child of a top-level widget.

- `GTK_UI_MANAGER_TOOLBAR`: Add a `GtkMenuBar`. The location of the placeholder should be a direct child of a `<ui>` tag.

- `GTK_UI_MANAGER_PLACEHOLDER`: Add a new placeholder, which can be added at any location in the user interface.

- `GTK_UI_MANAGER_POPUP`: Add a `GtkMenuBar`. This requires that the placeholder is located as a direct child of a `<ui>` tag.

- `GTK_UI_MANAGER_MENUITEM`: Add a `GtkMenuItem` as a child of a top-level widget.

- `GTK_UI_MANAGER_TOOLITEM`: Add a `GtkToolItem` as a child of a top-level `GtkToolbar` widget.

- `GTK_UI_MANAGER_SEPARATOR`: Add a separator into any type of top-level widget.

- `GTK_UI_MANAGER_ACCELERATOR`: Add a keyboard accelerator to a menu or toolbar.

The last parameter of gtk_ui_manager_add_ui() is a Boolean variable that positions the new UI element with respect to the given path. If set to TRUE, the UI element is inserted before the path. Otherwise, it is inserted after the path.

Custom Stock Items

From the last section, you will notice that GtkActionEntry accepts a stock identifier to add an image to the item. Because of this, you will, at some point, need to create your own custom stock icons that can be used for nonstandard menu and toolbar items. New stock items are created with three objects: GtkIconSource, GtkIconSet, and GtkIconFactory. Let us work from the bottom up.

GtkIconSource is an object that holds a GdkPixbuf or an image filename. It is meant to hold one variant of an image. For example, if you have an image that will be displayed differently when it is enabled or disabled, you would need to have multiple icon sources, one for each state. You may need multiple icon sources for different icon sizes, different languages, or different icon states.

Multiple icon sources are organized with GtkIconSet, which holds all of the GtkIconSource objects for one stock image. In some cases, your icon set may only have one image. While this is usually not the case, you can use gtk_icon_set_new_from_pixbuf() to skip the step of creating an icon source.

```
GtkIconSet* gtk_icon_set_new_from_pixbuf (GdkPixbuf *pixbuf);
```

After you have created all of the necessary icon sets, they are added to a GtkIconFactory, which is used to organize all of the stock items for a particular theme. Icon factories are added to a global list that GTK+ searches through to find stock items.

In this section, a number of new stock items are going to be created. Figure 9-8 is a screenshot of the new stock items that are created in Listing 9-12.

Figure 9-8. *Custom images added to the global icon factory*

In Listing 9-12, five new stock items are created including "check-list", "calculator", "screenshot", "cpu", and "desktop". A toolbar item is then created from each of the new stock items and displayed on the screen.

Listing 9-12. *Using GtkIconFactory (iconfactory.c)*

```c
#include <gtk/gtk.h>

#define ICON_LOCATION "/path/to/icons/"

typedef struct
{
  gchar *location;
  gchar *stock_id;
  gchar *label;
} NewStockIcon;

const NewStockIcon list[] =
{
  { ICON_LOCATION"checklist.png", "check-list", "Check _List" },
  { ICON_LOCATION"calculator.png", "calculator", "_Calculator" },
  { ICON_LOCATION"camera.png", "screenshot", "_Screenshots" },
  { ICON_LOCATION"cpu.png", "cpu", "CPU _Info" },
  { ICON_LOCATION"desktop.png", "desktop", "View _Desktop" },
  { NULL, NULL, NULL }
};

static void add_stock_icon (GtkIconFactory*, gchar*, gchar*);

int main (int argc,
          char *argv[])
{
  GtkWidget *window, *toolbar;
  GtkIconFactory *factory;
  gint i = 0;

  gtk_init (&argc, &argv);

  window = gtk_window_new (GTK_WINDOW_TOPLEVEL);
  gtk_window_set_title (GTK_WINDOW (window), "Icon Factory");
  gtk_container_set_border_width (GTK_CONTAINER (window), 10);

  factory = gtk_icon_factory_new ();
  toolbar = gtk_toolbar_new ();
```

```
/* Loop through the list of items and add new stock items. */
while (list[i].location != NULL)
{
  GtkToolItem *item;

  add_stock_icon (factory, list[i].location, list[i].stock_id);
  item = gtk_tool_button_new_from_stock (list[i].stock_id);
  gtk_tool_button_set_label (GTK_TOOL_BUTTON (item), list[i].label);
  gtk_tool_button_set_use_underline (GTK_TOOL_BUTTON (item), TRUE);
  gtk_toolbar_insert (GTK_TOOLBAR (toolbar), item, i);
  i++;
}

gtk_icon_factory_add_default (factory);
gtk_toolbar_set_style (GTK_TOOLBAR (toolbar), GTK_TOOLBAR_BOTH);
gtk_toolbar_set_show_arrow (GTK_TOOLBAR (toolbar), FALSE);
gtk_container_add (GTK_CONTAINER (window), toolbar);

gtk_widget_show_all (window);
gtk_main ();
return 0;
}

/* Add a new stock icon from the given location and with the given stock id. */
static void
add_stock_icon (GtkIconFactory *factory,
                gchar *location,
                gchar *stock_id)
{
  GtkIconSource *source;
  GtkIconSet *set;

  source = gtk_icon_source_new ();
  set = gtk_icon_set_new ();

  gtk_icon_source_set_filename (source, location);
  gtk_icon_set_add_source (set, source);
  gtk_icon_factory_add (factory, stock_id, set);
}
```

Creating a new icon factory, source, or set is as simple as calling gtk_icon_factory_new(), gtk_icon_source_new(), or gtk_icon_set_new(). Each of these functions creates an empty object that is not of any use in its current state.

In Listing 9-12, the icon source is initialized to an image found at the specified filename with gtk_icon_source_set_filename(). Alternatively, you can create the icon source out of a GdkPixbuf object with gtk_icon_source_set_pixbuf().

Since we only needed one icon source in Listing 9-12 for each stock item, there was no need for further customization. However, it is possible to set the icon to be displayed for a specific size with gtk_icon_source_set_size(). This will tell GTK+ to only use this icon if the application needs the specified size.

```
void gtk_icon_source_set_size (GtkIconSource *source,
                               GtkIconSize size);
```

■Caution If you need to set the icon source size, it will have no effect unless you pass FALSE to gtk_icon_source_set_size_wildcarded(). Otherwise, the icon source will be used for all sizes. This also goes for icon states, which must be unset with gtk_icon_source_set_state_wildcarded().

Additionally, you can define the icon to be shown during a specific state defined by the GtkIconState. If you use gtk_icon_source_set_state(), you will want to make sure to define icons for all five states defined by the enumeration.

```
void gtk_icon_source_set_state (GtkIconSource *source,
                                GtkIconState state);
```

After you create your icon sources, you will need to add them all to an icon set with gtk_icon_set_add_source(). This function accepts the GtkIconSet and the icon source that will be added.

```
Void gtk_icon_set_add_source (GtkIconSet *iconset,
                              const GtkIconSource *source)
```

If you unset any wildcards in the icon sources, you will want to make sure to define stock icons for every possible state or size. Adding a single icon source with both the state and the size indicated as the wildcards usually does this. If there is a more specific icon, it will be used. If the appropriate icon is not found, the wildcard icon will be used. This wildcard image may be lightened or altered in some other way to fit the occasion.

Next, you need to add each GtkIconSet to the icon factory with gtk_icon_factory_add(). This function accepts the stock identifier that will be used to reference the icon. Normally, you will want to name this "myapp-iconname", where "myapp" is replaced by the name of your application.

```
void gtk_icon_factory_add (GtkIconFactory *factory,
                           const gchar *stock_id,
                           GtkIconSet *iconset);
```

If the stock identifier already exists, the new item will replace it, so by using your application name in the stock identifier, you avoid overriding any default stock items.

Any stock items added to your icon factory are not available until you add it to the global list of icon factories with gtk_icon_factory_add_default(). Normally, a separate icon factory will exist for each graphical library that includes its default icons.

Test Your Understanding

The following two exercises give an overview of what you have learned about menus and toolbars throughout the chapter.

In addition to completing them, you may want to create examples of pop-up menus with other widgets that do not support them by default. Also, after finishing both of these exercises, you should expand them by creating your own stock icons that are used in place of the default items.

Exercise 9-1. Toolbars

In Chapter 7, you created a simple text editor using the GtkTextView widget. In this exercise, expand on that application and provide a toolbar for actions instead of a vertical box filled with GtkButton widgets.

While manual toolbar creation is possible, in most applications, you will want to utilize the GtkUIManager method of toolbar creation. Therefore, use that method in this exercise. You should also make use of built-in stock items or create your own with GtkIconFactory.

Oftentimes, it is advantageous for an application to provide the toolbar as a child of a handle box. Do this for your text editor, placing the toolbar above the text view. Also, set up the toolbar so that the textual descriptor is shown below every tool button.

This first exercise taught you how to build your own toolbars. It also showed you how to use the GtkHandleBox container. In the next exercise, you will reimplement the Text Editor application with a menu bar.

Exercise 9-2. Menu Bars

In this exercise, implement the same application as in Exercise 9-1, except use a menu bar this time. You should continue to use GtkUIManager, but the menu does not need to be contained by a GtkHandleBox.

Since tooltips are not shown for menu items automatically, use a status bar to provide more information about each item. The menu bar should contain two menus: File and Edit. You should also provide a Quit menu item in the File menu.

Summary

In this chapter, you learned two methods for creating menus, toolbars, and menu bars. The first method was the manual method, which was more difficult but introduced you to all of the necessary widgets.

The first example showed you how to use basic menu items to implement a pop-up menu for a progress bar. This example was expanded on in order to provide keyboard accelerators and more information to the user with the GtkStatusbar widget. You also learned about submenus as well as image, toggle, and radio menu items.

The next section showed you how to use menu items with submenus to implement a menu bar with a GtkMenuShell. This menu bar could be displayed horizontally or vertically and forward or backward.

Toolbars are simply a horizontal or vertical list of buttons. Each button contains an icon and label text. You learned about three additional types of toolbar buttons: toggles, radio buttons, and tool buttons with a supplemental menu.

Then, after much hard work, you were taught how to create dynamically loadable menus. Each menu or toolbar is held in a UI definition file, which is loaded by the GtkUIManager class. The UI manager associates each object with the appropriate action and creates the widgets according to the UI definition.

Last, you learned how to create your own custom stock icons. It is necessary to create your own icons, because arrays of actions require a stock identifier to add an icon to an action.

In the next chapter, we are going to take a short break from coding and cover the design of graphical user interfaces with the Glade User Interface Builder. This application creates user interface XML files, which can be dynamically loaded when your application starts. You will then learn how to handle these files programmatically with Libglade.

CHAPTER 10

■ ■ ■

Dynamic User Interfaces

By now, you have learned a great deal about GTK+ and its supporting libraries and are able to create fairly complex applications. However, manually writing all of the code to create and configure the widgets and behavior for these applications can quickly become tedious.

The Glade User Interface Builder removes the need for you to write all of that code by allowing you to design your UI graphically. It supports the GTK+ library of widgets as well as various widgets from the GNOME libraries. User interfaces are saved as XML files, which can be used to dynamically build your application's user interface.

The last part of this chapter covers Libglade, a library that can be used to dynamically load the XML files. Libglade will create all of the necessary widgets and allow you to connect any signals defined in Glade.

Note This chapter covers the user interface of Glade that is current at the time of this writing. It is possible that this may change in the future, but any changes should be an easy transition from the instructions provided in this chapter. Also, in a future version of GTK+, Libglade is going to be moved into GTK+ as the `GtkBuilder` object. When this happens, a tutorial will be posted on this book's web site with more information on making the transition.

In this chapter, you will learn the following:

- Issues you should keep in mind when designing graphical user interfaces (GUIs)

- How to design custom graphical user interfaces with Glade

- How to dynamically load Glade user interfaces with Libglade

User Interface Design

In this chapter, you are going to learn how to use Glade 3 and Libglade to implement dynamic user interfaces. However, it is prudent to first learn a few concepts that you should keep in mind when designing graphical user interfaces. These concepts can help you to avoid confusing and frustrating users in the future.

You also have to realize that, while you will know how to use your application because you designed it, you need to do as much as possible to help the user make sense of it. Whether the user is an expert or a novice, each user should be able to use your application with the shortest possible learning curve. That said, the following sections include many tips and design decisions to help you achieve this level of intuitiveness. They will also improve the maintainability of your application.

Know Your Users

When designing a user interface, the most important thing to consider is your audience. Are they all experienced with the task at hand, or will some need more help than others? Can you model your user interface after one that they are already familiar with, or is this something completely new?

One of the biggest possible mistakes is to make rash generalizations about your users' skill level. You may think that the way you lay out your application makes sense, but that is because you designed it. You should place yourself in the users' position, understanding they will have no prior knowledge about how to use your application.

To avoid confusion, take time to study similar applications, taking note of what design decisions seem successful and which cause problems. For example, if you are creating an application to be used in the GNOME desktop environment, you should check out the GNOME Human Interface Guidelines, which will help you lay out a design that is used for other compliant applications. A copy of the GNOME Human Interface Guidelines can be found at http://developer.gnome.org/.

Another thing to consider when designing a user interface is accessibility. Users may have vision problems that could inhibit them from using an application. The Accessibility Toolkit provides many facilities for GTK+ applications to make them compatible with screen readers. GTK+ also relies heavily on themes, which is why you should avoid setting the font, when possible, or provide the user with a way to change it.

Your language is another consideration when designing the user interface. First, you should always use jargon that is familiar to the users. For example, you are free to use mathematical terms in an engineering application, but you should not do so in a web browser.

Many applications are translated into other languages when they become popular, which may cause problems if you use words or images that could be offensive in other cultures.

Keep the Design Simple

Once you know your audience, it becomes a lot simpler to design an effective user interface, but you can still run into problems if the interface is too difficult or cluttered. Always try to reduce the number of widgets on the screen to a reasonable number.

For example, if you need to provide many choices to the user where only one can be selected, you might be tempted to use a lot of radio buttons. However, a better solution may be to use a GtkComboBox, which will significantly decrease the number of required widgets.

The GtkNotebook container is extremely useful for grouping similar option groups that would otherwise clutter a huge page. In many applications, this widget is used to group widgets that relate or depend on each other into a preferences dialog.

Menu layout is also another problematic area, because it is not always done in a sensible manner. When possible, you should use standard menus such as File, Edit, View, Help, Format, and Window. These menus are familiar to users who are experienced with computing, and users will expect them. Because of this, these menus should contain standard items as well. For example, the File menu should contain items for manipulating files, printing, and exiting the application. You should investigate how other applications lay out their menu items if you are not sure where to place a particular item.

Repetitive jobs, or those that the user will be performing often, should always be made quick and easy. There are multiple ways to do this. The most important is to provide keyboard accelerators for many actions—pressing Ctrl+O on the keyboard is a lot faster than clicking the File menu and the Open menu item.

Note Whenever possible, you should always use standard keyboard accelerators, such as Ctrl+X for cutting and Ctrl+N for creating something new. This will significantly decrease the initial learning curve for users of your application. In fact, some keyboard accelerators are already built into many widgets, such as Ctrl+X for cutting the selection in text widgets.

It may take some time for your users to get accustomed to keyboard accelerators, which is why toolbars are also extremely useful for repetitive options. You need to find a balance between placing too few and too many items on a toolbar, though. A cluttered toolbar will scare and confuse the user, but a toolbar with too few items will be useless. If you have a large number of items that users might want on toolbars, it would make sense to allow the users to customize the toolbars themselves.

Always Be Consistent

Consistency is key when designing a graphical user interface, and GTK+ makes this extremely easy. First, GTK+ provides many stock items that should always be used in favor of homegrown items where possible. The user will already be familiar with the icons for the stock items and will know how to use them.

Caution Stock items can be very dangerous if you do not use them correctly. You should never use a stock item for an action for which it was not originally intended. For example, you should not use `GTK_STOCK_REMOVE` for a subtraction operation just because it looks like a "minus sign." The icons are defined by the user's theme and may not always look the way you assume.

Speaking of themes, you should fall back on the settings provided by a theme whenever possible. This will help you create a consistent look—not only throughout your application but across the whole desktop environment. Since themes are applied to all applications throughout a desktop, your application will be consistent with most other applications that the user runs.

In those few cases where you do need to deviate from the defaults provided by the user's theme, you should always give the user a way to change the settings or to just use the system defaults. This is especially important when dealing with fonts and colors, because your changes can render your application unusable with some themes.

Another advantage of consistency is that the user will learn how to use your application much faster. The user will need to learn only one design instead of many. If you do not use a consistent layout for your application and supplemental dialogs, the user will be presented with a brand new adventure with every new window.

Keep the User in the Loop

One thing that can turn a user off of your application very quickly is if it is not responsive for a long period of time. Most computer users are accustomed to a bug or two, but if your application is processing information and remains unresponsive for quite a while, the user may give up.

To avoid this, there are two possible solutions. The first is to make your application more efficient. However, if your application is not to blame, or there is no way to make it more efficient, you should use progress bars. A progress bar will tell the user that your application is still working. Just make sure to update your progress bar! If you do not know how long the process will take, another option would be to pulse the progress bar and provide messages that update the user on the process's progress.

Also, remember the following loop from Chapter 2:

```
while (gtk_events_pending ())
  gtk_main_iteration ();
```

This loop will make sure that the user interface is updated, even when the processor is busy processing another task. If you do not update the user interface during a CPU-intensive process, the application may be unresponsive to the user until it is finished!

You should also provide your users with feedback when actions are performed. If a document is being saved, you should mark it as unmodified or display a message in the status bar. If you do not provide feedback to the user when an action is performed, it may be assumed that the action was not performed.

Message dialogs are a very useful way to provide feedback, but they should be used only when necessary. The user will become frustrated if message dialogs appear too often, which is why only critical errors and warnings should be reported this way.

We All Make Mistakes

Whether you are an expert or a novice, we all make mistakes. Because of this, you should always forgive your users. After all, everyone has at one time or another pressed an incorrect button that resulted in losing a large amount of work. In a properly designed application, this should never occur.

For basic actions that cannot be easily undone by the user, you should provide the ability to undo the action. For example, these basic actions could include deleting an item from our Grocery List application or moving text within a text view.

For actions that cannot be undone, you should always provide a confirmation dialog. It should explicitly state that this action cannot be undone and ask whether the user wants to continue. For example, you should always ask the user whether the application should be closed when there are documents with unsaved changes. People have been using software for years and have come to expect a confirmation dialog box for actions that cannot be undone.

The Glade User Interface Builder

One factor that can make or break a GUI toolkit is whether it can be used to rapidly deploy applications. While the user interface is extremely important to the success of an application, it should not be the most consuming aspect of the development process.

Glade is a tool that allows you to quickly and efficiently design graphical user interfaces so that you can move onto other aspects of your code. User interfaces are saved as an XML file that describes the widget structure, the properties of each widget, and any signal handlers you associated with each. Libglade can then load the user interface file in order to dynamically build it on application load. This allows you to alter the user interface aesthetically without the need to recompile the application.

■**Note** Previous versions of Glade allowed you to generate source code instead of saving the user interface in an XML file. This method is depreciated, because it is difficult to manage when you want to change your user interface. Therefore, you should follow the method provided in this chapter.

You need to realize from the start what Glade is and what it is not. Glade is used to design the user interface of an application, set up signals that will be associated with callback functions implemented in your code, and take care of common widget properties. However, Glade is *not* a code editor or an integrated development environment. The files it outputs must be loaded by your application, and you must implement all of the callback functions in your code. Glade is just meant to simplify the process of initializing your application's graphical user interface and connecting signals.

■**Tip** Glade 3, the version used in this book, now allows integrated development environments such as Anjuta to embed it into their user interfaces. These IDEs provide a complete, start-to-finish solution for deploying GTK+ applications.

Another advantage of Glade is that, since the user interfaces are stored as XML files, they are independent of the language. Any language that has wrapped the functionality provided by Libglade can load user interfaces. This means that the same graphical user interface designer can be used regardless of the programming language you choose.

Before continuing with the rest of this chapter, you should install Glade, Libglade, and the development package for Libglade from your operating system's package manager. Alternatively, you can download and compile the sources from `http://glade.gnome.org/`.

Also, you should make sure to follow along and create this application while reading the rest of the chapter. This will give you a chance to learn your way around the Glade 3 application, so you can get as much practice as possible while you have this book to guide you.

The Glade Interface

When you launch Glade for the first time, you will see three windows: the main window, the widget palette, and the widget property editor. Figure 10-1 is a screenshot of the main Glade application window with a project opened from the file browser.glade.

Figure 10-1. *The main Glade window*

The main window facilitates Glade project management. The Projects menu shows a list of the currently open projects, allowing you to switch among them. The main window also includes the widget tree view, which shows the widget containment of the project with focus.

The widget tree view shows the parent-to-child container relationships within a project. It is possible to have multiple top-level widgets. However, in Figure 10-1, window is the only top-level widget of the browser.glade project.

This window is where you will specify project options, save the project, and load existing projects. The menus in this window also provide many other options that can help you when working with projects, such as undoing and redoing actions.

■**Note** If you decide to work with Glade 2 instead of Glade 3, make sure to save often. Undo and redo support was not implemented in the older versions of Glade, and it is very frustrating if you accidentally overwrite an hour of work with one wrong mouse click!

The second window shown when you launch Glade 3 is the widget palette, which lists all of the widgets available to you for designing your applications. A screenshot of the widget palette can be viewed in Figure 10-2.

Figure 10-2. *The Glade widget palette*

By default, there are four categories of widgets displayed: top-level widgets, containers, widgets used for control and display, and depreciated widgets. You should not use any widgets in the GTK+ Obsolete list in new applications, because they are depreciated and may be removed in future releases.

In addition to the default categories of widgets, you may find other categories that include additional widget libraries. These can be widgets added for the GNOME libraries or other custom widget libraries.

Through the View menu, you can change the layout of the widget palette. Figure 10-2 shows a widget palette that is set to show both icons and text. However, you can show only text or only icons depending on what style you are most comfortable with.

To create a new top-level widget, all you need to do is click the icon of the desired widget in the Toplevels section. A new top-level widget will then be displayed and added to the widget tree in the main window. To add non-top-level widgets, you need to first click the icon of the desired widget and then click your mouse where the widget should be placed. You must click an empty cell in a container widget for the non-top-level widget to be inserted into the user interface.

Creating the Window

In this chapter, you are going to be creating a simple file browser application with Glade and Libglade. You begin by creating a new project with File ➤ New or by using the blank project created for you when the application loads. You can open an existing project with File ➤ Open if you return to this tutorial at a later time.

After you have a blank project, you can begin by creating a new top-level GtkWindow by clicking the Window icon in the widget palette. In the new window, you will see a mesh pattern in the interior of the widget, as displayed in Figure 10-3. This pattern designates a region where a child widget can be added to a container. After selecting a non-top-level widget from the widget palette, you must click this region to add the widget to the container. Follow this method for adding all non-top-level widgets.

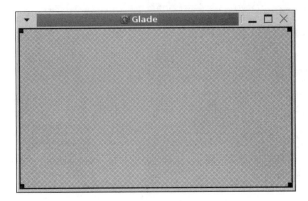

Figure 10-3. *The default GtkWindow widget*

After you create the top-level window, you will notice changes in the content of the widget Properties window, shown in Figure 10-4. In this window, you can customize all of the properties of each widget that is supported in Glade.

■**Note** While Glade allows you to edit many widget properties, some actions simply have to be performed in the code. Therefore, you should not view Glade as a replacement for everything that you have learned thus far in the book. You will still be doing a lot of GTK+ development in most applications.

The widget Properties window displayed in Figure 10-4 has five tabs filled with various options. The General tab provides basic options that are specific to the widget type that is currently selected. For example, the GtkWindow widget allows you to specify the window's type, title, ability to be resized, default size, and so on.

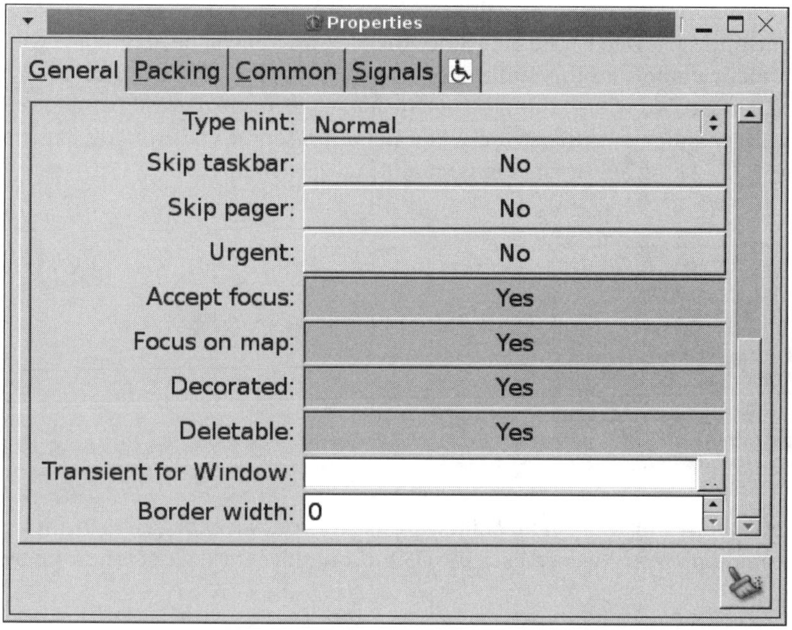

Figure 10-4. *A widget Properties dialog*

The Name field, which is scrolled beyond the bounds of the scrolled window in Figure 10-4, is used to give a unique name to the widget. Glade will automatically assign a name to each widget that is unique for the current project, but these are generic names. If you plan on referencing a widget from within your application, you should give it a name that means something. It can easily become confusing when you have to load three GtkTreeView widgets named treeview1, treeview2, and treeview3!

The Packing tab provides basic information about how the widget will react to changes in the size of its parent widget, such as expanding and filling. Common properties are those provided by GtkWidget and are available to all widgets. For example, you can provide a size request in this tab.

Note Packing options are a bit unintuitive when first working with Glade, because properties are set by the child instead of the parent container. For example, packing options for the children of a GtkVBox will be provided in the Packing tab of the children themselves instead of the parent container.

The Signals tab allows you to define signals for each widget that will be connected by Libglade. Lastly, the Accessibility tab, designated by the handicapped symbol, gives options that are used for accessibility support.

As you will recall from the first example in this book, an empty GtkWindow widget is not of any use except for illustrating how to create one. Since the file browser will need multiple widgets packed into the main window for this application, the next step is to add a vertical box container. Select the Vertical Box widget from the palette and click inside the grid pattern of window to insert a GtkVBox widget into the window. You will be presented with a dialog, like the one shown in Figure 10-5, asking how many items your GtkVBox will hold.

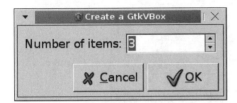

Figure 10-5. *Create a GtkVBox widget*

By default, three cells are created to hold child widgets, but you can change this to any number of items greater than zero. You can click the OK button, since the default is how many child widgets we need.

■**Note** Do not worry if you are not sure how many widgets the container will hold. You can add or remove cells in the General tab in the widget Properties window. You can then change the position of a widget within the box under the Packing tab. You are also still able to edit the user interface with your code after it is built by Libglade!

After adding the vertical box, you will see three separate, empty container meshes; notice the changes in the Properties window and the widget tree view. To these meshes, we will be adding a toolbar, an address bar, and a tree view.

Adding a Toolbar

It is usually a good idea when creating a toolbar to add it to a handle box so that the user can remove the toolbar from the window if desired. To do this, you need to select the Handle Box item from the widget palette, and click in the topmost GtkVBox cell. You can then add a toolbar widget to the handle box in the same way.

■**Note** If you want to create a toolbar in the way that was covered in the previous chapter, you should create the handle box but add no child widget to it. When you write the code for your application, you can programmatically add the toolbar to the handle box.

When the toolbar widget is selected, you will notice that an Edit button appears in the lower-left corner of the widget's Properties window. Clicking this button will open the toolbar editor shown in Figure 10-6. This toolbar editor creates new tool items that compose the toolbar. You will have to implement all of your callback functions for the tool items in your code.

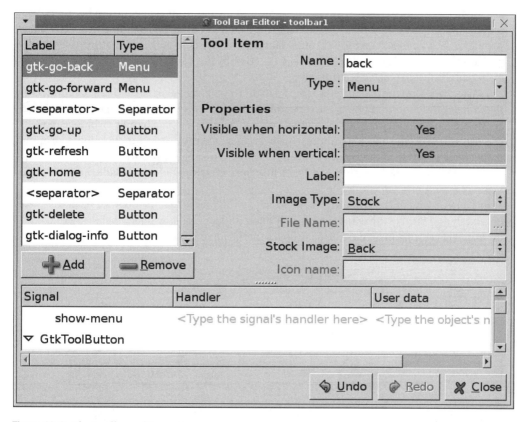

Figure 10-6. *The toolbar editor*

The toolbar editor allows you to add any supported type of item to a toolbar. To add a new item, you need only to click the Add button. This will insert a generic tool button, although you can change the type of item at a later time. On the right side, you will see many options that correspond to your new tool item.

After you add a new tool button, the next step is to choose what type of widget it should be by selecting an option from the Type combo box. The types of toolbar items included in the combo box are a generic tool button containing an image and a label, toggles, radio buttons, menu tool buttons, tool items, and separators. When you select a new type, the dialog will immediately be changed to allow you to edit properties for the chosen type.

For example, in Figure 10-6, the selected tool button is of the type GtkMenuToolButton. Every toolbar item gives you the option of whether it should be visible when the toolbar is horizontal or vertical. This allows you to hide the toolbar item when the toolbar has a vertical orientation but show it to the user when the toolbar is horizontal.

Menu tool buttons also allow you to choose a label and image to display in the tool item. An image can be a stock image, an existing image file, or an identifier of a custom icon theme depending on what option you choose in the Image Type combo box.

Along the bottom of the toolbar editor, you will see a tree view that allows you to connect signals to each tool button. Glade provides a number of named callback functions for you to choose from that are based on the signal name and the name you gave the toolbar item. You are also able to enter your own custom callback function name. It is possible to specify data to pass to each callback function through Libglade, so you can usually leave the "User data" parameter blank. In Figure 10-6, a callback function by the name on_back_clicked() was connected to GtkToolButton's clicked signal.

When you load the user interface with Libglade, you will have two choices for connecting the callback functions defined in the Glade file with those in your code. If you want to manually connect each and every callback function, you can name the signal handler whatever you choose, as long as the name is unique. However, Libglade provides a function that will automatically connect all of the signals by using GModule to find the appropriate symbols in your executable. To use this feature, the callback function name you define in Glade *must* match the name of the function in your code!

When you are finished editing the toolbar, you will notice that the handle box always takes up exactly one third of the window vertically because, by default, widgets are set to expand and fill. You will want to unset the expand property of the handle box, as shown in Figure 10-7.

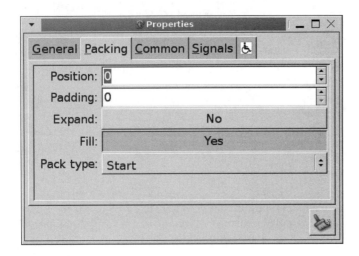

Figure 10-7. *Widget packing properties*

■**Tip** You should remember from Chapter 3 that a table was provided that illustrates what the expand and fill properties do to child widgets of a GtkBox widget. Glade is a perfect opportunity for you to experiment with packing options to gain a better understanding of how they affect the widget. Therefore, take a moment to experiment with the various packing options!

The Packing tab also includes options to determine padding around the widget, whether the packing is from the start or end of the box, and to determine the widget's position within the container. These properties are exactly equivalent to the settings you used when adding child widgets to GtkBox with gtk_box_pack_start() and friends.

After completing the toolbar and fixing packing preferences, your application should look like Figure 10-8. Notice that when you expand the size of the window vertically by dragging the window edge, the handle box no long expands to fill extra space!

Figure 10-8. *The toolbar in action*

The toolbar shown in Figure 10-8 contains two menu tool buttons used for moving forward and backward throughout the user's browsing history. There are also tool buttons for moving to the parent directory, refreshing the current view, removing a file, moving to the home directory, and viewing file information. Each of these tool buttons is connected to a callback function that you must implement in your code for the application.

Completing the File Browser

The next step in creating our file browser is to create the address bar that will show the users the current location and allow them to enter a new location. This means that we need a horizontal box with three widgets, as shown in Figure 10-9. The three widgets are a label describing the content held in the GtkEntry widget, the GtkEntry widget that holds the current location, and a button that will move to the location when pressed.

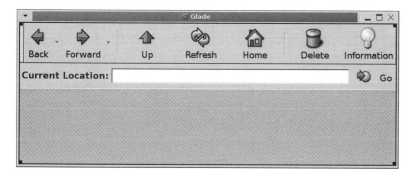

Figure 10-9. *The file browser*

We could easily just use the GTK_STOCK_JUMP_TO stock item for the button, but instead, I will show you how to use the button as a container. You first need to change the button type to a container in the Properties dialog. This will display an empty container mesh as the content of the button.

To create the button in Figure 10-9, a GtkHBox with two child widgets was added to the button: a GtkImage widget set to the GTK_STOCK_JUMP_TO stock image and a GtkLabel widget that says "Go."

Another important aspect of the address bar is the Current Location GtkLabel widget, which is set to bold. In Chapter 2, you learned about the Pango Text Markup Language. By selecting "Use markup" in a label's preferences dialog, as shown in Figure 10-10, you will be able to use Pango Text Markup Language tags in the label content. If you do not select this option, the markup tags will be rendered as text in the label.

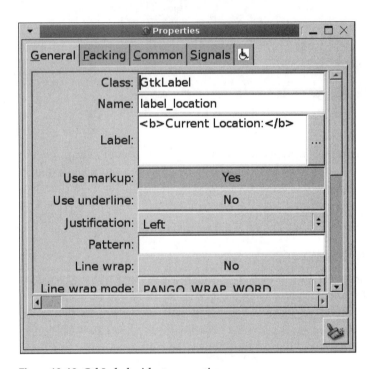

Figure 10-10. *GtkLabel widget properties*

Below the markup property, you can enable mnemonic labels by setting the "Use underline" property. In Figure 10-10, mnemonics are turned off, so underscore characters will be shown as text.

The last step is to add a GtkScrolledWindow widget to the last cell in the vertical box and a GtkTreeView widget to that container. The completed file browser user interface is shown in Figure 10-11. However, we are not yet finished editing the application in Glade.

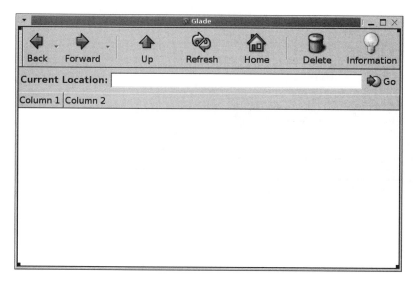

Figure 10-11. *The completed file browser*

Making Changes

The file browser is completely designed, but now I have decided that it should include a
GtkStatusBar widget along the bottom of the window! Making changes to the user interface
can be tricky, so this section will walk you through a few challenging actions.

The first step in adding the status bar is to extend the number of child widgets contained
by the main GtkVBox widget. To do this, choose the vertical box from the widget tree view. In the
Properties window, you can increase the number of children with the "Number of items" property in the General tab. This will add a new empty space at the end of the vertical box into which
you can add a status bar widget.

If you need to reorder the children of a vertical or horizontal box, you first need to select
the widget you want to move. Then, under the Packing tab in the Properties window, you can
choose a new position by changing the value of its spin button. You will be able to see the child
widget moving to its new position as you change spin button's value. The position of surrounding child widgets will automatically be adjusted to reflect the changes.

Another problematic task can result if you decide that you need to stuff a container into a
location where another widget is already added. For example, let us assume that you have
decided to place a horizontal pane in place of the scrolled window in the file browser application. You first need to select the widget from the widget tree view in the main window and
remove it by pressing Ctrl+X. After this, an empty box will be displayed, in which you can add
the horizontal pane. Next, select the pane where the scrolled window should be placed and
press Ctrl+V.

Making changes to a user interface used to be a touchy topic with Glade 2, because it did
not support undo and redo actions. It used to be very easy to make a mistake and lose hours of
work by accidentally deleting your top-level widget, since you could not undo any actions.
Now that Glade 3 includes undo and redo support, you do not have to worry as much.

Widget Signals

The last step for this application is to set up signals for all of the widgets. Figure 10-12 shows the Signals tab of the widget properties editor for the Go button. The GtkButton widget is connected to the clicked signal, which will call on_button_clicked() when emitted.

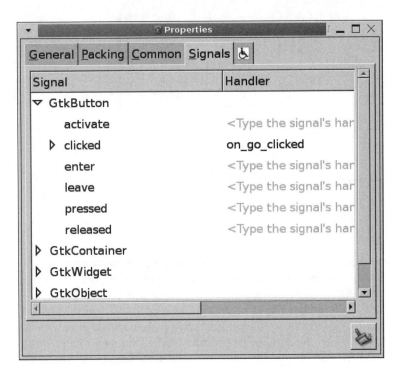

Figure 10-12. *A widget signal editor*

In addition to the clicked signal, you need to connect to a few others. Each of the tool items should be connected to GtkToolButton's clicked signal with the exception of the separators. Also, you should connect the GtkEntry to activate, which will be emitted when the user presses the Enter key when the entry has focus.

■Note This application is only a design for a simple file browser that is meant to show you how to design applications with Glade 3. The code needed for the application to be more than just a design will be implemented in Chapter 13.

As for the tree view, you should connect it to row-activated. When a row is activated, the user will be shown more information about the file or will navigate to the chosen directory. A list of the widgets along with their signals and callback functions is provided in Table 10-1 so that you can easily follow along with this example.

Table 10-1. *Widget Signals*

Widget	Description	Signal	Callback Function
GtkButton	Go button	clicked	on_go_clicked()
GtkEntry	Location entry	activate	on_location_activate()
GtkMenuToolButton	Back	clicked	on_back_clicked()
GtkMenuToolButton	Forward	clicked	on_forward_clicked()
GtkToolButton	Up	clicked	on_up_clicked()
GtkToolButton	Refresh	clicked	on_refresh_clicked()
GtkToolButton	Home	clicked	on_home_clicked()
GtkToolButton	Delete	clicked	on_delete_clicked()
GtkToolButton	Information	clicked	on_info_clicked()
GtkTreeView	File browser	row-activated	on_row_activated()
GtkWindow	Main window	destroy	gtk_main_quit()

Creating a Menu

In addition to toolbars, it is possible to create menus in Glade 3. Figure 10-13 shows the Menu Bar Editor, which is very similar to the toolbar editor. It supports normal menu items and those rendered with images, check buttons, radio buttons, and separators.

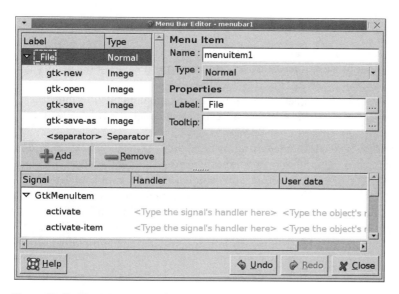

Figure 10-13. *The Menu Bar Editor*

You now know of three ways to create menus, which raises the question of which one is best. Every method has its advantages and disadvantages, so let us take a look at each method.

You first learned how to create menus manually, molding each object to your needs. This method is good to use with smaller menus, because the code will not take up a lot of space and the implementation is located entirely in one place. However, if your menu grows in size or contains more than just basic items, the code can become tedious to maintain and take up a lot of space.

Next, you learned how to use GtkUIManager with UI definitions to dynamically create menus. This method simplified menu creation, because you could define a large number of actions in a small amount of space. Also, since menus are constructed from UI definitions, allowing the user to edit a menu is extremely simple. This is clearly the preferred method of menu creation if you are not using Glade to design your application.

Glade also presents a very attractive method of menu creation, because after its initial design, maintenance is simple. It also requires no code to create the menu, since Libglade constructs it for you. However, one problem with this method is that it is not as easy to allow the user to alter the layout of menus and toolbars as with the UI file method.

One method that can easily be employed is to pack all of your widgets with respect to the end of the vertical box or whatever container you use as the child of the main window. Then, when your application loads, you can simply pack the menu created by GtkUIManager into the window with gtk_box_pack_start(). Nevertheless, if you do not need to allow your users to customize the menu, it makes sense to do all menu creation through Glade.

Now that you are finished creating the user interface, you can save it as a project.glade file, where project can be replaced by a name of your choice. This file can be loaded with respect to the location of the application or from an absolute path.

Using Libglade

After you design your application in Glade, the next step is to load the user interface with Libglade. This library is used to parse the Glade user interface and create all of the necessary widgets at runtime.

Libglade provides the GladeXML object that is used to create and hold the user interface loaded from an XML file. It can also be used to connect signals added in the Glade file to callback functions within your application.

Another advantage of Libglade is that overhead is added only during initialization, and this is negligible compared to an interface created directly from code. After initialization, there is virtually no overhead added to the application. For example, GladeXML connects signal handlers internally in the same way as your own code, so this will require no extra processing.

Since Libglade handles all of the widget initialization and the layout was already designed in Glade 3, the length of your code base can be significantly reduced. Take, for example, Listing 10-1, which would be significantly longer if you had to hand-code everything.

■**Note** The callback functions are not implemented in this example, because they are not relevant to the exercise. However, this application will be revisited in more detail in Chapter 13, which *will* include full implementation of the callback functions.

Listing 10-1. *Loading the User Interface (browser.c)*

```c
#include <gtk/gtk.h>
#include <glade/glade.h>

void on_back_clicked (GtkToolButton*);
void on_forward_clicked (GtkToolButton*);
void on_up_clicked (GtkToolButton*);
void on_refresh_clicked (GtkToolButton*);
void on_delete_clicked (GtkToolButton*);
void on_home_clicked (GtkToolButton*);
void on_info_clicked (GtkToolButton*);
void on_go_clicked (GtkButton*);
void on_location_activate (GtkEntry*);
void on_row_activated (GtkTreeView*, GtkTreePath*, GtkTreeViewColumn*);

int main (int argc,
          char *argv[])
{
  GtkWidget *window;
  GladeXML *xml;

  gtk_init (&argc, &argv);

  xml = glade_xml_new ("browser.glade", NULL, NULL);
  window = glade_xml_get_widget (xml, "window");

  glade_xml_signal_autoconnect (xml);

  gtk_widget_show_all (window);
  gtk_main ();

  return 0;
}
```

The code shown in Listing 10-1 will not compile with only GTK+ and its supporting librar-ies. You will need to include Libglade in the compile command, as follows:

```
gcc -export-dynamic browser.c -o browser `pkg-config --cflags --libs gtk+-2.0` \
    `pkg-config --cflags --libs libglade-2.0`
```

■**Caution** If you want to automatically connect signals in the main executable or any nonshared library, you will have to pass -export-dynamic to the linker. Otherwise, none of the signals will be able to be con-nected because GModule will not be able to open the application for introspection!

Loading a User Interface

Loading a Glade user interface is done with glade_xml_new(). This is the first GladeXML function you should call, although it should be called after gtk_init(). It parses the user interface provided by the XML file, creates all of the necessary widgets, and provides facilities for translation.

```
GladeXML* glade_xml_new (const char *glade_file_name,
                         const char *root_widget,
                         const char *translation_domain);
```

This function accepts three strings. The first is the location of the Glade user interface file. This path can be either relative or absolute, although you will usually want to use an absolute path since the executable could be installed in an alternative location on the user's system. This absolute path is usually defined by applications such as GNU Autotools during compila-tion. The relative path is with respect to the current working directory, which is initially set to the location of the executable but can be changed with g_chdir().

The second parameter accepted by glade_xml_new() is the widget name of the root node. You can specify a widget name so that only GladeXML loads a certain widget and its children. Passing NULL to this parameter will cause GladeXML to load every widget in the file.

■**Note** Every call to glade_xml_new() will build a new version of the user interface. Because of this, it is necessary to call this function only once for a single UI unless you destroy the widgets at some point in the application.

Lastly, you can provide a translation domain for the widgets, which will handle any wid-gets marked as translatable accordingly. If your application does not provide translations, it is safe to provide NULL to this parameter.

Once you have initialized the user interface by creating a new GladeXML object, you can retrieve widgets with glade_xml_get_widget(). This function returns a widget that is already instantiated, which is referred to by the name you gave it in Glade.

```
GtkWidget* glade_xml_get_widget (GladeXML *xml,
                                 const char *name);
```

The widget returned by glade_xml_get_widget() is already set up with all of the properties that you set in Glade. You can use this widget like any other GtkWidget that was created in your application using the functions provided in GTK+. This shows one of the main advantages of Libglade—you do not have to provide all of the monotonous code for setting up the user interface and can quickly get to developing more interesting aspects of the application.

Another useful function is glade_xml_get_widget_prefix(), which allows you to retrieve a list of widgets that have the same prefix as the given string. If you name all of your widgets according to their type or what window they belong to, this function can be very helpful.

```
GList* glade_xml_get_widget_prefix (GladeXML *xml,
                                    const char *name);
```

Connecting Signals

The next step in getting your application ready for use is to connect the signal handlers that you created in Glade. In Listing 10-1, glade_xml_signal_autoconnect() was used to connect all of the signals at once.

```
void glade_xml_signal_autoconnect (GladeXML *xml);
```

To autoconnect signals, Libglade opens a NULL version of GModule, which will provide access to your application's symbol table. The function then tries to find functions with the same signal handler name, which means that the names in the Glade file *must* match those of the callback functions in your application. This function will work only if GModule is supported on the user's system.

Another option for connecting signals is to use glade_xml_signal_autoconnect_full(). This function allows you to provide a callback function that will connect all of the signals for you. This way you can provide any necessary customization.

```
void glade_xml_signal_connect_full (GladeXML *self,
                                    const gchar *handler_name,
                                    GladeXMLConnectFunc connect_func,
                                    gpointer data);
```

Listing 10-2 presents a simple GladeXMLConnectFunc implementation that uses GModule in the same way as in glade_xml_signal_autoconnect(). This function is called for every signal in the Glade user interface file.

Listing 10-2. *Autoconnecting Signals*

```
static void
connect_func (const gchar *callback_name,
              GObject *object,
              const gchar *signal_name,
              const gchar *signal_data,
              GObject *connect_object,
              gboolean connect_after,
              gpointer data)
{
  static GModule *module_self = NULL;
  gpointer handler_func;

  module_self = g_module_open (NULL, 0);
  g_assert (module_self != NULL);

  if (g_module_symbol (module_self, callback_name, &handler_func))
  {
    if (connect_object && connect_after)
      g_signal_connect_object (object, signal_name, handler_func,
                               connect_object, G_CONNECT_AFTER);
    else if (connect_object && !connect_after)
      g_signal_connect_object (object, signal_name, handler_func,
                               connect_object, G_CONNECT_SWAPPED);
    else if (!connect_object && connect_after)
      g_signal_connect_after (object, signal_name, handler_func, data);
    else
      g_signal_connect (object, signal_name, handler_func, data);
  }
  else
    g_warning ("The callback function could not be found: %s", callback_name);
}
```

You already know how to use GModule, so the code in Listing 10-2 should be understandable to you. However, there are two new functions used for connecting signals that were introduced in Listing 10-2, which I will explain now.

When you connect a signal with g_signal_connect(), your callback function will be run before the standard callback function. This allows you to override the standard callback with your own in some cases. Alternatively, if you want your callback function to run after the default, you can connect the signal with g_signal_connect_after().

```
gulong g_signal_connect_after (gpointer object,
                               const gchar *signal_name,
                               GCallback handler,
                               gpointer data);
```

Another useful signal connection function is g_signal_connect_object(), but it temporarily increases the reference count to ensure that the GObject provided to the fourth parameter will remain for the duration of the callback function. Also, gobject is sent to the callback function instead of the object.

```
gulong g_signal_connect_object (gpointer object,
                                const gchar *signal_name,
                                GCallback handler,
                                gpointer gobject,
                                GConnectFlags flags);
```

The g_signal_connect_object() function accepts flags from the following GConnectFlags enumeration:

- G_CONNECT_AFTER: If this flag is set, the callback function will be called after the default signal handler. This is similar to calling g_signal_connect_after().

- G_CONNECT_SWAPPED: If this flag is set, the signal data will be sent to the callback function as the first parameter followed by the initiating GObject. This is similar to calling g_signal_connect_swapped().

■**Tip** G_CONNECT_SWAPPED may not seem useful at first, but it can be used to call a function on only the user data parameter. For example, if you use this flag when connecting a GTK_STOCK_QUIT menu item, you can connect it to gtk_widget_destroy() and pass the main window as the user data. This will cause the main window to be destroyed when the menu item is activated.

In addition to autoconnecting signals, you can connect a signal with glade_xml_signal_connect(). You need to specify the signal handler that you provided to Glade. The nice thing about this function is that the Glade signal handler and the actual function name do not need to be the same. This function is only for convenience and is equivalent to retrieving the widget and calling g_signal_connect() on it.

```
void glade_xml_signal_connect (GladeXML *xml,
                               const char *signal_name,
                               GCallback callback_func);
```

The problem with glade_xml_signal_connect() is that you cannot pass data to the callback function. To fix this, you can use glade_xml_signal_connect_data(), which allows you to specify a data parameter to pass to the callback function.

```
void glade_xml_signal_connect_data (GladeXML *xml,
                                    const char *signal_name,
                                    GCallback callback_func,
                                    gpointer data);
```

Unless you need to pass different data parameters to each function, it is a lot more convenient to simply allow Libglade to autoconnect all of the signals. Remember, though, that autoconnect will only work on systems that support GModule, so you should still know how to connect each signal one at a time!

Test Your Understanding

These two exercises are especially important for you to become a proficient GTK+ developer. It is not practical to programmatically design every aspect of large applications, because it takes too long.

Instead, you should be using Glade to design the user interface and Libglade to load that design and connect signals. By doing this, you will be able to quickly finish the graphical aspects of your applications and get to the backend code that makes your applications work.

Exercise 10-1. Glade Text Editor

In this exercise, implement the text editor from Exercise 9-1 in Glade. The toolbar in the text editor should be implemented completely in Glade.

This exercise should not require much extra coding if you still have the exercise solution from the previous chapter. You can also find the solution to Exercise 9-1 on the book's web site at www.gtkbook.com. This exercise will give you a chance to learn your way around Glade 3 and test out many widget properties.

After you design an application with a toolbar, it is an easy transition to add a menu bar. In larger applications, you should provide both of these options to the user. In the following exercise, you will add a menu bar to the text editor application.

Exercise 10-2. Glade Text Editor with Menus

In Exercise 9-2, you implemented the text editor with a menu bar. In this exercise, redesign the application from that exercise using Glade and Libglade. First, you should implement the menu with GtkUIManager, which will allow you to use both together. Second, you should implement the menu again in Glade.

As with the previous exercise, the solution for Exercise 9-2 can be found at www.gtkbook.com. Using the downloadable solution will allow you skip over coding the callback functions, since you have already done that in the previous chapter.

Summary

In this chapter, we took a short break from coding and looked into issues that you need to consider when designing a graphical user interface. In short, you must always keep your users in mind. You need to know what to expect of your users and cater to their needs in every aspect of the application.

Next, you learned how to design graphical user interfaces using Glade 3. The ability to quickly deploy the graphical aspects of an application is a must when considering a GUI toolkit, and GTK+ has Glade to fill this need.

Glade allows you to design every aspect of your user interface including widget properties, layout, and signal handlers. User interfaces are saved as readable XML files that are used to describe the structure of your application.

After designing an application in Glade 3, you can dynamically load the user interface with Libglade. This library is used to parse the Glade user interface and create all of the necessary widgets at runtime. It also provides functions for connecting signal handlers declared in Glade to callback functions within your application.

In the next chapter, we are going to get back to coding and delve into the complexities of the GObject system. You will learn how to create your own GObject classes by deriving new widgets and classes as well as how to create a widget from scratch.

CHAPTER 11

■■■

Creating Custom Widgets

By now, you have learned a great deal about GTK+ and its supporting libraries. You have enough knowledge to use the widgets provided by GTK+ to create complex applications of your own.

However, one thing that you have not yet learned is how to create your own widgets. Therefore, this chapter is dedicated to deriving new classes from GObject. You will be guided through three examples.

The first example derives a new widget called MyIPAddress from the GtkEntry widget. This widget allows the user to enter an IP address, controlling the placement of the cursor accordingly. The second example creates a new custom GtkWidget class called MyMarquee that scrolls a message at a specified speed. Lastly, you will learn how to implement and use custom interfaces.

In this chapter, you will learn the following:

- How to derive new classes and widgets from those that already exist.

- How to create custom widgets derived from GtkWidget. This method will require you to expose and draw the widget on the screen yourself.

- How to implement and use custom interfaces.

Deriving New Widgets

The purpose of this chapter is to teach you how to create new GObject types by deriving from those that already exist. The best way to learn how to derive new objects is by example. In this section, we will be creating a new widget called MyIPAddress, which will allow the user to enter an IP address. This allows you to restrict the user from entering anything but a valid IP address.

■Note While we are deriving a new widget in this section, the method outlined here applies to all objects derived from GObject. Therefore, you are not limited to deriving new widgets but can derive a new type from any other type that is derived directly or indirectly from GObject.

A screenshot of the GtkIPAddress widget created in this section is shown in Figure 11-1. Notice that all of the one-digit and two-digit numbers are aligned to the right.

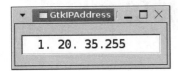

Figure 11-1. *A MyIPAddress widget*

Creating the MyIPAddress Header File

The first step in deriving any type of GObject is to create the header file. This file allows you to set up the basic function calls required by each object. It is also a good place to plan out your widget, since the header file will contain public functions that are available to any code using your new object.

In order to accommodate C++ compilers, you should bracket the content of your header file with G_BEGIN_DECLS and G_END_DECLS. These two macros add extern "C" around the content, which will force all functions to use their names for symbol names when compiled as in C. An example of the shell of the header file is shown in Listing 11-1.

Listing 11-1. *MyIPAddress Header File (myipaddress.h)*

```
#ifndef __MY_IP_ADDRESS_H__
#define __MY_IP_ADDRESS_H__

#include <glib.h>
#include <glib-object.h>
#include <gtk/gtkentry.h>

G_BEGIN_DECLS
...
G_END_DECLS

#endif /* __MY_IP_ADDRESS_H__ */
```

■Note Unlike most examples in this book, this chapter's examples have been split up into small parts instead of displaying them as a whole, because they span so many lines. You can download the full files of source code from the book's web site at www.gtkbook.com.

Along with the necessary structures and functions, you need to define five macros for every new widget, as shown in Listing 11-2. All of the function and structure declarations in the rest of the header file should be placed between G_BEGIN_DECLS and G_END_DECLS. The macros in Listing 11-2 follow a standard naming scheme that every GObject uses. Standard naming makes object inheritance a lot simpler.

Listing 11-2. *GObject Directives*

```
#define MY_IP_ADDRESS_TYPE            (my_ip_address_get_type ())
#define MY_IP_ADDRESS(obj)            (G_TYPE_CHECK_INSTANCE_CAST ((obj), \
                                      MY_IP_ADDRESS_TYPE, MyIPAddress))
#define MY_IP_ADDRESS_CLASS(klass)    (G_TYPE_CHECK_CLASS_CAST ((klass), \
                                      MY_IP_ADDRESS_TYPE, MyIPAddressClass))
#define IS_MY_IP_ADDRESS(obj)         (G_TYPE_CHECK_INSTANCE_TYPE ((obj), \
                                      MY_IP_ADDRESS_TYPE))
#define IS_MY_IP_ADDRESS_CLASS(klass) (G_TYPE_CHECK_CLASS_TYPE ((klass), \
                                      MY_IP_ADDRESS_TYPE))
```

All of the functions used by your new object should be prefixed with the library name such as GTK_ or GDK_, followed by the widget name. The first macro you need to define is MY_IP_ADDRESS_TYPE. This macro returns the GType structure corresponding to your object. We will define my_ip_address_get_type() later in the header file.

The next macro, MY_IP_ADDRESS(), is used to cast the object as MyIPAddress. This is similar to casting an object with functions such as GTK_WIDGET(), GTK_ENTRY(), or G_OBJECT(). G_TYPE_CHECK_INSTANCE_CAST() performs two tasks. It first checks whether the object is of the correct type. If it is not, a warning will be emitted. Otherwise, the object will be cast as a MyIPAddress widget and returned.

MY_IP_ADDRESS_CLASS() is used in the same way as MY_IP_ADDRESS(), except it is used to cast an object as MyIPAddressClass. You will soon learn the difference between these two types.

■Note Since your code may be compiled with a C++ compiler as well, you should always use klass instead of class to refer to the widget class type, since the latter is a C++ keyword.

The last two macros, IS_MY_IP_ADDRESS() and IS_MY_IP_ADDRESS_CLASS(), are used to check whether the object is the correct type. Each function will return TRUE if the object is of the specified type.

The next step is to define both the MyIPAddress and MyIPAddressClass structures, as in Listing 11-3. The widget content is held by _MyIPAddress. The first member in the new widget's structure should always be an instance of the type that you are deriving from. As you can see in the listing, the MyIPAddress widget is going to be derived from GtkEntry.

Listing 11-3. *The MyIPAddress Structure*

```
typedef struct _MyIPAddress        MyIPAddress;
typedef struct _MyIPAddressClass   MyIPAddressClass;

struct _MyIPAddress
{
  GtkEntry entry;
};

struct _MyIPAddressClass
{
  GtkEntryClass parent_class;

  void (* ip_changed) (MyIPAddress *ipaddress);
};
```

■**Caution** You should *not* define the parent GtkEntry object in MyIPAddress as a pointer! If you do, you will get an error stating that your new widget class is smaller than the parent and compilation will fail.

Notice that the GtkEntry child of MyIPAddress is not a pointer as with most widgets. This affirms the fact that a derived object *is* its parent structure in every way. It inherits not only signals, properties, and styles but also the whole object itself. This relationship is reaffirmed by the declaration of a nonpointer GtkEntryClass object in the MyIPAddressClass structure.

The MyIPAddress structure does not hold any other objects besides the GtkEntry object. The widget structure GtkEntry was originally used to hold private objects that the programmer was not supposed to access, but GObject provides a better way to implement private properties, which will be covered in the source file. You are also free to place any variables within the widget structure that you deem necessary, although you should consider whether the programmer should have direct access to the objects before doing this. Basically, if the widget needs to react to changes of a variable, it should be declared in the private class in the source file. Otherwise, it can be placed within the public widget structure.

In addition to MyIPAddress, you also need to define MyIPAddressClass, which first contains an instance of the parent class type, GtkEntryClass. Again, this should not be a pointer type, because it will allow parent properties, signals, and functions to be inherited by your widget class.

Furthermore, you should define callback function prototypes for signals in the widget class. In this example, the ip-changed signal will be added, which will be called when the IP address is successfully changed. This signal is provided so the developer does not need to monitor all four widget properties for changes, since each of the four numbers will be defined as its own widget property.

The last step in creating the header file is to define function prototypes for those functions that are available for the developer to call, as shown in Listing 11-4. We will also define private functions that will only be accessible in the myipaddress.c file.

Listing 11-4. *Header File Function Prototypes*

```
GType      my_ip_address_get_type (void) G_GNUC_CONST;
GtkWidget* my_ip_address_new      (void);

gchar* my_ip_address_get_address (MyIPAddress *ipaddress);
void   my_ip_address_set_address (MyIPAddress *ipaddress, gint address[4]);
```

The four functions in Listing 11-4 will return the GType associated with MyIPAddress, create a new MyIPAddress widget, return the IP address as a string, and provide new IP address values respectively. These will be discussed in more detail later in the chapter when their implementations are covered.

Creating the Source File

Now that the header file is completed, it is time to derive the new object and implement the functionality of MyIPAddress. The widget is going to have a number of properties and signals, which need to be tracked, which will be defined in the following listing.

Listing 11-5 defines a number of values and structures that will be needed throughout the MyIPAddress source file. This includes the private class as well as signal and property identifiers.

Listing 11-5. *Global Enumerations and Structures (myipaddress.c)*

```
#include <gtk/gtk.h>
#include <gdk/gdkkeysyms.h>
#include <stdlib.h>
#include <math.h>
#include "myipaddress.h"

#define MY_IP_ADDRESS_GET_PRIVATE(obj) (G_TYPE_INSTANCE_GET_PRIVATE ((obj), \
                                        MY_IP_ADDRESS_TYPE, MyIPAddressPrivate))

typedef struct _MyIPAddressPrivate  MyIPAddressPrivate;

struct _MyIPAddressPrivate
{
  guint address[4];
};
```

```
enum
{
  CHANGED_SIGNAL,
  LAST_SIGNAL
};

enum
{
  PROP_0,
  PROP_IP1,
  PROP_IP2,
  PROP_IP3,
  PROP_IP4
};

static guint my_ip_address_signals[LAST_SIGNAL] = { 0 };
```

The macro defined in Listing 11-5, MY_IP_ADDRESS_GET_PRIVATE(), retrieves the MyIPAddressPrivate structure associated with the current object instance. This structure is used to hold private properties of the object, which are unique to each instance. In this example, MyIPAddressPrivate holds each of the four IP address values. These values are kept private so that only functions defined in this file may alter them, since the widget must be updated when they change.

The next step is to define enumerations that will be used to refer to signals and properties installed on the widget. CHANGED_SIGNAL refers to the ip-changed signal that will be emitted when the user changes the content of the IP address or when it is programmatically changed. LAST_SIGNAL is used to figure out how many signals are installed on the widget and stored in my_ip_address_signals[]. By defining this as the last enumeration value, signals can easily be added in the future without worrying about updating the signal count.

The other enumeration holds property identifiers. Since all of your property identifiers must be greater than zero when declared, it is traditional to place an initial enumeration value of PROP_0. The other enumeration values refer to the four integers that will compose the IP address. These are only used when adding the signals to the widget class. Programmers using the new widget can use the property names that you will later define.

Registering a New GType

In the header file, we defined a function prototype for the my_ip_address_get_type() function that is implemented in Listing 11-6. This function returns a GType value, which is simply a numerical value that is unique to the registered type. In this case, the registered type is the MyIPAddress object.

Listing 11-6. *Creating the New MyIPAddress Type*

```
GType
my_ip_address_get_type (void)
{
  static GType entry_type = 0;

  if (!entry_type)
  {
    static const GTypeInfo entry_info =
    {
      sizeof (MyIPAddressClass),
      NULL,
      NULL,
      (GClassInitFunc) my_ip_address_class_init,
      NULL,
      NULL,
      sizeof (MyIPAddress),
      0,
      (GInstanceInitFunc) my_ip_address_init,
    };

    entry_type = g_type_register_static (GTK_TYPE_ENTRY, "MyIPAddress",
                                         &entry_info, 0);
  }

  return entry_type;
}
```

If the type has not yet been created, which means that the static identifier has yet to be set during the initialization of the object, we need to add it. When registering a new GType, we first need to declare a GTypeInfo object for the type. There are ten members in the GTypeInfo structure, as defined in Table 11-1, although not all of the members are required.

Table 11-1. *GTypeInfo Members*

Variable	Description
guint16 class_size	The size of the class structure, which is required when creating widgets. This is simply the size of the MyIPAddressClass structure.
GBaseInitFunc base_init	Optional location of the base initialization function. This callback function is used to reallocate all dynamic class members copied from the parent class.
GBaseFinalizeFunc base_finalize	Optional location of the base finalization function. This callback function is used to finalize things done by the GBaseInitFunc function.
GClassInitFunc class_init	Optional implementation of the class initialization function, which is used to fill in virtual functions for the class and register signals and object properties.
GClassFinalizeFunc class_finalize	Optional implementation of the class finalization function. This function is rarely needed, because dynamically allocated resources should be handled in the GBaseInitFunc and GBaseFinalizeFunc functions.
gconstpointer class_data	Pointer data that will be passed to the implementations of GClassInitFunc and GClassFinalizeFunc.
guint16 instance_size	Size of the widget or object that you are deriving. This is simply the size of the MyIPAddress structure.
guint16 n_preallocs	Since the release of GLib 2.10, this member is ignored, since memory allocation of instances is handled with the slice allocator.
GInstanceInitFunc instance_init	Optional function used to set up the instance. In the MyIPAddress example, this function connects the keypress-event and changed signals to each GtkEntry and packs the widget.
const GTypeValueTable *value_table	A function table that handles generic GValue objects for this type. This is usually only used when creating fundamental types, so in most cases it does not have to be defined.

There are four steps to initializing a new class: copying over members from the parent class, initializing remaining members to zero, calling the GBaseInitFunc initializer, and calling the GClassInitFunc initializer. These steps are followed each time a new instance of the object are instantiated. The GClassInitFunc function is required in GTypeInfo for the new GType to be valid.

After setting up a GTypeInfo object for your new type, the next step is to register the GType with g_type_register_static(). The first parameter of this function is the GType value referring to the parent type. For example, if you derive an object from MyIPAddress, this would be set to GTK_TYPE_IP_ADDRESS. You can use the GTK_TYPE_ENTRY macro to derive the new object from the GtkEntry widget.

```
GType g_type_register_static (GType parent_type,
                              const gchar *type_name,
                              const GTypeInfo *info,
                              GTypeFlags flags);
```

Next, you should specify a string that will be used as the name of the new type and the corresponding GTypeInfo object. In our example, the name of the widget, MyIPAddress, was used. This is generally a good idea, since it should be unique to your object. This name must be at least three characters long and begin with an alphabetic character.

The last parameter is a bitwise combination of GTypeFlags. There are two values defined by this enumeration. G_TYPE_FLAG_ABSTRACT indicates that the type is abstract. You will be prevented from creating instances of abstract types. The other flag, G_TYPE_FLAG_VALUE_ABSTRACT, indicates an abstract value type such as a value table, but it cannot be used with g_value_init(). The function returns a new GType for the given parameters.

The last step for setting up a new GType is to return the new value from my_ip_address_get_type(), whether it was just registered or simply stored by the static value. This function is used first to register the new type and then to retrieve the unique GType value. The returned value can be used in many places such as if you derive a new widget from MyIPAddress or when you create a new MyIPAddress widget.

Initializing the Widget Class

The next function in the source file is the implementation of the class initialization function (GClassInitFunc), provided by my_ip_address_class_init(). This function accepts a MyIPAddressClass object and the optional gpointer data parameter specified when registering the type. The second parameter is ignored in Listing 11-7, since the user data parameter was defined as NULL when defining the new GType.

Listing 11-7. *Initializing MyIPAddressClass*

```
static void
my_ip_address_class_init (MyIPAddressClass *klass)
{
  GObjectClass *gobject_class = G_OBJECT_CLASS (klass);

  /* Override the standard functions for setting and retrieving properties. */
  gobject_class->set_property = my_ip_address_set_property;
  gobject_class->get_property = my_ip_address_get_property;
```

```
/* Add MyIPAddressPrivate as a private data class of MyIPAddressClass. */
g_type_class_add_private (klass, sizeof (MyIPAddressPrivate));

/* Register the ip-changed signal, which will be emitted when the ip changes. */
my_ip_address_signals[CHANGED_SIGNAL] =
      g_signal_new ("ip-changed", G_TYPE_FROM_CLASS (klass),
                   G_SIGNAL_RUN_FIRST | G_SIGNAL_ACTION,
                   G_STRUCT_OFFSET (MyIPAddressClass, ip_changed),
                   NULL, NULL, g_cclosure_marshal_VOID__VOID, G_TYPE_NONE, 0);

/* Register four GObject properties, one for each ip address number. */
g_object_class_install_property (gobject_class, PROP_IP1,
              g_param_spec_int ("ip-number-1",
                               "IP Address Number 1",
                               "The first IP address number",
                               0, 255, 0,
                               G_PARAM_READWRITE));

g_object_class_install_property (gobject_class, PROP_IP2,
              g_param_spec_int ("ip-number-2",
                               "IP Address Number 2",
                               "The second IP address number",
                               0, 255, 0,
                               G_PARAM_READWRITE));

g_object_class_install_property (gobject_class, PROP_IP3,
              g_param_spec_int ("ip-number-3",
                               "IP Address Number 3",
                               "The third IP address number",
                               0, 255, 0,
                               G_PARAM_READWRITE));

g_object_class_install_property (gobject_class, PROP_IP4,
              g_param_spec_int ("ip-number-4",
                               "IP Address Number 1",
                               "The fourth IP address number",
                               0, 255, 0,
                               G_PARAM_READWRITE));
}
```

The first thing you should do in the class initialization function is override any necessary functions for the GObjectClass, from which your widget class derives. In this example, we needed to override the default implementations of set_property() and get_property(). These functions are called when the programmer calls g_object_set() and g_object_get() respectively. You must *always* override these functions if your new object will have any number of properties installed.

Note There are a number of other functions provided in GObjectClass including a constructor, notify signal callback, and finalization function. You can find a full list of functions that can be overridden in the GObject API documentation.

Next, an instance of the MyIPAddressPrivate is associated with the widget class with g_type_class_add_private(). This structure will hold the values for the four widget properties.

```
void g_type_class_add_private (gpointer klass,
                               gsize private_size);
```

The first parameter of this function is the widget class that the private class will be associated with. This is followed by the size of the private structure, which can be obtained with sizeof(). By implementing private data in this manner, GObject provides data hiding to the extent allowed by the C programming language.

Installing Signals

After you override any necessary virtual functions, the next step in the widget class initialization function is to set up any signals required by your object with g_signal_new(). This is a very long and complex function, so let us take it one parameter at a time.

```
guint g_signal_new (const gchar *signal_name,
                    GType class_type,
                    GSignalFlags signal_flags,
                    guint class_offset,
                    GSignalAccumulator accumulator,
                    gpointer accumulator_data,
                    GSignalCMarshaller c_marshaller,
                    GType return_type,
                    guint n_parameters,
                    ...);
```

The first parameter of g_signal_new() is the name of the new signal you are creating. In this example, we are adding the ip-address signal. This name will be used by the programmer in the g_signal_connect() family of functions to connect the signal to a callback function. It is important to make this name as descriptive as possible so that the programmer can discern its purpose from the name.

The next parameter of g_signal_new() provides the GType of the class that will contain the signal. You can retrieve this type by calling G_TYPE_FROM_CLASS() or G_OBJECT_CLASS_TYPE() on the instance. This is followed by a bitwise list of signal flags as defined by the GSignalFlags enumeration values that follow:

- G_SIGNAL_RUN_FIRST: Call the handler for this signal during the first emission stage. This will be run while other object signals with this flag set are run.

- G_SIGNAL_RUN_LAST: Call the handler for this signal during the third emission stage. This will be run while other object signals with this flag set are run.

- G_SIGNAL_RUN_CLEANUP: Call the handler for this signal during the last emission stage. This will be run while other object signals with this flag set are run.

- G_SIGNAL_NO_RECURSE: If a signal on this object is already being emitted, a recursive call will be prevented. Instead, the first emission will simply be restarted.

- G_SIGNAL_DETAILED: Add support for the ::detail descriptor added to the signal name upon connections and emissions of the signal.

- G_SIGNAL_ACTION: If set, this signal can be emitted with g_signal_emit() and friends without the need to perform pre- or post-emission adjustments to the object. This is meant to allow a signal to be emitted by code that uses this object.

- G_SIGNAL_NO_HOOKS: Do not support emission hooks for this signal.

The next parameter in g_signal_new() is the structure offset in your class of the signal prototype. For example, G_STRUCT_OFFSET() is used to get the offset of ip_changed() in MyIPAddressClass. This function is defined by GLib as shown in the following code snippet, which illustrates that the function simply returns the offset of member within struct_type. This allows g_signal_new() to find the callback function prototype.

```
#define G_STRUCT_OFFSET(struct_type, member) \
        ((glong) ((guint8*) &((struct_type*) 0)->member))
```

Next, you can specify an optional function of the type `GSignalAccumulator` that will be used for accumulation followed by data to pass to that function. In most cases, both of these parameters will be set to `NULL`.

The next parameter, `GSignalCMarshaller` is called a closure marshal function, which is used to translate arrays of parameters into callback invocations supported by C. There are a number of closure marshal functions provided by `GObject`, which follow a standard naming scheme. There should be no need to create your own in most cases.

The most basic type of closure marshal is `g_cclosure_marshal_VOID__VOID()`. Take note of the specific notation, where the function includes two consecutive underscore characters! The first `VOID` tells `GObject` that the return type of the callback function is void. The second `VOID` says that there are no additional parameters beyond the instance and user data sent to the callback function. The function prototype for this type of signal follows:

```
void (*callback) (gpointer instance, gpointer data);
```

Another example is `g_cclosure_marshal_VOID__BOOLEAN()`. The callback function prototype corresponding to this type of signal follows. It returns void and has an additional gboolean parameter located between the object instance and the user data.

```
void (*callback) (gpointer instance, gboolean arg, gpointer data);
```

In addition to these two closures, there are a number of others that return other fundamental types. `GObject` also provides a few with nonvoid return values. For example, `g_cclosure_marshal_STRING__OBJECT_POINTER()` returns a C string and accepts two additional parameters, a `GObject` and a pointer. A full list of closure marshal functions available in GLib 2.12 follows:

- `g_cclosure_marshal_VOID__*()`: These functions return nothing and accept only a single additional parameter of `BOOLEAN`, `CHAR`, `UCHAR`, `INT`, `UINT`, `LONG`, `ULONG`, `ENUM`, `FLAGS`, `FLOAT`, `DOUBLE`, `STRING`, `PARAM`, `BOXED`, `POINTER`, `OBJECT`, or `UINT_POINTER`. A value of `VOID` will cause the callback function to have only the two basic parameters.

- `g_cclosure_marshal_STRING__OBJECT_POINTER()`: This function type returns a string and accepts addition parameters of a `GObject` and a pointer.

- `g_cclosure_marshal_BOOLEAN__FLAGS()`: This function type returns a gboolean value and accepts bitwise fields defined by `G_TYPE_FLAGS`.

The next parameter of `g_signal_new()` gives the return type that will be used for the callback function. For example, the callback function in the `MyIPAddress` example has no return value, so it is referred to as `G_TYPE_NONE`. A full list of fundamental types that are registered by default is shown in Table 11-2.

Table 11-2. *Fundamental GLib Types*

GType	Definition
G_TYPE_BOOLEAN	A standard Boolean type that holds either TRUE or FALSE
G_TYPE_BOXED	A fundamental type referring to a boxed or structure type
G_TYPE_CHAR G_TYPE_UCHAR	Signed and unsigned versions of the standard C char type
G_TYPE_DOUBLE	A gdouble variable equivalent to the standard C double type
G_TYPE_ENUM	A standard enumeration equivalent to the C enum type
G_TYPE_FLAGS	Bitwise fields holding Boolean flags
G_TYPE_FLOAT	A gfloat variable equivalent to the standard C float type
G_TYPE_INT G_TYPE_UINT	Signed and unsigned versions of the standard C int type
G_TYPE_INT64 G_TYPE_UINT64	Signed and unsigned versions of GLib's implementation of a 64-bit integer
G_TYPE_INTERFACE	A fundamental type from which interfaces can be derived
G_TYPE_INVALID	An invalid GType that is used as an error return value by some functions
G_TYPE_LONG G_TYPE_ULONG	Signed and unsigned versions of the standard C long type
G_TYPE_NONE	An empty type equivalent to void
G_TYPE_OBJECT	A fundamental type that refers to any class derived from and cast as a GObject
G_TYPE_PARAM	A fundamental type that refers to any type derived from GParamSpec
G_TYPE_POINTER	An untyped pointer type that is implemented as a void pointer
G_TYPE_STRING	A NULL-terminated C string that is stored as a pointer to an array of gchar characters

The last parameters of g_signal_new() are the number of parameters accepted by the callback function excluding the instance and user data followed by a list of a types for each parameter. In our example, there were no extra types added, so the number of parameters was set to zero. Let us look at the following declaration for the populate-popup signal of the GtkEntry widget.

```
g_signal_new ("populate_popup",
              G_OBJECT_CLASS_TYPE (gobject_class), /* or G_TYPE_FROM_CLASS() */
              G_SIGNAL_RUN_LAST,
              G_STRUCT_OFFSET (GtkEntryClass, populate_popup),
              NULL, NULL,
              _gtk_marshal_VOID__OBJECT, /* defined in gtkmarshal.h */
              G_TYPE_NONE, 1,
              GTK_TYPE_MENU);
```

In this signal declaration, there was one additional parameter sent to the callback function, which is cast as a GtkMenu. The GtkMenu type is defined by GTK_TYPE_MENU. This gives you a more specific parameter cast type to use instead of the generic GObject defined by g_cclosure_marshal_VOID__OBJECT().

Installing Properties

The last thing you need to do in the class initialization function for this example is install any necessary properties. There are four properties installed in the MyIPAddress widget, all four of them integers.

Properties are installed on a GObjectClass with g_object_class_install_property(). The first two parameters of this function accept the GObjectClass corresponding to your new widget class and the property identifier. The identifier is simply a unique unsigned integer that refers to the specific property. These identifiers are normally defined in an enumeration, as was done for MyIPAddress, so that they are guaranteed to be unique to the object.

```
void g_object_class_install_property (GObjectClass *object_class,
                                      guint property_id,
                                      GParamSpec *pspec);
```

The last parameter of g_object_class_install_property() is a GParamSpec object, which stores information about what type of variable the property holds, its name, and various other characteristics. There are a number of functions for setting up GParamSpec objects.

In the MyIPAddress example, g_param_spec_int() is used to set up a new GParamSpecInt implementation for a property of the type G_TYPE_INT. The first three parameters of this function refer to the property name, a short nickname for the property, and a description of the property. The property name will be used to access it with calls to g_object_set() and g_object_get().

```
GParamSpec* g_param_spec_int (const gchar *name,
                             const gchar *nick,
                             const gchar *blurb,
                             gint minimum,
                             gint maximum,
                             gint default_value,
                             GParamFlags flags);
```

The next three parameters define the minimum and maximum possible values and the default value of the property. These are used to define the property bounds, as well as the initial state. The last parameter allows you to define flags from the following GParamFlags enumeration that can be applied to the property:

- G_PARAM_READABLE: It is possible to read the value of the parameter.

- G_PARAM_WRITABLE: It is possible to write a new value for the parameter.

- G_PARAM_CONSTRUCT: The parameter will be set when the object is constructed.

- G_PARAM_CONSTRUCT_ONLY: The parameter will be set only when the object is constructed.

- G_PARAM_LAX_VALIDATION: When g_param_value_convert() is used to convert a parameter, strict validation will not be required.

- G_PARAM_STATIC_NAME: The parameter name will never be altered and will remain valid during its whole existence.

- G_PARAM_STATIC_NICK: The parameter nickname will never be altered and will remain valid during its whole existence.

- G_PARAM_STATIC_BLURB: The parameter description will never be altered and will remain valid during its whole existence.

There is also an additional flag, G_PARAM_READWRITE, which is defined as a bitwise alias for (G_PARAM_READABLE | G_PARAM_WRITABLE). This is included as a macro instead of an enumeration value in GParamFlags.

There are GParamSpec structures available for all of the fundamental data types provided in GLib. For a full list of function prototypes for creating other types of properties, you should reference the GObject API documentation.

Parameter and Value Definitions

There are a number of GParamSpec and GValue functions defined for many fundamental types. The following list gives a description of each of these functions. The asterisk character can be replaced by boolean, char, uchar, int, uint, long, ulong, int64, uint64, float, double, enum, flags, string, param, boxed, pointer, object, or gtype in each of the following functions according to the function's case:

- G_IS_PARAM_SPEC_*(): Return TRUE if the given object is a valid parameter specification object for the given type.

- G_PARAM_SPEC_*(): Cast a GParamSpec object to the specific parameter specification type.

- G_VALUE_HOLDS_*(): Return TRUE if the given GValue can hold the type defined by the function.

- G_TYPE_PARAM_*(): Return GType for the given parameter specification type.

- g_param_spec_*(): Create a new parameter specification of the given type. This function is normally used when defining new properties for a GObject. Every function accepts the property name, nickname, a short description, and a bitwise list of GParamFlags values in addition to parameters that relate to the given type. It returns a new GParamSpec object.

- g_value_set_*(): Set the value stored by the GValue object to the given variable. This new value must be the same type as the function.

- g_value_get_*(): Retrieve the value stored by the GValue object, which is already cast to the given type.

Note In the previous list of functions, when you replace the asterisk character with a data type, you should match the case of the function. For example, the asterisk in G_IS_PARAM_SPEC_*() should be replaced by a data type in all upper case. For more examples, you should visit the API documentation.

Setting and Retrieving Object Properties

In the class initialization function, the default set_property() and get_property() functions were overridden in GObjectClass. These two functions *must* be overridden if your new GObject has one or more properties. Listing 11-8 is the implementation of the function that will be called for every property sent to g_object_set().

Listing 11-8. *Setting Object Properties*

```
static void
my_ip_address_set_property (GObject *object,
                            guint prop_id,
                            const GValue *value,
                            GParamSpec *pspec)
{
  MyIPAddress *ipaddress = MY_IP_ADDRESS (object);
  gint address[4] = { -1, -1, -1, -1 };

  switch (prop_id)
  {
    case PROP_IP1:
      address[0] = g_value_get_int (value);
      my_ip_address_set_address (ipaddress, address);
      break;
    case PROP_IP2:
      address[1] = g_value_get_int (value);
      my_ip_address_set_address (ipaddress, address);
      break;
    case PROP_IP3:
      address[2] = g_value_get_int (value);
      my_ip_address_set_address (ipaddress, address);
      break;
    case PROP_IP4:
      address[3] = g_value_get_int (value);
      my_ip_address_set_address (ipaddress, address);
      break;
    default:
      G_OBJECT_WARN_INVALID_PROPERTY_ID (object, prop_id, pspec);
      break;
  }
}
```

When the property arrives, it is stored as a GValue object, which is a generic container used to store any type of object. The g_value_get_int() function is used to retrieve the integer value stored by GValue. There are functions available for converting between all fundamental data types and GValue objects available, defined in the previous section.

The next step is to store the new value of the property if it is a valid property. The property identifier is stored in prop_id, which can be compared to the installed property to find the one that is being altered. The function my_ip_address_set_address() was used to apply the changes. You can view the implementation of this function later in this section.

It would also be possible to implement the same functionality provided by this function with the method shown in the following code snippet. However, it was given to you in the expanded form, because it is a rare case when every property of a widget is the same type and is stored in an array.

```
address[prop_id-1] = g_value_get_int (value);
my_ip_address_set_address (ipaddress, address);
```

The MyIPAddress example in this chapter is one of the simplest examples possible and could be greatly expanded. If you were implementing this widget for use in an application, you would want to provide further properties and signals, as well as provide further functionality. Keep this in mind as you continue to examine this example.

The default get_property() function of the object class was overridden. Therefore, when g_object_set() is called on a property of MyIPAddress, my_ip_address_get_property() will be called as shown in Listing 11-9.

Listing 11-9. *Retrieving Object Properties*

```
static void
my_ip_address_get_property (GObject *object,
                            guint prop_id,
                            GValue *value,
                            GParamSpec *pspec)
{
  MyIPAddress *ipaddress = MY_IP_ADDRESS (object);
  MyIPAddressPrivate *priv = MY_IP_ADDRESS_GET_PRIVATE (ipaddress);

  switch (prop_id)
  {
    case PROP_IP1:
      g_value_set_int (value, priv->address[0]);
      break;
    case PROP_IP2:
      g_value_set_int (value, priv->address[1]);
      break;
    case PROP_IP3:
      g_value_set_int (value, priv->address[2]);
      break;
    case PROP_IP4:
      g_value_set_int (value, priv->address[3]);
      break;
    default:
      G_OBJECT_WARN_INVALID_PROPERTY_ID (object, prop_id, pspec);
      break;
  }
}
```

The my_ip_address_get_property() function takes the appropriate property from the MyIPAddressPrivate structure and converts it to a GValue. The new value is then applied to the user's variable and cast to the correct variable type. The private structure is retrieved by using the MY_IP_ADDRESS_GET_PRIVATE() function that was defined at the top of the source file.

Instantiating the Widget

The other initialization function that needs to be implemented is my_ip_address_init(), which is called every time a new MyIPAddress widget is created. This differs from the class initialization function, which is only called in order to set up the object class, not every time the object is instantiated. This instance initialization function, displayed in Listing 11-10, sets the initial IP address values to zero, performs initial rendering, and connects the necessary signals.

Listing 11-10. *Instantiating a MyIPAddress Object*

```
static void
my_ip_address_init (MyIPAddress *ipaddress)
{
  MyIPAddressPrivate *priv = MY_IP_ADDRESS_GET_PRIVATE (ipaddress);
  PangoFontDescription *fd;
  guint i;

  for (i = 0; i < 4; i++)
    priv->address[i] = 0;

  fd = pango_font_description_from_string ("Monospace");
  gtk_widget_modify_font (GTK_WIDGET (ipaddress), fd);
  my_ip_address_render (ipaddress);
  pango_font_description_free (fd);

  /* The key-press-event signal will be used to filter out certain keys. We will
   * also monitor the cursor-position property so it can be moved correctly. */
  g_signal_connect (G_OBJECT (ipaddress), "key-press-event",
                    G_CALLBACK (my_ip_address_key_pressed), NULL);
  g_signal_connect (G_OBJECT (ipaddress), "notify::cursor-position",
                    G_CALLBACK (my_ip_address_move_cursor), NULL);
}
```

The my_ip_address_init() function accepts a MyIPAddress object that has already been created and cast. Your task is to do any further processing that needs to be performed on the widget before it is returned to the programmer and displayed to the user.

In this example, the function first initializes the four IP address values to zero. Then, the font of the widget is set to Monospace. Notice that the size is not specified, which allows the user's theme to dictate the size. This is done so that users with large fonts will still be able to read the content of the widget.

Lastly, the MyIPAddress widget is connected to two signals. The key-press-event callback function will filter the keys that the widget will react to. Then, when cursor-position changes, the position will be updated, so we can control where text is entered. Remember that, since MyIPAddress is derived from GtkEntry, it inherits all of its members, properties, signals, functions, and so on. It also inherits everything from GtkWidget, GtkObject, and GObject, since those classes are its ancestors.

Next, a few private functions are implemented that will handle how the widget interacts with the user. Listing 11-11 shows a function called my_ip_address_render(). This function builds a string out of the IP address values and adds it to the GtkEntry widget. This is the only function that will write to the GtkEntry widget.

Listing 11-11. *Rendering the MyIPAddress Widget*

```
/* Render the current content of the IP address in the GtkEntry widget. */
static void
my_ip_address_render (MyIPAddress *ipaddress)
{
  MyIPAddressPrivate *priv = MY_IP_ADDRESS_GET_PRIVATE (ipaddress);
  GString *text;
  guint i;

  /* Create a string that displays the IP address content, adding spaces if a
   * number cannot fill three characters. */
  text = g_string_new (NULL);
  for (i = 0; i < 4; i++)
  {
    gchar *temp = g_strdup_printf ("%3i.", priv->address[i]);
    text = g_string_append (text, temp);
    g_free (temp);
  }

  /* Remove the trailing decimal place and add the string to the GtkEntry. */
  text = g_string_truncate (text, 15);
  gtk_entry_set_text (GTK_ENTRY (ipaddress), text->str);
  g_string_free (text, TRUE);
}
```

This function uses GString to build a fifteen-character IP address string out of three periods and the four integers that are currently stored in the instance of MyIPAddressPrivate. This string will be displayed to the user in the GtkEntry widget. If an integer does not fill up three spaces, it is padded with one or two space characters so that the IP address will always have a width of fifteen characters. This allows us to know exactly where the cursor should be placed at all times, since the width is guaranteed.

The MyIPAddress widget is built so that the cursor is forced to one of four positions. Each number is always aligned to the right and padded with spaces on the left if necessary. Because of this, the cursor is forced into the position on the right of one of the four numbers. This is done in the notify::cursor-position callback function displayed in Listing 11-12.

Listing 11-12. *Callback Functions for MyIPAddress*

```
/* Force the cursor to always be at the end of one of the four numbers. */
static void
my_ip_address_move_cursor (GObject *entry,
                           GParamSpec *spec)
{
  gint cursor = gtk_editable_get_position (GTK_EDITABLE (entry));

  if (cursor <= 3)
    gtk_editable_set_position (GTK_EDITABLE (entry), 3);
  else if (cursor <= 7)
    gtk_editable_set_position (GTK_EDITABLE (entry), 7);
  else if (cursor <= 11)
    gtk_editable_set_position (GTK_EDITABLE (entry), 11);
  else
    gtk_editable_set_position (GTK_EDITABLE (entry), 15);

}

/* Handle key presses of numbers, tabs, backspaces and returns. */
static gboolean
my_ip_address_key_pressed (GtkEntry *entry,
                           GdkEventKey *event)
{
  MyIPAddressPrivate *priv = MY_IP_ADDRESS_GET_PRIVATE (entry);
  guint k = event->keyval;
  gint cursor, value;

  /* If the key is an integer, append the new number to the address. This is only
   * done if the resulting number will be less than 255. */
  if ((k >= GDK_0 && k <= GDK_9) || (k >= GDK_KP_0 && k <= GDK_KP_9))
  {
    cursor = floor (gtk_editable_get_position (GTK_EDITABLE (entry)) / 4);
    value = g_ascii_digit_value (event->string[0]);

    if ((priv->address[cursor] == 25) && (value > 5))
      return TRUE;
```

```
    if (priv->address[cursor] < 26)
    {
      priv->address[cursor] *= 10;
      priv->address[cursor] += value;
      my_ip_address_render (MY_IP_ADDRESS (entry));
      gtk_editable_set_position (GTK_EDITABLE (entry), (4 * cursor) + 3);
      g_signal_emit_by_name ((gpointer) entry, "ip-changed");
    }
  }

  /* Move to the next number or wrap around to the first. */
  else if (k == GDK_Tab)
  {
    cursor = (floor (gtk_editable_get_position (GTK_EDITABLE (entry)) / 4) + 1);
    gtk_editable_set_position (GTK_EDITABLE (entry), (4 * (cursor % 4)) + 3);
  }

  /* Delete the last digit of the current number. This just divides the number by
   * 10, relying on the fact that any remainder will be ignored. */
  else if (k == GDK_BackSpace)
  {
    cursor = floor (gtk_editable_get_position (GTK_EDITABLE (entry)) / 4);
    priv->address[cursor] /= 10;
    my_ip_address_render (MY_IP_ADDRESS (entry));
    gtk_editable_set_position (GTK_EDITABLE (entry), (4 * cursor) + 3);
    g_signal_emit_by_name ((gpointer) entry, "ip-changed");
  }

  /* Activate the GtkEntry widget, which corresponds to the activate signal. */
  else if ((k == GDK_Return) || (k == GDK_KP_Enter))
    gtk_widget_activate (GTK_WIDGET (entry));

  return TRUE;
}
```

Listing 11-12 also includes a second function, my_ip_address_key_pressed(), which is called when the key-press-event signal is emitted. It handles specific keys, ignoring all of the rest. For example, number keys are handled, but all letters and symbols are ignored. We will walk through each set of keys that is handled one at a time.

The first conditional handles numbers pressed on the keyboard, whether along the top or in the keypad, as defined in <gdk/gdkkeysyms.h>. GDK_KP_# corresponds to the digit keys on the number pad, and GDK_# corresponds to the digit keys along the top of the keyboard, both of which must be accounted for in the conditional statement.

The floor() function is used to convert the cursor position into a number between zero and three, which represents what IP address value should be edited. The event string is also converted into an integer with g_ascii_digit_value().

Now that you have all of the necessary values, two conditionals check the validity of the new value. The new integer will only be appended to the current value if the new value will not exceed 255. If the number is within bounds, the current value is scaled, and the new integer is appended. Next, the new IP address is rendered in the GtkEntry widget, and the cursor position refreshed. Lastly, g_signal_emit_by_name() is used to inform the user that the IP address was changed.

The second conditional handles the Tab key, which will cycle through each of the four numbers when pressed. This could be altered in another implementation of the widget to cycle to the next widget in the tab order when the end of the widget is reached.

Next, the Backspace key divides the current value by ten. Since you are dividing an integer by an integer, the remainder is ignored, and the last digit is dropped off. Then, the widget is rendered, and the ip-changed signal emitted.

Lastly, the Return and Enter keys call gtk_widget_activate() when pressed. This allows the user to press these keys to activate the default widget of the window from within the MyIPAddress widget. All other key presses besides those covered in this section are ignored.

Implementing Public MyIPAddress Functions

The last step to create the widget is to implement the public functions declared in the widget's header file. The first function is my_ip_address_new(), which creates a new MyIPAddress widget in Listing 11-13.

Listing 11-13. *Creating a New MyIPAddress Widget*

```
GtkWidget*
my_ip_address_new ()
{
  return GTK_WIDGET (g_object_new (my_ip_address_get_type (), NULL));
}
```

You should notice that the only task this function provides is casting to a GtkWidget the object returned by g_object_new(). This is simply a convenience function for many widgets, so the programmer does not need to create the GObject instance itself. If you are using widgets that accept parameters into their initialization functions, you would handle those here.

The my_ip_address_get_address() function in Listing 11-14 returns a string representation of the IP address that is currently stored by the widget. This returned string must be freed when the programmer is finished with it, since it is created with g_strdup_printf(). While the user can construct this programmatically, most widgets usually provide a number of convenient functions that perform tasks that will be needed often.

Listing 11-14. *Retrieving the Current IP Address*

```
gchar*
my_ip_address_get_address (MyIPAddress *ipaddress)
{
  MyIPAddressPrivate *priv = MY_IP_ADDRESS_GET_PRIVATE (ipaddress);

  return g_strdup_printf ("%d.%d.%d.%d", priv->address[0], priv->address[1],
                          priv->address[2], priv->address[3]);
}
```

The last function, my_ip_address_set_address(), applies programmatic changes to the IP address and is displayed in Listing 11-15. You will notice that the function filters out numbers that are less than 0 or greater than 255. By doing this, the programmer does not have to provide new values for every IP address number. This means that we only need to provide one function for programmatically updating the IP address, since the programmer can update a single value with it.

Listing 11-15. *Setting a New IP Address*

```
void
my_ip_address_set_address (MyIPAddress *ipaddress,
                           gint address[4])
{
  MyIPAddressPrivate *priv = MY_IP_ADDRESS_GET_PRIVATE (ipaddress);
  guint i;

  for (i = 0; i < 4; i++)
  {
    if (address[i] >= 0 && address[i] <= 255)
    {
      priv->address[i] = address[i];
    }
  }

  my_ip_address_render (ipaddress);
  g_signal_emit_by_name ((gpointer) ipaddress, "ip-changed");
}
```

Testing the Widget

The last step in this example is to test whether the widget works. The code in Listing 11-16 creates a window with a new MyIPAddress widget. An initial IP address of 1.20.35.255 is added, and the ip-changed signal is connected to a callback function that prints the current state of the IP address.

Listing 11-16. *Test the MyIPAddress Widget (ipaddresstest.c)*

```c
#include <gtk/gtk.h>
#include "myipaddress.h"

static void ip_address_changed (MyIPAddress*);

int main (int argc,
          char *argv[])
{
  GtkWidget *window, *ipaddress;
  gint address[4] = { 1, 20, 35, 255 };

  gtk_init (&argc, &argv);

  window = gtk_window_new (GTK_WINDOW_TOPLEVEL);
  gtk_window_set_title (GTK_WINDOW (window), "MyIPAddress");
  gtk_container_set_border_width (GTK_CONTAINER (window), 10);

  g_signal_connect (G_OBJECT (window), "destroy",
                    G_CALLBACK (gtk_main_quit), NULL);

  ipaddress = my_ip_address_new ();
  my_ip_address_set_address (MY_IP_ADDRESS (ipaddress), address);
  g_signal_connect (G_OBJECT (ipaddress), "ip-changed",
                    G_CALLBACK (ip_address_changed), NULL);

  gtk_container_add (GTK_CONTAINER (window), ipaddress);
  gtk_widget_show_all (window);

  gtk_main ();
  return 0;
}

/* When the IP address is changed, print the new value to the screen. */
static void
ip_address_changed (MyIPAddress *ipaddress)
{
  gchar *address = my_ip_address_get_address (ipaddress);
  g_print ("%s\n", address);
  g_free (address);
}
```

This `MyIPAddress` widget is a very simple example of creating a new widget. For use in an actual application, it would have to be expanded greatly. For example, you would want to customize the pop-up menu that is displayed when the user right-clicks the widget. Another enhancement would be to allow the programmer to define custom IP address formats. You may want to try expanding the `MyIPAddress` widget before continuing on to the next section so that you can better understand what was covered in this section.

Creating a Widget from Scratch

Now that you have learned how to derive a new widget from one that already exists, it is time to learn how to create a widget from scratch. You will notice that a lot of the code in this section is similar to that in the previous. This is because new widgets are implemented in the same way as those that are derived, since they both have a base type of `GObject`; it just takes a little more work.

In this section, you will learn how to implement a widget called `MyMarquee`. This widget scrolls a message from the right side of the widget to the left side, over and over. Make sure you understand this widget, because it will be your job to extend it in this chapter's exercise.

You can view a screenshot of the `MyMarquee` widget in Figure 11-2. As with all of the examples in this book, you can download the full source code for this example on the book's web site.

Figure 11-2. *The MyMarquee widget*

Creating the MyMarquee Header File

The first step in setting up a new widget is to create the header file. This allows you to define the programmatic interface that will be used to control the widget. Listing 11-7 gives the full header file for the `MyMarquee` widget, which should appear very similar to the `MyIPAddress` header file.

Listing 11-17. *MyMarquee Widget Header (mymarquee.h)*

```
#ifndef __MY_MARQUEE_H__
#define __MY_MARQUEE_H__

#include <glib.h>
#include <gdk/gdk.h>
#include <gtk/gtkwidget.h>
```

```
G_BEGIN_DECLS

#define MY_MARQUEE_TYPE          (my_marquee_get_type ())
#define MY_MARQUEE(obj)          (G_TYPE_CHECK_INSTANCE_CAST ((obj), \
                                  MY_MARQUEE_TYPE, MyMarquee))
#define MY_MARQUEE_CLASS(klass)  (G_TYPE_CHECK_CLASS_CAST ((klass), \
                                  MY_MARQUEE_TYPE, MyMarqueeClass))
#define IS_MY_MARQUEE(obj)       (G_TYPE_CHECK_INSTANCE_TYPE ((obj), \
                                  MY_MARQUEE_TYPE))
#define IS_MY_MARQUEE_CLASS(klass) (G_TYPE_CHECK_CLASS_TYPE ((klass), \
                                  MY_MARQUEE_TYPE))

typedef struct _MyMarquee       MyMarquee;
typedef struct _MyMarqueeClass  MyMarqueeClass;

struct _MyMarquee
{
  GtkWidget widget;
};

struct _MyMarqueeClass
{
  GtkWidgetClass parent_class;
};

GType      my_marquee_get_type (void) G_GNUC_CONST;
GtkWidget* my_marquee_new      (void);

void   my_marquee_set_message (MyMarquee *marquee, const gchar *message);
gchar* my_marquee_get_message (MyMarquee *marquee);

void my_marquee_set_speed (MyMarquee *marquee, gint speed);
gint my_marquee_get_speed (MyMarquee *marquee);

void my_marquee_slide (MyMarquee *marquee);

G_END_DECLS

#endif /* __MY_MARQUEE_H__ */
```

Since MyMarquee is a new widget, it will be directly derived from GtkWidget. This is shown by the fact that MyMarquee contains a GtkWidget object and MyMarqueeClass contains a GtkWidgetClass class. Recall that neither of these members should be declared as pointers! Deriving the widget from GtkWidget allows you to take advantage of all of the signals and properties that are common to every widget, including event handling.

The widget will have two properties that the programmer can set and retrieve. The user can use my_marquee_set_message() to change the message that is scrolled by the widget. The speed is an integer between 1 and 50. The message will be moved this many pixels to the left every time my_marquee_slide() is called.

Creating the MyMarquee Widget

Now that the header file is created, Listing 11-18 performs basic initialization such as declaring the private class, enumerating properties, and creating a new GType. There are no new signals associated with this widget, so the signal enumeration and array of signal identifiers are omitted.

Listing 11-18. *Defining MyMarqueePrivate and MyMarquee GType (mymarquee.c)*

```
#include "mymarquee.h"

#define MARQUEE_MIN_WIDTH 300

#define MY_MARQUEE_GET_PRIVATE(obj) (G_TYPE_INSTANCE_GET_PRIVATE ((obj), \
                                    MY_MARQUEE_TYPE, MyMarqueePrivate))

typedef struct _MyMarqueePrivate  MyMarqueePrivate;

struct _MyMarqueePrivate
{
  gchar *message;
  gint speed;
  gint current_x;
};

enum
{
  PROP_0,
  PROP_MESSAGE,
  PROP_SPEED
};

/* Get a GType that corresponds to MyMarquee. The first time this function is
 * called (on object instantiation), the type is registered. */
GType
my_marquee_get_type ()
{
  static GType marquee_type = 0;
```

```
  if (!marquee_type)
  {
    static const GTypeInfo marquee_info =
    {
      sizeof (MyMarqueeClass),
      NULL,
      NULL,
      (GClassInitFunc) my_marquee_class_init,
      NULL,
      NULL,
      sizeof (MyMarquee),
      0,
      (GInstanceInitFunc) my_marquee_init,
    };

    marquee_type = g_type_register_static (GTK_TYPE_WIDGET, "MyMarquee",
                                           &marquee_info, 0);
  }

  return marquee_type;
}
```

Listing 11-18 shows the first part of the implementation of the MyMarquee widget. We begin this file by creating the MyMarqueePrivate structure, which will be used to hold the values of necessary widget properties. This includes the displayed message, the scrolling speed, and the current horizontal position of the message. The next position of the message will be calculated based on this position, which allows us to easily handle resizing of the widget.

Since MyMarquee is derived directly from GtkWidget, you will need to register the widget with a parent class type of GTK_TYPE_WIDGET, as shown in the implementation of my_marquee_get_type(). The implementation of this function is almost an exact replica of my_ip_address_get_type().

Listing 11-19 shows the MyMarquee class and instance initialization functions. In my_marquee_class_init(), you will notice that we not only override functions in the GObjectClass but also in the GtkWidgetClass.

Listing 11-19. *Initializing the MyMarquee Class and Structure*

```
/* Initialize the MyMarqueeClass class by overriding standard functions,
 * registering a private class and setting up signals and properties. */
static void
my_marquee_class_init (MyMarqueeClass *klass)
{
  GObjectClass *gobject_class;
  GtkWidgetClass *widget_class;

  gobject_class = (GObjectClass*) klass;
  widget_class = (GtkWidgetClass*) klass;
```

```
/* Override the standard functions for setting and retrieving properties. */
gobject_class->set_property = my_marquee_set_property;
gobject_class->get_property = my_marquee_get_property;

/* Override the standard functions for realize, expose, and size changes. */
widget_class->realize = my_marquee_realize;
widget_class->expose_event = my_marquee_expose;
widget_class->size_request = my_marquee_size_request;
widget_class->size_allocate = my_marquee_size_allocate;

/* Add MyMarqueePrivate as a private data class of MyMarqueeClass. */
g_type_class_add_private (klass, sizeof (MyMarqueePrivate));

/* Register four GObject properties, the message and the speed. */
g_object_class_install_property (gobject_class, PROP_MESSAGE,
           g_param_spec_string ("message",
                                "Marquee Message",
                                "The message to scroll",
                                "",
                                G_PARAM_READWRITE));

g_object_class_install_property (gobject_class, PROP_SPEED,
              g_param_spec_int ("speed",
                                "Speed of the Marquee",
                                "The percentage of movement every second",
                                1, 50, 25,
                                G_PARAM_READWRITE));
}

/* Initialize the actual MyMarquee widget. This function is used to set up
 * the initial view of the widget and set necessary properties. */
static void
my_marquee_init (MyMarquee *marquee)
{
  MyMarqueePrivate *priv = MY_MARQUEE_GET_PRIVATE (marquee);

  priv->current_x = MARQUEE_MIN_WIDTH;
  priv->speed = 25;
}
```

The next step is to implement the class and instance initialization functions that were referenced by the GTypeInfo object. In this example, in addition to overriding functions in the parent GObjectClass, we also need to override a few in GtkWidgetClass. These include overriding calls for realizing and exposing the widget as well as size requests and allocations.

You need to be especially careful when overriding functions in GtkWidgetClass, because they perform crucial tasks for the widget. You can render the widget unusable if you do not perform all of the necessary functions. I would recommend that you view how other GTK+ widgets implement overridden functions when you do it yourself. For a full list of functions that can be overridden, you should view the GtkWidgetClass structure in <gtk/gtkwidget.h>.

The MyMarqueePrivate structure was also added in the class initialization function to MyMarqueeClass with g_type_class_add_private(). Since the object is not stored as a member of the MyMarqueeClass structure, you need to use the definition of MY_MARQUEE_GET_PRIVATE() to retrieve the MyMarqueePrivate object, as shown in the instance initialization function.

In my_marquee_init(), the current position of the message is set to be displayed beyond the right side of the widget. By default, the message will then be scrolled 25 pixels to the left when my_marquee_slide() is programmatically called.

The implementations of the overridden set_property() and get_property() functions are similar to the previous example. These functions are displayed in Listing 11-20, which allow the user to set and retrieve the message and speed properties of the widget.

Listing 11-20. *Setting and Retrieving MyMarquee Properties*

```
/* This function is called when the programmer gives a new value for a widget
 * property with g_object_set(). */
static void
my_marquee_set_property (GObject *object,
                         guint prop_id,
                         const GValue *value,
                         GParamSpec *pspec)
{
  MyMarquee *marquee = MY_MARQUEE (object);

  switch (prop_id)
  {
    case PROP_MESSAGE:
      my_marquee_set_message (marquee, g_value_get_string (value));
      break;
    case PROP_SPEED:
      my_marquee_set_speed (marquee, g_value_get_int (value));
      break;
    default:
      G_OBJECT_WARN_INVALID_PROPERTY_ID (object, prop_id, pspec);
      break;
  }
}

/* This function is called when the programmer requests the value of a widget
 * property with g_object_get(). */
static void
my_marquee_get_property (GObject *object,
                         guint prop_id,
                         GValue *value,
                         GParamSpec *pspec)
```

```
{
  MyMarquee *marquee = MY_MARQUEE (object);
  MyMarqueePrivate *priv = MY_MARQUEE_GET_PRIVATE (marquee);

  switch (prop_id)
  {
    case PROP_MESSAGE:
      g_value_set_string (value, priv->message);
      break;
    case PROP_SPEED:
      g_value_set_int (value, priv->speed);
      break;
    default:
      G_OBJECT_WARN_INVALID_PROPERTY_ID (object, prop_id, pspec);
      break;
  }
}
```

Listing 11-21 shows the implementation of my_marquee_new(). This is the function that the programmer can call to create a new MyMarquee widget. It is simply a convenience function, so you do not have to call g_object_new() directly.

Listing 11-21. *Creating a New MyMarquee Widget*

```
GtkWidget*
my_marquee_new ()
{
  return GTK_WIDGET (g_object_new (my_marquee_get_type (), NULL));
}
```

Realizing the Widget

Where the implementation of this widget is different from MyIPAddress is the overridden GtkWidgetClass functions. The first of these functions is my_marquee_realize(), shown in Listing 11-22. This function is called when the MyMarquee instance is first realized.

Listing 11-22. *Realizing the MyMarquee Widget*

```
static void
my_marquee_realize (GtkWidget *widget)
{
  MyMarquee *marquee;
  GdkWindowAttr attributes;
  gint attr_mask;

  g_return_if_fail (widget != NULL);
  g_return_if_fail (IS_MY_MARQUEE (widget));
```

```
    /* Set the GTK_REALIZED flag so it is marked as realized. */
    GTK_WIDGET_SET_FLAGS (widget, GTK_REALIZED);
    marquee = MY_MARQUEE (widget);

    /* Create a new GtkWindowAttr object that will hold info about the GdkWindow. */
    attributes.x = widget->allocation.x;
    attributes.y = widget->allocation.y;
    attributes.width = widget->allocation.width;
    attributes.height = widget->allocation.height;
    attributes.wclass = GDK_INPUT_OUTPUT;
    attributes.window_type = GDK_WINDOW_CHILD;
    attributes.event_mask = gtk_widget_get_events (widget);
    attributes.event_mask |= (GDK_EXPOSURE_MASK);
    attributes.visual = gtk_widget_get_visual (widget);
    attributes.colormap = gtk_widget_get_colormap (widget);

    /* Create a new GdkWindow for the widget. */
    attr_mask = GDK_WA_X | GDK_WA_Y | GDK_WA_VISUAL | GDK_WA_COLORMAP;
    widget->window = gdk_window_new (widget->parent->window, &attributes, attr_mask);
    gdk_window_set_user_data (widget->window, marquee);

    /* Attach a style to the GdkWindow and draw a background color. */
    widget->style = gtk_style_attach (widget->style, widget->window);
    gtk_style_set_background (widget->style, widget->window, GTK_STATE_NORMAL);
    gdk_window_show (widget->window);
}
```

The first tasks performed by my_marquee_realize() are to check whether the widget is non-NULL and whether it is a MyMarquee widget. The gtk_return_if_fail() function is used to return from the function if either test returns FALSE. You should always perform these tests, because your program can respond unexpectedly otherwise.

The purpose of the realization function is to set up a GdkWindow for the instance of the widget so that it can be rendered to the screen. To do this, you first need a GdkWindowAttr object that holds the desired properties of the new GdkWindow. Table 11-3 describes all of the GtkWindowAttr structure's members.

Table 11-3. *GtkWindowAttr Members*

Variable	Description
gchar *title	The title of the window or NULL if the window is not a top-level window. This usually does not need to be set.
gint event_mask	A bitmask of GDK events that will be recognized by the widget. You can use gtk_widget_get_events() to retrieve all of the events that are currently associated with the widget and then add your own.

Variable	Description
gint x, y	The x and y coordinates of the GdkWindow object with respect to the parent window. You can retrieve these values from the widget's allocation.
gint width, height	The width and height of the GdkWindow object. You can retrieve these values from the widget's allocation.
GdkWindowClass wclass	This should be set to GDK_INPUT_OUTPUT for most GdkWindow objects or GDK_INPUT_ONLY if the window will be invisible.
GdkVisual *visual	A GdkVisual object to use for the window. The default can be retrieved with gtk_widget_get_visual().
GdkColormap *colormap	A GdkColormap object to use for the window. The default can be retrieved with gtk_widget_get_colormap().
GdkWindowType window_type	The type of window that will be displayed as defined by the GdkWindowType enumeration.
GdkCursor *cursor	An optional GdkCursor object that will be displayed when the mouse is over the top of the widget.
gchar *wmclass_name	This property should be ignored. For more information, view the documentation on gtk_window_set_wmclass().
gchar *wmclass_class	This property should be ignored. For more information, view the documentation on gtk_window_set_wmclass().
gboolean override_redirect	If set to TRUE, the widget will bypass the window manager.

In our implementation of my_marquee_realize(), we first set the horizontal and vertical positions of the widget, which are relative to the top-left corner of the parent window. This is easy, since they are already provided by the widget's allocation. The allocation also provides the initial width and height of the widget.

The next member, wclass, is set to one of two values. GDK_INPUT_OUTPUT refers to a normal GdkWindow widget, which should be used for most widgets. GDK_INPUT_ONLY is an invisible GdkWindow widget that is used to receive events. Next, you can set the window type, which is determined by a value from the following GdkWindowType enumeration:

- GDK_WINDOW_ROOT: A window that has no parent window and will cover the whole screen. This is usually only used by the window manager.

- GDK_WINDOW_TOPLEVEL: A top-level window that will usually have decorations. For example, GtkWindow uses this window type.

- GDK_WINDOW_CHILD: A child window of a top-level window or another child window. This is used for most widgets that are not top-level windows themselves.

- GDK_WINDOW_DIALOG: This window type is depreciated and should not be used.

- GDK_WINDOW_TEMP: A window that is only going to be displayed temporarily, such as a GtkMenu widget.

- GDK_WINDOW_FOREIGN: A foreign window type implemented by another library that needs to be wrapped as a GdkWindow widget.

The next call sets the event mask for the GdkWindow. A call to gtk_widget_get_events() returns all events that are already installed on the widget, and then we add GDK_EXPOSURE_MASK to the list. This will make sure that our exposure function will be called.

Next, we set the GdkVisual object that will be used for the GdkWindow widget. This object is used to describe specific information about the video hardware. In most cases, you should use the default GdkVisual assigned to the widget, which you can retrieve with gtk_widget_get_visual().

The last property set in the GdkWindowAttr structure is the color map. Again, we use gtk_widget_get_colormap() to retrieve the default color map for the widget, since you will usually not need to edit this.

The next step is to create a mask of specific GdkWindowAttributesType values, which indicate which fields in the GdkWindowAttr should be honored. In this example, the specified x and y coordinates, GdkVisual, and GdkColormap will be used.

```
attributes_mask = GDK_WA_X | GDK_WA_Y | GDK_WA_VISUAL | GDK_WA_COLORMAP;
```

We now have enough information to create a new GdkWindow for the widget with gdk_window_new(). This function accepts the parent GdkWindow, a GdkWindowAttr object, and a mask of attributes to honor.

```
GdkWindow* gdk_window_new (GdkWindow *parent,
                           GdkWindowAttr *attributes,
                           gint attributes_mask);
```

Next, the GtkWidget should be stored as the user data of the GdkWindow for custom widgets with gdk_window_set_user_data(). This ensures that widget events such as expose-event are recognized. If you do not call this, events will not be recognized.

```
void gdk_window_set_user_data (GdkWindow *window,
                               gpointer user_data);
```

The window's style is then attached to the window with gtk_style_attach(), which will begin the process of creating graphics contexts for the style. You should always make sure to store the returned value, since it may be a new style.

```
GtkStyle* gtk_style_attach (GtkStyle *style,
                            GdkWindow *window);
```

Once the style is attached to the window, the background of the window is set. The gtk_style_set_background() sets the background color of the GdkWindow to the color specified by the GtkStyle in the given state.

```
void gtk_style_set_background (GtkStyle *style,
                               GdkWindow *window,
                               GtkStyleType state_type);
```

Lastly, the window is displayed to the user with a call to gdk_window_show(). If you do not call this function, the widget will never be visible to the user. This function will also make sure that all of the necessary initialization has been performed.

Specifying Size Requests and Allocations

We also overrode the size request and allocation functions of the parent GtkWindowClass. The my_marquee_size_request() function in Listing 11-23 was simply used to specify default width and height values to the requisition.

Listing 11-23. *Handling Size Requests and Allocations*

```
/* Handle size requests for the widget. This function forces the widget to have
 * an initial size set according to the predefined width and the font size. */
static void
my_marquee_size_request (GtkWidget *widget,
                         GtkRequisition *requisition)
{
  PangoFontDescription *fd;

  g_return_if_fail (widget != NULL || requisition != NULL);
  g_return_if_fail (IS_MY_MARQUEE (widget));

  fd = widget->style->font_desc;
  requisition->width = MARQUEE_MIN_WIDTH;
  requisition->height = (pango_font_description_get_size (fd) / PANGO_SCALE) + 10;
}

/* Handle size allocations for the widget. This does the actual resizing of the
 * widget to the requested allocation. */
static void
my_marquee_size_allocate (GtkWidget *widget,
                          GtkAllocation *allocation)
{
  MyMarquee *marquee;

  g_return_if_fail (widget != NULL || allocation != NULL);
  g_return_if_fail (IS_MY_MARQUEE (widget));

  widget->allocation = *allocation;
  marquee = MY_MARQUEE (widget);

  if (GTK_WIDGET_REALIZED (widget))
  {
    gdk_window_move_resize (widget->window, allocation->x, allocation->y,
                            allocation->width, allocation->height);
  }
}
```

The size request function sets the initial width to MARQUEE_MIN_WIDTH, which was set at the top of the file. It also forces the height to be at least the height of the font plus 10 pixels. This will make sure that the whole message can be displayed in the widget along with some padding.

The allocation function in Listing 11-23 begins by assigning the given allocation to the widget. Then, if the widget is realized, it calls gdk_window_move_resize(). This function can be used to resize a GdkWindow and move it in a single call. It accepts the GdkWindow to work on as well as the new x coordinate, y coordinate, width, and height of the window.

```
void gdk_window_move_resize (GdkWindow *window,
                             gint x,
                             gint y,
                             gint width,
                             gint height);
```

Exposing the Widget

The my_marquee_expose() function is where things become especially interesting. This function is called when the widget is first shown to the user, when the widget is resized, and when a part of the window is shown that was previously hidden. It is displayed in Listing 11-24.

Listing 11-24. *Exposing the MyMarquee Widget*

```
static gint
my_marquee_expose (GtkWidget *widget,
                   GdkEventExpose *event)
{
  PangoFontDescription *fd;
  MyMarquee *marquee;
  MyMarqueePrivate *priv;
  PangoLayout *layout;
  PangoContext *context;
  gint width, height;

  g_return_val_if_fail (widget != NULL || event != NULL, FALSE);
  g_return_val_if_fail (IS_MY_MARQUEE (widget), FALSE);

  if (event->count > 0)
    return TRUE;

  marquee = MY_MARQUEE (widget);
  priv = MY_MARQUEE_GET_PRIVATE (marquee);
  fd = widget->style->font_desc;
  context = gdk_pango_context_get ();
  layout = pango_layout_new (context);
  g_object_unref (context);
```

```
/* Create a new PangoLayout out of the message with the given font. */
pango_layout_set_font_description (layout, fd);
pango_layout_set_text (layout, priv->message, -1);
pango_layout_get_size (layout, &width, &height);

/* Clear the text from the background of the widget. */
gdk_window_clear_area (widget->window, 0, 0, widget->allocation.width,
                       widget->allocation.height);

/* Draw the PangoLayout on the widget, which is the message text. */
gdk_draw_layout (widget->window,
                 widget->style->fg_gc[widget->state],
                 priv->current_x,
                 (widget->allocation.height - (height / PANGO_SCALE)) / 2,
                 layout);

return TRUE;
}
```

We begin by creating a new PangoLayout with pango_layout_new(). This layout will be used to draw text onto the widget. This function accepts a PangoContext object; the default context was retrieved with gdk_pango_context_get().

```
PangoLayout* pango_layout_new (PangoContext *context);
```

This implementation of PangoLayout is extremely simple. A call to pango_layout_set_text() sets the textual content of the layout to the message property of the MyMarquee widget. The width and height of the text are then retrieved with a call to pango_layout_get_size().

■**Note** The width and height values returned by pango_layout_get_size() are scaled by PANGO_SCALE. Therefore, you will need to divide these integers by the scale in order to obtain their values in pixels.

After the PangoLayout is set up, the whole widget is cleared, which readies the widget to be drawn. This is performed with gdk_window_clear_area(), which clears the area from the coordinates (x,y) to (x + width,y + height).

```
void gdk_window_clear_area (GdkWindow *window,
                            gint x,
                            gint y,
                            gint width,
                            gint height);
```

Once we clear the area, the layout can be drawn on the screen with gdk_draw_layout(). This function first accepts the GdkDrawable object to draw on, which is the GdkWindow. The second parameter is the graphics context to use, which is stored by the GtkStyle member of the class.

```
void gdk_draw_layout (GdkDrawable *drawable,
                      GdkGC *gc,
                      gint x,
                      gint y,
                      PangoLayout *layout);
```

Lastly, you need to specify the x and y positions at which to draw the layout. You should note that these positions do *not* have to be in the window. Initially, the layout is drawn off the right side of the widget, so that it can scroll to the left. Also, it will not be reset to the initial position until it is completely hidden from view on the left side. Therefore, at the end of a scrolling cycle, the x coordinate will actually be negative.

Drawing Functions

In addition to the ability to draw a PangoLayout object to a GdkWindow object, GDK provides a number of other primitive drawing functions through the GdkDrawable object. A full list of these can be found in the GDK API documentation. Table 11-4 lists these functions, so that you can easily find the one that you need.

Table 11-4. *GdkDrawable Functions*

Function	Description
gdk_draw_arc()	Draw an arc beginning at (x,y) and ending at (x + width,y + height). You have the option of whether to fill in the arc with color or not. You also need to specify starting and ending angles to 1/64 of a degree.
gdk_draw_drawable()	At times, it may be desirable to copy a specific portion of another drawable area into your GdkDrawable. This function will allow you to specify an area of the source drawable from which to copy.
gdk_draw_image()	Draw a portion of a source GdkImage object onto the drawable area. You can convert a GdkDrawable object into a GdkImage one, so this can actually be a source drawable.
gdk_draw_layout()	Draw a specific number of characters of text as defined by a PangoLayout. This is used to place text on a GdkDrawable.
gdk_draw_layout_line()	This is similar to gdk_draw_layout(), except it is only capable of drawing a single line from a PangoLayout called a PangoLayoutLine.
gdk_draw_line()	Draw a straight line from a starting point to an ending point. This line will be drawn using the foreground color of the graphics context.
gdk_draw_lines()	Draw a series of lines with endpoints specified in a GdkPoint array. You must specify the number of points in the array.

Function	Description
gdk_draw_pixbuf()	Draw a portion of a GdkPixbuf image on a GdkDrawable object. You must also specify additional parameters, which will be used when rendering the image.
gdk_draw_point()	Draw a single point on the screen using the foreground color specified in the graphics context. You simply need to provide the x and y coordinates for the point.
gdk_draw_points()	Draw a number of points on the screen specified in an array of GdkPoint objects. The GdkPoint structure holds an x and a y coordinate. You must also specify the number of points in the array.
gdk_draw_polygon()	Draw a polygon that connects the points listed in an array of GdkPoint objects. If necessary, the last point will be connected to the first. You also have the option of whether or not to fill in the polygon.
gdk_draw_rectangle()	This is similar to gdk_draw_polygon(), except the resulting shape is always a rectangle. You need to specify the x coordinate, y coordinate, width, and height, as well as whether or not to fill in the rectangle.
gdk_draw_segments()	Draw a number of unconnected line segments. Each of these line segments is stored in a GdkSegment object that holds a start coordinate and end coordinate. An array of GdkSegment objects is provided to this function.
gdk_draw_trapezoids()	Draw a number of trapezoids stored in an array of GdkTrapezoid objects. The GdkTrapezoid structure holds y coordinates for the start point and the end point. It also holds four x coordinates, one for each corner of the trapezoid.

Implementing Public Functions

The MyMarquee widget includes a number of public functions. The most important is my_marquee_slide(), which will move the message speed pixels to the left when called. The programmer can cause a marquee effect by adding this function as a timeout, calling it at a specified interval of time.

Listing 11-25. *Sliding the MyMarquee Message*

```
void
my_marquee_slide (MyMarquee *marquee)
{
  PangoFontDescription *fd;
  GtkWidget *widget;
  MyMarqueePrivate *priv;
  PangoLayout *layout;
  PangoContext *context;
  gint width, height;
```

```
    g_return_if_fail (marquee != NULL);
    g_return_if_fail (IS_MY_MARQUEE (marquee));

    widget = GTK_WIDGET (marquee);
    priv = MY_MARQUEE_GET_PRIVATE (marquee);
    fd = widget->style->font_desc;
    context = gdk_pango_context_get ();
    layout = pango_layout_new (context);
    g_object_unref (context);

    /* Create a new PangoLayout out of the message with the given font. */
    pango_layout_set_font_description (layout, fd);
    pango_layout_set_text (layout, priv->message, -1);
    pango_layout_get_size (layout, &width, &height);

    /* Clear the text from the background of the widget. */
    gdk_window_clear_area (widget->window, 0, 0, widget->allocation.width,
                           widget->allocation.height);

    /* Scroll the message "speed" pixels to the left or wrap around. */
    priv->current_x = priv->current_x - priv->speed;
    if ((priv->current_x + (width / PANGO_SCALE)) <= 0)
      priv->current_x = widget->allocation.width;

    /* Draw the PangoLayout on the widget, which is the message text. */
    gdk_draw_layout (widget->window,
                     widget->style->fg_gc[widget->state],
                     priv->current_x,
                     (widget->allocation.height - (height / PANGO_SCALE)) / 2,
                     layout);
}
```

You will notice that this function is very similar to the expose function that was previously implemented. Let us look at the differences between the two functions.

This function must calculate the new position of the text, which is the current location minus the speed property value. We then need to check whether the message is still visible on the screen. If it has moved beyond the left bound of the widget, the position will be reset to the right side of the widget, which loops the scrolling message. At this point, the drawing can be done just like it was in my_marquee_expose().

■**Tip** Remember that height and width values retrieved from the PangoLayout are not in pixels. You must divide the values by PANGO_SCALE in order to retrieve the values in pixels!

Lastly, we should provide the ability to set and retrieve the speed and message properties of the MyMarquee widget. You should note that we have to retrieve the private data structure with MY_MARQUEE_GET_PRIVATE() to access these properties.

Listing 11-26. *Setting and Retrieving the Message and Speed*

```
/* Set the message that is displayed by the widget. */
void
my_marquee_set_message (MyMarquee *marquee,
                            const gchar *message)
{
  MyMarqueePrivate *priv = MY_MARQUEE_GET_PRIVATE (marquee);

  if (priv->message)
  {
    g_free (priv->message);
    priv->message = NULL;
  }

  priv->message = g_strdup (message);
}

/* Retrieve the message that is displayed by the widget. You must free this
 * string after you are done using it! */
gchar*
my_marquee_get_message (MyMarquee *marquee)
{
  return g_strdup (MY_MARQUEE_GET_PRIVATE (marquee)->message);
}

/* Set the number of pixels that the message will scroll. */
void
my_marquee_set_speed (MyMarquee *marquee,
                        gint speed)
{
  MyMarqueePrivate *priv = MY_MARQUEE_GET_PRIVATE (marquee);
  priv->speed = speed;
}

/* Retrieve the number of pixels that the message will scroll. */
gint
my_marquee_get_speed (MyMarquee *marquee)
{
  return MY_MARQUEE_GET_PRIVATE (marquee)->speed;
}
```

Testing the Widget

Now that the widget sources are written, it is time to test the widget. A small test application can be viewed in Listing 11-27. A timeout is added, which will make a call to my_marquee_slide() about every 150 milliseconds.

The marquee is set with an initial message to display of "Wheeeee!" and will move 10 pixels to the left every time my_marquee_slide() is called.

Listing 11-27. *Test the MyMarquee Widget (marqueetest.c)*

```
#include <gtk/gtk.h>
#include "mymarquee.h"

int main (int argc,
          char *argv[])
{
  GtkWidget *window, *marquee;
  PangoFontDescription *fd;

  gtk_init (&argc, &argv);

  window = gtk_window_new (GTK_WINDOW_TOPLEVEL);
  gtk_window_set_title (GTK_WINDOW (window), "MyMarquee");
  gtk_container_set_border_width (GTK_CONTAINER (window), 10);

  g_signal_connect (G_OBJECT (window), "destroy",
                    G_CALLBACK (gtk_main_quit), NULL);

  fd = pango_font_description_from_string ("Monospace 30");
  marquee = my_marquee_new ();
  gtk_widget_modify_font (marquee, fd);
  my_marquee_set_message (MY_MARQUEE (marquee), "Wheeeee!");
  my_marquee_set_speed (MY_MARQUEE (marquee), 10);
  pango_font_description_free (fd);

  g_timeout_add (150, (GSourceFunc) my_marquee_slide, (gpointer) marquee);

  gtk_container_add (GTK_CONTAINER (window), marquee);
  gtk_widget_show_all (window);

  gtk_main ();
  return 0;
}
```

Implementing Interfaces

In past chapters, you have been introduced to a number of interfaces including GtkCellEditable, GtkEditable, GtkFileChooser, GtkTreeModel, and GtkRecentChooser. Interfaces in GObject are very similar to those in Java. New interfaces are derived from GTypeInterface as shown in Listing 11-28.

■**Note** The code in this section simply implements a very basic interface and object to illustrate what is necessary to use interfaces. For any practical purposes, it would need to be greatly expanded to include much more API.

Listing 11-28. *The Interface Header File (myiface.h)*

```
#ifndef __MY_IFACE_H__
#define __MY_IFACE_H__

#include <gtk/gtk.h>

G_BEGIN_DECLS

#define MY_TYPE_IFACE                (my_iface_get_type ())
#define MY_IFACE(obj)                (G_TYPE_CHECK_INSTANCE_CAST ((obj), \
                                      GTK_TYPE_IFACE, MyIFace))
#define MY_IS_IFACE(obj)             (G_TYPE_CHECK_INSTANCE_TYPE ((obj), \
                                      GTK_TYPE_IFACE))
#define MY_IFACE_GET_INTERFACE(inst) (G_TYPE_INSTANCE_GET_INTERFACE ((inst), \
                                      MY_TYPE_IFACE, MyIFaceInterface))

typedef struct _MyIFace          MyIFace;
typedef struct _MyIFaceInterface  MyIFaceInterface;

struct _MyIFaceInterface
{
  GTypeInterface parent;

  void (*print_message) (MyIFace *obj, gchar *message);
};

GType my_iface_get_type ();
void my_iface_print_message (MyIFace *obj, gchar *message);

G_END_DECLS

#endif /* __MY_IFACE_H__ */
```

You will notice that the myiface.h header file contains much of the same functions and structures as when we were creating new widgets. There are four definitions; they return the interface's GType, cast the interface, check whether it is a valid GTK_TYPE_IFACE, and return the associated interface.

When declaring interfaces, you must declare a type definition for the MyIFace structure, but this is merely an opaque type that allows MY_IFACE() to work. The MyIFaceInterface is the actual content of the interface. It should include a GTypeInterface object, which is the parent type of every interface.

It also includes one or more function pointers. The programmer overrides these functions when an object implements the given interface. This allows each object to implement the interface in its own way, while still providing the consistency of naming across multiple objects.

Implementing the Interface

Listing 11-29 is a very basic implementation of the MyIFace source file. It provides functions for registering a new interface GType, initializing the interface class, and calling the member function.

Listing 11-29. *The Interface Source File (myiface.c)*

```
#include "myiface.h"

static void my_iface_class_init (gpointer iface);

GType
my_iface_get_type ()
{
  static GType type = 0;

  if (!type)
  {
    type = g_type_register_static_simple (G_TYPE_INTERFACE, "MyIFace",
                                          sizeof (MyIFaceInterface),
                                          (GClassInitFunc) my_iface_class_init,
                                          0, NULL, 0);

    g_type_interface_add_prerequisite (type, GTK_TYPE_WIDGET);
  }

  return type;
}
```

```
static void
my_iface_class_init (gpointer iface)
{
  GType iface_type = G_TYPE_FROM_INTERFACE (iface);

  /* Install signals & properties here ... */
}

void
my_iface_print_message (MyIFace *obj,
                        gchar *message)
{
  MY_IFACE_GET_INTERFACE (obj)->print_message (obj, message);
}
```

The first function in Listing 11-29 is used to register the MyIFace type. This is done with g_type_register_static_simple(). It first accepts the GType corresponding to the parent and a name for the new type. The parent type is G_TYPE_INTERFACE for interfaces. The third parameter is the size of the interface structure, which can be obtained with the sizeof() function.

```
GType g_type_register_static_simple (GType parent_type,
                                     const gchar *type_name,
                                     guint class_size,
                                     GClassInitFunc class_init,
                                     guint instance_size,
                                     GInstanceInitFunc instance_init,
                                     GTypeFlags flags);
```

Next, you need to specify a class initialization function. Both the instance size and the instance initialization function can be ignored, since the instance structure is an opaque type. The last parameter is a bitwise field of GTypeFlags, which can safely be set to zero for interfaces.

The other function, g_type_interface_add_prerequisite(), is used to force any object that implements the interface to also implement prerequisite_type. Interfaces can have only one prerequisite at most.

```
void g_type_interface_add_prerequisite (GType interface_type,
                                        GType prerequisite_type);
```

The class initialization function is similar to any other GObject class initialization function. It should be used to set up any signals and properties that are needed by the interface. Adding these to the interface means they will be available to any class that implements this interface.

The last function, my_iface_print_message(), is a public function that simply calls the function located in the current MyIFaceInterface instance. This means that it will call the instance of the function that was added by the object that is implementing the interface.

Using the Interface

Implementing the interface in an object is actually very simple. The first step is to add two things to your GType registration function. Listing 11-30 shows an instance of this function for an imaginary class called MyObject. This object includes only the bare essentials of an object in order to show you how easy it is to use interfaces.

Listing 11-30. *Creating the Object's GType*

```
GType
my_object_get_type (void)
{
  static GType type = 0;

  if (!type)
  {
    static const GTypeInfo info =
    {
      sizeof (MyObjectClass),
      NULL,
      NULL,
      (GClassInitFunc) my_object_class_init,
      NULL,
      NULL,
      sizeof (MyObject),
      0,
      (GInstanceInitFunc) my_object_init,
    };

    static const GInterfaceInfo iface_info =
    {
      (GInterfaceInitFunc) my_object_interface_init,
      NULL,
      NULL
    };

    type = g_type_register_static (GTK_TYPE_WIDGET, "MyObject", &info, 0);
    g_type_add_interface_static (type, MY_TYPE_INTERFACE, &iface_info);
  }

  return type;
}
```

The first thing this function does differently is declare a GInterfaceInfo object. This structure holds three pieces of information. The first two are GInterfaceInitFunc and GInterfaceFinalizeFunc functions that are called when the interface is initialized and finalized. The third member is a pointer of data that will be passed to each function. The second two members can be safely ignored.

The second difference is a call to g_type_add_interface_static(), which is used to add an interface to an instance type. This function accepts three parameters: the instance GType, the interface GType, and the GInterfaceInfo object that was previously defined.

```
void g_type_add_interface_static (GType instance_type,
                                  GType interface_type,
                                  const GInterfaceInfo *info);
```

Listing 11-31 shows the last two steps for implementing the MyIFace interface. The first function, my_object_print_message(), is the actual implementation of the print_message() function that will be pointed to by the MyIFaceInterface member. This function will be called when the programmer calls my_iface_print_message().

Listing 11-31. *Initializing the Interface*

```
static void
my_object_print_message (MyObject *object,
                         gchar *message)
{
  g_print (message);
}

static void
my_object_interface_init (gpointer iface,
                          gpointer data)
{
  MyIFaceInteface *iface = (MyIFaceInterface*) iface;
  iface->print_message =
        (void (*) (MyIFace *obj, gchar *message)) my_object_print_message;
}
```

The second function in Listing 11-31 is the implementation of the object's interface initialization function. It simply points MyIFaceInterface's print_message() member to the object's implementation of the function.

This was a very simple example of implementing an interface, but it taught you all of the essentials that you will need when creating more complex examples. By this point, you should be able to derive your own objects from any other GObject as well as create and implement your own interfaces, which is quite an accomplishment! In the next chapter, you will get back to learning about widgets that are already built into GTK+.

Test Your Understanding

In this chapter's exercise, you will be expanding on the MyMarquee widget to include new features. This will require you to edit many parts of the code and explore new functions in the API documentation. You should also consider adding your own enhancements to the widget that are not mentioned in the exercise, such as a message-changed signal!

Exercise 11-1. Expanding MyMarquee

In this exercise, expand the MyMarquee with a few new abilities. First, the programmer should be able to specify the scroll direction, whether it is to the left or to the right. Also, place a rectangular border around the widget. The other property, the message, should now be a list of messages that are cycled. The initial message should be able to be set in my_marquee_new().

Also, implement an override function that is called when the mouse enters the proximity of the widget. When this happens, the message should stop scrolling until the mouse cursor leaves the proximity. To do this, you will have to add new event masks to the GdkWindow object.

Summary

In this chapter, we walked through two examples that taught you how to derive new objects. The first created a new widget called MyIPAddress, which was derived from GtkEntry. The second new widget was MyMarquee, which scrolls a message across the screen. This example taught you how to create a new widget from scratch, literally drawing it part by part on the screen.

Next, you were introduced to how interfaces are implemented and used in GTK+. This allows you to create your own interfaces or to use those that already exist for new widgets that you create.

In the next chapter, you will be learning about a number of widgets that did not fit into previous chapters. These include printing widgets, recent file support, calendars, automatic completion entries, status icons, and drawing areas.

■ ■ ■

Additional GTK+ Widgets

You have learned, by now, almost everything this book has to teach you. However, there are a number of widgets that did not quite fit into previous chapters. Therefore, this chapter will cover those widgets.

The first two widgets are used for drawing and are named GtkDrawingArea and GtkLayout. These two widgets are very similar except the GtkLayout widget allows you to embed arbitrary widgets into it in addition to using functions for drawing.

In addition, you will learn about GtkEntry widgets that support automatic completion and calendars. Lastly, you will be introduced to widgets that were added in GTK+ 2.10 including status icons, printing support, and recent file managers.

In this chapter, you will learn the following:

- How to use the drawing widgets GtkDrawingArea and GtkLayout

- How to use the GtkCalendar widget to track information about months of the year

- How to use widgets introduced in GTK+ 2.10 that provide recent file tracking, printing support, and status icons

- How to implement automatic completion in a GtkEntry widget by applying a GtkEntryCompletion object

Drawing Widgets

In the previous chapter, you learned about the GdkDrawable object that allows you to draw shapes and text on a GdkWindow. GTK+ provides the GtkDrawingArea widget, which is simply a blank slate on which you can draw.

GtkDrawingArea only provides one nondeprecated function—gtk_drawing_area_new(), which accepts no parameters and returns a new drawing area widget.

```
GtkWidget* gtk_drawing_area_new ();
```

To begin using the widget, you only need to use the functions covered in the last chapter to draw on the widget's GdkWindow. Remember that a GdkWindow object is also a GdkDrawable object.

One advantage of GtkDrawingArea is that it derives from GtkWidget, which means that it can be connected to GDK events. There are a number of events to which you will want to connect your drawing area. You will first want to connect to realize so that you can handle any tasks that need to be performed when the widget is instantiated, such as creating GDK resources. The configure-event signal will notify you when you have to handle a change in the size of the widget. Also, expose-event will allow you to redraw the widget when a portion is exposed that was previously hidden. The expose-event signal is especially important, because if you want the content of the drawing area to persist over expose-event callbacks, you will have to redraw its content. Lastly, you can connect to button and mouse click events so that the user can interact with the widget.

Note In order to receive certain types of events, you will need to add them to the list of widget events that are supported with gtk_widget_add_events(). Also, to receive keyboard input from the user, you will need to set the GTK_CAN_FOCUS flag, since only focused widgets can detect key presses.

A Drawing Area Example

Listing 12-1 implements a simple drawing program using the GtkDrawingArea widget. Points will be drawn on the screen when the user clicks a mouse button and when the pointer is dragged while a button is clicked. A screenshot of this application can be viewed in Figure 12-1.

Figure 12-1. *A drawing area widget with text drawn with the mouse*

The current content of the drawing area's GdkWindow object is cleared when the user presses the Delete key. While this is a very simple program, it nonetheless shows how to interact with the GtkDrawingArea widget and use events with it.

Listing 12-1. *A Simple Drawing Program (drawingareas.c)*

```
#include <gtk/gtk.h>
#include <gdk/gdkkeysyms.h>

static gboolean button_pressed (GtkWidget*, GdkEventButton*, GPtrArray*);
static gboolean motion_notify (GtkWidget*, GdkEventMotion*, GPtrArray*);
static gboolean key_pressed (GtkWidget*, GdkEventKey*, GPtrArray*);
static gboolean expose_event (GtkWidget*, GdkEventExpose*, GPtrArray*);

int main (int argc,
          char *argv[])
{
  GtkWidget *window, *area;
  GPtrArray *parray;

  gtk_init (&argc, &argv);

  window = gtk_window_new (GTK_WINDOW_TOPLEVEL);
  gtk_window_set_title (GTK_WINDOW (window), "Drawing Areas");
  gtk_widget_set_size_request (window, 400, 300);

  g_signal_connect (G_OBJECT (window), "destroy",
                    G_CALLBACK (gtk_main_quit), NULL);

  /* Create a pointer array to hold image data. Then, add event masks to the new
   * drawing area widget. */
  parray = g_ptr_array_sized_new (5000);
  area = gtk_drawing_area_new ();
  GTK_WIDGET_SET_FLAGS (area, GTK_CAN_FOCUS);
  gtk_widget_add_events (area, GDK_BUTTON_PRESS_MASK |
                               GDK_BUTTON_MOTION_MASK |
                               GDK_KEY_PRESS_MASK);

  g_signal_connect (G_OBJECT (area), "button_press_event",
                    G_CALLBACK (button_pressed), parray);
  g_signal_connect (G_OBJECT (area), "motion_notify_event",
                    G_CALLBACK (motion_notify), parray);
  g_signal_connect (G_OBJECT (area), "key_press_event",
                    G_CALLBACK (key_pressed), parray);
  g_signal_connect (G_OBJECT (area), "expose_event",
                    G_CALLBACK (expose_event), parray);
```

```
  gtk_container_add (GTK_CONTAINER (window), area);
  gtk_widget_show_all (window);

  /* You must do this after the widget is visible because it must first
   * be realized for the GdkWindow to be valid! */
  gdk_window_set_cursor (area->window, gdk_cursor_new (GDK_PENCIL));

  gtk_main ();
  return 0;
}

/* Redraw all of the points when an expose-event occurs. If you do not do this,
 * the drawing area will be cleared. */
static gboolean
expose_event (GtkWidget *area,
              GdkEventExpose *event,
              GPtrArray *parray)
{
  guint i, x, y;
  GdkPoint points[5];

  /* Loop through the coordinates, redrawing them onto the drawing area. */
  for (i = 0; i < parray->len; i = i + 2)
  {
    x = GPOINTER_TO_INT (parray->pdata[i]);
    y = GPOINTER_TO_INT (parray->pdata[i+1]);

    points[0].x = x;   points[0].y = y;
    points[1].x = x+1; points[1].y = y;
    points[2].x = x-1; points[2].y = y;
    points[3].x = x;   points[3].y = y+1;
    points[4].x = x;   points[4].y = y-1;

    gdk_draw_points (area->window,
                     area->style->fg_gc[GTK_WIDGET_STATE (area)],
                     points, 5);
  }

  return TRUE;
}
```

```
/* Draw a point where the user clicked the mouse and points on each of the
 * four sides of that point. */
static gboolean
button_pressed (GtkWidget *area,
                GdkEventButton *event,
                GPtrArray *parray)
{
  gint x = event->x, y = event->y;
  GdkPoint points[5] = { {x,y}, {x+1,y}, {x-1,y}, {x,y+1}, {x,y-1} };

  gdk_draw_points (area->window,
                   area->style->fg_gc[GTK_WIDGET_STATE (area)],
                   points, 5);

  g_ptr_array_add (parray, GINT_TO_POINTER (x));
  g_ptr_array_add (parray, GINT_TO_POINTER (y));

  return FALSE;
}

/* Draw a point where the moved the mouse pointer while a button was
 * clicked along with points on each of the four sides of that point. */
static gboolean
motion_notify (GtkWidget *area,
               GdkEventMotion *event,
               GPtrArray *parray)
{
  gint x = event->x, y = event->y;
  GdkPoint points[5] = { {x,y}, {x+1,y}, {x-1,y}, {x,y+1}, {x,y-1} };

  gdk_draw_points (area->window,
                   area->style->fg_gc[GTK_WIDGET_STATE (area)],
                   points, 5);

  g_ptr_array_add (parray, GINT_TO_POINTER (x));
  g_ptr_array_add (parray, GINT_TO_POINTER (y));

  return FALSE;
}
```

```
/* Clear the drawing area when the user presses the Delete key. */
static gboolean

key_pressed (GtkWidget *area,
             GdkEventKey *event,
             GPtrArray *parray)
{
  if (event->keyval == GDK_Delete)
  {
    gdk_window_clear (area->window);
    g_ptr_array_remove_range (parray, 0, parray->len);
  }

  return FALSE;
}
```

You should notice a few things about Listing 12-1. First, a GPtrArray is used to track points that are added to the drawing area. When a point is added to the screen, the points on all four sides of the initial point are also activated. Then, the horizontal and vertical positions are added to the array. When the expose-event callback function is called, all of the points are redrawn. If you do not redraw the content of a drawing area, it will be cleared during expose-event emissions.

To draw the points, this application uses gdk_draw_points(). This function draws an array of npoints points onto the drawable object. It uses the default foreground color of the current state of the widget.

```
void gdk_draw_points (GdkDrawable *drawable,
                      GdkGC *gc,
                      GdkPoint *points,
                      gint npoints);
```

In addition to gdk_draw_points(), it is also possible to use any of the drawing functions that were listed in Chapter 11 with drawing areas.

The Layout Widget

In addition to GtkDrawingArea, GTK+ provides another drawing widget called GtkLayout. This widget is actually a container and differs from GtkDrawingArea in that it supports not only drawing primitives but also child widgets. In addition, GtkLayout provides scrolling support natively, so it does not need a viewport when added to a scrolled window.

Note One important distinction to note with layouts is that you should draw to GtkLayout's bin_window member instead of GtkWidget's window. For example, you would draw to GTK_LAYOUT(layout)->bin_window instead of GTK_WIDGET(layout)->window. This allows child widgets to be correctly embedded into the widget.

CHAPTER 12 ■ ADDITIONAL GTK+ WIDGETS

New GtkLayout widgets are created with gtk_layout_new(), which accepts horizontal and vertical adjustments. Adjustments will be created for you if you pass NULL to both function parameters. Since GtkLayout has native scrolling support, it can be much more useful than GtkDrawingArea when you need to use it with a scrolled window.

```
GtkWidget* gtk_layout_new (GtkAdjustment *hadjustment,
                           GtkAdjustment *vadjustment);
```

However, GtkLayout does add some overhead, since it is capable of containing widgets as well. Because of this, GtkDrawingArea is a better choice if you only need to draw on the widget's GdkWindow.

Child widgets are added to a GtkLayout container with gtk_layout_put(), which will place the child with respect to the top-left corner of the container. Since GtkLayout is derived directly from GtkContainer, it is able to support multiple children.

```
void gtk_layout_put (GtkLayout *layout,
                     GtkWidget *child_widget,
                     gint x,
                     gint y);
```

A call to gtk_layout_move() can be used at a later time to relocate the child widget to another location in the GtkLayout container.

■**Caution** Because you place child widgets at specific horizontal and vertical locations, GtkLayout presents the same problems as GtkFixed. You need to be careful of these when using the layout widget! You can read more about the problems with the GtkFixed widget in Chapter 3.

Lastly, if you want to force the layout to be a specific size, you can send new width and height parameters to gtk_layout_set_size(). You should use this function instead of gtk_widget_set_size_request(), because it will adjust the adjustment parameters as well.

```
void gtk_layout_set_size (GtkLayout *layout,
                          guint width,
                          guint height);
```

Also, unlike size requests, the layout sizing function requires unsigned numbers. This means that you must specify an absolute size for the layout widget. This size should be the total size of the layout, including portions of the widget that will not be visible on the screen because they are beyond the bounds of the scrolling area! The size of a GtkLayout widget defaults to 100 pixels by 100 pixels.

Calendars

GTK+ provides the GtkCalendar widget, which is a widget that displays one month of a calendar. It allows the user to move among months and years with scroll arrows, as shown in Figure 12-2.

You can also display three-letter abbreviations of the day names and week numbers for the chosen year.

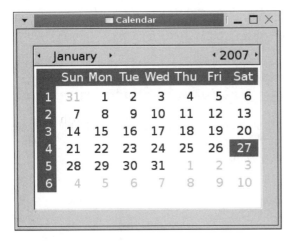

Figure 12-2. *GtkCalendar widget*

There are number of members in the GtkCalendar structure that can be used but are read only; these objects are explained in the following list. You should note that when the current month or year is changed programmatically or by the user, all of these values would be reset. Therefore, you will have to handle all changes.

- num_marked_dates: The number of days in the current month that are marked. This value should be between zero and the number of days in the current month.

- marked_date: An array of unsigned integers containing num_marked_dates of days that are marked for the current month.

- month: The current month the user is viewing. Month values are within the range of 0 to 11. When the month changes, the month-changed signal will be emitted. Also, if the calendar is moved to the next or previous month, the next-month or previous-month signal will be emitted.

- year: The current year for the month that is displayed. If the calendar is moved to the next or previous year, the next-year or previous-year signal will be emitted.

- selected_day: The currently selected day, which is always a single day, although more than one day can be marked. Days are within the range of one to the number of days in the month.

New GtkCalendar widgets are created with gtk_calendar_new(). By default, the current date is selected. Therefore, the current month and year stored by the computer will also be displayed. You can retrieve the selected date with gtk_calendar_get_date() or select a new day with gtk_calendar_select_day(). To deselect the currently selected day, you should use gtk_calendar_select_day() with a date value of zero.

To customize how the GtkCalendar widget is displayed and how it interacts with the user, you should use gtk_calendar_set_display_options() to set a bitwise list of GtkCalendarDisplayOptions values. The nondeprecated values of this enumeration follow:

- GTK_CALENDAR_SHOW_HEADING: If set, the name of the month and the year will be displayed.

- GTK_CALENDAR_SHOW_DAY_NAMES: If set, a three letter abbreviation of each day will be shown above the corresponding column of dates. They are rendered between the heading and the main calendar content.

- GTK_CALENDAR_NO_MONTH_CHANGE: Stop the user from changing the current month of the calendar. If this flag is not set, arrows will be displayed that allow you to go to the next or previous month. By default, the arrows are enabled.

- GTK_CALENDAR_SHOW_WEEK_NUMBERS: Display the week number along the left side of the calendar for the current year. The week numbers are hidden by default.

In addition to selecting a single day, you can mark as many days in the month as you want one at a time with gtk_calendar_mark_day(). This function will return TRUE if the day was successfully marked.

```
gboolean gtk_calendar_mark_day (GtkCalendar *calendar,
                                guint day);
```

Marks have a number of uses, such as selecting all days in the month that have events associated with them. When marked, the date will be added to the marked_date array.

In addition to marking days, you can unmark one day with gtk_calendar_unmark_day(), which will return TRUE if the day was successfully unmarked. You can also unmark every day with gtk_calendar_clear_marks().

```
gboolean gtk_calendar_unmark_day (GtkCalendar *calendar,
                                  guint day);
```

There are two signals available for detecting when the user selects a day. The first signal, day-selected, will be emitted when the user selects a new day with the mouse or the keyboard. The day-selected-double-click signal will be emitted when the user selects a day by double-clicking it. This means that you should not need the button-press-event signal with the GtkCalendar widget in most cases.

Status Icons

The GtkStatusIcon widget was introduced in GTK+ 2.10 and is used to display an icon in the system tray (notification area) in a platform-independent manner. System tray icons are often used to notify the user of some type of event in a nonintrusive way or provide easy access to a minimized application.

The GtkStatusIcon implementation of the system tray icon provides the ability to add a tooltip, add a pop-up menu for interaction with the icon, and make the icon blink to notify the user of some type of event. It is also possible for the user to activate the icon by clicking it.

■**Note** GtkStatusIcon is *not* derived from GtkWidget; it is a GObject! This is necessary because on Microsoft Windows, system tray icons are not allowed to be added as widgets.

Five functions are provided for creating a new status icon. An empty GtkStatusIcon instance is created with gtk_status_icon_new(). You will need to specify an image for the system tray icon before setting the object as visible if you use that initialization function.

```
GtkStatusIcon* gtk_status_icon_new ();
GtkStatusIcon* gtk_status_icon_new_from_pixbuf    (GdkPixbuf *pixbuf);
GtkStatusIcon* gtk_status_icon_new_from_file      (const gchar *filename);
GtkStatusIcon* gtk_status_icon_new_from_stock     (const gchar *stock_id);
GtkStatusIcon* gtk_status_icon_new_from_icon_name (const gchar *icon_name);
```

The other four functions create a status icon out of a GdkPixbuf object, from a file on the system, a stock item, or an image in the current icon theme. All of these functions will scale the image to fit in the notification area if necessary.

If you initialized the status icon with gtk_status_icon_new(), you can then set the image with gtk_status_icon_set_from_pixbuf() and friends. Functions are provided for setting the image from a GdkPixbuf object, file, stock item, or an image from the current icon theme. These functions can also be used to change the image at a later time to reflect the current state of the application. For example, if your application is an e-mail client, you could change the system tray icon from your application's icon to an envelope to show that a new message has arrived.

■**Tip** By default, the status icon is set as visible. You can hide the icon from view or set it as visible with gtk_status_icon_set_visible().

When the user hovers over the system tray icon, it is possible to display a tooltip that gives further information with gtk_status_icon_set_tooltip(). For example, this information could be the number of new messages in an e-mail client or the percentage of progress that has been made in a downloading application.

```
void gtk_status_icon_set_tooltip (GtkStatusIcon *icon,
                                  const gchar *tooltip_text);
```

If some event has occurred in your application that the user should know about, you can make the status icon blink with gtk_status_icon_set_blinking(). Depending on the user's preferences, this feature may be disabled. In this case, this function will have no effect. When using this function, *do not forget to turn off blinking*! Not turning off blinking when it is no longer necessary is enough of an annoyance for some people to stop using your application.

```
void gtk_status_icon_set_blinking (GtkStatusIcon *icon,
                                   gboolean blinking);
```

GtkStatusIcon provides three signals. The activate signal is emitted when the user activates the status icon. The size-changed signal is emitted when the available size for the icon changes. This allows you to resize the icon or load a new icon to fit the new size, in which case you should return TRUE. If you return FALSE, GTK+ will scale the current icon to fit the new size.

Lastly, the popup-menu signal is emitted when the user has indicated that a menu should be shown. Usually right-clicking the icon does this, but this is also dependent on the user's platform. This function accepts the two unsigned integers indicating which button was pressed and at what time it was activated. These two values should be sent to gtk_menu_popup() to display the menu. For the fourth parameter of gtk_menu_popup(), you will want to use gtk_status_icon_position_menu(). This is a menu positioning function that will calculate where to place the menu on the screen.

Printing Support

GTK+ 2.10 introduced a number of new widgets and objects that add printing support to the library. While there are many objects in this API, in most instances, you will only need to directly interact with GtkPrintOperation, which is a high-level printing API that can be used across multiple platforms. It acts as a front-end interface for handling most print operations.

In this section, we are going to implement an application that will print the content of a text file that the user selects in a GtkFileChooserButton widget. A screenshot of the default print dialog on a Linux system can be viewed in Figure 12-3. The user will select a file from the disk using a GtkFileChooserButton widget and click the Print button in the main window to open this dialog.

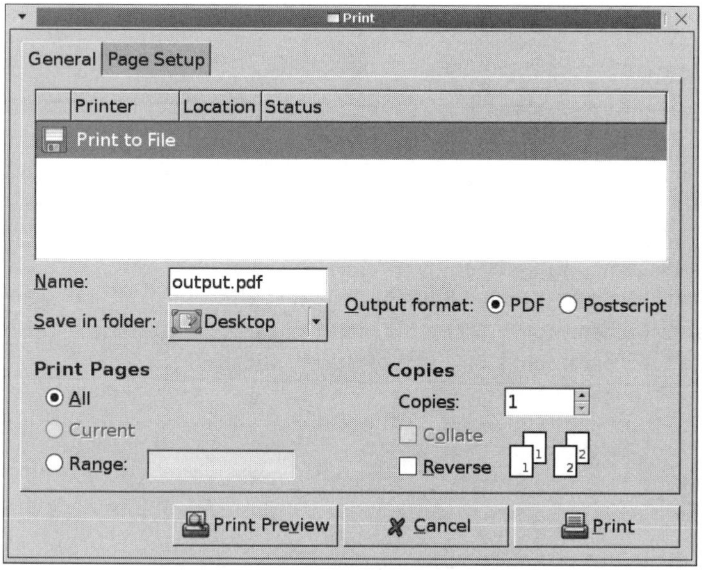

Figure 12-3. *Print dialog on a Linux system*

Listing 12-2 begins by defining the necessary data structures for the application and setting up the user interface. The PrintData structure will be used to hold information about the current print job that will help with rendering the final product. Widgets is a simple structure that provides us with access to multiple widgets and the print job information in callback functions.

Listing 12-2. *GTK+ Printing Example (printing.c)*

```
#include <gtk/gtk.h>
#include <math.h>

#define HEADER_HEIGHT 20.0
#define HEADER_GAP 8.5

/* A structure that will hold information about the current print job. */
typedef struct
{
  gchar *filename;
  gdouble font_size;
  gint lines_per_page;
  gchar **lines;
  gint total_lines;
  gint total_pages;
} PrintData;

typedef struct
{
  GtkWidget *window, *chooser;
  PrintData *data;
} Widgets;

GtkPrintSettings *settings;

static void print_file (GtkButton*, Widgets*);
static void begin_print (GtkPrintOperation*, GtkPrintContext*, Widgets*);
static void draw_page (GtkPrintOperation*, GtkPrintContext*, gint, Widgets*);
static void end_print (GtkPrintOperation*, GtkPrintContext*, Widgets*);

int main (int argc,
          char *argv[])
{
  GtkWidget *hbox, *print;
  Widgets *w;
```

```
  gtk_init (&argc, &argv);

  w = g_slice_new (Widgets);
  w->window = gtk_window_new (GTK_WINDOW_TOPLEVEL);
  gtk_window_set_title (GTK_WINDOW (w->window), "Printing");
  gtk_container_set_border_width (GTK_CONTAINER (w->window), 10);

  g_signal_connect (G_OBJECT (w->window), "destroy",
                    G_CALLBACK (gtk_main_quit), NULL);

  w->chooser = gtk_file_chooser_button_new ("Select a File",
                                            GTK_FILE_CHOOSER_ACTION_OPEN);
  gtk_file_chooser_set_current_folder (GTK_FILE_CHOOSER (w->chooser),
                                       g_get_home_dir ());

  print = gtk_button_new_from_stock (GTK_STOCK_PRINT);

  g_signal_connect (G_OBJECT (print), "clicked",
                    G_CALLBACK (print_file), (gpointer) w);

  hbox = gtk_hbox_new (FALSE, 5);
  gtk_box_pack_start (GTK_BOX (hbox), w->chooser, FALSE, FALSE, 0);
  gtk_box_pack_start (GTK_BOX (hbox), print, FALSE, FALSE, 0);

  gtk_container_add (GTK_CONTAINER (w->window), hbox);
  gtk_widget_show_all (w->window);

  gtk_main ();
  return 0;
}
```

Two values are defined at the top of Listing 12-2 called HEADER_HEIGHT and HEADER_GAP. HEADER_HEIGHT is the amount of space that will be available for the header text to be rendered. This will be used to display information such as the file name and page number. HEADER_GAP is padding that will be placed between the header and the actual page content.

The PrintData structure will be used to store information about the current print job. This includes the location of the file on the disk, the size of the font, the number of lines that can be rendered on a single page, the file's content, the total number of lines, and the total number of pages.

Print Operations

The next step is to implement the callback function that will be run when the GTK_STOCK_PRINT button is clicked. This function is implemented in Listing 12-3. It will take care of creating the PrintData object, connecting all of the necessary signals, and creating the print operation.

Listing 12-3. *Print and Print Preview*

```
/* Print the selected file with a font of "Monospace 10". */
static void
print_file (GtkButton *button,
            Widgets *w)
{
  GtkPrintOperation *operation;
  GtkWidget *dialog;
  GError *error = NULL;
  gchar *filename;
  gint res;

  /* Return if a file has not been selected because there is nothing to print. */
  filename = gtk_file_chooser_get_filename (GTK_FILE_CHOOSER (w->chooser));
  if (filename == NULL)
    return;

  /* Create a new print operation, applying saved print settings if they exist. */H
  operation = gtk_print_operation_new ();
  if (settings != NULL)
    gtk_print_operation_set_print_settings (operation, settings);

  w->data = g_slice_new (PrintData);
  w->data->filename = g_strdup (filename);
  w->data->font_size = 10.0;

  g_signal_connect (G_OBJECT (operation), "begin_print",
                    G_CALLBACK (begin_print), (gpointer) w);
  g_signal_connect (G_OBJECT (operation), "draw_page",
                    G_CALLBACK (draw_page), (gpointer) w);
  g_signal_connect (G_OBJECT (operation), "end_print",
                    G_CALLBACK (end_print), (gpointer) w);

  /* Run the default print operation that will print the selected file. */
  res = gtk_print_operation_run (operation, GTK_PRINT_OPERATION_ACTION_PRINT_DIALOG,
                                 GTK_WINDOW (w->window), &error);

  /* If the print operation was accepted, save the new print settings. */
  if (res == GTK_PRINT_OPERATION_RESULT_APPLY)
  {
    if (settings != NULL)
      g_object_unref (settings);
    settings = g_object_ref (gtk_print_operation_get_print_settings (operation));
  }
  /* Otherwise, report that the print operation has failed. */
  else if (error)
```

```
{
  dialog = gtk_message_dialog_new (GTK_WINDOW (w->window),
                                   GTK_DIALOG_DESTROY_WITH_PARENT,
                                   GTK_MESSAGE_ERROR, GTK_BUTTONS_CLOSE,
                                   error->message);

  g_error_free (error);
  gtk_dialog_run (GTK_DIALOG (dialog));
  gtk_widget_destroy (dialog);
}

  g_object_unref (operation);
  g_free (filename);
}
```

The first step in printing is to create a new print operation, which is done by calling gtk_print_operation_new(). What makes GtkPrintOperation unique is that it will use the platform's native print dialog if there is one available. On platforms like UNIX that do not provide such a dialog, GtkPrintUnixDialog will be used.

■Note For most applications, you should use the GtkPrintOperation API when possible instead of directly interacting with the print objects. GtkPrintOperation was created as a platform-independent printing solution, which cannot be easily reimplemented without a lot of code.

The next step is to call gtk_print_operation_print_settings() to apply print settings to the operation. In this application, the GtkPrintSettings object is stored as a global variable called settings. If the print operation is successful, you should store the current print settings so that these same settings can be applied to future print jobs.

You then set up the PrintData structure by allocating a new object with g_slice_new(). The file name is set to the currently selected file in the GtkFileChooserButton, which was already confirmed to exist. The print font size is also set to 10.0 points. In text editing applications, you would usually retrieve this font from the current font of GtkTextView. In more complex printing applications, the font size may vary throughout a document, but this is a simple example meant only to get you started.

Next, we connect to three GtkPrintOperation signals, which will be discussed in detail later in this section. In short, begin-print is called before the pages are rendered and can be used for setting the number of pages and doing necessary preparation. The draw-page signal is called for every page in the print job so that it can be rendered. Lastly, the end-print signal is called after the print operation has completed, regardless of whether it succeeded or failed. This callback function is used to clean up after the print job. There are a number of other signals that can be used throughout the print operation; a full list can be found in Appendix B.

Once the print operation has been set up, the next step is to begin the printing by calling gtk_print_operation_run(). This function is where you define what task the print operation will perform.

```
GtkPrintOperationResult gtk_print_operation_run (GtkPrintOperation *operation,
                                                 GtkPrintOperationAction action,
                                                 GtkWindow *parent,
                                                 GError **error);
```

The GtkPrintOperationAction enumeration, shown in the following list, defines what printing task the print operation will perform. To print the document, you should use GTK_PRINT_OPERATION_ACTION_PRINT_DIALOG.

- GTK_PRINT_OPERATION_ACTION_PRINT_DIALOG: Show the default print dialog for the platform, or use GtkPrintUnixDialog if one is not available. This is the usual action for most print operations.

- GTK_PRINT_OPERATION_ACTION_PRINT: Start printing using the current printing settings without presenting the print dialog. You should only do this if you are 100 percent sure that the user approves of this action. For example, you should have already presented a confirmation dialog to the user.

- GTK_PRINT_OPERATION_ACTION_PREVIEW: Preview the print job that will be performed with the current settings. This uses the same callbacks for rendering as the print operation, so it should take little work to get it up and running.

- GTK_PRINT_OPERATION_ACTION_EXPORT: Export the print job to a file. In order to use this setting, you will have to set the export-filename property prior to running the operation.

The last two parameters of gtk_print_operation_run() allow you to define a parent window to use for the print dialog and a GError structure or to use NULL to ignore either parameter. This function will not return until all of the pages have been rendered and are sent to the printer.

When the function does give back control, it will return a GtkPrintOperationResult enumeration value. These values give you instructions on what task you should perform next, and whether the print operation succeeded or failed. The four enumeration values are shown in the following list:

- GTK_PRINT_OPERATION_RESULT_ERROR: Some type of error has occurred in the print operation. You should use the GError object for more information.

- GTK_PRINT_OPERATION_RESULT_APPLY: Print settings were changed. Therefore, they should be stored immediately, so changes will not be lost.

- GTK_PRINT_OPERATION_RESULT_CANCEL: The user cancelled the print operation, and you should not save the changes to the print settings.

- GTK_PRINT_OPERATION_RESULT_IN_PROGRESS: The print operation has yet to be completed. You will only get this value if you are running the task asynchronously.

It is possible to run the print operation asynchronously, which means that gtk_print_ operation_run() may return before the pages have been rendered. This is set with gtk_print_operation_set_allow_async(). You should note that not all platforms allow this operation, so you should be prepared for this not to work!

If you run the print operation asynchronously, you can use the done signal to retrieve notification when the printing has completed. At this point, you will be given the print operation result and will need to handle it accordingly.

After handling the print operation result, you should also handle the resulting error if it was set and exists. A full list of possible errors under the GtkPrintError domain can be found in Appendix E. Also, gtk_print_operation_get_error() can be used to retrieve the most recent GError that occurred, if any, for the print operation. This can be used when running the print operation asynchronously to retrieve more information about a print job that returned GTK_ PRINT_OPERATION_RESULT_ERROR.

One unique feature provided by GtkPrintOperation is the ability to show a progress dialog while the print operation is running. This is turned off by default, but it can be turned on with gtk_print_operation_set_show_progress(). This is especially useful if you allow the user to run multiple print operations at the same time.

```
void gtk_print_operation_set_show_progress (GtkPrintOperation *operation,
                                            gboolean show_progress);
```

It may be necessary at times to cancel a current print job, which can be done by calling gtk_print_operation_cancel(). This function is usually used within a begin-print, paginate, or draw-page callback function. It also allows you to provide a Cancel button so that the user can stop in the middle of an active print operation.

```
void gtk_print_operation_cancel (GtkPrintOperation *operation);
```

It is also possible to give a unique name to the print job, which will be used to identify it within an external print monitoring application. Print jobs are given names with gtk_print_ operation_set_job_name(). If this is not set, GTK+ will automatically designate a name for the print job and number consecutive print jobs accordingly.

If you are running the print job asynchronously, you may want to retrieve the current status of the print job. By calling gtk_print_operation_get_status(), a GtkPrintStatus enumeration value will be returned that gives more information about the status of the print job. A list of possible print job status values follows:

- GTK_PRINT_STATUS_INITIAL: The print operation has yet to begin. This status will be returned while the print dialog is still visible because it is the default initial value.

- GTK_PRINT_STATUS_PREPARING: The print operation is being split into pages, and the begin-print signal was emitted.

- GTK_PRINT_STATUS_GENERATING_DATA: The pages are being rendered. This will be set while the draw-page signal is being emitted. No data will have been sent to the printer at this point.

- GTK_PRINT_STATUS_SENDING_DATA: Data about the print job is being sent to the printer.

- GTK_PRINT_STATUS_PENDING: All of the data has been sent to the printer, but the job has yet to be processed. It is possible that the printer may be stopped.

- GTK_PRINT_STATUS_PENDING_ISSUE: There was a problem during the printing. For example, the printer could be out of paper, or there could be a paper jam.

- GTK_PRINT_STATUS_PRINTING: The printer is currently processing the print job.

- GTK_PRINT_STATUS_FINISHED: The print job has been successfully completed.

- GTK_PRINT_STATUS_FINISHED_ABORTED: The print job was aborted. No further action will be taken unless you run the job again.

The value returned by gtk_print_operation_get_status() can be used within applications, since it is a numerical value. However, GTK+ also provides the ability to retrieve a string with gtk_print_operation_get_status_string(), which is a human-readable description of the print job status. This can be used for debugging output or displaying more information to the user about the print job. For example, it could be displayed on a status bar or in a message dialog.

Beginning the Print Operation

Now that the print operation is set up, it is time to implement the necessary signal callback functions. The begin-print signal is emitted when the user initiates printing, which means that all settings have been finalized from the user's point of view.

In Listing 12-4, the begin_print() callback function is used to first retrieve the contents of the file and split it into the number of lines. The total number of lines is then calculated, which can be used to retrieve the number of pages.

Listing 12-4. *Callback Function for the begin-print Signal*

```
/* Begin the printing by retrieving the contents of the selected files and
 * splitting it into single lines of text. */
static void
begin_print (GtkPrintOperation *operation,
             GtkPrintContext *context,
             Widgets *w)
{
  gchar *contents;
  gdouble height;
  gsize length;

  /* Retrieve the file contents and split it into lines of text. */
  g_file_get_contents (w->data->filename, &contents, &length, NULL);
  w->data->lines = g_strsplit (contents, "\n", 0);

  /* Count the total number of lines in the file. */
  w->data->total_lines = 0;
  while (w->data->lines[w->data->total_lines] != NULL)
    w->data->total_lines++;
```

```
/* Based on the height of the page and font size, calculate how many lines can be
 * rendered on a single page. A padding of 3 is placed between lines as well. */
height = gtk_print_context_get_height (context) - HEADER_HEIGHT - HEADER_GAP;
w->data->lines_per_page = floor (height / (w->data->font_size + 3));
w->data->total_pages = (w->data->total_lines - 1) / w->data->lines_per_page + 1;
gtk_print_operation_set_n_pages (operation, w->data->total_pages);
g_free (contents);
}
```

To calculate the number of pages required by the print operation, you need to figure out how many lines can be rendered on every page. The total height of every page is retrieved with gtk_print_context_get_height(), which is stored in a GtkPrintContext object. GtkPrintContext is used to store information about how to draw the page. For example, it stores the page setup, width and height dimensions, and dots per inch in both directions. We will go into more detail in the draw-page callback function later in this chapter.

Once you have the total height of the page that will be available for rendering text, the next step is to divide that height by the font size of the text plus 3 pixels of spacing to be added between each line. The floor() function was used to round down the number of lines per page so that clipping will not occur along the bottom of every full page.

Once you have the number of lines per page, you can calculate the number of pages. Then, you must send this value to gtk_print_operation_set_n_pages() by the end of this callback function. The number of pages will be used so that GTK+ knows how many times to call the draw-page callback function. This *must* be set to a positive value, so rendering will not begin until it is changed from its default value of -1.

Rendering Pages

The next step is to implement the draw-page callback function, which will be called once for every page that needs to be rendered. This callback function requires the introduction of another library called Cairo. Cairo is a vector graphics library that is used to render print operations, among other things.

Listing 12-5 begins by retrieving the Cairo drawing context for the current GtkPrintContext with gtk_print_context_get_cairo_context(). The cairo_t object will be used to render print content and then apply it to the PangoLayout.

At the beginning of this callback function, we also need to retrieve two other values from the GtkPrintContext. The first is gtk_print_context_get_width(), which returns the width of the document. Notice that we do not need to retrieve the height of the page, since we have already calculated the number of lines that will fit on each page. If the text is wider than the page, it will be clipped. You will have to alter this example in order to avoid clipping the document.

■**Caution** The width returned by the GtkPrintContext is in pixels. You need to be careful because different functions may use alternative scales such as Pango units or points!

The next step is to create a `PangoLayout` with `gtk_print_context_create_layout()`, which can be used for the print context. You should create Pango layouts in this manner for print operations, because the print context will already have the correct font metrics applied.

Listing 12-5. *Callback Function for the draw-page Signal*

```
/* Draw the page, which includes a header with the file name and page number along
 * with one page of text with a font of "Monospace 10". */
static void
draw_page (GtkPrintOperation *operation,
           GtkPrintContext *context,
           gint page_nr,
           Widgets *w)
{
  cairo_t *cr;
  PangoLayout *layout;
  gdouble width, text_height;
  gint line, i, text_width, layout_height;
  PangoFontDescription *desc;
  gchar *page_str;

  cr = gtk_print_context_get_cairo_context (context);
  width = gtk_print_context_get_width (context);
  layout = gtk_print_context_create_pango_layout (context);
  desc = pango_font_description_from_string ("Monospace");
  pango_font_description_set_size (desc, w->data->font_size * PANGO_SCALE);

  /* Render the page header with the filename and page number. */
  pango_layout_set_font_description (layout, desc);
  pango_layout_set_text (layout, w->data->filename, -1);
  pango_layout_set_width (layout, -1);
  pango_layout_set_alignment (layout, PANGO_ALIGN_LEFT);
  pango_layout_get_size (layout, NULL, &layout_height);
  text_height = (gdouble) layout_height / PANGO_SCALE;

  cairo_move_to (cr, 0, (HEADER_HEIGHT - text_height) / 2);
  pango_cairo_show_layout (cr, layout);

  page_str = g_strdup_printf ("%d of %d", page_nr + 1, w->data->total_pages);
  pango_layout_set_text (layout, page_str, -1);
  pango_layout_get_size (layout, &text_width, NULL);
  pango_layout_set_alignment (layout, PANGO_ALIGN_RIGHT);

  cairo_move_to (cr, width - (text_width / PANGO_SCALE),
                 (HEADER_HEIGHT - text_height) / 2);
  pango_cairo_show_layout (cr, layout);
```

```
/* Render the page text with the specified font and size. */
cairo_move_to (cr, 0, HEADER_HEIGHT + HEADER_GAP);
line = page_nr * w->data->lines_per_page;
for (i = 0; i < w->data->lines_per_page && line < w->data->total_lines; i++)
{
  pango_layout_set_text (layout, w->data->lines[line], -1);
  pango_cairo_show_layout (cr, layout);
  cairo_rel_move_to (cr, 0, w->data->font_size + 3);
  line++;
}

g_free (page_str);
g_object_unref (layout);
pango_font_description_free (desc);
}
```

The next operation performed by this function is to add the file name to the top-left corner of the page. To start, pango_layout_set_text() sets the current text stored by the layout to the file name. The width of the layout is set to -1 so that the file name does not wrap at forward slash characters. The text is also aligned to the left of the layout with pango_layout_set_alignment().

Now that the text is added to the layout, cairo_move_to() is used to move the current point in the Cairo context to the left of the page and the center of the header. Note that the height of the PangoLayout must first be reduced by a factor of PANGO_SCALE!

```
void cairo_move_to (cairo_t *cairo_context,
                    double x,
                    double y);
```

Next, we call pango_cairo_show_layout() in order to draw the PangoLayout on the Cairo context. The top-left corner of the layout is rendered at the current point in the Cairo context. This is why it was first necessary to move to the desired position with cairo_move_to().

```
void pango_cairo_show_layout (cairo_t *cairo_context,
                             PangoLayout *layout);
```

After rendering the file name, the same method is used to add the page count to the top-right corner of each page. You should again note that the width returned by the PangoLayout had to be scaled down by PANGO_SCALE so that it would be in the same units as other Cairo values.

The next step is to render all of the lines for the current page. We begin by moving to the left of the page, HEADER_GAP units below the header. Then, each line is incrementally rendered to the Cairo context with pango_cairo_show_layout(). One interesting thing to note is that the cursor position in the loop is moved with cairo_rel_move_to().

```
void cairo_rel_move_to (cairo_t *cairo_context),
                        double dx,
                        double dy);
```

This function is used to move the current position relative to the previous position. Therefore, after a line is rendered, the current position is moved down one line, which is equal to the font size of the text since the font is Monospace.

Tip By moving the cursor relative to the previous position, it is easy to add an arbitrary amount of spacing between each line of text and the adjacent one as long as this additional height was previously taken into consideration when calculating the number of pages in the `begin-print` callback function.

When developing with GTK+, you have the whole Cairo library available to you. Some more basics will be covered in the Cairo section of this chapter. However, if you are implementing printing in your own applications, you should take the time to learn more about this library from the Cairo API documentation.

Finalizing the Print Operation

After all of the pages have been rendered, the `end-print` signal will be emitted. Listing 12-6 shows a callback function that will be used for this signal. It frees all dynamically allocated memory in the `PrintData` object and then frees the object itself.

Listing 12-6. *Callback Function for the end-print Signal*

```
/* Clean up after the printing operation since it is done. */
static void
end_print (GtkPrintOperation *operation,
           GtkPrintContext *context,
           Widgets *w)
{
  g_strfreev (w->data->lines);
  g_slice_free1 (sizeof (PrintData), w->data);
  w->data = NULL;
}
```

The printing API provided by GTK+ is very large, even without taking into consideration the large APIs for `PangoLayout` and Cairo. Therefore, this example is obviously only a simple one that is meant to get you started and help relieve the learning curve that the API presents. You can use this example to get started with implementing printing in your own applications, but you will need to delve further into the topic in most cases.

Cairo Drawing Context

Cairo is a graphics rendering library that is used throughout the GTK+ library. In the context of this book, Cairo is used to render pages during a print operation. This section will introduce you to the `cairo_t` object and some of the drawing functions associated with it.

Pages of a print operation in GTK+ are rendered as `cairo_t` objects. This object allows you to render text, draw various shapes and lines, and fill clipped areas with color. Let us look at a few functions provided by Cairo for manipulating Cairo drawing contexts.

Drawing Paths

Shapes in Cairo contexts are rendered with paths. A new path is created with `cairo_new_path()`. You can then retrieve a copy of the new path with `cairo_copy_path()` and add new lines and shapes to the path.

```
cairo_path_t* cairo_copy_path (cairo_t *cairo_context);
```

There are a number of functions provided for drawing paths, which are listed in Table 12-1. More information about each function can be found in the Cairo API documentation.

Table 12-1. *Cairo Path-Drawing Functions*

Function	Description
cairo_arc()	Draw an arc in the current path. You must provide the radius of the arc, horizontal and vertical positions of its center, and the start and end angle of the curve in radians.
cairo_curve_to()	Create a Bezier curve in the current path. You must provide the end position of the curve and two control points that will be used to calculate the curve.
cairo_line_to()	Draw a line from the current position to the specified point. The current position will simply be moved if an initial point does not exist.
cairo_move_to()	Move to a new position in the context, which will cause a new subpath to be created.
cairo_rectangle()	Draw a rectangle in the current path. You must provide the coordinates of the top-left corner of the rectangle, its width, and its height.
cairo_rel_curve_to()	This function is the same as `cairo_curve_to()`, except it is drawn with respect to the current position.
cairo_rel_line_to()	This function is the same as `cairo_line_to()`, except it is drawn with respect to the current position.
cairo_rel_move_to()	This function is the same as `cairo_move_to()`, except it is drawn with respect to the current position.

When you are finished with a subpath, you can close it with `cairo_path_close()`. This will enclose the current path so that it can be filled with a color if necessary.

Rendering Options

The current color used for drawing operations on a source is `cairo_set_source_rgb()`. The color will be used until a new color is set. In addition to choosing a color, you can use `cairo_set_source_rgba()`, which accepts a fifth alpha parameter. Each of the color parameters is a floating point number between 0.0 and 1.0.

```
void cairo_set_source_rgb (cairo_t *cairo_context,
                           double red,
                           double green,
                           double blue);
```

After you have moved to a specific point and set the source color, you can fill the current path with `cairo_fill()`, which accepts only the context. Alternatively, you can fill a rectangular area with `cairo_fill_extents()`. This function will calculate an area with corners of (x1,y1) and (x2,y2), filling all of the area that is in between those points that is also contained by the current path.

```
void cairo_fill_extents (cairo_t *cairo_context,
                         double *x1,
                         double *y1,
                         double *x2,
                         double *y2);
```

Drawing operations such as curves can cause edges to become jagged. To fix this, Cairo provides antialiasing to drawings with `cairo_set_antialias()`.

```
void cairo_set_antialias (cairo_t *cairo_context,
                          cairo_antialias_t antialias);
```

Antialiasing settings are provided by the `cairo_antialias_t` enumeration. A list of values provided by this enumeration follows:

- `CAIRO_ANTIALIAS_DEFAULT`: The default antialiasing algorithm will be used.

- `CAIRO_ANTIALIAS_NONE`: No antialiasing will occur; instead, an alpha mask will be used.

- `CAIRO_ANTIALIAS_GRAY`: Use only a single color for antialiasing. This color is not necessarily gray but is chosen based on the foreground and background colors.

- `CAIRO_ANTIALIAS_SUBPIXEL`: Use subpixel shading that is provided by LCD screens.

This is simply a short introduction to Cairo drawing contexts that is provided to give you a taste of the topic. For further information on using Cairo, you should reference its API documentation, available at `www.cairographics.org`.

Recent Files

In GTK+ 2.10, a new API was introduced that allows you to keep track of recently opened files across applications. In this section, we are going to implement this functionality in the simple text editing application. This application with a recent file chooser is shown in Figure 12-4. Later, in this chapter's exercise, you are going to add recent file support to your text editor.

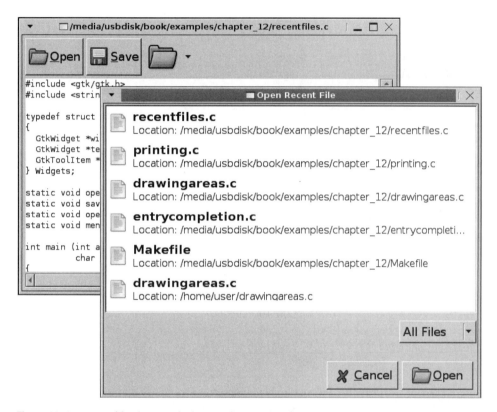

Figure 12-4. *Recent file chooser dialog used in a text editor*

The code in Listing 12-7 sets up the text editing application. Two buttons allow you to open an existing file using a GtkFileChooserDialog and save your changes. Then, there is a GtkMenuToolButton that provides two functions. When the button is clicked, a GtkRecentChooserDialog is displayed that allows you to select a recent file from the list. The menu in the GtkMenuToolButton widget is of the type GtkRecentChooserMenu, which shows the ten most recent files.

Listing 12-7. *Remembering Recently Opened Files (recentfiles.c)*

```c
#include <gtk/gtk.h>

typedef struct
{
  GtkWidget *window;
  GtkWidget *textview;
} Widgets;

static void open_file (GtkButton*, Widgets*);
static void save_file (GtkButton*, Widgets*);
static void open_recent_file (GtkButton*, Widgets*);
static void menu_activated (GtkMenuShell*, Widgets*);

int main (int argc,
          char *argv[])
{
  GtkWidget *vbox, *hbox, *open, *save, *swin, *icon, *menu;
  PangoFontDescription *fd;
  GtkRecentManager *manager;
  Widgets *w;

  gtk_init (&argc, &argv);

  w = g_slice_new (Widgets);
  w->window = gtk_window_new (GTK_WINDOW_TOPLEVEL);
  gtk_window_set_title (GTK_WINDOW (w->window), "Recent Files");
  gtk_container_set_border_width (GTK_CONTAINER (w->window), 5);
  gtk_widget_set_size_request (w->window, 600, 400);

  g_signal_connect (G_OBJECT (w->window), "destroy",
                    G_CALLBACK (gtk_main_quit), NULL);

  w->textview = gtk_text_view_new ();
  fd = pango_font_description_from_string ("Monospace 10");
  gtk_widget_modify_font (w->textview, fd);
  pango_font_description_free (fd);

  swin = gtk_scrolled_window_new (NULL, NULL);
  open = gtk_button_new_from_stock (GTK_STOCK_OPEN);
  save = gtk_button_new_from_stock (GTK_STOCK_SAVE);
  icon = gtk_image_new_from_stock (GTK_STOCK_OPEN, GTK_ICON_SIZE_BUTTON);
  w->recent = gtk_menu_tool_button_new (icon, "Recent Files");
```

```
  /* Load the default recent chooser menu and create a menu from it. */
  manager = gtk_recent_manager_get_default ();
  menu = gtk_recent_chooser_menu_new_for_manager (manager);
  gtk_menu_tool_button_set_menu (GTK_MENU_TOOL_BUTTON (w->recent), menu);

  gtk_recent_chooser_set_show_not_found (GTK_RECENT_CHOOSER (menu), FALSE);
  gtk_recent_chooser_set_local_only (GTK_RECENT_CHOOSER (menu), TRUE);
  gtk_recent_chooser_set_limit (GTK_RECENT_CHOOSER (menu), 10);
  gtk_recent_chooser_set_sort_type (GTK_RECENT_CHOOSER (menu),
                                    GTK_RECENT_SORT_MRU);

  g_signal_connect (G_OBJECT (menu), "selection-done",
                    G_CALLBACK (menu_activated), (gpointer) w);

  /* ... Connect other signals and populate the window ... */

  gtk_container_add (GTK_CONTAINER (w->window), vbox);
  gtk_widget_show_all (w->window);

  gtk_main ();
  return 0;
}

/* Save the changes that the user made to the file to disk. */
static void
save_file (GtkButton *save,
           Widgets *w)
{
  const gchar *filename;
  gchar *content;
  GtkTextBuffer *buffer;
  GtkTextIter start, end;

  filename = gtk_window_get_title (GTK_WINDOW (w->window));
  buffer = gtk_text_view_get_buffer (GTK_TEXT_VIEW (w->textview));
  gtk_text_buffer_get_bounds (buffer, &start, &end);
  content = gtk_text_buffer_get_text (buffer, &start, &end, FALSE);

  if (!g_file_set_contents (filename, content, -1, NULL))
    g_warning ("The file '%s' could not be written!", filename);
  g_free (content);
}
```

A central class called GtkRecentManager handles recent file information. It is possible to create your own from scratch, but if you want to share recent files across applications, you can retrieve the default with gtk_recent_manager_get_default(). This will allow you to share recent files with applications such as GEdit, GNOME's recent documents menu, and others that take advantage of the GtkRecentManager API.

We next create a new GtkRecentChooserMenu widget from the default GtkRecentManager. This menu displays recent files and will optionally number the menu items created with gtk_recent_chooser_menu_new_for_manager(). The files are not numbered by default, but this property can be changed by setting show-numbers to TRUE or by calling gtk_recent_chooser_menu_set_show_numbers().

GtkRecentChooserMenu implements the GtkRecentChooser interface, which provides the functionality you will need for interacting with the widget. In Listing 12-7, a number of GtkRecentChooser properties are used to customize the menu. These also apply to two other widgets that implement the GtkRecentChooser interface: GtkRecentChooserDialog and GtkRecentChooserWidget.

It is possible that recent files in the list have been removed since they were added. In this case, you may not want to display them in the list. You can hide recent files that no longer exist with gtk_recent_chooser_set_show_not_found(). This property will only work with files that are located on the local machine.

■**Tip** You may actually want to show files that are not found to the user. If the user selects a file that does not exist, you can then easily remove it from the list after informing the user about the problem.

By default, only local files are shown, which means that they will have a Uniform Resource Identifier (URI) prefix of file://. A URI is used to refer to things such as file locations or Internet addresses based on their prefixes. Using only the file:// prefix will guarantee that they are located on the local machine. You can set this property to FALSE in order to show recent files that are located at a remote location. You should note that remote files are not filtered out if they no longer exist!

If the list includes a large number of recent files, you will probably not want to list all of them in the menu. A menu with a hundred items is quite large! Therefore, you can use gtk_recent_chooser_set_limit() to set a maximum number of recent items that will be displayed in the menu.

```
void gtk_recent_chooser_set_limit (GtkRecentChooser *chooser,
                                   gint limit);
```

When you set a limit on the number of elements, which files are shown depends on the sort type you defined with gtk_recent_chooser_set_sort_type(). By default, this is set to GTK_RECENT_SORT_NONE. The available values in the GtkRecentSortType enumeration follow:

- GTK_RECENT_SORT_NONE: The list of recent files is not sorted at all and will be returned in the order that they appear. This should not be used when you are limiting the number of elements that are displayed, because you cannot predict which files will be displayed!

- GTK_RECENT_SORT_MRU: Sort the most recently added files first in the list. This is most likely the sorting method you will want to use, because it places the most recent file at the beginning of the list.

- GTK_RECENT_SORT_LRU: Sort the least-recently added files first in the list.

- GTK_RECENT_SORT_CUSTOM: Use a custom sorting function to sort the recent files. To use this, you will need to use gtk_recent_manager_set_sort_func() to define the sorting function to use.

The last part of this example saves the file under the specified name. When a file is opened in this text editor, the window title is set to the file name. This file name is used to save the file. Therefore, be careful because this simple text editor cannot be used to create new files!

Recent Chooser Menu

You have just learned about the GtkRecentChooserMenu widget. Listing 12-8 implements the selection-done callback function that was connected in Listing 12-7. This function retrieves the selected URI and opens the file if it exists.

Listing 12-8. *Using GtkRecentChooserMenu*

```
/* A menu item was activated. So, retrieve the file URI and open it. */
static void
menu_activated (GtkMenuShell *menu,
                Widgets *w)
{
  GtkTextBuffer *buffer;
  gchar *filename, *content, *fn;
  gsize length;

  filename = gtk_recent_chooser_get_current_uri (GTK_RECENT_CHOOSER (menu));
```

```
  if (filename != NULL)
  {
    /* Remove the "file://" prefix from the beginning of the URI if it exists. */
    fn = g_filename_from_uri (filename, NULL, NULL);

    if (g_file_get_contents (fn, &content, &length, NULL))
    {
      gtk_window_set_title (GTK_WINDOW (w->window), fn);
      buffer = gtk_text_view_get_buffer (GTK_TEXT_VIEW (w->textview));
      gtk_text_buffer_set_text (buffer, content, -1);
      g_free (content);
    }
    else
      g_warning ("The file '%s' could not be read!", filename);

    g_free (filename);
    g_free (fn);
  }
}
```

You can use gtk_recent_chooser_get_current_uri() to retrieve the currently selected recent file, since only one item can be selected. Since we restricted the menu to only displaying local files, we need to remove the file:// prefix from the URI. If you are allowing remote files to be displayed, you may need to remove different prefixes from the URI such as http://. You can use g_filename_from_uri() to remove URI prefixes.

```
gchar* g_filename_from_uri (const gchar *uri,
                            gchar **hostname,
                            GError **error);
```

After the prefix is removed, GLib attempts to open the file. If the file was successfully opened, the window title is set to the file name and the file is opened. Otherwise, a warning is presented to the user that the file could not be opened.

Adding Recent Files

When the Open button is pressed, we want to allow the user to select a file to open from a GtkFileChooserDialog. If the file is opened, it will be added to the default GtkRecentManager, which is shown in Listing 12-9.

Listing 12-9. *Open a File and Add It to the List of Recent Files*

```
/* Open a file selected by the user and add it as a new recent file. */
static void
open_file (GtkButton *open,
           Widgets *w)
{
  GtkWidget *dialog;
  GtkRecentManager *manager;
  GtkRecentData *data;
  GtkTextBuffer *buffer;
  gchar *filename, *content, *uri;
  gsize length;

  static gchar *groups[2] = {
    "testapp",
    NULL
  };

  dialog = gtk_file_chooser_dialog_new ("Open File", GTK_WINDOW (w->window),
                                        GTK_FILE_CHOOSER_ACTION_OPEN,
                                        GTK_STOCK_CANCEL, GTK_RESPONSE_CANCEL,
                                        GTK_STOCK_OPEN, GTK_RESPONSE_OK,
                                        NULL);

  if (gtk_dialog_run (GTK_DIALOG (dialog)) == GTK_RESPONSE_OK)
  {
    filename = gtk_file_chooser_get_filename (GTK_FILE_CHOOSER (dialog));

    if (g_file_get_contents (filename, &content, &length, NULL))
    {
      /* Create a new recently used resource. */
      data = g_slice_new (GtkRecentData);
      data->display_name = NULL;
      data->description = NULL;
      data->mime_type = "text/plain";
      data->app_name = (gchar*) g_get_application_name ();
      data->app_exec = g_strjoin (" ", g_get_prgname (), "%u", NULL);
      data->groups = groups;
      data->is_private = FALSE;
      uri = g_filename_to_uri (filename, NULL, NULL);
```

```
      /* Add the recently used resource to the default recent manager. */
      manager = gtk_recent_manager_get_default ();
      gtk_recent_manager_add_full (manager, uri, data);

      /* Load the file and set the filename as the title of the window. */
      gtk_window_set_title (GTK_WINDOW (w->window), filename);
      buffer = gtk_text_view_get_buffer (GTK_TEXT_VIEW (w->textview));
      gtk_text_buffer_set_text (buffer, content, -1);

      g_free (content);
      g_free (uri);
      g_free (data->app_exec);
      g_slice_free (GtkRecentData, data);
    }
    else
      g_warning ("The file '%s' could not be read!", filename);

    g_free (filename);
  }

  gtk_widget_destroy (dialog);
}
```

If the file is successfully opened, gtk_recent_manager_add_full() is used to add it as a new recent item to the default GtkRecentManager. In order to use this function, you need two items. First, you need the URI, which is created by appending the file name to file:// to show that it is a local file. This filename can be built with g_filename_to_uri().

```
gchar* g_filename_to_uri (const gchar *filename,
                          const gchar *hostname,
                          GError **error);
```

Secondly, you need an instance of the GtkRecentData structure. The content of this structure is shown in the following code snippet, which contains seven parameters. The display_name is a short name to display instead of the file name and description is a short description of the file. Both of these values can safely be set to NULL.

```
typedef struct
{
  gchar *display_name;
  gchar *description;
  gchar *mime_type;
  gchar *app_name;
  gchar *app_exec;
  gchar **groups;
  gboolean is_private;
} GtkRecentData;
```

You then have to specify a MIME type for the file, the name of your application, and the command line used to open the file. The name of your application can be retrieved by calling g_get_application_name(). Then, g_get_prgname() can be used to get the program name. The %f and %u characters can be used to get the file path to the resource and the URI respectively.

Next, groups is a list of strings that designate what groups the resource belongs to. You are able to use this to filter out files that do not belong to a specific group. For example, if a filter for the group testapp is added to a GtkRecentChooser, only recent files added by this application will be displayed.

The last member, is_private, specifies whether this resource will be available to applications that did not register it. By setting this to TRUE, you can prevent other applications that use the GtkRecentManager API from displaying this recent file.

Once you construct the GtkRecentData instance, it can be added along with the recent file URI as a new resource with gtk_recent_manager_add_full(). You can also add a new recent item with gtk_recent_manager_add_item(), which will create a GtkRecentData object for you.

To remove a recent item, call gtk_recent_manager_remove_item(). This function will return TRUE if a file with the specified URI is successfully removed. If not, an error under the GtkRecentManagerError domain will be set. You can also remove all recent items from the list with gtk_recent_manager_purge_items().

```
gboolean gtk_recent_manager_remove_item (GtkRecentManager *manager,
                                         const gchar *uri,
                                         GError **error);
```

■**Caution** You should avoid purging all of the items in the default GtkRecentManager! This will remove recent items that are registered by every application, which the user probably does not want since your application should usually not be altering recent resources from other applications.

Recent Chooser Dialog

GTK+ also provides another widget called GtkRecentChooserDialog, which displays recent files in a convenient dialog. This widget implements the GtkRecentChooser interface, so it is very similar in functionality to GtkRecentChooserMenu. Listing 12-10 shows you how to use this widget to allow the user to choose a recent file to open.

Listing 12-10. *Using GtkRecentChooserDialog*

```
/* Allow the user to choose a recent file from the list in the dialog. */
static void
open_recent_file (GtkButton *recent,
                  Widgets *w)
{
  GtkWidget *dialog;
  GtkRecentManager *manager;
```

```
GtkTextBuffer *buffer;
GtkRecentFilter *filter;
gchar *filename, *content, *fn;
gsize length;

manager = gtk_recent_manager_get_default ();
dialog = gtk_recent_chooser_dialog_new_for_manager ("Open Recent File",
                                    GTK_WINDOW (w->window), manager,
                                    GTK_STOCK_CANCEL, GTK_RESPONSE_CANCEL,
                                    GTK_STOCK_OPEN, GTK_RESPONSE_OK, NULL);

/* Add a filter that will display all of the files in the dialog. */
filter = gtk_recent_filter_new ();
gtk_recent_filter_set_name (filter, "All Files");
gtk_recent_filter_add_pattern (filter, "*");
gtk_recent_chooser_add_filter (GTK_RECENT_CHOOSER (dialog), filter);

/* Add another filter that will only display plain text files. */
filter = gtk_recent_filter_new ();
gtk_recent_filter_set_name (filter, "Plain Text");
gtk_recent_filter_add_mime_type (filter, "text/plain");
gtk_recent_chooser_add_filter (GTK_RECENT_CHOOSER (dialog), filter);

gtk_recent_chooser_set_show_not_found (GTK_RECENT_CHOOSER (dialog), FALSE);
gtk_recent_chooser_set_local_only (GTK_RECENT_CHOOSER (dialog), TRUE);
gtk_recent_chooser_set_limit (GTK_RECENT_CHOOSER (dialog), 10);
gtk_recent_chooser_set_sort_type (GTK_RECENT_CHOOSER (dialog),
                                  GTK_RECENT_SORT_MRU);

if (gtk_dialog_run (GTK_DIALOG (dialog)) == GTK_RESPONSE_OK)
{
  filename = gtk_recent_chooser_get_current_uri (GTK_RECENT_CHOOSER (dialog));

  if (filename != NULL)
  {
    /* Remove the "file://" prefix from the beginning of the URI if it exists. */
    fn = g_filename_from_uri (filename, NULL, NULL);
```

```
      if (g_file_get_contents (fn, &content, &length, NULL))
      {
        gtk_window_set_title (GTK_WINDOW (w->window), fn);
        buffer = gtk_text_view_get_buffer (GTK_TEXT_VIEW (w->textview));
        gtk_text_buffer_set_text (buffer, content, -1);
        g_free (content);
      }
      else
        g_warning ("The file '%s' could not be read!", filename);

      g_free (filename);
      g_free (fn);
    }
  }

  gtk_widget_destroy (dialog);
}
```

New GtkRecentChooserDialog widgets are created in a similar way to dialogs with gtk_recent_chooser_dialog_new_for_manager(). This function accepts a title for the dialog, a parent window, a GtkRecentManager widget to display, and pairs of buttons and response identifiers.

Listing 12-10 then introduces recent file filters. New GtkRecentFilter objects are created with gtk_recent_chooser_new(). Filters are used to display only recent files that follow installed patterns.

```
gtk_recent_filter_set_name (filter, "All Files");
gtk_recent_filter_add_pattern (filter, "*");
gtk_recent_chooser_add_filter (GTK_RECENT_CHOOSER (dialog), filter);
```

The next step is to set the name of the filter. This name will be displayed in the combo box where the user will choose which filter to use. There are many ways to create filters, including with gtk_recent_filter_add_pattern(), which finds filters with matching patterns. The asterisk character can be used as the wildcard. There are also functions for matching MIME types, image file types, application names, group names, and ages in days. Next, use gtk_recent_chooser_add_filter() to add the GtkRecentFilter to the recent chooser.

With the GtkRecentChooserDialog widgets, it is possible to choose multiple files with gtk_recent_chooser_set_select_multiple(). If the user can select multiple files, you will want to use gtk_recent_chooser_get_uris() to retrieve all of the selected files.

```
gchar** gtk_recent_chooser_get_uris (GtkRecentChooser *chooser,
                                     gsize *length);
```

This function also returns the number of elements in the NULL-terminated list of strings. You should free the list with g_strfreev() after you are finished using it.

Automatic Completion

You learned about the GtkEntry widget in Chapter 4, but GTK+ also provides the GtkEntryCompletion object. GtkEntryCompletion is derived from GObject and can be used to provide the user with automatic completion in a GtkEntry widget. Figure 12-5 shows an example GtkEntry that is providing the user with multiple selections. Note that the user also has the option of ignoring the choices and entering an arbitrary string.

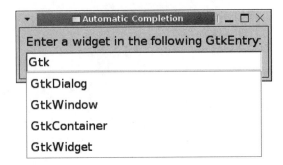

Figure 12-5. *GtkEntryCompletion automatic completion*

Listing 12-11 implements a GtkEntry widget that asks you to enter the name of a GTK+ widget. All of the strings in the GtkEntryCompletion widget that have the same prefix as the entered text are displayed as choices. This example shows just how easy it is to get automatic completion up and running.

Listing 12-11. *Automatic Completion (entrycompletion.c)*

```
#include <gtk/gtk.h>

#define NUM_ELEMENTS 4

static gchar *widgets[] = { "GtkDialog", "GtkWindow", "GtkContainer", "GtkWidget" };

int main (int argc,
          char *argv[])
```

```
{
  GtkWidget *window, *vbox, *label, *entry;
  GtkEntryCompletion *completion;
  GtkListStore *store;
  GtkTreeIter iter;
  unsigned int i;

  gtk_init (&argc, &argv);

  window = gtk_window_new (GTK_WINDOW_TOPLEVEL);
  gtk_window_set_title (GTK_WINDOW (window), "Automatic Completion");
  gtk_container_set_border_width (GTK_CONTAINER (window), 10);

  label = gtk_label_new ("Enter a widget in the following GtkEntry:");
  entry = gtk_entry_new ();

  /* Create a GtkListStore that will hold autocompletion possibilities. */
  store = gtk_list_store_new (1, G_TYPE_STRING);
  for (i = 0; i < NUM_ELEMENTS; i++)
  {
    gtk_list_store_append (store, &iter);
    gtk_list_store_set (store, &iter, 0, widgets[i], -1);
  }

  completion = gtk_entry_completion_new ();
  gtk_entry_set_completion (GTK_ENTRY (entry), completion);
  gtk_entry_completion_set_model (completion, GTK_TREE_MODEL (store));
  gtk_entry_completion_set_text_column (completion, 0);

  vbox = gtk_vbox_new (FALSE, 5);
  gtk_box_pack_start (GTK_BOX (vbox), label, FALSE, FALSE, 0);
  gtk_box_pack_start (GTK_BOX (vbox), entry, FALSE, FALSE, 0);

  gtk_container_add (GTK_CONTAINER (window), vbox);
  gtk_widget_show_all (window);

  g_object_unref (completion);
  g_object_unref (store);

  gtk_main ();
  return 0;
}
```

To implement a GtkEntryCompletion, you need to first create a new GtkListStore that will display the choices. The model in this example only has one textual column, but it is acceptable to provide a more complex GtkListStore as long as one column is of the type G_TYPE_STRING.

New GtkEntryCompletion objects are created with gtk_entry_completion_new(). You can then apply it to an existing GtkEntry widget with gtk_entry_set_completion(). GTK+ will take care of displaying matches and applying the choices by default.

Next, gtk_entry_completion_set_model() is used to apply the tree model to the GtkEntryCompletion object. If there was already a model applied to the object, it will be replaced. You will also have to use gtk_entry_completion_set_text_column() to designate which column contains the string, since models do not have to be only a single column. If you do not set the text column, automatic completion will not work because the text column is set to -1 by default.

It is possible to display as much of the prefix as is common to all of the matches with gtk_entry_completion_set_inline_completion(). You should note that inline completion is case sensitive, but automatic completion is not! If you are using this, you may want to set gtk_entry_completion_set_popup_single_match(), which will prevent the pop-up menu from being displayed when there is only a single match.

You can use gtk_entry_completion_set_popup_set_width() to force the pop-up menu to be the same width as the GtkEntry widget. This corresponds to GtkEntryCompletion's popup-set-width property.

If there are a lot of matches, you may want to set the minimum match length with gtk_entry_completion_set_minimum_key_length(). This is useful when there is such a large number of elements in the list that it would take a long time for the list to be rendered on the screen.

Test Your Understanding

In this chapter's exercise, you will be finishing the text editing application that has been the focus of multiple exercises in past chapters. It will require you to integrate the automatic completion, printing, and recent file capabilities into your application.

Exercise 12-1. Creating a Full Text Editor

In this exercise, you are going to complete the text editor that you have been creating the last few chapters. You will add three new features to the application.

First, add the automatic completion feature, which should be implemented to remember past searches in the search toolbar. The application has to remember the past searches for only the current instance of the application runtimes. Next, add printing support, which includes printing and print preview abilities. Printing support can be easily implemented with the high-level GtkPrintOperation API. Lastly, instruct the text editor to remember the last five files loaded using the GtkRecentManager API.

So that you do not have to rewrite previous aspects of the application, you should use the solution to a Chapter 10 exercise or download that solution from this book's official web site.

Summary

In this chapter, you learned about a number of widgets that did not quite fit into previous chapters. These widgets and objects are summarized in the following list:

- GtkDrawingArea: An empty widget that is meant to allow you to draw on its GdkWindow object, which is also a GdkDrawable object.

- GtkLayout: This widget is like GtkDrawingArea, except it allows you to embed widgets within its interface as well. It introduces overhead, so you should not use this widget if you want only drawing capabilities.

- GtkCalendar: Display a single month for the chosen year. This widget allows the user to select a date, and you can mark multiple dates programmatically.

- GtkStatusIcon: Display an icon in the task bar on supported platforms to provide a message to the user. You can also provide a pop-up menu or tooltip and detect when the icon is activated.

- GtkPrintOperation: A high-level printing API that is platform independent. There are many other objects provided for implementing printing support, but most actions should be handled with the GtkPrintOperation API so that it will function across multiple platforms.

- GtkRecentManager: A simple API for managing lists of recent files. These lists can be shared across applications. Menu and dialog widgets are provided for displaying recent files.

- GtkEntryCompletion: Provide automatic completion support to GtkEntry widgets. The choices are composed of a GtkListStore object filled with possible matches.

You have now learned all of the topics that this book intended to introduce. In the next chapter, you will be presented with five complete applications that take advantage of topics that were covered in the past twelve chapters.

CHAPTER 13

■■■

Putting It All Together

Throughout the past twelve chapters you have been given an in-depth view of everything you can do with GTK+ and associated technologies. In this chapter, we're going to put this knowledge to work by building a few applications.

This chapter introduces five full applications: the file browser that was designed in Chapter 10, a calculator, a ping utility, a Hangman game, and a calendar. However, the source code for the examples is not contained in this chapter. The code for each of the applications in this chapter can be downloaded from www.gtkbook.com.

Finally, I will conclude the final chapter of this book by offering some pointers to other learning resources, so you can continue expanding your GTK+ knowledge.

File Browser

In Chapter 10, you implemented the user interface for a file browser application in Glade. That user interface was then dynamically loaded with Libglade and all of the signals were autoconnected with glade_xml_signal_autoconnect().

At the end of that chapter, you were told that the callback functions would be implemented in Chapter 13, and we will do so now. Figure 13-1 shows the file browser application when it is first launched and is displaying the root folder.

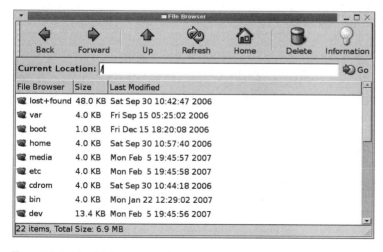

Figure 13-1. *The file browser using GtkTreeView*

471

Of special interest in this application are the actual file browsing abilities. These are very similar to those in Exercise 8-1. In that exercise, you created a simple application using a GtkTreeView widget that could browse throughout the user's file system. The current location of the file browser is stored in a linked list from which the full path can be built. Each node in the list is one part of the path, and the directory separator is placed between each string to build the full path. A GtkEntry widget is also provided to allow the user to edit the path with the keyboard.

Navigation through the file system can be done using a few different methods. As previously mentioned, a location can be entered into the address bar, although the validity of the location must be verified when the GtkEntry widget is activated. In addition to this method, the user can use the Back, Forward, Up, or Home toolbar buttons to navigate throughout the browsing history, move to the parent directory, or go to the home directory respectively. Lastly, GtkTreeView's row-activated signal allows the user to move into the selected directory or view information about the selected file.

A GtkStatusBar widget is placed along the bottom of the window. It is used to keep track of the total number of items in the current directory and the total size of these items. The sources for this example, along with the four other applications in this chapter, can be downloaded from www.gtkbook.com.

Calculator

A calculator is a simple application that is implemented in most GUI programming books. This example is meant to show you just how easy it is to implement a calculator. A screenshot of the application can be viewed in Figure 13-2.

Figure 13-2. *A simple calculator application*

This calculator application was designed in Glade, so the user interface was already completed with absolutely no code. Next, glade_xml_signal_autoconnect() was used to connect all of the buttons to their signals. Since most of the widgets in this example are GtkButton widgets, the clicked and destroy signals were the only two needed.

The calculator allows the user to enter numbers with an optional decimal point, perform the four basic operations (add, subtract, multiply, and divide), negate numbers, and calculate square roots and exponents. In order to cut down on the number of callback functions needed, all of the numbers and the decimal place were connected to a single callback function called num_clicked(), and the four basic operations and the power operations were connected to another. This allows you to take advantage of the fact that these groups of operations need a lot of similar code to work.

When a number or the decimal point button is clicked, the character is appended to the end of the current value, although the length of the number is restricted to ten digits. When an operation button is clicked, the operation is performed, and the new value is stored. It also sets a flag called clear_flag that tells the calculator that a new number should be started when the user presses a number or decimal place.

The square root operation is not grouped with the other operations, because it is immediately performed on the displayed value in the sqrt_clicked() callback function. In order to do this, it simply takes the current value displayed in the GtkEntry widget, calculates the square root of the number, and stores the result back in the GtkEntry widget. Likewise, the negate operation also takes effect immediately. The exponential operation, on the other hand, asks for the power after it is clicked.

Hangman

The hangman application, shown in Figure 3-3, takes advantage of the GtkDrawingArea widget that you learned about in the previous chapter. The character, border, and current puzzle are drawn on the GtkDrawingArea widget. Next, a table of buttons, one for each of the alphabetic characters, is placed along the bottom of the window. Each button becomes insensitive when clicked.

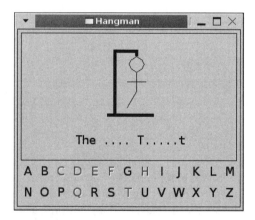

Figure 13-3. *A hangman game using GtkDrawingArea*

The important thing to remember about drawing areas is that you will want to connect the widget to the expose-event signal. Every time the user resizes the window, changes focus, or moves the window, the widget will be cleared. In the hangman application, the drawing area had to be reconstructed every time an expose-event occurred.

Within this callback function, gdk_draw_lines() was used to draw the border around the window from a set of points. Next, gdk_draw_polygon() was used to draw the scaffolding from a set of points. Notice in the solution that the third parameter of this function is set to TRUE, which causes the polygon to be filled in with the color specified in the widget's style.

Then, the current puzzle string is added to a PangoLayout, where any characters that are not yet discovered are set as the period character. The puzzle is aligned in the center of the border according to its width, since its size will vary depending on the current puzzle. The layout is drawn to the drawing area's GdkWindow with gdk_draw_layout().

Lastly, gdk_draw_line() and gdk_draw_polygon() are again used to draw the actual character, although what is drawn depends on how many wrong guesses the user has made.

When a letter is clicked, the callback function loops through the current puzzle, revealing any of the characters that have been found. If no matches are found, another appendage is added to the hangman. If the state reaches 5, the user loses. If the whole solution was filled, then the user wins.

Ping Utility

In Chapter 6, you learned how to use GIOChannel to communicate with applications through pipes. A ping utility application is displayed in Figure 13-4; it allows the user to ping an address a specific number of times or continually until the application is stopped.

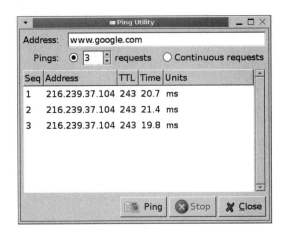

Figure 13-4. *A ping utility application*

In this application, g_spawn_async_with_pipes() is used to fork an instance of the ping application with the specified address. The shell command received by this function was parsed with g_shell_parse_argv() so that it was in the correct format. The Ping button is also disabled, which prevents the user from running multiple instances of the child process.

After spawning the child process, the output pipe is used to create a new GIOChannel object that watches the pipe for read data. When data is ready to be read, it is parsed so that statistics for each ping can be displayed in a GtkTreeView widget. This will continue the specified number of times or until the user stops the child.

When a child process is running, a Stop button is enabled, which allows the user to kill the child process before it completes. This function simply calls the following instance of the kill() function, which forces the child process to close:

```
kill (pid, SIGINT);
```

When the process is killed, the pipe will be destroyed, which will cause the GIOChannel to be shut down in the watch function. This ensures that we will be able to reuse the same GIOChannel object for the next child process.

Calendar

The last application in this chapter creates a calendar that organizes events for the user. It uses the GtkCalendar widget to allow the user to browse throughout dates and GtkTreeView to display events for the given day. Figure 13-5 shows this calendar application.

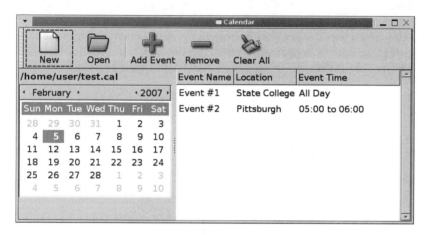

Figure 13-5. *A calendar application with two events*

Most of the code that was used to create the calendar application should look very familiar, because it uses functions introduced in previous chapters. In addition to the familiar functions, the application uses the XML parser provided by GLib to open calendar files, which are stored as XML files. An example calendar file that contains one event is shown in Listing 13-1.

Listing 13-1. *Calendar File (test.cal)*

```
<calendar>
  <event>
    <name>Release of the Book</name>
    <location>Everywhere</location>
    <day>16</day>
    <month>3</month>
    <year>2007</year>
    <start>All Day</start>
    <end></end>
  </event>
</calendar>
```

A new calendar is created by clicking the New toolbar button, which will ask for a calendar file name and location. The calendar is saved every time you add or remove an event, so a Save button is not provided. You can also open an existing calendar by pressing the Open toolbar button.

Markup Parser Functions

To open a calendar, this application uses GLib's XML parser to retrieve the content of the file. This parser is very easy to use and supports basic XML files. The first thing you need to do to use the parser is to define a new GMarkupParser structure. This structure contains five functions, which I will cover one at a time. Any of these functions can be set to NULL except error().

The first function, start_element() is called for every open tag such as <calendar> and <event>. This function receives the name of the tag element along with arrays of attribute names and values. This allows you to differentiate between starting elements, checking for attributes when appropriate. In the calendar application, this function is used to free all of the temporary data stored for the previous event, creating a clean slate for the next event.

```
void (*start_element) (GMarkupParseContext *context,
                       const gchar *element_name,
                       const gchar **attribute_names,
                       const gchar **attribute_values,
                       gpointer data,
                       GError **error);
```

The next function, end_element(), is called for every close tag such as </calendar> and </event>. It is also called for tags that have no close tag such as <tag/>. Similar to the previous function, it accepts the tag name. In the calendar application, it is used to add the event to the global tree if the </event> tag has been reached.

```
void (*end_element) (GMarkupParseContext *context,
                     const gchar *element_name,
                     gpointer data,
                     GError **error);
```

The text() function is called for the data found between start_element() and end_element() calls. It accepts the text between the two tags as well as the length of the text. You should note that the text string is *not* NULL-terminated! This function is called in the calendar application to read the content of an event.

```
void (*text) (GMarkupParseContext *context,
              const gchar *text,
              gsize text_len,
              gpointer data,
              GError **error);
```

Note The text() function is not only called for tags that contain strings but also for tags that call other tags. Therefore, this function may have a text parameter filled with spaces and new line characters! You can use g_markup_parse_context_get_element() to retrieve the tag that contains the string.

The passthrough() function is not used in the calendar application. It is called for elements that are not XML and should retain their current position such as comments. As with text(), the passthrough_text string is *not* NULL-terminated!

```
void (*passthrough) (GMarkupParseContext *context,
                     const gchar *passthrough_text,
                     gsize text_len,
                     gpointer data,
                     GError **error);
```

Lastly, the error() function is called when an error occurs in the parsing. This is the only function that must be set within GMarkupParser.

```
void (*error) (GMarkupParseContext *context,
               GError *error,
               gpointer data);
```

Parsing the XML File

The actual parsing of the XML text is done with a GMarkupParseContext object. You can create a new parser with g_markup_parse_context_new():

```
GMarkupParseContext* g_markup_parse_context_new (const GMarkupParser *parser,
                                                 GMarkupParseFlags flags,
                                                 gpointer data,
                                                 GDestroyNotify user_data_dnotify);
```

This function first accepts a GMarkupParser object, which contains functions that will be called for elements within the XML file. Then, it accepts flags defined by GMarkupParseFlags. There is only one available flag—G_MARKUP_TREAT_CDATA_AS_TEXT. If this flag is set, sections marked as CDATA will be passed to your implementation of text() instead of passthrough(). The last two parameters of g_markup_parse_context_new() allow you to pass data to the GMarkupParser functions and provide a function to call when the parser is freed.

Parsing of XML is performed with g_markup_parse_context_parse(). When you call this function, it will step through all of the tags in the provided text string, calling the appropriate GMarkupParser functions. This function will return TRUE if the parsing was successful.

```
gboolean g_markup_parse_context_parse (GMarkupParseContext *context,
                                       const gchar *text,
                                       gssize text_len,
                                       GError **error);
```

You should call g_markup_parse_context_free() when you are finished with the parse context. This function cannot be called from within one of your GMarkupParser functions.

Further Resources

Congratulations! You have now completed reading this book and know enough to develop and manage complex GTK+ applications. However, you may be wondering where you should go from here. There are a number of libraries and resources that will become indispensable as you begin developing applications on your own.

The first resource, as mentioned throughout this book, is the official web site of this book, which you can find at www.gtkbook.com. This site includes links to online resources for GTK+ developers as well as tutorials on topics that did not fit in this book. You can use it as a starting point for finding help with GTK+ application development.

Another great resource is the GTK+ web site, found at www.gtk.org. This site includes information about mailing lists, downloads, and bug tracking for GTK+. You can find up-to-date documentation on this site as well. The GNOME developer's home page, found at http://developer.gnome.org is also an ideal place to learn more.

In addition to GTK+ and its supporting libraries, there are a number of other libraries used to develop applications for GNOME that you will continually run across. The following list gives a brief summary of the purposes of a few of these libraries; you can find more information about these libraries at http://developer.gnome.org:

- Libgnome: Usually distributed with Libgnomeui, these libraries provide a number of other objects and widgets that expand the functionality of current GTK+ widgets. In recent releases, the most frequently used widgets from these libraries have been consolidated into GTK+. For example, Libgnomeprint and Libgnomeprintui are now implemented as printing support in GTK+.

- GConf: A system used by GNOME to store various settings for applications and the desktop environment itself. You can use the GConf library to store many types of settings for your application and watch for changes so that your application can immediately be updated. This is especially useful if multiple instances of your application are being run at the same time.

- GnomeVFS: Short for the GNOME Virtual File System, this library is simply an abstraction layer for reading, writing, and executing local or remote files. It can also be used to handle MIME file types and retrieve the MIME type of a specific file.

- ORBit: A library compliant with the Common Object Request Broker Architecture (CORBA) that is used to allow your code to make program calls between computers. It uses a standard definition that allows multiple programming languages to work together.

- Libart: A vector-based graphics library used for rendering various widgets such as GnomeCanvas. It handles complex drawing actions for the GNOME desktop environment.

- Bonobo: A set of libraries based on CORBA used by GNOME for modeling compound documents.

- VTE: A terminal emulator widget that is used by many applications in GNOME. It allows you to embed a terminal into any application as a GtkWidget.

Summary

In the past thirteen chapters, you have become familiar with a large portion of GTK+ and its supporting libraries. This knowledge can be used to implement graphical user interfaces for applications on many platforms.

This book is intended to give you a thorough understanding of GTK+, and I hope that it will continue to be a valuable resource as you develop applications. The first five appendixes are indispensable references for topics that are not always thoroughly documented in the API documentation and can be used even when you become an expert. The sixth appendix provides short descriptions of exercise solutions along with tips on how to complete them.

Now that you have this knowledge, practice and experience will help you become a great graphical application developer. You have everything you need to continue on your own. I hope you have had as much fun reading this book as I have had writing it!

APPENDIX A

■■■

GTK+ Properties

GObject provides a property system, which allows you to customize how widgets interact with the user and how they are drawn on the screen. In the following sections, you will be provided with a complete reference to widget and child properties available in GTK+ 2.10.

GTK+ Properties

Every class derived from GObject can create any number of properties. In GTK+, these properties store information about the current state of the widget. For example, GtkButton has a property called relief that defines the type of relief border used by the button in its normal state.

In the following code, g_object_get() was used to retrieve the current value stored by the button's relief property. This function accepts a NULL-terminated list of properties and variables to store the returned value. You can also use g_object_set() to set each object property as well.

```
g_object_get (button, "relief", &value, NULL);
```

There are a great number of properties available to widgets; Tables A-1 to A-90 provide a full properties list for each widget and object in GTK+ 2.10. Remember that object properties are inherited from parent widgets, so you should investigate a widget's hierarchy for a full list of properties. For more information on each object, you should reference the API documentation.

Table A-1. *GtkAboutDialog Properties*

Property	Type	Description
artists	GStrv	A list of individuals who helped create the artwork used by the application. This often includes information such as an e-mail address or URL for each artist, which will be displayed as a link.
authors	GStrv	A list of individuals who helped program the application. This often includes information such as an e-mail address or URL for each programmer, which will be displayed as a link.

Continued

Table A-1. *Continued*

Property	Type	Description
comments	gchararray	A short string that describes the general functionality of the program. This is displayed in the main dialog window, so it should not be too long.
copyright	gchararray	Copyright information about the application. This is displayed in the main dialog window, so it should not be too long. An example copyright string would be "(C) Copyright 2007 Author".
documenters	GStrv	A list of individuals who helped write documentation for the application. This often includes information such as an e-mail address or URL for each documenter, which will be displayed as a link.
license	gchararray	The content of the license for the application. This is displayed with a GtkTextView widget in a secondary dialog, so the length of the string does not matter.
logo	GdkPixbuf	An image that will be displayed as the application's logo in the main window. If this is not set, gtk_window_get_default_icon_list() will be used.
logo-icon-name	gchararray	An icon name from the icon theme to use as the logo in the main About dialog. If this is set, it will take precedence over the logo property.
name	gchararray	The name of the application to display in the main About dialog. If you do not set this property, g_get_application_name() will be used.
translator-credits	gchararray	A string that holds information about the translator(s) for the current language. It should be set as translatable, so each translator can provide a custom string. This often includes information such as an e-mail address or URL for each translator, which will be displayed as a link.
version	gchararray	The version of the application that the user is running.
website	gchararray	A URL to the homepage for the application. This string must be prefixed with http://.

Property	Type	Description
website-label	gchararray	A label to display in place of the web site URL. If this is not set, website will be set as the URL label.
wrap-license	gboolean	If set to TRUE, the license content will be wrapped.

Table A-2. *GtkAccelLabel Properties*

Property	Type	Description
accel-closure	GClosure	The closure that should be watched for changes to the keyboard accelerator.
accel-widget	GtkWidget	The widget that should be watched for changes to the keyboard accelerator.

Table A-3. *GtkAction Properties*

Property	Type	Description
action-group	GtkActionGroup	An action group that the action belongs to. You can set this to NULL if the action does not belong to an action group.
hide-if-empty	gboolean	If set to TRUE, menu proxies that are empty will be hidden from view.
icon-name	gchararray	The name of the icon to use from the icon theme. This property is overridden by the stock-id property.
is-important	gboolean	If a toolbar is in GTK_TOOLBAR_BOTH_HORIZ mode, this property will display the label for the item when set to TRUE. Otherwise, it will have no effect.
label	gchararray	The text to display in the menu item or button. Toolbar items use the short-label property.
name	gchararray	A unique string that distinguishes the action.
sensitive	gboolean	If set to TRUE, the action will be enabled. Otherwise, the user will not be able to interact with it.
short-label	gchararray	The text to display in the tool item. Menu items and buttons use the label property.

Continued

Table A-3. *Continued*

Property	Type	Description
stock-id	gchararray	The stock icon to display for widgets using the action. This property takes precedence over icon-name.
tooltip	gchararray	A tooltip for the action that will be displayed when the user hovers over a toolbar item.
visible	gboolean	If set to TRUE, the action will be visible to the user.
visible-horizontal	gboolean	If set to TRUE, the action will be visible in toolbars when the toolbar orientation is set as horizontal.
visible-overflown	gboolean	If set to TRUE, the action will be displayed in the toolbar overflow menu. Otherwise, it will be hidden from view.
visible-vertical	gboolean	If set to TRUE, the action will be visible in toolbars when the toolbar orientation is set as vertical.

Table A-4. *GtkActionGroup Properties*

Property	Type	Description
name	gchararray	A string that distinguishes the action group.
sensitive	gboolean	If set to TRUE, the action group is set as active or enabled.
visible	gboolean	If set to TRUE, the action group will be visible to the user.

Table A-5. *GtkAdjustment Properties*

Property	Type	Description
lower	gdouble	The minimum gdouble value that the adjustment can reach.
page-increment	gdouble	The increment that will be shifted when moving one page forward or backward.

Property	Type	Description
page-size	gdouble	The size of a page of the adjustment. You should set this to zero when you use GtkAdjustment for GtkSpinButton.
step-increment	gdouble	The increment that will be moved in an individual step. For example, with GtkSpinButton, a single step will be taken when an arrow button is pressed.
upper	gdouble	The maximum gdouble value that the adjustment can reach.
value	gdouble	The current value of the adjustment, which is always between lower and upper.

Table A-6. *GtkAlignment Properties*

Property	Type	Description
bottom-padding	guint	Padding added along the bottom of the child widget
left-padding	guint	Padding added along the left side of the child widget
right-padding	guint	Padding added along the right side of the child widget
top-padding	guint	Padding added along the top of the child widget
xalign (yalign)	gfloat	A number between 0.0 and 1.0 used to align the child widget, where 1.0 is aligned to the right side or bottom of the container
xscale (yscale)	gfloat	A number between 0.0 and 1.0 used to expand the child to fill extra space

Table A-7. *GtkArrow Properties*

Property	Type	Description
arrow-type	GtkArrowType	The direction the GtkArrow will point
shadow-type	GtkShadowType	The type of shadow to place around the arrow

Table A-8. *GtkAspectFrame Properties*

Property	Type	Description
obey-child	gboolean	If set to TRUE, use the aspect ratio defined by the child widget instead of the ratio property.
ratio	gfloat	A number between 0.0001 and 10,000 that defines the aspect ratio.
xalign (yalign)	gfloat	The alignment of the child within the container as defined by a number between 0.0 and 1.0, where 0.5 is centered.

Table A-9. *GtkBox Properties*

Property	Type	Description
homogeneous	gboolean	If set to TRUE, all of the children will be set to the same size.
spacing	gint	The spacing to add between each child and its neighbors.

Table A-10. *GtkButton Properties*

Property	Type	Description
focus-on-click	gboolean	If set to TRUE, the button will grab focus when it is clicked by the mouse.
image	GtkWidget	A widget to display beside the button's text.
image-position	GtkPositionType	The position of image with respect to the label.
label	gchararray	A text label to display within the button if the button contains a label.
relief	GtkReliefStyle	The type of border to place around the button.
use-stock	gboolean	If set to TRUE, a stock item will be used as the button's content.
use-underline	gboolean	If set to TRUE, a mnemonic keyboard accelerator will be used for the character following an underscore.
xalign (yalign)	gfloat	A floating point number between 0.0 and 1.0 that aligns the child widget if it is a GtkMisc or GtkAlignment widget, where 0.5 is centered.

Table A-11. *GtkButtonBox Properties*

Property	Type	Description
layout-style	GtkButtonBoxStyle	The type of layout that is used for the child buttons

Table A-12. *GtkCalendar Properties*

Property	Type	Description
day	gint	The currently selected day between 1 and 31. A day of 0 will deselect the current day.
month	gint	The currently selected month between 0 and 11, where 0 is January.
no-month-change	gboolean	If set to TRUE, the user will be prevented from changing the month.
show-day-names	gboolean	If set to TRUE, the day names will be displayed above the days.
show-heading	gboolean	If set to TRUE, the calendar heading will be displayed.
show-week-numbers	gboolean	If set to TRUE, the week numbers for the current month and year will be displayed along the left side of the calendar.
year	gint	The currently selected year.

Table A-13. *GtkCellRenderer Properties*

Property	Type	Description
cell-background	gchararray	A string that represents the background color such as "Red" or "#00CC00". For this property to take effect, you have to also set cell-background-set to TRUE.
cell-background-gdk	GdkColor	The background color of the cell.
height	gint	The height of the cell. Set this property to -1 to use the default height of the cell.
is-expanded	gboolean	If the row has children, this property will be set to TRUE if the row is expanded.
is-expander	gboolean	Set to TRUE if the row has child rows.

Continued

Table A-13. *Continued*

Property	Type	Description
mode	GtkCellRendererMode	The interactivity mode of the cell.
sensitive	gboolean	If set to TRUE, the user will be able to interact with the cell.
visible	gboolean	If set the TRUE, the cell will be visible to the user.
width	gint	The width of the cell. Set this property to -1 to use the default width of the cell.
xalign (yalign)	gfloat	The alignment of the content within the cell as defined by a number between 0.0 and 1.0, where 0.5 is centered.
xpad (ypad)	guint	Horizontal and vertical padding to place on either side of the child content of the cell.

Table A-14. *GtkCellRendererAccel Properties*

Property	Type	Description
accel-key	guint	The key value for the accelerator. A list of key codes can be found in gdkkeysyms.h.
accel-mode	GtkCellRendererAccelMode	A flag value that determines whether the accelerators are GTK+ accelerators. A value of GTK_CELL_RENDERER_ ACCEL_MODE_GTK will stop accelerators that are already used from being entered.
accel-mods	GdkModifierType	A modifier to use for the accelerator.
keycode	guint	The hardware key code for the keyboard accelerator. The accel-key property should be used when the key has a key value available.

Table A-15. *GtkCellRendererCombo Properties*

Property	Type	Description
has-entry	gboolean	If set to TRUE, a GtkComboBoxEntry widget will be displayed when the cell is being edited.
model	GtkTreeModel	The tree model that defines the choices in the GtkComboBox widget.
text-column	gint	The column number in model that will be displayed when the cell is not being edited.

Table A-16. *GtkCellRendererPixbuf Properties*

Property	Type	Description
follow-state	gboolean	If set to TRUE, the pixbuf will be colored based on GtkCellRendererState.
icon-name	gchararray	An icon to display from the icon theme. The stock-id and pixbuf properties take precedence over this setting.
pixbuf	GdkPixbuf	An image to display in the cell. This property takes precedence over icon-name.
pixbuf-expander-closed	GdkPixbuf	An image to display as the expander when the child rows are hidden.
pixbuf-expander-open	GdkPixbuf	An image to display as the expander when the child rows are visible.
stock-detail	gchararray	A string that is sent to the theme engine that gives more information about rendering a stock item.
stock-id	gchararray	A stock identifier to use as the icon. This property takes precedence over icon-name.
stock-size	guint	The size of the stock icon to render.

Table A-17. *GtkCellRendererProgress Properties*

Property	Type	Description
text	gchararray	A text string that will be drawn over the progress bar. If this is set to NULL, the default string will be displayed.
value	gint	The amount of the progress bar that is filled in as defined by a number between 0 and 100, where 100 is completely filled.

Table A-18. *GtkCellRendererSpin Properties*

Property	Type	Description
adjustment	GtkAdjustment	The adjustment that holds information about the spin button when it is being edited. This property must be set for it to be editable.
climb-rate	gdouble	The rate of acceleration when an arrow button is held down.
digits	guint	The number of decimal places to display in the spin button when the cell is being edited. Note that this does not affect the number of decimal places being displayed when the cell is not being edited. You should use a cell data function to set the normal state digits.

Table A-19. *GtkCellRendererText Properties*

Property	Type	Description
alignment	PangoAlignment	The alignment of lines of text. You must set align-set to TRUE for this property to take effect.
attributes	PangoAttrList	A list of attributes that are applied to the renderer's text.
background	gchararray	The background color of the cell as a string. You must set background-set to TRUE for this property to take effect.
background-gdk	GdkColor	The background color of the cell.
editable	gboolean	If set to TRUE, the user will be able to edit the text. You must set editable-set to TRUE for this property to take effect.

Property	Type	Description
ellipsize	PangoEllipsizeMode	The place within the string to replace text with ellipses if there is not enough space to display the whole string. You must set ellipsize-set to TRUE for this property to take effect.
family	gchararray	The font family name such as Arial or Monospace. You must set family-set to TRUE for this property to take effect.
font	gchararray	The font description string such as "Monospace Bold 10". You must set font-set to TRUE for this property to take effect.
font-desc	PangoFontDescription	A font description that defines the font for the cell.
foreground	gchararray	The foreground color of the cell as a string. You must set foreground-set to TRUE for this property to take effect.
foreground-gdk	GdkColor	The foreground color of the cell.
language	gchararray	The language of the cell's text as an ISO code. In most cases, you will not need to use this property. You must set language-set to TRUE for this property to take effect.
markup	gchararray	Text that will be rendered by the cell that contains Pango markup.
rise	gint	The positive or negative offset of the text. You must set rise-set to TRUE for this property to take effect.
scale	gdouble	The scaling factor for the font as a gdouble value. You must set scale-set to TRUE for this property to take effect.
single-paragraph-mode	gboolean	If set to TRUE, all text will be forced into one paragraph.
size	gint	The font size of the text, scaled by a factor of PANGO_UNITS. You must set size-set to TRUE for this property to take effect.
size-points	gdouble	The font size of the text in points.
stretch	PangoStretch	A flag that is used to add or remove spacing between text characters. You must set stretch-set to TRUE for this property to take effect.

Continued

Table A-19. *Continued*

Property	Type	Description
strikethrough	gboolean	If set to TRUE, a single line will be placed through the text. You must set strikethrough-set to TRUE for this property to take effect.
style	PangoStyle	The style of the font such as italics or oblique. You must set style-set to TRUE for this property to take effect.
text	gchararray	The text to display in the cell.
underline	PangoUnderline	The style of underline to place below the text. You must set underline-set to TRUE for this property to take effect.
variant	PangoVariant	Set to PANGO_VARIANT_SMALL_CAPS to render lower case characters as small upper case characters. You must set variant-set to TRUE for this property to take effect.
weight	gint	The font weight. You must set weight-set to TRUE for this property to take effect.
width-chars	gint	The width of the cell in characters. If you set this property to -1, GTK+ will calculate the width.
wrap-mode	PangoWrapMode	The type of wrap to use for the text. By default, this is set to PANGO_WRAP_CHAR.
wrap-width	gint	The width at which text will be wrapped. If this property is set to -1, then wrapping will be disabled.

Table A-20. *GtkCellRendererToggle Properties*

Property	Type	Description
activatable	gboolean	If set to TRUE, the toggle button can be activated by the user. Otherwise, the toggle button can only be used to display a setting.
active	gboolean	If set to TRUE, the toggle button will be set as activated.
inconsistent	gboolean	If set to TRUE, the toggle button is in a state that is neither active nor inactive.

Property	Type	Description
indicator-size	gint	The size of the check button or radio button. By default, this is set to 12 pixels.
radio	gboolean	If set to TRUE, the toggle will be drawn as a radio button. However, you will have to implement the functionality of the radio buttons yourself.

Table A-21. *GtkCellView Properties*

Property	Type	Description
background	gchararray	The background color of the cell as a string. You must set background-set to TRUE for this property to take effect.
background-gdk	GdkColor	The background color of the cell.
model	GtkTreeModel	The tree model associated with the cell view. GtkCellView is used to display one column of a model.

Table A-22. *GtkCheckMenuItem Properties*

Property	Type	Description
active	gboolean	If set to TRUE, the check menu item is set as active.
draw-as-radio	gboolean	If set to TRUE, the menu item will be drawn as a radio button. However, you will have to implement the functionality of the radio buttons yourself.
inconsistent	gboolean	If set to TRUE, the toggle button will display an in-between state that is neither active nor inactive.

Table A-23. *GtkColorButton Properties*

Property	Type	Description
alpha	guint	The transparency of the selected color, where 0 is transparent and 65,535 is opaque.
color	GdkColor	The currently selected color.
title	gchararray	The title to give the GtkColorSelectionDialog displayed when the user clicks the button.
use-alpha	gboolean	If set to TRUE, the user will be given the option to select transparency.

Table A-24. *GtkColorSelection Properties*

Property	Type	Description
current-alpha	guint	The transparency of the selected color, where 0 is transparent and 65,535 is opaque.
current-color	GdkColor	The currently selected color.
has-opacity-control	gboolean	If set to TRUE, the user will be given the option to select transparency.
has-palette	gboolean	If set to TRUE, a color palette will be displayed to the user.

Table A-25. *GtkComboBox Properties*

Property	Type	Description
active	gint	The index of the current item that is activated. This item will be equal to the value returned by gtk_tree_path_get_indices() for the selected row if it is not a root element.
add-tearoffs	gboolean	If set to TRUE, menus will have tear-off menu items if the combo box is using a menu style.
column-span-column	gint	If you want a value to span multiple columns in the list, set this to a non-negative integer that points to a model column with the type G_TYPE_INT. This integer defines how many columns the value will span.
focus-on-click	gboolean	If set to TRUE, the combo box will grab focus when the user clicks it.
has-frame	gboolean	If set to TRUE, a frame will be drawn around the selected item.
model	GtkTreeModel	The tree model that holds the choices for the combo box.
popup-shown	gboolean	If set to TRUE, the combo box is currently displaying choices. You can connect to this with the notify signal to receive notification of when the user is shown the pop-up window.
row-span-column	gint	This property performs the same functionality as column-span-column except in the vertical direction.

Property	Type	Description
tearoff-title	gchararray	The title to display when the pop-up window of combo box choices is torn from its original placement.
wrap-width	gint	You can set this property to a positive integer so that a list can be displayed in multiple columns. This property defines the number of columns.

Table A-26. *GtkComboBoxEntry Properties*

Property	Type	Description
text-column	gint	The column number in the GtkTreeModel that holds data with a GType of G_TYPE_STRING

Table A-27. *GtkContainer Properties*

Property	Type	Description
border-width	guint	An integer defining the number of pixels to place along the outside of a container's children.
child	GtkWidget	A child widget of the container. You can add a new child to the container with this property. However, this property should not be used if the container holds multiple children.
resize-mode	GtkResizeMode	Defines how to handle resize requests of a container and its children.

Table A-28. *GtkCurve Properties*

Property	Type	Description
curve-type	GtkCurveType	The type of curve. For example, types of curves are linear, spline interpolated, and freeform.
max-x (max-y)	gfloat	Numbers that define the maximum x or y values.
min-x (min-y)	gfloat	Numbers that define the minimum x or y values.

Table A-29. *GtkDialog Properties*

Property	Type	Description
has-separator	gboolean	If set to TRUE, a separator will be placed between the dialog's GtkVBox widget and its action area.

Table A-30. *GtkEntry Properties*

Property	Type	Description
activates-default	gboolean	If set to TRUE, the default widget for the window will be activated when the user presses the Enter key.
cursor-position	gint	An integer between 0 and 65,535 that defines the current cursor position within the GtkEntry widget.
editable	gboolean	If set to TRUE, the user will be able to edit the content of the GtkEntry widget.
has-frame	gboolean	If set to TRUE, a border will be placed around the widget.
inner-border	GtkBorder	An object that defines spacing to add on all four sides of the text.
invisible-char	guint	When visibility is set to FALSE, this character will be shown instead of the actual text. This property is often used to implement password entries.
max-length	gint	The maximum length of text that the GtkEntry will accept; use 0 if there should be no limit. GtkEntry is only capable of handling strings up to 65,535 characters long.
scroll-offset	gint	An integer describing the number of pixels of GtkEntry content that is scrolled off the left of the widget.
selection-bound	gint	The integer index of the other end of the selection from cursor-position in the number of characters.
text	gchararray	The current content of GtkEntry.
truncate-multiline	gboolean	If set to TRUE, when the user pastes text that spans multiple lines into a GtkEntry widget, only the first line will be inserted.
visibility	gboolean	If set to FALSE, all of the characters in the GtkEntry widget will be replaced by invisibility-char.

Property	Type	Description
width-chars	gint	The number of characters that will be visible to the user. GtkEntry will usually be resized to accommodate this property.
xalign	gfloat	The alignment of the text within the GtkEntry widget described by a number between 0.0 and 1.0, where 0.5 is centered.

Table A-31. *GtkEntryCompletion Properties*

Property	Type	Description
inline-completion	gboolean	If set to TRUE, the prefix that is common to all choices will be added to the text. For this property to work, text-column must be set.
minimum-key-length	gint	The minimum number of characters that need to be entered into the GtkEntry widget before matches will be displayed.
model	GtkTreeModel	A tree model that holds all possible choices. One of the columns should have a GType of G_TYPE_STRING.
popup-completion	gboolean	If set to TRUE, all possible matches will be displayed in a pop-up window.
popup-set-width	gboolean	If set to TRUE, the width of the pop-up window will be the same as the GtkEntry widget.
popup-single-match	gboolean	If set to TRUE, the pop-up window will be displayed even if there is only one choice. You should set this to FALSE if inline-completion is set to TRUE.
text-column	gint	The index of the column in the model property that has a GType of G_TYPE_STRING. This column will provide the content for matches.

Table A-32. *GtkEventBox Properties*

Property	Type	Description
above-child	gboolean	If set to TRUE, the event box will receive all events that occur within it. Otherwise, events will first go to the children and then to the event box.
visible-window	gboolean	If set to TRUE, the event box will be visible to the user.

Table A-33. *GtkExpander Properties*

Property	Type	Description
expanded	gboolean	If set to TRUE, the expander is currently displaying its child widget.
label	gchararray	A text string to display beside the expander's arrow.
label-widget	GtkWidget	A GtkWidget to display beside the expander's arrow instead of the text defined by label.
spacing	gint	An integer amount of spacing to place between the expander's label and its child widget.
use-markup	gboolean	If set to TRUE, any Pango markup in label will be parsed and applied.
use-underline	gboolean	If set to TRUE, mnemonic keyboard accelerators will be supported in label.

Table A-34. *GtkFileChooser Properties*

Property	Type	Description
action	GtkFileChooserAction	The functionality performed by the file chooser.
do-overwrite-confirmation	gboolean	If set to TRUE, a file chooser with an action of GTK_FILE_CHOOSER_ACTION_SAVE will ask the user for confirmation if a file already exists.
extra-widget	GtkWidget	A supplementary widget that can be used to provide extra options to the user.
file-system-backend	gchararray	A name that refers to the file system backend.
filter	GtkFileFilter	The currently selected file filter, which is used to filter what files are displayed.
local-only	gboolean	If set to TRUE, only local files will be displayed as choices.
preview-widget	GtkWidget	A widget to use for previewing the content of a selected file.
preview-widget-active	gboolean	If you want to use preview-widget, this property must be set to TRUE for it to be displayed.

Property	Type	Description
select-multiple	gboolean	If set to TRUE, the user will be able to select multiple files.
show-hidden	gboolean	If set to TRUE, hidden files and folders will be visible in the file chooser.
use-preview-label	gboolean	If set to TRUE, a label will be displayed with the name of the file currently being previewed.

Table A-35. *GtkFileChooserButton Properties*

Property	Type	Description
dialog	GtkFileChooserDialog	The file chooser dialog that will be displayed when the user clicks the button.
focus-on-click	gboolean	If set to TRUE, the GtkFileChooserButton widget will grab focus when the user clicks it.
title	gchararray	The title of the GtkFileChoooserDialog widget that is displayed when the user clicks the button.
width-chars	gint	The width of the label within the file chooser button, in characters.

Table A-36. *GtkFontButton Properties*

Property	Type	Description
font-name	gchararray	The name of the font that is currently selected such as "Monospace Bold 10".
show-size	gboolean	If set to TRUE, the font size will be displayed in the font button's label.
show-style	gboolean	If set to TRUE, the font style will be displayed in the font button's label.
title	gchararray	The title of the GtkFontSelectionDialog widget that is displayed when the user clicks the button.
use-font	gboolean	If set to TRUE, the font button's label will use the selected font when drawn.
use-size	gboolean	If set to TRUE, the font button's label will use the selected size when drawn.

Table A-37. *GtkFontSelection Properties*

Property	Type	Description
font	GdkFont	The font that is currently selected in the GtkFontSelection.
font-name	gchararray	A string that represents the currently selected font.
preview-text	gchararray	Text that will be displayed as a preview of the currently selected font.

Table A-38. *GtkFrame Properties*

Property	Type	Description
label	gchararray	Text to display along the label of the GtkFrame
label-widget	GtkWidget	A widget to use instead of the text set in the label property
label-xalign	gfloat	The horizontal alignment of the label within the label, defined by a number between 0.0 and 1.0
label-yalign	gfloat	The vertical alignment of the label within the label, defined by a number between 0.0 and 1.0
shadow-type	GtkShadowType	A flag that defines what shadow type the GtkFrame uses

Table A-39. *GtkHandleBox Properties*

Property	Type	Description
handle-position	GtkPositionType	The position of the handle with respect to the child widget.
shadow-type	GtkShadowType	A flag that defines what shadow type the GtkHandleBox widget uses.
snap-edge	GtkPositionType	The position of the snap edge that will be used to dock the GtkHandleBox widget. You must set snap-edge-set to TRUE for this property to take effect.

Table A-40. *GtkIconView Properties*

Property	Type	Description
column-spacing	gint	The amount of spacing to place between columns of icons.
columns	gint	The number of columns that the icons will be sorted into. Setting this to -1 will tell GTK+ to choose this value for you.
item-width	gint	The width of each item in pixels. Setting this to -1 will tell GTK+ to choose this value for you.
margin	gint	The number of pixels of padding to place along the edges of GtkIconView.
markup-column	gint	The column in the GtkTreeModel widget that contains information about markup. This column must have a GType of G_TYPE_STRING.
model	GtkTreeModel	A tree model that defines the data displayed by the GtkIconView.
orientation	GtkOrientation	The horizontal or vertical orientation of the icon and text with respect to each other.
pixbuf-column	gint	The column in the GtkTreeModel widget that contains the icon. This column must have a GType of GDK_TYPE_PIXBUF.
reorderable	gboolean	If set to TRUE, the items in a GtkIconView widget can be reordered with drag and drop.
row-spacing	gint	The amount of spacing to place between rows of icons.
selection-mode	GtkSelectionMode	The selection mode of the icon view.
spacing	gint	The number of pixels of spacing to place between items and their neighbors.
text-column	gint	The column in GtkTreeModel that contains each item's text. This column must have a GType of G_TYPE_STRING.

Table A-41. *GtkImage Properties*

Property	Type	Description
file	gchararray	A filename that specifies the location of the icon image.
icon-name	gchararray	An icon from the current icon theme. This will automatically be updated if the icon theme changes. The size of this icon is defined by icon-size.
icon-set	GtkIconSet	A GtkIconSet to display as the icon. The size of this icon is defined by icon-size.
icon-size	gint	When using icon-name, icon-set, or stock, you can use this property to specify an icon size, defined by GtkIconSize.
image	GdkImage	An image to display as the icon. If you want to mask the icon with a GdkPixbuf, use mask.
mask	GdkPixmap	A pixmap that is used to mask the icon provided by image or pixmap.
pixbuf	GdkPixbuf	A pixbuf to display as the icon.
pixbuf-animation	GdkPixbufAnimation	An animated image to display as the icon, which is an animated pixbuf object.
pixel-size	gint	The size that should be used for pixels. This property takes precedence over icon-size if the image is specified with icon-name.
pixmap	GdkPixmap	A pixmap to display as the image. If you want to mask the icon with a GdkPixbuf, use mask.
stock	gchararray	The stock identifier for the image to display as the icon. The size of this icon is defined by icon-size.
storage-type	GtkImageType	The type of image storage type that is being used by the GtkImage.

Table A-42. *GtkImageMenuItem Properties*

Property	Type	Description
image	GtkWidget	The widget that will appear beside the menu item's label

Table A-43. *GtkInvisible Properties*

Property	Type	Description
screen	GdkScreen	The screen on which the GtkInvisible window is displayed

Table A-44. *GtkLabel Properties*

Property	Type	Description
angle	gdouble	The angle of the text between 0.0 and 360.0 with respect to the x axis, rotating counterclockwise. For example, with a value of 90.0, the bottom of the text will be on the right side of the screen. This property is ignored if you set ellipsize, selectable, or wrapped.
attributes	PangoAttrList	A list of attributes that are applied to the label's text.
cursor-position	gint	If selectable is set to TRUE, this property will be set the position of the cursor within the label's text.
ellipsize	PangoEllipsizeMode	The place within the string to replace text with ellipses if there is not enough space to display the whole string. You must set ellipsize-set to TRUE for this property to take effect.
justify	GtkJustification	The justification of the label. This is used to justify labels that span multiple lines, not to align the label within its child!
label	gchararray	The text string displayed by the label.
max-width-chars	gint	The maximum number of characters that will be displayed in a single line. If you set this to -1, it will be calculated automatically for you. This property is overridden by max-chars.
mnemonic-keyval	guint	The key value for the label's mnemonic keyboard accelerator.
mnemonic-widget	GtkWidget	The widget that is activated when the label's mnemonic keyboard accelerator is activated.
pattern	gchararray	A text string to display, where the underscore character designates which characters to underline.

Continued

Table A-44. *Continued*

Property	Type	Description
selectable	gboolean	If set to TRUE, the user will be able to select the label with the mouse.
selection-bound	gint	The location of the other end of the selected text, opposite of cursor-position. If there is no selected text, this will be equal to cursor-position.
single-line-mode	gboolean	If set to TRUE, the label will be forced into one line of text.
use-markup	gboolean	If set to TRUE, Pango markup in the label text will be parsed.
use-underline	gboolean	If set to TRUE, the underscore character will be used to designate the key to use for the mnemonic keyboard accelerator.
width-chars	gint	The width of the label in characters. Set this property to -1 to have it automatically calculated by GTK+. This property takes precedence over max-width-chars.
wrap	gboolean	If set to TRUE, the label will be wrapped if it cannot fit on one line.
wrap-mode	PangoWrapMode	The type of wrapping to perform if wrap is set to TRUE.

Table A-45. *GtkLayout Properties*

Property	Type	Description
hadjustment	GtkAdjustment	The horizontal adjustment that is used when scrolling the widget.
height	guint	The height of the GtkLayout widget, in pixels. Since the widget supports scrolling natively, the height can be larger than the height of the screen.
vadjustment	GtkAdjustment	The vertical adjustment that is used when scrolling the widget.
width	guint	The width of the GtkLayout widget in pixels. Since the widget supports scrolling natively, the height can be larger than the width of the screen.

Table A-46. *GtkLinkButton Properties*

Property	Type	Description
uri	gchararray	The URI of the web site that the link button visits. This must be a full URI such as http://www.gtkbook.com.

Table A-47. *GtkMenu Properties*

Property	Type	Description
tearoff-state	gboolean	If set to TRUE, the menu will be able to be torn from its attached widget.
tearoff-title	gchararray	The title that will be displayed when the menu is torn from its attached widget.

Table A-48. *GtkMenuBar Properties*

Property	Type	Description
child-pack-direction	GtkPackDirection	The direction that menu items of children will be packed
pack-direction	GtkPackDirection	The direction that child menu items will be packed

Table A-49. *GtkMenuShell Properties*

Property	Type	Description
take-focus	gboolean	If set to TRUE, menus and submenus will grab focus from the keyboard.

Table A-50. *GtkMenuToolButton Properties*

Property	Type	Description
menu	GtkMenu	The menu that will be displayed when the user clicks the arrow beside the tool button

Table A-51. *GtkMessageDialog Properties*

Property	Type	Description
buttons	GtkButtonsType	The button or buttons shown in the action area of the message dialog.
image	GtkWidget	The widget image to display in the GtkMessageDialog.
message-type	GtkMessageType	The type of message that is reported by the GtkMessageDialog. The message type defines what image is displayed in the dialog unless image is set.
secondary-text	gchararray	Secondary text that is displayed below the string defined in text.
secondary-use-markup	gboolean	If set to TRUE, markup in secondary-text will be parsed.
text	gchararray	The main text displayed by the dialog, which will appear above any secondary text.
use-markup	gboolean	If set to TRUE, markup in text will be parsed.

Table A-52. *GtkMisc Properties*

Property	Type	Description
xalign (yalign)	gfloat	Horizontal or vertical alignment defined by a number between 0.0 and 1.0, where 0.5 is centered
xpad (ypad)	gint	The padding to add on either side of the widget, in pixels

Table A-53. *GtkNotebook Properties*

Property	Type	Description
enable-popup	gboolean	If set to TRUE, a pop-up menu to allow navigation to other pages will be displayed when the user clicks the right mouse button over a tab.
group-id	gint	An integer group identifier used for drag-and-drop operations on GtkNotebook tabs.

Property	Type	Description
homogeneous	gboolean	If set to TRUE, all GtkNotebook tabs will have the same width.
page	gint	The index of the currently selected page, indexed starting with zero.
scrollable	gboolean	If set to TRUE, arrows will be drawn to all the user to scroll tabs if there is not enough space for them.
show-border	gboolean	If set to TRUE, a border will be displayed.
show-tabs	gboolean	If set to TRUE, the tabs will be visible to the user.
tab-border	guint	The width of the border placed around each tab label.
tab-hborder	guint	The width of the horizontal border placed around each tab label.
tab-pos	GtkPositionType	The position of the tabs with respect to the GtkNotebook children.
tab-vborder	guint	The width of the vertical border placed around each tab label.

Table A-54. *GtkObject Properties*

Property	Type	Description
user-data	gpointer	A piece of data with the type gpointer associated with the GtkObject

Table A-55. *GtkPaned Properties*

Property	Type	Description
max-position	gint	The maximum position of the pane, which is calculated based on the sizes and types of its children.
min-position	gint	The minimum position of the pane, which is calculated based on the sizes and types of its children.
position	gint	A property used to explicitly set the position of the separator, where 0 refers to the top or left side. You must set position-set to TRUE for this property to take effect.

Table A-56. *GtkPrinter Properties*

Property	Type	Description
accepts-pdf	gboolean	If set to TRUE, the printer will be able to accept PDF files.
accepts-ps	gboolean	If set to TRUE, the printer will be able to accept PostScript files.
backend	GtkPrintBackend	The print backend used by the GtkPrinter.
icon-name	gchararray	The name of the icon to use for the GtkPrinter.
is-virtual	gboolean	If set to TRUE, GtkPrinter is a virtual printer, which means that it may not represent real hardware.
job-count	gint	The number of print jobs that are currently waiting for GtkPrinter to become available.
location	gchararray	A string that describes the location of the printer.
name	gchararray	A unique name that identifies the printer.
state-message	gchararray	A string that gives more information about the current state of the printer.

Table A-57. *GtkPrintJob Properties*

Property	Type	Description
page-setup	GtkPageSetup	The page setup associated with the print job. This property holds information such as the page orientation and size of the paper.
printer	GtkPrinter	The printer that was selected to process the print job.
settings	GtkPrintSettings	The print settings associated with the print job. This property holds information such as the number of copies, print quality, and resolution.
title	gchararray	A title given to the print job so that it can be recognized. This usually differentiates print jobs set up by your application from those set up by others.
track-print-settings	gboolean	If set to TRUE, the status-changed signal will continue to be emitted even after the print job is sent to the printer.

Table A-58. *GtkPrintUnixDialog Properties*

Property	Type	Description
current-page	gint	The current page from the document. Set this property to -1 to enable the Range option.
page-setup	GtkPageSetup	The page setup associated with the print dialog. This property holds information such as the page orientation and size of the paper.
print-settings	GtkPrintSettings	The print settings associated with the print dialog. This property holds information such as the number of copies, print quality, and resolution.
selected-printer	GtkPrinter	The printer that is selected in the print dialog.

Table A-59. *GtkProgressBar Properties*

Property	Type	Description
ellipsize	PangoEllipsizeMode	The place within the string to replace text with ellipses if there is not enough space to display the whole string. You must set ellipsize-set to TRUE for this property to take effect.
fraction	gdouble	The amount of the status bar that is filled, defined by a number between 0.0 and 1.0, where 1.0 is completely filled.
orientation	GtkProgressBarOrientation	The direction that the progress bar fills.
pulse-step	gdouble	Sets the distance along the progress bar to move when the progress bar is being pulsed. For example, a progress bar will have to be pulsed 10 times for the block to travel from one end to the other if pulse-step is set to 0.1.
text	gchararray	The text to print on top of the progress bar.

Table A-60. *GtkRadioAction Properties*

Property	Type	Description
current-value	gint	The value of the member of the action group that is currently activated.
group	GtkRadioAction	A radio action that specifies the radio group to which the radio action belongs.
value	gint	An integer that is unique to the GtkRadioAction in its radio group. This property can be used along with current-value to find the radio action that is currently activated.

Table A-61. *GtkRadioButton, GtkRadioMenuItem, and GtkRadioToolButton Properties*

Property	Type	Description
group	GtkWidget	A radio button, radio menu item, or radio tool button that links the radio widget to others in the same radio group

Table A-62. *GtkRange Properties*

Property	Type	Description
adjustment	GtkAdjustment	An adjustment that holds the current value of the GtkRange as well as bound information.
inverted	gboolean	If set to TRUE, the slider will switch the locations of the larger and smaller values.
lower-stepper-sensitivity	GtkSensitivityType	The sensitivity associated with the button that decreases the GtkAdjustment object's value when activated.
update-policy	GtkUpdateType	Defines how the GtkRange should be updated on the screen.
upper-stepper-sensitivity	GtkSensitivityType	The sensitivity associated with the button that increases the GtkAdjustment object's value when activated.

Table A-63. *GtkRecentChooser Properties*

Property	Type	Description
filter	GtkRecentFilter	The currently selected file filter, which is used to decide what resources are displayed to the user.
limit	gint	The maximum number of items that are shown in the GtkRecentChooser. Use -1 for no limit. This property should be set when using GtkRecentChooserMenu so that the pop-up menu does not become unwieldy.
local-only	gboolean	If set to TRUE, only resources with a prefix of file:// will be displayed.
recent-manager	GtkRecentManager	The manager that holds the recently used resources to display. You can use gtk_recent_manager_get_default() to retrieve the default GtkRecentManager for the current screen.
select-multiple	gboolean	If set to TRUE, the user will be able to select multiple resources from the list.
show-icons	gboolean	If set to TRUE, an icon will be displayed beside each resource that gives more information about it, such as the MIME type.
show-not-found	gboolean	This property can be set to FALSE to hide files that are no longer available. You should note that this will only affect local resources.
show-private	gboolean	If set to TRUE, items that are set as private to a specific application will be displayed.
show-tips	gboolean	If set to TRUE, a tooltip will be displayed for each item if available.
sort-type	GtkRecentSortType	The method that will be used for sorting the recent resource list, if any.

Table A-64. *GtkRecentChooserMenu Properties*

Property	Type	Description
show-numbers	gboolean	If set to TRUE, a number will be prepended to the first ten recent resources in the menu.

Table A-65. *GtkRecentManager Properties*

Property	Type	Description
filename	gchararray	The location of the file that stores the list of recently used resources
limit	gint	The greatest number of recently used resources that will be returned by GtkRecentManager when gtk_recent_manager_get_items() is called
size	gint	The total number of items in the list of recently used resources

Table A-66. *GtkRuler Properties*

Property	Type	Description
lower	gdouble	The smallest value displayed by the ruler.
max-size	gdouble	The maximum size of the ruler. Set this property to 0.0 so that it is not restricted.
metric	GtkMetricType	The type of units used by the ruler, such as pixels, inches, or centimeters.
position	gdouble	The current position of the ruler's marker.
upper	gdouble	The largest value displayed by the ruler.

Table A-67. *GtkScale Properties*

Property	Type	Description
digits	gint	The maximum number, up to 64, of decimal places of the value that are displayed. Setting this property to -1 will tell GTK+ to choose for you.
draw-value	gboolean	If set to TRUE, the value will be drawn beside the slider.
value-pos	GtkPositionType	The position of the GtkScale value with respect to the slider.

Table A-68. *GtkScrolledWindow Properties*

Property	Type	Description
hadjustment	GtkAdjustment	The adjustment for the horizontal scrollbar.
hscrollbar-policy	GtkPolicyType	Defines whether the horizontal scroll-bar is always shown, always hidden, or only displayed when needed.
shadow-type	GtkShadowType	The type of shadow to place around the child widget.
vadjustment	GtkAdjustment	The adjustment for the vertical scrollbar.
vscrollbar-policy	GtkPolicyType	Defines whether the vertical scrollbar is always shown, always hidden, or only displayed when needed.
window-placement (set)	GtkCornerType	The placement of the child widget with respect to the scrollbars. You must set window-placement-set to TRUE for this property to take effect.

Table A-69. *GtkSeparatorToolItem Properties*

Property	Type	Description
draw	gboolean	If set to TRUE, the separator tool item will be drawn on the screen. Otherwise, blank space will be added in its place.

Table A-70. *GtkSizeGroup Properties*

Property	Type	Description
ignore-hidden	gboolean	If set to TRUE, widgets that are not visible on the screen will be ignored when the size of the group is calculated.
mode	GtkSizeGroupMode	A flag that defines how the size group will determine its size and the sizes of its children.

Table A-71. *GtkSpinButton Properties*

Property	Type	Description
adjustment	GtkAdjustment	The adjustment that holds information about the spin button's value and bounds.
climb-rate	gdouble	The rate of acceleration when an arrow button is held down.
digits	guint	The number, between 0 and 20, of decimal places of the value to display.
numeric	gboolean	If set to TRUE, only numeric characters will be recognized by the spin button.
snap-to-ticks	gboolean	If set to TRUE, the value will automatically be updated to align with the closest step increment.
update-policy	GtkSpinButtonUpdatePolicy	A flag that determines how often and when the spin button will update.
value	gdouble	The current value stored by the spin button. You can read and write this value instead of interacting with the spin button's adjustment.
wrap	gboolean	If the spin button reaches its upper or lower bound and this property is set to TRUE, the spin button value will wrap to the opposite end.

Table A-72. *GtkStatusbar Properties*

Property	Type	Description
has-resize-grip	gboolean	If this property is set to TRUE, the GtkStatusbar widget will display a graphic that allows the user to resize the window by dragging it with the mouse.

Table A-73. *GtkStatusIcon Properties*

Property	Type	Description
blinking	gboolean	If set to TRUE, the status icon will blink on platforms where this behavior is supported.
file	gchararray	The location of the icon to display as the status icon.
icon-name	gchararray	An icon from the icon theme to display as the status icon.
pixbuf	GdkPixbuf	An image to display as the status icon.
size	gint	The size of the icon to display.
stock	gchararray	A stock identifier that defines the icon to display as the status icon.
storage-type	GtkImageType	The image type to display. This is used to identify whether to use file, icon-name, pixbuf, or stock.
visible	gboolean	If set to TRUE, the status icon will be visible to the user in the system tray.

Table A-74. *GtkTable Properties*

Property	Type	Description
column-spacing	guint	The number of pixels of spacing to add between a column and each of its neighbors.
homogeneous	gboolean	If set to TRUE, every cell will be given the same height and width.
n-columns	guint	The total number of columns in the GtkTable.
n-rows	guint	The total number of rows in the GtkTable.
row-spacing	guint	The number of pixels of spacing to add between a row and each of its neighbors.

Table A-75. *GtkTextBuffer Properties*

Property	Type	Description
copy-target-list	GtkTargetList	A target list for the buffer that is used to store information about copying from clipboards and other drag-and-drop sources.
cursor-position	gint	The current position of the cursor within the buffer. You can monitor this property with the notify signal to know when the cursor is moved.
has-selection	gboolean	If set to TRUE, the text buffer currently has selected text.
paste-target-list	GtkTargetList	A target list for the buffer that is used to store information about pasting to clipboards and drag-and-drop destinations.
tag-table	GtkTextTagTable	A text tag table that holds all text tags that are used by the text buffer.
text	gchararray	The text currently contained by the text buffer excluding embedded images and child widgets.

Table A-76. *GtkTextView Properties*

Property	Type	Description
accepts-tab	gboolean	If set to TRUE, the text view will insert a tab character when the Tab key is pressed instead of giving focus to the next widget in the tab order.
buffer	GtkTextBuffer	The text buffer that is currently displayed by the text view.
cursor-visible	gboolean	If set to TRUE, the cursor will be visible to the user.
editable	gboolean	If set to TRUE, the user will be able to edit the content of the text view.
indent	gint	The number of pixels to indent each paragraph, which is set to zero by default.
justification	GtkJustification	The justification of the text to the left, right, or center.

Property	Type	Description
left-margin	gint	The number of pixels of spacing to add between the left side of the text view and the content.
overwrite	gboolean	If set to TRUE, new characters will overwrite those that already exist. Otherwise, they will be inserted.
pixels-above-lines	gint	The number of pixels of padding to place above each paragraph.
pixels-below-lines	gint	The number of pixels of padding to place below each paragraph.
pixels-inside-wrap	gint	The number of pixels of padding to place between lines that are wrapped within a paragraph.
right-margin	gint	The number of pixels of spacing to add between the right side of the text view and the content.
tabs	PangoTabArray	A tab array that defines the content that will be added when the user presses the Tab key.
wrap-mode	GtkWrapMode	The type of wrapping to perform.

Table A-77. *GtkToggleAction Properties*

Property	Type	Description
active	gboolean	If set to TRUE, the GtkToggleAction will be drawn as checked.
draw-as-radio	gboolean	If set to TRUE, the GtkToggleAction will be drawn as a radio button.

Table A-78. *GtkToggleButton Properties*

Property	Type	Description
active	gboolean	If set to TRUE, the GtkToggleButton will be drawn as checked.
draw-indicator	gboolean	If set to TRUE, the toggle aspect of the GtkToggleButton will be displayed.
inconsistent	gboolean	If set to TRUE, the toggle button will have an in-between state that is neither active nor inactive.

Table A-79. *GtkToggleToolButton Properties*

Property	Type	Description
active	gboolean	If set to TRUE, the GtkToggleToolButton will be drawn as checked.

Table A-80. *GtkToolbar Properties*

Property	Type	Description
icon-size	GtkIconSize	The size of the toolbar icons. You should only use this property for specialty toolbars. In most cases, you should follow the user's choice of theme. You must set icon-size-set to TRUE for the property to take effect.
orientation	GtkOrientation	The orientation of the toolbar—horizontal or vertical.
show-arrow	gboolean	If set to TRUE, an arrow will be displayed if all of the toolbar items do not fit. The arrow will give access to a pop-up menu displaying the overflow toolbar items.
toolbar-style	GtkToolbarStyle	The toolbar style that states whether text or icons are displayed.
tooltips	gboolean	If set to TRUE, tooltips will be displayed for toolbar items.

Table A-81. *GtkToolButton Properties*

Property	Type	Description
icon-name	gchararray	The name of an icon from the icon theme to display. The label, icon-widget, and stock-id properties take precedence over icon-name.
icon-widget	GtkWidget	A widget to display as the tool button's icon.
label	gchararray	A text string to display as a label for the tool button.
label-widget	GtkWidget	A widget to use as the tool button's label instead of label.
stock-id	gchararray	The stock icon to display for widgets using the action. This property takes precedence over icon-name.
use-underline	gboolean	If set to TRUE, the underscore character will designate the character that follows the underline as a mnemonic keyboard accelerator.

Table A-82. *GtkToolItem Properties*

Property	Type	Description
is-important	gboolean	When a toolbar uses a toolbar-style of GTK_TOOLBAR_BOTH_HORIZ, setting this property to TRUE will tell GTK+ to display the tool button's label. Otherwise, only the icon will be displayed.
visible-horizontal	gboolean	If set to TRUE, the tool item will be visible when the toolbar's orientation is set to GTK_ORIENTATION_HORIZONTAL.
visible-vertical	gboolean	If set to TRUE, the tool item will be visible when the toolbar's orientation is set to GTK_ORIENTATION_VERTICAL.

Table A-83. *GtkTreeModelFilter Properties*

Property	Type	Description
child-model	GtkTreeModel	A tree model that holds the content that is filtered by GtkTreeModelFilter.
virtual-root	GtkTreePath	A tree path that points to the root row to use in child-model. This does not have to be the absolute root path of the tree model.

Table A-84. *GtkTreeModelSort Properties*

Property	Type	Description
model	GtkTreeModel	A tree model that holds the content that is sorted by GtkModelSort

Table A-85. *GtkTreeView Properties*

Property	Type	Description
enable-grid-lines	GtkTreeViewGridLines	A flag to place horizontal or vertical grid lines.
enable-search	gboolean	If set to TRUE, the user will be able to search the content of GtkTreeView with the keyboard.
enable-tree-lines	gboolean	If set to TRUE, lines will be drawn that define the hierarchy of the tree view content.
expander-column	GtkTreeViewColumn	The tree view column where the expander is displayed for tree views using GtkTreeStore.

Continued

Table A-85. *Continued*

Property	Type	Description
fixed-height-mode	gboolean	If set to TRUE, GTK+ will assume that every row is the same height, which speeds up rendering. You should only use this property if you are sure that every row will have the same height.
hadjustment	GtkAdjustment	The horizontal adjustment used for scrolling the widget.
headers-clickable	gboolean	If set to TRUE, the user will be able to click the column headers.
headers-visible	gboolean	If set to TRUE, the column headers will be visible to the user.
hover-expand	gboolean	If set to TRUE, a row will expand or collapse if the mouse pointer hovers over it.
hover-selection	gboolean	If set to TRUE, a row will be selected if the mouse pointer hovers over it with a selection mode of GTK_SELECTION_SINGLE or GTK_SELECTION_BROWSE.
level-indentation	gint	The number of pixels to add as extra indentation for child rows. Even if this is set to zero, child rows will still be indented with the default padding.
model	GtkTreeModel	The tree model that is currently displayed by the tree view.
reoderable	gboolean	If set to TRUE, the tree view is reorderable by user interaction. For example, you will be able to implement drag-and-drop support.
rubber-banding	gboolean	If set to TRUE, the user will be able to drag the mouse pointer to select multiple items.
rules-hint	gboolean	If set to TRUE, the theme engine will be instructed to draw alternating rows in different colors. You should note that this is a hint and may not be honored by the theme. Also, some themes color alternating rows by default.
search-column	gint	The column number to search when enable-search is set to TRUE.
show-expanders	gboolean	If set to TRUE, expanders will be displayed beside rows that have one or more children.
vadjustment	GtkAdjustment	The vertical adjustment used for scrolling the widget.

Table A-86. *GtkTreeViewColumn Properties*

Property	Type	Description
alignment	gfloat	The horizontal alignment of the column title within the header, defined by a number between 0.0 and 1.0, where 0.5 is centered.
clickable	gboolean	If set to TRUE, the user will be able to click the column header.
expand	gboolean	If set to TRUE, the column will expand to fill extra space allocated to the GtkTreeView to which it belongs.
fixed-width	gint	A number of pixels that defines the fixed width of the column.
max-width	gint	The maximum width, in pixels, to which the column can be expanded .
min-width	gint	The minimum width, in pixels, to which the column can be shrunk.
reorderable	gboolean	If set to TRUE, the column can be reordered by using a method such as drag and drop.
resizable	gboolean	If set to TRUE, the user will be able to resize the column.
sizing	GtkTreeViewColumnSizing	A flag that sets the resizing mode for the column.
sort-indicator	gboolean	If set to TRUE, an arrow will be displayed in the column header that designates that the tree view is sorted according to its content.
sort-order	GtkSortType	A flag that defines in which direction the sort indicator will be displayed.
spacing	gint	The number of pixels of spacing that is added between a row and each of its neighbors.
title	gchararray	The title of the column that appears in the header.
visible	gboolean	If set to TRUE, the column will be visible to the user.
widget	GtkWidget	Instead of placing the title string in the column header, you can use this property to place a widget in the header instead.
width	gint	The width of the tree view column, in pixels.

Table A-87. *GtkUIManager Properties*

Property	Type	Description
add-tearoffs	gboolean	If set to TRUE, menus generated by the GtkUIManager will have tear-off menu items unless they are pop-up menus.
ui	gchararray	The XML string that is used to generate the menu or toolbar user interface. This was either explicitly set or loaded from a file.

Table A-88. *GtkViewport Properties*

Property	Type	Description
hadjustment	GtkAdjustment	The horizontal adjustment of the viewport used for native scrolling support.
shadow-type	GtkShadowType	The type of shadow that is drawn around the viewport's child widget.
vadjustment	GtkAdjustment	The vertical adjustment of the viewport used for native scrolling support.

Table A-89. *GtkWidget Properties*

Property	Type	Description
app-paintable	gboolean	If set to TRUE, GTK+ will draw directly on the GtkWidget.
can-default	gboolean	If set to TRUE, the GtkWidget will be able to become the window's default widget.
can-focus	gboolean	If set to TRUE, the GtkWidget will be able to accept the window's focus.
composite-child	gboolean	If set to TRUE, the widget is not derived directly from GtkWidget.
events	GdkEventMask	A bitmask of all of the events from GdkEventMask that the widget will receive.
extension-events	GdkExtensionMode	A bitmask of all extension events from GdkExtensionMode that the widget will receive.
has-default	gboolean	If set to TRUE, the GtkWidget is currently the default widget of its parent window.
has-focus	gboolean	If set to TRUE, the GtkWidget is currently the widget with focus.

Property	Type	Description
height-request	gint	The requested height of the widget. Use -1 to allow GTK+ to set the widget's height. This is a request and may not be honored in some cases.
is-focus	gboolean	If set to TRUE, the widget has focus within the top-level window.
name	gchararray	A unique name that can be used to distinguish widgets of the same type. This is often used to set widget styles in resource files.
no-show-all	gboolean	If set to TRUE, the widget will not be affected by calls to gtk_widget_show_all().
parent	GtkContainer	The parent container of the widget.
receives-default	gboolean	If set to TRUE, when the widget has focus, it will receive the default action.
sensitive	gboolean	If set to TRUE, the user will be able to interact with the widget.
style	GtkStyle	The style associated with the widget that is used to customize how it is drawn.
visible	gboolean	If set to TRUE, the widget will be displayed on the screen.
width-request	gint	The requested width of the widget. Use -1 to allow GTK+ to set the widget's width. This is a request and may not be honored in some cases.

Table A-90. *GtkWindow Properties*

Property	Type	Description
accept-focus	gboolean	If set to TRUE, the window will be able to receive focus for input.
allow-grow	gboolean	If set to TRUE, the user will be able to resize the window larger than its initial size.
allow-shrink	gboolean	If set to TRUE, there will be no minimum size for the window.
decorated	gboolean	If set to TRUE, the window will be drawn with a title bar by the window manager.
default-height	gint	The default height of the window. This height is used when the window is first mapped to the screen.

Continued

Table A-90. *Continued*

Property	Type	Description
default-width	gint	The default width of the window. This width is used when the window is first mapped to the screen.
deletable	gboolean	If set to TRUE, the window's title bar will display a close button.
destroy-with-parent	gboolean	If set to TRUE, the window will be destroyed along with its parent.
focus-on-map	gboolean	If set to TRUE, the window will receive focus when it is mapped.
gravity	GdkGravity	The reference point of the window when using gtk_window_move().
has-toplevel-focus	gboolean	This property will be set to TRUE when a child of the window has focus.
icon	GdkPixbuf	An image that is shown as the window icon on window managers that use this property.
icon-name	gchararray	A named icon from the icon theme that is shown as the window icon on window managers that use this property.
is-active	gboolean	If set to TRUE, the window is the current window with focus.
modal	gboolean	If set to TRUE, the user will be prevented from interacting with parent windows until this one returns. The parent window is set with transient-for.
resizable	gboolean	If set to TRUE, the user will be able to resize the window when it is not prevented by other GTK+ settings.
role	gchararray	A unique string that distinguishes the window that is used when the window manager restores a past session.
screen	GdkScreen	The screen on which the window is drawn.
skip-pager-hint	gboolean	If set to TRUE, the window manager will recognize the window in its pager.

Property	Type	Description
skip-taskbar-hint	gboolean	If set to TRUE, the window manager will display the window in the task bar.
title	gchararray	The title of the window to display in the title bar and task bar of the window manager.
transient-for	GtkWindow	The parent window of the current window. This allows your window to become modal.
type	GtkWindowType	The type of window, either top-level or pop-up.
type-hint	GdkWindowTypeHint	A hint given to the window manager about the purpose of the window. This may affect how the window is drawn on various window managers.
urgency-hint	gboolean	If set to TRUE, the user will be notified that the window needs attention.
window-position	GtkWindowPosition	The position of the window when originally mapped. This is a hint and may not be honored by all window managers.

Child Widget Properties

A few containers in GTK+ have properties that are assigned to every child of the container. Tables A-91 through A-100 list these properties.

Table A-91. GtkAssistant Child Properties

Property	Type	Description
complete	gboolean	If set to TRUE, the page is set as complete, and navigation buttons will be set as sensitive.
header-image	GdkPixbuf	An image that is displayed next to the page header.
page-type	GtkAssistantPageType	The type of buttons to use.
sidebar-image	GdkPixbuf	An image that is displayed next to the page as the sidebar.
title	gchararray	A string that is displayed as the title of the page in the header.

Table A-92. *GtkBox Child Properties*

Property	Type	Description
expand	gboolean	If set to TRUE, the child widget will get extra space when the box grows. The child can either fill the extra space with itself or padding.
fill	gboolean	If set to TRUE, extra space allocated to the child will be filled with the widget. Otherwise, it will be filled with padding.
pack-type	GtkPackType	The type of packing used by the child.
padding	guint	The number of pixels of padding placed between the child widget and its neighbors.
position	gint	The position of the child within the box, indexed from zero.

Table A-93. *GtkButtonBox Child Properties*

Property	Type	Description
secondary	gboolean	If set to TRUE, the child button will be placed in a secondary group of buttons.

Table A-94. *GtkFixed Child Properties*

Property	Type	Description
x (y)	gint	The horizontal and vertical position of the child widget within the GtkFixed widget

Table A-95. *GtkLayout Child Properties*

Property	Type	Description
x (y)	gint	The horizontal and vertical position of the child widget within the GtkLayout widget

Table A-96. *GtkMenu Child Properties*

Property	Type	Description
bottom-attach	gint	The row that the bottom of the child widget is attached to.
left-attach	gint	The column that the left side of the child widget is attached to.
right-attach	gint	The column that the right side of the child widget is attached to.
top-attach	gint	The row that the top of the child widget is attached to.

Table A-97. *GtkNotebook Child Properties*

Property	Type	Description
detachable	gboolean	If set to TRUE, the user will be able to detach the tab from the parent notebook.
menu-label	gchararray	The string to display for the tab in the notebook's tab selection menu.
position	gint	The current position of the child within the notebook, indexed from zero.
reorderable	gboolean	If set to TRUE, the user will be able to change the position of the current tab.
tab-expand	gboolean	If set to TRUE, the child's tab will expand to fill extra space allocated to the notebook.
tab-fill	gboolean	If set to TRUE, the child's tab will fill extra space allocated to it.
tab-label	gchararray	The string to display as the child's tab label. This can be left unset if you want to provide your own label widget.
tab-pack	GtkPackType	They type of packing that was used to add the child.

Table A-98. *GtkPaned Child Properties*

Property	Type	Description
resize	gboolean	If set to TRUE, the child widget will be resized to fill the whole pane.
shrink	gboolean	If set to TRUE, the child's pane can be resized smaller than the requested size of the child widget.

Table A-99. *GtkTable Child Properties*

Property	Type	Description
bottom-attach	guint	The row that the bottom of the child widget is attached to.
left-attach	guint	The column that the left side of the child widget is attached to.
right-attach	guint	The column that the right side of the child widget is attached to.
top-attach	guint	The row that the top of the child widget is attached to.
x-options (y-options)	GtkAttachOptions	Horizontal and vertical attach options provided for the widget.
x-padding (y-padding)	guint	Horizontal and vertical padding to add on either side of the child widget.

Table A-100. *GtkToolbar Child Properties*

Property	Type	Description
expand	gboolean	If set to TRUE, the tool item will receive extra space if the toolbar is enlarged.
homogeneous	gboolean	If set to TRUE, the tool item will be forced to the same size as all other items with this property set.

APPENDIX B

■ ■ ■

GTK+ Signals

GTK+ is a system that relies on signals and callback functions. A signal is a notification to your application that the user has performed some action. When a signal is emitted, you can tell GTK+ to run a function named a callback function.

To connect a signal, you can use g_signal_connect(). This function accepts four parameters. The first is the GObject you are watching for the signal. The signal_name is a string representing the signal; a list of signal names can be found in the tables throughout this appendix.

```
gulong g_signal_connect (gpointer object,
                         const gchar *signal_name,
                         GCallback handler,
                         gpointer data);
```

The third parameter is the name of the callback function that will be called when the signal is emitted. The form for each callback function can be found in the GTK+ API documentation. However, many of the function prototypes have incomplete documentation, so you can find more information about nonstandard parameters in the signal reference tables throughout this appendix.

The last parameter of g_signal_connect() allows you to send data of an arbitrary pointer type to the callback function. You can do this because gpointer is equivalent to C's void pointer type.

You can also use g_signal_connect_swapped(), which works the same way as g_signal_connect(), except the order of the object and data parameters is switched. This allows you to call a function on the data parameter pointer.

This appendix provides a complete list of events and signals available to GTK+ objects and widgets. The first section provides information about the GDK event types available to GtkWidget and derivative classes. The sections that follow provide a complete list of signals' names and a description for every object with signals in GTK+.

Events

Events are a special type of signal that are emitted by the X Window System. Once emitted, they are sent from the window manager to your application to be interpreted by the signal system provided by GLib.

In doing this, you can use the same signal connection and callback function methods as with normal signals. One difference is that event callback functions return a gboolean value.

If you return TRUE, no further action will happen. If you return the default value of FALSE, GTK+ will continue to handle the event.

Table B-1. *GtkWidget Event Types*

Signal Name	GdkEventType Value	Description
delete-event	GDK_DELETE	The window manager requested that the top-level window be destroyed. This can be used to confirm the deletion of the window.
destroy-event	GDK_DESTROY	The widget's GdkWindow was destroyed. You should not use this signal, because the widget will usually be disconnected before it can be emitted.
expose-event	GDK_EXPOSE	A new part of the widget was shown and needs to be drawn. This is emitted when the window was previously obscured by another object.
motion-notify-event	GDK_MOTION_NOTIFY	The mouse cursor has moved while within the proximity of the widget.
button-press-event	GDK_BUTTON_PRESS	A mouse button was clicked once. This is emitted along with GDK_2BUTTON_PRESS and GDK_3BUTTON_PRESS events.
button-press-event	GDK_2BUTTON_PRESS	A mouse button was clicked twice. This will also emit GDK_BUTTON_PRESS, so you need to check the event type in the callback function.
button-press-event	GDK_3BUTTON_PRESS	A mouse button was clicked three times. This will also emit GDK_BUTTON_PRESS, so you need to check the event type in the callback function.
button-release-event	GDK_BUTTON_RELEASE	A previously clicked mouse button was released.
key-press-event	GDK_KEY_PRESS	A keyboard key was pressed. You can return TRUE to prevent any text from being entered or actions being taken because of the key press.

Signal Name	GdkEventType Value	Description
key-release-event	GDK_KEY_RELEASE	A previously pressed keyboard key was released. This is usually not as useful as key-press-event.
enter-notify-event	GDK_ENTER_NOTIFY	The mouse cursor entered the proximity of the widget.
leave-notify-event	GDK_LEAVE_NOTIFY	The mouse cursor exited the proximity of the widget.
focus-in-event	GDK_FOCUS_CHANGE	Keyboard focus entered the widget from another widget within the window.
focus-out-event	GDK_FOCUS_CHANGE	Keyboard focus left the widget for another widget within the window.
configure-event	GDK_CONFIGURE	The size, position, or stacking order of the widget changed. This is normally emitted when a new size is allocated for the widget.
map-event	GDK_MAP	The widget was mapped onto the display. It also means that the widget was realized.
unmap-event	GDK_UNMAP	The widget was unmapped from the display.
property-notify-event	GDK_PROPERTY_NOTIFY	A property of the widget has been changed or deleted. You can use this to track changes to a specific widget property stored by GObject.
selection-clear-event	GDK_SELECTION_CLEAR	The application no longer has ownership of a selection, so it needs to be cleared.
selection-request-event	GDK_SELECTION_REQUEST	The selection of the widget was requested by another application.
selection-notify-event	GDK_SELECTION_NOTIFY	The owner of a selection responded to a selection conversion request.
proximity-in-event	GDK_PROXIMITY_IN	An input device has come in contact with a sensing surface, such as a pen on a touch screen.

Continued

Table B-1. *Continued*

Signal Name	GdkEventType Value	Description
proximity-out-event	GDK_PROXIMITY_OUT	An input device, such as a pen on a touch screen, has broken off contact with a sensing surface.
event	GDK_DRAG_ENTER	The mouse pointer entered the widget while a drag action was in progress.
event	GDK_DRAG_LEAVE	The mouse pointer left the widget while a drag action was in progress.
event	GDK_DRAG_MOTION	The mouse pointer moved within the widget while a drag action was in progress.
event	GDK_DRAG_STATUS	The current status of a drag action was changed.
event	GDK_DROP_START	A drop action on the widget began.
event	GDK_DROP_FINISHED	A drop action on the widget completed.
client-event	GDK_CLIENT_EVENT	An event for the widget was received from another application.
visibility-notify-event	GDK_VISIBILITY_NOTIFY	The visibility of the widget changed. For example, some portion of it has been covered or uncovered.
no-expose-event	GDK_NO_EXPOSE	The source region was completely available when parts of a drawable area were copied.
scroll-event	GDK_SCROLL	The widget has been scrolled in one direction or another. This allows you to update the widget's visible area.
window-state-event	GDK_WINDOW_STATE	The state of the widget has changed. If the widget is a top-level window, this can happen when it is minimized, maximized, made sticky, made into an icon, and so forth.
event	GDK_SETTING	A setting was added, removed, or modified for the widget.

Signal Name	GdkEventType Value	Description
event	GDK_OWNER_CHANGE	The owner of the widget has changed. This event was introduced in GTK+ 2.6.
grab-broken-event	GDK_GRAB_BROKEN	The widget was grabbed by the pointer or the keyboard, but it was broken. This can happen when the window becomes invisible or when a user attempts to repeat a grab. This event was introduced in GTK+ 2.8.

Widget Signals

Tables B-2 through B-69 provide a complete list of signals for each class in GTK+ that has signals. In addition to signal names, a description is provided for each item. If the signal does not follow the standard signal prototype, the additional parameters are listed; these additional parameters do not include the object itself and the user data pointer.

Table B-2. *GtkAction Signals*

Signal Name	Description
activate	The associated menu or toolbar item was triggered.

Table B-3. *GtkActionGroup Signals*

Signal Name	Additional Parameters	Description
connect-proxy	GtkAction *action GtkWidget *proxy	A proxy that is used to synchronize properties between a GtkAction object and an associated widget was added.
disconnect-proxy	GtkAction *action GtkWidget *proxy	A proxy that is used to synchronize properties between a GtkAction and an associated widget was removed.
post-activate	GtkAction *action	An action contained by the action group was activated after the signal was emitted.
pre-activate	GtkAction *action	An action contained by the action group will be activated right after this signal is emitted.

Table B-4. *GtkAdjustment Signals*

Signal Name	Description
changed	One or more properties of the adjustment were changed, excluding the value property.
value-changed	The value property of the adjustment was changed.

Table B-5. *GtkAssistant Signals*

Signal Name	Additional Parameters	Description
apply	None	The Apply button or the Forward button was clicked on any GtkAssistant page.
cancel	None	The Cancel button was clicked on any GtkAssistant page.
close	None	The Close button or the Apply button was clicked on the last page in the GtkAssistant.
prepare	GtkWidget *page	A new page is about to become visible. This signal was emitted so that you can perform any preparation tasks before it is visible to the user.

Table B-6. *GtkButton Signals*

Signal Name	Description
activate	This signal is used to animate a button. You should never connect to it! Instead, use the clicked signal.
clicked	The button was clicked or released.

Table B-7. *GtkCalendar Signals*

Signal Name	Description
day-selected	The user selected a day on the calendar.
day-selected-double-click	The user selected a day by double-clicking it. This should be used to force an update of any supplementary widgets if they exist.
month-changed	The user selected a new month on the calendar by using one of the arrow buttons.
next-month	The displayed month was incremented. This will only be called when the user manually changes the month.

Signal Name	Description
next-year	The displayed year was incremented. This will only be called when the user manually changes the year.
prev-month	The displayed month was decremented. This will only be called when the user manually changes the month.
prev-year	The displayed year was decremented. This will only be called when the user manually changes the year.

Table B-8. *GtkCellEditable Signals*

Signal Name	Description
editing-done	The user finished editing the textual content of the cell. This signal tells the cell renderer to update its value.
remove-widget	The cell is finished editing, so the text editing widget can now be destroyed.

Table B-9. *GtkCellRenderer Signals*

Signal Name	Additional Parameters	Description
editing-canceled	None	The user chose to cancel the editing of a cell. You can set this up to occur in any case, such as when the Escape key is pressed.
editing-started	GtkCellEditable *editable gchar *path	A cell has become editable. You can use this signal to add a different type of editing widget instead of the default associated with the cell content.

Table B-10. *GtkCellRendererAccel Signals*

Signal Name	Additional Parameters	Description
accel-cleared	gchar *path_string	The accelerator was removed from the cell. The cell should be reset to some type of default text that tells the user that it is empty, or it should return to the default value.
accel-edited	gchar *path_string guint accel_key GdkModifierType accel_mods	The accelerator chosen by the user changed. The callback function provides enough information for you to apply the new selection immediately.

Table B-11. *GtkCellRendererText Signals*

Signal Name	Description	
edited	gchar *path_string gchar *new_text	The textual content of the renderer was changed. The callback function receives the path to the cell and the new content of the cell.

Table B-12. *GtkCellRendererToggle Signals*

Signal Name	Additional Parameters	Description
toggled	gchar *path_string	The cell was activated or deactivated. If you set the renderer to display as a radio button, you will need to update the renderer that was originally activated.

Table B-13. *GtkCheckMenuItem Signals*

Signal Name	Description
toggled	The state of the check box changed. You will have to check the active property of the GtkCheckMenuItem class to discover the current status.

Table B-14. *GtkColorButton Signals*

Signal Name	Description
color-set	The user chose a new color. This signal is *not* emitted when you change the color programmatically! You need to track GtkColorButton's color and alpha properties to detect all changes.

Table B-15. *GtkColorSelection Signals*

Signal Name	Description
color-changed	The selected color changed. This signal is emitted whether it was the user or your code that initiated the alteration.

Table B-16. *GtkComboBox Signals*

Signal Name	Description
changed	The user selected a different item from the list, or your code made a call to gtk_combo_box_set_active_iter(). This signal will also be emitted when the user types into a GtkComboBoxEntry.

Table B-17. *GtkContainer Signals*

Signal Name	Additional Parameters	Description
add	GtkWidget *child	A child widget was added or packed into the container. This signal will be emitted even if you do not explicitly call gtk_container_add() but use the widget's built-in packing functions instead.
check-resize	None	The container checked whether it needs to be resized before adding a child widget.
remove	GtkWidget *child	A child widget was removed from the container.
set-focus-child	GtkWidget *child	A container's child widget gained focus from the window manager.

Table B-18. *GtkCurve Signals*

Signal Name	Description
curve-type-changed	A call was made to gtk_curve_set_gamma(), gtk_curve_reset(), or gtk_curve_set_curve_type().

Table B-19. *GtkDialog Signals*

Signal Name	Additional Parameters	Description
close	None	The GtkDialog object was closed.
response	gint response	A button in the GtkDialog's action area was activated; the dialog received a delete event, or you made a call to gtk_dialog_response(). Delete events cause a response identifier of GTK_RESPONSE_NONE to be emitted. Otherwise, the response identifier will already be defined.

Table B-20. *GtkEditable Signals*

Signal Name	Additional Parameters	Description
changed	None	The user changed the contents of the editable widget.
delete-text	gint start_pos gint end_pos	Text was deleted from the widget by the user between the two positions.
insert-text	gchar *new_text gint text_length gint *position	Text was inserted into the widget by the user at the given position.

Table B-21. *GtkEntry Signals*

Signal Name	Additional Parameters	Description
activate	None	The Enter key was pressed while the GtkEntry widget had focus. You should run the dialog's default button associated with GtkEntry when activated.
backspace	None	The Backspace key was pressed. The character located to the left of the cursor was deleted, if it existed.
copy-clipboard	None	Selected text was copied to the clipboard.
cut-clipboard	None	Selected text was copied to the clipboard and then removed from the GtkEntry widget.
delete-from-cursor	GtkDeleteType type gint num_deletions	Text was deleted from around the cursor.
insert-at-cursor	gchar *new_text	Text was inserted at the location of the cursor.
move-cursor	GtkMovementStep step gint num_steps gboolean extended	The cursor moved a specified distance. The callback function receives whether the selection was extended.
paste-clipboard	None	Text from the clipboard was inserted into the GtkEntry.

Signal Name	Additional Parameters	Description
populate-popup	GtkMenu *popup_menu	The pop-up menu was shown, because the user clicked the right mouse button.
toggle-overwrite	None	The Insert key was pressed, which toggles the overwrite property, or the property was explicitly changed.

Table B-22. *GtkEntryCompletion Signals*

Signal Name	Additional Parameters	Description
action-activated	gint index	An action item with the given index was chosen from the pop-up list.
insert-prefix	gchar *prefix	The automatic completion provided by GtkEntryCompletion was activated. This allows you to change the default prefix shown by the widget.
match-selected	GtkTreeModel *model GtkTreeIter *match	The user chose a match from the list of items, which is defined by the given GtkTreeModel.

Table B-23. *GtkExpander Signals*

Signal Name	Description
activate	The expander was toggled. This signal is emitted both when the widget is expanded and when it is retracted.

Table B-24. *GtkFileChooser Signals*

Signal Name	Description
confirm-overwrite	The user wants to save a file with a name of a file that already exists. You need to return GTK_FILE_CHOOSER_CONFIRMATION_ ACCEPT_FILENAME to accept the user's choice, GTK_FILE_CHOOSER_ CONFIRMATION_CONFIRM to present the default dialog to confirm the overwriting, or GTK_FILE_CHOOSER_CONFIRMATION_SELECT_AGAIN to make the user select a different name.
current-folder-changed	The current folder shown by the GtkFileChooser was changed. Examples of this can be when the user changes the folder, a bookmark is clicked, or a function call explicitly changes the folder.

Continued

Table B-24. *Continued*

Signal Name	Description
file-activated	The user either double-clicked a file from the list or pressed the Enter key. This is usually only used internally by GtkFileChooserDialog.
selection-changed	The selected file was changed within GtkFileChooser. Examples of this can be when the mouse or keyboard changes the selection or when the code explicitly changes it.
update-preview	The user performed some action, so the preview widget in the file chooser should be re-created. You need to use this signal if the file chooser has a preview widget.

Table B-25. *GtkFontButton Signals*

Signal Name	Description
font-set	The user selected a new font. This signal is not emitted when you change the font explicitly. To monitor all changes to the font, you need to use the notify signal on GtkFontButton's font-name property.

Table B-26. *GtkHandleBox Signals*

Signal Name	Additional Parameters	Description
child-attached	GtkWidget *child	The handle box was re-attached to the main window.
child-detached	GtkWidget *child	The handle box was detached from the main window.

Table B-27. *GtkIconView Signals*

Signal Name	Additional Parameters	Description
activate-cursor-item	None	The user pressed the Enter key while an icon was selected.
item-activated	GtkTreePath *path	The user double-clicked an icon item or pressed the Enter key. You can force this signal to be emitted by calling gtk_icon_view_item_activated().

Signal Name	Additional Parameters	Description
move-cursor	GtkMovementStep step gint num_steps	The user selected a different icon with the mouse cursor. This can also be done with the Up, Down, Ctrl+P, Ctrl+N, Home, End, Page Up, Page Down, Right, or Left keys or a few other Shift and Ctrl keyboard combinations.
select-all	None	All of the items were selected by pressing Ctrl+A on the keyboard.
select-cursor-item	None	The user selected an icon item by pressing the space bar on the keyboard.
selection-changed	None	The selected icons were changed by a user action or a call by your application.
set-scroll-adjustments	GtkAdjustment *hadj GtkAdjustment *vadj	The scroll adjustments of GtkIconView were changed.
toggle-cursor-item	None	The user pressed Ctrl+space bar on the keyboard.
unselect-all	None	All of the icon items were deselected when the user pressed Ctrl+Shift+A on the keyboard.

Table B-28. *GtkIMContext Signals*

Signal Name	Additional Parameters	Description
commit	gchar *str	The string is ready to be displayed by your application.
delete-surrounding	gint offset gint delete_chars	The input method needs to delete the context text. TRUE should be returned if the signal was handled.
preedit-changed	None	The preedited text was changed.
preedit-end	None	The preedited text change was completed.

Continued

Table B-28. *Continued*

Signal Name	Additional Parameters	Description
preedit-start	None	A preedited text change has begun.
retrieve-surrounding	None	The input method needs to know the context surrounding the cursor. You need to use this signal to set the surrounding context with gtk_im_context_set_surrounding(), returning TRUE if it was successfully handled.

Table B-29. *GtkInputDialog Signals*

Signal Name	Additional Parameters	Description
disable-device	GdkDevice *deviceid	The user changed the mode of the input device from GDK_MODE_SCREEN or GDK_MODE_WINDOW to GDK_MODE_DISABLED.
enable-device	GdkDevice *deviceid	The user changed the mode of the input device from GDK_MODE_DISABLED to GDK_MODE_SCREEN or GDK_MODE_WINDOW.

Table B-30. *GtkItem Signals*

Signal Name	Description
deselect	The GtkItem widget was deselected by the user, or gtk_item_deselect() was called.
select	The GtkItem widget was selected by the user, or gtk_item_select() was called.
toggle	The GtkItem widget was toggled by the user, or gtk_item_toggle() was called.

Table B-31. *GtkLabel Signals*

Signal Name	Additional Parameters	Description
copy-clipboard	None	The text from a GtkLabel widget was copied to the GtkClipboard. You can make a GtkLabel widget selectable so that portions of the label can be copied as well as the whole.
move-cursor	GtkMovementStep step gint num_steps gboolean extended	If you have allowed the GtkLabel to be selected with the mouse, a cursor will be shown. You can then move the cursor around the label, which will emit this signal. The callback function receives whether the selection range was extended.
populate-popup	GtkMenu *popup_menu	The user right-clicked the GtkLabel widget, and you need to populate a new menu.

Table B-32. *GtkLayout Signals*

Signal Name	Additional Parameters	Description
set-scroll-adjustments	GtkAdjustment *hadj GtkAdjustment *vadj	The scroll adjustments of the layout were changed.

Table B-33. *GtkMenu Signals*

Signal Name	Additional Parameters	Description
move-scroll	GtkScrollType type	The user scrolled the menu with one of the GtkScrollType values.

Table B-34. *GtkMenuItem Signals*

Signal Name	Additional Parameters	Description
activate	None	The menu item was activated. If you need to catch activation of a submenu, you should use the activate-item signal.
activate-item	None	The menu item was activated, or the menu item has a submenu that was activated.
toggle-size-allocate	gint new_size	The menu item was allocated with a new size.
toggle-size-request	gpointer size	The menu item requested a new size.

Table B-35. *GtkMenuShell Signals*

Signal Name	Additional Parameters	Description
activate-current	gboolean force_hide	Activate the current menu item contained by GtkMenuShell.
cancel	None	Cancel the selection of the selected menu item. This will cause the selection-done signal to be emitted.
cycle-focus	GtkDirectionType type	The focus moved to another menu bar in the given direction.
deactivate	None	The GtkMenuShell was deactivated, which usually means that it was erased from the screen.
move-current	GtkMenuDirectionType type	The current menu item moved within the menu shell in the given direction.
selection-done	None	The selection within the menu shell was completed.

Table B-36. *GtkMenuToolButton Signals*

Signal Name	Description
show-menu	This signal is emitted right before the menu is shown, giving you a chance to update it before the user sees it.

Table B-37. *GtkNotebook Signals*

Signal Name	Additional Parameters	Description
change-current-page	gint pages_moved	The page currently shown by GtkNotebook was changed.
focus-tab	GtkNotebookTab type	The focus was moved by changing the current tab. The callback function returns TRUE if the signal was handled.
move-focus-out	GtkDirectionType type	The focus was moved out of the GtkNotebook widget in the given direction.
page-added	GtkWidget *child guint page_num	A page was added to the GtkNotebook widget. This signal was added in GTK+ 2.10.
page-removed	GtkWidget *child guint page_num	A page was removed from the GtkNotebook widget. This signal was added in GTK+ 2.10.
page-reordered	GtkWidget *child guint page_num	The GtkNotebook widget pages were reordered. This signal was added in GTK+ 2.10.
select-page	gboolean focus_moved	A new page was selected for the child widget. The callback function returns TRUE if the signal was handled.
switch-page	GtkNotebookPage *page guint page_num	The notebook page was changed to the given page.

Table B-38. *GtkObject Signals*

Signal Name	Description
destroy	When the GtkObject widget has released all of its references, it will be destroyed. This will result in finalization of the object when you release all of the references.

Table B-39. *GtkPaned Signals*

Signal Name	Additional Parameters	Description
accept-position	None	Resizing of the pane was completed, and the user pressed the Return key, Enter key, or space bar. This signal will give focus and activate the child widget. The callback function should return TRUE if the signal was handled.
cancel-position	None	Resizing the pane was stopped, because the user pressed the Escape key to cancel the change. The callback function should return TRUE if the signal was handled.
cycle-child-focus	gboolean reversed	The user changed the child focus by pressing F6 or Shift+F6 while the GtkPaned widget had focus. The callback function returns TRUE if the signal was handled.
cycle-handle-focus	gboolean reversed	If the GtkPaned widget had focus and the user presses Tab, Ctrl+Tab, Shift+Tab, or Ctrl+Shift+Tab, the signal is emitted. The callback function should return TRUE if the signal was handled.
move-handle	GtkScrollType type	The handle was moved, and one of the following keys was pressed while it was in focus: Left, Right, Up, Down, Page Up, Page Down, Home, or End. The callback function should return TRUE if the signal was handled.
toggle-handle-focus	None	The GtkPaned widget was within focus, and F8 was pressed to give or take away focus from the handle. The callback function should return TRUE if the signal was handled.

Table B-40. *GtkPlug Signals*

Signal Name	Description
embedded	The GtkPlug window was assigned to the socket window as its parent. GtkPlug allows top-level widgets to be embedded into other processes.

Table B-41. *GtkPrinter Signals*

Signal Name	Additional Parameters	Description
details-acquired	gboolean success	Detailed information about the printer was requested from the print backend.

Table B-42. *GtkPrintJob Signals*

Signal Name	Description
status-changed	The current status of the print job changed. You should use gtk_print_job_get_status() to check the new status of the print job.

Table B-43. *GtkPrintOperation Signals*

Signal Name	Additional Parameters	Description
begin-print	GtkPrintContext *context	The user just finished changing printer settings but rendering has not yet begun.
create-custom-widget	None	The dialog was just displayed. You can return a widget or a container widget containing multiple widgets from the callback function so that it will be added as a custom page to the dialog's GtkNotebook.
custom-widget-apply	GtkWidget *widget	Right before begin-print is emitted, this signal is emitted if a custom widget was added in the create-custom-widget signal handler.

Continued

Table B-43. *Continued*

Signal Name	Additional Parameters	Description
done	GtkPrintOperationResult result	Printing completed, and you can now view the result. You should use gtk_print_operation_get_error() to check the error message if the result was GTK_PRINT_OPERATION_RESULT_ERROR.
draw-page	GtkPrintContext *context gint page_num	Each page must be converted into a Cairo context. You can use this callback to render a page manually.
end-print	GtkPrintContext *context	All of the pages were rendered.
paginate	GtkPrintContext *context	This signal is emitted after begin-print but before page rendering begins. It will continue to be emitted until FALSE is returned or until it is not handled. This allows you to split the document into pages in steps so that the user interface is not noticeably blocked.
preview	GtkPrintOperationPreview *preview GtkPrintContext *context GtkWindow *parent	The user requested a preview of the document from the main printing dialog. This signal allows you to create your own preview dialog. If this signal is not handled, the default handler will be used. The callback function returns TRUE if you are handling the print preview.
request-page-setup	GtkPrintContext *context gint page_num GtkPageSetup *setup	This signal is emitted for every page, which gives you one last chance to edit the setup of a page before it is printed. Any changes will be applied to *only* the current page!
status-changed	None	The status of the print operation changed. Possible values are defined by the GtkPrintStatus enumeration, and the current value can be retrieved with gtk_print_operation_get_status().

Table B-44. *GtkRadioAction Signals*

Signal Name	Additional Parameters	Description
changed	GtkRadioAction *current	The states of two radio buttons in a group were changed. This signal is emitted on every member of a radio group when the selection is changed.

Table B-45. *GtkRadioButton and GtkRadioMenuItem Signals*

Signal Name	Description
group-changed	The radio button switched to a new group, or it was removed from a radio group altogether.

Table B-46. *GtkRange Signals*

Signal Name	Additional Parameters	Description
adjust-bounds	gdouble value	The bounds of a GtkRange were altered by some type of user action.
change-value	GtkScrollType type gdouble value	The current value of the range was changed. You can prevent the range from being updated by returning TRUE, but you will have to manually round the displayed value to the desired number of decimal places.
move-slider	GtkScrollType type	The user pressed a keyboard key such as Page Up, Page Down, Home, End, or an arrow key that caused the slider to move.
value-changed	None	The range value was changed. This can be caused by user action or a call within your code.

Table B-47. *GtkScale Signals*

Signal Name	Additional Parameters	Description
format-value	gdouble value	A scale is about to be displayed, but GTK+ first gives you an opportunity to customize how it is displayed. The callback function returns a customized string displaying the value created by you.

Table B-48. *GtkScrolledWindow Signals*

Signal Name	Additional Parameters	Description
move-focus-out	GtkDirectionType type	The user moved focus from the scrolled window by pressing Ctrl+Tab or Ctrl+Shift+Tab. The given direction is always either GTK_DIR_TAB_FORWARD or GTK_DIR_TAB_BACKWARD.
scroll-child	GtkScrollType type gboolean horizontal	The child widget was scrolled in one direction. This could be caused by the mouse or one of the following default key bindings: Ctrl+Left, Ctrl+Right, Ctrl+Up, Ctrl+Down, Ctrl+Page Up, Ctrl+Page Down, Page Up, Page Down, Ctrl +Home, Ctrl+End, Home, or End.

Table B-49. *GtkSocket Signals*

Signal Name	Description
plug-added	A client was successfully added to the socket.
plug-removed	A client was removed from the socket. Usually, you will want to destroy the GtkSocket widget, which is the default. To prevent this, you can return TRUE from the callback function.

Table B-50. *GtkSpinButton Signals*

Signal Name	Additional Parameters	Description
change-value	GtkScrollType type	The displayed value of the spin button was changed. This was done by pressing one of the following keyboard bindings: Up, Down, Page Up, Page Down, Ctrl+Page Up, or Ctrl+Page Down.
input	gpointer value	The displayed value was changed.
output	None	The displayed value of the spin button was changed by either setting a new value or changing the digits property of a realized widget. You should return TRUE if you successfully handle the signal so that no further action is taken.

Signal Name	Additional Parameters	Description
value-changed	None	Any one of the properties that require the spin button value to be changed (e.g., value or digits) of the spin button was changed.
wrapped	None	The spin button wrapped from the maximum to the minimum value or vice versa. This signal was introduced in GTK+ 2.10.

Table B-51. *GtkStatusbar Signals*

Signal Name	Additional Parameters	Description
text-popped	guint context_id gchar *message	The top message was removed from the status bar's stack. The next message will be displayed.
text-pushed	guint context_id gchar *message	A message was added to the top of the status bar's stack.

Table B-52. *GtkStatusIcon Signals*

Signal Name	Additional Parameters	Description
activate	None	The status icon was activated. How the status icon was activated is dependent on the user's platform. In any case, you should take appropriate action.
popup-menu	guint button guint activate_time	The pop-up menu of the status icon was shown. The function parameters can be passed to gtk_menu_popup(). The pop-up menu feature is not available on every platform, so you should always provide alternative functionality!
size-changed	gint size	The area available to the status icon was changed. The callback function returns TRUE if you scaled the icon. Otherwise, GTK+ will take care of scaling for you.

Table B-53. *GtkTextBuffer Signals*

Signal Name	Additional Parameters	Description
apply-tag	GtkTextTag *tag GtkTextIter *start GtkTextIter *end	A GtkTextTag widget was applied to a section of the text buffer.
begin-user-action	None	The user began some type of action on the text buffer.
changed	None	The text buffer was changed in some way, which resulted in a change of visible or invisible text, images, or widgets.
delete-range	GtkTextIter *start GtkTextIter *end	Text was deleted from the text buffer.
end-user-action	None	Some type of user action on the text buffer ended.
insert-child-anchor	GtkTextIter *location GtkTextChildAnchor *anchor	An anchor was inserted, which allows the text buffer to contain other widgets.
insert-pixbuf	GtkTextIter *location GdkPixbuf *pixbuf	A GdkPixbuf object was inserted into the text buffer.
insert-text	GtkTextIter *location gchar *new_text gint text_length	Text was inserted into the text buffer.
mark-deleted	GtkTextMark *mark	A GtkTextMark object was deleted from the text buffer.
mark-set	GtkTextIter *location GtkTextMark *mark	A GtkTextMark object was added to the text buffer.
modified-changed	None	The text buffer was set as modified or unmodified.
remove-tag	GtkTextTag *tag GtkTextIter *start GtkTextIter *end	A tag was removed from the text buffer between the given iterators.

Table B-54. *GtkTextTag Signals*

Signal Name	Additional Parameters	Description
event	GObject *object GdkEvent *event GtkTextIter *location	An event occurred that was within the range of the text encompassed by GtkTextTag.

Table B-55. *GtkTextTagTable Signals*

Signal Name	Additional Parameters	Description
tag-added	GtkTextTag *tag	A GtkTextTag object was added to the tag table.
tag-changed	GtkTextTag *tag gboolean size_changed	A property of a tag contained by the tag table was changed. The size of the displayed text can be changed by other properties besides the size, such as weight and font family.
tag-removed	GtkTextTag *tag	A GtkTextTag object was removed from the tag table.

Table B-56. *GtkTextView Signals*

Signal Name	Additional Parameters	Description
backspace	None	One character was deleted from the document from behind the cursor.
copy-clipboard	None	Selected text was copied to the clipboard.
cut-clipboard	None	Selected text was copied to the clipboard and removed from the document.
delete-from-cursor	GtkDeleteType type gint length	Text was deleted from around the cursor.
insert-at-cursor	gchar *text	Text was inserted at the current cursor position.
move-cursor	GtkMovementStep step gint num_steps gboolean extended	The cursor was moved to a new position, possibly extending the current selection.
move-focus	GtkDirectionType type	Focus has been moved in the given direction.
move-viewport	GtkScrollStep step gint num_steps	Some type of scrolling occurred, which is described by the given step.
paste-clipboard	None	Text from the clipboard was inserted into the document.

Continued

Table B-56. *Continued*

Signal Name	Additional Parameters	Description
populate-popup	GtkMenu *menu	The pop-up menu was shown and is available for editing.
select-all	gboolean selected	All of the text in the document was selected or deselected.
set-anchor	None	An anchor was added to the text view.
set-scroll-adjustments	GtkAdjustment *hadj GtkAdjustment *vadj	The adjustments of the text view were set.
toggle-overwrite	None	The overwrite key was toggled on or off.

Table B-57. *GtkToggleAction, GtkToggleButton, and GtkToggleToolButton Signals*

Signal Name	Description
toggled	The state of the toggle was changed. You should connect to this signal if you want to take some type of action when the toggle is activated or deactivated.

Table B-58. *GtkToolbar Signals*

Signal Name	Additional Parameters	Description
focus-home-or-end	gboolean focus_home	This signal is used internally by GTK+ to move to the first or last element in the toolbar and cannot be used in application code. The callback function returns TRUE if the signal was handled.
move-focus	GtkDirectionType type	This signal is used internally by GTK+ to move the focused item and cannot be used in application code.
orientation-changed	GtkOrientation dir	The orientation of the toolbar was changed to horizontal or vertical.

Signal Name	Additional Parameters	Description
popup-context-menu	gint x_position gint y_position gint button	The user right-clicked the toolbar or pressed a key binding that causes a pop-up menu to be displayed. You can use this to display a custom context menu for the toolbar. You should return TRUE if the signal was handled.
style-changed	GtkToolbarStyle style	The style of the toolbar was changed.

Table B-59. *GtkToolButton Signals*

Signal Name	Description
changed	The tool button was clicked with the mouse. This signal can also be emitted if the tool button was activated with a keyboard binding.

Table B-60. *GtkToolItem Signals*

Signal Name	Additional Parameters	Description
create-menu-proxy	None	The toolbar needs to know whether the item should appear in an overflow menu. To handle this signal, you should either call gtk_tool_item_set_proxy_menu_item() or return FALSE to prevent it from appearing in the overflow menu. You should return TRUE if the signal was handled.
set-tooltip	GtkTooltips *tooltips gchar *tip_text gchar *tip_private	The tooltip of an item was changed to the given configuration.
toolbar-reconfigured	None	Some property of the tool item's parent was changed that requires the child to be changed. This is caused by a change in the orientation, style, icon size, or relief style of the toolbar.

Table B-61. *GtkTreeModel Signals*

Signal Name	Additional Parameters	Description
row-changed	GtkTreePath *path GtkTreeIter *iter	A row in the tree model at the given location was changed.
row-deleted	GtkTreePath *path	A row was removed from the tree model at the given location.
row-has-child-toggled	GtkTreePath *path GtkTreeIter *iter	A row at the given location was given its first child, or its last remaining child was removed.
row-inserted	GtkTreePath *path GtkTreeIter *iter	A row was added to the tree model. This signal is called immediately after the row is added, so it may not yet contain any data.
rows-reordered	GtkTreePath *path GtkTreeIter *iter gpointer row_nums	Rows within a tree model were reordered by some method besides drag and drop. The callback function receives an array of reordered row numbers.

Table B-62. *GtkTreeSelection Signals*

Signal Name	Description
changed	The selection may have been changed. This signal is not always reliable, because it is only emitted once when multiple rows are selected with the Shift key and can be emitted when nothing at all has occurred. You should build error protection into callback functions for this signal.

Table B-63. *GtkTreeSortable Signals*

Signal Name	Description
sort-column-changed	The sort column is the column that will be used to sort all of the rows within a GtkTreeSortable model. This signal is emitted when the chosen sort column is changed.

Table B-64. *GtkTreeView Signals*

Signal Name	Additional Parameters	Description
columns-changed	None	Columns were added or removed from the tree view, which caused the number of columns to change.
cursor-changed	None	The position of the cursor within a cell with focus changed.
expand-collapse-cursor-row	gboolean logical gboolean expanded expand_children	A row located at the cursor position needs to expanded or collapsed. You should return TRUE if the signal is handled.
move-cursor	GtkMovementStep step gint num_steps	The cursor was moved by using one of the following key bindings: Right, Left, Up, Down, Page Up, Page Down, Home, or End. You should return TRUE if the signal was handled.
row-activated	GtkTreePath *path GtkTreeViewColumn *column	The user double-clicked a row, or gtk_tree_view_row_activated() was called. It can also be emitted with the following key bindings: Space, Shift+space bar, Return, or Enter.
row-collapsed	GtkTreeIter *iter GtkTreePath *path	The child nodes of the given row were hidden.
row-expanded	GtkTreeIter *iter GtkTreePath *path	The child nodes of the given row were shown.
select-all	None	All of the rows within the tree view were selected. This can be done by pressing Ctrl+A or Ctrl+/.
select-cursor-parent	None	The user pressed the Backspace key while the row had cursor focus. The callback function should return TRUE if the signal was handled.

Continued

Table B-64. *Continued*

Signal Name	Additional Parameters	Description
select-cursor-row	gboolean editing	A noneditable row was selected by pressing one of the following key bindings: space bar, Shift+space bar, Return, or Enter. The callback function should return TRUE if the signal was handled.
set-scroll-adjustments	GtkAdjustment *hadj GtkAdjustment *vadj	Horizontal and vertical scroll adjustments were set for the tree view. The callback function should return TRUE if the signal was handled.
start-interactive-search	None	The user pressed Crtl+F while the tree view had focus. You should return TRUE if the signal was handled.
test-collapse-row	GtkTreeIter *iter GtkTreePath *path	A row is about to be collapsed. The callback function should return TRUE to go forward with the collapse.
test-expand-row	GtkTreeIter *iter GtkTreePath *path	A row is about to be expanded. The callback function should return TRUE to go forward with the expansion.
toggle-cursor-row	None	The user pressed Ctrl+space bar while a row had focus. You should return TRUE if the signal was handled.
unselect-all	None	All of the rows in a tree view were deselected by pressing Shift+Ctrl+A or Shift+Ctrl+/. You should return TRUE if the signal was handled.

Table B-65. *GtkTreeViewColumn Signals*

Signal Name	Description
clicked	The user pressed the tree view column's header button. This usually causes the tree view's rows to be sorted according to that column in views that support sorting.

Table B-66. *GtkUIManager Signals*

Signal Name	Additional Parameters	Description
actions-changed	None	A set of actions within the UI manager were changed.
add-widget	GtkWidget *widget	A menu bar or toolbar was generated. This signal is not emitted for pop-up menus, so you will have to use gtk_ui_manager_get_widget() to retrieve those.
connect-proxy	GtkAction *action GtkWidget *proxy	A proxy was connected to an action within the group. You can use this signal for customizations that are used by many actions.
disconnect-proxy	GtkAction *action GtkWidget *proxy	A proxy was connected to an action within the group.
post-activate	GtkAction *action	An action was just activated. This signal can be used to retrieve notice of activation of all actions.
pre-activate	GtkAction *action	An action is about to be activated. This signal can be used to retrieve notice of activation of all actions.

Table B-67. *GtkViewport Signals*

Signal Name	Additional Parameters	Description
set-scroll-adjustments	GtkAdjustment *hadj GtkAdjustment *vadj	The adjustments for the viewport were changed.

Table B-68. *GtkWidget Signals with Events Removed*

Signal Name	Additional Parameters	Description
accel-closures-changed	None	An accelerator was added or removed from the widget's accelerator group. This signal is also emitted when an accelerator path is set up.
can-activate-accel	guint signal_id	You can use this signal to override the default handler for whether an accelerator can be activated. You should return TRUE if the signal can be activated.
child-notify	GParamSpec *pspec	A child property was changed for the widget. This signal can be used to monitor a signal property.
composited-changed	None	The composited status of the widget was changed; composited is a property that determines whether the widget's alpha channel will be honored.
direction-changed	GtkTextDirection dir	The direction of the text within the widget was changed. This is usually initiated by a call to gtk_widget_set_direction().
drag-begin	GdkDragContext *context	A drag action began. This signal is emitted on the drag source. You can use this signal to set up a custom icon to display when dragging.
drag-data-delete	GdkDragContext *context	A drag action was successfully completed. This signal is used to delete the data that was being dragged when the action is completed.
drag-data-get	GdkDragContext *context GtkSelectionData *data guint info guint timestamp	The drop site requested the data that was dragged.
drag-data-received	GdkDragContext *context gint x_position gint y_position GtkSelectionData *data guint int guint timestamp	The drag data was received by the drop site.

Signal Name	Additional Parameters	Description
drag-drop	GdkDragContext *context gint x_position gint y_position guint timestamp	The user dropped data onto a widget. You must determine whether the cursor position is within the accepted drop region. You should return TRUE if the drop is acceptable.
drag-end	GdkDragContext *context	A drag action was completed, which can be used to undo actions performed in the drag-begin callback.
drag-leave	GdkDragContext *context guint timestamp	The cursor left the proximity of the drop site. This signal can be used to undo actions performed in the drag-motion callback.
drag-motion	GdkDragContext *context gint x_position gint y_position guint timestamp	The cursor was moved over the drop site during a drag. You should return TRUE if the cursor is within an acceptable drop area.
focus	GtkDirectionType type	The widget received focus. You should return TRUE if the signal was handled.
grab-focus	None	The widget forced focus on itself by calling gtk_widget_grab_focus(). This signal can also be initiated with mnemonic accelerators.
grab-notify	gboolean was_grabbed	The widget became shadowed because of an explicit call to gtk_grab_add() on another widget, or it became unshadowed because of a removed grab.
hide	None	The widget was hidden from the user's view. The user interface will be redrawn to accommodate for the missing widget.
hierarchy-changed	GtkWidget *toplevel	The widget is considered to be anchored when its top-level ancestor is a GtkWindow widget. This signal is emitted when the child becomes anchored or unanchored.

Continued

Table B-68. *Continued*

Signal Name	Additional Parameters	Description
map	None	The widget requested to be mapped. This can be initiated by calling gtk_widget_show() or gtk_widget_map().
mnemonic-activate	gboolean shift_focus	A mnemonic accelerator was used to activate the widget.
parent-set	GtkObject *old_parent	The parent widget was changed.
popup-menu	None	The user requested a pop-up menu to be shown. This call-back function returns TRUE if it was handled.
realize	None	The widget requested to be realized because of a call to gtk_widget_realize(). This is not usually explicitly called by your code unless you are creating your own custom widget.
screen-changed	GdkScreen *screen	The widget was moved to a new screen.
selection-get	GtkSelectionData *data guint info guint timestamp	Selection data was requested from the widget.
selection-received	GtkSelectionData *data guint timestamp	The owner of a selection responded to a request for selection data for the widget.
show	None	The widget was set as visible. The user interface will be redrawn to accommodate the newly visible widget.
show-help	GtkWidgetHelpType type	The user requested help with the widget by pressing Ctrl+F1. Help types are defined by GtkWidgetHelpType, which is composed of GTK_WIDGET_HELP_TOOLTIP and GTK_WIDGET_HELP_WHATS_THIS.
size-allocate	GtkAllocation *alloc	The widget was given a new size allocation.
size-request	GtkRequisition *req	The widget requested a new size by using gtk_widget_set_size_request().

Signal Name	Additional Parameters	Description
state-changed	GtkStateType state	The current state of the widget changed to the given state.
style-set	GtkStyle *prev_style	The widget's style was modified. This is caused by changing the whole style or by changing specific elements of the style.
unmap	None	The widget requested to be unmapped. This can be initiated by calling gtk_widget_unmap().
unrealize	None	The widget requested to be unrealized. This will cause all of its associated resources and the resources of any child widgets to be freed.

Table B-69. *GtkWindow Signals*

Signal Name	Additional Parameters	Description
activate-default	None	The default widget of the window was activated. This is usually because the user pressed the Return or Enter key.
activate-focus	None	The child widget of the window that has focus was activated. This is usually because the user pressed the space bar.
frame-event	GdkEvent *event	An event other than key-press-event, key-release-event, or a change in focus was received on the window's frame.
keys-changed	None	A mnemonic accelerator was added, removed, or changed within the window. This can also be caused by setting a mnemonic modifier.
move-focus	GtkDirectionType type	The focus was changed within the child widgets of the window. This usually happens when the user presses one of the following key bindings: Tab, Shift+Tab, Up, Down, Left, or Right.
set-focus	GtkWidget *widget	The focus was changed to a different child in the window.

■■■

GTK+ Styles

GTK+ provides many ways to customize the styles of widgets. Most customization of widget styles is done through style properties and resource (RC) files, which were covered in the Widget Styles section of Chapter 4.

In addition to the information in Chapter 4, this appendix provides a reference to default RC file elements that can be applied to any widget, the Pango Text Markup Language, and GtkTextTag styles.

Default RC File Styles

Resource files are introduced in Chapter 4, but this section can be used as a reference of the default styles supported by every widget.

Along with the background, foreground, base, and text color styles, you need to specify a widget state for which many styles will be attributed. States are also required when specifying stock icons for some functions. The five widget states follow:

- NORMAL: The state of the widget during normal operation.

- ACTIVE: The state of an active widget, such as when a toggle is depressed.

- PRELIGHT: The mouse pointer is over the widget, which will respond to button clicks.

- SELECTED: The widget or widget text has been selected.

- INSENSITIVE: The widget is deactivated and will not respond to the user.

Colors can be specified in multiple formats. These may include hexadecimal formats like #RGB, #RRGGBB, #RRRGGGBBB, and #RRRRGGGGBBBB where R, G, and B are hexadecimal digits representing red, green, and blue values respectively. You can also specify colors as { R, G, B } where the values are given as integers between 0 and 65,535 or floating point values between 0.0 and 1.0.

Table C-1 gives a complete list of the default RC file styles that are supported as of GTK+ 2.10. Some of the style descriptions also include examples of how they are implemented.

Table C-1. *RC File Styles*

Style	Description
base[state]	Set the background color of widgets that allow text to be edited (e.g., GtkEntry) in one of the five states. Example: base[ACTIVE] = { 0.5, 0.3, 1.0 }
bg[state]	Set the background color for most widgets in one of the five states. Example: bg[NORMAL] = "#036"
bg_pixmap[state]	Set an image to use as the background for the widget in one of the five states. If the image file is relative, it will be searched for in one of the paths specified by pixmap_path. Example: bg_pixmap[SELECTED] = "image.xpm"
class::property	Set a style property for the specific widget class. For example, GtkWidget properties include cursor-aspect-ratio, cursor-color, and draw-border. Example: class::cursor-aspect-ratio = 0.1
color["color_name"]	As of GTK+ 2.10, you can define your own colors. A color is referred to as @color_name. More information can be found immediately after this table.
engine	Theme engines allow you to define your own widget styles from an RC file. More information about using engines can be found in the GTK+ documentation.
fg	Set the foreground color for most widgets in one of the five states. Example: fg[PRELIGHT] = "#123456"
font_name	The font and fontset styles are ignored as of GTK+ 2.10 in favor of this style. You should specify this font name as you would to a Pango Font Description string. Example: font_name = "Sans Bold 12"
stock["stockid"]	Define a new stock item that can be used by the application. The stock item accepts the image filename, text direction (left to right or right to left), widget state, and size. Sizes include gtk-menu, gtk-small-toolbar, gtk-large-toolbar, gtk-button, and gtk-dialog. The asterisk (*) character can be used as a wildcard for any of the last three parameters. Example: stock["myitem"] = { "myitem.png", LTR, NORMAL, "gtk-menu" }
text[state]	Set the text color for widgets such as GtkEntry. Example: fg[PRELIGHT] = { 0, 65535, 0 }
xthickness	Set horizontal padding for various values in GTK+. This value is specified as an integer.
ythickness	Set vertical padding for various values in GTK+. This value is specified as an integer.

As of GTK+ 2.10, you can define your own colors. Four functions are provided that allow you to alter existing colors. Each of the following methods accepts any of the supported color expressions:

- shade (factor, color): Make the specified color lighter or darker. The factor can be a floating point number, where 1.0 leaves the color as it is. A smaller factor will darken the color, while larger factors will lighten it.

- darker (color): This expression is equivalent to shade (0.7, color).

- lighter (color): This expression is equivalent to shade (1.3, color).

- mix (factor, color1, color2): Create a new color by mixing the two colors, where a factor of 0.0 outputs color2 and a factor of 1.0 outputs color1.

These methods can also be used together to create colors. To help you understand, a few examples of color creation expressions follow:

```
color["blackwhite"] = mix (0.5, "#000000", "#FFFFFF")
color["darker"] = shade (0.5, @blackwhite)
color["multiple"] = shade (1.4, mix (0.1, "#369", { 0, 1.0, 0 }))
```

Pango Text Markup Language

The Pango Text Markup Language allows you to change the styles of text with XML tags in some widgets, such as GtkLabel.

The <span> tag can be used with many attributes to define the styles of text. For example, <span font_desc='Sans Bold 12'>Text</span> sets the text between the tags with the specified font. Table C-2 gives a list of supported attributes for the <span> tag.

Table C-2. *Span Tag Attributes*

Attribute	Description
background	A value that describes the background color. Possible values include the hexadecimal RGB value in the form #RRGGBB or a supported color name like blue.
face	A font family name such as Sans or Monospace. This tag is the same thing as font_family.

Continued

Table C-2. *Continued*

Attribute	Description
fallback	When enabled, which is the default, the system will try to find the font that most closely matches the specified font. You should not turn this off, but if it is necessary, you should use a value of false.
font_desc	A font description string that would be supported by PangoFontDescription such as "Sans Bold 12".
font_family	A font family name such as Sans or Monospace. This tag is the same thing as face.
foreground	A value that describes the foreground color. Possible values include the hexadecimal RGB value in the form #RRGGBB or a supported color name like blue.
lang	A language code that states what language the text string is in.
rise	This value allows you to create superscripts and subscripts by specifying a vertical displacement, in 10,000ths of an em unit. Negative values create a subscript, and positive values create a superscript.
size	The size of the font, in 1,024ths of a point. You can also use xx-small, x-small, small, medium, large, x-large, xx-large, larger, or smaller. Absolute sizes are usually easier to specify by using font_desc.
stretch	How much the text will be stretched. Possible values include ultracondensed, extracondensed, condensed, semicondensed, normal, semiexpanded, expanded, extraexpanded, and ultraexpanded.
strikethrough	You should specify true to place a single line through the text or false to turn it off.
strikethrough_color	A value that describes the strikethrough line color. Possible values include the hexadecimal RGB value in the form #RRGGBB or a supported color name like blue.
style	The italicized style of the text. Possible values include normal, oblique, and italic.
underline	A value describing how the text will be underlined. Possible values include single, double, low, and none.
underline_color	A value that describes the underline color. Possible values include the hexadecimal RGB value in the form #RRGGBB or a supported color name like blue.
variant	A value of normal or smallcaps, which allows text to be rendered as all capital letters.
weight	The weight of the text. Possible values include ultralight, light, normal, bold, ultrabold, heavy, and a numeric weight value.

The Pango Text Markup Language also provides a number of convenience tags. These tags can be used in place of various `<span>` attributes. As with the `<span>` tag, you must always provide a closing tag (e.g., `</span>`).

- `<b>`: Make the font bold, which is equivalent to `<span weight="bold">`.

- `<big>`: Make the font larger than the current font, which is equivalent to `<span size="larger">`.

- `<i>`: Equivalent to `<span style="italic">`, which makes the font italic.

- `<s>`: Strike through the text, which is equivalent to `<span strikethrough="true">`.

- `<sub>`: Make the text string subscript. This uses the default value for subscript text.

- `<sup>`: Make the text string superscript. This uses the default value for superscript text.

- `<small>`: Make the font larger than the current font, which is equivalent to `<span size="smaller">`.

- `<tt>`: Make the font a monospace font. This can be used for code segments or other strings that require monospaced characters.

- `<u>`: Underline the text, which is equivalent to `<span underline="single">`.

GtkTextTag Styles

Text tags allow you to define styles for specific sections of a `GtkTextBuffer`. Table C-3 is a complete list of styles supported by `GtkTextTag` along with a description of what type of values each style supports.

Table C-3. *GtkTextTag Style Properties*

Property	Type	Description
background	gchararray	The background color as a hexadecimal string. Strings should be specified in the following format: #RRGGBB.
background-full-height	gboolean	Indicates whether the background color fills the entire line height or only the height of each individual character.
background-gdk	GdkColor	The background color.

Continued

Table C-3. *Continued*

Property	Type	Description
background-stipple	GdkPixmap	A bitmap to draw as the background of the widget.
direction	GtkTextDirection	The default text direction, set as GTK_TEXT_DIR_NONE, GTK_TEXT_DIR_LTR, or GTK_TEXT_DIR_RTL.
editable	gboolean	Indicates whether the text can be modified.
family	gchararray	The formal name of the font family such as Sans or Monospace.
font	gchararray	A string describing the full font in the form accepted by PangoFontDescription.
font-desc	PangoFontDescription	A font to apply to the widget. You can also use font to specify the actual font string.
foreground	gchararray	The foreground color as a hexadecimal string. Strings should be specified in the following format: #RRGGBB.
foreground-gdk	GdkColor	The foreground color.
foreground-stipple	GdkPixmap	A bitmap to use as a foreground mask.
indent	gint	Integer that sets the number of pixels to indent the paragraph.
invisible	gboolean	Indicates whether the text is hidden.
justification	GtkJustification	The type of justification, set as GTK_JUSTIFY_LEFT, GTK_JUSTIFY_RIGHT, or GTK_JUSTIFY_CENTER.
language	gchararray	The ISO code of the default language. Use NULL to remove a previous setting.
left-margin	gint	The width of the left margin in pixels.
name	gchararray	A string that can be used as the name of the text tag. Use NULL to remove a previous setting.
paragraph-background	gchararray	Paragraph background color as a hexadecimal string. Strings should be specified in the following format: #RRGGBB.
paragraph-background-gdk	GdkColor	The paragraph's background color.
pixels-above-lines	gint	The number of pixels of space to add above paragraphs.
pixels-below-lines	gint	The number of pixels of space to add below paragraphs.

Property	Type	Description
pixels-inside-wrap	gint	The number of pixels of space to add between wrapped lines.
right-margin	gint	The width of the right margin in pixels.
rise	gint	The offset of text above the bottom of the line.
scale	gdouble	The font size as a Pango scale value, set as PANGO_SCALE_XX_SMALL, PANGO_SCALE_X_SMALL, PANGO_SCALE_SMALL, PANGO_SCALE_MEDIUM, PANGO_SCALE_LARGE, PANGO_SCALE_X_LARGE or PANGO_SCALE_XX_LARGE.
size	gint	The font size in Pango units.
size-points	gdouble	The font size in points.
stretch	PangoStretch	A value defining how much the text will be stretched, set as PANGO_STRETCH_ULTRA_CONDENSED, PANGO_STRETCH_EXTRA_CONDENSED, PANGO_STRETCH_CONDENSED, PANGO_STRETCH_SEMI_CONDENSED, PANGO_STRETCH_NORMAL, PANGO_STRETCH_SEMI_EXPANDED, PANGO_STRETCH_EXPANDED, PANGO_STRETCH_EXTRA_EXPANDED, or PANGO_STRETCH_ULTRA_EXPANDED.
strikethrough	gboolean	Indicates whether a line should be placed through the text.
style	PangoStyle	A font style value, set as PANGO_STYLE_NORMAL, PANGO_STYLE_OBLIQUE, or PANGO_STYLE_ITALIC.
tabs	PangoTabArray	A custom tab array to use for all tab characters within the tag's range.
underline	PangoUnderline	An underline style, set as PANGO_UNDERLINE_NONE, PANGO_UNDERLINE_SINGLE, PANGO_UNDERLINE_DOUBLE, PANGO_UNDERLINE_LOW, or PANGO_UNDERLINE_ERROR.
variant	PangoVariant	All of the text should be rendered as all capital letters (PANGO_VARIANT_SMALL_CAPS) or normally (PANGO_VARIANT_NORMAL).

Continued

Table C-3. *Continued*

Property	Type	Description
weight	gint	Font weight, set as PANGO_WEIGHT_ULTRALIGHT, PANGO_WEIGHT_LIGHT, PANGO_WEIGHT_NORMAL, PANGO_WEIGHT_SEMIBOLD, PANGO_WEIGHT_BOLD, PANGO_WEIGHT_ULTRABOLD, or PANGO_WEIGHT_HEAVY.
wrap-mode	GtkWrapMode	The wrap mode, set as GTK_WRAP_NONE, GTK_WRAP_CHAR, GTK_WRAP_WORD, or GTK_WRAP_WORD_CHAR.

Widget Style Properties

Many widgets have style properties that can be altered with RC files. Tables C-4 through C-32 give a complete listing of the style properties provided by those widgets that can be customized using this method.

Table C-4. *GtkArrow Style Properties*

Property	Type	Description
arrow-scaling	gfloat	A number between 0.0 and 1.0 used for scaling the arrow size, where the default is 0.7

Table C-5. *GtkAssistant Style Properties*

Property	Type	Description
content-padding	gint	The number of pixels of padding that are added around the content of each page
header-padding	gint	The number of pixels of padding that are added around the header of each page

Table C-6. *GtkButton Style Properties*

Property	Type	Description
child-displacement-x	gint	Horizontal displacement of the button's child widget that will occur when the button is pressed.
child-displacement-y	gint	Vertical displacement of the button's child widget that will occur when the button is pressed.
default-border	GtkBorder	Extra border to add along the button when it is capable of becoming the default widget.
default-outside-border	GtkBorder	Extra border to add along the outside of the button when it is capable of becoming the default widget.
displace-focus	gboolean	If set to TRUE, the child displacement style properties will be used.
image-spacing	gint	The number of pixels of spacing that are added between the image and text contained by the button.
inner-border	GtkBorder	The border to place along the edges of the button and its child widget.

Table C-7. *GtkButtonBox Style Properties*

Property	Type	Description
child-internal-pad-x	gint	Padding that is placed on either side of each child widget
child-internal-pad-y	gint	Padding that is placed above and below each child widget
child-min-height	gint	The minimum height of each button within the container
child-min-width	gint	The minimum width of each button within the container

Table C-8. *GtkCheckButton Style Properties*

Property	Type	Description
indicator-size	gint	The size of the check or radio button in pixels
indicator-spacing	gint	Padding to add around the check button indicator

Table C-9. *GtkCheckMenuItem Style Properties*

Property	Type	Description
indicator-size	gint	The size of the check button indicator in pixels

Table C-10. *GtkComboBox Style Properties*

Property	Type	Description
appears-as-list	gboolean	If set to TRUE, the drop-down window that is shown when the widget is activated will appear like a list instead of a menu.
arrow-size	gint	The size, in pixels, of the arrow displayed by the combo box. This is the minimum value and will be enlarged if the font size is set larger.

Table C-11. *GtkDialog Style Properties*

Property	Type	Description
action-area-border	gint	The number of pixels of padding to place around the action area, which is found along the bottom of the dialog
button-spacing	gint	Spacing to add between buttons in the dialog's action area
content-area-border	gint	The number of pixels of padding to place around the dialog's main content

Table C-12. *GtkEntry Style Properties*

Property	Type	Description
inner-border	GtkBorder	The number of pixels of padding to place between the GtkEntry widget's text and its edges

Table C-13. *GtkExpander Style Properties*

Property	Type	Description
expander-size	gint	The size of the expander's arrow in pixels
expander-spacing	gint	Padding to place around the expander's arrow in pixels

Table C-14. *GtkIconView Style Properties*

Property	Type	Description
selection-box-alpha	guchar	The alpha value of the selection box, which is set to 64 by default
selection-box-color	GdkColor	The color displayed by the selection box

Table C-15. *GtkMenu Style Properties*

Property	Type	Description
double-arrow	gboolean	If set to TRUE, both arrows will be displayed when scrolling through a menu.
horizontal-offset	gint	The horizontal offset, in pixels, of a submenu from its original position. This value can be either positive or negative! In fact, the default value is -2.
horizontal-padding	gint	The number of pixels of padding to add along the left and right sides of the menu.
vertical-offset	gint	The horizontal offset, in pixels, of a submenu from its original position. This value can be either positive or negative!
vertical-padding	gint	The number of pixels of padding to add along the top and bottom edges of the menu.

Table C-16. *GtkMenuBar Style Properties*

Property	Type	Description
internal-padding	gint	Padding to place between the menu items and the edge of the menu bar
shadow-type	GtkShadowType	The type of shadow to place around the edges of the menu bar

Table C-17. *GtkMenuItem Style Properties*

Property	Type	Description
arrow-spacing	gint	Padding that is added between the menu item's label and its arrow when the item contains a submenu
horizontal-padding	gint	The number of pixels of padding placed on either side of the menu item

Continued

Table C-17. *Continued*

Property	Type	Description
selected-shadow-type	GtkShadowType	The type of shadow to place around the edges of the menu item
toggle-spacing	gint	The number of pixels of padding placed between the icon and text of a menu item

Table C-18. *GtkMessageDialog Style Properties*

Property	Type	Description
message-border	gint	Padding to add around both the image and label in the message dialog.
use-separator	gboolean	If set to TRUE, a separator will be drawn between the content of the message dialog and its buttons.

Table C-19. *GtkNotebook Style Properties*

Property	Type	Description
arrow-spacing	gint	Padding to place between the scrolling arrows and the GtkNotebook widget's tabs.
has-backward-stepper	gboolean	If set to TRUE, the backward scroll arrow will be displayed.
has-forward-stepper	gboolean	If set to TRUE, the forward scroll arrow will be displayed.
has-secondary-backward-stepper	gboolean	If set to TRUE, a second backward scroll arrow will be placed on the other side of the tabs.
has-secondary-forward-stepper	gboolean	If set to TRUE, a second forward scroll arrow will be placed on the other side of the tabs.
tab-curvature	gint	The size difference between the selected tab and the deselected tabs.
tab-overlap	gint	The number of pixels by which adjacent tabs will overlap.

Table C-20. *GtkPaned Style Properties*

Property	Type	Description
handle-size	gint	The width or height of the separator placed between the two panes

Table C-21. *GtkProgressBar Style Properties*

Property	Type	Description
xspacing	gint	Horizontal spacing to add to the width of the widget
yspacing	gint	Vertical spacing to add to the height of the widget

Table C-22. *GtkRange Style Properties*

Property	Type	Description
activate-slider	gboolean	If set to TRUE, the slider will be drawn as active when it is dragged, which will cause the shadow to be drawn inwards.
arrow-displacement-x	gint	When the horizontal arrow is pressed, the range will move this far in the direction that the arrow points.
arrow-displacement-y	gint	When the vertical arrow is pressed, the range will move this far in the direction that the arrow points.
slider-width	gint	The width or height of the actual scrollbar or the scale area, depending on the orientation of the widget.
stepper-size	gint	The size of the stepper buttons, depending on the type of range widget.
stepper-spacing	gint	The amount of padding to add between the stepper buttons and the thumb. If this is set to a positive number, it will cause trough-under-steppers to be set.
trough-border	gint	Padding added between the steppers and the outer trough.
trough-side-details	gboolean	If set to TRUE, details will be placed on the side of the stepper.
trough-upper-steppers	gboolean	If set to TRUE, the trough will be drawn along the whole range.

Table C-23. *GtkScale Style Properties*

Property	Type	Description
slider-length	gint	The length of the GtkScale's slider in pixels
value-spacing	gint	Padding to place between the scale's value and trough, if it is displayed

Table C-24. *GtkScrollbar Style Properties*

Property	Type	Description
fixed-slider-length	gboolean	If set to TRUE, the slider will be forced to remain the minimum length, regardless of the size of the range.
has-backward-stepper	gboolean	If set to TRUE, the backward arrow will be displayed.
has-forward-stepper	gboolean	If set to TRUE, the forward arrow will be displayed.
has-secondary-backward-stepper	gboolean	If set to TRUE, a second backward arrow will be placed on the other side of the scrollbar.
has-secondary-forward-stepper	gboolean	If set to TRUE, a second forward arrow will be placed on the other side of the scrollbar.
min-slider-length	gint	The minimum length of the slider. This will be the constant size of the scroller if fixed-slider-length is set to TRUE.

Table C-25. *GtkScrolledWindow Style Properties*

Property	Type	Description
scrollbar-spacing	gint	The number of pixels of padding to place between the scrollbars and the content of the scrolled window

Table C-26. *GtkSpinButton Style Properties*

Property	Type	Description
shadow-type	GtkShadowType	The type of shadow to draw around the spin button. By default, the shadow type is GTK_SHADOW_IN.

Table C-27. *GtkStatusbar Style Properties*

Property	Type	Description
shadow-type	GtkShadowType	The type of shadow to draw around the status bar's content. By default, the shadow type is GTK_SHADOW_IN.

Table C-28. *GtkTextView Style Properties*

Property	Type	Description
error-underline-color	GdkColor	The color that will be used to draw underlines below text marked with errors.

Table C-29. *GtkToolbar Style Properties*

Property	Type	Description
button-relief	GtkReliefStyle	The type of border to place around toolbar buttons.
internal-padding	gint	The number of pixels of padding to place between the toolbar's border and the tool buttons.
max-child-expand	gint	The maximum width or height that each tool item can resize to.
shadow-type	GtkShadowType	The type of shadow to draw around the toolbar. By default, the shadow type is GTK_SHADOW_OUT.
space-size	gint	The width or height of spacers found on the toolbar.
space-style	GtkToolbarSpaceStyle	The type of spacer that will be displayed by the toolbar. This can be set to GTK_TOOLBAR_SPACE_EMPTY or GTK_TOOLBAR_SPACE_LINE, which will display empty padding or a line respectively.

Table C-30. *GtkToolButton Style Properties*

Property	Type	Description
icon-spacing	gint	The number of pixels of padding to place between the icon and label of the tool button

Table C-31. *GtkTreeView Style Properties*

Property	Type	Description
allow-rules	gboolean	If set to TRUE, rows can be drawn in alternating colors. Note that this does *not* enable this feature, it simply allows it to be done!
even-row-color	GdkColor	The background color of even-numbered rows when alternating rows are drawn with different colors.

Continued

Table C-31. *Continued*

Property	Type	Description
expander-size	gint	The size of the row expander, in pixels, where the default value is 12.
grid-line-pattern	gchararray	The pattern to use for grid lines drawn in the tree view.
grid-line-width	gint	The width of grid lines drawn in the tree view.
horizontal-separator	gint	Horizontal spacing to place between cells, which must be a positive, even integer.
indent-expanders	gboolean	If set to TRUE, expanders will be indented when the row content is expanded.
odd-row-color	GdkColor	The background color of odd-numbered rows when alternating rows are drawn with different colors.
row-ending-details	gboolean	If set to TRUE, row background theming will be enabled.
tree-line-pattern	gchararray	A string that describes the pattern used for drawing tree view lines.
tree-line-width	gint	The width of tree view lines, in pixels.
vertical-separator	gint	Vertical spacing to place between cells, which must be a positive, even integer.

Table C-32. *GtkWidget Style Properties*

Property	Type	Description
cursor-aspect-ratio	gfloat	The aspect ratio to draw the insertion cursor, between 0.0 and 1.0, where the default value is 0.04.
cursor-color	GdkColor	The color that will be used to draw the insertion cursor.
draw-border	GtkBorder	The amount of border that will be placed beyond the widget's initial allocation.
focus-line-pattern	gchararray	A string that describes the pattern that is drawn around the widget when it has focus.
focus-line-width	gint	The width of the line that is drawn when the widget has focus.
focus-padding	gint	The number of pixels of padding to place between the focus line and the widget's edge.
interior-focus	gboolean	If set to TRUE, the focus line will be drawn for widgets.

Property	Type	Description
link-color	GdkColor	The color that will be used to draw unvisited links.
scroll-arrow-hlength	gint	The length of horizontal scroll arrows in widgets that have them.
scroll-arrow-vlength	gint	The length of vertical scroll arrows in widgets that have them.
secondary-cursor-color	GdkColor	The color that will be used to draw the secondary insertion cursor. This cursor is displayed when you are editing both left-to-right and right-to-left text at the same time.
separator-height	gint	The height of many types of separators displayed in different widgets. This property will only work if wide-separators is set.
separator-width	gint	The width of many types of separators displayed in different widgets. This property will only work if wide-separators is set.
visited-link-color	GdkColor	The color that will be used to draw visited links.
wide-separators	gboolean	If set to TRUE, separator width and height properties can be set with separator-width and separator-height. They will be drawn as boxes instead of lines in this case.

APPENDIX D

■ ■ ■

GTK+ Stock Items

Stock items are commonly used items that provide an image and some accompanying text. They are used for items in menus, toolbars, and buttons as well as in a few other places. A stock string identifies each stock item, but preprocessor macros are provided for convenience.

Stock items may have right-to-left variants, which are used for locales that prefer them. These include GTK_STOCK_GOTO_FIRST, GTK_STOCK_GOTO_LAST, GTK_STOCK_GO_BACK, GTK_STOCK_GO_FORWARD, GTK_STOCK_INDENT, GTK_STOCK_JUMP_TO, GTK_STOCK_MEDIA_FORWARD, GTK_STOCK_MEDIA_NEXT, GTK_STOCK_MEDIA_PLAY, GTK_STOCK_MEDIA_PREVIOUS, GTK_STOCK_REWIND, GTK_STOCK_REDO, GTK_STOCK_REVERT_TO_SAVED, GTK_STOCK_UNDELETE, GTK_STOCK_UNDO, and GTK_STOCK_UNINDENT.

It is also possible for you to register your own stock items in applications. Table D-1 lists the 98 items available as of GTK+ 2.10. Some of the items have been introduced since the release of GTK+ 2.0; the introduction date of each item has been specified.

Table D-1. *GTK+ Stock Items*

Stock ID	Display	Introduced
GTK_STOCK_ABOUT	About	GTK+ 2.6
GTK_STOCK_ADD	Add	GTK+ 2.0
GTK_STOCK_APPLY	Apply	GTK+ 2.0
GTK_STOCK_BOLD	Bold	GTK+ 2.0
GTK_STOCK_CANCEL	Cancel	GTK+ 2.0
GTK_STOCK_CDROM	CD-Rom	GTK+ 2.0
GTK_STOCK_CLEAR	Clear	GTK+ 2.0
GTK_STOCK_CLOSE	Close	GTK+ 2.0
GTK_STOCK_COLOR_PICKER	Color picker	GTK+ 2.2
GTK_STOCK_CONNECT	Connect	GTK+ 2.6
GTK_STOCK_CONVERT	Convert	GTK+ 2.0
GTK_STOCK_COPY	Copy	GTK+ 2.0
GTK_STOCK_CUT	Cut	GTK+ 2.0
GTK_STOCK_DELETE	Delete	GTK+ 2.0

Continued

Table D-1. *Continued*

Stock ID	Display	Introduced
GTK_STOCK_DIALOG_AUTHENTICATION	Authentication	GTK+ 2.4
GTK_STOCK_DIALOG_ERROR	Error	GTK+ 2.0
GTK_STOCK_DIALOG_INFO	Information	GTK+ 2.0
GTK_STOCK_DIALOG_QUESTION	Question	GTK+ 2.0
GTK_STOCK_DIALOG_WARNING	Warning	GTK+ 2.0
GTK_STOCK_DIRECTORY	Directory	GTK+ 2.6
GTK_STOCK_DISCONNECT	Disconnect	GTK+ 2.6
GTK_STOCK_DND	Drag-And-Drop	GTK+ 2.0
GTK_STOCK_DND_MULTIPLE	Drag-And-Drop multiple	GTK+ 2.0
GTK_STOCK_EDIT	Edit	GTK+ 2.6
GTK_STOCK_EXECUTE	Execute	GTK+ 2.0
GTK_STOCK_FILE	File	GTK+ 2.6
GTK_STOCK_FIND	Find	GTK+ 2.0
GTK_STOCK_FIND_AND_REPLACE	Find and Replace	GTK+ 2.0
GTK_STOCK_FLOPPY	Floppy	GTK+ 2.0
GTK_STOCK_FULLSCREEN	Fullscreen	GTK+ 2.8
GTK_STOCK_GO_BACK	Back	GTK+ 2.0
GTK_STOCK_GO_DOWN	Down	GTK+ 2.0
GTK_STOCK_GO_FORWARD	Forward	GTK+ 2.0
GTK_STOCK_GO_UP	Up	GTK+ 2.0
GTK_STOCK_GOTO_BOTTOM	Bottom	GTK+ 2.0
GTK_STOCK_GOTO_FIRST	First	GTK+ 2.0
GTK_STOCK_GOTO_LAST	Last	GTK+ 2.0
GTK_STOCK_GOTO_TOP	Top	GTK+ 2.0
GTK_STOCK_HARDDISK	Harddisk	GTK+ 2.4
GTK_STOCK_HELP	Help	GTK+ 2.0
GTK_STOCK_HOME	Home	GTK+ 2.0
GTK_STOCK_INDENT	Increase Indent	GTK+ 2.4
GTK_STOCK_INDEX	Index	GTK+ 2.0
GTK_STOCK_INFO	Information	GTK+ 2.8
GTK_STOCK_ITALIC	Italic	GTK+ 2.0
GTK_STOCK_JUMP_TO	Jump to	GTK+ 2.0

Stock ID	Display	Introduced
GTK_STOCK_JUSTIFY_CENTER	Center	GTK+ 2.0
GTK_STOCK_JUSTIFY_FILL	Fill	GTK+ 2.0
GTK_STOCK_JUSTIFY_LEFT	Left	GTK+ 2.0
GTK_STOCK_JUSTIFY_RIGHT	Right	GTK+ 2.0
GTK_STOCK_LEAVE_FULLSCREEN	Leave Fullscreen	GTK+ 2.8
GTK_STOCK_MEDIA_FORWARD	Forward	GTK+ 2.6
GTK_STOCK_MEDIA_NEXT	Next	GTK+ 2.6
GTK_STOCK_MEDIA_PAUSE	Pause	GTK+ 2.6
GTK_STOCK_MEDIA_PLAY	Play	GTK+ 2.6
GTK_STOCK_MEDIA_PREVIOUS	Previous	GTK+ 2.6
GTK_STOCK_MEDIA_RECORD	Record	GTK+ 2.6
GTK_STOCK_MEDIA_REWIND	Rewind	GTK+ 2.6
GTK_STOCK_MEDIA_STOP	Stop	GTK+ 2.6
GTK_STOCK_MISSING_IMAGE	Missing Image	GTK+ 2.0
GTK_STOCK_NETWORK	Network	GTK+ 2.4
GTK_STOCK_NEW	New	GTK+ 2.0
GTK_STOCK_NO	No	GTK+ 2.0
GTK_STOCK_OK	OK	GTK+ 2.0
GTK_STOCK_OPEN	Open	GTK+ 2.0
GTK_STOCK_ORIENTATION_LANDSCAPE	Landscape	GTK+ 2.10
GTK_STOCK_ORIENTATION_PORTRAIT	Portrait	GTK+ 2.10
GTK_STOCK_ORIENTATION_REVERSE_LANDSCAPE	Reverse Landscape	GTK+ 2.10
GTK_STOCK_ORIENTATION_REVERSE_PORTRAIT	Reverse Portrait	GTK+ 2.10
GTK_STOCK_PASTE	Paste	GTK+ 2.0
GTK_STOCK_PREFERENCES	Preferences	GTK+ 2.0
GTK_STOCK_PRINT	Print	GTK+ 2.0
GTK_STOCK_PRINT_PREVIEW	Print Preview	GTK+ 2.0
GTK_STOCK_PROPERTIES	Properties	GTK+ 2.0
GTK_STOCK_QUIT	Quit	GTK+ 2.0
GTK_STOCK_REDO	Redo	GTK+ 2.0
GTK_STOCK_REFRESH	Refresh	GTK+ 2.0
GTK_STOCK_REMOVE	Remove	GTK+ 2.0

Continued

Table D-1. *Continued*

Stock ID	Display	Introduced
GTK_STOCK_REVERT_TO_SAVED	Revert	GTK+ 2.0
GTK_STOCK_SAVE	Save	GTK+ 2.0
GTK_STOCK_SAVE_AS	Save As	GTK+ 2.0
GTK_STOCK_SELECT_ALL	Select All	GTK+ 2.10
GTK_STOCK_SELECT_COLOR	Color	GTK+ 2.0
GTK_STOCK_SELECT_FONT	Font	GTK+ 2.0
GTK_STOCK_SORT_ASCENDING	Ascending	GTK+ 2.0
GTK_STOCK_SORT_DESCENDING	Descending	GTK+ 2.0
GTK_STOCK_SPELL_CHECK	Spell Check	GTK+ 2.0
GTK_STOCK_STOP	Stop	GTK+ 2.0
GTK_STOCK_STRIKETHROUGH	Strikethrough	GTK+ 2.0
GTK_STOCK_UNDELETE	Undelete	GTK+ 2.0
GTK_STOCK_UNDERLINE	Underline	GTK+ 2.0
GTK_STOCK_UNDO	Undo	GTK+ 2.0
GTK_STOCK_UNINDENT	Decrease Indent	GTK+ 2.4
GTK_STOCK_YES	Yes	GTK+ 2.0
GTK_STOCK_ZOOM_100	Normal Size	GTK+ 2.0
GTK_STOCK_ZOOM_FIT	Best Fit	GTK+ 2.0
GTK_STOCK_ZOOM_IN	Zoom In	GTK+ 2.0
GTK_STOCK_ZOOM_OUT	Zoom Out	GTK+ 2.0

■ ■ ■

GError Types

GLib provides a standard method for error propagation called GError. In this appendix, you will find a complete list of the GError domains, as of GTK+ 2.10, along with the error types that correspond to each domain.

The GError structure provides three elements: the error domain, a message string, and an error code.

```
struct GError
{
  GQuark domain;
  gchar *message;
  gint code;
};
```

Each error domain represents a group of similar error types. Example error domains include G_BOOKMARK_FILE_ERROR, GDK_PIXBUF_ERROR, and G_FILE_ERROR. They are always named as <NAMESPACE>_<MODULE>_ERROR, where the namespace is the library containing the function, and the module is the widget or object type.

The message is a human-readable string that describes the error. If the user would expect visual feedback for the type of error that occurred, you should output message. It is also very useful when debugging your code.

The error code is specific to the error that occurred under the domain. Each error code consists of the domain name with the error type appended to it. For example, the error type G_BOOKMARK_FILE_ERROR_INVALID_URI falls under the G_BOOKMARK_FILE_ERROR domain.

Most error code domains also include <NAMESPACE>_<MODULE>_ERROR_FAILED, a generic fail code. This will be returned if a specific error is not available.

Tables E-1 to E-14 provide a complete reference to GError enumerations found throughout GTK+ and its supporting libraries. Along with each error is a description of what has occurred.

Table E-1. *GBookmarkFileError Enumeration Values*

Error Value	Description
G_BOOKMARK_FILE_ERROR_INVALID_URI	The URI provided to the function was not formatted correctly.
G_BOOKMARK_FILE_ERROR_INVALID_VALUE	The requested field was not found.

Continued

Table E-1. *Continued*

Error Value	Description
G_BOOKMARK_FILE_ERROR_APP_NOT_REGISTERED	The requested application did not register the bookmark.
G_BOOKMARK_FILE_ERROR_URI_NOT_FOUND	The requested URI provided to the function was not found.
G_BOOKMARK_FILE_ERROR_READ	The document was not formatted correctly.
G_BOOKMARK_FILE_ERROR_UNKNOWN_ENCODING	An unknown encoding was attributed to the document being parsed.
G_BOOKMARK_FILE_ERROR_WRITE	The bookmark could not be successfully written. Some type of write error occurred.
G_BOOKMARK_FILE_ERROR_FILE_NOT_FOUND	The requested bookmark file was not found.

Table E-2. *GdkPixbufError Enumeration Values*

Error Value	Description
GDK_PIXBUF_ERROR_CORRUPT_IMAGE	The image file is broken in some way.
GDK_PIXBUF_ERROR_INSUFFICIENT_MEMORY	Not enough memory is available to store the image.
GDK_PIXBUF_ERROR_BAD_OPTION	A bad option was passed. This error can occur while saving an image.
GDK_PIXBUF_ERROR_UNKNOWN_TYPE	The function is unable to detect the image type.
GDK_PIXBUF_ERROR_UNSUPPORTED_OPERATION	This function is unable to perform the operation on the specified image.
GDK_PIXBUF_ERROR_FAILED	This is the generic failure code for all other errors.

Table E-3. *GFileError Enumeration Values*

Error Value	Description
G_FILE_ERROR_EXIST	The application does not have permissions to perform the operation.
G_FILE_ERROR_ISDIR	The file is a directory, which cannot be opened for writing.
G_FILE_ERROR_ACCESS	File permissions do not allow the current operation.
G_FILE_ERROR_NAMETOOLONG	The specified filename is too long.
G_FILE_ERROR_NOENT	The file or directory does not exist.
G_FILE_ERROR_NOTDIR	The specified location is not a directory, but the option requires a directory.

Error Value	Description
G_FILE_ERROR_NXIO	The device on which the file is located cannot be found.
G_FILE_ERROR_NODEV	The file type does not support mapping.
G_FILE_ERROR_ROFS	The file system is read-only.
G_FILE_ERROR_TXTBSY	The text file is currently busy.
G_FILE_ERROR_FAULT	A pointer to a bad memory location was passed.
G_FILE_ERROR_LOOP	Circular symbolic links have been detected.
G_FILE_ERROR_NOSPC	The disk is full; no space is available.
G_FILE_ERROR_NOMEM	No memory is available, and virtual memory is full.
G_FILE_ERROR_MFILE	The current process already has too many open files.
G_FILE_ERROR_NFILE	Too many files are open on the entire system.
G_FILE_ERROR_BADF	A reading file descriptor has been specified for writing or vice versa.
G_FILE_ERROR_INVAL	The wrong argument has been passed.
G_FILE_ERROR_PIPE	The pipe is broken or has been blocked.
G_FILE_ERROR_AGAIN	Resources are broken but may work if you try again later.
G_FILE_ERROR_INTR	The function call has been interrupted.
G_FILE_ERROR_IO	A read or write error has occurred on the disk.
G_FILE_ERROR_PERM	The operation is not permitted.
G_FILE_ERROR_NOSYS	The function has not been implemented for your operating system.
G_FILE_ERROR_FAILED	The operation failed for an unspecified reason.

Table E-4. *GKeyFileError Enumeration Values*

Error Value	Description
G_KEY_FILE_ERROR_UNKNOWN_ENCODING	An unknown encoding was attributed to the document being parsed.
G_KEY_FILE_ERROR_PARSE	The document that was being parsed was not formatted correctly.
G_KEY_FILE_ERROR_NOT_FOUND	The file provided to the function was not found.
G_KEY_FILE_ERROR_KEY_NOT_FOUND	The key requested by the function was not found.

Continued

Table E-4. *Continued*

Error Value	Description
G_KEY_FILE_ERROR_GROUP_NOT_FOUND	The group requested by the function was not found.
G_KEY_FILE_ERROR_INVALID_VALUE	The value provided to the function could not be successfully parsed.

Table E-5. *GMarkupError Enumeration Values*

Error Value	Description
G_MARKUP_ERROR_BAD_UTF8	The text being parsed was not specified in valid UTF-8 format. You need to change the formatting and try again.
G_MARKUP_ERROR_EMPTY	The document did not have any content or it contained only whitespace.
G_MARKUP_ERROR_PARSE	The document that was being parsed was not formatted correctly.
G_MARKUP_ERROR_UNKNOWN_ELEMENT	The element specified to the function was not found. This value should only be set by GMarkupParser functions.
G_MARKUP_ERROR_UNKNOWN_ATTRIBUTE	The attribute specified to the function was not found. This value should only be set by GMarkupParser functions.
G_MARKUP_ERROR_INVALID_CONTENT	The document caused an error because of a problem with its contents. This value should only be set by GMarkupParser functions.

Table E-6. *GOptionError Enumeration Values*

Error Value	Description
G_OPTION_ERROR_UNKNOWN_OPTION	The parser did not recognize the option provided to the function. This will only be reported if you have configured GOptionContext so that is does not ignore unknown options.
G_OPTION_ERROR_BAD_VALUE	A value could not be correctly parsed.
G_OPTION_ERROR_FAILED	A callback function of type GOptionArgFunc failed.

Table E-7. *GShellError Enumeration Values*

Error Value	Description
G_SHELL_ERROR_BAD_QUOTING	Quoting was not matched correctly, or it was garbled.
G_SHELL_ERROR_EMPTY_STRING	The string to be parsed was completely empty.
G_SHELL_ERROR_FAILED	Some other type of GShellError occurred. You should reference error->message for more information.

Table E-8. *GSpawnError Enumeration Values*

Error Value	Description
G_SPAWN_ERROR_FORK	The fork failed because there was not enough memory available.
G_SPAWN_ERROR_READ	The pipe could not be selected or read from.
G_SPAWN_ERROR_CHDIR	The working directory could not be successfully changed.
G_SPAWN_ERROR_ACCES	Search permission was denied for the path prefix, the new file was not an ordinary file, execute permissions were denied, or the file was mounted on a file system with execution disabled (execv() failed with EACCES).
G_SPAWN_ERROR_PERM	The operation was not permitted because the process did not have the correct permissions (execv() failed with EPERM).
G_SPAWN_ERROR_2BIG	The process's argument list was too long according to the limits set by the system (execv() failed with E2BIG).
G_SPAWN_ERROR_NOEXEC	The file does not have permissions to be executed (execv() failed with ENOEXEC).
G_SPAWN_ERROR_NAMETOOLONG	The length of a component of the path or of the whole path exceeded the maximum (execv() failed with ENAMETOOLONG).
G_SPAWN_ERROR_NOENT	The process file did not exist (execv() failed with ENOENT).
G_SPAWN_ERROR_NOMEM	There is a maximum virtual memory allocation for processes, and more memory was required than the maximum (execv() failed with ENOMEM).

Continued

Table E-8. *Continued*

Error Value	Description
G_SPAWN_ERROR_NOTDIR	The path prefix did not point to a valid directory (execv() failed with ENOTDIR).
G_SPAWN_ERROR_LOOP	The function detected too many symbolic links to the path (execv() failed with ELOOP).
G_SPAWN_ERROR_TXTBUSY	The process cannot be opened because it was already opened by another process (execv() failed with ETXTBUSY).
G_SPAWN_ERROR_IO	An input or output error occurred while reading (execv() failed with EIO).
G_SPAWN_ERROR_NFILE	The maximum number of open files supported by the system was reached (execv() failed with ENFILE).
G_SPAWN_ERROR_MFILE	The maximum number of open files for one process supported by the system was reached (execv() failed with EMFILE).
G_SPAWN_ERROR_INVAL	A parameter passed to the function was not formatted correctly (execv() failed with EINVAL).
G_SPAWN_ERROR_ISDIR	The file was found to be a directory, and you were trying to perform a nonsupported operation on it (execv() failed with EISDIR).
G_SPAWN_ERROR_LIBBAD	The shared library you tried to access was corrupted (execv() failed with ELIBBAD).
G_SPAWN_ERROR_FAILED	Some other fatal error occurred. You should reference error->message for more information.

Table E-9. *GThreadError Enumeration Values*

Error Value	Description
G_THREAD_ERROR_AGAIN	There were not enough resources available to create the thread. In this case, you should try again at a later time.

Table E-10. *GtkFileChooserError Enumeration Values*

Error Value	Description
GTK_FILE_CHOOSER_ERROR_NONEXISTENT	A file specified to GtkFileChooser does not exist.
GTK_FILE_CHOOSER_ERROR_BAD_FILENAME	The filename specified to the function was not formatted correctly.
GTK_FILE_CHOOSER_ERROR_ALREADY_EXISTS	The filename specified to the function already exists.

Table E-11. *GtkIconThemeError Enumeration Values*

Error Value	Description
GTK_ICON_THEME_NOT_FOUND	The icon specified as a parameter to the function does not exist within GtkIconTheme.
GTK_ICON_THEME_FAILED	Some other type of GtkIconTheme error occurred. You should use error->message for more information.

Table E-12. *GtkPrintError Enumeration Values*

Error Value	Description
GTK_PRINT_ERROR_GENERAL	A general printing error occurred. You should use error->message for more information.
GTK_PRINT_ERROR_INTERNAL_ERROR	An error occurred internally in the printing system. This signifies a problem on the user's system.
GTK_PRINT_ERROR_NOMEM	Not enough memory was found to continue the printing operation.

Table E-13. *GtkRecentChooserError Enumeration Values*

Error Value	Description
GTK_RECENT_CHOOSER_ERROR_NOT_FOUND	The file specified to the function does not exist.
GTK_RECENT_CHOOSER_ERROR_INVALID_URI	The URI specified to the function was not formatted correctly.

Table E-14. *GtkRecentManagerError Enumeration Values*

Error Value	Description
GTK_RECENT_MANAGER_ERROR_NOT_FOUND	The URI specified to the function did not exist within the list.
GTK_RECENT_MANAGER_ERROR_INVALID_URI	The URI specified to the function was not formatted correctly.
GTK_RECENT_MANAGER_ERROR_INVALID_ENCODING	The specified string was not provided in UTF-8 encoding.
GTK_RECENT_MANAGER_ERROR_NOT_REGISTERED	The item specified to the function was not registered by any application.
GTK_RECENT_MANAGER_ERROR_READ	Reading the recently used resources file failed.
GTK_RECENT_MANAGER_ERROR_WRITE	Writing the recently used resources file failed.
GTK_RECENT_MANAGER_ERROR_UNKNOWN	Some other type of error occurred. You should use error->message for more information.

APPENDIX F

■ ■ ■

Exercise Solutions and Hints

This last appendix will walk you through the solutions for each of the exercises found in this book, although the full code for the solutions can be downloaded at www.gtkbook.com. If you get stuck, this appendix will give you the tools to solve the exercises before you look at the code. You can then reference the downloadable solutions to see how I implemented each of the exercise applications.

Note As the exercises become more complex, the solutions may differ greatly from your implementations. Even if your application works successfully, you should check out the downloadable solutions for comparison.

Exercise 2-1. Using Events and Properties

The solution for this exercise should appear very similar to the exercises found throughout Chapter 2. To begin, your application should include the following four basic steps that are required by every GTK+ application:

1. Initialize GTK+ with `gtk_init()`.

2. Create your top-level `GtkWindow` widget.

3. Show the `GtkWindow` widget to the user.

4. Move into the main loop with `gtk_main()`.

In addition to these basic steps, you must also add a `GtkLabel` widget to the top-level window. This label widget can be set as selectable with `gtk_label_set_selectable()`. Next, you should connect the `GtkWindow` widget to the `key-press-event` signal, which will be called every time the user presses a key when the window has focus.

Note The `key-press-event` will not work if it is connected to the `GtkLabel` widget! You will learn in Chapter 3 that the label widget cannot receive GDK events, since it does not have its own `GdkWindow`.

In the key-press-event callback function, you can use g_ascii_strcasecmp() to determine whether the label is currently displaying the first or last name. The window and label text should be switched accordingly. You should then return FALSE so that the application will continue to handle the key-press-event.

The last step in creating this first application is to connect the top-level window to the destroy signal. Calling gtk_main_quit() from within the destroy signal's callback function will quit the application. You do not need to use the delete-event signal, since you want to destroy the window on all delete-event emissions.

Exercise 2-2. GObject Property System

This exercise is very similar to Exercise 2-1, except you need to use the functions provided by the GObject library for changing properties. For example, in the main() function, the title, width, height, and resizability of the GtkWindow widget should be set with g_object_set().

In addition, within the key-press-event callback function, you should use g_object_get() and g_object_set() to interact with the title property of the GtkWindow and the label property of the GtkLabel.

You are also instructed to provide notification when the window's title property is changed. Connecting the window to the notify::title signal, which will monitor the value of the given property, can do this. Then, g_message() will output the new window title to standard output. You should see the message in the terminal output if you launch your application from a terminal emulator.

Exercise 3-1. Using Multiple Containers

This exercise helps you gain experience using a variety of container widgets that were covered in Chapter 3, including GtkNotebook, GtkVBox, and GtkHBox. Let us analyze the content of each of these containers one at a time.

The GtkNotebook container should contain four tabs. Each tab in a notebook is associated with a label widget and a child widget. The gtk_notebook_append_page() function can be used to add new pages to a notebook. Each of these tabs should contain a GtkButton widget that is connected to the clicked signal. When a button is clicked, the notebook should move to the next page, wrapping around when the last page is reached. Connecting each clicked signal to the same callback function can do this.

Within the callback function, which is called next_tab() in the downloadable solution, you first need to check the page number. If the page number is less than three, you can simply call gtk_notebook_next_page() to move to the next page. Otherwise, you can use gtk_notebook_set_page() to set the page number to zero. This same method can be used for moving to the previous page in the notebook.

The next container is a GtkHBox that holds two buttons. The first button should move to the previous page in the GtkNotebook container when pressed. As previously stated, you can use the same method that was used for moving to the next page for moving to the previous page, although it will have to be reversed. The other button should close the window and exit the application when clicked. These buttons can be packed with gtk_box_pack_end() so that they appear against the right side of the horizontal box instead of the left side.

The last container in the application is a GtkVBox widget that should hold the GtkNotebook and GtkHBox widgets. This vertical box can be packed into the top-level GtkWindow widget to complete the application's user interface.

Exercise 3-2. Even More Containers

This exercise solution is very similar to the previous exercise. The first difference is that the GtkNotebook tabs should be hidden with gtk_notebook_set_show_tabs(). Then, a GtkExpander container should be placed between each GtkButton widget and the notebook tab. This will allow you to show and hide the button found in each tab. The expander's label can also be used to tell you which tab is currently displayed.

The last difference is that, instead of using a GtkVBox widget to pack the notebook and horizontal box, you should use a GtkVPaned widget. This container will allow you to redistribute the allocated space for each of its two children by dragging the horizontal separator located between the two widgets.

Exercise 4-1. Renaming Files

In this exercise, you need to use several widgets that you learned about in Chapter 4, including the stock buttons GtkEntry and GtkFileChooserButton. The purpose of this exercise is to allow the user to rename the selected file with a function built into GLib.

The first step is to set up your user interface, which includes three interactive widgets. The first is a file chooser button, created with gtk_file_chooser_button_new(). The chooser's action should be set to GTK_FILE_CHOOSER_ACTION_OPEN. This will allow you to select only a single file. The gtk_file_chooser_set_current_folder() function can be used to set the current folder of the file chooser button to the user's home directory, found at g_get_home_dir().

This GtkFileChooserButton widget should be connected to the selection-changed signal. Within its callback function, you need to verify whether the file can be renamed. This can be done with a GLib function called g_access(). The following call can use used within your application:

```
gint mode = g_access (fn, W_OK);
```

If the file cannot be accessed or changed by the current user, the GtkEntry and GtkButton widgets should be disabled. This can be done by sending the opposite Boolean value as mode to gtk_widget_set_sensitive().

The next widget in the exercise is a GtkEntry, which allows the user to enter a new name for the widget. This is a new name for the file excluding the location, since this file name will be appended to the GtkFileChooserButton's location when the file is renamed. The last widget, the GtkButton, should call the renaming function when clicked.

Within the button's callback function, you first need to retrieve the current file and location from the file chooser button. The location, along with the content of the GtkEntry widget, can be used to build a new absolute path for the file. Lastly, you should use the g_rename() function to rename the file. You should note that you must include <glib/gstdio.h> for g_rename() to work!

Exercise 4-2. Spin Buttons and Scales

This exercise is very different from the previous exercise; it gives you practice with the GtkCheckButton, GtkSpinButton, and GtkHScale widgets. When the check button is activated, the values of the spin button and horizontal scale should be synchronized. Otherwise, they can move independently of each other.

To do this, the first step is to create two identical adjustments, one for each range widget. The toggle button in the solution is active on application launch so that the values will be immediately synced.

The next step is to connect each of the range widgets to the same callback function for the value-changed signal. Within this function, the first step is to retrieve the current values of the spin button and scale. If the toggle button is active, these values are compared. Action is only taken if the values are not the same so that the value-changed signal is not repeatedly emitted.

Lastly, the callback function can use GTK_IS_SPIN_BUTTON() to figure out which type of widget holds the new value. Based on the result of the test, the other widget should be given the new value.

Exercise 5-1. Implementing File Chooser Dialogs

In this chapter's only exercise, you are supposed to re-create the four types of file chooser dialogs by embedding a GtkFileChooserWidget widget into a GtkDialog widget. The results of each action can simply be printed to standard output.

The main application window will include four buttons, one for each of the GtkFileChooser action types, where the GTK_FILE_CHOOSER_ACTION_OPEN action will allow you to select multiple files. These buttons can be packed into a vertical box and then into the top-level window.

Each of the callback functions follows the same pattern. It first creates a GtkDialog widget and packs a GtkFileChooserWidget above the dialog's action area by packing the dialog's vbox member with gtk_box_pack_start().

The next step is to run the dialog with gtk_dialog_run(). If the returned result is the response associated with acceptance of the action, you should output what would occur with g_print(). For example, you should tell the user that the file will be saved,; the folder has been created; the files will be opened; or the folder was selected. In the case of a GTK_FILE_CHOOSER_ACTION_OPEN action, you should output all of the selected files.

Exercise 6-1. Working with Files

This exercise is meant to take what you have learned about file manipulation in Chapter 6 and integrate it with the widgets from previous chapters. The user interface for this exercise should include three widgets: GtkEntry, GtkFileChooserButton, and GtkButton.

The GtkEntry widget will allow the user to enter a single line of text that will be saved in a file on the system. The location of the file is chosen in the GtkFileChooserButton widget with an action of GTK_FILE_CHOOSER_ACTION_SELECT_FOLDER. Lastly, the GtkButton widget will initiate the saving of the file when it is clicked. In the downloadable exercise solution, the text will be saved to a file named arbitrary_file at the selected location when the user clicks the button.

In the button's callback function, you can first build the file path out of the selected location and the file name that you choose. Then, g_file_set_contents() can be used to save the contents of the GtkEntry widget to the file. If an error occurs when writing the file, you should report it to the user with the message reporting system covered in Chapter 6. For example, the write operation will fail if the user does not have write access to the chosen location.

Exercise 6-2. Timeout Functions

In this exercise, you are using a timeout function to create a timer, which is actually a very simple thing to do. First, you need to create two widgets, a GtkLabel that will output the current count and a GtkButton that will reset the count to zero when clicked. The timeout should be created with g_timeout_add_full() as follows:

```
g_timeout_add_full (G_PRIORITY_DEFAULT, 1000,
                    (GSourceFunc) timeout_function,
                    (gpointer) widget, NULL);
```

The previous timeout will call timeout_function() every 1,000 milliseconds. Within this function, the count of seconds is incremented and the label updated.

The second part of the exercise is to reimplement the timer's creation using GTimer. Try doing this by placing a second label within your previous solution so that the counts can be compared. You should notice that the timeout counts slower than GTimer, which keeps accurate time. This is because of the fact that timeout_function() is called every 1,000 milliseconds *plus* the time it takes to run the function! The next counting period for a timeout does not begin until the previous call is complete, which prevents the overlap of function calls. This is why timeout functions should *never* be used to keep track of time, which is what this exercise has illustrated.

Exercise 7-1. Text Editor

This exercise is the first instance of the text editor application that you will encounter. It asks you to implement all of the functionality of the text editor.

■**Note** The downloadable exercise solution includes only very basic functionality of a text editor. It is meant to get you started if you are having trouble. However, you are encouraged to continue to expand your text editor implementation beyond the provided solution!

There are a number of callback functions implemented for the text editor. These are the ability to create a new file; open an existing file; save the file; cut, copy, and paste selected text; and search for text in the document.

To create a new document, you should first ask the user whether or not the application should continue with a GtkMessageDialog widget. If the user chooses to continue, the downloadable exercise solution simply clears the GtkTextBuffer object and destroys the dialog. Otherwise, the dialog is just destroyed.

Opening a document in the provided solution does not ask the user for confirmation, since it is easy to cancel the operation from the GtkFileChooserDialog widget. The file chooser dialog has an action type of GTK_FILE_CHOOSER_ACTION_OPEN. When a file is selected, its contents are read with g_file_get_contents() and written into the text buffer. Saving in the exercise solution asks for a new file name every time the button is pressed. It calls g_file_set_contents() to save the text to the selected file.

The clipboard functions are similar to those provided in Chapter 7's clipboard example. It uses the built-in text buffer functions for cut, copy, and paste actions. These actions are performed on the default clipboard, GDK_SELECTION_CLIPBOARD.

The last callback function searches the current text for a case-sensitive string. The solution used is similar to the function shown in Listing 7-6 in Chapter 7, so you should refer to its description for more information.

Exercise 8-1. File Browser

In this chapter's exercise, you will be implementing a very simple file browser. It will allow the user to browse throughout the system's file structure and will differentiate between files and folders. This exercise is meant to give you practice using the GtkTreeView widget. It will be greatly expanded in Chapter 13 into a more functional file browser.

The first step is to configure the tree view, which will include a single column. This column will include two cell renderers, one for a GdkPixbuf and one for the file or folder name, so you will have to use the expanded method of tree view column creation that was discussed in Chapter 8. The first cell renderer should use GtkCellRendererPixbuf and the second, GtkCellRendererText.

The tree model, a GtkListStore is created with two columns with types of GDK_TYPE_PIXBUF and G_TYPE_STRING. Remember that the list store should be unreferenced with g_object_unref() after you add it to the tree view so that it will be destroyed along with the tree view widget.

After the tree model is created in the downloadable exercise solution, the populate_tree_model() function is called, which displays the root folder of the file system on startup. The current path displayed by the file browser is stored in a global linked list called current_path. If the list is empty, the root folder is displayed. Otherwise, a path is built out of the list's content, and the ".." directory entry is added to the tree model.

Then, GDir is used to walk through the contents of the directory, adding each file or folder to the tree model. You can use g_file_test() along with G_FILE_TEST_IS_DIR to check whether each is a file or folder, displaying the correct icon depending on the result.

The last step is to handle directory moves, which is done with GtkTreeView's row-activated signal. If the selection is the ".." entry, then the last element in the path is removed, and the tree model repopulated. Otherwise, the new path is built out of the current location and the selection. If the selection is a folder, then the tree model is repopulated in the new directory. If it is a file, then the action is ignored and nothing else is done.

Exercise 9-1. Toolbars

This exercise alters Exercise 7-1 replacing the buttons along the side with a GtkToolbar created with GtkUIManager. The following UI file can be used for creating the toolbar:

```
<ui>
  <toolbar name="Toolbar">
    <toolitem name="FileNew" action="New"/>
    <toolitem name="FileOpen" action="Open"/>
    <toolitem name="FileSave" action="Save"/>
    <separator/>
    <toolitem name="EditCut" action="Cut"/>
    <toolitem name="EditCopy" action="Copy"/>
    <toolitem name="EditPaste" action="Paste"/>
  </toolbar>
</ui>
```

Within your application, you next need to create an array of GtkActionEntry objects that will be associated with each of the toolbar items in the UI file. These actions are organized in a GtkActionGroup object, and then the toolbar is created with a GtkUIManager object. The rest of the text editor's implementation is the same as in Exercise 7-1.

Exercise 9-2. Menu Bars

This exercise is an alteration of Exercise 7-1 where the buttons along the side are replaced by a GtkMenuBar widget created with GtkUIManager. The following UI file can be used for creating the toolbar:

```
<ui>
  <menubar name="MenuBar">
    <menu name="FileMenu" action="File">
      <menuitem name="FileNew" action="New"/>
      <menuitem name="FileOpen" action="Open"/>
      <menuitem name="FileSave" action="Save"/>
    </menu>
    <menu name="EditMenu" action="Edit">
      <menuitem name="EditCut" action="Cut"/>
      <menuitem name="EditCopy" action="Copy"/>
      <menuitem name="EditPaste" action="Paste"/>
    </menu>
  </menubar>
</ui>
```

Within your application, you next need to create an array of GtkActionEntry objects that will be associated with each of the toolbar items in the UI file. These actions are organized in a GtkActionGroup object, and then the menu bar is created with a GtkUIManager object. The rest of the text editor's implementation is the same as in Exercise 7-1.

Exercise 10-1. Glade Text Editor

This exercise expands on Exercise 7-1 yet again by asking you to redesign the whole user interface in Glade. Instead of using buttons, you should implement a toolbar for text editing functions. You can then use Libglade to load the graphical user interface and connect the necessary signals. Figure F-1 is a screenshot of the application for this exercise using a toolbar.

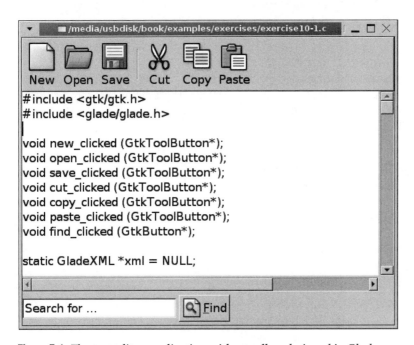

Figure F-1. *The text editor application with a toolbar designed in Glade*

Exercise 10-2. Glade Text Editor with Menus

This exercise also expands on Exercise 7-1 by asking you to redesign the whole user interface in Glade. This time, though, instead of using buttons, you should implement a menu bar for text editing functions. You can then use Libglade to load the graphical user interface and connect the necessary signals. Figure F-2 is a screenshot of the application for this exercise using a menu bar.

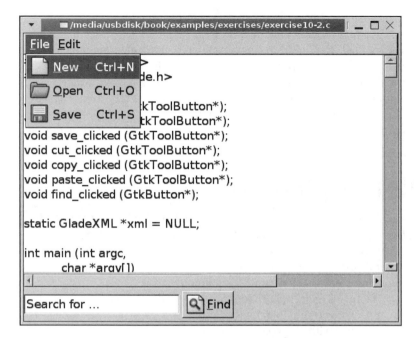

Figure F-2. *The text editor application with a menu bar in Glade*

Exercise 11-1. Expanding MyMarquee

In this exercise, you will be extending the MyMarquee widget that was built in Chapter 11. This section contains a number of tips for implementing the extra features required by the exercise.

The first extension is to add a border around the widget. This can be done with the gdk_draw_rectangle() function. The following function draws a rectangular border with the given width and height and the top-left corner positioned at (x,y):

```
void gdk_draw_rectangle (GdkDrawable *drawable,
                         GdkGC *gc,
                         gboolean filled,
                         gint x,
                         gint y,
                         gint width,
                         gint height);
```

The next thing you need to do is provide the ability to scroll through multiple messages. To do this, you need to store the messages as a private, linked list. You should then provide functions for adding and removing a message. When a message has scrolled beyond the bounds of the widget, the next message in the list should begin to scroll.

Next, you need to provide the ability to scroll the message in either direction, whether left or right. This is handled in your slide function, moving speed pixels in the correct direction every time the function is called. The only thing you need to be careful of is that the message will scroll off of the widget in the direction specified by the scroll direction!

Lastly, the message should stop scrolling when the mouse pointer is over the widget. This is accomplished by overriding the default enter-notify-event and leave-notify-event callback functions. You should use a gboolean flag to specify whether the message should be scrolled. You can check this in my_marquee_slide() to decide whether the message should be moved during that call.

Exercise 12-1. Full Text Editor

This last text editor exercise is an extension of Exercise 10-1. In it, you should add two additional features. The first is printing support, which allows the user to print the current text in the GtkTextBuffer widget. The printing support in the downloadable solution for this exercise is very similar to the printing example built in Chapter 12, so you should check out that example's description for more information about how this solution works.

The other additional feature is a recent file chooser menu for the Open toolbar item. In order to create this, you must convert the Open toolbar item to a GtkMenuToolItem widget. The default recent manager, obtained with gtk_recent_manager_get_default(), can be used to provide the recent files. Then, you can create the recent file chooser menu with gtk_recent_choose_menu_new_for_manager(). This menu should be added to the Open menu tool button's GtkMenu. You can use the selection-done signal to figure out which menu item is selected and what file should be opened.

Index

Find it faster at http://superindex.apress.com

Find it faster at http://superindex.apress.com

Find it faster at http://superindex.apress.com

Find it faster at http://superindex.apress.com

You Need the Companion eBook

Your purchase of this book entitles you to buy the companion PDF-version eBook for only $10. Take the weightless companion with you anywhere.

We believe this Apress title will prove so indispensable that you'll want to carry it with you everywhere, which is why we are offering the companion eBook (in PDF format) for $10 to customers who purchase this book now. Convenient and fully searchable, the PDF version of any content-rich, page-heavy Apress book makes a valuable addition to your programming library. You can easily find and copy code—or perform examples by quickly toggling between instructions and the application. Even simultaneously tackling a donut, diet soda, and complex code becomes simplified with hands-free eBooks!

Once you purchase your book, getting the $10 companion eBook is simple:

❶ Visit **www.apress.com/promo/tendollars/**.

❷ Complete a basic registration form to receive a randomly generated question about this title.

❸ Answer the question correctly in 60 seconds, and you will receive a promotional code to redeem for the $10.00 eBook.

2560 Ninth Street • Suite 219 • Berkeley, CA 94710

eBookshop

THE EXPERT'S VOICE™